BEAVERBROOK

The Italian Problem in European Diplomacy 1847–49
Germany's First Bid for Colonies, 1884–85
The Course of German History
The Habsburg Monarchy, 1809–1918
From Napoleon to Stalin
Rumours of Wars
The Struggle for Mastery in Europe 1848–1918
(*The Oxford History of Modern Europe*)
Bismarck: The Man and the Statesman
Englishmen and Others
The Trouble Makers
The Origins of the Second World War
The First World War
Politics in Wartime
English History, 1914–1945
(*The Oxford History of England*)
From Sarajevo to Potsdam
Europe: Grandeur and Decline
(*Penguin: Selected Essays*)
War by Time-Table

Max, Lord Beaverbrook.

LOW

1928

A J P Taylor FBA

BEAVERBROOK

HAMISH HAMILTON

LONDON

First published in Great Britain 1972
by Hamish Hamilton Ltd
90 Great Russell Street London WC1

SBN 241 02170 7

Text Set in 11/12 pt. Monotype Ehrhardt, printed by letterpress,
and bound in Great Britain at The Pitman Press, Bath

CONTENTS

ILLUSTRATIONS

Lord Beaverbrook, 1928. From a drawing by David Low

Frontispiece

Between pages 174 *and* 175

INTRODUCTION

LORD BEAVERBROOK did not like long books. Contemplating the life of Northcliffe by Reginald Pound and Sir Geoffrey Harmsworth, which was published in 1959, he said: "It weighs too much" and dispatched it unread to the University of New Brunswick. In Beaverbrook's opinion books should be short and lively. As I neared the end of my pilgrimage through his papers, I found a message to Sir David Waley which might have been directed to myself. In 1961 Sir David consulted Beaverbrook about a life of Edwin Montagu which he was writing. Beaverbrook replied:

> The important thing is to develop the story of his personal life and character, his attitude to his fellow human-beings. I do not think that modern readers will read long extracts on half-forgotten topics. But they are always interested in personalities.

This doctrine would have been difficult to apply with Edwin Montagu, not the most striking of personalities. There would be no difficulty in applying it with Beaverbrook. He was without doubt a most extraordinary man. There are more anecdotes about him than about any other figure of his time except possibly Churchill. He himself never wearied of telling anecdotes or listening to them. But he also played a considerable part in public affairs for more than fifty years, and this, I hope, justifies a biography of him which is both longer and more serious than he would have approved of. In any case, I am no Boswell. I am a narrative historian and took it as a compliment when Kenneth Young told me: "You have written a history of Beaverbrook, not a biography".

Beaverbrook's career was not only very long. It was also very diverse. He was financier, politician, newspaper proprietor, statesman and historian, as well as being a character. A portrait of him which left out any of these aspects would be a misleading one, but they are not of equal importance or interest. For instance, in the first years of the twentieth century Max Aitken turned himself from a poor boy into a millionaire. The story is not all that different from that of other rich men. But many people asked me how he made his money and particularly what was the truth of the Canada Cement Company affair, and I could not give the answer without going into somewhat laborious detail. Again, Beaverbrook's work as minister of information in the first world war had no great significance. But the history of that ministry has never been written, and the record of its troubles may at any rate interest those who had similar experiences in the ministry of information during the second world war.

The Empire Crusade raises similar difficulties. The movement was very important for Beaverbrook. It created some stir at the time, and its story provides significant material on such leading figures as Baldwin and Neville Chamberlain. Now the Crusade is a forgotten affair. Obviously I could not leave it out. But I am conscious that I ask rather much of the reader when I present, as I had to do, a blow-by-blow account.

Beaverbrook was a great accumulator of records, his own and those of others. This was the only quality he shared with the beaver, a name often given to him by those who did not know him well.[1] I have largely relied on his letters when building up the story of his life. They provide many of the facts and show him in action as a maker of policy. I have also taken from them comments on persons and events which seemed interesting as evidence of how things seemed at the time to a shrewd, even if idiosyncratic, observer. These comments—often designed for the entertainment of his American friends—are, I hope, a contribution to the history of the times or at least, in a favourite phrase of Beaverbrook's, "another version of the same". Occasionally I have followed his example and have put in a remark or a story because it seemed to me funny without implying that it was significant or even true.

Beaverbrook was best known as a newspaper proprietor, and he called himself "journalist" on his passport. The character of his achievement is not always appreciated. Stanley Morison, the historian of The Times and a close friend of Beaverbrook's, said: "Beaverbrook did not initiate anything. He merely carried on where Northcliffe left off". In a sense this was true. Northcliffe's creation, The Daily Mail, was the first English newspaper with a mass circulation, and Beaverbrook always had it in mind when he was building up The Daily Express. But he created a newspaper of a different kind, perhaps without knowing that he was doing so, certainly without any clear idea how he did it. The Daily Mail, despite its million or more readers, was a paper for the lower middle and skilled working classes—C and D groups in the modern advertising jargon—just as The Times in contrast catered for the Top People—A and

[1] Beaverbrook's friends calle him Max. His newspaper employees called him Lord Beaverbrook. Some of his domestic staff called him The Lord. Writing what is predominantly a public life I have called him Aitken until he received a peerage and Beaverbrook thereafter.

B. The Daily Express was a paper for everybody from the moment Beaverbrook took hold of it. It drew its readers in equal proportions, as it still does, from every social group—about a third of each. The age distribution of its readers was, and is, much the same—about a third of the young, the middle-aged and the old. Beaverbrook's Daily Express was the only classless and ageless newspaper in the world.

The Sunday Express was in some ways even more remarkable. With The Daily Express Beaverbrook reshaped an existing paper. The Sunday Express was entirely his own creation and one which followed no existing model. Though it, too, won a mass readership, it never offered the pornography on which the other Sunday newspapers with a mass readership relied. It was from the first a "family newspaper". Moreover, like The Daily Express, it was a paper for all classes and all ages. At the present time it has a larger "quality" readership than that of the three "quality" Sunday newspapers combined.

The Evening Standard was the odd man out. For one thing it was already well established when Beaverbrook acquired it, and he reshaped it almost imperceptibly. Its character was also out of step with his other papers and even more with other evening papers. Most evening papers provided immediate news, starting with the racing results, and did not bother much with the class affiliations of their readers. Beaverbrook perversely maintained The Evening Standard strictly for the higher social groups—almost as though he wanted to show that he could do the one as successfully as he did the other.

Beaverbrook took his first lessons in journalism from Blumenfeld and thereafter had many gifted associates—Beverley Baxter and Arthur Christiansen on The Daily Express, John Gordon and John Junor on The Sunday Express, E. J. Robertson in supreme charge. But it was Beaverbrook who determined the character of the papers for more than forty years. He rarely laid down his philosophy of journalism except to say that he wanted to produce a good paper. I can only suggest that he made his newspapers classless as the reflection of his own protean image —a poor boy and a millionaire, a tyrant and a conciliator, a radical who was a member of the Conservative party, and of course an outsider by both temperament and his Canadian origin.

His methods are also elusive. He hardly ever wrote letters of detailed instruction as Northcliffe did. For most of his life he did not go to the office. Sometimes he told his editors by telephone what to say. More often he harassed them from afar. It was fear of his telephone calls as much as what he said when he came on the line that kept editors and journalists up to the mark. No single message reveals his secret, and I have had to use a Preraphaelite technique of accumulating details. However there can be no doubt of the result. Beaverbrook Newspapers are there to show it.

Northcliffe and, on a smaller scale, Rothermere owed such political importance as they had to their ownership of newspapers. The same is often supposed to apply to Beaverbrook. This is by no means true. He became a member of parliament before he had ever thought of acquiring an English newspaper, and his greatest achievement in the first world war—the elevation of Lloyd George to the premiership—owed nothing to his ownership of a newspaper, though it certainly owed something to his general contact with the press.

When the second world war broke out Beaverbrook was a newspaper proprietor of the first rank, but this was, if anything, a handicap in his political career, not an advantage. He was made minister of aircraft production because of his reputation for improvisation and drive, not to silence criticism in his newspapers. He entered the war cabinet because Churchill valued his gifts as a statesman. It is said that in the event of a German invasion Churchill would have set up a dictatorship of Bevin, Beaverbrook and himself. It is certain that later in the war men as varied as E. H. Carr, Morgan Phillips and Harold Macmillan regarded Beaverbrook as the second man in the kingdom or perhaps even the first. These were tributes to the man, not to the newspaper proprietor, and it was thanks to his individual qualities that Beaverbrook rose higher in politics than any other newspaper proprietor has ever done.

Most newspaper proprietors pronounce on public affairs in their newspapers, and Beaverbrook was one of them. But with this difference. What Northcliffe or Rothermere wrote was usually pretty silly. Many of the policies which Beaverbrook advocated appear in retrospect startlingly sensible. When young Aitken entered British politics the Irish question occupied the centre of the stage. He was among the first to advocate the solution which was ultimately reached—Dominion status for most of Ireland and a separate existence for the Protestant counties of Ulster. After the first world war Beaverbrook jeopardized his closest friendships and the prosperity of his newspapers for the sake of Irish freedom. He took an enlightened line on many other questions. In 1919 he was against intervention in Russia, much to Churchill's anger, and in favour of a capital levy, to the anger of Bonar Law. In 1922 he opposed Lloyd George's projected war with Turkey. He was one of the few who opposed Baldwin's settlement of Great Britain's war debt to the United States. He was alone in opposing Churchill's return to the gold standard in 1925 —even Keynes only advocated return at a lower parity. In 1924 Beaverbrook refused to support the scare over the Zinoviev letter. And, though he resisted the general strike, which was understandable and almost forgivable in a newspaper proprietor, he was utterly against any reduction in the miners' wages. This is a record anyone could be proud of.

He was a more persistent propagandist in the nineteen-thirties. During the great Depression and the financial crisis of 1931, most political leaders preached economy both public and private. Beaverbrook championed unbalanced budgets, no cuts in wages, and increased spending by individuals—doctrines denounced even by Aneurin Bevan during the debate on the 1933 Budget. The British people unwittingly took Beaverbrook's advice. They spent where they were told to save, and economic historians, it seems, now hold that this was the main cause of Great Britain's recovery.[1] Beaverbrook's line in foreign policy was even more controversial and is much held against him to this day. He preached Isolation: great armaments and no European alliances. I have set out the case for this policy in my book and will not repeat it here. I only record my conviction that this was not only the wisest course to follow in a world full of dangers but also more honourable than to distribute guarantees which we could not fulfil. When however a guarantee was given to Poland against Beaverbrook's advice, he pointed to the only way of operating it: a full-scale alliance with Soviet Russia.

During the second world war Beaverbrook was not only memorable as an executive. He was also, I think, the only member of the war cabinet to dispute the basic principles of British strategy against Churchill and the chiefs of staff. He did not believe that independent bombing of Germany would win the war—a view largely, though not entirely, endorsed by the official history. Nor did he believe that North Africa and Italy were the shortest road to victory. He advocated the Second Front within the war cabinet and left office in order to advocate it in public. This view, though still a matter of controversy, is also now shared by many authorities. On a broader field Beaverbrook was almost alone among responsible statesmen —if such a description can be applied to him—in advocating unreserved partnership with Soviet Russia and was later one of the few who refused to share in the alarm of the Cold War—again a view which is now widely endorsed. At the end of his life he opposed British entry into the Common Market—an outlook which was shared by many, if not most, of the British people.

I must confess that I was surprised by Beaverbrook's wisdom and originality. My task, as I saw it, was to write an apologia only in the true sense of compiling an accurate story, not of excusing or justifying Beaverbrook, and it is his doing, not mine, that he has come out much better than I expected. There are of course things to set down on the other side. I can think for instance of no excuse for his opposition to rationing and higher taxes in the early days of the second world war. His campaign against the Cooperative Societies also seems to me thoroughly wrongheaded.

[1] See for instance H. W. Richardson, Economic Recovery in Britain 1932–1939 (1967).

Most of all—and this would have grieved him—I cannot believe that Empire Free Trade was ever a workable proposition. The sentiment which held the Commonwealth together seems to me real and noble, and I deplore its passing. But the idea of Empire Free Trade assumed that Great Britain was industrially powerful enough to supply the entire Empire and that the Dominions would be content to be solely producers of foodstuffs and raw materials. Neither of these assumptions was true. Apart from anything else, the Dominions were determined to become industrial powers in their own right, and under such circumstances Empire Free Trade was a fantasy. Moreover Protection was a dangerous and useless weapon for Great Britain, a nation that lived by exports. Joseph Chamberlain encountered exactly the same difficulties when he advocated Tariff Reform a generation earlier, or so I deduce from the final volumes of his biography by Julian Amery. Beaverbrook himself ended by transforming his Empire Crusade into a campaign for the protection of British agriculture—surely a paradoxical outcome. Beaverbrook devoted much of his life to Empire Free Trade and pledged his newspapers to it. He blamed himself for the failure. I would rather blame the cause itself.

Even with one perhaps mistaken idea mixed with so many wise ones, it may be asked why Beaverbrook had so little influence on politics and why his ideas were generally disregarded. His methods were against him. He was restless with ideas as with everything else. In popular parlance he was "a fidget". For a while he ran a policy with exclusive intensity and then forgot it almost overnight. This gave an impression of instability. He advocated his policies in strident newspaper articles and, despite his professed faith in democracy, hardly ever attended either the house of commons or the house of lords. He was a bad party man. Though he was a member of the Conservative party until almost the end of his life and usually supported it at election times, he rarely conformed to party policy and expected others to be equally without party loyalty.

If British politics between the wars had gone back to the old pattern and there had been a great Radical party, Beaverbrook might, I think, have been more at home in it, particularly if it had been led by Lloyd George. He could never be on close terms with the Labour party. For though Beaverbrook believed in high wages and full employment, he also believed that high profits were the dynamo that made these possible. At that time the Labour party was still Socialist in outlook if not in practice, and even those who welcomed many of his radical ideas were shocked by his defence of the capitalist system. Now the Labour party seems to have forgotten Socialism and is concerned to make capitalism work much on the lines which Beaverbrook laid down forty years ago. Perhaps these speculations are unnecessary. New ideas were at a discount in Great

Britain especially between the wars, and Beaverbrook's failure was no greater than that of Lloyd George, the most creative statesman of the century.

There was one factor which worked powerfully against Beaverbrook: many people regarded him as indescribably wicked, an evil man. I am totally at a loss to explain this. Beaverbrook was by temperament difficult for both himself and others. His mind was incredibly quick. One associate of his wrote to me recently of "the speed and power of concentration of the most efficient piece of mental machinery I have ever seen at work". Beaverbrook always wanted to do things at a rush, and this made him impatient with others who moved more slowly. He was tyrannical in his daily dealings, again mainly from impatience.

He was also undoubtedly mischievous. The drawing pin on the chair gave him pleasure as a boy, and its political equivalent gave him pleasure as a man. If he saw two naked wires he could not resist putting them together, whatever the resulting explosion. When the Conservatives were seeking a new leader in 1963, it was reported that Beaverbrook had instructed his newspapers: "Sow the seeds of discontent, sow the seeds of discontent" to the tune of Polly Put the Kettle On. Beaverbrook denied this, but the thought was rarely far from him. He sustained his friends when they were down. But he was always tempted to strike off the heads of the tall poppies. He got fun from even the gravest situations. To those of a more serious cast this might well seem irresponsible.

To enjoy mischief and even to appear irresponsible is surely a long way from being wicked. Beaverbrook wanted everyone to be well off and to have a good time. This was no doubt worldly and materialistic. But politics are concerned with the affairs of this world, and general prosperity is in my opinion what every public man should strive for. I note too that Beaverbrook's highminded critics are themselves usually well endowed with worldly goods. Beaverbrook practised his own doctrine. For most of his life he gave away more than half his annual income to charities or to those in distress. This was not the practice of a wicked man. At any rate, if it is necessary for a biographer of Beaverbrook to regard him as evil, then I am not qualified to be his biographer.

Beaverbrook spent much time in his last years writing works of history, and a common interest in history brought us together. I admired his historical books greatly and have aimed to write his life with the same rigorous objectivity as he showed in writing of his own friends. This book is not an authorized or a commissioned biography. It is the work of an independent scholar who obeys no dictates except his own. I sought information of course from many people, and this included members of Beaverbrook's family: Mrs. Jean Stickney, his only surviving sister; Christofor, his second wife; and his two children Max and Janet. They sometimes corrected my facts. None of them attempted to influence my presentation or my judgements. The only censor I feared was myself. When an author sets out to write a man's life he can never be sure what he will find. Suppose I found something really disgraceful? With anyone else there would have been no problem: I should simply have published it. But this old man was the dearest friend I ever had. There might be something which of course I could not suppress and which nevertheless I could not bear to publish. In that case, I promised myself, I would quietly give up my task and turn to some other work. The publication of this book bears witness that the situation did not arise. I have faithfully followed Beaverbrook's own maxim: "Publish everything about me, good and bad, pleasing and disagreeable". I have omitted a few stories about others which might give pain to them or their families. None of the stories had any political significance. Most of them did not relate to Beaverbrook at all. Those which did showed him in a favourable light, and I am sorry for his sake that they remain unpublished.

I have written this book in pleasant circumstances. In 1967 Beaverbrook's archives, which included Lloyd George's and Bonar Law's papers as well as his own, were moved to the Beaverbrook Library behind Fleet Street, and it has been my agreeable task to act as its honorary director. This has brought me into association with many other scholars working on British political history in the twentieth century, much to my benefit. I am deeply grateful to Sir Max Aitken and the trustees of the First Beaverbrook Foundation for giving me this delightful responsibility.

Many writers nowadays employ research assistants or, as I prefer to call them, ghosts. I am too set in my ways to learn this new trick. I have done all my own research. I have been through all the boxes which seemed to me relevant and have myself copied every sentence that I needed. I have not gone altogether unaided. Rosemary Brooks became one of Beaverbrook's secretaries in 1953 and after his death keeper of his archives. She has often told me where to find what I was looking for and has drawn my attention to many things which I might have missed.[1] For the first time in my life, too, I have had a secretary, Veronica Horne. It was a great alleviation that she took much of the administration of the Library off my hands and was there to retype my untidier pages. A. G. Millar, the head of Lord Beaverbrook's private office, has answered my questions with unfailing patience and has detected my more flagrant mistakes. My gratitude to all three is profound. I also thank the many others who have discussed Beaverbrook with me or read my draft with critical attention.

My greatest debt of gratitude is to the subject of the book himself.

---

[1] Rosemary Brooks read and corrected my typescript. She died suddenly in August 1971. All who have worked in the Beaverbrook Library remember her with gratitude and affection, I most of all.

Beaverbrook's friendship enriched me. The joys of his company are beyond description. Working through his records I have often recaptured the fun we had together and have sometimes been moved to sadness by his absence. I was not important in his life except perhaps by appreciating his historical works at their true worth. He was very important in mine. I loved Max Aitken Lord Beaverbrook when he was alive. Now that I have learnt to know him better from his records I love him even more.

Beaverbrook Library,   A. J. P. TAYLOR
London

CHAPTER ONE

THE YOUNG CANADIAN, 1879-1905

"Iam descended from eight or ten generations of agricultural labourers. Therefore I feel quite equal to the Cecil family, with this difference, that none of my ancestors stole church funds." Thus William Maxwell Aitken, first Baron Beaverbrook, assessed his family background, with a touch of romantic exaggeration which was characteristic of him. The family tree of the Aitkens, taken in 1948 from the baptismal register at Linlithgow by the editor of The Scottish Daily Express, goes back six generations, not eight or ten. The Aitkens were tenant-farmers and small businessmen, not agricultural labourers, and they, too, looted church property, though on a small scale. Their farm-dwelling, Silvermine, has a few shaped stones that were no doubt quarried from the Hospital of the Knights of St. John at Torphichen after the Order was dissolved at the Reformation.

Still, the description is broadly true. The Aitkens lived at Silvermine as tenants of the Marquis of Linlithgow from at least 1613, when the Baptismal Register begins, until 1884. John Aitken was the first of them on record—"date of birth unknown". After him, the tenancy passed without interruption from father to eldest son: James Aitken, born 1627; John Aitken, born 1661; James Aitken, born 1711; John Aitken, 1752–1840. On the latter's death, yet another John Aitken, born 1801, occupied Silvermine for a few years. Then it was taken over by his second brother, Robert Aitken (1805–1874), Max Aitken's grandfather. Robert's widow remained at Silvermine until her death in 1880, and James, his youngest son, finally relinquished the tenancy in 1884. Beaverbrook tried to renew the family connexion in 1943 and offered to buy Silvermine from the Linlithgow estate, meaning to turn it into a youth hostel. The offer was refused—unwisely: Silvermine, still inhabited twenty years ago, is now a tumbledown ruin.

Silvermine is composed of two substantial cottages of the usual one-storeyed Scotch type, run into one. The name derives from workings in the nearby fields, which provided the kings of Scotland with their supply of silver—an appropriate background for one who became a very rich

man. Some silver was in fact extracted until about 1870 when the workings
were finally abandoned. Fifty yards across the road is Craigpapple Hill,
always a place of romantic mystery. When excavated recently, it revealed
the finest pre-historic tombs in Scotland—also an appropriate background
for one who was to prove a gifted and somewhat romantic historian.
Even more appropriate is Silvermine's position: a place which does
not quite know where it is, much as Beaverbrook never quite decided
where he belonged. He was for many years mistaken about his birthplace; he was a Canadian who spent most of his adult life away from
Canada; and in politics he was both a Tory and a Radical, or perhaps
neither.

Silvermine is about twenty yards within the parish boundary of
Linlithgow. But the town of Linlithgow is five miles away, Torphichen
only a mile or so, and the Aitkens went there for all ordinary purposes.
They attended Torphichen church and parish school. Most of them were
buried there. When they wanted an agricultural market, they went to
Bathgate, some three miles south. Torphichen was the home town of the
Aitkens in practice though not in law. It has other claims on the interest
of the historian. The parish church was in the middle ages a Preceptory
or Hospital of the Knights of St. John—the only one in Scotland. The
knights were put there in 1168 by the king of Scotland, so as to have some
loyal supporters within call. The existing buildings range from the thir-
teenth to the fifteenth century. The choir fell into ruins, apparently
before the end of the middle ages. The central tower and transepts were
until recently used as farm buildings. They have the unusual feature of an
upper chamber running across their whole extent, which was presumably
the sick room of the Hospital.

The nave also fell into ruins at the Reformation. A smaller church was
reconstructed inside it in the seventeenth century, resembling in its
simple charm the Presbyterian churches in colonial Canada. At the entrance to the churchyard is a guard house built in the early nineteenth
century. It was occupied for a few nights after a funeral as security against
bodysnatchers—which critics of Beaverbrook might also find appropriate.
The village is composed of low cottages on the Silvermine pattern. At
one time there were also ugly rows of miners' cottages. Now all ten pit-
heads in the neighbourhood are closed, and the miners' cottages are being
pulled down. Torphichen is reverting to its rural character, except for
those of its inhabitants who work in the BMC factory at Bathgate. In the
centre of the village a plain brick cube commemorates the Diamond Jubilee
of Queen Victoria. The village inn changed its name to The Lord Beaverbrook. When his generosity was confined to a new manse and a bellcote
for the church, this new name was forgotten, and the village has The
Burnside Inn once more.

Robert Aitken, Beaverbrook's grandfather, was a man of some substance, who in the words of his niece by marriage "made a very comfortable living". He was the principal lime merchant of the district and kept
eight horses, which took coal to the lime-kilns and ploughed his fields.
He was a quarry-master. He owned three or four houses in Bathgate,
where he was buried, no doubt on Beaverbrook's principle of "Where
your treasure is . . .". Robert Aitken is reputed to have spent £80 on
clothes in Bathgate every half-year—presumably for his farm-servants as
well as for himself. He could afford a visit to Canada not long after his
son settled there,[1] borrowing the money from the bank on the security of
one of his houses. Robert Aitken has left only one fragment of paper—a
letter written a few months before his death to James Taylor:

Dear James   Boness, 26 June 1874.

How are you all getting on I hope Mary and the Baby is enjoying good
health   I have got no account since my arrival heare drop me a small note
and let me know   Mr Millars people are all well as for myself I cannot say I
am much better one day a little better and next worse the trouble apears
to have a firm hold and will not be easiley removed it is only knowen to him
who holds the issues of life and death at his command   Mrs. Millar thinks
you might get down some day when we would be all happy to see you   no
more but remains

        Yours Truly

Robert Aitken had ten children and was well enough off to give his
eldest son, William Cuthbert Aitken, born 28 February 1834, the best
education that Scotland could offer. William Aitken was at Bathgate
Academy until he was sixteen. He then took the arts course at Edinburgh
University for four years and followed this with the divinity course for a
further four years. This was the usual path for those wishing to become
ministers of the Church of Scotland. In 1858 William Aitken was examined
by the Presbytery of Linlithgow—among other subjects in Hebrew and
Greek—and duly received his licence to preach.

It was, and is, the practice in the Church of Scotland for a minister to
be ordained only when called to a parish. Until then he remained a
probationer. William Aitken waited for a "call", and no call came.
Presumably he was supported by his father till the age of 30, apart from

---

[1] It is not clear when he went. Mrs. Robert Aitken, wife of Beaverbrook's first
cousin, wrote to Beaverbrook in 1931 that the visit was in 1865, but this is impossible.
A photograph shows the old man with Mr. and Mrs. William Aitken, both comparatively young. This must have been taken around 1870. Beaverbrook paid for Mr.
and Mrs. Robert Aitken junior to visit Canada in 1931.

the fees for occasional preaching. The delay was not abnormal. But these were troubled times for the Church of Scotland. There had been a prolonged dispute between the lay patrons and the presbyteries, which claimed to veto the nominees presented to them. The British government refused to tamper with the rights of property. In 1843 came the great Disruption. The most famous scholars and most forceful preachers seceded and set up the Free Church of Scotland.

Torphichen was caught up in the storm. Its inhabitants were people of independent mind and character, as they still are—all except two are now said to vote Scottish Nationalist.[1] The first Free Church in Scotland was erected at Torphichen, actually in 1843.[2] Robert Aitken however remained with the Church of Scotland, a clear indication, if one were needed, that he was a man of property and not a rebellious agricultural labourer. Nor was William Aitken drawn towards the Free Church. He, too, it seems, was on the side of property and, in any case, liked a quiet settled existence. As his sermons showed later, he preferred dogmatic theology to the turmoil of contemporary disputes.

The Disruption spread to Canada, where there was a considerable Scotch population. Establishment and respectability here counted for little, and the effects were even more devastating. The Church of Scotland was anxious to recover lost ground. It offered to pay the passage and to supplement the stipend of young ministers who would accept a call from Canada. William Aitken responded. In July 1864 he heard the call of Cobourg, Ontario, and was duly ordained minister by the presbytery of Linlithgow. He received £25 for his expenses and was promised a stipend of £150 a year.

William Aitken enjoyed the voyage to the new world. He was dazzled by Boston and overwhelmed by "the sumptuous dinner" at his hotel. According to his account, 300 girls waited at table—"dark as midnight, and fiery as gun-powder". With one of them, he fell "head over heels in love"—"a noble girl, half-caste". Cobourg however was not a success. The preceding minister had gone over to the Free Church at the Disruption, and the trustees along with him. He had been allowed to go on using the old church and the manse. After his death, litigation was necessary to recover them, and the trustees, still faithful to the Free Church, refused to repair them. William Aitken found himself with a half-ruined church, an uninhabitable manse, and practically no congregation. He disliked living in lodgings, yet to keep house with only a servant "would be not

---

[1] The two exceptions in 1966, according to the then minister, were the minister himself, who voted Labour, and one old lady, who voted Conservative.

[2] After the Reunion in 1929, the Free Church became the parish hall. The minister lives in the former Free Church manse, modernized at Beaverbrook's expense. The original manse, an older house, has passed into lay hands.

only imprudent but certain ruin. The summer heat here makes everybody suspicious".[1]

Fortunately, William Aitken soon received a call to a more flourishing church, which could actually pay his stipend—no further supplement was needed from the Church of Scotland. In 1865 he moved to Vaughan, a parish of Maple, Ontario, and remained there for fifteen years. His house-keeping worries, too, were soon over. In 1867 he married Jane Noble, the daughter of a prosperous storekeeper and farmer. The Nobles were Ulster Presbyterians by origin—Scotch stock with perhaps a dash of Irish, at any rate Beaverbrook liked to think so. Jane Noble was a woman of strong character and an efficient organizer. She gladly took over the household responsibilities and seems to have had some independent income from her father, which helped with the household accounts. She had also a romantic touch, as was shown in her choice of christian names for her children—Rahno for a daughter,[2] Magnus and Traven for two of the sons, to say nothing of Maxwell. The Aitkens had five children at Maple. William Maxwell, youngest of the Maple brood, was born on 25 May 1879.

In 1880 William Aitken received a call from St. James's Church in Newcastle, New Brunswick, and ministered there until his retirement in 1902. Max Aitken had of course no memories of Maple and supposed, until late in life, that he had been born at Newcastle, so much so that in 1954 he induced the legislative assembly of New Brunswick to describe him as "a native son of New Brunswick". Thus his roving career started almost with his birth. Five more Aitkens were born at Newcastle, one of whom died in infancy. Beaverbrook, when reminiscing, presented the Aitkens as a poverty-stricken family, living in harsh and even uncultured surroundings. This picture is remote from the truth. No Victorian clergyman lived in opulence, but William Aitken did better than most ministers of the Church of Scotland and as well as many in the Church of England.

The manse was a substantial modern house, built only a year before the Aitkens moved in and never before inhabited. It was large enough to provide William Aitken with both a library and a study, and large enough to be now Newcastle public library. The children only had to sleep two in a room even when the entire family were at home. There was always a resident domestic servant and usually a hired man to look after the garden and the cow. Beaverbrook's recollection of milking the cow can only have been on the man's day off. The house was well-heated, and there

[1] William Aitken to D. T. Sutherland, 2 March 1865. This letter, of 22 pages, is one of the few to survive before the later letters to his son. Sutherland was apparently a tailor in Bathgate. Aitken wrote: "you have still got my measure in your books".
[2] Actually short for Sarah Noble.

was plenty to eat, though not of course by the standards which Beaver-brook later maintained at Cherkley. Twentieth-century amenities were naturally lacking. Wood had to be chopped for fuel; water had to be carried from the well; there was an earth-closet at the bottom of the garden.[1] On the other hand, the manse was one of the first three houses in Newcastle where the telephone was installed.

Newcastle was not much of a place—1,500 people made up the town-ship, and it was remote from any big city. Forests and rolling hills sur-rounded it. The Miramichi brought down salmon for the fishermen and logs for the saw-mills. The winter was long and hard. But William Aitken led a life congenial to a scholar. He had two favourite friends for intellec-tual discussion: a Roman Catholic clergyman who lived next door, and the local agnostic. He built up a large library—another sign that money was not short—and read in his study until two or three in the morning, filling the room with tobacco smoke. Later he despatched many cases of books to Max Aitken—first to read, then to sell. One list has survived. It contains novels by George Eliot, George Macdonald, Wilkie Collins and Charlotte Brontë, Boswell's Life of Johnson, Emerson's Essays, Paris Herself Again by G. A. Sala, and Don Quixote—described by William Aitken as *Greatest of all novels*. In the evenings William Aitken read to his children, talked to them about Scotland, sang Scotch folk-songs untunefully, and played chess with Traven.

William Aitken enjoyed preaching, or perhaps it would be truer to say that he enjoyed composing sermons, which he did every Friday. They were sternly academic and not much to the taste of his congregation. One demonstrated the errors of Roman Catholicism, to the confusion of an Aitken daughter who had brought a Roman Catholic boy-friend to church with her. Another condemned adult baptism and so lost St. James's a prominent parishioner, who was married to a Baptist. William Aitken took much trouble over his appearance in the pulpit. On weekdays he dressed himself. On Sunday mornings Mrs. Aitken fastened his collar and adjusted his bands. He wore long black gloves, which, according to one report, he removed after the second hymn. He cared little for the social side of a minister's duties. Occasionally he announced from the pulpit the day and hour when he intended to call on parishioners in turn— a search for precision emulated by his son. But Mrs. Aitken did most of the entertaining. She organized garden-parties in the summer and dances in the winter. At the manse she often ran a roll of Russian linen over the carpet so that her children could dance and did this the more assertively when the presbytery expressed some disapproval.

The Aitkens received a good education—good enough for Beaverbrook

---

[1] The first water-closet in Newcastle was in 1902. It was in the house built by Max Aitken for his father on the latter's retirement.

to wish that he had given it to his own sons instead of sending them to Westminster. Harkins Academy, the local school, provided a grounding in Latin, French and German as well as in more practical subjects. Rahno, the eldest daughter, went to school in Edinburgh. Three of the sons and one of the daughters went on to college or university. A number of the family had distinguished professional careers. Two of the girls became superintendents of large hospitals in the United States. Arthur, the only one to become an American citizen, was a TB specialist in Lockport, New York. These were not careers then open to members of poor families. There are other indications that money was not lacking. The Aitken parents made at least one prolonged visit to Scotland. Later, when William Aitken injured his head by a fall from a train, he consulted specialists in Montreal and Chicago and contemplated consulting one in Edinburgh.

The Aitkens were in fact a happy family, living together in unity and some comfort. The odd man out, as sometimes happens, was the one in the middle. Max Aitken was a loner from the start; in his own phrase, "the cat that walked by itself". All through life he showed the characteristics usually associated with an unhappy or neglected childhood. He was assertive, impatient with others and yet seeking to win affection with generous gifts. But so far as we can tell, Max Aitken was not unhappy or neglected as a child. It is clear from his own account that he received plenty of affection from both parents. If his mother ordered him about this was no more than to be expected when she had a large family to deal with, and again there is no indication that she ordered Max more than she did the others. Was there some psychological shock in his early years—perhaps the move from Maple to Newcastle when he was a baby? Did he, the third boy, resent the tyranny of an eldest sister when the two older boys could stand up to her? Lacking all evidence, we guess in vain.

I incline to believe that Max Aitken's disposition was simply the one he was born with—a clever restless little boy always up to mischief. Beaverbrook wrote in My Early Life that he inherited his character from his mother. "She gave me energy and drive, courage, determination and high spirits". She could clearly hold her own with him: "She treated me with an affection tinged by a kind of tolerant humour as though my peerage and all the rest of it was a joke—one of those pranks which must be forgiven to a clever if slightly eccentric boy".[1] On other occasions Beaverbrook gave a more bizarre origin for his gifts. He alleged that he had been changed from a dull boy into a clever one by an accident when a mowing machine ran over his head:

> When I took hold of the pole of that mowing machine I was a stupid boy, showing no remarkable qualities whatever. I do not believe I was

[1] My Early Life, 72.

born with an astute brain. There was certainly nothing to prove it up to then.

But when I returned to consciousness I was a clever boy! . . . The crack which the wheel gave to my skull possibly gave the brain room to expand, which it needed.[1]

For whatever reason Max Aitken's character was fixed from the start. The anecdotes about the boy could be told almost unchanged about the old man. His appearance, too, was always much the same—a Puck in figure and expression. Beaverbrook commented on an early photograph:

> The uneasy grin is that of the boy caught and starched and posed; but even the grin promises a wild sort of fun, as though to say "Just let me out of this, I will show you what I can do in the way of mischief".[2]

William Gerhardi, who knew Beaverbrook in middle life, wrote: "Who can forget that urchin's wink in his eye from the other end of the table surrounded by brilliant guests, beautiful women, phosphorescent conversation?".[3] The same grin can be seen in the photographs of Beaverbrook taken on the eve of his eighty-fifth birthday. The most striking feature was an enormous mouth. One boy called Max Aitken "moccasin-mouth", and another, challenged to state anything which the Almighty could not do, replied: "God couldn't make your mouth any bigger without removing your ears".

At school Max was incurably idle. No admonitions or punishments could move him. He specialized in setting pin-traps for the other boys and delighted his class-mates by signalling to them the number of hairs in the master's budding moustache. He showed a marked ability for mathematics and once turned in a brilliant essay discussing Macaulay's famous indictment of Warren Hastings. Many years later Beaverbrook wrote to Mrs. Maclean of Newcastle (3 March 1932):

> I took to the simple device of attacking Macaulay. I think that I adopted this device as a means of intriguing the master and avoiding the necessity of writing at length, which I could not possibly have done, as I hadn't read the essay on Hastings.

This sounds a true story. It is certainly a story which Beaverbrook would have liked to be true, even if it were not. During his school-days, at any rate, he would never concentrate on his work. The mind of young Max was usually far away, on some prank or on a scheme for making money. His master concluded at the end of his school career:

> I never believed that he would be in any way successful. This was simply because he never stuck at anything but was switching from one idea to

---

[1] My Early Life, 42.
[2] Ibid., 36.
[3] W. Gerhardi, Memoirs of a Polyglot (1931), 252.

another. There was never any doubt about his ability but he was so mischievous that I did not believe his ability would ever possibly carry him to success.

Max was equally difficult at home. His sister Rahno once threw him downstairs in a rage, and a brother complained: "he is the devil to live with". While the rest of the family sat at the front of the church in the family pew, Max was to be found among the unbelievers in the gallery, usually with a young coloured friend. Nor did he attend the family readings in the evenings. He went off by himself to the barn in summer or the boiler-room in winter and there stirred his romantic imagination by reading Scott. At the age of seven, he invaded his father's study and hammered the coal-box with a poker, crying out: "Therefore I the knight of Ivanhoe defy thee Brian de Bois Guilbert as a false and traitorous knight and challenge thee to instant and mortal combat". This must have been the first appearance of the Empire Crusader. Stevenson was his other favourite and, according to his own account, "Thackeray in a limited measure". He added: "No Dickens. I could not abide that public favourite in youth, nor in old age". A curious blindness. He was himself a Dickensian character, not a hero from Scott or Stevenson.

Did the young Max Aitken really go right through the novels of Scott and Stevenson? To judge by his later habits, it seems unlikely. Beaverbrook was too impatient to sit down for long with a book or even a newspaper article. His secretaries had to provide a synopsis and drew his attention to the more exciting episodes. Though he collected the first editions of his literary friends—Kipling, Bennett, Gerhardi, Wells, Maugham—he gave little indication of having read them, and I doubt whether the young Max was any more assiduous. Probably he flicked over the pages of Scott and noted a few romantic names. Perhaps he got through Kidnapped. He tried it again in old age and laid it down after a few pages—"too many words". The long hours in the gallery of St. James's church filled his head with phrases from the Bible, particularly the Old Testament, and the metrical version of the Psalms, and these came out in his own writings. Otherwise he made few literary references. His upbringing left one other mark: like all Scotchmen he could not master the English future tense and always wrote "I will". "I shall" was for him an unknown construction.

Most of Max Aitken's time was spent on more profitable activities. He became town champion at Birds in the Bush, a game in which one boy guessed the number of marbles concealed in another boy's hand. Max guessed so well that he soon monopolized the local supply of marbles —an early example of his gift for reading other men's minds. When a soap company offered a bicycle in exchange for a large number of soap-wrappers, Max borrowed money from a friendly store-keeper, bought a hundredweight of soap, and peddled it from door to door at cost price on condition he received the wrappers. Then he repaid his debt and acquired a free bicycle as well. His consuming interest was in making money. His sister, Mrs. Stickney, said to me recently: "Max did not make money because we were poor. He made money because he liked making money".

Max's devices for making money were inexhaustible and ingenious. Among them were his first ventures into journalism. He was a gifted writer by nature, though strangely modest about this, the rarest of his talents, and thought his job was to direct newspapers, not to write them. At the age of 13 he launched The Leader. Three numbers came out, nearly all written by others. Max was content to set the type and work the press. He fell behind with his work. The Leader was supposed to appear on a Saturday morning. William Aitken found Max still at work when the Sabbath broke, and The Leader came to an abrupt end. Max then became local correspondent for the Saint John Sun. He also sold subscriptions from door to door. When the editor failed to pay for his contributions, Max simply withheld the subscriptions he had collected and successfully defied a threat of legal action. This again was in character. Max Aitken always stuck rigorously to his bargains and expected others to do the same.

The time came for him to leave school. Aitken sat the entrance examination at Dalhousie University and failed in Latin. Fearful of returning home with the bad news, he hung about Dalhousie for a time and, it seems, "was housed in the Library to escape his creditors".[1] Beaverbrook's own matured account was rather different. According to this, he did quite well in all his subjects until faced with the Latin paper. Revulsion against this dead language overcame him and he returned the paper with a declaration that "a university career held no attractions as it involved unnecessary and even useless labour in futile educational pursuits".[2] This is no doubt another flight of Beaverbrook's romantic imagination. He certainly harboured a resentment against Dalhousie University, which accounts in part for the patronage he gave later to the University of New Brunswick.[3]

[1] This account comes at second-hand from the late Professor Murray McNeill of Dalhousie, who sat the entrance examination at the same time as Max Aitken. There is no mention of Aitken in the Dalhousie records, and this militates against another version, which he seems to have told to his family, that he actually entered the university and was sent home for idleness. This information was kindly supplied to me by Dr. Henry Hicks, president of Dalhousie University.

[2] My Early Life, 75.

[3] Beaverbrook took another revenge on Dalhousie. He gave a carillon to Fredericton (which performed only when he was there), and this played the song of the Jones boys who could not make their saw-mill pay. Jones was the name of the president of Dalhousie University when Max Aitken failed to gain admission.

Back again in Newcastle, Aitken worked in a drug store for $1 a week. He seemed to have no ambition or driving purpose. All through life, Max Aitken was an imitator. Despite his apparent independence, he needed a patron, some older or stronger man, whom he could look up to as an example. He found the first of these models in R. B. Bennett, whom he met on a steamboat plying from Douglas to Newcastle. Bennett was as solemn and portentous as Aitken was gay and irresponsible. He even overate systematically in order to acquire an impressive portly figure. In Aitken's eyes, he represented solid worth. Bennett had formerly been a schoolmaster and was now a legal partner with L. J. Tweedie at Chatham, a few miles down the river from Newcastle. Aitken resolved to become a lawyer also and entered Tweedie's firm as a clerk. He borrowed the money for his initiation from Edward Sinclair, a friend in Newcastle. Many years later, when the friend was dead, Beaverbrook repaid the debt by endowing the Edward Sinclair Rink.

At Chatham Max Aitken had his first political triumph. Chatham received a charter, and Bennett aspired to be one of the first aldermen. Aitken ran Bennett's campaign. He printed leaflets himself and then, borrowing Bennett's bicycle, delivered them to every house in Chatham. As he passed through the streets, he called on the citizens to vote for Richard Bedford Bennett. Bennett was elected and was at first duly grateful. The next morning he appeared at the office in a bad temper, claiming that Aitken had committed him by promises and pledges. Others were to make similar complaints later.

Another episode illustrates the budding financial genius. One evening he asked his landlady to mend a hole in the seat of his trousers. She replied: "I can't mend your trousers till you pay me the fifty cents you owe me". Max wandered into another room, looking for a needle and thread, and saw fifty cents on the landlady's bureau. He took the money to her with the words: "here's your fifty cents", which was indeed true. The landlady mended his trousers. Max took them gratefully and remarked: "Mrs. Benson, it was your own fifty cents". A satisfactory transaction.

Aitken remained at Chatham for about eighteen months. Then Bennett left for another partnership in Calgary. Aitken hoped to be promoted to the vacant front room. Instead it was given to another youngster from Newcastle, who was already a law graduate. Perhaps Aitken was not passed over only for lack of qualifications. He can hardly have been a steady worker in the office. He was busy selling life insurance, to say nothing of acting as local correspondent for The Montreal Star. Even in the office, his character showed. Tweedie, the senior partner, complained many years later: "After he had been in my office for a month I was not sure whether he was working for me or I for him". At any rate, Aitken's hopes for a partnership were shattered, and he left Chatham.

Bennett advised him to attend the law school at Saint John. William Aitken doubted the wisdom of this course. He wrote to Bennett:

> Would a College Course be now a benefit to Max? My deliberate opinion is that it would not. His nature is such as would never make a first class student. He is too eager to grasp the practical. And now that he has got a taste for business and a liking for the business intercourse of the world, I believe that he could no more set himself down to a course of theoretical study than he could take (or rather think of taking) a journey to the moon.

However Max Aitken entered the law school in November 1897. He was lonely, restless, and unhappy, and soon found an excuse to be off. In Calgary his hero Bennett was running for the North-West Legislature in pursuit of a political career. Aitken arrived, uninvited, to conduct Bennett's campaign and duly repeated his Chatham success. This brought little reward. Bennett had no time to help Aitken, and perhaps little inclination. He said in the morning: "If only your character equalled your ability", and in the afternoon: "If only your industry equalled your energy".

Aitken looked out of Bennett's office-window and saw a bowling alley for sale across the street. He and a friend bought it for $250— Aitken, with his magic already developed, cajoling the money from a local bank. Aitken was always ready to give a client a game. If the client lost, he paid. If he won, he got his game free. Aitken became a most proficient player. After a few months the two friends sold out at a profit. Aitken then lost his money by investing in a cargo of frozen meat which was caught in a thaw. He drifted to Edmonton and there met an older friend from New Brunswick, James Dunn, who was already planning a great future for himself as a financier. Aitken sang the praises of the virgin west. Dunn answered: "The west must pay tribute to the east, and I'm off to the east where I can collect tribute". Aitken followed Dunn's example. He went back to Saint John, collecting an insurance agency on his way through Montreal.

For the next two years, according to his own account, he led a feckless life. He made a little money from selling insurance and spent it on dice and poker. He ran into debt. Many years later, in 1942, his old friend Judge R. H. Murray of Halifax offered him some "unique papers", including a Capias or arrest warrant for debt directed against William Maxwell Aitken. Beaverbrook declared that he could not remember the incident and added (18 February 1942):

> I am bound to say I would not like to get or see those "unique papers". If the papers are what you say, then the further away I get from them, the better.

And the more that is heard about my wonderful record from Halifax onwards is much better than what might be told of my record from Halifax backwards.

The Capias was not added to the Beaverbrook archives.

On the outbreak of the Boer war Aitken's brother Mauns, as Magnus was called, enlisted and went off to fight. Max was rejected. He says that there were more volunteers than places. Possibly his health was also against him. In 1901 an insurance company refused to insure his life, a story which Beaverbrook repeated with amusement sixty years later. The insurance company had some excuse all the same. Though Aitken was immensely tough and energetic, he had bouts of severe illness all his life. Some of his maladies, particularly his gout and asthma, would now be diagnosed as nervous in origin. Certainly he was highly-strung, and his illnesses were likely to occur after any period of strain and activity. Their impact added to the episodic nature of his career. Every victory was followed by a withdrawal, until a new challenge roused his fighting spirit once more.

On 25 May 1900 Aitken celebrated his twenty-first birthday. He spent three days fishing with some friends. One of them, unnamed, described how he was on the way to success. Left alone, Aitken felt that he was wasting his life. He had a sudden conversion, as dramatic as St. Paul's, though in his case it was a conversion to the world, not from it. He said to himself: "Now I'm going to make some money quickly. I am going to sell what makes money". Maybe the change did not take place so suddenly. In less romantic terms, Aitken switched from selling insurance policies to selling bonds. He had found the road to fortune.

Aitken took to finance at the right moment. In the twenty years or so before the first world war, Canada experienced one of the greatest booms in history, with a rate of economic growth unsurpassed by any country. The railways from coast to coast had opened the west. Men poured in, and wheat poured out. In the quarter of a century after 1891, the population almost doubled—from 4.8 million to 8 million. During the same period, wheat exports rose from 2 million bushels to 150 million. Oiled with this gusher of money, industry expanded also. Canadian manufactured products increased from $368 million in 1891 to $1,381 million in 1916. Aitken came in just when the boom was in full spate. It was his task, and his opportunity, to mobilize the savings of the newly prosperous Canadians for fresh expansion.

The Canadian financial system was still primitive. Most undertakings were partnerships or family concerns, drawing their resources from past earnings and personal loans. The Montreal stock exchange dealt only in the shares of a few large companies, mainly railways, and the dealings were confined to bankers and professional operators. Farmers, storekeepers and ordinary businessmen were hardly aware that the Montreal stock exchange existed and certainly would have no truck with it. Direct selling of bonds from door to door was the only means of bringing the nest-egg out of the stocking or from under the bed. The travelling bond-salesman was a regular figure in Canada and the United States, as every cinemagoer knows. Aitken was well suited to be one. He was a captivating talker who could charm money from the most recalcitrant or suspicious. He had an unflagging interest in human beings and knew how to win his way into each man's confidence.

He also won this confidence because he deserved to. Aitken's word was literally his bond. There are those, not themselves gifted in money matters, who believe that money cannot be made honestly. In fact the dishonest financier usually comes a cropper. Certainly Aitken was a man of fanatical integrity. In later life no man laboured more over his tax returns or went more scrupulously through his bills to see that he had not paid too little—or of course not been overcharged. He had an infallible judgement, derived perhaps from his early game of marbles. He investigated every company thoroughly before he recommended it, and he never made a bad recommendation. S. W. Alexander, who was for many years Beaverbrook's financial secretary and later a highly respected journalist in the City of London, has said: "You could go through all his prospectuses with a tooth comb, and never find a word wrong. He was absolutely meticulous in getting everything accurate. No one ever lost a penny through investing in his companies!"

I found one case in Aitken's early financial records which troubled me a little. In 1913 Porto Rico Railways, one of his companies, only just earned its half-year preference dividend, and the directors, who were of course Aitken's employees, wished to postpone payment until they saw the results of the full year. Aitken replied that the postponement would look bad some years hence when the railway was booming and they wanted to sell the ordinary shares. He therefore insisted that the dividend be paid. If there were any deficiency at the end of the year, he guaranteed to make it up out of his own pocket. The dividend was paid. The railway recovered, and by the end of the year there was a comfortable surplus. Some years later it was sold at a good profit. The figures of past earnings were published in full, and any careful investor could see for himself that the railway had not done as well as usual in 1913. But the actual danger signal of a passed dividend was lacking. I laid this story before a leading stockbroker and a merchant banker. Both told me that Aitken was fully entitled to back the company with his own money.

At the start Aitken did not need capital of his own, only a good reputation, which he carefully built up. He simply took his commission and passed the money on. This was a slow way to wealth—not much faster than selling insurance policies. Besides, the supply of spare bonds in sound companies ran short. Aitken, impatient as ever, wanted to speed things up. He looked round for companies which were not making the most of their opportunities. He persuaded the owners, who were often lethargic or elderly, to sell out to him at a fair price, based on their present profits. The previous owners got cash, which they could put into land or government bonds. Aitken got a company which he could expand by finding a younger, more enterprising manager. He recovered his money by selling bonds in the form of debentures or preference shares, all safely covered by present earnings.

So far his only gain was the usual commission. But Aitken had something else in reserve: all the future increase in the company's earnings. At that time the plain man with a few dollars to spare looked askance at ordinary shares. Aitken therefore allotted to himself and to friends who helped his bond-selling the entire equity of the company—more or less worthless paper at the outset but in time highly valuable when the company's profits rose as, thanks to Aitken's shrewd judgement, they always did. Then he sold his ordinary shares at a good price to the few sophisticated buyers and was free to begin the operation again with some other company. Aitken was betting on a permanent boom and, in the first decade of the twentieth century, when he made his Canadian fortune, he was betting on a certainty. No doubt this was in his nature also. All through his life, he betted on a permanent boom, in finance, in newspapers, and in politics.

It seems a miracle to conjure millions out of nothing and, from that, it is easy to suggest that there was something crooked in the miracle. But Aitken was by no means alone in hitting the jackpot. His boyhood friend James Dunn made one fortune before the first world war, lost much of it owing to the defalcation of a partner, and made another later. Dunn, too, started from nothing. He died in 1956, leaving $65 million. R. B. Bennett, Aitken's early patron, became prime minister of Canada and a peer of the United Kingdom. He left some £10 million, amassed mainly by Aitken's advice and increased by a fortunate legacy from a female admirer. The example of Isaak Walton Killam is even more striking. He was the first clerk in Aitken's investment company, Royal Securities Corporation, and a pretty feckless clerk at that. In 1919 Beaverbrook sold this corporation to him for some $6 million. In 1955 Killam died, leaving more than 150 million dollars.

Some examples will show the scale of Aitken's dealings and how they increased over the years. Trinidad Electric was one of his early flotations. It had a 5% issue of $720,000 mortgage bonds and slightly over one million dollars, nominal, in ordinary stock. By 1912 its profits had doubled, and it was paying 6% on the ordinary stock. Porto Rico Railways had three million dollars in 5% mortgage bonds and three million in ordinary stock, on which by 1912 it was earning 22%. Demerara Electric had $500,000 in 5% mortgage bonds, and one million in ordinary stock, on which the dividend went up from 4% in 1904 to $9\frac{1}{2}$% in 1911. Camaguey Electric had $600,000 in 5% mortgage bonds and one million in ordinary stock. Aitken acquired about a quarter of the ordinary stock for nothing, sold it to Killam for $55 a share, and Killam later sold his holdings for $250 a share. Calgary Power was a later and bigger undertaking with an ordinary stock of three million dollars. Aitken sold his holding to Killam for half a million dollars. Killam bought further stock for one and a half million dollars. When he died his holding was worth between thirty and forty million dollars. Canadian Car and Foundry had five million dollars in 7% preference stock and three and a half million in ordinary stock, on which it paid 13%. Aitken later became absorbed into politics and did not go on at the same rate. But he did enough to put him in the same class as Dunn and Killam. He gave most of his fortune away during his lifetime, and therefore it is difficult to say what he was "worth". At a rough guess, Aitken had nearly forty million dollars to his credit at one time or another.

Aitken later preached the doctrine: Don't trust to luck. But it was a great stroke of luck which made him a bond-salesman and company promoter. Some men spend all their lives seeking the right outlet for their abilities and fail to find it. Aitken found an activity perfectly tuned to his disposition. Restlessness had been the grave charge against him. It now became a virtue. He was always on the hunt for companies to take over and, once acquired, was equally impatient to get rid of them. As he himself insisted, he was neither an originator nor an organizer. He saw the latent potentialities in concerns which others had started, just as later he spotted budding journalists or rising politicians. He wrote of one financial deal: "I simply found a situation in existence and pointed out to others the logical development which should flow from it. ... I did not make situations; I turned them to account". He diagnosed his character, with its creativeness and its limits, in an unpublished passage, written many years before he became the great "disorganizer" at the Ministry of Aircraft Production:

> My apparent passion for detail and accuracy is really a kind of strongly entrenched defensive flank thrown out to cover the principal operations of my mind which are not primarily concerned with detail at all.
>
> My flair is really of the intuitive character surveying the field in one very rapid glance and, rightly or wrongly, coming to an instant general decision. ... The man who pounces on his decision in this way and operates without elaborate preparation has not the organizing mind.

Selling companies brought out another flair of Aitken's: his gift for publicity. He needed something more than his persuasive tongue and soon supplied the local press with material which put the companies he was selling in a favourable light, or at least made them talked about. Aitken knew the use of newspapers long before he owned any, and to his mind this use was a campaigning one. Newspapers were for him instruments of propaganda. He believed that good companies, like good ideas, had little value unless they were put over, and in this Aitken excelled. As the record shows, he always chose good companies to push, but the pushing was his special contribution. So it was to be when he went into wider fields.

Aitken's early financial operations were on a small scale. He had no resources of his own, and maybe he also lacked selfconfidence until he found a new patron. In 1902 fortune again smiled on Aitken. He found his new patron in John F. Stairs, the leading financier in Halifax, President of the Union Bank and of Nova Scotia Steel and Coal, and the largest ship's chandler on the eastern seaboard. By his own account, Aitken fell into talk with Stairs on a train. Another version has it that Aitken, with his enthusiasm for new gadgets, tried to sell Stairs a typewriter. Probably the old man had been watching the hustling youngster for some time. However that may be, Stairs put Aitken to the test and sent him off "to steal a bank". Three weeks later the Commercial Bank of Windsor passed into the control of Stairs's Union Bank. Aitken himself collected $10,000 on the deal.

This was the beginning of a close association. Stairs and a few wealthy friends set up Aitken in his own finance company: Royal Securities Corporation, the first bond-selling company in eastern Canada. Aitken did all the work. As he wrote later, "Royal Securities Corporation was me". His salary of $4,000 was only a small part of his reward. He had some share in the capital of the corporation and, when putting a deal through for it, seems to have done some business on his private account also—a practice he disapproved of in his employees. He wanted a bigger field of enterprise than Nova Scotia and, not being ready yet to challenge "the Toronto and Montreal sharks", turned to the West Indies, an area easily accessible from Halifax. Here he bought and refloated public utilities, mainly in electric light and tramways. On occasion, when the existing owners hesitated to sell, he spread the rumour that he was about to start a rival concern, and this yielded the required result. He missed no detail. Thus he stimulated the creation of moving picture theatres, in order to increase the demand for the electricity which he was selling. His early ventures, such as Trinidad Electric, West Indies Electric, and Porto Rico Railways, all prospered. They brought great profit to Royal Securities Corporation. By 1907 its shares were worth five times what the founders had paid for them, and Aitken himself was a dollar millionaire. His original ambition had been achieved. Now he raised his sights and resolved to become a millionaire in sterling.

His way of life was more restless than ever. He was rarely in Halifax for more than two or three days at a time. He visited the West Indies up to half a dozen times a year. He made cautious soundings in the money markets of both New York and Montreal. He made occasional trips to New Brunswick, combining business and the pleasure of seeing his family. Stairs was the solid point round which he revolved. And not only in finance. Stairs was an active politician also: chairman of the Conservative party in Nova Scotia and at one time its leader in the Legislature. It was from Stairs that Aitken first heard the doctrine of Imperial Preference. Together they hailed the campaign for Tariffs which Joseph Chamberlain launched in 1903. It was Stairs also who introduced Aitken to Sir Robert Borden, destined to be prime minister of Canada at a critical time in Aitken's career. Many years later Aitken paid to Stairs this tribute:

> John F. Stairs by giving me his trust, by correcting my errors with patience, by providing in my formative years a shining example of good conduct and honest and upright dealings has conferred benefits beyond any other contact in my long life in finance, politics and journalism.

Stairs's influence was indeed greater than Aitken appreciated at the time or even afterwards. For it was Stairs who fixed Aitken's allegiance to the Conservative party. The Aitken family were Conservative, in the sense of attaching importance to the British connexion and being on the side of the Church of Scotland against the Free Church. But there was nothing practical behind this. Max Aitken learnt from Stairs that the Conservatives were the party of capitalist enterprise and Imperial Preference—the two causes in which he himself believed. Hence, when Aitken went to England later, he enrolled automatically as a Conservative without appreciating that Conservatism in the mother country stood also for causes in which he emphatically did not believe, such as inherited wealth and rank, respect for tradition, and all the outlook subsequently called the Establishment. Thanks to Stairs, Aitken found himself tangled up with causes repugnant to his radical nature. This was to give him trouble throughout his political career.

Aitken had little time for a private life in these first hectic years. Nevertheless he began to play Providence to his family. Max Aitken enjoyed making money and fought hard to make it. He also got pleasure from bestowing it on others, especially if they were in distress. There was in him a wide-ranging charity which more than offset the innocent malice of his tongue. The members of his family, childhood friends at Newcastle, and later even politicians who had displayed great hostility to him, learnt the depth of his bounty. No one will ever know the amount of money Aitken gave away, and he gave it without a touch of ostentation or self-praise. As his father wrote to him:

God has prospered your worldly efforts. But the world has evidently got no hold of you: for you seem ever ready to part with your means to your friends.

The Rev. William Aitken was himself the first to benefit. The old minister had been failing for some time. Often he lost the thread of his discourse in the pulpit. According to Beaverbrook's later recollection, the old man's faith was failing also:

> He told me that he had been troubled by orthodoxy for some years, and it would be a relief to him to preach no more. . . . He was ageing, failing—his heart was no longer in his work. Every sermon must have been produced in a panic, with endless fears and hesitations.[1]

His father's troubles made a great impression on Beaverbrook. In 1919 he described them to Arnold Bennett who saw in them the stuff for a novel: the old Calvinist with his faith crumbling, and consoled by the comfortable, even luxurious, life which his worldly son provided.[2]

The picture seems to have been another creation of Beaverbrook's romantic imagination. Having imagined, correctly, his father's physical failings, he went on to imagine how he himself would have felt if he had been a preacher who had lost his faith. There is good evidence that the Rev. William Aitken's faith remained secure. In the last years of his life, when he could no longer climb the hill to the Presbyterian church, he regularly took Holy Communion in the Episcopalian church near his house. It is inconceivable that, with his strict theological training, he would have done this if his faith had been shaken. His letters to his son also continue to show an orthodox devotion, though touched with a worldly wisdom which Max Aitken must have appreciated. Thus he wrote on 13 November 1903:

> I hope you are getting on well in Halifax, attending Church regularly, and in everything and at all times behaving as a good Christian. That is the only way, I am fully persuaded, to be trusted and loved in the secular life and in all its affairs.

Again, in almost his last letter, on 28 April 1911:

> I would earnestly advise you to join your Church and to attend your Church. This, above all else, will insure to you the esteem, confidence and trust of your fellow men.

Max Aitken did not take his father's advice and perhaps imagined his father's loss of faith as some consolation for himself. Probably the one bit of truth was in the remark of his father's which he reports: "I am grateful beyond telling that I will never have to preach another damn sermon"— though even here it is unlikely that the old minister used the word "damn".

[1] This passage from My Early Life does not appear in the published version.
[2] Bennett, Journals, ii, 254–55.

Nor, though he lived well, is it likely that he got through $55,000—the sum Beaverbrook mentioned to Bennett.

The congregation at St. James's were growing impatient with their minister. They could offer a retiring pension of only $200 a year. Max stepped in and added another $600. William Aitken doubted whether his son was a steady source of income and asked for a capital sum. Max first promised $10,000 and then urged that this sum—"the tools of my trade" —would be more profitably employed in his own concerns. The old man came to Halifax and was convinced. He wrote: "You are doing well— *that* I could plainly see". William Aitken retired and said to his son: "I am gazing into the evening mists, happy". Max did all he could to increase this happiness. He built a house for his father, who named it Torphichen.[1] Later he arranged for his parents to spend each winter in South Carolina or Florida and provided a private railway carriage—then the height of luxury and a mode of travel which his father particularly enjoyed. Amidst all his business activities, Max always found time to care for his parents. A cable to Miss de Gruchy, the first of his long-suffering secretaries, is characteristic: "Degruchy I rely upon you to see that my father and mother have everything they want and that their bank account is constantly maintained" (12 November 1910). And again: "Spare neither time nor effort and give them every attention in the world. I think you clearly understand this and I should like you to write to me saying that you do". (15 November 1910).

Aitken's charity extended to all the members of his family. He paid for the education of his two youngest sisters, Jean and Laura, and helped his brothers in their careers or maintained them when they fell ill. Though he never refused a request and indeed often anticipated one, he liked to know how his money was being spent and tried to impose on others a financial precision which he never achieved in his own private affairs. He wrote in his earliest surviving letter to Jean (23 December 1902):

> I think you had better perhaps keep a memorandum of your expenditure after you come back again and send it up to me once a month or so, as it is not well for little girls to become careless about the expenditure of money, although you understand I think you are an economical little girl, and it is not a question of amount but a matter of carefulness in making expenditures.

Beaverbrook himself commented on this in old age:

> My letter to her, not even written in my own hand, is interesting as an example of pomposity in prosperity and indeed early evidence of money-grubbing propensities not at all attractive in youth or old age either.

[1] The house cost Max Aitken $1,000. After his parents' death, he sold it for $7,000 and distributed the money among the Presbyterian churches of Newcastle.

His letters to his brothers and sisters are all of this pattern. All contain gifts of money; all are signed Yours faithfully W. M. Aitken; all demand precise accounts which he never received, and on which he never in fact insisted. Thus to Rahno, on 11 December 1905, after complaining that he had had to provide extra money for Laura's schooling:

I do not wish you to take this letter as meaning that I wish Laura to cut down any expenses at all but I wish to be kept more fully informed of matters of this nature than I have been in the past.

To Arthur, at the end of 1906:

Of course, you understand that I do not wish to assist you to extravagances.

To Allan, 11 March 1907:

Please make ample allowance for your living expenses, after you have investigated the cost, but on no account indulge in extravagances.

Miss de Gruchy writes to Allan, 19 December 1908:

Mr. Aitken wishes you to understand that you are only to go to California, subject to the following condition:
You must write Mr. Aitken once a week, keeping him fully advised of your condition.
Mr. Aitken will supply you with what money you require, and you *must* send an accounting of same every week. In this connection, Mr. Aitken does not wish you to do without things as you did in Toronto, but to call on him for all necessary expenses.

These admonitions bore little fruit. Miss de Gruchy was soon writing to Allan, 11 March 1909:

With regard to the disbursements which Mr. Aitken is making from time to time on behalf of the several members of the family, on making an approximate estimate per year, we find that this totals about $5,000. Now, it would appear that for this amount of money more could be obtained than at present.

Then another letter of complaint (Miss de Gruchy to Allan, 10 May 1909):

The last letter I have received from you is dated April 19. Mr. Aitken understood when you left Montreal that you were to write to me once a week, even if you had no expense account to enclose.

Max Aitken himself broke out to Miss de Gruchy in despair (12 November 1910):

All I can say is—it costs me per minute more than anybody else to live. Is there no way of cutting down this enormous expense? I am quite sure I spend very little of it myself. Good management will save a great deal of money.

Aitken never achieved this good management. Though he loved every kind of new device, he had the opposite of green fingers with them. His cars broke down; his telephone wires got crossed. His office expenses mounted, despite his insistence on using cheap stationery. His servants were for ever going off. His suits did not fit. He wrote to a Montreal tailor on 20 September 1904:

I have decided to pay you for this suit, and if you will send me your account I will forward a cheque, but do not send the suit back again because ill-fitting clothes only worry me, and I have enough things which one has to worry about without worrying about things which are not absolutely necessary.

Max Aitken had plenty to worry about in 1904. John F. Stairs had started him on the road to success and had set him a shining example. But the example did not last long—perhaps Aitken treasured it afterwards for that reason. In the autumn of 1904 Stairs died suddenly from a heart attack. He had been planning a merger of local banks and had invested heavily in the People's Bank of Halifax. Its affairs were in bad shape, partly owing to forgeries and frauds by one considerable client. Those associated with Stairs seemed to be in danger. A friend said to Aitken: "Get back to the Insurance Rate Book. There is your hope for years to come". Aitken refused to surrender. He and Stairs's executors offered the People's Bank to the Bank of Montreal, the senior and most powerful bank in the Dominion. Sir Edward Clouston, the general manager, bid a ruinous price. Then he relented and said: "Send me back the little fellow with the big head". Clouston and Aitken made a satisfactory bargain. Stairs's estate was saved. Aitken himself shouldered over one quarter of his dead patron's liabilities—a gesture which enhanced his reputation in Halifax. The meeting with Clouston was of great importance for Aitken's future. The Bank of Montreal was the stronghold of financial orthodoxy. A little later when Aitken burst into Montreal as an outsider, it was no small advantage for him to have in Clouston an ally within the walls.

Despite this success, Aitken's position in Halifax and at Royal Securities Corporation changed markedly for the worse with Stairs's death. John F. Stairs had given Aitken a free hand. Stairs's brother and other associates, who now took over his holdings, did not show the same patience. They were stolid elderly men who would not treat Aitken as an equal. They disliked his pushing irregular ways. Beaverbrook wrote towards the end of his life:

I was too fond of using the shillelagh in business when milder methods would have served my purpose as well. Intolerant of opposition, I sometimes rode roughshod over obstacles when there might have been an easy way round. Hence that myth of stern methods and a merciless nature, which sometimes shrouded the peak of my reputation with a cloud of mist.[1]

Here indeed is the explanation of the distrust and hostility which Aitken so often aroused in Halifax, as Beaverbrook did in later life.

Aitken's associates were constantly demanding higher dividends from Royal Securities Corporation, whereas Aitken, already true to a practice which he followed all his life, wanted to keep the money in the corporation for further investment. Nova Scotia Steel and Iron, their principal undertaking, was itself short of money. R. E. Harris, one of the Halifax group, suggested that Aitken should agree to raise the money and couple this with the condition that Harris should succeed John F. Stairs as President. In exchange, Harris would make Aitken a director. Aitken kept his bargain. Harris became President and did not keep his. He did not make Aitken a director.

Harris's ingratitude threw Aitken into "a real bout of depression and dismay". But he completed his bargain. He raised over one million dollars for Nova Scotia at a profit to himself of $200,000. This was an unusual sort of revenge. Beaverbrook wrote in his autobiography: "My confidence was restored". This was not true. Aitken had lost his sure support. He was never happy in the society of men who criticized and depreciated him. Not surprisingly he had his first serious bout of illness. He imagined he had heart disease. His doctor told him firmly:

> Your condition is wholly brought about by overwork and hallucinations, with possibly too great business strain at the time of the death of the late Mr. Stairs and events which followed it that winter.

Aitken had in fact again reached a dead end. Once more luck, or his own unconscious genius, favoured him. 1905 was a barren exasperating year. When it ended, he found the way to greater adventure in new company and new surroundings.

[1] My Early Life, 135.

CHAPTER TWO

MONTREAL MILLIONAIRE, 1906–10

On 1 January 1906 Max Aitken began to keep a diary. There is little of interest in it except for entries that he had drunk too much champagne—not a complaint ever heard later from Beaverbrook. Like most diaries, Aitken's was not maintained for long. The last entry was on 29 January:

> Will be married at 6 and a half in the Garrison Church. Leaving tonight at nine o'clock. . . . I hope the experiment will be successful. It rests with me. Gladys may pull it through, but she will have a hard time with my terrible temper and stubbornness. She knows what she has undertaken and is confident of the future. Years will tell.

Such doubts often assail men on the eve of matrimony. In Aitken's case they were more justified than usual. He knew in his heart that he would not make a good orthodox husband. The stumbling block was not so much his temper or his stubbornness, though both existed. It was the fault in what was also his greatest virtue: his capacity for intense, though short-lived, concentration.

He could not help switching people on and off according to his mood, just as he switched absolutely from one business or political deal to another. When he needed someone, no trouble was too great for him. When he turned to something else, his closest friends and even his wife ceased to exist for him. He always remained a loner, and marriage did not change his nature. Some twenty years later, Beaverbrook had another shot at defining why he had been unsuited to marriage. He wrote:

> My wife had a more lively interest in me than I had in her. I had my business, my affairs, my liabilities, my difficulties, all pressing on me every hour of the day. I had no time for pleasure, no chance for recreation, and a nervous system under so much pressure that it was by no means attuned to pleasure. In these circumstances, my wife undertook to make my life as easy as possible.

Even more ruthlessly, he made out that he had not been in love:

> I had not married under any very compelling desire for marriage. It had been to some extent a matter of convenience with me. I had been

24

moved by two factors, (1) I was eligible as it is called, and a good deal sought after, and (2) a statement by I. C. Mackintosh that if I was to have a permanent place in Montreal, I must have a family. And so I had made what I thought to be the best marriage. I do not say that I made her life easier for her but I can claim that I made it more interesting and exciting.[1]

Beaverbrook was being unfair to his younger self. His wife, Gladys Drury, was a lovely person in both looks and character; Aitken, always impressionable so far as women were concerned, was surely swept off his feet by her. No doubt there were also practical considerations. From Aitken's point of view, Gladys Drury was a good match. Her father, Colonel (later General) Charles Drury, belonged to one of the most distinguished families in Canada and was the first Canadian to command the Halifax garrison. Gladys Drury, though only nineteen, had a social experience far beyond the range of a Newcastle manse or the financial circles of Halifax. In England the entry of the Aitkens into high society would not have been won so easily without her charm and social gifts. There is also some evidence that the Drury family did not welcome the rough young adventurer at all warmly, until softened later by the flow of his bounty. Such opposition must have heightened Max Aitken's zest.

The honeymoon showed Aitken at his characteristic best and worst. He overwhelmed his bride with lavish gifts such as she had never known before. He gave her a brief taste of gay life in New York. Then he carried her off to the West Indies and spent his time looking at business propositions. A letter of 5 May 1906 to a friend gives some idea of this curious honeymoon:

> While in Cuba, I bought the Puerto Principe Electric Light Co., for the sum of $300,000. I bought 200 acres of land in the City of Camaguey, and 217 acres to the north of Sir Wm. Van Horne's car works. I bought the old Mule Tram franchise, and I acquired the electric railway franchise in an almost completed condition. . . . When the tram lines are constructed they will pass through the lands I have purchased. On account of the congested condition of the population of the City, I expect to make a very large profit out of selling business lots.

On his return, Aitken gave an early example of his capacity to switch his wife on and off. He again fell ill, this time with an inflamed appendix. Fifty years later, he wrote: "My wife watched over me devotedly", and this is what one would expect with any normal married couple. It did not happen with the Aitkens. In 1907 Aitken wrote to a friend who was also ill:

> If anybody worries you, you will have to part with that person for a time until the worry and annoyance passes away. My wife worried me

---

[1] Thirty more years passed. When Beaverbrook came to publish his autobiography, he suppressed entirely the second passage and gave the opening sentence of the first an innocuous form: "My wife had a lively interest in me".

and the worry was entirely caused by her solicitude for my well being, but this got on my nerves, and my doctor was wise enough to send her away while I was left without anything to grumble over and I am satisfied that this hastened my recovery. Subsequently I was mighty glad to have her back again.

Marriage was not the only new departure Aitken made in 1906. He also took the plunge into the greater financial world of Montreal. He had grown too big for the modest pond of Halifax, which offered only the local enterprises of Nova Scotia and the tramways of the West Indies. In Montreal Aitken could really ride the great Canadian boom. Also he resented the staid financiers of Halifax and their disapproval of his push-fulness, resented it all the more when they demanded a large share of his profits. He wanted to break loose from the Stairs and perhaps from the Drurys as well.

The Aitkens established themselves in an apartment house at Montreal. This did not mean that they had a settled married life. Though Aitken made no more business visits to the West Indies, he was constantly on the move between the various financial centres of Canada and the United States: off to Halifax or New York in one direction, and to Toronto or Calgary in the other. Early in 1909 he recorded that he had not spent more than two nights together in Montreal for the last four months. Aitken had built himself a country house across the bay, or Arm, at Halifax, and Gladys was liable to be consigned here for long solitary stretches during the summer months. Even when Max Aitken arrived at the Arm, he soon sailed away on the yacht which he had rented as a sign of his millionaire status—cruises brusquely interrupted in their turn when Aitken was overcome by the boredom of the sea.

Janet, their first child, was born across the Arm in the early summer of 1908. Beaverbrook asserts that Gladys "had insisted on this out-of-the-way place for the birth of her baby". It is more likely that Aitken did not want the turmoil of childbirth added to his business worries in Montreal. He seems also to have assumed that the company of a baby made his own less necessary. On one occasion, Gladys rebelled and cabled that she had moved into an hotel at Halifax. Aitken wired: "What is wrong? Is baby ill?" Gladys replied: "Nothing wrong. Too lonely across the Arm". After this, her stays in Montreal became more prolonged.

Even so, Aitken could never understand that people, especially those close to him, wanted steady, quiet affection rather than a shower of gifts and the occasional excitement of his stimulating company. Gladys Aitken had a rich house with plenty of servants, a motor car, and credit accounts at the principal stores. But she saw little of her husband and, when he appeared, had usually to entertain some tedious Montreal financier also. His flow of generosity still ran over and was now extended to the Drury family. The Rev. William Aitken remained the one on whom Max bestowed the most attention and often in ingenious ways. The old man complained of feeling useless. Max set up a hospital in Newcastle and paid $1,000 a year towards its upkeep on condition his father was made honorary superintendent. By 1909 the old man was also complaining that he was too old and deaf to go south for the winter. Max was determined that he should go. He therefore made out that Allan Aitken, one of his brothers, who was ill, must go south and needed a father's care. At the same time, he told Allan that he must go south in order to look after his father.

Allan duly took charge. William Aitken, though he went south, was less taken in. The friend in Newcastle, Allan Davidson, who conducted these negotiations and after whom Allan Aitken was named, reported of Max's father: "Words and their real meaning have always been a plaything for him". Davidson, too, benefited from Max's kindly subterfuges, without being deceived by them. He repeatedly received cheques for $1500 or $2000, with the explanation that this was the profit on some share dealing which Max had conducted for him. Finally Davidson broke out:

> Max, what am I to do with you? I know perfectly well that, if the transaction had lost money, I should never have heard of it.

The affectionate expostulation was of no use. Aitken continued to make these profitable deals for the benefit of others. Later, in England, it became his favourite method of bestowing money on his political and literary friends. After all, it is difficult to refuse money which has actually been made on the stock exchange in your name.

When Aitken moved to Montreal, he evidently intended to continue his previous activities by means of Royal Securities Corporation on a larger scale. He soon discovered that he had not escaped from his difficulties by leaving Halifax, had indeed enhanced them. The Halifax shareholders, particularly "that podgy gentleman" R. E. Harris, continued to complain and criticize. They still wanted higher dividends and fuller accounts. They objected that meetings of directors were not held or were abruptly called at Montreal before they had proper notice to attend. Aitken therefore withdrew from Royal Securities Corporation. The Halifax assets and good will were handed over to a new administrator, Gerald Farrell. Aitken's own assets and those of his Montreal associates were transferred to a new body entitled the Bond and Share Company.

At the end of 1906 Aitken also changed his profession, temporarily as it turned out. He ceased to be a company promoter and became instead an investment banker. He acquired the Montreal Trust Company, an old-established and respected house. In this way, he entered more solid banking circles. He now had a considerable concern to administer. According to his own account, he tried to settle down. He worked long hours at the office and took papers home with him in the evening. His surviving records do not confirm this picture. The files are swollen with letters stating: "Mr. Aitken is not at present in the City. He will give an answer on his return". Even when he was in the office, he did not stay long. His letters have another constant refrain of a postscript by his secretary: "Mr. Aitken left the office before the letter was completed, and consequently I have signed same". However even the attempt to observe a routine wore Aitken down, and he later called this "the most absolutely wasted time in my whole career".

Aitken's worries were the greater because he was now handling other people's money instead of his own, and that moreover at an unpropitious time. In the autumn of 1907 there was a brief depression in the United States. Aitken happened to be in New York. He saw queues of depositors outside the banks, and the banks closing their doors. He resolved that he would not run the risk of being harassed himself in the same way. "I did not want to be the victim of caprice, and panic, and rumour and mass fear. . . . It was more comfortable to be in the queue, not behind the grille". His resolve was strengthened when the Montreal Trust Company stagnated throughout 1908. Letters to his three principal employees show his impatience:

> I cannot stand the present disgraceful manner in which we are all handling one of the greatest earning capacities in Canada, and I would rather go out of business than keep in our present career.

> I have had a very bad pain ever since I received the statement of Profit and Loss. . . . All flags are at half mast and I feel the end of the world is at hand.

> If you expect me to remain quiet until such time as the Montreal Trust Company is doing the best bond business at least in Montreal you are very much mistaken.

Sometimes Aitken tried to make light of his anxieties. He wrote to his good banker friend, W. D. Ross, at Toronto:

> The only pleasure I get out of life is the schemeing and planning which goes on from day to day. If there were not bitter disappointments and dogged opposition the game wouldn't be worth playing.

Despite this, he soon finished with the game of banking. In the late summer of 1908 he sold the Montreal Trust Company to a group associated with the Royal Bank. He had paid $400,000. He received $600,000. One episode in the sale showed his rigid integrity. When Aitken bought the company, he examined its assets, but did not look into all those of the trusts which it administered. A little later, he found that the funds in one of these were being misapplied and insisted on putting things right at the cost of an angry dispute with the former President. When Aitken sold the company, he reminded the purchasers that they had not investigated the subsidiary trusts and refused to accept their money until this was done.

Aitken was now again his own master, free to play a lone hand as a company promoter. He reacquired Royal Securities Corporation which had not been doing well since he left it and, with his increased assets, was able to buy out the Halifax shareholders—by 1910 none of them was left. He still had the Bond and Share Company. Another subsidiary, the Montreal Engineering Company, administered the electrical undertakings and tramways which he controlled in the West Indies. He seems however to have conducted much of his affairs for the benefit of a private account, entitled "Aitken special", which he kept at Toronto away from the prying eyes of Montreal. There was nothing sinister about this. Aitken was operating in a tough world and against all the established powers. Whatever bankers might say about respecting the confidence of their clients, the state of Aitken's credit balance was known in Montreal, and his rivals soon learnt when he had drawn on it or built it up. Aitken could take them by surprise when he used funds known only to his friend W. D. Ross of Toronto.

As well Aitken kept money in various accounts for his own convenience in the usual way of financiers. It is after all not an offence, or even a questionable operation, for a financier to run more than one concern. After all these years, it is impossible to disentangle the financial relations of Aitken's various companies, and he himself does not seem to have been clear about it. For instance, in 1911, when the Bond and Share Company had come in for some criticism, Aitken wrote to Dr. Morison of Ashton-under-Lyne:

> Upon going over my books this morning, I find I am not and never was a shareholder in the Bond and Share Company. I thought I had some shares in that Company at one time, but I was wrong. I never had any.

Presumably the Bond and Share Company was controlled by some other Aitken enterprise, and these complications really do not matter. Probably Aitken enjoyed them, as most financiers do. He was the man who made the money whatever the name on the door.

Aitken's activities were now on a larger scale. He had more resources of his own, and his Montreal associates were wealthier and more adventurous men than those in Halifax had been. Aitken also broke into new fields. He had already moved rather cautiously into the New York market. Later in 1908 he went to London for the first time. The initiative for this came from Ion Hamilton Benn, a leading figure in the City and a keen Unionist politician. As an Imperialist and strong Tariff Reformer, Benn was among the first British financiers to appreciate the potentialities of Canada. He came over to survey the prospects. Many years later, he told William Kilbourn, historian of the Steel Company of Canada: "I decided Max was a brainy fellow, so I told him to look me up when he came to London and I would introduce him about, and get him a seat in the House of Commons".[1] Benn was in his nineties when he told this story—he survived to a hale 98 and died only in 1961—and claimed more credit than he deserved. He did not find a seat for himself until 1910, and, if Aitken did indeed offer himself to the Unionist party in 1908 as he alleged to Law in 1910, he met with no response.

However, Benn's patronage was a big break for Aitken even if it had no political significance attached to it. At this time, and even later, London financiers looked askance at Canadian enterprises. When I showed Aitken's early prospectuses to a stockbroker, he replied: "I would not have put a penny into them then, and I doubt if I would now". Hamilton Benn was more far-sighted. He opened the London money market to Aitken and gave him valuable backing. Aitken equipped himself with introductions to wealthy English people and to a few French ones as well. He secured a London quotation for a dozen of his various enterprises. He also followed his old trade of selling bonds—principally Porto Rico Electric and Nova Scotia Steel and Coal. As these were left-overs from his Halifax days, he was presumably clearing his desk of old commitments. Among his many letters of introduction was one to Bonar Law, a powerful figure in the Unionist party. Law, too, was a Canadian by birth, with an Ulster Scot father and a Scotch mother. He too was the son of a New Brunswick manse. Aitken thought this a useful opening and spoke of the Augmentation Fund which had brought his own father to Canada, assuming that James Law had come in the same way. This was a mistake. Apparently Aitken did not appreciate the feud between the Church of Scotland and the Free Church. James Law was in fact a Free Church minister, and Bonar Law was not touched by a reference to the Fund which had been directed against the labours of such men as his father.

The meeting between Aitken and Law therefore was not a success, though Aitken did not understand the cause. He supposed only that Law was bored. He consoled himself with the reflection that Bonar Law's head was the wrong shape and that he could not possibly go far. Law was however more impressed than Aitken later made out. He bought $5000 of Nova Scotia bonds—a larger sum than a shrewd man like Law would pay merely in order to get rid of an unwelcome visitor. Moreover Law

[1] Kilbourn, The Elements Combined, 69.

showed further signs of interest after Aitken had returned to Canada. Hamilton Benn wrote on 25 February 1909:

> I have had some discussion with Mr. Bonar Law lately. He would like to be in with you and me, but he thinks that the General Election is so imminent that it would be impossible for him to join the Board. You know he is sure to get one of the important posts in the next Ministry, and ministers in England are not allowed to hold any directorships. He wishes, however, to take a substantial interest in the Company, and both he and I would like to have a share with you in the Royal Securities Corporation on the lines that you discussed with me in December—that is to say, we would like to be in your inner circle.

The letter is incidentally evidence of Unionist hopes early in 1909. With the great dispute over the building of more dreadnoughts at its height, they were confident of electoral victory—a confidence in fact belied when the general election of January 1910 was fought instead on the issue of the People's Budget. It is not surprising that the Unionists were thereafter embittered and violent.

Benn's proposal was an awkward one for Aitken to be faced with. His enthusiasm had run away with him, as often happened. When Aitken was putting over a proposition, the sky was the limit. Anyone whom Aitken was trying to captivate was taken up to a high place and shown all the kingdoms of the earth. Many a journalist in later years heard from Beaverbrook the phrase: "If you work for me, your wife will soon be wearing mink". Of course this only meant that Beaverbrook paid good salaries. Similarly, in his financial dealings, Aitken always offered attractive bargains, but not the limitless wealth which he spoke of in his opening remarks. He could not resist putting a romantic glow on every transaction and was then caught out when others took him seriously. Benn himself often experienced this and was bewildered by it. Throughout 1909 and 1910 his firm received a good deal of Aitken's London business. At the same time, his correspondence with Aitken is full of complaints that other London firms were receiving more, whereas he had expected that he would have more or less a monopoly. Aitken could only reply that he had worked satisfactorily with the other firms for a long time and could not break with them as Benn wanted. Later on, the break came in fact with Benn, though in an amicable way.

In 1909 Aitken was eager to be associated with Benn and still more with Law. He could not afford to offend or disappoint them. On the other hand, he did not want anyone breaking into his newly-established control of Royal Securities Corporation and perhaps repeating the interference which he had suffered from the financiers of Halifax. He devised an ingenious escape. He set up yet another concern, Utility Securities Corporation. Aitken, Benn, and Law each put in $100,000, and Aitken

ensured that profitable business came its way. Two years later, the
Corporation had served its turn. Aitken was now securely established in
Law's friendship, and the Corporation was wound up. Each partner
received $200,000, all of it really earned by Aitken. He had talked himself
into a difficult situation and got out of it by paying Danegeld, though
with some profit for himself.

There were other episodes of the same kind in Aitken's career at this
time. Both Nesbitt and Killam, Aitken's principal agents in Royal
Securities Corporation, were aggrieved that the prospect of their becoming partners was not fulfilled, though in Killam's case it ultimately was
to his very great profit. R. B. Bennett, who did much work for Aitken in
western Canada, also complained that he was poorly rewarded compared
to others. He wrote to Aitken on 17 February 1914:

> I really do not propose to continue my business relations with your
> corporation on the basis of receiving anything from you as a matter of
> grace and favour. Business is business and is always best conducted upon
> the understanding that definite promises involve definite results. . . . I
> am more concerned about having a good name and big assets than a big
> name and small assets.

Aitken did not reply to this letter, and Bennett continued to work for
him.

The case of C. H. Cahan is of special interest, in view of Beaverbrook's
comments on it at the end of his life. Cahan was a leading lawyer in
Halifax and one of the men who had started Aitken off in Royal Securities
Corporation. Later he became secretary of state in a Conservative Canadian government. Clearly he was a man of both judgement and capacity.
During 1909 Cahan handled all the legal work for Aitken's dealings which
were then at their height. He was well paid for his work, but believed
that he had been promised more—a share in the profits or even a partnership in Royal Securities Corporation. In 1911 he pursued Aitken to
England and wrote long, aggrieved letters from his hotel. Aitken gave no
answer beyond a brief acknowledgement. When the two met, Cahan
could produce no firm evidence to justify his claims. He had to fall back
on the impressions of lavish reward which he had received. Ultimately
Aitken paid him $50,000, debiting half to Royal Securities Corporation
and finding the rest from his own pocket. In 1964 Beaverbrook reviewed
the file and wrote on it:

> He was well paid.
> His legal fees were large—too large for that age.
> After I left Canada for the House of Commons here, he made this black-
> mailing attempt on me.
> His demand represented claims to many millions of dollars.

He accepted $50,000. . . . I paid this amount, as it was evident costs would run far beyond the small sum I proposed to pay Cahan.

He often tried to find a way to restore himself to our favour again—but once was enough.

Actually, Aitken's bark was worse than his bite, particularly when he only barked fifty years afterwards. Cahan continued to do Aitken's work in Halifax, and their correspondence was maintained on a friendly basis. Essentially Aitken was a fixer, a man of negotiation and compromise. He often stormed in private, but on the day of action he preferred to settle.

1909 and the early part of 1910 were the heyday of Aitken's financial achievements. These brought him great wealth and also some opprobrium. Where previously he had been content with the West Indies and Nova Scotia, all Canada now became his field of operations. His ceaseless travels taught him that Canada could be treated as an economic unit instead of being a collection of separate provinces. Existing concerns of the same kind could be brought together with immediate economies in specialization, purchase of raw materials, and division of markets. Increased profits would follow almost at once. Moreover these new larger concerns would at last be able to face the competition from their greater American rivals, particularly if they were protected by Canadian tariffs. Here was the case for the mergers which Aitken inspired. He ranged wide. He merged the cast-iron trade and said: "Everyone who buys an enamelled iron pan in Canada pays tribute to me". He merged the manufacture of freight cars. He merged grain elevators and hydro-electric stations in the west. His agent here was none other than R. B. Bennett, his former mentor, who now himself became a rich man thanks to Aitken's patronage.

Aitken profited from these mergers in three ways. He acquired options to buy the existing companies and sold these options at a profit to the new amalgamation which he created. He sold the bonds and preferred stock of the new company, again with a good commission. He held on to the ordinary stock which had at first little market value and gradually sold it as the profits rose. Of course he did not retain all the ordinary stock. In a single year he created companies with a capital of over one hundred million dollars, and these transactions were too big for him to handle alone. He worked with syndicates of friends, and his associates also received a good bonus of ordinary stock on their sales. Still, it is a fair guess that Aitken secured something like a third of the ordinary stock for himself. He rarely sat on the board of any company which he had created, though he usually took care to put on some reliable nominees. He himself wanted fresh action. In his own words: "I am a builder. When the building is finished I do not stay in it but move on to another".

Aitken denied that he was the J. P. Morgan of Canada. He said: "Morgan had failures. I have had none". There was another, more important difference. Morgan promoted monopolies and aroused the United States to an orgy of trust-busting. Aitken promoted mergers. He always left some leading companies outside his amalgamation. He said that he did so in order to stimulate competition and to have some standard of comparison. He was also anxious to keep out of political trouble, though in this he did not succeed. The economic life of Canada was divided into two conflicting factions, which corresponded roughly to the two political parties, Liberal and Conservative. The Liberals were the party of wheat-farmers, merchants, railwaymen, and shippers: all those who looked for profit to Canada's world market. They wanted cheap industrial goods at home and did not mind if these were American. Hence the Liberals favoured low tariffs or none at all and were advocating Reciprocity with the United States.

The Conservatives were the party of Canadian industry and, in so far as it was concerned with industry, of Canadian finance. They wanted tariff protection against the United States and did not repine if this put up the price of industrial goods in Canada. They needed something more than a selfish appeal and therefore had to talk "British". They were indeed traditionally the party of the British connection. In practice this meant little to them. Of course they welcomed easy access to the London capital market, but they had no more desire to be under-cut by British goods than by American. "Imperial Preference" was a slogan they used against the United States, not in favour of Great Britain. The Liberals, on the other hand, might really have been captured for Imperial Preference if only this had involved a British tariff on foreign wheat. Beaverbrook was to learn these complications at bitter cost in his later days, when he launched his campaign for Empire Free Trade.

In 1909 Aitken had no difficulty in bestowing his political allegiance. His early associates had been Conservative: John F. Stairs, Bennett, and Borden. He now moved among Conservative industrialists. The Liberals made him a target for their criticism. They used the jealousy of humble men against the wealth which he was amassing. They alleged that his mergers forced up Canadian prices. Aitken answered that he was defending Canadian independence against American encroachments. His British patriotism was undoubtedly genuine. New Brunswick had been founded by United Empire Loyalists who left the United States after the American revolution, and Aitken had been nourished among their traditions. His family links were with Scotland, not with the United States, and his sister Rahno sacrificed an important position rather than fly the Stars and Stripes over her hospital. Aitken did not in fact know much about the British Empire, most of which he never visited. For that matter, he exaggerated the British character even of Canada. His Empire was really an association between Newcastle and Torphichen. It had a reality in his mind all the same.

At any rate Aitken wished to justify himself on an anti-American ticket. His first political venture was in the battle over Reciprocity which was now beginning. He founded The Canadian Century, a rather ineffective intellectual weekly. He also sought to buy The Montreal Gazette, the only morning newspaper in Montreal printed in English. Later Beaverbrook alleged that he had already a vision of himself as a great newspaper proprietor and speculated what might have been if he had fulfilled this vision in Canada instead of in London. However these visions do not seem to have occurred to him at the time. He simply wanted an instrument of publicity in which he could preach the cause of Canadian independence and the value of mergers. The Montreal Gazette was controlled by the Bank of Montreal and the Canadian Pacific Railway, and these two forbade the sale to Aitken. The Bank of Montreal was itself largely controlled by the CPR, or at least a number of CPR directors sat on its board. The opposition of the CPR was decisive.

This opposition was not surprising. The CPR was by far the greatest undertaking in Canada. Not only was it a great railway. It also owned much land adjoining its tracks. Included in this land were coal mines, mineral deposits, power plants, and railway workshops, to say nothing of building lots. The CPR looked with a jealous eye on the new mergers and on the thrusting adventurer who had created them. Moreover, unlike most Canadian industry, the CPR was Liberal. Despite its many industrial undertakings, its greatest wealth came from the transport of wheat. In its view, there should be only one great concern in Canada: the Canadian Pacific Railway. Apart from this, the CPR and its great men were on the side of the farmers against the industrialists and financiers.

The CPR was a formidable antagonist for Aitken to face. In April 1909 something like a miracle occurred. The gates of the CPR citadel opened before him. The son of Sir Sandford Fleming and two associates invited Aitken to arrange a merger of three cement companies in which they were interested. Sir Sandford Fleming, though now a very old man, was still the greatest figure in the CPR and a great figure in Canadian politics also. He had directed the construction and financing of the railway; he had led the movement for confederation in 1867; he had championed Standard Time. Now this legendary figure was actually asking Aitken to perform a service. Aitken saw himself secure in the favour of the CPR. He also reflected that Sir Sandford Fleming's name would make the floating of the merger easier and more profitable. Aitken agreed to carry through the merger if the financial conditions were satisfactory, and C. H. Cahan began the necessary enquiries.

In August 1909 Aitken received further encouragement, this time from Sir Edward Clouston, manager of the Bank of Montreal. Clouston, too, was interested in the cement merger and would support it if Aitken vouched that everything was satisfactory. This was a stroke of fortune more miraculous still. Aitken would be organizing a merger with the backing of the Bank of Montreal. The terms would be still more favourable, and the approval of respectable Montreal for Aitken would be thrown in as a bonus. Aitken turned all his attention to the cement affair. Naturally he regarded it as a Fleming venture and indeed proposed to make one of the Fleming group general manager of the new concern.

At this moment Cahan returned from the west with grave news: there was something wrong on the Fleming side. One of the three companies which they wished to sell, at Exshaw in Alberta, was in bad shape. It had been floated in 1905 at an excessive figure. Among other things, land bought by one of Fleming's associates for $40,000 had been credited to him for $1,250,000 in the belief that it contained coal. It contained none. Exshaw had run consistently at a loss. To meet the interest on its mortgage bonds, Fleming and his associates had borrowed $100,000 from the Bank of Montreal on their personal security and, when the bank refused any further advance, had got the CPR to back them in obtaining $200,000 more. Now they were calculating that the merger would take over both the bankrupt company and its debts. Fleming, the experienced old financier, perhaps himself now the cat's paw of others, was proposing to take the young financier Aitken for a ride.

A terrible situation. If Aitken backed down, he would offend Fleming and his friends in the CPR. He would forfeit the patronage of the Bank of Montreal. He would also lose a highly profitable operation. On the other hand, to bring Exshaw into the merger would be a swindle on the public, totally against Aitken's financial code and disastrous for his reputation when the true situation came out as it was bound to do. Aitken faced the crisis with remarkable ingenuity. He swamped the Fleming interests by bringing into the merger virtually every cement company in Canada outside British Columbia—thirteen companies all told instead of the original three. He quietly forgot his earlier proposal to make a Fleming associate general manager and secured instead Frank P. Jones, then manager of a steel works in Nova Scotia. Jones was a man of outstanding ability who subsequently became, in Beaverbrook's words, "the leader of industry in Canada". He was promised the then fabulous salary of $50,000 a year. By November 1909 Aitken held options on all the cement companies. The ensuing issue of bonds and stock in the Canada Cement Company, which of course Aitken handled, was the largest to have been made in Canada. The issue went over, though only just. It was a great help that Sir Sandford Fleming had agreed to become president of the

Company. Aitken thus made skilful use of Fleming's name, and Fleming no doubt assumed on his side that he had brought off his shady deal.

The new board met early in 1910. On it were representatives of the old companies and also leading industrialists and bankers. Aitken was not a member of the board. Jones duly reviewed the options which Aitken had acquired. The board took them all with one exception. Exshaw was turned down. The decision was unanimous. Even Fleming at first acquiesced. After all, he too was making a good profit from the sale of his other companies and in the bond and stock issue. Aitken had probably prepared the stroke with Jones beforehand or maybe he relied on its emerging of itself from the figures. At any rate he had done what he had set out to do: he had used Fleming's prestige and had not been gulled over Exshaw. Moreover Aitken, in his usual way, was ready to temper the blow. When Fleming began to grumble, Aitken persuaded the board to offer a compromise: the Canada Cement Company would take over Exshaw, though at a lower figure than that proposed in the option, and would pay Fleming $50,000 if he would sign a letter declaring that he was completely satisfied. Fleming signed the letter and then repudiated it.

Even now the board was conciliatory. They offered Fleming an investigation by two independent lawyers. The investigation was made, and the lawyers reported that everything had been done correctly. At this Fleming resigned from the board, pushed into action by his younger associates. He was in a difficult position. His grievance, however unfounded, was against the board of the Canada Cement Company, in that it had refused to take up the option on Exshaw. There was nothing he could do about this. Therefore he tried to blackmail Aitken by exploiting the general unpopularity of mergers. He alleged that Aitken, by organizing the merger, had raised the price of cement—a cry which appealed to the Canadian farmers. He further alleged that Aitken had made an excessive profit—a cry which appealed to everyone except those who had shared in the profit.

It is impossible to give a clear answer about the price of cement. What the merger did was to make the price uniform throughout Canada. It therefore raised the price in some districts and lowered it in others. Moreover the merger lessened the fluctuations in price over the years. The price was higher than it had been in 1908, a year of depression, but it remained stable in the boom years which followed. Some consumers suffered in the short run. Over a longer period everyone benefited.

The allegation about excessive profit is easier to answer. For once Aitken left a precise record, when provoked to do so by the storm which broke later. On the initial acquisition of options and their subsequent sale to the new company, he made $76,000, though some of this went on legal expenses. On the sale of bonds and stock, he made $272,000, and his associates in the syndicate made some $400,000 more. This was not an unreasonable profit by the standards of the time, on a turnover of $16,500,000. Aitken's profit however seemed much larger to the financially-innocent who did not appreciate, as many people still do not, that the value of a share is what a buyer will pay for it and not the nominal sum inscribed on its face. Aitken bought the companies for $16,500,000 and issued bonds and stock to the nominal value of $30,000,000. It could therefore be alleged that he had made an undisclosed profit of $13,500,000. This profit was imaginary. Jones, when challenged, gave the following figures:

Bonds $5,000,000 issued at 90	$4,500,000
Preferred Stock $10,500,000 issued at 85–90	$8,925,000
Ordinary Stock $13,500,000 issued at 30	$3,600,000
	$17,025,000

It is clear what had happened. It had been intended that the bonds and preferred stock would be almost enough to meet the purchase price of the old companies. The ordinary stock was designed as a free bonus, according to the usual practice of the time, issued to those who helped with the selling of the bonds and preferred stock. But these proved impossible to sell at par. The underwriters, Aitken and his associates, had to fill the gap out of their own pockets and thus often paid $30 for each $100 of ordinary stock instead of getting it free. Even this put too good a face on things. The bonds and preferred stock absorbed all the current profits. Nothing was left over for a dividend on the ordinary stock. In 1911 this stock was quoted at $15, and there were few buyers. Of course Aitken and his friends made big profits later when the Canada Cement Company prospered. Aitken himself sold his ordinary stock in 1928 at prices ranging between $500 and $800. Such, under capitalism, are the rewards of risk and enterprise. These rewards could have been shared by anyone prepared to risk $15 in 1911—and no one was. Aitken did not make an excessive profit in the present. He gambled on Canada's future and won.

In the early months of 1910 these controversies were still far off. The Canada Cement Company was in its first glow, and Sir Sandford Fleming was its president. But the general grumble against Aitken's mergers was already starting. A leading member of the Canadian Liberal government warned Aitken that, if he conducted further mergers, he would "incur strictures". Aitken resolved to lie low for a time. He even told his friends that, being now a rich man, he was giving up business altogether. He was often to make similar declarations later. Once more however an opportunity was thrust upon him, and he could not resist taking it. The opening came in an even greater industry than cement. It was in the world of steel.

Montreal Rolling Mills was the leading firm in the steel-finishing industry, controlled by William McMaster, now an old man. It was a strong, flourishing company, but it had increasing difficulties in acquiring adequate supplies of steel from the primary producers. McMaster tried half-heartedly at a link with one such producer and failed to get it. He could not understand this new talk of mergers and was anxious to sell out. Sir Edward Clouston heard the news and passed it to Aitken. Aitken was the more stirred into action when he learnt that United States Steel Corporation were also in the market. He determined to save the Canadian steel industry from American control. He knew nothing about steel himself, as indeed he knew nothing about any of the industries he merged. He knew only how to assess a bargain and where to go for the right advice. He borrowed Frank P. Jones from cement for the week-end, and together they inspected Montreal Rolling Mills. After two days of enquiry, Aitken bought the company at McMaster's price: $4,200,000.

This was not an option. It was a firm purchase. Aitken had to raise the money. Where should he raise it? Sir Edward Clouston, manager of the Bank of Montreal, said to him: "We will loan you the money. But don't take it. Borrow the whole of the purchase price in Great Britain". Aitken did not need this warning. He knew that there were forces hostile to him in the Bank of Montreal, particularly among those directors who were friends of Sir Sandford Fleming's. Besides, he wanted to keep his control of Montreal Rolling Mills a secret until he sat down with other steel magnates at the conference table and, if he borrowed a large sum from the Bank of Montreal, someone would be sure to talk. He therefore took Sir Edward Clouston's advice. Evidently he felt he needed some moral support. Though their son Max had been born in February, he proposed that his wife should accompany him. His account is characteristically complacent:

> She informed me that her duty to her husband conflicted with her devotion to her young daughter and newborn son. She must make a sacrifice. And I was not the victim.

Max and Gladys Aitken sailed for England late in April 1910. They remained in London only a week. Aitken duly borrowed $5,000,000 from Parr's Bank—later a constituent of the Westminster Bank. He pledged his personal securities and showed his gratitude by keeping his account at Westminster Bank until 1955.[1] He also found time to call again on Bonar Law. Their meeting was however little warmer than their previous one.

[1] Westminster Bank then refused Beaverbrook a temporary overdraft of £40,000 on the plea that a credit squeeze was in operation. Beaverbrook at once transferred all his London business, including a deposit account of £700,000 in the Jersey branch of the Westminster Bank, to the Royal Bank of Canada.

At this moment Aitken's mind was too full of financial matters for him
to think of anything else.

In May he was back in Montreal and ready to bargain with the other
steel companies. This was a new sort of merger for him. Previously he
had been on the outside of the industry he was merging and merely
cajoled others into coming together. This time he was himself a principal
and wanted a good price for Montreal Rolling Mills as well as the profit
from subsequent selling of bonds. The steel-masters had been trained in a
hard school. Two of the most powerful were associated also with the CPR
and were determined not to be outsmarted by the young interloper,
Aitken, as Fleming had been. The bargaining was long and rough. At
one moment, the participants moved to an hotel in New York, so as to
escape the distractions of Montreal society. Aitken demanded for his
mills one-third of the equity and $5,000,000, to be met of course from the
sale of bonds. Failing this, he threatened to negotiate with other steel
firms or even with United States Steel.

His prospective partners were outraged. They made no difficulty about
the third of the equity—this was mere speculation on the future. But they
complained that Aitken was demanding a million dollars profit for a
company which he had only owned for a couple of months. He should be
content to recover what he had paid and make his usual profits from the
sale of bonds and shares. Aitken waited for the storm to subside and then
offered what seemed to be an attractive compromise. He would accept
four million dollars on account—actually less than he had paid—and the
Montreal Rolling Mills should be examined by independent valuers.
Then the new company would pay him the difference or, if the valuation
proved to be less than four million dollars, he would repay the company.
The others were delighted. They imagined that they had won. Agreement was duly signed. In reality Aitken had made a sure-fire bargain.
He knew that the Mills could not conceivably be valued at less than four
million dollars and, even if he only got his money back, he would still
have the prospect of selling bonds profitably on a big scale. But he also
had a shrewd idea that the Mills were worth more than four million dollars,
particularly as the merger could not flourish without them.

Late in June the steel men met again to receive the valuers' report.
The answer: a little over six million dollars.[1] Most of them agreed wryly
that they must pay this sum. The two CPR men were determined to fight.
They knew that Aitken had not sold securities largely on the market.
Therefore, they argued, he must have obtained a credit from the Bank of
Montreal, and there were enough CPR directors of the bank to have his

---

[1] In telling the story later, Beaverbrook varied from saying that he had bought at
four million dollars and sold at seven to saying that he had bought at five million and
sold at six. The correct figures are as stated in the text.

credit withdrawn. Then Aitken would be unable to complete his purchase of the Montreal Rolling Mills and would have to moderate his terms. The directors of the bank met. They called for Aitken's account. There they discovered that, far from being overdrawn, Aitken had a credit balance of five million dollars. Due to legal delays, the transfer of ownership had not been completed and Aitken had not yet paid over the money, but Montreal Rolling Mills were indisputably his. The CPR men were beaten. Aitken's terms were met, and on 17 July 1910 the Steel Company of Canada came into existence. It proved a profitable venture, like all Aitken's undertakings. Fifty years later, its shares were worth sixty times their original price. In addition Aitken at the outset had made two million dollars in cash without actually owning the Montreal Rolling Mills for a single day.

On the evening of 17 July 1910 Aitken and his wife left Montreal for New York on their way to England. This was momentous. They were never to take up permanent residence in Canada again. In later years, the move came to appear conscious and premeditated. On the one side, Aitken was alleged to have fled from the storm which had been provoked by his mergers, particularly in cement. Lord Northcliffe is reported to have said: "Max only just got away in time from the arm of the law". On the other side, Beaverbrook made out that he had taken a clear decision to abandon finance for politics and to become the champion of Empire Free Trade in Great Britain. Both stories are mythical. Far from being unpopular in Canada, Aitken was greatly admired and respected, even by the financiers whom he had worsted. The row over cement came into the open only in 1911 and even then was confined to a few Liberals. The most preposterous version has it that Aitken dared not return to Canada for many years. In fact, he made repeated business visits between 1911 and 1914 and—a further proof of his standing in Canada—became Canadian military representative in Great Britain during the first world war.

Beaverbrook's own claim that he knew what he intended to do is equally unfounded. There is not a shadow of contemporary evidence that he meant to leave finance or to enter British politics. He was certainly in a hurry to leave Montreal on 17 July 1910. This was not because he was leaving business. It was because he had an appointment at Saratoga on the following day with Sir William Price, head of a great pulp and paper concern. At this meeting, Aitken agreed to sell five million dollars of Price Brothers bonds in London—hardly a withdrawal from business. For that matter, Aitken's financial initiatives in Canada between 1912 and 1914, though less publicized, were larger than either the cement or the steel merger.

Nor did this appear a suitable moment to enter British politics. A general election had been held in January 1910 and, in the ordinary course

of events, another would not be held for four or five years. If Aitken had
his eye on politics at all, it was in Canada, where a general election was
impending in 1911. Even this cannot be sustained from the record: he
had made no political contacts at all except with his old friends such as
Bennett. It seems far more likely that Aitken went to London, as he had
done before, simply to sell bonds, though on a bigger scale. He once
said as much himself to William Kilbourn: "I walked much about the
City of London that summer telling over and over the story of the Steel
Company of Canada. A bond issue wasn't sold in five minutes in those
days".[1] As he also had Price Brothers to sell, he must have been kept
busy. He clearly meant to return to Montreal. He had kept his house there,
and his wife went home in September. Events took an unexpected turn
only in the autumn, and Aitken was caught up in them. Once more: "I
did not make situations; I turned them to account".

[1] Kilbourn, The Elements Combined, 79.

CHAPTER THREE

UNIONIST MP, 1910–11

In July 1910 Max Aitken was unknown in England except among a small circle of financiers. By the end of the year he had made a sensational entry into British politics. His finances merged into politics almost by accident. While threshing around in lonely boredom during the summer, he bought the controlling shares in Rolls-Royce, which were on offer after the death of Charles Rolls, one of the founders, in an air accident. Aitken, in his usual fashion, kept off the board. To represent him, he put on a city acquaintance, Edward Goulding, later Lord Wargrave and at this time MP for Worcester—a nomination which he had won against the competition of the then unknown Stanley Baldwin.

Aitken's control of Rolls-Royce brought him an unexpected acquaintance, the full importance of which he did not then appreciate. Northcliffe, the greatest press lord of the time, was interested in Rolls-Royce as he was in Westminster Abbey or The Times newspaper—a great British institution which must, he thought, be preserved. He at once arranged to meet Aitken and offered his cooperation in Rolls-Royce affairs. Their early correspondence was entirely devoted to this topic. Northcliffe did not foresee that Aitken himself would ever become a press man, nor for that matter did Aitken himself. But Northcliffe noted Aitken's quick judgement and grasp of politics and was soon quoting him as an authority on Canadian matters.

Apart from this Rolls-Royce played no great part in Aitken's life. A couple of years later, he grew impatient with the company's leisurely output of luxury motor cars and demanded that it go over to mass production. When the board resisted, Aitken sold out at a considerable profit to J. B. Duke, the American tobacco magnate, who in time made a greater profit still. Goulding remained chairman of Rolls-Royce until his death in 1936 and was duly grateful to Aitken. The political connection between the two men had more permanent results. Goulding, though primarily a financier, was also a keen politician and at this time head of the Tariff Reform League. Like other back-bench Unionists, he was impatient with the negations of official policy—"anti-Parliament Bill, anti-Home

43

Rule, anti-Welsh Disestablishment". He wanted to revive Joseph Chamberlain's combination of Imperial Preference and Social Reform. Aitken echoed him: "The Radical section of the Unionist party must prevail or Lloyd George will predominate".

It is impossible to trace more precisely how Aitken added politics to his financial activities. City men at this time often went into parliament as a side-line. Hamilton Benn was in, Goulding was in, and Aitken's first political promotion seems to have been for Otto Kahn, an American banker-friend of his, not for himself. Aitken negotiated with the Unionist party in Gorton on Kahn's behalf and apparently also projected that Kahn, not himself, should become a backer of The Daily Express. When Kahn changed his mind and departed for New York, Aitken took over this unfinished business.

Nor was it unusual for men from the Dominions to sit at Westminster. After all they were then just as British as those who spent all their lives in the home country, and often more so. Even foreign origin was no bar to Westminster. Trebitsch Lincoln was there, and when Aitken became a member of parliament he saw on the Radical benches opposite Baron de Forest, heir and natural son of Baron Hirsch, builder of the Orient Railway.[1] Maybe Aitken pushed into British politics more quickly than most new arrivals. But he had already political interests. He had promoted Bennett's political career in Canada. He was friendly with Borden, the Canadian Conservative leader, to whom in his usual way he brought financial benefit. Aitken's first intimate friend in England was Rudyard Kipling. Again it is impossible to tell how they met, but there is no doubt of their early intimacy. They went round England together. The Kiplings often spent weekends at Aitken's house, and Kipling was godfather to Aitken's younger son, Peter. Though Aitken professed to be interested in Kipling's writings, the real link between them was enthusiasm for the British Empire—an enthusiasm which ultimately destroyed their friendship. For Kipling never forgave Aitken's support later on for Irish freedom.

It was however Goulding who gave the practical push. He tempted Aitken to try for a constituency. Aitken was flattered though not deluded. He wrote to R. B. Bennett on 22 October 1910: "I believe I am being selected on my merits or supposed merits. They say money does not count but I am sometimes suspicious". Goulding's suggestion was North Cumberland. Aitken went and looked at it. He did not like what he saw.

[1] Baron de Forest was my first political acquaintance. I shook hands with him when he was Liberal candidate for Southport in January 1910. The Unionists complained that land was being valued at an excessive figure, preparatory to the taxation of land values. De Forest announced that he would buy all the land of Southport at the official figure and deposited the necessary money in a Southport bank. No landowner accepted his offer.

It was far from London and, being a rambling county constituency, not easily swayed by the barnstorming tactics which Aitken was likely to employ. Aitken in his impulsive way was eager to enter politics and did not know how to do it.

The solution came from another financial acquaintance, Bonar Law. Aitken and he had done business together ever since 1908, but they do not seem to have drawn closer. When Aitken called on Law in August 1910, he found the house shut up. Their next meeting was at a lunch in Law's honour, organized appropriately by Goulding. Here Aitken also met others who were to shape his destiny in a different way. They were three outstanding Unionist journalists: H. A. Gwynne, editor of The Standard and later of The Morning Post; J. L. Garvin, editor of The Observer; and, most significant of all, R. D. Blumenfeld, American-born editor of The Daily Express. All three favoured Radical Unionism, Gwynne perhaps less than the other two. All three were coming to believe that Law was the man to lead it. Aitken was excited by their company and told Blumenfeld: "I am going to pick out a good, sound Liberal seat and turn it over to the Unionist party".

Aitken soon found his way again to Law's house, this time with more lasting effect. Law put down £100,000 and entered a syndicate with Aitken and others for selling Price Brothers bonds. Thereafter their dealings were incessant, even when Law became a cabinet minister. Nine-tenths of their considerable correspondence between 1910 and 1923 was on financial matters, much to Law's profit. Thus he wrote in September 1917: "I see that I have made £8,000 on an investment of £2,200, so that the want of money is not one of my worries". Probably he benefited to the extent of some £10,000 a year, of course tax-free. The dealings were not altogether one-sided. While Aitken ran the stock exchange transactions, Law, as a former member of the Glasgow iron ring, speculated in iron futures for their joint account.[1]

The association soon turned into personal intimacy. Law's wife had died the previous year. He was melancholy and solitary. Aitken gave him

---

[1] The financial cooperation between Law and Aitken sheds a comical light on a recollection recorded by Lord Davidson (Memoirs of a Conservative, 26–27). When Law became colonial secretary in 1915, he inherited Davidson as his private secretary. One day, Aitken came out of Law's room and asked to use the office telephone. Davidson asked why, and Aitken answered: "I am going to ring up some friends in the City". Davidson said: "I am afraid you can't use our exchange for that—it is never permitted". Aitken went off in a temper, and Davidson hastened to tell Law what he had done. Law answered: "You were completely right—it's just like Max". But of course Aitken was intending to put through a deal on Law's account. Law must have been considerably embarrassed. Aitken no doubt was amused when he talked over the story with Law later. So much for Davidson's claim that he knew Law's secrets and Aitken did not.

gay company, the talk of the day, and unstinted admiration. In his own words: "Bonar pinned me down and kept me ever after. . . . I loved him more than any other human being". Others thought that Aitken rated Law too highly. Birkenhead wrote many years later, in 1928: "I think and have always thought—much though I loved him—that you greatly over-rated Bonar". Aitken would admit no doubts. He praised Law's political judgement, his resolution, and above all his honesty—"he was without guile".

Aitken had been looking for a hero and father-figure ever since the death of John F. Stairs. Now he had found one and clung to his hero for ever. Beaverbrook said shortly before his death: "I have been a court favourite twice in my life. I have served two masters. One was faithful unto death; the other betrayed me". Whether this judgement was unduly harsh on Churchill will be considered later. That on Law was unduly kind. Law often failed Aitken, and Aitken knew it. Perhaps his devotion became wholehearted only after Law's death and then grew more intense with the passing of the years. Much the same had happened with Aitken's posthumous exaltation of John F. Stairs and was to happen also with Beaverbrook's tardy resurrection of R. B. Bennett.

The intimacy between Law and Aitken was not quite so immediate as Aitken later implied. Law did not drop the Mr. in writing to Aitken until 24 April 1911, and his first letter beginning "My dear Max" was on 9 August 1912. Probably Law's appreciation grew gradually from finance into politics and from that into personal attachment. Aitken had fewer reserves. Law was the only Unionist of the front rank to whom he had access—both from their common Canadian background and their financial associations. Law's political outlook corresponded closely with Aitken's. Law, too, had no connection with the aristocratic wing of the Unionist party, little concern with Ireland outside Ulster, and a strong belief in Tariff Reform. Historians sometimes suggest that Law was an almost unknown backbencher until his surprising election as leader of the Unionist party in November 1911. This is not so. Law was a first-rate debater and had already established a personal ascendancy over many Tariff Reformers. Like them, he was "hard", or seemed to be. Aitken was right in describing Law to Bennett as "one of the first four men in the Unionist party".

Aitken's attachment to Law was not merely political calculation. There was in it always a strong element of personal affection. Many people are surprised by this. They ask: "How could Aitken be attracted by a dull man like Bonar Law?" The answer is simple. Law was not a dull man. He was quiet and reserved. He had no sophisticated talk. He was not an amateur philosopher like Balfour. He did not have Asquith's taste for classical literature. But he was shrewd and not without a sense of fun. Aitken wa not alone in his devotion. Love for Bonar Law was the one thing Aitken and Baldwin had in common. Lloyd George who had no time for dull men prized Law's company. A passage from Lady Lloyd-George's diary provides independent and compelling evidence. It was written on 12 May 1921 when Law had left Lloyd George's cabinet and been replaced by Austen Chamberlain:

> We had dinner in D's [Lloyd George's] room in the House again on Tuesday night. This is becoming an institution. He just asks one or two people with whom he can let himself go, and it is a great relief for him. Since Bonar left, he has lost an ideal companion with whom he could laugh and joke and enjoy himself. He cannot do that with Chamberlain, who is pompous to the last degree, and has become increasingly so since he took Bonar's place.

There is another indication of Law's true character. He came to appreciate Aitken as much as Aitken appreciated him. He often referred to Aitken publicly as "my most intimate friend", and when his sister Mary expressed some disapproval, answered: "Do let me like him". Thereafter Mary Law, too, loved Max Aitken.

At all events, Aitken bowed down before Law, and Law promoted Aitken's entry into politics. Early in October, Law asked the central office to look out "for any suitable seats available". Later in the month, Lord Derby, on Law's prompting, suggested him for West Salford. These were fairly remote speculations. Events speeded up unexpectedly. There had been a general election as recently as January 1910. The Liberals secured a majority of 120 with Irish and Labour support. They seemed safe for another five years. A principal element in their programme was a bill to curb the powers of the house of lords. King George V, who had come to the throne in May, promoted a conference between the party leaders to reach an agreed solution. The conference broke down, mainly over Irish Home Rule. The Liberal cabinet then demanded that the king should pledge himself to create peers if the Lords threw out the Parliament Bill. The king secretly gave the pledge on condition that a general election was held first. In November the country was plunged into its second general election within a year.

Law had a safe seat at Dulwich. But he was anxious to enhance his position as the leader of Tariff Reform and resolved to challenge Free Trade in its traditional Lancashire home. He chose North West Manchester, a seat which Winston Churchill had won as a Liberal in 1906 and lost at a by-election in 1908 to Joynson-Hicks, who in his turn lost it to a Liberal in January 1910. Law's move left Dulwich vacant, and Aitken tried to push himself in, though it is not clear with what success. Then a more exciting prospect opened. At Ashton-under-Lyne, a textile town six miles outside Manchester, the Unionist candidate, who had been narrowly defeated in January, quarrelled with his committee. Beaverbrook gives a dramatic account of what followed. A deputation of Ashton Unionists came to lunch with Law and urged him to contest the seat. He remained faithful to North West Manchester. Aitken, in the background, could not restrain himself. He exclaimed: "Why not me?" The deputation agreed, "possibly influenced by the very audacity of the question". The next morning Aitken had cold feet and hankered after the safety of Dulwich. Law was adamant: "Ashton it was yesterday. Ashton it must be tomorrow".

This is a good instance, repeated at many high moments in Aitken's life, of his romantic imagination at work. Though his stories were all basically true, he could not resist throwing in an extra element of drama, and they thus became, in a favourite phrase of his, "another version of the same". It is true that Aitken was on the look-out for a parliamentary seat. It is also true that Law helped him to find one. The rest of Aitken's story is embroidery.

Law was offered Ashton by letter. He wrote back on 14 November, declining, and instead suggested "a young friend of mine":

> He is a young Canadian, not much over 30; he is a man of really exceptional ability, who, without any outside help, has made a large fortune; he is a keen Imperialist, and for that reason, now wants to stand for Parliament.

Also: "If I should happen to go to Manchester I should prefer to have him in Lancashire". The Ashton Unionists, no doubt desperate for a candidate, accepted Law's suggestion. Aitken, surprisingly enough, refused the offer. He claimed to have learnt that the nomination had already been offered to a Tory workingman and resented being second choice. He wrote, undated, to Law:

> The central office has ignored my offer to serve the party in the interests of Tariff Reform and Preference from the period of my first visit until three days ago. . . .
> Now that the election is impending I am offered a seat intended by the office for a labour candidate.[1] . . .
> I cannot accept further humiliation at the hands of a body which cannot accept proffered services in the spirit in which I approached the subject.

Law evidently silenced these objections or perhaps convinced Aitken that his suspicions were unfounded. Aitken still hesitated. He telegraphed to Goulding on 20 November:

> I am ready to accept if you and F. E. Smith will guarantee to address a meeting. Unless you and Smith give me a warranty the deal is off.

---

[1] If Aitken had meant what we now call a Labour candidate, he would have written "Socialist". It is however inconceivable that the Unionist central office did not mean to run a Unionist candidate at all. Tory workingman seems the most likely explanation.

Goulding replied that he could not leave Worcester. Aitken went on despite this, as no doubt he had intended to do all along.

This hesitation before action was to be repeated again and again in Aitken's life. His records do not show whether he was really as decisive and confident in financial affairs as he appeared to be. Before political action he was for ever consulting others and trying to make them push him into doing what he wanted to do, culminating in the second world war when he saddled his secretaries with the task of deciding whether he should resign. Like Lloyd George, Aitken trembled before he acted. Unlike Lloyd George, he went on trembling even when he had acted. Under his assertive exterior, he was all nerves and, if he could not find others to share the responsibility for his decisions, would be brought low with asthma. One kind of brave man does not know fear. Another kind has fear as his companion and acts bravely all the same. Aitken, when brave, was a brave man of the second sort.

Things were soon moving at Ashton-under-Lyne. Aitken had mastered the methods of propaganda when he was a company-promoter and now "sold" himself as he had once sold companies and bonds. He planted articles in Canadian newspapers so that they could be reproduced for the electors of Ashton as independent tributes to his worth. He telegraphed to Miss de Gruchy in Montreal on 14 November:

> Get articles privately prepared dealing with constructive work tramways water power industrials. Omit combines financial operations. Do not deal in figures. Riches beneficial. . . . Do not omit Mrs. Aitken who is very important. Do not intend to accept North Cumberland but intend to make difficult run likely to result in considerable acrimony.

For once Miss de Gruchy's work was less than satisfactory. Aitken wrote to her on 21 November:

> The book of newspapers clippings is perfectly disgraceful. Probably for the first time in my life I have found you wanting when I called on you unexpectedly. It is true under my own statement of conditions I have not, but if you persist in doing all your work perfectly, you must be prepared to be criticized whenever the occasion arises.

Aitken was now impatient for action. Gladys Aitken was hastily summoned from Canada and had to abandon her children once more. She arrived in London on a Monday and was carried off to Manchester on the Tuesday. "It turned out that she was a good speaker, better than the Conservative candidate for Ashton, about to embark upon the uncharted waters of an election in a British constituency". Law advised her not to wear her best clothes on the public platform. This was one of the few

occasions when Aitken firmly decided that Law was wrong. Nor did he
scruple to invoke Law's aid in an unusual way. He telegraphed to Law
on 21 November:

> Midland Hotel state can give me accommodation for one night only.
> Will you send for Manager and compel accommodation. I sincerely hope
> you will introduce me on Thursday night. My motor will rush you back
> to your own meeting. I have two motors. Shall I send one up for your use?

Law compelled accommodation. Max and Gladys Aitken established
themselves at the Midland Hotel, Manchester, with a staff of secretaries,
and swept into Ashton by car each morning.

The Ashton election has been held up as something of a marvel.
Aitken claimed that he had performed prodigies of organization and had
seized the seat in defiance of Lord Derby, the dominant figure of Lancashire Unionism. He made out also that it was an unparalleled achievement to defeat the Liberals after only a ten days' campaign. His Liberal
opponent talked darkly of corruption, and even a biographer of Aitken's
"doubts whether there had been an election in Britain to compare with it
for years, unless one went back to the days of Eatanswill".[1]

There is little truth in these stories. Constituency organization could
not be improvised in ten days, though no doubt party workers were
keener and perhaps better rewarded than when party and candidate were
on bad terms, as they had been in the January election. Lord Derby was
not yet a rigid Free Trader and resented the incursion of Aitken no more
than he did that of Law himself, which indeed he had actively promoted.
Ashton, like its neighbour Stalybridge, had a bad reputation for corrupt
practices by both Liberals and Unionists, and Aitken had to work the
accepted system. He hired brass bands, and three days before the poll
he and Gladys Aitken gave an At Home for three thousand women—
had they been men this would have constituted treating. Aitken did nothing which the Liberals did not do also. Even so, he strongly disliked these
practices and after the election forced his local agents to abandon them.
By 1912 his leading Ashton representative was writing to him about the
municipal elections: "It is generally admitted that this is the purest
election ever fought in Ashton-under-Lyne".

Aitken's publicity was perhaps more than usual. There were two
newspapers in Ashton, both weeklies. Aitken arranged, and no doubt
paid for, a daily edition of the Unionist Herald, which was distributed
free during the election. The proprietors of the Liberal Reporter were
softened, if not won over, by Aitken's flattery and charm, so much so that
within a year one of them was playing hymns at Aitken's house. As well,

[1] Alan Wood, True History of Lord Beaverbrook, 55.

both papers were glad to reprint the material from Canada with which
Aitken fed them.

Aitken's meetings were not particularly sensational. They were only
well-reported—again at his own expense. He had no exceptional run of
speakers despite his cajoling. Law came over once from Manchester and
advised the audience not to judge Aitken from his first speech. F. E.
Smith came from Liverpool and asserted that there was no discredit in
Aitken's being a millionaire—"a man's a man for a' that". Gwynne came,
though only to announce that he was no speaker. Rudyard Kipling failed
to come because of the death of his mother. Even so, he received his
reward: Aitken gave him $50,000 underwriting in Steel Company of
Canada.[1] Aitken's own speeches had one unusual feature, apart from his
Canadian accent. He waved aside the ostensible issue of the election, the
house of lords, with the confession that he neither knew nor cared anything about it. This fence cleared, he swept into passionate advocacy of
tariffs and Imperial unity.

Aitken's ignorance brought advantage in another way. Both candidates
were asked whether they would be prepared to reverse the Osborne
judgement, which prevented trade unions from contributing to the
Labour party. The Liberal high-mindedly replied that he would insist
on a conscience clause allowing contracting out (which was in fact included in the 1913 act). Aitken made no such reservation. Cocker, the
representative of the trades council who interviewed him, remarked:
"Yon fellow will promise to vote for anything, but he doesn't understand
what he's promising. He asked us not to be too hard on him, as he'd
'only been in politics a week!'" However Aitken's answer was good
enough. Cocker rushed the Ashton and Dukinfield Trades and Labour
Council into recommending all trade unionists to vote for Aitken.[2]
In this way Ashton provided "the only example of the recognized
Labour organization preferring a Conservative to a Liberal candidate".[3]
The recommendation may have had a decisive effect. A Socialist had
stood at the January election and polled 413 votes. No Socialist stood in
December. If trade unionists followed the advice of their council, the

[1] Kipling got $50,000 preferred stock to sell among his friends. He paid $94
for each $100 of stock, sold at $97 and also received a 50% bonus in ordinary stock.
[2] Cocker reported back to the trades council executive. Only seven out of sixty
members were present. The recommendation of Aitken was carried by three votes to
two. Cocker strengthened the recommendation when he issued it to the press. After the
election Liberal trade unionists protested, and the motion recommending Aitken was
expunged by 32 votes to 18. Some of those who supported Aitken were later entertained
by him in London.
[3] P. F. Clarke, Lancashire and the New Liberalism, 336. Dr. Clarke gives a full
account of the affair, based on Aitken's Ashton-under-Lyne papers, in his Appendix F.
I am grateful for his guidance.

four hundred Socialist votes, now going a-begging, were enough to turn the scale.[1]

These speculations are hardly necessary. There was, it seems, a general swing in Lancashire from Liberal to Unionist between January and December 1910, perhaps caused by a depression in the cotton trade. Eight Lancashire seats went over to Unionists. North West Manchester was not among them. Ashton-under-Lyne was:

Aitken, W. Max (Unionist)	4,044
Scott, A. H. (Liberal)	3,848
Unionist majority	196

Aitken made a brief comment on his success: "Victory due to brilliant organization and Tariff Reform". His exaltation did not last. As usual with Aitken, nervous collapse followed triumph, and he was additionally weighed down by Law's defeat. He spent a gloomy weekend in the Midland Hotel and then returned to London, where he consulted Horder, the favourite medical man of the wealthy. Aitken told Horder that he had hardening of the arteries. Horder replied that there was nothing wrong with him which a holiday in the south of France would not cure. This was the beginning of a remedy which Aitken was to apply often over the next fifty years.

Max and Gladys Aitken spent Christmas 1910 in Nice. Here Aitken increased his political knowledge from an unexpected source. An elderly bearded Englishman of distinguished appearance was staying at their hotel. He was Sir Charles Dilke, a man whose political experience—not all of it fortunate—went back over forty years. He had been, at various times, a future foreign secretary, a future prime minister, and a future leader of the Labour party. In 1884 he had devised the redistribution of constituencies almost single-handed. Aitken introduced himself. Dilke refused to believe that this abrupt young man, with his harsh Canadian voice, was a member of the British house of commons, and Aitken had to get the hotel porter to vouch for him. Thereafter Aitken and Dilke

[1] The January figures were:

Scott, A. H. (Liberal)	4,039
Whiteley, H. J. (Unionist)	3,746
Gee, W. (Socialist)	413
Liberal majority	293

The bill reversing the Osborne judgement was not officially opposed by the Unionist party. Aitken did not vote either for or against it.

walked on the Promenade des Anglais by the hour, Aitken seeking instruction in British political ways, as he had earlier sought instruction in Canadian cement or steel. It is unlikely that Aitken learnt much of practical value. Fifty years afterwards he could only remember that Dilke walked very slowly and talked very solemnly. His real interest was the historian's. Dilke was for him a collector's piece, taking him back to the days when Gladstone was in his prime and Joseph Chamberlain a Radical. Nor, looking at Dilke, did he forget the Crawford divorce case and three in a bed.

On 2 January 1911 Aitken began another association which was to prove far more significant for his future. As he was going down the steps of the Casino at Monte Carlo, he was approached by R. D. Blumenfeld, who bore with him a note of recommendation from Bonar Law. Blumenfeld was editor of The Daily Express and told a troubled story. Sir Arthur Pearson, the founder of The Daily Express, had been stricken with blindness and in 1908 withdrew his interest from the paper. The circulation was beginning to get off the ground, but Blumenfeld was saddled with out-of-date presses and had pledged all his own financial resources. He was heavily in debt to the supplier of newsprint. The Unionist party had offered to take over The Express, but Blumenfeld, being a keen Tariff Reformer, was reluctant to be shackled to a party which was still equivocating over this issue. One evening he consulted Law at the Carlton Club. Law said: "I know the man for you. Max Aitken is enormously rich. He knows nothing about newspapers and is not interested in them. But he wants to have a big political career, and he'll be glad of a paper which will back him". Blumenfeld left at once for the south of France. Aitken listened to his story, walked over to the Hotel de Paris and wrote out a cheque for £25,000 as a personal loan.[1]

The Aitkens returned to England in time for the opening of parliament on 6 February 1911. Aitken was no longer the glamorous winner of a seat. He was merely a backbench MP, condemned to hours of waiting and listening—not occupations at which he ever excelled. He slipped into the House almost unobserved, as he recalled many years later. On 10 September 1935 Beaverbrook wrote to Sir Samuel Hoare, who also entered parliament at this time:

> On the morning when I went to the House of Commons to be sworn for the first time, I was in a state of intense anxiety and nervous to a degree. I expected to find a full Chamber. Instead there was not a soul in the place except you. We carried on a brief conversation.

[1] Information from Sir John Elliot, Blumenfeld's son. The meeting at Monte Carlo on 2 January 1911 is confirmed in a letter from Beaverbrook to Blumenfeld of 24 April 1937.

Hoare replied on 14 September 1935:

> I was rather frightened of you. My friends told me, what was perfectly true, that you had a quicker brain than anyone else in the House and that Bonar, the coming man from Glasgow, was completely under your influence.

The friendship, thus begun, lasted until Hoare's death.

Another introduction, with very different consequences, came from Kipling, who wrote on 9 March 1911:

> I do hope you have made acquaintance with my cousin Stanley Baldwin. I think you'll find him a delightful fellow as well as a man of business.

Aitken also consolidated his friendship with F. E. Smith, who said of him: "Max is a very clever fellow and a very good fellow—and a very rich fellow too". Aitken conducted stock exchange transactions on Smith's behalf, of course without informing him, and paid over winnings of about £1000 a time. Smith, like Allan Davidson before him and Arnold Bennett after him, enquired what would happen if the speculation showed a loss. He enquired in vain. The winnings continued to flow in. The losses, if any, were never mentioned.

Aitken's political friendships were not confined to the Unionist benches. As Law commented sourly a little later (15 August 1911): "You seem to be very thick with George and Churchill—have you found out yet what the latter wants or is it only love of your beaux yeux". Of course it was Aitken who wanted entry into the highest and most exciting political circles. Lloyd George, it seems, was the one who spotted Aitken first. He told Churchill that "a Canadian had appeared on the scene and the politicians would hear of him". But Aitken did not become at all intimate with Lloyd George until later. He early pushed himself on Churchill's attention, aided by F. E. Smith, who was very close to Churchill despite their political antagonism.

There are no detailed accounts of Aitken's impact on English political society, and we can only judge from events. He was young, intensely curious, and with an inexhaustible fund of gaiety and energy. He sought out the brilliant men of the time without regard to party and won their friendship. He even played bridge for their sake, a diversion from conversation which he inwardly detested. As he said: "Business is more exciting than any game". With only a flat in London and as yet no country house, he was always available for a lively social evening. It was not long before he knew everyone worth knowing.

He also performed services for his friends. Some time early in May 1911[1] Aitken offered to organize a visit to Canada for Churchill.

---

[1] Aitken's letter is undated. Churchill's "very reluctant" refusal, to "My dear Aitkin", is dated 5 May 1911.

He wrote: "I don't think any other person can arrange your reception as efficiently as I can". He then added:

> There is an objection to me you must know about. I created al the big trusts in Canada. None of them are bad trusts but the Western farmers attack me very often and sometimes very offensively. I don't care. But you might not like an intimate connection. I can best illustrate the position when I tell you that my relation to Canada was in a small way the same as Morgan's relation to America. I'm done now and in fact for eighteen months past I have steadily pulled out. . . .
>
> If you don't mind the objection I would take care to relieve you from the incubus if it developed. And if you are to be my guest it won't so appear. Probably it doesn't make any difference at all, and I exaggerate it.
>
> . . . .
>
> Please don't tell anybody I admitted I organized any trusts.

Churchill had to refuse the invitation for reasons which were not stated.

This was the only direct exchange between Aitken and Churchill before 1916. Churchill's correspondence records however a curious initiative which he took a little later on Aitken's behalf. On 20 December 1911 Churchill informed the Master of Elibank, the Liberal chief whip, that Aitken would like to be appointed one of the British Commissioners on the Imperial commission to investigate the trade resources of the Empire. Churchill continued:

> If Aitken were appointed he would vacate his seat at Ashton-under-Lyne and retire for the time being from politics altogether. He is really a very advanced Liberal and it is only accident that sent him into politics on the Tory side. . . . I have talked it over with the Chancellor of the Exchequer and he thinks very highly of the project. I like Aitken myself personally, and he is certainly a man of very high commercial ability as well as being thoroughly patriotic and public spirited.

The suggestion was sharply rejected by Asquith. He wrote to Churchill on 26 December 1911:

> Aitken is quite impossible. I take it that his Canadian record is of the shadiest, and when (at the instance of the Tories) he was made a Coronation knight, Albert Grey wrote to us that throughout the Dominion there was a howl of indignation and disgust.[1]

If Churchill meant by "a very advanced Liberal" that Aitken had a radical outlook, he was right. But Aitken had no sympathy with the softness and do-good sentiment of much Liberal policy. Asquith's judgement, though quite unjustified, shows the prejudice against which Aitken had to contend. Albert, Earl Grey, governor general of Canada from 1904 to

---

[1] Randolph Churchill, Winston Churchill, companion Volume II, Part 2, 1362–64.

1911, was deeply committed to the Canadian Liberal government and retailed, in exaggerated form, the mud which the Liberals threw at Aitken. The Canadian Conservatives had nothing against Aitken, but much against Earl Grey, and it was fortunate for him that his term of office ran out just when the Conservatives won the general election of 1911. Otherwise they would have asked for his recall.[1]

Aitken was the despair of the Whips. He preferred to meet his political friends at private dinner-parties, not in the smoking room, and was particularly indifferent to the House while Law was not a member. Six weeks later Law was returned at Bootle in a by-election, but even this did not make Aitken's attendance much more frequent. He rarely bothered to vote, and his record of silence surpassed even that achieved by Group-Captain Max Aitken, DSO, DFC, in the parliament of 1945–50. The debates seemed to Aitken both boring and futile. He regarded a general election as a take-over bid. If the bid succeeded, he went on to organize the ensuing merger, just as he had expected the Unionists to form a government. If the bid failed, he turned to something else and waited for a more favourable opportunity. He certainly did not go on hammering at a door which he knew was firmly closed, and this is what parliamentary opposition seemed to be.

Aitken had lost interest in British politics until the next general election or, at the very least, some upheaval in one party or the other. He wrote to a friend in Canada on 4 March 1911: "After all, there can be no further success here until the Irishmen and Radicals disagree, which will not be for two or three years anyway". And a little later to Steel-Maitland, chairman of the newly-created Unionist central office:

> I am not at all interested in wasting time in futile opposition to Radical measures in the House of Commons. Also I think that if our back-benchers would pay as much attention to their neighbouring constituencies as to discussion of politics, we would probably win the next election.

In this mood, Aitken was ready to turn elsewhere, and events in Canada gave the necessary push. The Liberal government in Canada had negotiated a Reciprocity Treaty with the United States, which provided for a mutual lowering of tariffs. This opened the Canadian market to American industrial goods and, still worse, established Free Trade in wheat between the two countries. Here was a deadly blow against Imperial Preference and particularly against the proposed British food taxes which were an essential part of the Chamberlain programme. Canadian farmers would

---

[1] Earl Grey was of course an authority on the manipulation of politics for financial reasons. He was earlier a principal London agent of Cecil Rhodes's Chartered Company of South Africa and sent to Rhodes the "Hurry up" telegram which touched off the Jameson raid.

be little impressed by a preference in Great Britain when all the United States market was open to them. What was more, with the establishment of Free Trade, American wheat could enter Great Britain in the guise of Canadian and thus receive the Imperial Preference.

This new development reinforced in England the outcry against food taxes which had harassed Joseph Chamberlain from the start of his campaign in 1903 and was to harass Aitken all his life. Imperial Preference started as a matter of sentiment. British people all over the world were to be brought into a Zollverein, mightier than its German original. Tariffs on foreign manufactured goods were welcome to many British industrialists, though in fact they would bring no help to Great Britain as an exporting nation. Taxes on foreign foodstuffs were the real stumbling block. They were essential in order to win over the Dominions, which were regarded, rightly or wrongly, as in the main producers of raw materials and foodstuffs. Tariffs on raw materials, raising the costs of production, were out. Food taxes were therefore the miraculous stroke which would bind the Empire together.

But food taxes provoked an answering storm of sentiment—the cry against dear food. The bad old days of the Corn Laws would be revived. It was useless for Tariff Reformers to argue that dearer food would be counterbalanced by the higher wages which tariffs on manufactured goods would produce. "Your food will cost you more" was a death-dealing slogan. There can be little doubt that British opinion was set against food taxes, as it has remained to this day. For this very reason Tariff Reformers pushed them so hard. Food taxes, and only food taxes, would be the decisive symbol that the cause of Empire had triumphed. It is pointless to speculate whether food taxes would really have won over the Dominions or raised the cost of living without compensation. They were the shibboleth, dividing the saints of Empire from the sinners. In the end, insistence on food taxes ruined the British Empire. Imperial sentiment existed, but the desire for cheap food proved stronger.

When Canada made the Reciprocity Treaty with the United States, food taxes seemed on the way out. The treaty was published on 28 January 1911. Northcliffe had always been against "stomach taxes" and now grasped that the Reciprocity Treaty made nonsense of them. He struck immediately against the devoted Tariff Reformer, Garvin, editor of The Observer which Northcliffe then owned. Northcliffe ordered Garvin to abandon food taxes. When Garvin refused, Northcliffe declared that he must either find another proprietor for The Observer or else leave the editorial chair. Garvin ultimately found a proprietor and protector in the American expatriate, Waldorf Astor, after offering the paper to many others including Aitken. The surprising part of the story is that Northcliffe's ally and adviser in turning against food taxes was none other than Aitken, who had just won his seat in parliament as a wholehearted Tariff Reformer.

On 2 February Northcliffe telegraphed to Garvin: "I am sending to you tonight the only Canadian in England who I believe understands the present position on both sides of the border". This authority was of course Aitken. No record survives of his meeting with Garvin, but evidently it was to no purpose. Northcliffe then appealed directly to Aitken: "Our party is in the clouds and many will be grateful if it is brought to solid earth". Aitken in his turn appealed to Law and reported on 5 February: "Privately Bonar frankly favours our views but apprehensive for serious opposition". Northcliffe met Law at Aitken's flat, and their support hardened him against Garvin. Otherwise Law remained cautiously silent. Aitken was less discreet. On 20 February he attended a Tariff Reform dinner and expounded the implications of the Reciprocity Treaty: food taxes, he declared, should be abandoned by the Unionist party. Two days later, he wrote to Northcliffe that a substitute for food taxes should be found by giving a preference for Colonial stocks and shares on the London market. This suggestion had its attractions for a financier. It had none for the ordinary Tariff Reformer, and Aitken fell into disrepute with his political friends such as Goulding, to say nothing of Garvin.

This is at first sight a puzzling story. In later years, Aitken was to stake his political life on food taxes time and time again. Yet here, it seems, he was abandoning them at the very outset. Did he really despair because of the Reciprocity Treaty? Was he flattered by attentions from the great Northcliffe? A more subtle explanation can be found in Aitken's subsequent conduct. He was on occasion a man of guile and had perhaps seen a way of trapping Northcliffe, the opponent of food taxes, into supporting them after all. Northcliffe argued that the Reciprocity Treaty made nonsense of British food taxes. Aitken agreed with him. But a general election was approaching in Canada. It would be fought over the Reciprocity Treaty. If the treaty were defeated, Northcliffe would have to admit that the stumbling block against food taxes had been removed. Aitken overlooked the flaw in this plan: Northcliffe was not a man amenable to logical argument.

Aitken was not content to wait passively while his Conservative friends in Canada campaigned against the Reciprocity Treaty. He was eager to enter the fight himself. This had the added advantage that he would be able to escape the dreary round of the British house of commons. In Montreal Miss de Gruchy was winding up Aitken's Canadian base. His house was relinquished in March, and the furniture sold. The two children, Janet and Max, were dispatched to England in the care of their nurses. Yet at this very moment Aitken was proposing to return to

Canada, apparently for good. He wrote to Northcliffe on 4 March: "I have decided to leave for Canada on Saturday next in order to study the situation first-hand". He had decided a good deal more than this. On the same 4 March, he wrote to G. S. Foster, a Canadian MP:

> If I thought that my connection with the mergers and trusts would not interfere with my party, I would resign from the Parliament here and go to Northumberland, NB, as an Imperial Preference anti-American agreement candidate.

He wrote still more urgently and precisely to Allan Davidson, his friend and agent in Newcastle:

> I have got to get back to Canada as soon as possible ... I would like to have the nomination in Northumberland if there is a fighting chance. ... Of course it means resigning from my seat in England, and I would therefore like to have the nomination thrown at me for that reason, and not appear to seek it in any way.
> If I accept the nomination I would not be prepared to run as a Liberal or as a Conservative, but entirely as an Imperial Preference candidate, and unless I can get an independent nomination and win on Imperial lines only, I would not undertake the job.
> Of course, if I could win under these conditions, the victory would be very important to the Unionist party in England.
> Of course, as there would be a considerable amount of expenditure in connection with my plans, I would expect you to undertake it on my behalf. Unless the town is ready to receive me in a non-political way, and in a whole-hearted way, I don't want to come.

A letter from Aitken to R. B. Bennett on 4 March is still more extraordinary, for it contains the suggestion that, having first used British politics as a jumping-off ground into Canadian, he (and Bennett) should then use Canadian politics as a jumping-off ground into British. Restlessness could hardly go further:

> Are you ready to give up business, and if so, shall we try to organize an Imperial Preference party, determined to oppose all American negotiations and to extend the preference to 50 per cent as and when England is prepared to act.
> I think it is quite time we made something move, and as you know, life is brief, and there will not be such another Canadian opportunity for years. Even if we don't do any more good than carry ourselves into Parliament in Canada, we can subsequently retire from the Canadian Parliament and be welcomed in England. ... All England is intensely concerned over the possible loss of Canadian trade, and a Canadian demand for Imperial Preference would now result in acceptance of the policy. It is an absolute fact that Lloyd George and Winston Churchill are favourable, and that Asquith, Haldane and Grey alone oppose. Samuel is being put up as

Asquith's hope against Lloyd George and Winston. Asquith's "hope" is
doomed to dismal failure.

This is a great chance to carry on the fight in Canada, and force England's
hand.

Bennett did not join Aitken's proposed, and non-existent, party,
though he subsequently ran in Calgary as a Conservative. Davidson,
however, operated effectively. With $10,000 to spend, he soon controlled
the patronage in Northumberland county. Newcastle, the county town
and Aitken's supposed birthplace, was eager to welcome its famous son.
On 20 March Aitken arrived in Newcastle and received the freedom of
the town. In his speech of thanks, he announced, among other things, that
he had given up finance and business for politics. Aitken returned to
England, confident that he had secured the Conservative nomination at
Northumberland. His wealth and local influence could be relied on to do
the rest.

All seemed to be going well. On 5 April Sir Robert Borden, leader of
the Conservative party in Canada, wrote to Aitken:

> It is possible, even probable, that we shall have a general Election in
> Canada within a few months. . . . It is a vital necessity that the forces opposed
> to the mischievous Reciprocity pact should be strengthened in every possible
> way. I realize that you owe a duty to your constituents in Great Britain;
> but you owe a closer duty to Canada at this juncture . . . . . . Do not hesitate
> for one moment.

Aitken hesitated all the same. It was no light matter to leave the British
parliament so soon after he had entered it, and he wanted to be pushed.
He did not consult Law, who would certainly have pressed him to stay.
Instead he sought approval from Balfour, the leader of the Unionist
party, and to little result. Balfour evaded all political discussion and displayed instead an interest, as enthusiastic as it was ignorant, in financial
speculations. Beaverbrook recorded later: "I was not only disappointed.
I was startled. He would talk of nothing but the stock markets, with
special reference to the chances of making a big killing on the New York
stock exchange". Aitken reported to Borden: "Mr. Balfour is playing
hide and seek with me as he usually does until he makes up his mind".
Aitken only learnt later that Balfour rarely made up his mind.

Aitken's letter to Borden of 21 April 1911 had more striking news.
Acland-Hood, the Unionist chief whip, had called the night before with
the information that he had "two peerages, two P.C.'s, two baronetcies,
and six knighthoods in his giving for the coronation". He offered a knighthood to Aitken "for the purpose of rewarding me for services to come and
to the Unionist party and not to the Canadian party". This was a surprising offer. Aitken had only been in British politics for a few months.

Though he had won a seat for the Unionists at the general election, so had some forty others, and he had played no part in the house of commons. Later, in writing to Canadian friends, he made out that he had distinguished himself as a constituency organizer in Lancashire and that he was due to be appointed chief of the new Unionist central office. These claims have little foundation. Aitken had perhaps enlivened the Unionist organization in Ashton-under-Lyne, but he had visited his constituency only once since the election, and he had no dealings with any other constituency, except to send £30 to the Unionist party in Gorton on behalf of Otto Kahn. As to the Unionist central office, Balfour and Acland-Hood had already decided to appoint Steel-Maitland, and he, as correspondence shows, decidedly did not welcome Aitken's advice or assistance.

"Services to come" therefore might simply mean, as it no doubt often did, a large subscription to party funds. There is naturally no trace of this in Aitken's records. Instead there is evidence of a more complicated transaction. Historians have often speculated where the political parties got their money from at this time, itself a difficult enough topic. They have not gone on to enquire what the parties did with the money when they got it. Constituency parties could usually fend for themselves, particularly on the Unionist side. There were of course objects for national expenditure during a general election, but the parties also spent money between elections. It appears from Aitken's files that one such expenditure was in subsidy to various newspapers. The subsidy was disguised in the form of investment in the paper's shares by some individual, who had himself to be a man of substance so as to make the transaction plausible; and the individual usually added some genuine investment of his own.

The "recognized channel", in Steel-Maitland's phrase, for this Unionist money was Sir Alexander Henderson of Glasgow, later Lord Faringdon. It seems that through this and other channels The Observer, The Standard, The Globe, and The Pall Mall Gazette were each receiving aid from the Unionist funds, sometimes as much as £10,000 a year. Further channels were obviously desirable, and Aitken, as a Canadian millionaire, was an appropriate one. Aitken kept his bargain. In a roundabout way it was connected with The Daily Express, which was still in trouble and seemed on the point of closing down. The Unionist central office was anxious to find a refuge for Blumenfeld if The Express went, and one lay close to hand: The Globe, an almost moribund evening paper, owned by Hildebrand Harmsworth, one of Northcliffe's brothers. Aitken duly bought The Globe for £40,000. Only £15,000 was in fact provided by him. The rest came from other Unionists and the party fund. Aitken was acting as a sort of trustee, and this explains why he could not honourably shake off The Globe even when it proved a financial burden. He had to carry this burden until he found someone, also on the look-out for an honour, who would relieve him. Aitken displayed no interest in the running of The Globe. He was not yet aspiring to become a press lord. Apart from pleasing Acland-Hood and keeping the editorial chair available for Blumenfeld, he was only concerned to secure new outlets for a little harmless propaganda about himself.

Aitken hesitated long before accepting the knighthood. At heart he had a plain radical contempt for the glitter of rank and title. Later on, he admired those friends of his, such as Arnold Bennett and Rudyard Kipling, who refused all honours, and laughed good-naturedly at those, such as John Buchan, who ran after them. On the other hand he was fascinated by the romance of his own career; first poor boy to millionaire and now son of the manse to knight, perhaps even in time to peer of the realm. Later in life he often described his knighthood as the one honour he really prized and even talked of returning to it if he could renounce his peerage. Characteristically he wanted to give the impression that he had been reluctant to accept and had been pushed into it by others. H. A. Gwynne, of The Morning Post, recalled one such attempt:

> You rang me up in 1911 and asked me most urgently to come and see you at the Hyde Park Hotel. I dropped everthing and came. You showed me a letter from Asquith offering you a knighthood and asked my advice as to the answer you should give. I thought I had convinced you that it was best to refuse for we drafted the letter declining the honour. Later I learnt that the matter had been arranged some time before. Although now I am quite convinced that you were just having a lark, I thought then that you were doing a somewhat unfriendly thing.[1]

Gwynne was in fact deeply estranged and refused to have any dealings with Aitken for years afterwards.

Aitken tried the same tactics with Borden. He wrote: "None of the persons who expect to get Front Bench rank in England will accept Knighthoods or Baronetcies, and I must modestly admit that I am generally regarded as a Front Bench probable". However the situation would be different if Borden pushed him: "I imagine a Knighthood is of enormous political benefit in Canada, and for that reason I have really signified my acceptance. . . . If you write in opposition to my accepting,

[1] Gwynne to Beaverbrook, 21 August 1928. The letter contains some minor inaccuracies. Aitken did not move to the Hyde Park Hotel until after the outbreak of war, and the offer came from Acland-Hood, not from Asquith. Gwynne's letter was a comment on the first volume of Politicians and the War (p. 83–84), where Beaverbrook gave a different, and apparently mistaken, explanation of the fact that he and Gwynne did not cooperate during the political crisis which led to the fall of the Asquith coalition government. Gwynne's estrangement went so deep that he wrote, in a letter to Goulding, of "Aitken's dirty peerage". Distrust of Aitken was by no means confined to the Liberal side.

please put your letter in such a shape that I can show it to Sir Alexander Acland-Hood".

Borden refused to make Aitken's mind up for him. He replied on 1 May: "I do not think the acceptance or non-acceptance of the Knighthood would materially affect the Canadian situation". Borden's concern lay elsewhere: "It will be entirely mischievous and perhaps fatal if you are prevented from fighting with us in the coming struggle. . . . It is the plain duty of the Unionist party to release you from any obligation which would prevent you from joining us at the first signal". Aitken accepted the knighthood, as no doubt he had intended to do all along. He apologized to his Canadian friends that it had been forced on him for British reasons, and to his British friends the other way round. He consoled himself that the proposal had really come from Law, of which again there is no evidence. Aitken wrote to Law:

> Hood did me the kindness but you made it possible and in my selfish way I want you to know that I am always ready to serve you, not because of what you've done but because you are yourself.

Aitken duly received his knighthood in the Coronation honours, along with Roger Casement among others.

It is said that Lord Derby, the leader of Lancashire Unionism, objected to this honour going to Aitken instead of to some other Lancashire Unionist MP nominated by himself. This cannot be confirmed from the records. But Derby undoubtedly resented Aitken's activities. This is shown in a letter which he addressed to the Unionist agent at Gorton on 10 September 1911:

> I am not in the habit of writing one thing and meaning another and your mention of a substantial donation from Sir Max Aitken leaves me quite unmoved and it gives me an opportunity of saying what I think.
>
> The other day you asked me to try and secure you a candidate. I at once set to work and I think I might have been able to get one for you, but I heard that you had privately consulted Sir Max Aitken and asked him to find you one. Under the circumstances I naturally decline to take any further interest in your constituency and must ask you to allow me to withdraw from any participation in your political affairs. I am sure Sir Max Aitken will do well by you and on the principle of "too many cooks spoiling the broth" it is better for me not to interfere.

Aitken's mind was not set on the affairs of Gorton in the early summer of 1911. A general election in Canada had now been proclaimed, and undoubtedly Aitken meant to return to Canada immediately after the Coronation. At this moment, a catastrophe intervened, which changed the whole course of Aitken's career. The affair of the Canada Cement Company exploded. Sir Sandford Fleming had continued to sit on the board until February 1911. He made repeated attempts to unload his derelict company, Exshaw, on to the company. These attempts were firmly rebuffed by the board. Finally he resigned. Private pressure had failed. Fleming determined to try public blackmail. There was already strong feeling against mergers, as everyone knew. Fleming exploited this feeling, even though he had inspired the cement merger in the first place. He made out that there had been excessive profits and even dishonesty by Aitken in the watering of stock. Fleming pointed to the disparity between the 16½ million dollars for which the old companies had been acquired and the 30 million dollars at which shares in the new company had been nominally issued, and alleged that Aitken had pocketed 13½ million dollars for himself.

These charges were without foundation, as has already been shown in detail, and Fleming, who had issued plenty of watered stock in his time, must have known it. The ordinary stock had gone as bonus "sweeteners" to the buyers of the bonds and preferred stock, in what was then the usual Canadian and American way. Those who paid real money got real value in the shape of interest and dividends, secured on the existing profits. Those who got water were speculating on future growth. The ordinary stock of Canada Cement, though nominally valued at 13½ million dollars, was at this time not worth more than one million dollars on the market. Fleming himself had received over one million dollars of the ordinary stock for nothing. However the Canadian farmers welcomed a grievance against the mergers, and the Liberals welcomed a grievance against the Conservatives. Fleming marshalled his charges in a pamphlet which caused a sensation. There was even talk of a parliamentary enquiry.

The storm fell on Aitken. He had promoted the merger and taken the credit for it. Now he got all the blame. Jones and the Cement board were unruffled. They challenged Fleming to appeal to the courts. He did not take up the challenge. Aitken suggested yielding over Exshaw, or as he put it, "buying off the Norseman". The Cement board refused. Jones wrote sternly: "There can be no half measures for you. You must either sit down and grow a good tough skin or fight with every tool". The latter course was impossible. Aitken would have had to sue thirty Liberal newspapers as well as Fleming. Moreover, if the case had come to court, he would have had to reveal the names of all those who had received ordinary stock as bonus. Many were men in high places who had recommended the Canada Cement Company to their friends and customers. They included the leaders of the Conservative party and also the general managers of the Bank of Montreal and of the Royal Bank of Canada. Though there was nothing illegal or improper in their action, they had no desire to be caught in the storm of political abuse. They relied on Aitken to respect their confidence, and he did so. Honour bound him to silence.

A good tough skin however was also beyond him. He wrote to Goulding on 25 May:

> I am feeling rather blue. I am under very heavy fire, and must forget everything for the moment, so that I can keep a good return going. . . . Don't let anybody know I am taking the slightest notice of it, because I must keep an undisturbed exterior.

To make matters worse, Aitken's knighthood was announced in England just when the Canadian newspapers were full of the Cement affair. The Canadian Liberals pointed at Aitken as typical of the men whom Conservatives delighted to honour. Liberal newspapers in England then reproduced the Canadian attacks and pilloried Aitken again, this time as typical of the men who would come to the front if Tariff Reform triumphed. A. G. Gardiner wrote a particularly vicious article in The Daily News, the statements in which are still taken seriously by some historians, and sandwichmen advertised the article in the streets of Ashton-under-Lyne. Aitken trembled at the prospect of yet graver rebuke from The Manchester Guardian. He wrote in exasperation of the English Radicals:

> They are a crowd of little Englanders, anti-Navy and Army fellows, who agitate for universal peace based on the love of God. It is a very devout policy, but unfortunately God is on the side of the big warships.

Friends told Aitken not to worry. Thus Law wrote on 17 June:

> I think it would be a great mistake for you to take notice of the articles. . . . The evident object of the articles is to attack Tariff Reform. . . . Unless you do take notice they will simply die away and attention will not be directed to them at all.

Aitken did not take this wise advice. He urged his friends and agents in Canada to hit out against Fleming: "Is it not possible to furnish me with some ammunition? . . . I am being deliberately attacked by Fleming and his cohorts. I need not reply, but at least I should give as much as I get". He himself prepared to attack and then constantly backed away. Thus when B. F. Pearson, a newspaper proprietor of Halifax, printed an article reproducing the Fleming charges, Aitken wrote to another Halifax newspaper proprietor, W. R. McCurdy, on 25 July:

> I wish you to know that it is my intention to relentlessly pursue Pearson's newspapers, and Pearson, until I have revenged myself for the scandals Pearson's newspaper published.

However he did nothing of the kind. He merely wrote to Pearson privately, reminding him that "You and I have both been concerned in creation of watered capital". Pearson more or less apologized, blaming an inexperienced editor, much as Aitken was often to do later, and by the end of the year Aitken was writing a letter of good wishes in which he assured Pearson: "No man has done as much for the building up of the Maritime Provinces as yourself".

Another little episode was even more characteristic. Aitken learnt that a certain E. W. Thomson was supplying British and American newspapers with material against him. He therefore wrote to V. M. Drury, who had succeeded Miss de Gruchy as his secretary in Montreal, on 21 July:

> Will you find out who E. W. Thomson is. He wrote a vicious personal attack on me for The Boston Transcript.
>
> Find out in what manner I can punish him. I do not propose to let things of this nature go unpunished.

A postscript was inserted by hand:

> Understand he is a professional writer for Liberal party and lives in Ottawa. Better retain him.

The Fleming campaign turned out to be a nine-days' wonder. There was no parliamentary enquiry. Fleming did not appeal to the courts. The Canada Cement Company quietly took a more effective revenge than anything Aitken could do. It bought up the mortgage debentures of Exshaw, the interest on which was in arrears. It then foreclosed on behalf of the bondholders and took over Exshaw as a bankrupt concern. After reorganization, Exshaw became a useful, though minor, member of the Cement Company. The Bank of Montreal later took action against Fleming and his associates to recover the money which they had borrowed in order to meet earlier instalments of the debenture interest. Fleming and his friends had no defence. The case was ultimately settled out of court. The Bank wrote off a quarter of its claim and accepted $75,000. Aitken provided $20,000 of this on condition that Fleming withdrew his charges and promised not to repeat them. Thus Aitken paid Danegeld after all. It is impossible to discover what happened to the further $200,000, which the CPR had guaranteed. Presumably it was lost in the wild Canadian west. Frank Jones commented: "Max refused to take Exshaw at the wrong price and then got it at the right one". This was a fair, though not entirely accurate, summary of the affair.

This final settlement was not reached until 1912. It was of no use to Aitken in 1911. A general election was proclaimed in Canada just when the Fleming stir was at its height. The Conservative leaders evidently did not take the stir very seriously, certainly not seriously enough to jeopardize Aitken's political standing. Borden himself urged Aitken to come and contest Northumberland county as soon as the Coronation was over. But Aitken could not face another mud-slinging campaign. He had found the attacks on him at Ashton as a rich man bad enough. Detailed misrepresentations were even more laborious to combat, particularly when this involved explaining the ethics of bonus stock to an audience ignorant of finance.

Allan Davidson was hastily told to stop the Aitken campaign in Northumberland. He was even told to conceal the fact that the money, which he continued to pour out for the substituted Conservative candidate, came from Aitken. Ostensibly this was to preserve the substitute from any Aitken smear. Actually it was to protect Aitken from the accusation that he was taking any part in the Canadian election. Aitken did not want to give the impression that he had run away. He therefore discovered that it was important for him to stay in British politics after all. He wrote to Davidson on 12 June:

> I am very much afraid we are going to have an election in England in August. The Liberal Whip has warned his agents. Of course if an election comes on here I cannot leave.

This was an unlikely and unconvincing excuse. Aitken soon did better. He telegraphed to Law on 1 August:

> Will you write me letter early tomorrow morning that my obligations to my constituents and to yourself politically are such that will not justify resigning from parliament at this time to join Conservatives in Canada.

Law did as requested. He wrote on 2 August:

> I do not think it would be right for you to take any action which would make it impossible for you to fulfil your duties as a Member of the British Parliament. It is only a few months since you were elected. The political situation here is very serious and it is certainly of the utmost importance that every Unionist Member should be at his post.

Even this was not quite satisfactory. After all, the need for Aitken in the British parliament must have been equally clear when he was pushing himself for Northumberland county. Aitken's ingenuity covered this point also. He claimed that he was expecting to get office in the next Conservative government and that a Canadian Liberal government would be offended by this if he had played any part in Canadian politics. He presented this complicated argument to Allan Davidson on 30 August:

> The Liberals [presumably Canadian?] have kicked up a great row here and have stated that if Conservatives subsequently come into office they would refuse to accept a continuance of a relation with the Colonial Office in the event that I should happen to be Under-Secretary for the Colonies which is of course the appointment I am expecting to get.

With this Aitken's connection with Northumberland ended, except that Davidson spent $26,000 as covertly as he could.

The Canadian Conservatives triumphed at the general election, though Donald Morrison, the last-minute substitute for Aitken, was beaten in Northumberland. Aitken's friends were confident that he would have won. Now he had missed his chance. Borden formed a government and Aitken was not in it. But opportunity of another sort again opened before him. The new Canadian government repudiated the Reciprocity Treaty with the United States, and therewith the hopes for Imperial Preference revived. Aitken had again a part to play as intermediary—this time between Canada and the mother country.

CHAPTER FOUR

BONAR LAW'S INTIMATE FRIEND, 1911–14

In October 1911 Aitken went to Canada in order to assess the political situation there after the election. He wanted to extract from Borden a clear request for British food taxes. He took with him his business associate and political mentor, Edward Goulding. Canadian politics were not their only topic of conversation on the boat. The leadership of the Unionist party was uppermost in their minds. Goulding himself had launched a campaign against Balfour's elegant conduct of affairs, and it was a reasonable guess that Balfour would give up now that the struggle over the house of lords was concluded. Who would succeed him? The obvious figure was Austen Chamberlain, heir to his father's policy and reputation. But, despite an appearance of firmness, Austen was weak within. Balfour said cruelly: "If only Austen was what he looked how splendid he would be". Those who lacked confidence in Chamberlain turned to Walter Long, an alternative of despair. Long had the good qualities of a country gentleman, but neither the character nor the ability of a leader. Unionists gloomily contemplated the coming choice and lamented that there was no third man.

The third man existed. Law had the qualities which Chamberlain ought to have had. He was a clear-headed Tariff Reformer and a man of cool political judgement. He was to prove himself a most successful Unionist leader. He took over a party torn by conflict and distrust. He reunited it and finally headed the first Conservative government since 1874 to win an independent majority. It is strange in retrospect that the Unionists had not recognized Law already as their predestined leader. But his background and comparative lack of experience were against him: a Scotch Canadian with no university education, a Presbyterian, a metal-broker, who had never sat in a cabinet. Law himself knew what he was doing when he championed Tariff Reform in Lancashire, but despite his intense ambition he liked to be pushed. Aitken pushed him. He also preached the cause of Law to others. He wrote to Law from the Lusitania while in mid-ocean:

> Goulding and I have had a row, first night on board, and none since. . . .
> Our quarrel was over politics. He is canvassing agent for Austin—or was.

told him Smith had no chance at all. He agreed. I then said you had some chance even if only an offchance. He agreed. Then I charged him with disloyalty. . . .

I have stated that you told me you would take the leadership if the chance offered. That your present line of conduct was your best plan for winning &c &c. He urged you promised Austin you wouldn't contest first place with him. I ridiculed this statement, if made, having any effect on your friends &c using the obvious arguments.

Goulding, it seems, was converted and wrote to Garvin, who was not. Aitken assumed that there was plenty of time. On his return to England, he intended to organize a careful campaign for Law, beginning with the capture of F. E. Smith.

Events moved too fast. Aitken arrived back in England on 7 November. On 8 November Balfour announced his resignation and departed to Bad Gastein. A meeting of Unionist MPs to elect a new leader in the house of commons[1] was summoned for 13 November. Aitken had only five days in which to work. The later stories of his elaborate lobbying are mythical, even when originated by Aitken himself. Aitken's real task was to hold Law steady. The rest followed of itself. With the Unionists irrevocably split between Chamberlain and Long, they would inevitably turn to the third man, once Law made his resolution clear. Law shook off his earlier pledge to Chamberlain that he would not contest the leadership with the ingenious argument, provided by Aitken, that he was running against Long, not against Chamberlain. Even so, he hesitated. On 10 November he drafted a letter, stating that he would refuse to run if he thought that his nomination would "damage C and help L". Law called on Aitken and showed him the letter. Aitken threw it on the fire.

Law angrily upbraided him, and their relations were strained up to the very moment when Law became leader—much as William I of Prussia refused to acknowledge Bismarck on the day he became German emperor. But the deed was done. Law yielded and drafted another letter, saying that he would accept the position if it were offered to him. There was no need for Aitken to manoeuvre. He was content to wait and even retired to the country for the weekend. On Monday, 13 November, Chamberlain and Long both withdrew. Law was elected leader. Kipling commented sardonically to Aitken:

I confess I wonder that our Party did not plump for Long. He would have been more immaculately useless and genteely incompetent than anything in sight. Austen—alas! is a son of a Father and when the Father is dead, the son's stock will drop heavily.

[1] The Unionists elected a leader of the party, at a joint meeting of peers and MPs, only when he became prime minister. Until that happened, they had separate and, in theory, equal leaders in the Lords and Commons. Lansdowne was at this time Unionist leader in the Lords.

A curious epilogue showed that Aitken could hesitate as much as Law. Aitken's first impulse was to collect some reward for himself. He could not ask Law directly. He therefore telegraphed on 18 November to his friend Hazen, formerly prime minister of Nova Scotia and now a minister in Borden's government:

I am very anxious to obtain appointment as Parliamentary Secretary. Will you ask Borden to send private and personal message to Bonar Law recommending me.

Borden took the hint. He wrote to Law on 22 November:

Several of my friends have asked me to write to you with regard to Sir W. M. Aitken. I hesitate to offer any suggestion, as obviously it should have little weight in such a matter; but, perhaps, I may venture to say that if he should be chosen as your Parliamentary Secretary, the selection would be favourably regarded here.

Aitken had already had second thoughts. He telegraphed to Hazen on 23 November that he had declined the appointment (which can by then hardly have been offered to him) "account of uncertainty concerning Fleming". Law replied to Borden in similar terms on 9 December:

As regards Sir Max Aitken, he is the most intimate personal friend I have in the House of Commons (in spite of the comparatively short time I have known him) and not only for that reason but because of his remarkable force and ability, I should have preferred him as my Secretary to any one else. Since I got my appointment also he has been assisting me in the most effective way, but he does not himself wish to be publicly announced as one of my secretaries, and he desires to continue to help me without any public announcement.

Possibly Aitken fought shy of the drudgery in regular attendance at the house of commons. Possibly Law was less eager to appoint Aitken than he made out. At any rate Aitken did not get the position. He made a virtue of necessity and said of his intimacy with Law: "If I use the key for myself where should I be then?"

In one way and another, Aitken had become more bound to England than he had originally intended. He had missed his chance in Canada, at least for some years and as events turned out for ever. He had a moral commitment to the man he had made Unionist leader. He began to put down roots as much as was in his nature. In his first enthusiasm for his constituency, he actually proposed to settle in Ashton-under-Lyne. He wrote to one of his supporters there: "Just as I had a house in Montreal when I was domiciled in Canada, so I want a house in Ashton now I am domiciled in England".[1] He inspected one or two six-bedroomed houses

[1] This sentence, though no doubt not meant legalistically, would have disturbed Beaverbrook's executors, when they were seeking to establish that he had never ceased to be domiciled in Canada.

and then, not surprisingly, lost interest. He found something more suitable on a sudden impulse. Driving back from Rottingdean one day with the Kiplings,[1] the Aitkens saw a for sale notice at Cherkley Court just outside Leatherhead. Aitken went in at once and bought the house after a single inspection. The cost was £30,000.

Cherkley Court was a harsh square block of a house, built by a Birmingham ironmaster called Dixon. It had no architectural merit and was, as one of Aitken's friends described it, an overgrown suburban villa rather than a country house. However it had wonderful views over the Surrey hills. Aitken added the amenities of a swimming pool, a tennis court, and later a private cinema. Gladstone had once called and had been angered at the number of people who came to meet him—not a complaint often heard from its new owner. The local people pronounced the name "Charkley" in the usual English way. Aitken insisted on "Churkley", just as he said "Durby", not "Darby", for Lord Derby—or rather, as Jean Norton remarked: "Max always says Durby when he remembers to do so".

The Aitkens gave up their London house soon after the birth of their second son, who was named Peter Rudyard Aitken and had Kipling as his godfather. Henceforth Cherkley was to be the most stable element in Aitken's life.[2] Characteristically he hesitated to commit himself. The house was bought in Lady Aitken's name. Though the arrangement may have had some financial advantage, it mainly represented a side of Aitken's nature. Just as he always used other men to preside over his companies and himself usually kept off the board, so now there was an implication that Gladys Aitken was tied to Cherkley, while Max Aitken remained free. At any rate this was how it worked out.[3]

Gladys Aitken did the furnishing with the assistance of Mrs. Kipling. Aitken gave a bulk order for prints of famous statesmen with which to line the corridors. Law supplied most of the books. He wrote to Aitken:

In our relationship all the giving has been on your side that is quite right for you have plenty to spare but I wanted to give you something to note the fact that you have taken possession of your estate. I could think of nothing better than books and I have sent some to Cherkley. They bulk large but are not of much value. They are all however books which I like & if you have any of them already bring them in and I shall change them.

Cherkley was without modern conveniences. There was no electricity, no central heating, and very little running water. Aitken spent £10,000

[1] Leatherhead is not on the direct road from Rottingdean to London, so perhaps Aitken already had his eye on Cherkley Court and used Kipling's approval as a cover.
[2] Beaverbrook always spoke of "Cherkley", never of "Cherkley Court".
[3] Beaverbrook acquired Cherkley from his wife before her death. I have not been able to ascertain when and why this took place.

on domestic improvements. One might have expected him to employ a big London firm or a local contractor from Leatherhead. Instead he called in G. H. Coop, leader of the Ashton-under-Lyne Unionist party, who was a master plumber and electrician. Similarly new fireplaces were installed by Buckley, the Unionist agent at Ashton. Aitken always liked to employ people he knew. Also, no doubt, the considerable profit involved increased the readiness of Coop and Buckley to promote his interests at Ashton.

Aitken was a hard, or rather an impatient employer. Sharp letters were addressed to Coop from Aitken's London office: "Sir Max has no more wish to criticize than anybody has to be criticized", but he found plenty to criticize. More surprisingly, after a complaint against the high estimates: "Sir Max only proposes to use Cherkley Court for a year or two". Aitken would not wait for the central boiler to be installed and ordered one himself. He was then angry at receiving the bill for it.

He was equally impatient over constituency affairs. He paid for Buckley's holiday at the seaside. In return, he expected prompt service. He wrote to Buckley: "I want to get answers by return of post. If you cannot do this, I would prefer to employ a local solicitor". Questions flowed in for Buckley nearly every day. Which charities should Aitken support? Which of them had Unionist governors or were in doubtful wards? Which hospitals should Lady Aitken patronize? Should this clergyman receive financial help for his parish-room, or that one have a message for his school on prizegiving day? Should Aitken buy cigars from a factory in Dukinfield? (Answer: no, it is not in the constituency.) Aitken resisted appeals to his charity from individuals with one exception: he always assisted anyone wishing to emigrate to Canada.

Aitken took great care over his publicity at Ashton. He scrutinized each issue of The Ashton Herald and advised on the make-up of its pages. When he finally broke silence in the house of commons, he instructed Buckley to put a full report of his speech in both Ashton papers at a cost of £20. This care for publicity had a remarkable result on Aitken's future. Accidentally it opened the door for him as a press lord. It has long been known that Aitken acquired the controlling shares of The Daily Express in November 1916. It was also known that his connection with The Express began earlier, but no trace of this could be found in his financial records. The executors looked in vain after Beaverbrook's death. Yet the story was there. It was in the boxes labelled "Ashton-under-Lyne".

The Daily Express was still in financial difficulties, despite the loan which Aitken had made to Blumenfeld in January 1911. Blumenfeld might be a lively politician and, according to Aitken, the only editor of the time who was universally beloved. He did not know how to make his paper prosper. The leading shareholders, who had taken the paper over from

Pearson, were indifferent to its fate and would not support it further. In 1912 Blumenfeld had to accept official Unionist help after all—perhaps less reluctantly now that Law was leader. Unionist party funds subscribed £10,000 for Express ordinary shares, nominally held by Aitken and two other wealthy Unionists. Unknown to the party organization, Aitken also slipped in ahead on his own account. He provided £40,000 as a first mortgage, thus establishing a prior claim over the ordinary shareholders. He also made a condition. The Daily Express was to insert paragraphs about Sir Max Aitken, the rising young MP for Ashton-under-Lyne, so that these could be reproduced in the two Ashton papers. Aitken further arranged for The Daily Express paragraphs to be reproduced in Canadian papers, from which again they returned to Ashton at third-hand. Thus, Aitken's association with The Daily Express, which later shaped his life, began as a by-product of his constituency propaganda.

Aitken's business concerns were also employed on his publicity. The officials of Royal Securities Corporation in Montreal were instructed to organize a Canadian Ashton-under-Lyne association. They reported proudly that the association had 80 members, whereas the similar association for all Yorkshire had only 150. No doubt the free parties and excursions for the Ashton men were more lavish. On one occasion, however, the Montreal office blundered. It hired a touring brass band from Ashton at considerable expense and only learnt afterwards that it was a Liberal offshoot.

Aitken knew well how to run publicity for himself. He was more at a loss in national politics. Indeed he often talked of leaving them altogether. Thus, he wrote to Lord Elcho on 22 November 1911:

> My interest in politics is not as great as my interest in business. I will always gladly run elections in the hope that I may be of some use in furthering the foremost policy of the Conservative party. . . . If our policy is successful in the near future I may possibly retire from politics and devote my time to developing the enterprises in which I take so much interest.

Admittedly, this letter was to excuse himself for not taking Elcho's son as his secretary. But it also reflected his genuine doubts. His friends assured him that he would become a good speaker in the House if only he spoke more often. He would not do it. Sometimes he said that he found routine attendance at the House boring. At other times he pleaded that he lacked the courage to speak to a critical audience. Both excuses were true. In particular Aitken was always racked by nerves unless he had a packed audience of enthusiastic supporters, such as the Ashton Unionists provided.

More than this, Aitken did not know what to say in regard to Home Rule, the great issue of the day between 1912 and 1914. Canada was loyal to the Empire, despite having self-government, and Aitken did not see why the Irish should be denied their national freedom, if that was what they wanted. On top of this, his closest friend in the house of commons was now Tim Healy, the Independent Irish Nationalist, and from him Aitken learnt to admire both the Irish and the Roman Catholic church. Against this, Aitken, as a Presbyterian, was ready to champion the demand of the Ulster Protestants not to be put under Rome rule. Once more he turned to publicity. He instructed Royal Securities Corporation to organize Orange demonstrations in Montreal: "Ulster is fighting against Rome rule in Ireland and is entitled to support of all God-fearing Protestants". Aitken's friend, R. B. Bennett, received the same instruction and with it a more extraordinary suggestion. Aitken wrote to him on 22 December 1911:

> I expected to make an arrangement with you by which you would abandon the Canadian House and go into politics here, campaigning against Home Rule. Here we are all Protestants, and no man is at a disadvantage on account of his anti-Roman views.

Aitken soon lost interest in Irish affairs. His Radical friends, Churchill and Lloyd George, assured him that the claims of Ulster would ultimately be met, and he assumed that this would happen without much fuss. Besides, his heart lay elsewhere. His only real interest in British politics was in food taxes for the sake of drawing Canada and Great Britain closer. Here things were not going well. Law, a sound Tariff Reformer, had become Unionist leader. Canada had rejected the Reciprocity Treaty with the United States. Nevertheless, Law hesitated. The Unionist party was still committed to Balfour's pledge of 1910 that it would hold a referendum before introducing food taxes. There was a condition: the Liberals should hold a similar referendum before introducing a Home Rule bill. The Liberals had not fulfilled the condition, and technically Law was free. But he knew that food taxes would split the Unionist party, and unlike Aitken, put the unity of the party even before Tariff Reform.

Law hit on a way out, or possibly Aitken suggested it for him. If the Canadians would insist on food taxes, he could put the responsibility on them and perhaps silence Unionist doubters in the name of imperial sentiment. Aitken tried to operate this plan. In June 1912 he invited Borden, the Canadian prime minister, to England. Borden and Law had long talks at Cherkley, where Borden duly emphasized that food taxes were essential for Imperial Preference in Canada. But he refused to express his opinion in public: he would not interfere in British politics, just as he would not tolerate British interference in Canadian.

Reluctantly, Law had to make up his mind for himself. In August the Unionist shadow cabinet decided to repudiate the referendum pledge.

But they still hoped for Canadian aid. Aitken was dispatched to Canada
as emissary, taking F. E. Smith with him. Law sent him urgent instructions on 3 September 1912:

> What Borden does is of the utmost importance. . . . What I should
> like to impress upon him is what I said to him at your house, that after all,
> this question of preference is his battle quite as much as ours; and, indeed,
> in a sense, more than ours, for it would help him in Canada; while, of
> course, the food taxes are only a handicap to us here.

Borden stuck to his old line: though food taxes were essential, he would
not meddle in British politics. Aitken returned empty-handed, but not
discouraged. He had thought of a new plan: if Law championed food taxes
publicly, the Free Trade Unionists would have to conform for the sake
of party unity.

Law allowed himself to be persuaded, or seemed to be so. At the
Albert Hall on 14 November, the two Unionist leaders, Lansdowne and
Law, repudiated Balfour's pledge of a referendum. To clinch matters,
Aitken carried Law off to Ashton-under-Lyne, where he repeated the
repudiation of the referendum on 16 December. But Law remained
evasive. He still intended to put the responsibility on the colonies. He
therefore declared that a Unionist government would not introduce food
taxes. It would call a colonial conference and would agree to food taxes
only if the colonies insisted. However, Aitken was triumphant. He believed
that Law's authority as leader would silence all opposition. He confessed
later:

> The advice given by me, to nail the colours to the mast, was mistaken.
> I gave it in the belief that a statement by him would end the agitation.
> There I was far wrong. The opposition grew more furious and more
> determined.

Law and his family spent Christmas at Cherkley with the Aitkens and
the Kiplings. This was only a brief lull in the political storm. Encouragement came from Austen Chamberlain: "Courage and a fine faith will
bring you triumphantly through". H. A. Gwynne wrote to Aitken: "Do
your damndest with Canada. Their declaration will save the situation and
make the enemy sit up". Aitken knew that this expedient would not work:
Borden remained silent. Instead Aitken tried to threaten the Free Trade
Unionists. He warned them that if they opposed food taxes, then the
Tariff Reformers would cease to resist Irish Home Rule and Welsh
Disestablishment. This was a threat without substance.

Gwynne's letter to Aitken had also the sinister sentence: "What price
your pal Alfred now? He's doing his best to ruin the party and the
Empire". Alfred was of course Lord Northcliffe, and the Northcliffe press
was in full cry against the stomach taxes. Northcliffe made repeated

attempts to see Law, using Aitken as intermediary. Aitken refused to take Northcliffe's telephone calls and did not answer his letters. But it was impossible to ignore his newspapers. Still worse, the Lancashire Unionist MPs mobilized against food taxes, and Lord Derby went along with them, if only to preserve his position as uncrowned king of Lancashire.

Law consulted Lansdowne. Faced with this powerful revolt in their party, the two leaders determined to resign. At the last moment, a way out was found. Carson, who cared much for the Union with Ireland and little for food taxes, drafted a memorial, requesting Law and Lansdowne to abandon food taxes and yet to remain the leaders. The backbench Unionists were invited to sign the memorial. All but six did so. One of those who refused was Max Aitken. He did not waver even when Law accepted the memorial and so abandoned food taxes. Instead he went off to Ashton-under-Lyne and declared that he still supported food taxes. If Ashton did not want them, they had better turn him out. He wrote later:

> For the first time in my life I could not march with Law ... I should have been false to my lifelong convictions and to my public if I had "ratted" on Imperial Preference like the bulk of the London Conservative press.

This was the version which Aitken gave throughout his life. Was it the whole truth? Some Tariff Reformers did not think so. They believed that Aitken himself had devised the way of escape for Law, though maintaining his opposition in public. Goulding wrote to Garvin on 11 January 1913: "B.L. has under the ... influence of his young Canadian friend lost his nerve", and Garvin, improving on this, wrote to Waldorf Astor two days later:

> It becomes pretty clear that we have been played with, and that Aitken is our leader. . . . Morally—that is in respect of will and decision—there is no B.L., but only a receptacle which must always be inhabited by another personality. The Hermit Crab in this case is Aitken, always putting himself into the other man's ear, and swaying in his sinister, insistent way as he likes that strange unfixed feeble mass of timidity and ambition.[1]

Goulding and Garvin were keen food taxers. They were passionately resentful at failure, and their testimony is by no means reliable. Law clearly did not need much prompting from Aitken to run away. He put the unity of the party first and had been apprehensive about the effect of food taxes all along. The situation was more or less repeated in 1922 when Law became prime minister and virtually abandoned Tariff Reform in order to hold the Conservative party together—this time undoubtedly to Beaverbrook's disappointment.

Aitken's actions in 1913, if indeed he took them, were perfectly defensible. Food taxes were lost for the time being. Law's resignation would

[1] A. M. Gollin, The Observer and J. L. Garvin, 383–85.

plunge the Unionist party into confusion without helping the Tariff Reform cause. Rather it would make food taxes more disliked than ever. Aitken therefore found a way out for Law and preserved his own political integrity at the same time. All this is no more than surmise. In 1959 when A. M. Gollin wished to print the hermit crab letter in his book on The Observer and J. L. Garvin, the Oxford University Press told him to leave it out for fear of an action for libel by Beaverbrook. Gollin appealed to Beaverbrook who laughed loudly and said: "Publish it. Publish the lot. Always publish everything about me good or bad". Beaverbrook made no further comment whereas usually he was eager to explain his past actions and live them over again. Gollin is convinced that the hermit crab story is true. I think it possible that Beaverbrook was amused and gratified as being credited with greater machiavellianism than he had in fact shown.

When the crisis was over, Aitken at last admitted Northcliffe to Law's presence. Law said: "You are my worst enemy". Northcliffe replied: "Oh, no! I am your best friend. I have taken the millstone of food taxes off your shoulders. You could never have won an election on the food tax".

Whatever part Aitken had played during the conflict, he was undoubtedly depressed when it was over. 1913 was a bad year for him. He was ill, he was disappointed, he had no firm objective. Towards the end of the year his father died. He talked repeatedly of resigning his seat in the house of commons. In March 1913 this got so far that the Ashton Unionists began to consider fresh candidates. However an enthusiastic meeting or two, with cries of "Buck up" and "You are good enough", made him change his mind, though not to the extent of appearing often at Westminster.

In May Aitken announced that he proposed to seek health in Canada. On the voyage he tried to sell Cherkley to J. B. Duke, who bought Rolls-Royce instead. Aitken's health cure in Canada took the form of buying over two hundred grain elevators in the west and promoting the largest real estate deal Montreal had known. He also launched a scheme, never carried out, for diverting the St. Lawrence river and supplying Montreal with hydro-electric power. He began, too, his lavish record of educational endowments in New Brunswick. He instituted prizes at Harkins Academy, Newcastle, his old school. Allan Davidson proposed that they should be $25 each. Aitken answered: "Make them $100". As well, he instituted scholarships of $250 to the University of New Brunswick and looked forward to the time when it would achieve a world-wide reputation. Beating off other appeals, he grumbled: "Last year cost me £27,000 to live. This is entirely too much and is due to the extent to which I contributed to projects here, there and everywhere".

Canada did not restore Aitken to health. He returned to England and decided that he was seriously ill. He broke off all business and political activities and departed to the continent, leaving an instruction that no letters were to be forwarded. Even Law did not know where he was and had to enquire of Blumenfeld, who naturally knew everything. Aitken was actually at Munich, consulting a specialist in the belief that he suffered from Bright's disease in an advanced form. The specialist found nothing wrong with him except nervous exhaustion. This was also Law's opinion. He wrote on 8 July: "I always thought that what was wrong with you was chiefly nervous and I still think that is at the bottom of it". The Munich specialist prescribed a long stay at St. Moritz. Aitken went there and left after a week. Boredom had effected a complete cure.

Aitken now resumed his business activities on a larger scale than ever. Royal Securities Corporation was well established in the City. Earlier in 1912 Montreal newspapers had announced Aitken's resignation as president in favour of A. R. Doble, head of the Montreal office. It is impossible to discover whether this resignation took place. But Aitken was certainly back as president in 1914, and he did not end his connection with Royal Securities Corporation until 1919, when he sold it to Killam, one of his subordinates. Even then he continued to act as chief and as late as 1935 was writing to Killam in such terms as: "Now be a good boy and do as I tell you. You know it has always been for your good". This does not prove that Beaverbrook still controlled Royal Securities Corporation. It is only one example among many of the domination which he continued to exert over those who had served him even when he had ostensibly relinquished financial control.

Royal Securities Corporation by no means exhausted Aitken's activities. He also acquired about this time the Colonial Bank—"the second oldest bank in the City", as he liked to boast—which had a large business in the West Indies, Aitken's original hunting-ground. He continued to run this bank until after the first world war, when it amalgamated with other similar institutions and became Barclays Bank, DC & O. His greatest financial worry was The Globe, which continued to lose money. This exasperated Aitken who as yet lacked either the time or the skill to put it right. In 1914 he disposed of responsibility for The Globe to Dudley Docker, a Birmingham industrialist. This was a curious transaction. Far from receiving money for the paper, Aitken paid Docker £5,000 on condition he kept The Globe going for six months. Docker in fact kept it going for longer, though he, too, could not make it pay, and Aitken won £500 by betting that he would not.[1] Aitken continued to have some connection with the paper, both financial and personal, though he did not draw

---

[1] Docker ultimately sold The Globe to Sir John Leach, who merged it in The Pall Mall Gazette. In 1923 Beaverbrook bought the latter for £7,500 and merged it in The Evening Standard.

4

attention to this later. In Politicians and the War Beaverbrook tells how
in November 1915 The Globe revealed that Kitchener was about to be
overthrown and was suppressed for a fortnight as a result.[1] Few readers
of this entertaining story would guess that the leak came from Aitken or
that he was among the proprietors of The Globe who reluctantly lost the
services of the peccant editor.

Aitken's life was now beginning to settle into the form which it followed
thereafter. Cherkley was the family home, where he spent his weekends,
usually with a party of friends—the Laws, the Kiplings, Tim Healy, and
visitors from Canada or Ashton-under-Lyne. Instead of a house in town,
Aitken established himself in the Temple, conveniently situated halfway
between Westminster and Lombard Street, his financial headquarters.
He rarely went into society, except when some publicity could be gained
from it, and preferred intimate parties at his chambers, where the talk
ranged from politics and finance to personalities. His friends were not all
men. Fifty years afterwards, a mention of Kühlmann, first secretary at
the German embassy before 1914 and subsequently secretary of state,
brought from Beaverbrook the remark: "He was a clever fellow. He and
I ran after the same girls".

In the autumn of 1913 Aitken returned to political life and in the form
which most suited him. He became the go-between, the man who tried
to arrange compromise between the contending political leaders. In his
own words: "I acted as an intermediary in practically all the negotiations
for a compromise settlement which took place between the two party
leaders, during the months when the United Kingdom seemed to be
drifting towards civil war".[2] The conflict was of course over Ireland.
The Liberals were determined to grant Home Rule. The Unionists were
determined that Ulster, or at any rate the predominantly Protestant
counties of Ulster, should be left out. Compromise on this basis was
favoured by many leading Unionists, including Carson the leader of the
Irish Unionists, and also by the most resolute Radicals, including Lloyd
George and Churchill. Aitken himself favoured it from the moment he
entered British political life and perhaps helped to win over Law.
Asquith's real opinion is impossible to ascertain. Probably he welcomed
compromise, but not if it lost him the votes of the Irish Nationalists.

Aitken's part was to bring the two leaders together. The suggestion for
a meeting came from Asquith. Law answered by proposing Cherkley
as the meeting-place. On 14 October Asquith drove down secretly, in
one of Aitken's cars. He found Law and Aitken playing double dummy—
not the only occasion when bridge entered into their relations. The two
leaders were constrained and hostile. "Bonar Law was harsh and Asquith

[1] Politicians and the War, i, 199–200.
[2] Ibid., 48.

subsided into silence". Aitken relieved the tension by telling a comical story about Blumenfeld. His hearers laughed "and a contact of personality was instantly established". Aitken drew the moral that "negotiations proceed better and national interests are more readily served when the negotiators on both sides are not too serious". Aitken always acted on this principle. It is unlikely that either Asquith or Law shared it. But it seems to have worked on this occasion.

Asquith and Law had three meetings, all at Cherkley, on 14 October, 6 November and 10 December. Aitken did not leave any record, other than the story of how he broke the ice, and the two leaders, perhaps naturally, did not mention him in their respective accounts.[1] Considering his ability as an intermediary and also his eagerness for a compromise on this particular issue, it is likely that he helped the conversations along a good deal. However, no agreement was reached. Law would not retreat from the principle that the Protestant counties of Ulster should be entirely excluded from Home Rule; Asquith would not go further than Home Rule for Ulster within a Home Rule Ireland. The negotiations broke down, fated to be an episode without significance in British history.

The meetings between Law and Asquith were however a remarkable tribute to Aitken, evidence that he was far from being an unimportant figure in British politics. Here were the prime minister and the leader of the Opposition engaged in secret negotiations behind the backs of their respective followers at a time of unparalleled political tension. A revelation of their meetings, let alone of what they talked about, would have been political dynamite. Yet both Asquith and Law trusted Aitken absolutely. Both spoke freely before him and listened to his suggestions. Law's reliance on Aitken's silence needs no explanation. But Asquith's reliance was equally complete. Whatever Asquith might say to others, he put his political life in Aitken's hands without the slightest hesitation. This was not treatment he would have accorded to anyone else. Aitken's behaviour on this occasion was true to his character throughout life: though he liked to know all the secrets of the day, he also knew how to keep them.

It is a melancholy reflection that the compromise originally urged by Aitken was in fact achieved eight years later, though only after much bitterness and bloodshed and on worse terms for all parties. Ireland lost six counties instead of losing probably four, and British Unionists had to accept Dominion status for Ireland instead of a much more limited Home Rule. There are many occasions on which to admire Aitken's statesmanship as well as his agility. The negotiations over Ireland before the first world war rank high on the list.

[1] Law's account is in Blake, The Unknown Prime Minister, 161–67; Asquith's in Jenkins, Asquith, 288–95.

There were no further meetings between Asquith and Law. Negotiations for a compromise went on at a lower level, and Aitken was apparently involved in them. Beaverbrook told me that he and the Master of Elibank, the former Liberal chief whip, cleared the way for the abortive Buckingham Palace conference on Irish affairs which met in July 1914. Nothing of this has survived in his records. At the end of his life Beaverbrook meant to return to the subject. He sent a researcher to Edinburgh to examine the Elibank papers; he enquired of W. T. Cosgrave, an old and valued friend, whether the papers of Dillon, Redmond, O'Higgins and Collins were for sale; and he wrote to Lord Rugby on 9 December 1963:

> I have thought for some time that I ought to do a story of the negotiations leading up to the Irish Treaty. The years of 1913 and 1914 were exceedingly interesting, with immense efforts to reach a settlement.

Nothing came of this. Beaverbrook had only another six months to live.

To judge from later correspondence, Aitken was seen much more in the house of commons at this time. Forty or even fifty years afterwards, Beaverbrook was writing to this old gentleman or that: "How vividly I remember sitting beside you in the house of commons in those far-off days before August 1914". This sounds impressive until one notices Beaverbrook's instruction to his secretary, attached to such letters: "Look up this fellow and see whether he was in the house of commons before 1914. I can't remember him".

Beaverbrook told me one story that sounds genuine and that I have not seen in any account. At the time of the Curragh mutiny, Seely, the secretary for war, gave foolish promises to Gough, the cavalry general in Ireland. The house of commons met in high excitement, the Unionists exclaiming: "Now we've got him". Asquith averted the storm by announcing that he had taken over the war office himself. The baffled Unionists roared: "Cromwell! Cromwell!" Beaverbrook added: "Good fun". Evidently he really was present at the house on this occasion.

He was again called into Unionist counsels on Irish affairs when the Buckingham Palace conference broke down. The call came on Friday, 31 July 1914. Aitken was invited to Edward Goulding's house at Wargrave—Cherkley's older rival as a political meeting place—in order to spend the weekend with Law, Carson, and F. E. Smith. He assumed that Ulster and Home Rule were on the agenda. His own mind was full of other things. As a financier, he had noticed a strange situation in the City. His observations, never published before,[1] are of some interest as

---

[1] There are many valuable passages which Beaverbrook carried as far as the galleys of Politicians and the War and then cut out. These excisions were usually made on Boswell's principle that they related too much to himself and not enough to the other characters in the book.

illustrating the atmosphere immediately before the outbreak of the first world war:

> It was clear to anyone with a real knowledge of markets that some obscure and colossal movement was on foot for a fortnight before the declaration of war—a "hold-up" indicating that some one somewhere knew of a definite intention. There was no ordinary panic in the sense of a sudden and tremendous fall in prices; it simply became almost impossible to find buyers at all.
> Presumably the financiers in touch with the German and Austrian Government knew either that war had been decided on or, at least, that the war party in Berlin and Vienna were so strong as to make war almost a certainty.

Aitken had received a telegram from R. B. Bennett in Canada: "Is there going to be a war?" He wanted to give Bennett the best opinion he could obtain. Not knowing Grey, he asked Healy to sound Grey. Healy returned with the answer: "it is a toss-up". Aitken had to express a definite opinion to Bennett and therefore telegraphed: "Everything points to war". However, as Beaverbrook recorded later: "I was too much of an optimist to believe at heart in the deliberate insanity which would precipitate a general war".

Arrived at Wargrave, Aitken noticed in Carson and Law "a reluctance to turn from Ireland to confront the realities of war". He has left no record of his own outlook beyond the remark that he, too, "found it hard to grasp that the war peril was an actual thing". In verbal recollection Beaverbrook said that he had intended to champion British non-intervention and was overawed by the warlike resolve of the others. This may be a case of jobbing backwards when he had come to believe that Great Britain would have done better to keep out of both wars. At any rate, the Unionist leaders were clear that Great Britain ought to support France and Russia.

There was a more urgent question before them. At this moment on 31 July, the German intention to march through Belgium was not yet known, and the Liberal government was sharply divided. It seemed that eight or perhaps even more ministers would resign from the cabinet. The Liberal party would be split, with possibly a majority supporting the opponents of war. Churchill, who was on the side of war, foresaw the need for a coalition government. Never one to hold back or to leave the initiative to the prime minister, he had asked F. E. Smith to find out whether the Unionists would join a coalition if the Liberal government broke up. Law refused to discuss the subject. He distrusted Churchill and held that any proposal for a coalition should be made directly from Asquith to himself. The most he would allow was a general agreement that the Unionists would support the government if it decided on war.

The following morning, Saturday, 1 August, Smith and Aitken were eager to return to London in order to be near the centre of events. Law insisted on their all remaining in the country unless summoned to London by Asquith. In the afternoon he weakened, and the party motored to London in Aitken's cars. Churchill invited Law to have dinner with himself and Grey, presumably to renew his attempt at coalition. Law refused. Instead he spent the evening with Lansdowne and Balfour, discussing what the Unionist attitude should be. They decided to inform Asquith that they would be ready to see him whenever he wished to see them.

Aitken was apparently not admitted to this conclave of Unionist leaders. Unable to resist the chance of being the intermediary in a political merger, he decided to act on his own despite Law's disapproval and after dinner went to Admiralty House with Smith. There they found Churchill with two Liberal friends. While waiting for news and for the Liberals to go away, four of them played bridge—seemingly a universal habit among politicians at this time. Aitken, as usual, was the odd man out. A dispatch box was brought in. It contained the news that Germany had declared war on Russia. Churchill pulled off his dress coat, called for a lounge jacket, and went off to mobilize the fleet. Aitken took over Churchill's partly-played hand, finding himself "in an extremely unfavourable tactical position". Smith and Aitken remained at Admiralty House until it was almost morning, but Churchill did not return.

On Sunday, 2 August, Aitken went at once to Law's house, Pembroke Lodge. There the Unionist leaders were meeting again. Aitken drafted a letter to Asquith at Law's dictation. Law declared, on behalf of Lansdowne and himself, that "it would be fatal to the honour and security of the United Kingdom to hesitate in supporting France and Russia at this present juncture; and we offer our unhesitating support to the Government in any measures they may consider necessary for that object". This was a skilful letter. It defined the Unionist position and left Asquith to make any further approach. Coalition was not proposed or even mentioned. Aitken himself took the letter to No. 10 Downing Street. He had there a conversation with Asquith's private secretary which he did not record.

Aitken did not weary in well-doing. Eager to promote a coalition, he went down to the house of commons, which was unusual for him, and actually dined there, which was more unusual still. He has recorded the event:

> I dined with Liberal politicians for the first time in my experience. . . .
> Sunday's dinner, in fact, registered the end of an epoch. There were not
> only Liberals there, but actually official Liberals, and one endeavoured
> to conform in one's demeanour to association with so many public virtues.

This was the beginning of the breaking of many bonds and of the binding of new ones—associations were formed which led men into strange paths never before contemplated.

Aitken's manoeuvres lost their immediate purpose on the following day, when it became known that the Germans were proposing to march through Belgium. Some members of the Liberal cabinet later claimed that they had been waiting for this all along, and Frances Stevenson, Lloyd George's secretary, declares that she prayed for a German invasion of Belgium every night.[1] However that may be, the threat to Belgium virtually reunited the Liberal cabinet. Only Lord Morley and John Burns resigned. The Liberal cabinet agreed to oppose the German demand. On 4 August Grey sent an ultimatum to Berlin. No answer was received, and at 11 p.m. Great Britain declared war. The Liberal party in parliament and the Liberal newspapers supported the war almost unanimously. The Liberal cabinet was unshaken. Coalition ceased to be talked of. But Aitken had developed zest and experience as a political intermediary.

[1] Lady Lloyd-George, The Years that are Past, 74.

CHAPTER FIVE

THE EYE WITNESS, 1914-16

After the British declaration of war, the life went out of politics. Liberals no longer debated whether they would support the war. Unionists no longer debated whether they would enter a coalition government. Events had settled their debates for them. Politicians, and even ministers, stood aside and waited for decisive battles on land and sea. The house of commons passed a vote of credit on 6 August and then adjourned. In the general burst of patriotic enthusiasm, politicians were hardly needed even on recruiting platforms. Aitken felt more unemployed and restless than most of them.

His first thought was for his friends. Kipling, down at Burwash, feared a collapse of civilized life. Aitken reassured him with £50 in gold, a sack of flour, and a ham. F. E. Smith, snatched from his rich career at the bar to the unrewarding labours of the Press Bureau, was anxious over his finances. Aitken guaranteed his bank account for £7,000. On a more public level, Aitken went down to Ashton-under-Lyne and flamboyantly placed £5,000 in the local trustee savings bank, as a gesture to restore the confidence of other depositors.[1] These were small activities for a financier of international standing.

Aitken had hoped to be consulted on the financial measures made necessary by the outbreak of war. Lloyd George and the great bankers somehow managed without him. He was also rebuffed in another enterprise. With his wide-ranging vision, he grasped at once that the ordinary channels of trade would be inadequate in wartime. He offered the Alberta Grain Company, which he and R. B. Bennett controlled, to the British government free of charge, as agent for the collection and transhipment of grain from the Canadian west. Asquith expressed gratitude and ignored the offer. No doubt Asquith did not appreciate the generous side of Aitken's nature, from which he himself was to benefit at the end of his life. To him, Aitken was simply a little Canadian adventurer on the make.

[1] I was told this story by Professor T. S. Ashton, the economic historian and son of the bank's manager, who much appreciated the gesture.

Aitken was also out of sympathy with his Unionist friends, even with Bonar Law. Parliament reassembled in September, but only to put Irish Home Rule on the statute book, along with an act postponing its operation for the duration of the war. The Unionists were indignant that the exclusion of Ulster was not enacted at the same time. They complained loudly of a breach of faith. Bitterness between the parties was revived. Aitken foresaw that many things would be changed by the storms of war and thought the Unionist outcry foolish. He said: "It did not matter a rap whether bills were put on the statute-book or not. They would be only sand castles against the sweeping tide of change". Aitken told Law that he had lost his sense of proportion. Law was angry, and Aitken fell out of favour.

Not surprisingly, he retreated to the land of his birth. Late in September he crossed the Atlantic, with Tim Healy as companion. This proved to be his last visit until after the war, and then he came as a stranger to Canadian politics. Healy and Aitken appeared together on recruiting platforms. Aitken had also long talks with Borden, the prime minister, and with Sam Hughes, the minister of militia, whom Aitken had helped financially during the general election of 1911. Now the Canadian ministers needed Aitken in a different way. Canadians were eager to help the mother country. Recruits poured in. The British authorities treated the Canadian contingents merely as reinforcements for the British army. Canadian ministers wished to maintain their soldiers as a distinct force. For them, the war was an opportunity to assert Imperial solidarity and the independence of Canada at the same time. Aitken was the right man to become the voice of Canada in Great Britain. He would be less official and more adroit than the High Commissioner.

Borden and Hughes told Aitken that he would be of more use to them in Great Britain than in Canada, though they did not want to lose him for good. Aitken promised that he would contest Northumberland county at the next election and actually spent $20,000 on preparing his way. However, when the election came in 1917, Aitken was otherwise engaged and bought himself out for another $20,000.

Meanwhile, Aitken returned to England on his allotted task. It was one after his own heart: he was now a go-between who could write his own instructions. No one knew how he was to assert Canadian independence. Aitken had to make up his duties and his posts as he went along. He became in time publicist, diplomatist, and organizer rolled into one. He even threw in the role of historian. In a curious way, he anticipated every facet of his later career.

Aitken's first invention, as befitted a believer in publicity, was to make himself Canadian Eye Witness. He acquired the rank of lieutenant-colonel in the Canadian militia and was authorized to attend GHQ in France.

Transport was no problem, since he sent over one of his own private cars. It would be interesting to know what Sir John French's staff officers made of him. He assembled vivid stories which he circulated to the Canadian press. There were as yet no recognized war correspondents, and Aitken was regarded with disapproval, the more because of his military rank. As he subsequently recorded, "the spirit was willing but the censorship was by no means weak". After the second battle of Ypres in April 1915, when the Canadians were heavily engaged, Aitken appealed to his government and got their firm support. Henceforth, he enjoyed more freedom than any British correspondent and gave, for instance, names of units and individual officers in defiance of the censorship rules.

There were complaints also in England. Americans saw the Canadian newspapers and got the impression that the Canadians were doing all the fighting in France. Aitken answered sharply that the British government should take up publicity also. As Eye Witness, he soon accumulated further tasks. He wrote an official weekly communiqué from the Canadian forces in France. He put together his journalistic pieces and published a historical narrative, entitled Canada in Flanders. He wrote the first two volumes of this himself. The later ones he left to others, as he became more committed elsewhere. He paid for this literary venture from his own pocket and gave the profits, which were considerable, to charity. Canada in Flanders is a fine piece of war reporting, the more striking because it had then few examples to follow. Kipling, calling himself a "wordsmith", helped Aitken with the style, but this help was hardly necessary. The inspiration came partly from the Old Testament and partly from Stevenson.

Aitken wrote a report to the Canadian government and described the spirit in which he had performed his work as a publicist. Unconsciously, his words looked forward to the time when he showed the same spirit as a newspaper proprietor:

> It is the popular demand which is the strongest factor in producing stories and pictures of the war. And the demand is natural, for the texture of the war has become ingrained in the whole fabric of the national life, and the people are asking for news, not of some small, distant and almost alien army, but of themselves, and of events personal to their interest, comfort and happiness. . . .
>
> The policy of this office has always been based on the firm belief that no propaganda reaches the hearts and minds of the people unless it is so convincing that the public is ready and anxious to pay a price to see or read it. What is given for nothing is in the eyes of the recipient worth nothing; what he is prepared to make a sacrifice for must in the nature of the case be worth something in his eyes.

Aitken also started a daily newspaper for the Canadian troops in Great Britain and France. It was called The Canadian Daily Record and ran until 31 July 1919. Nor was he content with the printed word. In 1916 he secured the appointment of an official Canadian photographer at the front. The first photographs of tanks were Canadian, and when British newspapers wanted to show a tank they had to borrow the picture from Aitken's office. This was followed by an official cinema team and again Canadians were the first to see actual films of the war. Aitken wrote of these films with romantic enthusiasm:

> The new generation will see the Battle of the Somme as though we saw the Egyptian Wars of the Eighties, the Fall of Khartoum, the assault of the Canadians at Paardeburg, or the combatants at the Battle of Mukden; and Courcelette and La Mouquet will be as vivid to them in fact as any of the great events of history are to us in imagination.

Aitken's final stroke of visual recording was the Canadian war memorials fund, a charitable endowment with Lord Rothermere as chairman. This commissioned artists to paint the scenes of war. Wyndham Lewis, Muirhead Bone, William Orpen, C. R. W. Nevinson and Augustus John all received their first commissions as war artists from this fund.[1]

This was not Aitken's only activity. In May 1915 he bestowed upon himself the title of Canadian record officer and in January 1916 created the Canadian war records office. This was designed to rival and surpass what the historical section of the committee of Imperial defence was doing for the British forces. Aitken's office accumulated every scrap of military information from divisional orders to the diaries of units and the letters of individual soldiers. All this material was arranged and catalogued, so that by the end of the war Canada had a military archive second to none. Again, this had all sprung from Aitken's private enterprise, so much so that the war records office was housed at first in rooms partitioned off from his business quarters in Lombard Street. In later years, Aitken followed his own example. As Lord Beaverbrook, he became an assiduous squirrel in pursuit of contemporary records and stored at Cherkley the remarkable archive which is now in the Beaverbrook library.

Aitken's third stroke was to set himself up as Canadian military representative overseas. Once more, he had no defined commission. He merely carried messages from the Canadian government to the British authorities in London and at the front, and they accepted him as a useful intermediary. His most remarkable achievement was to change the command of the Canadian corps in France. In April 1916 General Alderson, a British officer who held this command, quarrelled with two of his Canadian subordinates and proposed to dismiss them. Aitken foresaw trouble and asked for an interview with Sir Douglas Haig, the commander-in-chief, whom he had never met. The constitutional position was, as Aitken

---

[1] The paintings specifically commissioned by the war memorials fund were sent to Ottawa, where they have never been worthily displayed.

remarks, a peculiar one: "I was speaking on behalf of the civil power of the Dominion to a British commander in the field on a matter relating to generals directly under his command". Haig, however, "showed himself the essentially broad-minded man he was". He recognized that a Dominion must have a say in the higher command of its own forces. At his suggestion, Alderson was removed to the empty post of inspector-general of the Canadian forces in England. It was characteristic that Aitken received Borden's authority to intervene with Haig only after the entire operation had been concluded.[1]

Ultimately, Aitken came near to disaster from this habit of undertaking tasks without securing precise authority beforehand. In the autumn of 1916 Sam Hughes came to England. He succumbed to illusions of grandeur. He insisted on being made a lieutenant-general to the dismay of the Imperial authorities. He proposed to set up a military council in England, which would exercise the sole control over the Canadian forces at his order. Worst of all, he announced that he intended to appoint Aitken as Canadian high commissioner, a post which was not vacant and which was not in Hughes's gift. Aitken at first went along with Hughes and his wild ways. Then sensing trouble, he pleaded that he could not be high commissioner while still a British MP. Aitken had judged rightly. When Hughes returned to Canada, Borden dismissed him. Hughes complained loudly of a conspiracy and declared that Borden, deprived of his support, would soon fall from power. But it was Hughes whose political days were over.

Aitken emerged unscathed. He had shown discretion and moderation.[2]

[1] Aitken was later accused of nominating Byng to succeed Alderson instead of insisting on a Canadian general. This is not quite accurate. Aitken had ventured far enough in criticizing Alderson and when asked about a successor, replied that that was Haig's affair. Haig then appointed Byng. This action of Aitken's was also approved by Borden.

[2] Aitken's innocence in this affair is confirmed by a letter from J. C. C. Davidson in the Harcourt papers. On 17 November 1916 Davidson wrote to Harcourt:

In fairness to Sir Max Aitken I think I ought to tell you that the construction which one would naturally put upon the telegrams from Canada, viz: that Sam would not carry on without Max and that Max had probably pressed strongly for the post of Overseas Minister here, is wrong. Max was offered the post by Sam and refused it some three weeks ago and Borden then telegraphed saying that Sam would only agree to Max being appointed and asking whether, for the sake of peace, he would accept, to which Max replied that he could not do so as he did not feel that he was qualified for the post and must be independent of Sam which no one could be.

I think you ought to know this because, whatever one's private opinion may be of Sir Max, he was not out in this particular instance for gain and never for one moment entertained the suggestion.

Davidson was at this time Law's private secretary at the colonial office. The grudging nature of his testimony makes it the more telling.

Indeed Borden praised him for the unfailing tact with which he had transmitted Hughes's impetuous instructions. Nevertheless, Aitken's situation was changed. Hughes's successor, Sir Edward Kemp, took the title of minister of overseas forces and dealt directly with the Imperial authorities himself. Aitken ceased to be military representative. He remained record officer until the end of the war, but it was no longer his principal activity. The organization which he had created was running smoothly, and, as usual, he was ready to move on. By an expected oscillation he returned to British politics.

The change over was not of course clear-cut. Throughout 1915 he was greatly absorbed by his Canadian affairs. The visitors' book at Cherkley bears witness to this. For the only time between 1912 and 1964 there was a prolonged break with no entry between 21 February 1915 and 11 March 1916, when the first visitor is recorded as "W. M. Aitken", perhaps further evidence of his long absence. In 1915 he seems to have spent days together in France and continued to make short visits until the autumn of 1916. Even so his main work was in London. He still ran his financial enterprises in the intervals of writing up Eye Witness and was particularly involved with the Colonial Bank—a useful contact with the colonial secretary, who after the middle of May 1915 happened to be Bonar Law. Aitken also drew closer to Law by moving his London quarters from the Temple to the Hyde Park Hotel,[1] which was within easy reach of Law's house in Edwardes Square.

When Aitken was appointed Canadian military representative at the end of 1915, he also acquired a room at the war office, which brought him even nearer to the centre of affairs. He became intimate with Sir Reginald Brade, the secretary to the war office, and in private correspondence bestowed on him the title of "Captain". He was also on surprisingly friendly terms with Sir William Robertson, chief of the Imperial general staff, a relationship which could not be guessed from Beaverbrook's later portrayal of generals in the first world war. As an added stroke of luck, Lloyd George became secretary for war in July 1916 and found Aitken already sitting two doors down the corridor. Fate certainly arranged things well for the go-between.

[1] Beaverbrook told me that he bought the controlling shares in this hotel in order to ensure his comfort. His papers contain no record of this, and maybe he mistook the Hyde Park Hotel for the Grand Babylon. (Perhaps Arnold Bennett's novel, The Grand Babylon Hotel, is no longer read. In it an American millionaire buys the hotel because his daughter cannot get steak and a bottle of beer otherwise.) Beaverbrook did acquire some shares in the hotel at a later date. He had become friendly with the manager and in 1924, when there was some talk of changing the management, bought 10,000 shares. These, though only 6.6% of the total, presumably enabled him to defend his friend's interest. When the manager retired in 1946 Beaverbrook sold his shares.

Aitken's key-relationship was with Bonar Law. This had its ups-and-downs, the more so when Aitken fell foul of the Unionist central office. In January 1915 The Daily Express was again in trouble. It owed £9,000 for newsprint, and the merchant refused to supply more unless a receiver was appointed. Steel-Maitland suggested that the ordinary shareholders, including Aitken, who were in fact nominees of the Unionist central office, should propose as receiver three safe Unionist MPs. Aitken replied that the mortgage holders were entitled to appoint the receiver, an argument which Steel-Maitland accepted. He was however less acquiescent when he learnt that Aitken himself was the mortgage holder and that he proposed to appoint Blumenfeld, the editor, as receiver. Steel-Maitland appealed to Bonar Law against Aitken's "extraordinary" proposal. Law took his usual line that Aitken was his close friend and therefore refused to be involved. Aitken got his way. Steel-Maitland had tried to use Aitken much as Sir Sandford Fleming had done. Instead Aitken used him. Aitken moved a stage nearer towards controlling The Daily Express, though at this time more in Blumenfeld's interest than his own.[1] He also moved further away from being an acceptable figure in respectable Unionist circles.

Law continued to listen to his advice and rarely took it. In the middle of May 1915 there was a political crisis. Backbench Unionists were already raging against the alleged shortage of shells, an agitation which, as Aitken knew from his vantage point at GHQ, was being fanned by Sir John French. The crisis however exploded when Lord Fisher, the first sea lord, resigned in protest against sending further warships to the Dardanelles. Law was determined to prevent a conflict between the parties. He therefore anticipated the Unionist outcry by proposing coalition to Lloyd George, and the two men then pressed it on Asquith. Aitken was in France when the crisis came to a head. An urgent telegram from Blumenfeld recalled him to London. Unlike Law, he wanted a conflict in the belief that this would end by making Law prime minister. He arrived in London too late: Law had already agreed to coalition. When Beaverbrook later wrote the story of this crisis, at second hand,

---

[1] Aitken certainly took an active interest in Express affairs, presumably out of friendship for Blumenfeld. Thus he wrote to Runciman, the president of the board of trade on 5 May 1916:

The Daily Express, in which I am interested, is short of paper. I should like to have the opportunity of discussing with you the means by which I could secure the release of a ship to bring over a cargo of paper from the mills of Price Brothers and Company Ltd. of Quebec.

Aitken had an interview with Runciman, the outcome of which is not stated. Aitken's letter is in the Runciman papers at Newcastle and was kindly brought to my notice by Christopher Wrigley.

he emphasized the mistake of those who thought that shells, not Fisher, had killed the Liberal government. This emphasis was to conceal his own expectation that shells would do the trick. For once he had misjudged a situation, though no one could have foreseen Fisher's strange behaviour.

Aitken was determined that Law should at least assert his position as leader of the largest single party in the coalition. Law, as Aitken pointed out, had entered the government "not as an ordinary subordinate, but as an independent potentate, capable of dealing on almost equal terms with the prime minister". As second in command, Law must demand the exchequer for himself or, if Lloyd George held on to this, the newly-created ministry of munitions. Law agreed and went to see Asquith, promising Aitken that he would not give way. Asquith produced the remarkable plan that Lloyd George was to become minister of munitions on a temporary basis and that therefore a Liberal, McKenna in fact, should be put at the exchequer until Lloyd George chose to return. Law acquiesced without complaint. He said to Asquith: "I know very well I can have what I want by lifting my little finger. But I won't fight. I am here to show you how to run a Coalition Government by forbearance and concession". At least this is Aitken's story. Perhaps it is really what he wished Law had said.

The indisputable fact was that Law did not fight. Nor did his Unionist colleagues fight for him, though Aitken tried to stir them into doing so. Aitken was grieved. But he refused to be disheartened. He had determined to make Law a great man, and nothing would turn him from this task. Having failed once, he prepared to try again. He concealed Law's weakness from the public and hardly confessed it even to himself. When he published his account of wartime politics, he gave only one sentence of complaint: "Over and over again in his career Bonar Law would have given rein to this passion for self-abnegation if others had not held up his hands".[1] Beaverbrook's first draft was much fuller:

> This tendency points to a very real defect and a very dangerous weakness in character. It makes him undependable and incalculable at moments of crisis, for if you are going into action under a man, the one thing you want to be sure of is what he is going to do.
>
> What must be the moral of a garrison if it suspects that its commander may suddenly be convinced that self-surrender is a Christian virtue? Again, a statesman ought not to be content to take up his duty and shoulder his responsibilities when men or events simply thrust them upon him; he ought to go out boldly and take them up of his own courage and volition.

Law not only sacrificed himself. He also sacrificed Aitken. When the government was being formed there was some talk of giving Aitken a

[1] Politicians and the War, i, 141.

minor office, probably as postmaster general. Aitken was not interested. He always hesitated to push himself forward for fear of being criticized by others. At this time there was also a conflict of ambitions in him between the politician and the historian, or possibly he used history to console himself for his political failure. He recorded his two motives:

> The lions roaring after their prey were many, and the provender pitiably small. I thought perchance if I snatch the meat from them they will make a meal of me.
>
> I really preferred the other extreme—the task of laying down the bed-rock of war history which awaited me at the Canadian war records office. The appeal to a remote future attracted me only less than vital work in the immediate present. Anything between the two seemed to lack the savour of interest.

There were however other ways of rewarding Aitken, with the June honours list approaching. These were the first nominations in which the Unionists had a share for ten years, except for the Coronation honours in 1911. There was a long list of eager claimants, most of whom had presumably contributed to party funds, and as well there was a black mark against Aitken at the Unionist central office for his adroitness over The Daily Express. Law therefore sang his usual tune: Aitken is my closest friend, therefore I should like to do something for him. But because he is my closest friend, it is undesirable that I should.

Law tried to shift the responsibility on to Borden, as he had done on more important matters. He suggested that the Canadian government nominate Aitken for a KCMG on the colonial office list. Borden replied that he, too, had many prior claimants. Law then reluctantly nominated Aitken for a baronetcy. Aitken refused. He wrote to Law on 2 June:

> I need not say how much obliged I am to you for the proposal made in your letter today but, as I feel certain that the honour would be criticized on the ground that it was given to me on account of personal friendship, I must definitely decline it, because I think even a small thing like this might weaken your position at the present time.

Aitken also told the Canadian high commissioner, for Borden's benefit, that he had been offered a baronetcy and "had the good judgement to refuse".

The transaction was not really so simple. It appears from Law's correspondence that Asquith expostulated against Aitken's nomination and that Law then asked Aitken to write the letter of refusal. His own letter to Aitken on 2 June shows his embarrassment:

> I really feel that I have acted like a fool and a weak fool throughout this business and that it has ended in sacrificing you to make things easier for myself.

I can only say that I honestly believe, if my judgement is worth anything, that so far as the opinion of all your friends here is concerned you will gain by what you have done and understanding your nature a little I feel that your liking for me must be very strong indeed to have stood the test of what I am sure has seemed to you and probably rightly my unnecessary timidity.

Many years later, Beaverbrook allowed his letter of refusal to be published.[1] He suppressed the letter from Law which had inspired it. Beaverbrook at any rate was faithful unto death.

The political crisis of May 1915 revealed another side of Aitken's character. Nothing was deeper or more constant in him than to be a foul-weather friend. Many spurned him when they were Up and yet received consolation from him when they were Down. So it was now. The making of the coalition government produced two great victims: Churchill and Haldane. The Unionists were determined to exclude Churchill from the admiralty, and many Liberals, including Asquith, were not sorry to see him go. In vain Aitken pleaded with Law: Law's distrust of Churchill was and remained absolute. Nevertheless Aitken went to Churchill, sought to enliven him, and actually stirred him to write a letter of defence and appeal to Law. The letter failed of its effect, as Aitken knew it would. But the effort of justification helped to restore Churchill's spirits, which again Aitken had foreseen.

Haldane was excluded from the government altogether, on the absurd charge of being pro-German. Asquith and Grey had long professed to be his close friends. Both let him go without a word of sympathy or regret. Kitchener, it is often said, was the only man who brought consolation to Haldane at this moment of downfall. There was in fact another. On 28 May 1915 Aitken wrote this letter in his own hand:

Dear Lord Haldane

I have received several letters about my account of the Canadian battle but I value none so highly as yours, on account of the work you have done at the War Office in preparing the Nation in the struggle.

But for your preparations the victorious advance of Germany would today have submerged Calis, Boulogne and Dunkirk and the existence of England as a power independent of Germany would have been menaced by mortal peril. But for the firm stand you and two or three of your colleagues in the Cabinet took, our hold upon honour would have been considerably less than our hold upon existence.[2]

[1] By Robert Blake in The Unknown Prime Minister, 256.
[2] The original of this letter is in the Haldane collection at the National Library of Scotland, the librarian of which kindly gave me a copy. There is no truth in the story that Aitken inspired The Daily Express campaign against Haldane. On the contrary, as Stephen Koss has shown (Lord Haldane: Scapegoat for Liberalism, 145–6), Blumenfeld was deterred from pursuing this campaign by his financial obligations to Aitken.

Aitken had nothing to gain by writing this letter. His nature compelled him to hold out a hand to one who was in distress.

Once the new government had been made, Aitken returned to his work as Canadian Eye Witness and war records officer. He played no part in British politics except for occasional attempts to stiffen Law. All of them failed. In the summer of 1915, with Asquith increasingly absent, it became necessary to appoint a deputy leader of the house of commons. Law reasonably claimed the place and again promised Aitken that he would not give way. Lloyd George pleaded that he had been virtually deputy leader for years, and Law dropped his claim. Asquith set up a cabinet committee on conscription and omitted to include Law. Law, stirred on by Aitken, sent a letter of expostulation, which Aitken drafted, but he did not become a member of the committee.

In November 1915 the cabinet had to decide whether to go on with the Gallipoli campaign. Law was for evacuation. The cabinet evaded the issue by sending Kitchener out to report—Asquith in the hope that he would not return. Law acquiesced and then came to Aitken in distress. He thought the decision wrong. What should he do? Aitken answered: resign. Law agreed. According to Beaverbrook, "he never flinched again".[1] But, though Law repeatedly threatened to resign—indeed carrying his letter of resignation round from one member of the cabinet to another— he did not do so. He allowed himself to be silenced by the argument that the cabinet ought to wait for Kitchener's report, if only out of politeness. Asquith promised that he would support evacuation when the question came up again. In the end, evacuation came about, though no one at the time gave the credit to Law. Beaverbrook made up for this later.

Law certainly had no faith in Kitchener, and Lloyd George agreed with him, though the two men also lacked faith in each other. It was at their suggestion that Sir William Robertson was brought back from France as chief of the imperial general staff with increased powers, which enabled him to supersede Kitchener in the conduct of the war. In making this suggestion, Law was influenced by Aitken, who had formed a favour-able opinion of Robertson while at GHQ in France—an opinion which he revised later. Law's favourite soldier, however, was Sir Henry Wilson, perhaps because of the readiness with which Wilson had leaked war office secrets to Law in 1914. Here Aitken disagreed. He recorded this judge-ment:

> I never found Wilson's military ideas much good—but an expert has a right to an opinion on his own subject. What I confess irritated me was that Wilson, who was a mere child in politics, fancied himself as a politician.

[1] Politicians and the War, i, 164.

He used to give Bonar Law the most nonsensical political advice—to which the statesman would listen with a tolerance he would never have shown to a civilian who talked so foolishly.

Aitken was drawn back into political activity because of the room he occupied at the war office. On 5 June 1916 Kitchener was drowned off the north of Scotland, while on his way to Russia. Aitken listened to the talk of the generals at the war office and learnt with alarm that they were going to propose Walter Long or "some second rate politician who could be trusted not to have a mind of his own" as Kitchener's successor. Aitken believed that the nation would not tolerate a man of straw at the war office. Besides, he saw an opening for Law. Aitken told General Whigham, then Robertson's deputy, that the soldiers could not have Walter Long and that if they did not want Lloyd George their only chance was to ask for Bonar Law. Whigham and Robertson rejected this advice out of hand. Aitken then went to Law and told him he ought to demand the war office for himself. Asquith, Aitken insisted, would agree if only to keep Lloyd George out. Law, as usual, could not be persuaded to push himself forward. He answered that Lloyd George was the better appointment. Aitken arranged for Law and Lloyd George to meet for lunch at Cherkley on Sunday, 11 June.[1] After much discussion, not all of it friendly, Law resolved to recommend Lloyd George to the prime minister. Aitken, ever mindful of his patron's interests, insisted that Lloyd George should in return relinquish the leadership of the house of commons to Law.

It was Whit weekend, and Asquith, not surprisingly, was at The Wharf, Sutton Courtenay, his country home. Early on the Monday morning Law and Aitken went there by motor. Law went in to see Asquith while Aitken waited impatiently outside. Asquith offered the war office to Law, who replied that it was too late. Asquith then reluctantly agreed to Lloyd George. Law came out in some irritation. He was always overawed by Asquith, who treated him with condescending superiority,[2] and he asserted his own opinion with difficulty. Perhaps also he was angry with himself for renouncing the great appointment at the war office. He certainly expressed to Aitken his annoyance at having to chase the prime minister into the country instead of seeing him in London. He may also have reported disapprovingly that he had been asked to wait while Asquith finished a rubber of bridge with three ladies. The disapproval, if expressed, was rather unreasonable, in view of the addiction to bridge of all politicians, including Law himself, at this time. In any case there

[1] Curiously, Lloyd George who only came to lunch signed the visitors' book. So did his daughter Megan. Law who stayed the night did not.
[2] Asquith told Lloyd George that it was not worth while having Law to dinner because his conversation was that of a third-class Glasgow baillie.

was not much else even for a prime minister to do on a Whit Monday when all the government offices were closed.[1]

Law and Aitken then crossed to France, where Law spent the night at Canadian headquarters. Aitken sent Lloyd George a telegram telling him, in vague language, what had been decided. The telegram was held up by the military censorship, which thus implicitly tried to assert its authority against the secretary of state for war. In the end, Lloyd George learnt that he had reached his goal. Actually, in the excitement of battling with Asquith, Lloyd George forgot to assert himself against Robertson and went to the war office only with the diminished powers which had made Kitchener a figurehead.

In June 1916 the birthday honours came round again. Once more Law sought Canadian support for Aitken, and this time Borden could reply in all sincerity that Aitken's work as Eye Witness and Canadian military representative had been invaluable. Borden duly recommended Aitken to the duke of Connaught, the governor general, who was the channel for such communications to the king. The duke, however, was at open war with Sam Hughes and regarded Aitken as one of Hughes's men. He therefore accompanied the official recommendation with a private letter to George V, in which he alleged that Borden himself "regretted an honour being conferred on a man with a Canadian reputation such as the particular individual possessed".[2] This is most unlikely. Borden had not only promoted Aitken's various appointments himself. He was also pressing Aitken to return to Canadian politics. The duke in fact was not over scrupulous when his personal feelings were involved.

King George V was naturally reluctant to accept such a half-hearted recommendation. Law had, after all, to take action himself. A KCMG was the highest honour which could appear on the colonial list, and Aitken had already been promised a baronetcy. Law therefore put Aitken's name on the prime minister's list, which as leader of one of the coalition parties he shared with Asquith. The king objected that Aitken should

[1] Did the game of bridge ever happen? Beaverbrook never told the story in print, though it provided a good anecdote in conversation. Robert Blake more rashly published it in his life of Bonar Law. There was an uproar from the Asquith family and much controversy. Beaverbrook was annoyed at being drawn into the controversy, and Blake fell from favour. The matter is otherwise of no conceivable importance.

[2] This story comes from an unsigned note (probably by Davidson) to Sir George Fiddes in the Bonar Law papers, 84/6/40. This refers to Borden's "double faced action in connection with a certain honour (the story of which for personal reasons I have never told the Chancellor) when he told Mr. Bonar Law, through Perley, how greatly a baronetcy given to a certain individual would be appreciated in Canada and at the same time told the Duke of Connaught how much he regretted etc. . . .". See also Memoirs of a Conservative, 31–32.

appear on the Canadian list or not at all[1]—again slightly sharp practice, since the king knew well why this was not possible. George V's objection was somehow overcome, as it usually was in such cases. The short biography circulated to the newspapers made clear that the honour was given for Aitken's wartime services to Canada. The Times alone added the sentence: "Politically he is the close friend and adviser of Mr. Bonar Law". Who inspired this addition? Aitken? Northcliffe? surely not Law? There is no means of knowing.

There was another change in Aitken's private affairs at this time which he took less care to record, indeed some pains to conceal. In the autumn of 1916 there were again difficulties over The Daily Express. Sir George Lawson Johnston, the largest private shareholder, grew weary of shares which gave him neither profit nor power. He offered his controlling shares to Aitken. Otherwise he threatened to close the paper, in which case Aitken would lose the considerable sums he had earlier advanced on mortgage. On 14 November 1916 Aitken bought out Lawson Johnston for £17,500. The purchase made little practical difference at first. Aitken had already influence over the paper from his friendship with Blumenfeld and exerted himself later as controlling shareholder only when he wished to rescue the money he had sunk in the paper and so set out to make it pay.

However Aitken always concealed the exact time when he acquired control of The Daily Express. And for a simple reason. At the very moment when he acquired control, he became involved in the great political upheaval which led to the fall of Asquith and the elevation of Lloyd George. The coincidence of dates was almost exact: the political crisis opened on 8 November when Law was threatened with loss of control over the Unionist party, and Aitken acquired control of The Daily Express on 14 November. The deal was formally completed on 2 December, an even closer coincidence. Yet this coincidence was pure accident, provoked simply by Lawson Johnston's impatience to have done with the paper. At most Aitken was rushed into concluding the deal so as to be free for his political activities. Certainly he frequently "inspired" The Daily Express during the crisis, but he inspired The Daily Chronicle just as much without having any financial link there at all, and he inspired other papers only a little less. Blumenfeld accepted Aitken's suggestions, as he had often done before, because he agreed with them, not because Aitken now had power over him.

---

[1] The royal archives at Windsor, otherwise a model of generosity, do not reveal correspondence over honours. I learnt from an irregular source that there was a query by George V why Aitken could not be put on the Canadian list. It is unlikely that this was made in 1911, and the king's expostulation against Beaverbrook's peerage in 1917 was, as we know, for different reasons. The wish to put the blame for Aitken on to Canada must therefore have been expressed on this occasion.

Still, the coincidence, if known, would have brought joy to those who alleged that Asquith had been overthrown by a conspiracy of press lords. Here, it would have been said, was Aitken acquiring a weapon for immediate use against Asquith. Aitken therefore equivocated over the moment when he got control. In Politicians and the War, he wrote of The Daily Express: "I did not at that time own the controlling shares of this newspaper, but I was on intimate terms with the editor".[1] This was true only until 14 November, though the transfer was not completed until 2 December. On another occasion, when writing about Northcliffe, Beaverbrook placed his acquisition of control in "November 1917"—correct about the month, wrong about the year. Usually Beaverbrook said that he did not concern himself intimately with The Daily Express until after the war, and this was undoubtedly true. Though he acquired control in November 1916, he had better things to do than to exercise it. He plunged into the greatest merger operation of his life.

[1] Politicians and the War, ii, 194.

CHAPTER SIX

THE KINGMAKER, 1916

In the autumn of 1916 Asquith's position as prime minister seemed beyond challenge. His authority in cabinet was unquestioned. The public looked to him for firm olympian guidance. His coalition government had the official support of the Liberal, Unionist and Labour parties. There was no open dissent except from a few Radicals and Socialists, and occasionally from the Irish Nationalists. Even when criticism grew behind the scenes, it was never voiced in the house of commons except on the seemingly trivial issue of whether foreigners should be allowed to buy confiscated enemy property in Nigeria. Yet in the course of a few days Asquith was swept from power, almost before the public were aware that a crisis existed.

On 5 December 1916 Asquith resigned, never to hold office again. Lloyd George became prime minister with new men and new methods. The old cabinet was replaced by a war cabinet or directorate of five. The Liberal party was rent asunder and never recovered from this division. Here was the great step towards what later came to be known as "total war". Lloyd George became prime minister under the standard of the Knock Out Blow. There was to be no more talk of waging war half-heartedly or of a compromise peace. Such, at least, was the theory.

This upheaval has sometimes been dismissed as a palace revolution, engineered by a few ambitious politicians and inspired from behind the scenes by Northcliffe the megalomaniac press lord. Asquith and those who fell with him often propounded this view. In reality Asquith's overthrow was only one among many such episodes in the winter of 1916–17. There was a spirit of unrest and discontent in every belligerent country after the fruitless slaughter of 1916, typified by Verdun and the Somme. Sometimes this spirit turned against the war. Often it produced a demand that the war be waged more energetically. The discontent which made Lloyd George prime minister in Great Britain was repeated in France until Clemenceau became virtual dictator. In Russia the demand for a more energetic conduct of the war brought about the fall of the tsar in

March 1917. In Germany a similar demand caused the fall of Bethmann as chancellor in July 1917.

Some great change in British politics was impending during the winter of 1916–17. Northcliffe voiced the dissatisfaction with Asquith in his newspapers, but his agitation was effective only because the dissatisfaction was so widespread. In this sense Northcliffe provided the driving force behind the political upheaval. He had no clear idea what would emerge from it. This was Aitken's doing. Aitken did not cause the storm. He did not foresee it. When it began to blow, he took advantage of it and turned it in a particular direction. This was Aitken's contribution to British affairs in the first world war.

He appreciated this himself. When asked by Sir Evelyn Wrench in 1934: "What is the biggest thing you have ever done?", he replied:

> The destruction of the Asquith Government which was brought about by an honest intrigue. If the Asquith Government had gone on, the country would have gone down.

Aitken was anxious to record this great stroke and set down the story almost at once. The original narrative, entitled History of the Crisis, was drafted during January 1917. This began only with the Nigerian debate, which is now chapter VII in the second volume of Politicians and the War.[1] Later, earlier bits and pieces were worked together, some in 1917 and the rest in 1919, as a general account of political happenings from the outbreak of the war until November 1916. Beaverbrook constantly revised his draft, partly as new ideas came to him, partly as he acquired information from the biographies and memoirs of others, such as Asquith, Churchill, Austen Chamberlain, and Sir William Robertson.

Beaverbrook's original intention was to publish his work in two volumes, as A Political History of the War. The title was changed to the more appropriate one of Politicians and the War at the publisher's suggestion. This was Beaverbrook's most considerable, indeed for many years his only, historical work.[2] Professional historians at first refused to acknowledge that one whom they dismissed as a press lord could be either a brilliant writer or a serious scholar. The enduring merits of the book are really beyond cavil. It provides essential testimony for events during a great political crisis—perhaps the most detailed account of such a crisis ever written from the inside. It contains character sketches worthy

---

[1] When Beaverbrook republished his book as a single volume in 1960, he tiresomely made the numbering of chapters and pages continuous. Thus the Nigerian debate became chapter XXIII. All references here are to the first edition.

[2] The first volume of Politicians and the War was published in 1928, the second in 1932. Men and Power, Beaverbrook's next historical work, was not published until 1956. Politicians and the Press (1925), though interesting, is too slight to count.

of Aubrey.[1] On a wider canvas, it displays the behaviour of political leaders in wartime. The narrative is carried along by rare zest and wit, yet with the detached impartiality of the true scholar.

The textual criticism of the book makes a fascinating exercise. It is a mixture of autobiography, based on personal recollection, and historical narrative, built from the evidence of others. The autobiographical element is slight down to chapter VII of the second volume. Aitken was busy with his Canadian work and played little part in British politics except for such occasional incursions as helping to make Lloyd George secretary for war. No doubt he observed events and formed his own opinion of the men involved. But he derived a great deal from others. The long account of Fisher's resignation, for instance—including even the final maxim, "Don't draw down the blinds"—reproduces almost word for word a narrative written by J. L. Garvin.[2] Beaverbrook merely enlivened it with a few characteristic phrases. Edwin Montagu supplied an even longer narrative covering the various stages of the Gallipoli campaign. Most of the details about Kitchener came from Sir Reginald Brade, the secretary to the war office.[3] Blumenfeld, editor of The Daily Express, gave much information, though in the form of letters and not as a continuous narrative.

One source is peculiarly interesting and valuable. It is now a matter of common knowledge that Asquith wrote long letters of political gossip to Venetia Stanley, until she married Edwin Montagu in May 1915. Roy Jenkins, Asquith's biographer, is supposed to have been the first to make use of these letters, a use still restricted by Asquith's family. Beaverbrook had in fact used the best bits long before, though without mentioning the source. They were supplied to him by Mrs. Montagu in the early nineteen twenties, and the excerpts in her handwriting survive.[4] When Asquith fell out with Mrs. Montagu, he found a new recipient for his indiscretions in Mrs. Pamela McKenna, and she, too, passed her material to Beaverbrook.[5]

[1] Beaverbrook did not read any Aubrey until 1930 when Politicians and the War was already complete.

[2] Beaverbrook paid his debt by including a character sketch of Garvin. Garvin queried some of the remarks, and Beaverbrook impatiently struck out the whole.

[3] Brade's manuscript provides the dull solution to one little puzzle. Kitchener is said to have remarked (Politicians and the War, i, 69): "My colleagues tell military secrets to their wives, all except ——, who tells them to other people's wives". Whose name should fill the blank? Some historians have suggested Lloyd George, some even Asquith. The correct answer is "the Q.M.", i.e. Sir John Cowans, the quartermaster general. As Cowans was notoriously carrying on with another man's wife, the remark was not surprising.

[4] This is the source, for instance, of the story about Lloyd George preferring to break stones, dig potatoes, be hanged, drawn and quartered rather than cabal against Asquith. Politicians and the War, i, 70.

[5] Asquith's letters of 3 and 6 December 1916 (Politicians and the War, ii, 233 and 299) were addressed to Mrs. McKenna.

Beaverbrook called in reinforcements even for the autobiographical part of his book. At his request, Law, Edwin Montagu, and Robert Donald, editor of The Daily Chronicle, wrote accounts of the crisis almost as soon as it was over. Law's narrative, which comes to nearly four thousand words, is dated 30 December 1916 and was presumably written at Cherkley, where Law and his family spent Christmas. Beaverbrook also grabbed at the letters of compromise or defiance as they went to and fro. In those days people did not assert their property rights in letters as rigorously as they do nowadays. Law and Lloyd George were no doubt flattered by Beaverbrook's interest and may also have given him the letters as some compensation for the political reward which they had failed to provide. At any rate Beaverbrook pocketed immediately the short dynamic letter which Lloyd George wrote to Law on 2 December 1916. He carried off the entire correspondence between Law and Asquith and in January 1917 secured the letters between Lloyd George and Asquith also.

When the book was expanded in order to cover the entire period from the beginning of the war, Beaverbrook accumulated material for this also, and not always in the most scrupulous manner. When Churchill read the proofs, he was surprised to discover the telegram which he had sent from Antwerp on 5 October 1914, offering to resign the admiralty and to take command of the British forces there.[1] He himself had no copy of the telegram and wondered how it had come into Beaverbrook's possession. Beaverbrook replied on 24 March 1927:

> I have the original message annotated in Kitchener's own writing. It would bother me greatly to explain how the telegram reached me under the Official Secrets Act. But I fear it would bother other people more. And this is a world of bother.

This is the only explanation Beaverbrook ever gave of how his great collection of papers began its existence.

At various stages Beaverbrook showed his narrative to the leading actors and invited their comments. As might be expected, most of them were more concerned to improve their own images than to provide further information. Thus, Sir Henry Dalziel failed to indicate the source of the disruptive article in Reynolds on 3 December and instead objected to the phrase that he was too interested in *making money*. He would prefer *commercial affairs*. Law's comment showed his usual modesty. He wrote on 31 May 1919:

> I do think that the picture is so exaggerated as to be almost ridiculous but let me say that it is a real pleasure to me to think that you yourself

[1] Politicians and the War, i, 54.

should hold anything like such an opinion. I think it would be better to tone it down but you must decide. As regard L.G. I should much like not to have the contrast so blatant.

Beaverbrook did not take this advice. On the contrary he strengthened the build-up of Law as the hero with each draft.

Finally, Beaverbrook sent the galley proofs—always his favourite form of revision—to Birkenhead, Austen Chamberlain, Churchill, Robert Donald, and Lloyd George. All of them commented appreciatively. Most of them made corrections or additions, some of which Beaverbrook adopted. The memory of politicians is notoriously unreliable. Still it is worthy of record that most of those best qualified to judge approved Beaverbrook's narrative, though not of course his interpretations. The great exception was Asquith. On his side, only Montagu, at an early stage, and McKenna, at a late one, saw what Beaverbrook had written, and neither was an orthodox "Squiffite". In regard to Churchill and Lloyd George, Beaverbrook noted in 1928 with justified satisfaction:

> Politicians and the War passed under the scrutiny of two public men, the most important figures in the story and neither of them the hero of it. For of course Bonar Law was the hero.

This little note is itself an indication that Beaverbrook's memory was not infallible. For Churchill was by no means one of the most important figures in the story, and Law was not, in the early version, its hero.

It is possible, with some ingenuity, to dig through the accretions and changes of view to something like this early version, which is likely to be also the most accurate, though not of course the fullest. The first volume, which runs to the death of Kitchener, is clearly a later narrative, not a contemporary record, though Beaverbrook writes in the introduction: "my original story was written down very shortly after the circumstances it records". Actually it was written in 1917. For the second volume, which describes the fall of Asquith and the triumph of Lloyd George, Beaverbrook made greater claims. He presented it "in diary form", which was technically correct, if slightly misleading. The dustcover of the original edition asserted that he was giving "to the public his diary of the daily events of the crisis of 1916—the most sensational political document published since the war", and when the book was serialized in The Daily Express the first instalment, again referring to Lord Beaverbrook's diary, asserted: "This diary, in narrative form, was kept all through these dramatic days".

No diary has survived, and it is as certain as any negative can be that none ever existed.[1] In my opinion, when Beaverbrook wrote his historical

---

[1] No diary exists in the Beaverbrook archive except for that at the beginning of 1906, referred to on p. 24. In Men and Power, p. 271, Beaverbrook claims to be quoting from a diary of 1915, but this again has not survived, and it too, I believe, never existed.

narratives, he relied on his engagement books, his correspondence and his vivid memory. His first account of the crisis of 1916 was written in pencil on Cherkley letter-paper (embossed, by the way—a luxury Beaverbrook always deplored). Since the first typescript was drafted in January 1917, these notes were probably made over Christmas 1916, when Law was also writing or dictating his account.

The notes deserve reproduction in full:[1]

Nov. 13th Monday	met George.
14th Tuesday	George goes France.
Morning—saw BL re Nigeria.	
15th Wed.	Telegraphed George
	(See answer)
16th Thur.	Blum sees Carson.
17th Friday	George returns B.L. dines with Wilson.
	George declines dinner
	& goes to Walton Heath.
18th Saturday	George arrives at H.P. for Breakfast and remains until nearly twelve explaining difficulties with Robertson.
	I lunch with B.L. and develop George scheme.
	B.L. leaves for PMs place "The Wharf".
19th Sunday	George asks me lunch. I go at 5 p.m.
	After G. telephones second time.
	Long talk and decide on meeting at dinner Monday night at H.P.H.
20th Monday	Saw G. at war office. He says B.L. assists at Council and McKenna much improved.
	B.L. agrees to dinner. Also Carson.
	Dinner at 8 p.m. progress slow. G. and C. go home. BL stays and expresses doubt regarding George's sincerity and charges him with share of responsibility for disorganization of War Committee.
	Probably dinner on Tuesday or Wed with Carson & Thursday with George.
25th Nov. *Saturday*	Lunch at B.L. with Carson and George.
	B.L. goes to see PM. C and G to War Office.
	I go home BL calls at War Office & home & telephones me not having disclosed to G and C conversation with PM.

[1] The notes mostly explain themselves. "Blum" on Thursday, 16 November, is R. D. Blumenfeld. H.P. and H.P.H. mean the Hyde Park Hotel. Two of the entries are inaccurately dated. Aitken telephoned to The Daily Express on Friday, 1 December, not on Thursday, 30 November. The Unionist meetings, assigned to Monday, 4 December, were actually held on Tuesday, 5 December, and the first of them was at the India office, not at the colonial office.

26th Nov. *Sunday*		I see George that night at 9 p.m.
27th Nov. *Monday*		P.M.'s answer rec'd by BL and communicated to C. and G.
	Tuesday	
	Wed	
	Thur.	George dining with Cunliffe. I call for him & B.L. goes with me. Back to my rooms I talk to Daily Express on telephone.
	Friday	George writes to PM.
	Sat	
Dec.	3rd Sunday	To B.L. house at 11 AM. Unionist meeting. Lunch. Smith called in. BL to PM. I wait at Colonial Office after calling George to town War Office at Four. George goes to P.M. George and BL return at 6.30. To Smith's house with BL. To Pembroke Lodge. Home at 1 a.m.
	4th Monday	Unionist meeting at Foreign Office afterwards at Colonial Office. Dine with BL & reported P.M. will resign.
	5th Tuesday	Resignation. I see George at War Office—tell him of decision and much impressed by his attitude. BL sees King Dinner with F. E. Smith.
	6th Wed.	Meeting at BL house with G. & C.—Decide on Palace Conference.

From such small seeds do large trees grow.

These notes provided the framework for a brief narrative which was written almost at once. Not however by Beaverbrook himself. Only the notes are in his handwriting. The History of the Crisis was given literary form by Maurice Woods, who was to play a considerable part in Beaverbrook's historical work until his death twelve years later. Ironically, the first reference to him in the Beaverbrook archives was in 1912, when Aitken complained to the Unionist central office that Woods, although a paid Unionist speaker, was running a campaign in Herefordshire against Colonial Preference. However, Aitken, in his usual manner, preferred a merger to a battle and soon afterwards recruited Woods to his staff. On the outbreak of war Woods went to France as an infantry captain and returned late in 1915 as unfit for active service, when he joined the Canadian records office. Aitken had written his early reports as Eye Witness himself. Once Woods appeared, Aitken was content to sketch the general lines of a report and left the rest to Woods. The same thing happened with the History of the Crisis. Aitken made his notes and talked at large, after which Woods produced a draft. This is not surmise.

Woods could not type, and many extended passages survive in his un-
mistakable handwriting. This is not to say that the book, as finally produced, was predominantly his work. Woods was a fluent writer, capable
of turning out a well-argued leader or straightforward narrative. But he
was uninspired and pedestrian when left to himself, as may be seen from
the only book he wrote on his own, A History of the Tory Party in the
Seventeenth and Eighteenth Centuries, published in 1925. This could
have been written by any well-tutored Oxford graduate, which Woods
was, and is far inferior to his work as Beaverbrook's ghost. Even the title
is much longer than Beaverbrook would have tolerated.

Beaverbrook, like Churchill, could employ others to write his books
for him and yet set his stamp on every sentence. He worked especially
hard on the narrative of the crisis in Politicians and the War. He tore
practically every sentence apart. He gave an unexpected twist to the ends
of chapters.[1] He made a larger modification during the prolonged work of
revision. As the years went by, he cast himself more and more as Law's
armour bearer. Law became the clearsighted resolute hero and Aitken
his faithful adherent, concerned only to ensure that Law remained leader
of the Unionist party. This is why the detailed narrative in its published
version begins with the Nigerian debate on 8 November, when a minority
of the Unionist party voted against the government and so challenged
Law's leadership. But the original notes begin on 13 November and with
Lloyd George, not with Law. At this time Aitken was closer to Lloyd
George than he was to Law. He had practically fallen out of British
politics—the Hansard index for 1916 contains no reference to his name—
and he saw little of Law. His place as Law's political adviser had been
taken by Johnny Baird, later Lord Stonehaven, of whose judgement he
had a poor opinion. Aitken only realized the significance of the vote
after the Nigerian debate, when Blumenfeld warned him of trouble to
come. He went down to the house of commons almost as a stranger and
there found Law surrounded by men who disregarded his warnings.

On the other hand Aitken, himself seated in the war office, was seeing
Lloyd George practically every day, as he continued to do throughout the
crisis. At heart he knew that Lloyd George was a great man and that Law
was not. But he would not commit himself to Lloyd George, no doubt

---

[1] Thus chapter XIV originally ended with the dramatic and yet banal statement
that Law "was going forward at any cost". Beaverbrook added a final paragraph of gay
discomfiture:

"I came out happily into the cool air of the night and went home to the Hyde Park
Hotel—to find I had to climb four flights of stairs because the lift was not working."

Beaverbrook's literary adviser, Edward Shanks, urged him to remove the paragraph
as detracting from the high seriousness of the narrative. Beaverbrook took no notice.
This was the unconscious artistry of genius.

wisely as the fate of some of Lloyd George's faithful adherents suggests. Hence, as time went on, he modified his account in order to emphasize that support for Law, not for Lloyd George, was his driving motive. This was by no means so clear in his original narrative.

There the starting point for Aitken's initiative was not the threat to Law's leadership of the Unionist party but Lloyd George's discontent with the set-up at the war office where Robertson, chief of the imperial general staff, alone determined strategy. Lloyd George, though secretary of state for war, was virtually powerless. In his usual way he sought a way round. He proposed that the ineffective war committee of eight cabinet ministers should be swept away and replaced by a war council of three with himself in the chair. This council would be the supreme executive of the war, subject only to the final authority of the cabinet. Asquith would not be a member. Nevertheless the council, as Lloyd George originally projected it, was a weapon against Robertson, not against Asquith.

Beaverbrook emphasized this in a letter to Mrs. Asquith on 31 October 1918:

> It was not Mr. Asquith's judgement that I distrusted; it was that of the kind of barnacles, especially in the general staff, which had affixed themselves to his administration. I believed with good reason as the event showed, that Mr. Lloyd George's military opinions were better than those of Sir William Robertson and the War Office, and that the united command and all else was impossible unless the generals could be put under proper control by the Secretary of State for War and the Prime Minister. That was the real struggle and I regretted the dénouement as much as did the present Prime Minister. But we feel that we were battling for the National existence.

Beaverbrook wrote in similar terms to John Buchan on 17 November 1921:

> There was no deliberate intention on George's part to force Asquith out. I feel sure George would have been perfectly content to leave Asquith the titular supremacy as long as he was allowed to run the war, and not to be held up (rightly or wrongly) by the Generals and the Imperial Staff.

This is not the received version which regards Lloyd George as an unscrupulous schemer intent on supreme power. Yet Lloyd George showed again and again throughout his career that he would be content with second place—under Asquith or later under MacDonald—if he were left free to apply his unique gifts as a statesman.

At any rate on 13 November Lloyd George expressed his dissatisfaction to Aitken. The conversation made Aitken feel that great events were impending. His early draft has this passage:

> The War Secretary had passed beyond the phase of personal ambition: the smaller qualities had been swallowed up by a blaze of patriotism, and

with candour, sincerity, zeal, and ability—he was bending all these qualities to the service of the nation in the hour of supreme peril. The impression was a powerful one, and I came away determined to help him to the best of my ability in the task he had undertaken.

Lloyd George could make his discontent effective only by appealing to others who were discontented for more general reasons—Northcliffe, the press lord, and Carson, leader of the Unionist rebels. There seems to have been little direct contact between Lloyd George and Northcliffe, but Lloyd George was certainly in touch with Carson. Lloyd George did not turn up for the Nigerian debate. Instead he spent the evening in Carson's company. He claimed that this meeting was accidental and wrote on Beaverbrook's proof:

> I was dining with Sir Arthur Lee. Carson happened to be there. Not a word was said about the Nigerian debate and I knew nothing about it. I rarely appeared in the house as I was absorbed in the office work.

However Lloyd George also told Law that he had been paired, and Law rightly did not believe him.

Northcliffe and Carson, though formidable, were dangerous associates for Lloyd George. Their aims were different. Northcliffe and Carson wanted to overthrow Asquith and to elevate the generals. Lloyd George wished to diminish the generals and was ready to retain Asquith as prime minister. This is where Aitken came in. If Law were convinced that the government and his own control of the Unionist party were in danger from Carson, he might be persuaded to support Lloyd George's council of three despite his distrust of Lloyd George personally. Carson could be recruited, ostensibly as the driving force, really to render him harmless. This tactic was often an important element in Aitken's negotiations. So it had been with Sir Sandford Fleming. So it was now with Carson. Each of them planned to exploit Aitken. Instead he exploited them. Carson, too, was taken for a ride. He was less and less consulted as the crisis developed and, though—against the original expectation of Law and Lloyd George—Asquith was overthrown, Carson did not succeed to any portion of his inheritance.

Aitken now set out to manoeuvre Law as he had done in 1911 and 1912. This was a more difficult operation than appears from Aitken's final account. By then Law had become the hero, always clearly aware of what he was doing. In fact Law did not know what he was doing or, in so far as he did, was doing almost the exact opposite of what Aitken attributed to him. For Law was loyal to Asquith whom he regarded as the leader indispensable to national unity. Law certainly wanted to stave off the danger from Carson. He certainly wanted a more energetic conduct of the war, which he recognized Lloyd George could provide. But he believed, until the last moment, that this must be under Asquith's leadership. Moreover as leader of a party himself, he was really on Asquith's side against all rebels. It was Asquith's failure to appreciate this which caused his fall.

Aitken himself hoped from the first to bring down Asquith, presumably with the idea of putting Law in his place. Lloyd George was primarily concerned to shake off Robertson's control. But he also wanted effective strategic control of the war, and this turned him implicitly against Asquith almost without his knowing it. Law was willing to support Lloyd George against Robertson and had no inkling that this might grow into a move against Asquith. Aitken kept the discussion firmly limited to reform at the war office for as long as he could. On 14 November he was ill in bed, perhaps a convenient excuse for seeing Law away from his associates in the house of commons. At any rate, Law called twice. On the second occasion Aitken told of Lloyd George's troubles at the war office and suggested that Law should meet him.[1] Law agreed somewhat reluctantly, and the meeting was arranged for dinner on 17 November. Then Aitken learnt that Sir Henry Wilson was also to be present. This was an unwelcome interference, and Aitken advised Lloyd George to decline the invitation. The failure to bring Law and Lloyd George together forced Aitken's hand. On 18 November he revealed to Law Lloyd George's plan for a war council, and Law agreed to discuss it with Lloyd George and Carson on Monday, 20 November.

Law was determined not to be drawn into a conspiracy against Asquith. On the contrary, quite against Aitken's intention, he went to Asquith the next day and told the full story. Asquith did not believe that Lloyd George would be satisfied even if he got his way, and Law agreed. However Asquith did not reject the proposal out of hand. As usual with him, "the discussion led to no definite conclusion or result". Law therefore felt free to listen to Lloyd George's proposal. He still thought of the war council as a move solely against Robertson, and at the meeting on 20 November Lloyd George did not disillusion him. But on the following day Lloyd George revealed to Law that Asquith was not to be a member of the war council.[2] This revived Law's distrust, and there was deadlock

---

[1] In his published account (Politicians and the War, ii, 133), Aitken claimed that he told Law about the plan for a war council. His original narrative shows that he did this only when forced to do so by the failure of the dinner meeting on 17 November.
[2] Here again there is a discrepancy between the original narrative and the printed account. According to the draft, Aitken advised Lloyd George to keep quiet on this point in order to get the principle of the war council settled first: "then he would have a better chance of tackling the more difficult position of the Prime Minister". In the book (Politicians and the War, ii, 142), he writes: "I had not thought it necessary to tell of this demand to Bonar Law. I was not sure that Lloyd George would insist on this condition"—an unlikely story.

5

throughout the week. Unfortunately Aitken does not tell how he broke this deadlock. He writes that "there was a protracted and fruitful discussion", but he does not say with whom and "fruitless" seems a more appropriate word.

At last, Law, Lloyd George and Carson met again on 25 November. Aitken, as an experienced go-between, felt that the time had come to be more precise and had drafted a statement which Asquith was to be invited to publish. It was a skilful compromise: there was to be a war council of three, Lloyd George as chairman, and Asquith stuck in on top as a sort of honorary president who would rarely attend. It was a somewhat remarkable stroke that an obscure backbencher should draft a statement to be imposed on the prime minister. Law thought that the scheme should be acceptable to Asquith and communicated it to him the same evening. Asquith, after recounting the personal faults of Carson and Lloyd George, agreed to think it over. Lloyd George expected a rupture and, in conversation with Aitken, dwelt on "his strength with his own party both in the country and the House and with the wealthy classes of Liberalism if it came to a fight"—a revealing phrase which was later given a more innocuous form.

Sure enough, Asquith turned down the scheme. His letter of rejection must have been written almost as soon as Law left him. Law was a little annoyed at this treatment and, according to Aitken's first draft, "for the first time seemed to be leading the party for the reconstruction of the government rather than being dragged along with it". However he soon weakened and merely suggested that Lloyd George should himself negotiate with the prime minister. Aitken expected, or rather feared, that these negotiations would succeed. He wrote in his draft: "Although when Lloyd George asked my opinion I told him that I was not in favour of a compromise but of a complete break with the old regime I had no sort of doubt that the two men would come to terms". Asquith however became increasingly obstinate, and Law grew weaker, especially when he discovered on 30 November that all the leading Unionist ministers were opposed to Lloyd George.

The manoeuvring had now been going on for over a fortnight, and nothing had been achieved. Law seemed to have contracted out. He wrote to Lansdowne on 1 December: "I recommended both Asquith and George to have it out with each other and I consider therefore that for the moment the matter is out of my hands". Aitken is curiously modest about his activities at this point. Reading between the lines, it is a fair surmise that he resolved to give the wheel another shove. On the morning of 1 December he went to Lloyd George and urged him to threaten resignation if his scheme were not accepted. Lloyd George would not take the big jump. Instead he drafted a new curt statement of his scheme, or more probably Aitken drafted it for him.[1] Lloyd George then carried this statement to Asquith, who sent back later in the day his usual negative response.

This was poor material with which to force the crisis. But Aitken was undismayed. That evening he warned Law that battle was about to be joined. Law was embarrassed. According to Aitken's original account "He was clearly inclining in the Prime Minister's direction, and was therefore most anxious to see George and explain his position—lest George should think afterwards that he had gone back on him". Aitken pursued Lloyd George to the Berkeley where he was dining and carried him off to meet Law, warning him on the way of the difficulties to come. Thus briefed, Lloyd George tactfully declared that he did not consider Law committed to support his views. This generous attitude drew from Law the answer that he was committed to support the war council of three in principle, though not to insist on any particular names—still less (though he did not say so) on the exclusion of Asquith. Lloyd George then departed, and the first narrative concludes: "Bonar Law left me very pleased with George's attitude". The book[2] gives a longer and more dramatic picture of Law's reflections, ending: "He was going forward at any cost". This, too, is an unlikely story. Law continued to hesitate until 5 December. But this did not suit Beaverbrook's later presentation of him as the hero and was therefore obscured.

Unknown to Law and probably to Lloyd George also, Aitken had sprung another mine in the course of 1 December. He had resolved to bring the conflict into the open. He gave Blumenfeld the story of Lloyd George's proposal, with instructions to publish it in The Daily Express. He writes:[3] "I did not at that time own the controlling shares of this newspaper". In fact he did or was on the point of acquiring them. No doubt Blumenfeld would have published the story in any case, and the point is therefore of no great importance. Aitken found another outlet. The Daily Chronicle was the leading Radical newspaper in London which fully supported the war,[4] and Aitken was on good terms with Robert Donald, the editor. Aitken now "took pains", in his own words, to inform Donald what was going on. This innocent phrase conceals a complicated manoeuvre. Donald was not prepared to act solely on the basis of information from Aitken and Blumenfeld. He decided to explore the story on the

[1] Politicians and the War, ii, 185 says Lloyd George "indicated in conversation with Asquith that resignation was not far behind". The original draft has only a pencilled marginal note in Beaverbrook's handwriting beside the text of Lloyd George's statement: "Probably conversation?".

[2] Politicians and the War, ii, 193.

[3] Ibid., 194.

[4] The Daily News, the other Radical daily, was less wholehearted in its support for the war.

following day. This was too late for Aitken, who wanted an impact before the weekend.[1] An independent source was therefore provided. An American journalist, Bell of The Chicago Daily News, rang Donald with the story, claiming that he had received it from the war office. Donald in turn rang his office and instructed Harry Jones, an assistant editor, to make enquiries. Jones went to the war office, where he saw J. T. Davies, Lloyd George's principal private secretary, and William Sutherland, then or soon afterwards Lloyd George's press officer. Both confirmed Aitken's story, and on this Donald decided to go ahead. Thus the story broke in two important newspapers on the Saturday morning.

Here it seems is decisive evidence that Lloyd George was inspiring a press campaign against Asquith at the very moment when he claimed to be seeking agreement. Beaverbrook had full statements by both Donald and Jones in his archives and yet made no use of them. It is possible that he wished to shield Lloyd George, even years afterwards, from the charge of "trafficking" with the press. There is an alternative and more likely explanation: that he wished to shield himself from Lloyd George's disapproval. If Lloyd George, as seems likely, aimed at an amicable arrangement with Asquith, he would not want publicity which might provoke a crisis. Aitken, on the other hand, was pushing both Law and Lloyd George into a crisis which neither wanted. The independent evidence provided for Donald was a plant. Bell, the American, was a close friend of Aitken's and would not have acted without his prompting. Aitken was on intimate terms with Davies and worked with Sutherland on other journalistic affairs. No one knew better than Aitken how to keep a secret, and also no one knew better how to run a publicity campaign. What he had once done for himself at Ashton-under-Lyne and then for the Canadians in France, he now did for Lloyd George, and Davies and Sutherland were glad to work under his direction. Lloyd George would not have welcomed the discovery that he had been manipulated, and Beaverbrook therefore took care that he should not find out.

The publicity, launched by Aitken, transformed the political conflict. What had been previously a secret discussion between a few men at the top became common knowledge. The effect was enhanced on the Sunday morning when Reynolds News came out with the story in even greater detail. Sir Henry Dalziel, the proprietor, never revealed where he got his information from. Beaverbrook suggests that he pieced it together by simple journalistic intuition and further states his belief that Lloyd George had nothing to do with it. Perhaps Davies and Sutherland were again acting behind their master's back, just as chief whips sold honours without informing the prime minister. At any rate the Reynolds article put the

[1] 2 December was a Saturday.

Unionist ministers in a passion. They distrusted Lloyd George and were indignant that Law appeared to be working with him.

At 11 a.m. on Sunday morning they arrived at Law's house, each of them brandishing a copy of Reynolds News. Aitken, arriving a little later, found Law's sister Mary and John Baird sitting in an adjacent room. He withdrew into another. There followed a little episode which Beaverbrook naturally cut out when he had established friendly relations with Mary Law. "Presently Miss Law came in to me and began to abuse me, saying that I had entrapped Bonar Law into a morass and ruined him with my bad advice. I contented myself with replying that Johnny Baird was a fool."

Aitken was of course not present at Law's discussion with the Unionist ministers and could only record his second-hand impressions. According to him all the Unionist ministers were against Lloyd George. "Their attitude was summed up by Mr. Walter Long who remarked with great truth and equal oblivion of the tremendous issues involved that 'an English gentleman would not have behaved like George' and left for the country". The remaining ministers[1] then drafted a resolution which they wished Law to present to Asquith. Its essential clauses read:

> ... The publicity given to the intention of Mr. Lloyd George makes reconstruction from within no longer possible.
>
> We therefore urge the Prime Minister to tender the resignation of the Government.
>
> If he feels unable to take that step, we authorize Mr. Bonar Law to tender our resignations.

At this point, Law came out to consult Aitken. He did not show Aitken the resolution, which was perhaps still being drafted. But Aitken at once assumed that the Unionist ministers were backing Asquith against Lloyd George. They believed that, if Asquith resigned, Lloyd George would be unable to form a government and Asquith would return in triumph. Aitken, who was of course very much Lloyd George's man, seems to have exaggerated the Unionists' hostility towards him. For, according to Austen Chamberlain, one of the ministers involved, they did not care which Liberal won, Asquith or Lloyd George, so long as the crisis was ended somehow.[2]

Law's attitude is described quite differently in Beaverbrook's first narrative and in his later book. The book implies throughout that Law was firmly committed to Lloyd George at any rate from 1 December. Therefore Beaverbrook asserted that Law knew exactly what he was

[1] Lord Robert Cecil, Austen Chamberlain, and Lord Curzon, nicknamed by Beaverbrook "the three C's". Lansdowne was in the country, and Balfour was ill in bed.
[2] Austen Chamberlain, Down the Years, 117–18.

doing. Law did not come out "to ask for my advice, but to clear his own mind. . . . He fully grasped that the object of the resolution was hostile to Lloyd George". He argued to himself: "They hope the new Ministry will be formed on their pattern; I hope it will be formed on mine. So let us agree to have a clean sweep of the situation—and then let the best man win". He therefore returned to the other room and accepted the resolution, knowing full well that he was interpreting it in a sense of his own.[1] Churchill commented sagely on the proof: "If B.L.'s colleagues did not understand his all important difference from them there is ground of complaint". Beaverbrook however was determined to present Law as the hero, even though this meant crediting him with sharp practice.

The original narrative shows a less adroit and also a less heroic Law. According to this, "Bonar Law did not seem very clear himself as to what was meant" and later, "Bonar Law out of the simplicity and direct-ness of his character failed to understand that the whole resolution was nothing but an attempt to dish Lloyd George through the Prime Minis-ter". Unlike practically everyone else Law did not want a fight at all. "In fact his one desire was to keep both Asquith and George in the cabinet under a new relationship". Aitken, wanting a fight, welcomed the Unionist stand. Somehow he assured Law that the resolution would do no harm. Law returned happily to his colleagues and announced his agreement with them. In this version, there was no deception by Law. The deception, no doubt in a good cause, was of Law by Aitken, and this version is the more likely.

The Unionist ministers departed. Aitken stayed for lunch. He now saw for the first time the text of the resolution. The complaint about publicity greatly alarmed him. If it were insisted on, the truth would come out, and he himself, not Lloyd George, would be revealed as the culprit. He wrote a full account which survived to proof stage and was then suppressed:

> As a matter of fact the publicity campaign had been launched not by George, but by me—e.g. the articles in my own paper, the *Express* and[2] in the *Chronicle* on the day before. Bonar Law had a vague idea from being with me that I had put something into the Express, but he had no idea of the extent to which I had carried on the Press campaign. He was much startled and perturbed by my news. I pointed out to him that it was an odious task to take to the Prime Minister, in a document likely to become public, a charge which he now knew to be largely untrue.
>
> Furthermore, I was much opposed to this clause ever going out for another reason. It was practically certain to come to George's knowledge, and if it

---

[1] Politicians and the War, ii, 213–14.

[2] "To a minor extent" inserted later by hand, the beginning no doubt of Beaver-brook's attempt to conceal his responsibility for the leak to The Daily Chronicle.

did it might lead to a misunderstanding between Bonar Law and George, considering that George knew I had launched the publicity campaign.[1]

Aitken urged Law not to show the resolution to Asquith. Law hesitated and agreed to consult F. E. Smith. He, on arrival, proved to be of no help. He insisted that the resolution was definitely intended to be offensive to George and could not be modified.

After lunch, Law went off to see Asquith, Aitken harassing him to the last moment with arguments against communicating the resolution. This helps to explain Law's attitude during his meeting with Asquith, as an unpublished passage shows:

> It was the publicity question, and not the general problem which was uppermost in his mind during the interview. Thus, although he did tell the Prime Minister that his colleagues were against George, the fact was not so stated as to make any very strong impression on Asquith's mind; the latter, indeed, must have chiefly seen that Bonar Law was trying to defend Lloyd George. Be that as it may, Bonar Law read him the resolution without amendment, but did not give him a copy.

This failure to give the resolution to Asquith was later made a high count against Law. Asquith, it was asserted, thus did not learn that most of the Unionist ministers were on his side. The charge is without substance. For, exactly like Law, Asquith, "good, easy man" in Beaverbrook's unpublished phrase, did not want a fight. Law reported to Aitken:

> The Prime Minister had dissented very strongly from the resolution: he had never contemplated resignation: he had not the faintest intention of resigning now. He would see George at once; in the meantime, would Bonar Law and his Unionist colleagues hold over their resignations?

This is more likely than Beaverbrook's later picture of Asquith's being thrown into a panic by the word "resignation". Asquith, in his usual way, was seeking a compromise. Indeed, the previous day, according to Montagu, he had been down to Walmer in the hope of discussing compromise with Carson, who had in fact not left London. He now renewed his assurances of compromise to Law. Law was content. He and Asquith, the two men who did not want a fight, seemed again in agreement.

The compromise was in fact achieved. Lloyd George, summoned from Walton Heath, went to see Asquith, and they agreed on the war council in principle, though still with some doubt as to its membership. As Lloyd

---

[1] The truth was still worse. Lloyd George did not know that Aitken had launched the publicity campaign. Aitken was thus desperately covering up for himself, and it is easy to understand why he insisted so strongly that the resolution of the Unionist ministers should not be communicated to Asquith.

George left Asquith, he remarked to the Liberal chief whip: "You need not get your writ ready, Gulland, there will be no general election".

Lloyd George had gained what he regarded as his main aim. The war council of three would give him control over Robertson, or so he supposed. Asquith had agreed to accept a nominal presidency, and Lloyd George had never wished to eject him from the premiership. Law was even more delighted. He had retained Asquith; he had satisfied Lloyd George; he had restored his control over the Unionist party. Aitken recorded sadly: "I did not regard this, as Bonar Law did, as the ideal solution. . . . Yet a sense of pleasurable relief accompanied the idea of a peace". This was a curious end to Aitken's endeavours. He had embarked on his campaign in order to overthrow Asquith and to elevate Lloyd George. His main instrument had been Law and, as happened on other occasions, Law had failed him. Instead of conflict, there was a compromise which would enable Asquith to survive in glory until the end of the war. At the last moment, Law had outwitted Aitken, where Aitken had intended to manoeuvre Law.

So affairs stood on the night of Sunday, 3 December. Montagu, who was always for compromise, persuaded Asquith to issue a statement that the government was to be reconstructed. The next morning, Asquith repudiated the compromise and threw everything into the melting pot again. His ostensible ground for doing so was a hostile leader in The Times which he attributed to Lloyd George. In fact Lloyd George was entirely guiltless, as on this occasion was Aitken also. Geoffrey Dawson, the editor, picked up part of the story at Cliveden from Waldorf Astor, an associate of Lord Milner's, and learnt the rest in London from Carson.[1]

Was The Times leader the real, or the sole, cause of Asquith's action? According to Beaverbrook, a number of Liberal ministers came to Asquith and urged him to defy Lloyd George. There is no independent evidence for this. Beaverbrook also stated in his published account that the "three C's" saw Asquith on the Monday morning to much the same effect. Austen Chamberlain denied this and stated that he saw Asquith only on Tuesday when the battle had been lost. Chamberlain was undoubtedly correct. Beaverbrook's statement to the contrary derives only from a vague sentence by Lord Crewe, which associates the visit of the three C's

[1] In 1931, when the second volume of Politicians and the War was being serialized, Lady Oxford, Asquith's widow, wrote to Wickham Steed, who had been foreign editor of The Times in 1916, and urged him to make public Lloyd George's responsibility for The Times leader. Steed, who was a reliable witness, answered that Lloyd George was guiltless and gave the story as stated above. Carson did not know that Asquith and Lloyd George had reached agreement, or perhaps he did and wanted to wreck it. In 1952 Stanley Morison gave a copy of the correspondence between Lady Oxford and Steed to Beaverbrook, who placed it in his archives.

with The Times leader without giving a date.[1] Beaverbrook's first account says only:

Lord Robert Cecil had been for some time in communication with Asquith and he told him the full extent of the Tory hostility to George.

Later Beaverbrook added this note:

Harcourt told me Curzon said to Asquith in Cabinet room that Tories would not serve under George—except A.B.L.

There is other evidence that Curzon was playing with both sides. Nevertheless, it seems likely that Asquith took the resolve to fight more or less on his own, as he had done before. Each time he had offered a compromise and then withdrawn it. So he did now. It has been argued by his admirers that he was driven from office. This is not so. The compromise with Lloyd George made him perfectly safe, and he deliberately went back on it. When battle was joined, he lost, but this is not proof that he did not try to fight at all. Rather it shows that the spirit had gone from him, whether for political warfare or for any other, and this is the justification for those such as Aitken who sought to bring him down. Churchill commented wisely:

A fierce, resolute Asquith, fighting with all his powers would have conquered easily. But the whole trouble arose from the fact that there was no fierce resolute A. to win this war or any other.

Even now Law tried to resurrect the compromise. He pursued Asquith to the house of commons and again urged the project of the war council. Asquith, according to Law, "lapsed into a glum and obstinate silence". When Law had left, Asquith wrote to Lloyd George repudiating the compromise finally and decisively. This was too much for Law. He wrote in the margin of Beaverbrook's manuscript:

It was only when L.G. showed me Asquith's letter going back on the Sunday arrangement that I definitely decided to back L.G. and I at once told him so.

Lloyd George thus knew that he had Law behind him at last. On 5 December he wrote to Asquith and for the first time offered his

[1] Crewe's memorandum in Asquith, Memories and Reflections, ii, 173, mentions The Times leader and then states "At the same time . . . Lord Curzon, Lord Robert Cecil and Mr. Austen Chamberlain went to 10 Downing Street", which certainly implies 4 December, but does not say so. Beaverbrook however snatched at it as proof of the three C's hostility to Lloyd George. Confusion is enhanced by the fact that Beaverbrook, both in his pencilled notes and in his first narrative, ascribed the Unionist meetings at the India office and the colonial office to 4 December, when they undoubtedly took place on 5 December. They are correctly dated in Beaverbrook's book. No explanation for this confusion occurs to me.

resignation. He said to Aitken: "I did not will this" and then declared his readiness to go forward even if it was alone. Aitken commented: "I had never seen such strength in any man".

At about the same time Asquith learnt from the three C's, apparently to his surprise, that they were not prepared to go on if both Lloyd George and Law left the government. Law in fact proved stronger than all his colleagues put together and, by estranging Law, Asquith had lost the battle. On the afternoon of 5 December he went to the king and resigned. Law, Lloyd George and Aitken met at the war office. They discussed what Law should say when he was sent for by the king as leader of the alternative party. Law wished to propose Lloyd George. Lloyd George answered that he preferred to serve under Bonar Law. In the evening Law went to Buckingham Palace. He agreed to form a government if Asquith would serve under him. Asquith refused. He also refused to serve under Balfour.

On the following day a conference was held at Buckingham Palace, perhaps at the suggestion of Arthur Henderson, perhaps at that of Montagu. There attended Asquith, Balfour, Henderson, Law and Lloyd George. Balfour again put forward the idea that Asquith should serve under Law, and Law actually believed for a brief period that compromise of a different kind had been achieved. In the afternoon however Asquith again refused. Thus he, not Lloyd George or Law, destroyed national unity and the unity of the Liberal party. Law now returned his commission to the king. In the evening the king invited Lloyd George to form a government, and he agreed to try. The difficulties which Asquith had expected did not appear. Balfour at once agreed to become foreign secretary with the famous remark: "You put a pistol to my head—yes". Law had also anticipated the attitude of the other Unionist ministers: "If they think their refusal to serve will make it impossible to form a ministry, they will refuse; if they see it can be formed without them, they will come in".[1] In the evening of 7 December Lloyd George again went to Buckingham Palace and kissed hands as prime minister.

Aitken played little part in these later stages, nor was he much involved in the construction of the new government. In his own words:

> With the actual formation of the Ministry I was indeed little concerned, except to put forward claims on behalf of some of my friends who deserved recognition. As soon as it was apparent, and it was so very early in the proceedings, that George could form a strong Government I felt that my work was done and my judgement justified. The Asquith Administration had fallen, and nothing remained but to pick up some of the pieces, reject others, and import new elements to form a stable Ministry.

[1] In the published version Beaverbrook attributed this remark to "an outside observer".

Such had been his attitude towards other mergers which he had organized. Once they were successful, he left them to other men and moved off to fresh activities.

As the years went by, Aitken's activities during this crisis won legendary importance, and his own writings sustained the legend. It was supposed that his intrigues had caused Asquith's fall and thus more remotely the destruction of the Liberal party. Aitken's original account shows that he played a more modest role. He supported Lloyd George's war council of three and persuaded Law to support it also. He brought the two men into an uneasy partnership. But Asquith's fall was an unconvenanted benefit, provided only by Asquith himself. Law was wholeheartedly anxious to keep Asquith as prime minister, and Lloyd George not much less so. Both men doubted their ability to lead the nation without Asquith's prestige. If Aitken triumphed, this was due to the mistakes of his adversary, not to his own skill. This often happens in life.

The crisis had a curious epilogue for Aitken himself. He tells in his book that he expected to become president of the board of trade. "In fact I had been promised the place". This would involve a by-election, as in those days a newly appointed minister had to be re-elected. He therefore warned the Unionist chairman at Ashton-under-Lyne and on 6 December dispatched his wife "to begin the campaign for the inevitable fray". But no message or invitation came. In the late evening he wandered disconsolately to the war office, where Lloyd George, he supposed, was allotting offices. He hesitated to go in and walked round and round "like a lost soul". His friend Brade came out and informed him that Albert Stanley was to have the board of trade. Worse was to follow. On Saturday, 9 December, Lloyd George called on Aitken at the Hyde Park Hotel, accompanied by Law. He said that, rightly or wrongly, he had given Stanley the post and then offered a smaller place, which Aitken refused. Later that day, Lloyd George wrote to Aitken and offered him a peerage. Aitken retired to Cherkley and meditated on his answer. There Law swooped down on him and ordered him to refuse. Lord Derby had objected on behalf of other Lancashire members with a better claim. Law added: "It would be most embarrassing to see a peerage conferred on an intimate friend of his". Aitken obeyed, though worried as to the explanations he would have to make at Ashton. On the Monday morning, Law issued a fresh order. Aitken must accept the peerage after all: "we want your safe seat at Ashton for Albert Stanley". Thus Aitken became an unwilling peer, his only consolation that appearances would be saved at Ashton. Beaverbrook concludes:

> I would much rather have stayed in the house of commons with a suitable office. But I had been jockeyed, or had jockeyed myself, into a position in

which I thought I had no choice. The Peerage was a way of escape. I took it. It would be absurd to deny that it was a very foolish way of escape.

This is a good story in Beaverbrook's best vein, even though at his own expense, a price he was always prepared to pay for a good story. It is also a very unlikely one. Why should he anticipate a fray at Ashton? The by-election would most probably be uncontested in wartime, as Stanley's actually was. And how could Aitken have sent his wife to Ashton during the day of 6 December when it was not yet clear that Lloyd George, or even Law, was to be prime minister? There is no scrap of evidence in Aitken's archives that he communicated with the Unionist chairman at Ashton or that Gladys Aitken went there. Admittedly his records are very defective for this period. But the dates simply do not fit.

There is another problem. When was the board of trade promised to Aitken? Beaverbrook wrote at the end of his life that Lloyd George had given him the promise "under the trees at Cherkley".[1] But Lloyd George never came to Cherkley during the crisis, and in any case men do not walk or sit under the trees in November. Lloyd George was at Cherkley in June, no doubt under the trees, but he was there to discuss the succession to the war office with Law and was in no position to promise Aitken the board of trade or anything else. When Lloyd George read the story in Beaverbrook's proof years later, he wrote in the margin: "I knew nothing of your desire to go to the board of trade. Bonar never suggested it to me". Surely Lloyd George would not have written this, if Beaverbrook could have reminded him of his visit to the Hyde Park Hotel and so given him the lie direct. So perhaps Law made the promise? This, too, is unlikely. Law did not make such promises to his embarrassing "intimate friend", whom he had refused to acknowledge earlier even as his parliamentary private secretary.

There was never any doubt from the first that Stanley was to have the board of trade. The Lloyd George papers contain a number of proposed cabinet lists in the handwriting of Christopher Addison, Lloyd George's main Liberal adherent. All put Stanley at the board of trade. In one of them, Aitken's name is entered with a query as parliamentary secretary to the board of trade. Aitken was known in England only as a financier, not as a businessman, and he had played no part in politics since the outbreak of war. Parliamentary secretary was the most he could expect, just as earlier he had expected to become under-secretary at the colonial office. Perhaps the suggestion was made to him. In that case, with his dislike of parliamentary drudgery, he must surely have refused. On the other hand, he was delighted at the time to become a peer. This put him on a level with Northcliffe and Rothermere, just when he had acquired The Daily Express.

[1] Decline and Fall of Lloyd George, 305.

The peerage appealed also to his romantic imagination. From New Brunswick manse to British house of lords was almost as good as from log cabin to White House. Beaverbrook's first narrative contains not a word about his disappointment over the board of trade. Instead, he writes of his peerage:

> The two middle-aged Tories who were overpaid for their services were Derby and myself. Derby stormed at my getting a peerage, and I laughed at the idea of his being at the War Office, and the world laughed with me.[1]

Finally, Beaverbrook's records contain fairly clear proof that the story of Law's objection was a manufacture, transferred from earlier episodes: a mixture of Derby's complaints in 1911 when Aitken got a knighthood and of Law's embarrassment in 1915 which led to Aitken's not getting a baronetcy. Law was certainly urged not to give Aitken any office. On 7 December L. J. Maxse, the right-wing editor of The National Review, wrote to him:

> As the front benches are crowded with political charlatans of proved incompetence who speak vastly above their ability, and whose ignorance of vital national affairs is only surpassed by their self-sufficiency, why not take this golden opportunity of looking outside into the larger world and associating the following elements with the war government.
>
> (1) the Fighting Services,
> (2) the Dominions,
> (3) the business world.   Yrs. v. sincerely,
>   L. J. Maxse.

P.S. We are all terrified of having men like Max Aitken and F. E. Smith thrust upon us, or Winston Churchill. That way disaster lies as you start by chilling public confidence.

Law was angered by this advice. He scrawled on Maxse's letter:

> I never mind attacks on myself (and indeed considering your views you have been very generous to me through these trying times) but I really do not like what you say about Aitken. He is my most intimate friend. I know him as well as I know anyone and in my belief he is as honourable a man as I am and one of the ablest men I know.

Here is the story of Beaverbrook's peerage as it appears from the records. On Saturday, 9 December 1916 Lloyd George wrote to Aitken:

> My dear Max,
>   There are two or three important business Departments which have no representatives in the House of Lords and therefore no spokesman.
>   Would you allow me to recommend your name to the king for a Peerage. You could answer for these departments in the H.L.

[1] Derby, then under-secretary at the war office, was the only leading Unionist who supported Lloyd George throughout. His reward was to become secretary of state for war, though as much subordinated to Robertson as Lloyd George had been.

On the same day Aitken replied:

> My dear Prime Minister,
> I am grateful to you for your offer and I shall be glad if I can be of any help to you in the way you indicate.

Beaverbrook printed the letter from Lloyd George in his book. He did not print his own letter of acceptance. Instead he alleges that on the evening of Sunday, 10 December he wrote to Lloyd George declining the peerage. This letter has not survived in either the Lloyd George or the Beaverbrook collection. It is tempting to suggest that it never existed.

There are however two letters in the Beaverbrook collection which he did not give in his book. Both are from Law. The first is of 9 December:

> My dear Max,
> I hope you will accept L.G.'s offer.
>
> > Yrs
> > A.B.L.
>
> It would be a delight to me if I felt that this would give you pleasure.

The second is on Monday, 11 December:

> My dear Max,
> It is all arranged and Younger will see you about it at once. Talbot is also helping in it.[1]
> I must see you some time but I don't know when.
>
> > Yours
> > A.B.L.

The last sentence of this letter surely implies that the two had not met for some days. There was therefore no visit from Law to Cherkley on Sunday, 10 December, telling Aitken to refuse, and no meeting in London on Monday, 11 December, telling him to accept.[2]

---

[1] Younger and Talbot were Unionist whips, who would attend to the formalities of Aitken's elevation.

[2] Other legends have accumulated round Beaverbrook's peerage. Lord Davidson, then Law's private secretary (Memoirs of a Conservative, 28), says that he had a row with Beaverbrook over it "because it would ruin Bonar's career, because no one would believe that Bonar hadn't given him a peerage for services rendered". When did this row take place? Aitken was offered the peerage on 9 December and accepted it on 11 December. He did not meet Davidson during this time, and there was no point in the row thereafter. Davidson also states that he reminded Beaverbrook "of the fact that Canada had decided to refuse to every Canadian in future any hereditary honour". In fact two Canadians, actually resident in Canada, received an hereditary honour after Beaverbrook, and the decision against such honours for Canadians was made only in 1919. Even then it only applied to Canadians resident in Canada. Canadians resident in England continued to receive hereditary honours, as for instance R. B. Bennett became a viscount in 1941.

Why should Beaverbrook invent such a story against himself or at best blow it up from more trivial happenings? He seems to have done it to please a friend. For there was a true story of a leading figure being disappointed in his hope for office, a very good story, and one which appears in Beaverbrook's drafts from the beginning. On 5 December he dined at F. E. Smith's with Lloyd George and Churchill. After dinner Lloyd George went off to find out what had happened at Law's meetings with the king and Asquith. Aitken accompanied him, and on the way Lloyd George asked Aitken to warn Churchill that the Unionists would not tolerate him in the government. Aitken returned to Smith's house. Churchill was looking forward to his return to office after being in the wilderness. He probed Aitken for information. Aitken became increasingly embarrassed. Finally, Churchill realized the truth. He exclaimed in anger: "Smith, this man knows that I am not to be included in the new government" and stormed out into the night. There is no doubt that this happened. Churchill did not dispute the story when he read it in proof. But he did not like it. Evidently he argued with Beaverbrook. Then he wrote in the margin:

> I still think it is better not to tell this story, wh. only gives yr enemies and mine the chance of saying "Thank God both these intriguers were jolly well scored off". But you are evidently so much in love with it and if you still want to print it I submit. W.

This was in 1928. Later, hearing that the book was about to appear, Churchill wrote on 21 December 1930:

> The more I think over your account of the dinner at F.E.'s during the formation of the second Coalition, the more sure I am that this account ought not to appear.
> I cannot understand why you should wish to make a laughing stock of yourself and me before all our enemies, who are numerous and spiteful. This personal and private episode is in no way necessary to the profoundly interesting chapter on English constitutional history with which your book is concerned. How B[aldwin] wd chuckle over it—and Neville!
> Do have the strength of mind to draw your pen through it at once.

Beaverbrook did not yield. He had less interest than Churchill in English constitutional history. His great love was for stories about individuals, and he would not sacrifice a good one even for the sake of a friend. But it would be some consolation if he balanced this story with one at his own expense, particularly as this second story enabled him to end the book on a personal note without pushing himself forward. The artist in him triumphed over all lesser considerations. No doubt the vague memory of the parliamentary secretaryship came back into his mind, but this was too trivial to have caused disappointment, and therefore it became the

actual presidency of the board of trade.[1] Moreover when Beaverbrook
wrote the story of his peerage, he was aspiring to play a great part in
politics and was being told by his admirers that he, not Baldwin, would
have been Law's political heir, if he had not gone to the house of lords.
The peerage now appeared as a blunder, and in time Beaverbrook himself
came to believe that it had been forced on him against his will.

There was indeed one political consideration in his mind at the time,
but it worked in favour of his accepting the peerage, not against. In 1950
Beaverbrook prepared a statement justifying his claim to Canadian
domicile. In the course of this he wrote:

> One of the considerations which influenced me to accept a Peerage was
> that it would not prevent me from sitting for a parliamentary constituency
> in Canada, I made a particular point of this at the time of acceptance.

There was, it is true, an objection to Beaverbrook's peerage. It came
from King George V, not from Law, who was indeed Beaverbrook's
advocate. When Aitken's name was submitted, George V replied that he
did not "see his way" to approve, since he did not consider that the
"public services of Sir Max Aitken called for such special recognition".
Lloyd George replied that any refusal would "place him in a position of
great embarrassment" and asked Stamfordham, the king's private secretary, to discuss the matter with Law. Law explained that Aitken, and still
worse his constituency association, had been told of the intended honour
and that the by-election was already being prepared. The king reluctantly
gave way, though trying to obtain a promise from Lloyd George that in
future honours should not be offered until the king had been informally
consulted—a promise which, if given, Lloyd George did not keep.

It is impossible to tell whether Beaverbrook learnt of the king's objection at the time. Probably not, though it is curious that Law used the
argument about Ashton-under-Lyne, which Beaverbrook later transformed into the instrument for imposing the peerage upon him. At all
events, when Harold Nicolson published the story in his life of George V,[2]

[1] If Beaverbrook had any real resentment against being displaced by Albert Stanley,
he should have received consolation from a letter which he found in Law's papers.
On 29 January 1919 Lloyd George wrote to Law:

Concerning Stanley. . . . I have come to the conclusion from a long observation of
Stanley's work that he is much too weak and flabby a man for the difficult task which
confronts a President of the Board of Trade under present conditions. He has all the
glibness of Runciman and that is apt to take in innocent persons—like you and me!
It certainly misled me into the belief that he was a much better man than he has turned
out to be.

However, by the time Beaverbrook found this letter, he had forgotten all about Albert
Stanley and supposed quite wrongly that the passage referred to Stanley Baldwin
(Beaverbrook to Lloyd George, 2 May 1927).

[2] Nicolson, George V, 511–12.

without however mentioning Aitken's name, Beaverbrook at once authorized Robert Blake to reveal that "the individual in question" was Sir Max Aitken.[1]

The visitors' book at Cherkley contains this entry for 18 December 1916:

Beaverbrook formerly W. M. Aitken.

With this entry William Maxwell Aitken took his farewell. The prestigious figure of Lord Beaverbrook strode upon the scene. The title was taken from a stream near Newcastle where Aitken had fished when a boy.[2] Kipling devised Beaverbrook's coat of arms for him. On 14 February 1917 Baron Beaverbrook was introduced into the house of lords. His sponsors were Lord St. Audries and Lord Rothermere. This was a striking conjunction. St. Audries, when he was Sir Alexander Acland-Hood and Unionist chief whip, had given Aitken his first push into British journalism by inducing him to invest in The Globe. Rothermere was to be Beaverbrook's adviser, associate and friendly rival, when he embarked on his career as a newspaper magnate.

[1] Blake, The Unknown Prime Minister, 347.
[2] Beaverbrook for once mismanaged a joke. He writes (Politicians and the War, ii, 331) that The Morning Post epitomized the view that he was the inspirer and architect of Asquith's downfall by using the phrase "Bunty pulls the strings"—the name of a popular play running at the time. Actually The Morning Post suggested that Aitken should take the title of Lord Bunty.

CHAPTER SEVEN

TROUBLES OF A MINISTER, 1917–18

L loyd George was established as prime minister. He no longer needed to temporize in his plans for directing the war. His proposed war committee subordinate to the prime minister was forgotten. Instead Lloyd George superseded the traditional cabinet by a war cabinet of five men—himself, Law, Curzon, Milner, and Arthur Henderson, incidentally leaving out Carson and thus confirming the doubts which Asquith had expressed. There was no more talk of excluding the prime minister from the day-to-day conduct of the war. On the contrary, Lloyd George, as prime minister, now hoped to direct the war in every detail. The change was the other way round. Lloyd George ceased to concern himself with the house of commons. Law, as leader of the house, took over the representational role which had been originally allotted to Asquith. Nor did Lloyd George neglect Law as Asquith had done. He knew that Law's backing had made him prime minister and that he would be lost without it.

The intimacy between the two men became very close. Law, as chancellor of the exchequer, moved into No. 11 Downing Street, and Lloyd George came in for an hour's private talk practically every morning. Beaverbrook was no longer needed as the go-between. He had also less opportunity. He lost his room at the war office early in 1917 when he ceased to be Canadian military representative, and in any case Lloyd George had departed to the other end of Whitehall. Law, too, was less accessible than he had been at Pembroke Lodge. He found a reliable private secretary in J. C. C. Davidson, who served him almost to the end of his life. Ironically, Beaverbrook provided unwittingly a still more dangerous rival to himself. Law, who disliked social occasions, wanted a financial secretary who would do the entertaining necessary at the treasury. Beaverbrook knew the very man: "very amiable and popular in a colourless kind of way":

Mildness, amiability, caution, lack of self-assertiveness and ambition, such were his qualities at this period. He was written down as a good neighbour, a trustworthy friend, a man of all the domestic virtues—but for his public capacities no one cared a whit.

His name was Stanley Baldwin.[1]

Baldwin became Law's devoted servant and attendant. Where Beaverbrook offered wit and excitement, Baldwin gave Law rest, which perhaps the tired man required more. Many years later, Baldwin gave an indication of what he had done for Law. On 18 December 1928 he wrote to Beaverbrook, asking for some relic of Law's which could be placed in the London Museum. He added:

> Of course the most characteristic thing to those who knew him would be a ginger cake and a glass of milk, to which I brought him home pretty nearly every night for about four years!

This was not the sort of service which Beaverbrook was accustomed to perform.

Occasionally Beaverbrook could still make himself useful. When Law became chancellor, he found that a new loan was necessary. The treasury wanted to raise the money by 6% bonds, placed through the banks. Law preferred a public issue at 5%, and Beaverbrook organized the publicity for this, enlisting the powerful aid of Northcliffe. His campaign was a mighty success and brought in £1,000,000,000. Usually, however, Beaverbrook's activities towards Law were the other way round. He became Lloyd George's agent for putting to Law proposals which Lloyd George hesitated to put himself. This was curious and revealing. Lloyd George was in theory the all-powerful prime minister, and his relations with Law were, according to many observers, as close as those between man and wife. Yet time and again he shrank from Law's displeasure. Beaverbrook had to brave it and then to report either that Law had been softened or that the proposal had better not be made.

The first such episode came almost at once. It concerned Sir William Robertson, chief of the imperial general staff. Lloyd George's original object in demanding an effective war committee had been to diminish Robertson's sole control over strategy. In the excitement of fighting Asquith, this object had been forgotten, and when the new government was formed, Robertson remained as powerful as ever. Lloyd George had given a pledge to the Unionist ministers that he would retain Haig as commander-in-chief. He had given no such pledge about Robertson and was anxious to strike him down. Beaverbrook was commissioned to break the ice with Law. He was ready to undertake the task. After his experiences at the war office, he regarded Robertson as a dangerously

[1] These sentences are from an unpublished chapter that was originally intended as the conclusion of Politicians and the War. Later Beaverbrook took it out, reserving it for the Age of Baldwin, which he never completed.

political soldier. He was sustained by Brade, who had also turned against Robertson and wrote of him:

> He is a very clever man, but he has no nerve and is too "slim". I shall never forgive his consistent playing for his own hand which is the most marked characteristic of his nature. He can lay no claim to the real soldier-like quality of discipline.

Beaverbrook in his turn enlisted the aid of F. E. Smith, who listened to the story and then said of Robertson, "Sack him now". Armed with this advice, Beaverbrook went to Law. But Law was unmoved. He was favourable to Robertson and refused to believe that the generals were conspiring against Lloyd George. He dismissed F. E. Smith as "a man with the vision of an eagle but with a blind spot in his eye". Beaverbrook had to report to Lloyd George that there was nothing doing. Robertson survived untamed for another year.

Beaverbrook's next intervention was more successful, or maybe Lloyd George was more determined. This time the question was the return of Churchill to office. Churchill's political standing was low. He was universally, if unjustly, saddled with responsibility for the failure in Gallipoli. The Tories hated him both as a renegade and as the man who had supposedly plotted a "pogrom" in Ulster in 1914. Law shared this feeling to the full. Lloyd George had promised the Unionist ministers in December 1916 that he would not give Churchill office. Soon Lloyd George began to fear that Churchill might become the rallying point for those who were dissatisfied with the course of the war and yet had no faith in Asquith. On 10 May 1917, in secret session, Churchill delivered a masterly speech which Lloyd George found hard to equal. Lloyd George did not waste a moment. He caught Churchill behind the speaker's chair and recruited him at once as an intimate, though unofficial, colleague. This could not last. An office must be found for Churchill. A first attempt, to make him head of the air board, broke on Unionist outcry. On 17 July Lloyd George resolved to try again.

Beaverbrook was summoned to No. 10 Downing Street. He imagined, as he walked down sunny Whitehall, that he himself was about to be offered some important office at last. Instead Lloyd George informed him that Churchill was to be appointed minister of munitions. Lloyd George had not dared to tell Law. Beaverbrook was commissioned to do so. He found Law surrounded by official papers and smoking his pipe. Beaverbrook thought, "This will put his pipe out". And it did. Law was furious. Not only did he distrust Churchill. His opinion had not been asked before the appointment was made. Beaverbrook loyally diverted Law's anger from Lloyd George to himself. Law recognized that, whatever his feelings, he must support Lloyd George. Though he said rightly, "Lloyd

George's throne will shake", he beat down Unionist complaints. Churchill survived as minister of munitions. Thus did Beaverbrook reopen to Churchill the path to glory.

Beaverbrook laboured to secure favourable publicity for Lloyd George's government just as he had done earlier for the mergers which he promoted. In particular, he strove to reconcile Northcliffe and Lloyd George. In May 1917 he succeeded. He hit on the idea of placating Northcliffe by sending him as head of the British war mission in the United States. It gave Beaverbrook additional pleasure that the appointment greatly offended Balfour, the foreign secretary, whom Beaverbrook numbered, rightly or wrongly, among his enemies. As a still further advantage, Northcliffe now ceased to oppose Churchill's return to office and indeed welcomed it. Later in the year Northcliffe quarrelled once more with Lloyd George. Beaverbrook was not at a loss. He at once proposed the appointment of Lord Rothermere, Northcliffe's brother, as the first secretary of state for air. Rothermere accepted with fulsome gratitude, and the Harmsworth front against Lloyd George was broken.

Beaverbrook also acted occasionally as the channel through whom Lloyd George conveyed offers of honours, particularly to those connected with the press. One proposed honour made Beaverbrook again a mediator with Law. At the end of 1917, F. E. Smith, about to depart on a speaking tour in the United States, wrote to Beaverbrook from Liverpool:

> The PM is willing to give me a baronetcy but Bonar is making some fuss. Would you mind dropping him a note.
> I want it (1) for recognition of my work (2) if anything happened to me I think it an advantage to Freddy. Please act at once.

Beaverbrook acted. He pleaded with Law, and not in vain. Sir F. E. Smith became a baronet in the new year's honours.

Law rarely used Beaverbrook as go-between from his side. There was little he wished to propose. There was one interesting little intervention. On 10 January 1918 J. C. C. Davidson wrote:

> It would help us very much in preparing a statement in connection with the taxation of capital to know whether "the big beast in the field" came to any terms with the workingmen on this subject at this time last year. I expect you know what passed over the road and I do not like to ask the herdsmen next door. If he did promise capital levy so much the better![1]

The approach is the more curious in that later, when the capital levy was discussed seriously, Law was its sole, and successful opponent.

---

[1] The big beast is Lloyd George. The workingmen are the Labour delegation which Lloyd George met on 7 December 1916. He did not mention a capital levy. Beaverbrook had a verbatim report of this meeting in his files, but there is no record of any reply to Davidson.

These marginal intrusions into politics were clearly not a fulltime occupation. Beaverbrook certainly did not discharge the political functions in the house of lords for which he had ostensibly been given his peerage. Indeed he did not make a single appearance there throughout the year after his introduction. He worked fairly hard at the Colonial Bank, using it among other things to thwart the government's decision about enemy property in Nigeria, which had helped to touch off the political crisis in November 1916. In theory the property was to be offered to all comers. In practice the Colonial Bank bought in any property which was in danger of passing out of British hands. Despite this, F. C. Goodenough of Barclays, who took over the Colonial Bank in 1919, reported that Beaverbrook had been a first-rate banker, but "rather too orthodox".

It seems also that Beaverbrook now began to concern himself seriously, if sporadically, with The Daily Express. His own evidence on this is confused and contradictory. At one moment he dated his shouldering of responsibility as November 1917. At another he wrote, "I claim to have become a full-blooded journalist just before the general election of 1918". Probably there was nothing so clear-cut, only a gradual process of interference and direction. Beaverbrook consulted the two newspaper magnates whom he knew, Northcliffe and Rothermere, though there is again some doubt when he did it. He records that his conversation with Northcliffe took place at Broadstairs "some years before the war", which sounds unlikely. Northcliffe asked him what his private fortune was. Beaverbrook told him.[1] Northcliffe said: "You will lose it all in Fleet Street".

Rothermere was more encouraging. This time the conversation took place "on a black Saturday's winter evening"—presumably as an interlude during the manoeuvres against Asquith. Rothermere understood newspaper finance in a way his brother Northcliffe did not. Indeed it was the only subject he understood. Moreover he was already engaged in some joint financial ventures with Beaverbrook and was therefore more sympathetic towards him. Rothermere estimated with remarkable accuracy the money and time Beaverbrook would need to turn The Express into a profitable undertaking. It would take a good deal of courage. Nevertheless he advised Beaverbrook to go ahead. He even regretted that, out of loyalty towards his brother, he could not himself invest in what was likely to

---

[1] What figure did Beaverbrook name? His own account says only: "I answered directly just as I should do if the same question were asked me today. For I detest a man who conceals the extent of his wealth—it is as bad as leaving out the date of one's birth in 'Who's Who' ". Driberg says: "Over five million dollars" (Beaverbrook, 139). This is surely too moderate an estimate. In 1910 Aitken had borrowed five million dollars in London on the strength of securities which must have been worth much more. Since then he had made two million dollars in the Steel Company of Canada deal alone and far more in transactions afterwards. Perhaps five million pounds was the figure Aitken had in mind.

prove a formidable competitor to Northcliffe's Daily Mail. The contrast between the two brothers was revealing. Northcliffe did not recognize any magnate in Fleet Street except himself and treated Beaverbrook, as their correspondence shows, with a mixture of condescension and mistrust. Rothermere had no jealousy of this kind and was simply interested in finance, whether his own or another's.

At any rate Beaverbrook became involved with The Daily Express. Early in 1917 he secured a thousand tons of paper from Northcliffe on favourable terms when the stocks of The Express were running low. His direction was apparently conducted from afar. Only a few scraps of evidence survive from this period. They give a foretaste of the way in which Beaverbrook treated his editors later. On 7 September 1917 Blumenfeld wrote to Beaverbrook:

> Dear Max:
>
> Wilson[1] tells me that you say I have been dodging you. That is just the impression I have had of you since you have not been get-atable this week except over the telephone and this question is far too important to discuss in that way. This situation has become both impossible and intolerable and you, being possessed of more than usual intelligence must understand the mischief that is worked by the sending of the sort of messages I have received through subordinates. I am most anxious to have it out with you without loss of time and I wish you would send word at what hour we can meet this afternoon after 3.
>
> I can't in the least understand your sudden attitude of hostility.

And on 20 December 1917 Beaverbrook wrote to Blumenfeld from Cherkley:

> My dear Blum,
>
> I have had time this morning to make a critical examination of the Daily Express and I'm sure you won't mind my giving you the results of it.
>
> The Smaller Advts are either being eliminated or are not coming in in a satisfactory way. This requires treatment. The Theatre Advts don't pay well enough to be put on the Leader page and shld go on the back page.
>
> It is not good business to attack Lord Rothermere even by implication. We are in the middle of complex paper deals with him, and he has always been generous in these matters.
>
> On the front page there are frequently important news items from the night before. Surely there ought to be enough completely fresh matter for that page.
>
> I notice this morning that we missed the Boom Towers claim. There ought to be a man put on to read the other papers and check anyone responsible for missing these things on The Express.

[1] J. B. Wilson, longtime news editor of The Daily Express.

The By-the-Way column is worse than that of The Daily News or The Star.

As to the Editorials they are a strange mixture of good and bad. I attribute this to their being written by one hand and then altered by other. I sometimes notice a lack of consistency between the various parts. There is also on Wednesday a flat contradiction between the leader and the Parliamentary Correspondent: the former advising L-G to follow Borden and go for an election while the Correspondent pours cold water on the whole idea.

An arrangement cannot be a good one, if it produces these contradictions. I am entirely in favour of short leaders written in a simple and direct style, but it seems to me that the Editor ought to have someone competent to write these on his own without any help from the Editor, and if he has not such a man he ought to find him. Wilson, Dach, & Farthing are all men of first class capacity, and I believe that if they are given real responsibility they will deliver the goods.

But I gathered from a telephone conversation I had with Wilson the other night that when you are in retreat at Dunmow everything has to be telephoned through to you. My own view is that working at the pressure you do, you ought to have 2 or 3 nights off, but on those occasions the man on the spot ought to be in charge. If we havn't got men we can trust to do this—which I believe we have—we must get new ones. Please dont trouble to answer this letter which merely consists of suggestions I hope you may find useful.

On 15 May 1918 Lady Diana Manners wrote to her future husband Duff Cooper that she had met Beaverbrook at dinner with Edwin and Venetia Montagu:[1]

> Beaverbrook talked of the Daily Express and of how much of his interest he gave to it. Every night, he said, he rang up and told them to insert and to omit so and so, and put the fact that Lady Diana Manners has a great mastiff with a diamond collar on the front page, not the inside one.

It is not possible to judge whether Beaverbrook's admonitions took effect. At any rate the circulation of The Daily Express did not improve. In September 1918 Beaverbrook drew a rather idealized picture of what he had achieved, no doubt on his general principle that confidence brought its own reward. Rebecca West, a young writer whom he knew, had voiced some criticism of The Daily Express. Beaverbrook replied:

> The Daily Express is rapidly changing its character. It was originally a paper with a small, but firm, clientele, representing a pretty strong, if limited view. It is now becoming a paper with an enormous and infinitely varied circulation, and its political opinions probably approximate to those held by, shall I say, Arnold Bennett, or someone of that kind.

[1] Diana Cooper, The Rainbow Comes and Goes (1958), 171. Lady Diana stood high among Beaverbrook's favourites. He gave her a motor car when she married in the following year.

As Arnold Bennett professed himself a Liberal, the invocation of his name would not have brought much joy to the Unionist central office.

Whatever Beaverbrook's parade of detachment from The Daily Express, it was in 1917 that others began to number him among the press lords. This was then a term of opprobrium, as it was to remain for a generation afterwards. Politicians had always been jealous of the press, as the Wilkes affair had shown long ago. They came to tolerate great editors such as Delane or C. P. Scott (who successfully played down the fact that he was also a proprietor)—men of much the same world as themselves. The distrust of the politicians was turned against the newspaper proprietors, particularly of Northcliffe's type. In the politicians' view, a proprietor should put up money for a paper and appoint the editor, naturally of his own political persuasion. He should then give the editor a free hand. This was what the newspaper dynasties of the nineteenth century did, from the Walters of The Times downwards. This was what the respectable proprietors were still doing.

It was not what Northcliffe did. He ran his papers at a profit instead of subsidizing them. To ensure that they did so, he had to direct them himself. He was his own chief editor. Northcliffe's prime aim was not political influence or power. It was to make his papers the best of their kind in the world, and he succeeded. The Times was a special case. Northcliffe regarded The Times as a national monument much like Westminster Abbey. He wished to preserve it and believed that running it at a profit was the only way of doing so. Political influence followed inescapably, often to Northcliffe's embarrassment. He did not want office or honours. He was not a party man. He was an intense patriot, and his patriotism dragged him into politics, especially in wartime. Northcliffe imagined that he was merely serving the interests of his country. To the politicians, he appeared an irresponsible figure, seeking to dictate to parliament and the government. His financial independence made him uncontrollable: he did not need subsidies from party funds. In addition, journalists from less successful papers stoked the resentment of the politicians. Northcliffe became the symbol, in conventional circles, for all the corrupting forces which were at work in British society.

Beaverbrook was tarred with the same brush when he took over control of The Daily Express. In some ways, his position was worse than Northcliffe's. Northcliffe had at least started relatively poor and had made all his money out of newspapers. Beaverbrook arrived in England already a wealthy man and used his wealth, or so it seemed, to break first into politics and then into journalism. He was a perfect example of the new rich who provoked hostility in all the political parties. The Liberals had long been regaled by their Canadian colleagues with exaggerated versions of the cement affair. As well, Beaverbrook was now regarded by many

Liberals as the engineer of Asquith's overthrow, and no doubt he made no secret of this himself.

There was also hostility to Beaverbrook on the Unionist side. The Unionist central office looked on him with disfavour. He had started respectably by subsidizing derelict Unionist newspapers. Instead of continuing these subsidies, he had snatched The Daily Express from the control of the central office and now announced his intention of making it pay, so that it would become independent like The Daily Mail or, in the politicians' phrase, irresponsible. Old-style, aristocratic Unionists blamed Beaverbrook, quite mistakenly, for the overthrow of Balfour as party leader in 1911, a view held especially by Balfour himself and by his Cecil cousins, Lord Salisbury, Lord Robert Cecil and Lord Hugh. Some of the Unionists who had originally gone with Beaverbrook in backing Law also turned against him. They were the hard men of the party and wanted an extreme right-wing government, not one dominated by Lloyd George. They believed that Beaverbrook had cheated them. He had used their discontent in order to dislodge Asquith and had then captured Law as Lloyd George's loyal supporter instead of producing a right-wing government under Carson or Milner.

These various grievances were in part rationalizations. Throughout life Beaverbrook provoked in many people a distrust and dislike which bewildered him and, still more, those who loved him. He was wealthy, but so were other men in politics. Maybe he offended English puritanism by his open enjoyment of wealth, or rather of the things which wealth brought—champagne, cigars, large motor cars, and most of all, though few knew this, the endless opportunities of generosity towards those less fortunate than he was. No doubt also Beaverbrook was a bad party man. He had friends in all parties and often urged them into the fray, even when their views were different from his own. He believed in Empire Free Trade. Otherwise what he liked, in politics or in life, was action. Beaverbrook, with all his great qualities, was not a sticker. He operated in short bursts and had no sooner got one thing started than he wanted to be off on something else. This is why he was happiest as a newspaper man: in journalism something new was happening every day. But even when he was busiest with his papers, he was also half a dozen other men at the same time: politician, historian, financier, racehorse-owner, cinema-promoter, and general entertainer. In H. G. Wells's phrase, he had "a multi-track mind". Rebecca West said penetratingly "Max was a honey but he did not add up". This, though true, did not worry him.

The deepest charge against Beaverbrook was that he could never be wholly serious. Disraeli said that the English loved "grave statesmen". Beaverbrook was not grave, even at the most solemn moment. He himself often described his conduct and conversation as ribald, and there were many for whom this was a term of abuse. Mrs. Churchill, for instance, steadfastly deplored the influence which the "three B's"—Birkenhead, Beaverbrook, and Bracken—had on her husband: it brought out, she alleged, the worst in Winston. Wherever Beaverbrook was, there were always shouts of laughter. This was not a recommendation in political circles.

In 1918 the political resentment, however caused, was to fall upon Beaverbrook's head. He went into the storm innocently and unwittingly. He had been at a loose end during most of 1917 as his work for Canadian publicity declined. In January 1918 Churchill invited him to become director of finance at the ministry of munitions, possibly with the sinecure of paymaster general. Beaverbrook refused. If he had to look after finance, he preferred to look after his own.

Soon after this Lloyd George made a more attractive offer and on 10 February 1918 announced that he had appointed Beaverbrook minister of information and chancellor of the duchy of Lancaster. This was a sensible thing to do. Beaverbrook was the most experienced war propagandist in the country, thanks to the work he had done for the Canadian government. He had invented all the methods of publicity which were now being belatedly used in Great Britain. He had commissioned the first war artists, the first war photographers, and the first makers of war films. Their products, far from costing the Canadian government money, were being shown round the world at a considerable profit. When the British war office reluctantly went in for publicity, it had to enlist Beaverbrook's cooperation and took over most of his men, from Sir William Jury, his director of cinematograph, to his team of war artists.

This suited Beaverbrook well enough. As usual, he had initiated and was glad when others took over. Even Canadian publicity, for which he was still responsible, now more or less ran itself. He found one new activity during 1917. There was a general election in Canada, and Beaverbrook provided the election literature for the Canadian troops in Great Britain and France. Though ostensibly non-party, this literature certainly directed the attention of the serving voters to those candidates who supported the war most resolutely. In Canada Beaverbrook's reputation as a propagandist stood high. He did not appreciate that in Great Britain his work was little known and still less esteemed. Even the men at the war office who learnt from his work were annoyed at having to do so. Most politicians distrusted propaganda as much as they distrusted Beaverbrook himself.

Lloyd George was the great exception. If anything, he rated the influence of propaganda and the press too highly. When he became prime minister, he found half a dozen committees dealing haphazardly with British propaganda in foreign countries. There was little to show except

some elegant works on the British way of life. Lloyd George grouped the
committees into a department of information, nominally under his own
direction. He was too busy to pay further attention, and the department
drifted ineffectively. In August 1917 Carson, who had been dislodged
from the admiralty by being made a member of the war cabinet, was put
in charge of information in order to give him something to do. No action
followed. Lloyd George had also set up an advisory committee, composed
of press men—Lord Burnham, C. P. Scott, Robert Donald, and Beaverbrook. No one sought their advice. At the end of 1917 the advisory committee resigned in protest. Immediately afterwards Carson also resigned
for reasons which had nothing to do with propaganda.[1] Here was the
opportunity for Lloyd George to make a fresh start. He had a less avowed
motive. His conflict with Sir William Robertson was reaching its climax,
and he wanted to get the press lords on his side. Beaverbrook, besides
being a press lord himself, was the appropriate go-between to the others.

Beaverbrook naturally welcomed the task. Rothermere, being secretary
for air, was already hooked. Northcliffe was the real problem and the great
prize. He had reverted to hostile independence in the previous November,
when he returned from his war mission to the United States.[2] Beaverbrook surmised that Northcliffe would find propaganda an irresistible
bait. And so it proved. For Northcliffe, the great master of publicity,
believed that he could run propaganda better than anyone else. There
was one considerable obstacle. Northcliffe would not jeopardize his
prized independence by becoming a minister. On the other hand, he
refused to be subordinate to Beaverbrook. Beaverbrook, with his customary agility, devised a compromise. Nominally he would become the
responsible minister, but Northcliffe would have direct access to the prime
minister, and his department would be in fact independent. This agreement was drafted in grandiloquent terms tuned to Northcliffe's taste,
as though it were a treaty between two sovereign powers:

> The Lord Beaverbrook, in the event of taking office as Chancellor of the
> Duchy of Lancaster, shall have assigned to him control of propaganda.
> He shall forthwith recommend to the Prime Minister that the entire
> direction of foreign propaganda shall be taken over by the Viscount North-
> cliffe, who will report direct to the Prime Minister, and who, it will be
> stated, assumes these duties at the Prime Minister's request.

This arrangement would have left Beaverbrook only with propaganda
in the British Empire, not much more in fact than the work he was already

---

[1] Carson's ostensible reason for resigning was to have a free hand in regard to
Ireland. In reality he resigned in protest against the dismissal of Jellicoe as first sea
lord.
[2] Anomalously Northcliffe maintained until the end of the war a headquarters
entitled "London office of the British war mission",

doing for Canada. After some further bargaining, Northcliffe, who was only interested in propaganda against the enemy, relinquished allied and neutral countries to Beaverbrook. Northcliffe held on to Italy, the centre from which Wickham Steed, his principal adviser on these matters, proposed to dismember Austria–Hungary. In exchange, Beaverbrook grabbed Turkey and the Near East.

Beaverbrook had thus performed his work as a mediator successfully. Northcliffe was caught. Lloyd George however dallied. For Beaverbrook had also made a condition. He had learnt from previous experience that the director of propaganda needed ministerial rank if he were to achieve anything. He had also noted Neville Chamberlain's failure as director of national service, due to lack of such rank. Beaverbrook therefore insisted that he must be appointed chancellor of the duchy of Lancaster, a sinecure office clearly suited to his purpose. Lloyd George agreed and then failed to act. Hints were dropped to the press that Beaverbrook was to be chairman of propaganda and nothing else. The difficulties came from King George V. He objected to Beaverbrook's presiding over the Duchy, "which, as it were, is the personal property of the Sovereign and entailing closer relations between the King and its Chancellor than with many of his Ministers".[1] After ten days when nothing had happened, Northcliffe lost patience and told Beaverbrook, in a letter marked "Not private", that he withdrew. At this Beaverbrook also resigned before he had been appointed. He wrote to Lloyd George on 7 February 1918:

> You will, I am sure, realize that the apparent withdrawal of the promise of ministerial rank entirely alters my whole attitude, while the continued discussion of a new appointment, which has not yet been made or officially announced, and the terms of which vary in each paper, makes my position personally impossible, and prejudices in advance the success of the new post as such.
>
> Therefore with many regrets I feel myself bound to decline this honour.

Lloyd George was alarmed and acted resolutely at last. He swept aside the king's objections, even asserting that Beaverbrook, as "a first-rate business man", would administer the duchy well—an expectation that does not seem to have been fulfilled; at least there is no sign that Beaverbrook ever went near the duchy offices. Lloyd George now pursued Beaverbrook urgently. Beaverbrook, on his side, began to hesitate, as he did so often. He walked round Horseguards Parade for twenty minutes before going in to see Lloyd George and said to his companion (presumably Maurice Woods): "For a man of my health and disposition office is a dreadful tie and I shall not accept". He then entered No. 10 Downing Street and succumbed to Lloyd George's charms. There was one gesture

[1] *Men and Power*, 274–75.

of respectability. The shocking word "propaganda" disappeared, and Beaverbrook became the first minister of information. A week later, Northcliffe relented and agreed to become director of enemy propaganda. On the same day, no doubt by chance, Sir William Robertson was dismissed from his post as chief of the imperial general staff. Northcliffe's newspapers, previously vocal on behalf of the generals, made no complaint. Beaverbrook's work as go-between had again been successful.

There was a price to pay. Beaverbrook was warned that Northcliffe's appointment, on top of his own, would cause trouble. Lloyd George said gaily: "If we are going to have a row it may as well be a good one!" Law was gloomier: "One of you newspaper barons was too much. Now there are two. Well, you'll hear of this". Beaverbrook was full of his achievements with Canadian propaganda and expected people to say: "Of course Lord Beaverbrook is on his mere record as a propagandist the obvious appointment BUT—!" Instead his qualifications were ignored, and it was said that he had got the job because he was a newspaper proprietor or a friend of Law's or an opponent of Asquith's in 1916. Moreover many MPs and journalists thought that the new ministry would run propaganda at home, of course to boost Lloyd George. In fact home propaganda, other than films, paintings, and photographs, was not within its purview. However Northcliffe was the real stumbling block. Mention of his name always produced an outcry in political circles, and Beaverbrook was brought in on a side wind.

The Unionist war committee of backbenchers met in high indignation and resolved that "no one who controls a newspaper should be allowed to be a Member of the Government or to hold a responsible post under it so long as he retains control of that newspaper". Lord Salisbury, who was in the chair, remarked that Beaverbrook was a very wicked man and, when challenged by Goulding to substantiate his accusation, merely replied, "Oh, ask anyone in Canada". Beaverbrook commented privately: "What would Lord Salisbury say of me if I published a statement that he was a bad landlord and when asked to justify it replied 'oh, ask anyone in Hertfordshire' ". His public defence was to announce that he had resigned all his directorships, though, as he was never a director of The Daily Express, this was really irrelevant to his control. Northcliffe merely ignored the uproar, asserting that he was neither a member of the government nor holding a responsible post under it. In his view he was running enemy propaganda as a private venture.

Protests were also made in the house of commons, principally by Austen Chamberlain, who was out of office and seeking to get in again. His strongest complaint was not that the presence of a newspaper proprietor in the cabinet damaged the government but that it damaged his newspaper—a strangely altruistic care for the independence of the press.

Chamberlain made his criticism twice, on 19 February and again on 11 March. On the second occasion, despite an effective defence of Beaverbrook by Lloyd George, Law lost his nerve. He came to Beaverbrook and told him that in the interests of the administration he ought to resign. Law even wrote Beaverbrook's letter of resignation for him. Usually Beaverbrook drafted such letters for others, as he was to do when Rothermere resigned as secretary for air a month later, and this was a curious reversal of roles. The pencil draft survives in Beaverbrook's papers, perhaps as a reminder that Law was not quite the perfect patron of Beaverbrook's later imagination:

My dear Prime Minister,

As you know I was very reluctant to undertake the duty of minister of propaganda, and I was indeed doubtful as I explained to you whether the state of my health would make it possible for me to [perform] give continuous attendance to the duties of the office.

In view however of the belief expressed by you that I was specially qualified to do [the work] successfully a piece of work to which you attached great importance I thought it my duty to undertake it.

I did so in the hope that I might in this way be able to render some small public service but I am convinced after the expression by Mr. Chamberlain of hostility to any newspaper proprietor being a member of the Govt and the [evident support] strong support which this suggestion evidently received from the H of C that my continuance in the [Govt] administration of the dept would [not be in the public interest] be extremely difficult. In these circumstances I have to request that you permit me to resign the office.

This was by no means the first time that Beaverbrook had been called upon to sacrifice himself for the sake of his intimate friend Law. Previously he had always complied. This time he refused. This unexpected rebellion suggests that at the time Beaverbrook was more Lloyd George's man than Law's. Beaverbrook's resolve was stiffened by his friend Healy who advised: "Don't resign; wait until you are sacked". Law warned Beaverbrook that an attack was coming also in the house of lords. Beaverbrook determined to meet the challenge. Some years later he described to Arnold Bennett his feelings of anxiety before the debate and gave Bennett the speech of defence with which he had triumphed. Bennett put both the feelings and the speech into a political novel, Lord Raingo, which he was then writing.

Bennett, when correcting his proofs, looked up some point of the speech in The Times. To his surprise, the speech was not there. On 24 September 1925 he wrote to Beaverbrook:

You told me that
1. Beresford attacked you.
2. You replied.

3. Haldane criticized you favourably.
4. Curzon   „   „   unfavourably.

Your secretary tells me that this debate occurred on February 12th 1918.
I doubt this, as in the "Times" report of the 13th there is no mention at all
of a speech by you or of a speech by Lord Haldane.

Beaverbrook did not answer, and this was scarcely odd. For his alleged
speech was never delivered. On 12 February 1918 Lord Beresford
delivered a rambling speech, attacking the government and condemning
the two press lords, Rothermere and Northcliffe. He did not mention
Beaverbrook, who had therefore no occasion to speak. In a later debate
in May, both Beaverbrook and Haldane spoke during a foolish debate on
pacifist propaganda, but, as Beaverbrook was not being attacked, Haldane
did not need to defend him. Beaverbrook, like the true romantic he was,
had imagined the whole episode. No doubt his feelings of anxiety were real,
and no doubt he experienced the triumphs of oratory in his dreams. As
often happened with him, the imaginary became more real to him than
the reality. At any rate, despite Bennett's discovery, Beaverbrook repeated
the original story to me in the last year of his life with admirable embellish-
ments, and, like Bennett, I believed it.

There were no attacks in the Lords, and no further attacks in the
Commons until August. Austen Chamberlain was brought into the war
cabinet and, thus mollified, accepted the newspaper proprietors as colleagues without complaint. Beaverbrook's difficulties were not over when
he survived the political storm. They had only begun, and they lasted
throughout his ministerial career. He was an improviser, not an organizer,
as he often confessed, and now improvised more impatiently than ever.
He appointed men right and left, without considering how they would fit
in with each other. He inherited John Buchan and Charles Masterman
from the old set-up. Otherwise he simply called on his own circle of
acquaintances. Few journalists were available. Lord Burnham and C. P.
Scott both withdrew, perhaps preferring, as Beaverbrook remarked, "Not
to be involved in any catastrophe". Robert Donald remained and became
jealous of Buchan with unfortunate results.

The new appointments were a curious assortment of businessmen and
writers. Sir Roderick Jones, head of Reuters, became chief executive.
Among the others were Sir William Stavert, a Canadian banker; Sir
Harold Snagge, a director of Barclays Bank; Sir Hugo Cunliffe-Owen, a
tobacco magnate who was supposed to understand the near East; Sir Eric
Hambro, another banker; Arnold Bennett, Hugh Walpole, Ian Hay
Beith, and Sir Evelyn Wrench. Arnold Bennett, originally in charge of
propaganda in France, proved the most successful of these appointments.
Beaverbrook nominated him as acting head of the ministry when he

himself resigned in October. As well the two men established a friendship of deep and lasting affection.

None of the directors appointed by Beaverbrook accepted a salary, nor did Beaverbrook himself. This offended politicians and civil servants as a way of using private wealth in order to buy immunity from criticism. Beaverbrook also gave offence to the treasury by calling in a firm of chartered accountants to advise on the running of the ministry. The advice cut the departmental estimates by £600,000. The treasury was not impressed. It complained that a government department should take financial advice from itself and no one else. Beaverbrook did not believe in sticking to the rules and took no notice.

Beaverbrook ran this first ministry of his with the mixture of personal impatience and underlying loyalty which he showed later at the ministry of aircraft production or with his newspapers. Sir Roderick Jones has left an account which could have been paralleled by many of Beaverbrook's associates later. Sir Roderick writes:

> Sometimes a line of policy or a method of working which I advocated would not commend itself to him. If he failed to convert me to his view and I pressed mine, he would exclaim impatiently, but never angrily: "You are the specialist. You know your job better than I do; go to it; I will back you". Which he invariably did.[1]

Sir Roderick Jones also tells the story of their only row. One day Beaverbrook gave Hugh Walpole, who handled the Russian department, "a severe dressing down". After Walpole had retired, Jones spoke out:

> I proceeded to tell Beaverbrook in effect that if he preferred to have yes-men about him and to listen to sycophants from outside the ministry who fawned upon, and flattered, him, he was welcome to; in that case he could at once count me out! As my anger steadily mounted, stimulated no doubt by an exaggerated sense of the righteousness of my indignation, Beaverbrook patiently listened to me in astonishment, pale and with an ominous hardening of feature. At length I paused, and waited for the storm I had asked for. I had not minced my words and deserved all I was likely to get.
>
> Imagine my surprise at Lord Beaverbrook's: "Well, Roderick, have you finished?"
>
> "Yes".
>
> "Good" (putting out his hand); it's lunch-time; let's go out and have food and talk it over".
>
> With which we went to the Savoy Grill and made our peace.

---

[1] Sir Roderick Jones, A Life in Reuters, 209. Beaverbrook's copy is inscribed "To Max. With love—From Roderick".

Subsequently Lord Beaverbrook sent for Walpole and apologized handsomely to him, a characteristic and perfectly sincere gesture that completely won Walpole over.[1]

The ministry was most successful where Beaverbrook simply extended the work he had already been doing for Canada. Thus the film section distributed news reels throughout the United Kingdom, though Beaverbrook pitched his claims rather high when he wrote: "The Topical Budget shown in every picture palace was the decisive factor in maintaining the moral of the people during the black days of the early summer of 1918". The ministry promoted exhibitions of war photographs and war paintings. These collections subsequently passed to the Imperial War Museum, where they are now exhibited. Few who admire the paintings or use the photographs as historical material appreciate that they were all brought into existence at Beaverbrook's inspiration.

Beaverbrook also exploited to the full his old weapon of the personal approach. Foreign pressmen in London found their work aided, instead of being hampered as it had been before. The ministry set up an overseas press centre, where foreign correspondents could receive information and send their telegrams. Every few days a war office representative reviewed the progress of the war for them. Beaverbrook was not allowed to deal with the British army. He provided entertainment and hospitality all the more zestfully for the American and Dominion troops in England. His object was to see that they had "the time of their lives". He brought over parties of editors, politicians, and clergymen from the Dominions and the United States. The visitors were shown round munitions factories and taken to the western front. They were entertained at Cherkley. They were also, on occasion, brought to meet Lloyd George, a form of propaganda which the overworked prime minister did not appreciate. Beaverbrook's insistence caused an estrangement, which grew worse when Lloyd George was more forthcoming to Northcliffe than to his own minister of information.

In one field Beaverbrook showed remarkable discretion. He made no attempt to take over propaganda at home. This was in poor shape. In 1917 a national war aims committee had been set up. It was composed of representatives of the three political parties, and its only task was to combat pacifism. The committee was extremely ineffective, but any attempt to supersede it or to subordinate it to Beaverbrook would have raised an outcry from the politicians, particularly the Liberals. Beaverbrook therefore left the affair alone, though he occasionally slipped an article into the press that he would do the work better than any committee. Home propaganda was left to Guest, the coalition Liberal chief whip, as agent of the national war aims committee, and Irish propaganda fell into the

[1] A Life in Reuters, 210.

hands of Walter Long, the colonial secretary. Beaverbrook was not even allowed to act as agent for other departments, such as food or national service, when they had some message to deliver.[1]

The ministry of information was thus confined to propaganda in allied and neutral countries. This brought Beaverbrook battles enough. However Beaverbrook's real battle was with other government departments, and particularly with the foreign office. He had to employ a full-time secretary "simply and solely for the purpose of conducting the diplomatic correspondence with the Foreign Office, as with a neighbouring and none too friendly Power". He claims that the disputes were none of his doing. "I will swear that they were not fomented by any truculence of bearing on my part. On the contrary I exhibited a most Christian humility". This does not sound in character. Later ministers of information were to encounter the same difficulties during the second world war, when Beaverbrook was also battling against departmental jealousies as minister of aircraft production.

Beaverbrook had a somewhat romantic vision of propaganda as "the popular arm of diplomacy". The ministry of information should receive full intelligence from the war office, the admiralty, and the foreign office, and then feed it by underground means into the foreign press. This was what Beaverbrook had done when he was with the Canadian forces, but of course Canadian generals welcomed all the publicity he could provide. British authorities did not relish this cloak-and-dagger project. Beaverbrook was further handicapped by the fact that, in his impulsive way, he had rushed into office without receiving defined powers or clear instruction on what his ministry was supposed to do. He had not even been given accommodation and therefore moved into Carson's room at the war cabinet offices until the Norfolk Hotel was ready for him. On 23 February he received a letter in Hankey's schoolboy hand:

> As the Government official in charge of the interior economy of this office I learned with some surprise that, without any reference to me, you were occupying the room lately vacated by Sir Edward Carson. In the circumstances I have no alternative but to let you know that I have an instruction from the Prime Minister that the accommodation in these offices is reserved by members of the War Cabinet with their staffs and secretaries.

An appeal to Lloyd George ensured that Beaverbrook was left undisturbed.

Appeals on larger questions were not so effective. On 20 February Beaverbrook produced a memorandum, demanding that a representative

---

[1] The situation was thus the exact opposite of that in the second world war when the ministry of information was confined almost entirely to home propaganda. The second ministry overcame the political difficulties, or tried to do so, by setting up local committees of information which were carefully balanced politically.

of his ministry should be admitted to the intelligence departments of the war office and the admiralty, and also to the secret service. Balfour, the foreign secretary, became the spokesman of the old order. He replied on 28 February that Beaverbrook's proposal "involved the dislocation of all the arrangements made in this office, with cabinet authority, for organizing the intelligence branch as part of the Foreign Office work. . . . It is not only indefensible from the point of view of organization, but would render secrecy even more difficult to maintain than it is at present".

Thus provoked, Beaverbrook appealed to the war cabinet. It, like the prime minister, proved a broken reed, fearful of offending such a powerful minister as Balfour. Beaverbrook had "a strange nightmare feeling that while as an individual one still retained some power and influence, directly one acted as a Minister one became a kind of shadowy phantom whose blows could affect no material object". The war cabinet took the soft way out of asking Smuts to reconcile the conflicting parties. Smuts, in his turn, evasively suggested that the admiralty and war office should pass their intelligence to the foreign office, which would be responsible for supplying the ministry of information with "suitable intelligence". Beaverbrook protested and for the moment acquiesced. Immediately after this the foreign office stole the entire intelligence bureau which had previously been part of the department of information. When Beaverbrook complained that civil servants were not allowed to transfer from one department to another without the consent of their original chief, Lord Hardinge, permanent under-secretary at the foreign office, replied that the members of the bureau were not civil servants, but "independent experts voluntarily serving the country in war time".[1] As might be expected, these independent experts, who included such names of future note as Toynbee, Namier, and Seton-Watson, preferred the elegance of the foreign office to the rough and tumble of life under Beaverbrook. They all resigned from the bureau and were at once reconstituted as the political intelligence department of the foreign office.

On 18 March Beaverbrook again appealed to the war cabinet. In reply he was merely told to confer with Lord Robert Cecil, Balfour's deputy. Beaverbrook imagined that Cecil was his one friend at the foreign office. This is hardly borne out by the record. Cecil was generous only in words. Though privately disapproving of the ministry of information and probably of Beaverbrook also, he promised that the foreign office would do "everything possible" to help the ministry of information and also that it would not interfere in any dispute, not affecting the foreign office, between that ministry and the war office or the admiralty. Beaverbrook now thought, mistakenly, that he could open a campaign to breach the

[1] In fact, most of these independent experts had been released from the armed forces in order to serve in the bureau. This could hardly be described as "voluntary".

intelligence of these two departments. He turned to Lloyd George for support and wrote to him on 2 April:

> The long and the short of it is that after six weeks discussion and delay I still find it impossible to proceed with the organization of perhaps the most important branch of the Ministry on the lines which are essential to its success.

Lloyd George was no doubt fully occupied with stemming the German advance in France. He therefore told Eric Geddes, the first lord of the admiralty, to settle the matter direct with Beaverbrook.

A meeting was arranged at the admiralty for 12 April. On the previous day Cecil wrote to Geddes that he had disapproved of the creation of the ministry of information. He concluded: "It seems clear that all political information should, as far as possible, come in the first instance to this office, and I cannot understand why Beaverbrook should object to this arrangement". This was a curious idea of non-interference. Thus fortified, the intelligence heads at the war office and admiralty told Beaverbrook that they were forbidden to deal directly with his ministry and that he must address his enquiries through the foreign office. Beaverbrook stormed out, announcing that he would appeal to the war cabinet. Instead his energy flagged for the time being, and he did nothing.

It is possible that Beaverbrook temporarily lost interest in the ministry of information because he saw the opportunity of higher game. In March Lloyd George had got rid of Robertson as chief of the imperial general staff. He was also anxious to dislodge Lord Derby from the war office, and a month later he struck. On 18 April Derby was sent into exile as ambassador at Paris. By then Lloyd George had decided on a successor. Lord Milner became secretary of state for war. This was an adroit move. Henceforth Milner carried the burden of the conflicts with the generals, and at the same time Lloyd George removed from the war cabinet a colleague with whom he was no longer in sympathy. No doubt other names had been canvassed, though as usual on such occasions no evidence is to be found in Lloyd George's records. But Beaverbrook supplied his own reminiscence. In 1929 Hamilton Fyfe enquired of him whether Northcliffe had been offered the war office in 1918. Beaverbrook denied it and denied also any subsequent offer during the summer. He added this surprising information:

> Derby was driven out of the War Office by George.
> Milner got the job.
> I applied for it but received very little support although George said he would give me the post if I could carry the support of my colleagues.

Strange things happened in the tumult of 1918, but Beaverbrook never alluded to this story again. Perhaps it was another creation of his romantic imagination. At any rate he did not leave the ministry of information.

The dispute with Geddes gave Beaverbrook an unexpected insight into Churchill's character. He gave an account of it many years later:

> Both Churchill and myself were greatly hampered by the stubborn attitude of Sir Eric Geddes. He controlled steel[1] and was putting difficulties in the way of Churchill at the Ministry of Munitions. He was also withholding intelligence information from myself. We agreed that the obstinacy of Geddes must be broken by a concerted attack. Imagine my astonishment when a few days after this agreement Churchill rang me up and asked me to lunch for the purpose of reconciling me with an old friend. The old friend was Geddes—the man he had agreed to attack. He had forgotten all about his anger and frustration. He was a man who "carried anger as the flint bears fire". He was incapable of rancour.[2]

In mid-May, Beaverbrook came across a copy of the letter from Cecil to Geddes. He had caught Cecil out cheating and on 21 May wrote to tell him so. On the same day he wrote to Balfour, that, unless the foreign office were prepared to cooperate, it would be better to make the ministry of information a subordinate department of the foreign office. Balfour made no reply. Cecil continued to talk ambiguously. Beaverbrook therefore prepared another appeal to the war cabinet. A lengthy memorandum, dated 29 May, recounted his grievances over the past three months and insisted that the ministry of information could succeed only if it were put on a real equality with other departments of state. "We have a diplomacy of our own to conduct, a popular diplomacy. . . . Our Agents will work not through Chancelleries and Courts, but through channels through which no diplomat could safely or usefully venture". As to the conflict over intelligence, the memorandum observed with some indignation that secrets were apparently safe with members of the foreign office, but could not be entrusted to the ministry of information or even to the minister himself. This was a powerful document, and it ended with the old refrain: either give the ministry of information full powers or put it openly under the foreign office.

If Northcliffe had been in this intolerable position, he would have either resigned immediately or descended on No. 10 Downing Street in rage. Beaverbrook did neither. Having first decided to fight, he then temporized. He sent his memorandum to Cecil who commented on 4 June:

> If the Ministry of Information were to set up an entirely new network of officials all over the world to carry out this kind of diplomacy, the Ministry

---

[1] Actually Geddes, first lord of the admiralty, was insisting on the admiralty's absolute priority for steel supplies, ahead of the ministry of munitions and the civilian departments.

[2] This is from an unpublished manuscript of Beaverbrook's entitled Two War Leaders: Lloyd George and Churchill. Much of the material on Lloyd George was incorporated in Appendix 63 of The Decline and Fall of Lloyd George.

would become a new Foreign Office, with, very possibly, an independent policy. I am quite certain that no Minister for Foreign Affairs who respected himself would consent to hold office if such a system were created. I certainly should not.

In my view... the Ministry of Information ought to have great freedom of action in all methods of operation; but when any question arises affecting policy or our relations with other countries, then the Ministry ought to be guided and, ultimately, controlled by the Minister in charge of the foreign policy of the country.

Clearly there was no escaping a fight with the foreign office. Beaverbrook still moved slowly. He wrote to Lloyd George on 29 May and then recalled his letter. After his rebuff by Cecil, he tried again. On 13 June he wrote to Lloyd George, not however with an appeal to the war cabinet. On the contrary he suggested that Lloyd George should call Beaverbrook to meet his opponents one by one. In this way they could not combine against him. His reason for avoiding an open struggle was remarkable: it was that he would win, or so he alleged:

My case, contained in the memorandum, is so irrefutable that it is bound to win. Such a victory based purely on the logic of the situation would produce infinite soreness among the defeated parties and serious trouble for the government.

In an accompanying private letter, Beaverbrook produced a still more ingenious argument for preferring "an amicable settlement":

I am nearly worn out with my effort to put this Ministry on its legs, and I feel it might be hardly fair to you to force a struggle in the War Cabinet in which the arguments contained in the Memorandum are bound to win, if I myself were to leave office directly afterwards leaving you to deal with the consequences of the struggle.

Lloyd George was not moved by this solicitude for his welfare. At any rate, he made no response of any kind. Beaverbrook had to face a conflict after all. On 24 June he sent a letter of resignation to the prime minister. Once more he recited his grievances and his failures. Once more he urged that his ministry should operate abroad "on equal terms with the Foreign Office". He declared, somewhat disingenuously: "nothing could have been pleasanter than my relations with Mr. Balfour and Lord Robert Cecil", and he put all the blame for obstruction on Hardinge, the permanent under-secretary:

No matter what concessions I offered him, he would never abate one iota of his demands: nor do I believe this matter will ever be settled so long as he remains Permanent Under-Secretary.

Confessing defeat, Beaverbrook concluded: "Since I cannot make my view prevail, I must with sincere regret place my resignation in your hands and ask you to act on it immediately". He also sent a personal message through "a friend" (maybe Churchill or F. E. Smith): "My decision is not for discussion, but is final".

This was far from being the case. On the following day Beaverbrook sent a copy of his resignation letter to Cecil, together with an invitation that Cecil should draft a modified version for publication. Beaverbrook was even prepared to leave out the attack on Hardinge, but still insisted that his decision was final. "If I went back on my resignation now or refrained from stating my reasons I should be false both to myself and to the interests of the nation". Cecil coolly declined: "I should either have to be disloyal to my colleagues in this Office, or I should write a very ineffective letter for you. . . . My safest and straightest course is to stand aside and let you write whatever you think best". Beaverbrook thereupon did nothing for five days. On 30 June he at last had a conversation with Lloyd George. To no good purpose. On 1 July he therefore again offered his resignation, this time merely stating that he had submitted a memorandum of grievances on 13 June and his resignation on 24 June and that nothing had happened.

Again Lloyd George did not reply. On 9 July, without consulting Beaverbrook, he had a conversation with Balfour. After it he drafted what seemed to him, and indeed was, an acceptable compromise, at any rate from the ministry of information's point of view:

(1) The Ministry of Information is an independent Ministry for whose operations the Foreign Office has no responsibility.

(2) Inasmuch, however, as the work of the Ministry of Information comes into contact with that of the Foreign Office at many points, and questions of policy are bound to arise in both the Foreign Office and the Ministry of Information which affect the other Department, there ought to be constant conference and consultation between the two.

(3) Where differences of opinion arise these should be settled in the usual manner by reference either to the Prime Minister or to the War Cabinet.

(4) The Ministry of Information is to receive from the Foreign Office all the political information necessary to enable it to conduct its operations and similarly the Foreign Office is to receive from the Ministry of Information all the information necessary to enable it to conduct its operations.

Beaverbrook was satisfied. He assumed that, with the prime minister's authority behind him, he could now hold his own against the foreign office. He soon discovered that he was wrong. Balfour in fact rejected Lloyd George's proposed compromise from the start. He wrote to Lloyd George on 12 July:

As you will have realized from the discussion which took place on Tuesday afternoon I am very anxious to arrive at a solution of the unfortunate difficulties which have arisen between Lord Beaverbrook and my Department.

The conditions laid down in your memorandum would however I fear not only result in increased friction but might seriously affect the constitutional position of the Secretary of State for Foreign Affairs. We should end by having two Ministers responsible to the Cabinet for Foreign policy, each having its own officers.

I should however be quite content to agree to your proposals were the following points made clear:

1. The Foreign Office to be consulted and my advice followed where questions of foreign policy are concerned.

2. Officers engaged in propaganda work abroad to keep in touch with the Ambassador or Minister, sending him copies of their reports when they concern political conditions. It should be understood that if the action of any officer seems to our representative to interfere with the policy of the Secretary of State it shall be his duty to report on the matter to the Foreign Office.

3. The Foreign Office to be consulted before important British personages are sent to foreign countries in order that an opportunity may be given for ascertaining the views of our diplomatic representatives on the proposed visit.

I think you will agree with me that these requests are not unreasonable If the conditions I have outlined above are accepted, I should of course be most happy to leave all details of propaganda work entirely in Lord Beaverbrook's hands.

On 18 July Lloyd George's secretary forwarded this letter to Beaverbrook, who thus learnt that he had been defeated again. However he decided to rely on the prime minister's authority and to make out that he knew nothing of Balfour's continued resistance. Balfour was not so easily ignored. When the ministry of information tried to assert its independence, Balfour wrote to Lloyd George on 31 July:

I am afraid that the relations between the Foreign Office and the Ministry of Information are getting into some confusion.

If I rightly understand the activities of the latter Office they extend a good deal beyond anything which I, at least, have been accustomed to describe as propaganda, using that word even in the widest sense.

I hope therefore that the matter may soon be regularized on the lines suggested in my letter of July 12th, which I venture to think leaves the Ministry of Information the fullest scope for its ambitions!

Beaverbrook now had to admit that he had seen Balfour's letter, though giving the impression that this had only been within the last day or two. Evidently he realized that it was useless to invoke Lloyd George again. The only alternative was a direct appeal to Balfour. This Beaverbrook attempted in a letter which was dated 6 August:

The Prime Minister has forwarded to me your letter of the 12th July dealing with his memorandum re the relations between the Foreign Office and the Ministry of Information. This, you will remember, was drawn up by the Prime Minister as the result of our conversations with him.

I must confess that your letter appears to make even stronger claims for the control of this Ministry by the Foreign Office than have ever been put forward before, either in theory or in practice.

The first clause in the Prime Minister's memorandum states "that the Ministry of Information is an independent Ministry for whose operations the Foreign Office has no responsibility". The three conditions you insert all claim absolute suzerainty of one kind or another of the Foreign Office over the Ministry. The first condition says that when there is a difference of opinion on policy "your advice is to be followed", which hardly makes it worth while having a difference of opinion at all. The second clause gives the representatives of the Foreign Office abroad power to report adversely on the action of the representatives of the Ministry, and since such a report would presumably be treated as a difference of policy, and your advice must be followed, the meaning of the clause would be challenged and stopped by the foreign office, beyond appeal of any sort. Clause 3 in the Prime Minister's memorandum, therefore, falls to the ground, since the Foreign Office being given, according to your suggestion, suzerainty, the Ministry would be confronted with the agreement the moment it appealed to the War Cabinet.

On your third condition, relating to big Foreign Missions headed by an important personage, I agree that the Foreign Office ought to be consulted but not that they should have the power of absolute veto—two rather different things.

It seems to me then, that you reject entirely the compromise put forward by the Prime Minister and therefore it seems hardly worth while asking whether that compromise could be worked, or, if so, how it would work in practice.

If the claim to complete control put forward by the Foreign Office is to be admitted, then it would be better, as I have said throughout this controversy, that the Ministry should be made a Department formally and definitely under the Foreign Office. For it is useless to call a Ministry independent and responsible which can only operate by permission of another.

I do not consider this plan the best solution of the difficulty, but rather that the Ministry should be given power to act of itself on certain defined lines. Therefore, with the utmost regret I am unable to agree to the conditions laid down in your letter to the Prime Minister.

At the same time, although I think I have read aright the obvious sense and results of your three conditions, I am loath to believe that it is your real intention to refuse all possibility of accommodation over this regrettable dispute.

I honestly believe the difficulties between the two departments to be more of practice than of theory, and I will endeavour to restate my position in a way which may be more agreeable to the views of the Foreign Office.

What is the real point of dispute? That foreign policy must belong to the Foreign Secretary? I do not deny it for an instant. If you define Foreign policy as the general strategy of the British Empire in dealing with all foreign countries, that must clearly belong to the Foreign Office. But that there are a considerable number of tactical methods by which this general idea can be carried out, you will, I think, hardly deny. Among these is the semi-official influencing of public opinion in the direction of the general policy laid down by His Majesty's Government, for which the Foreign Secretary is primarily responsible. This task falls within the province of the Ministry of Information which is specially constructed for that purpose, and while the Ministry does not challenge this general direction of the Foreign Office, it ought to be allowed an absolutely free hand in carrying out the common policy in its own realm of practice. For much of this work the Foreign Office organization is not really a suitable instrument, while the Ministry of Information is.

I do not wish to make this letter any longer, but I would ask you, with the utmost earnestness and sincerity, whether this last statement of the situation does not offer some chance of reaching a working agreement acceptable to both parties.

This letter was a skilful blend of firmness and conciliation in Beaverbrook's best negotiating vein. It was also quite fruitless, as he himself appreciated on reflection. For the final draft is marked in his handwriting: "This letter was not sent. B."

Thus ended the great battle. No surrender by the foreign office, and no resignation by Beaverbrook. Guerrilla warfare continued, with the foreign office now on the offensive. Thus, the ministry of information, in its propaganda to America, made much of the Balfour declaration, which had promised a national home for the Jews in Palestine. Two leading Jews, Sir Charles Henry and Lionel de Rothschild, told Beaverbrook that Lloyd George had changed his mind and that therefore the Balfour declaration should be played down. Beaverbrook asked Lloyd George for instructions and received no answer. Balfour seized the opportunity to reassert his authority. He wrote sternly to Beaverbrook: "The policy of His Majesty's Government in Palestine is that laid down by the Foreign Secretary in his last speech". Balfour also wrote to Lloyd George, using the incident as a weapon against the ministry of information as well as against the anti-Zionist Jews. His letter concluded:

I think you will agree that an incident of this kind necessitates an immediate decision as to the distribution of functions of the Foreign Office and the Ministry of Information.

Lloyd George returned a soft answer from his Welsh home. He declared that he had always been a strong supporter of Zionism. As to propaganda:

I quite agree that the position must be regularized, otherwise friction and misunderstanding are inevitable. I hope to be back on Friday. We can discuss the question either that day or some early day next week.

There is no indication, in either Beaverbrook's or Lloyd George's papers, that the question was ever discussed. Lloyd George no doubt assessed the position correctly. Beaverbrook was unlikely to give up work which he enjoyed doing. Balfour, besides being the more important politically, was the harder character. The man who could ruin such rivals as Lord Randolph Churchill and Joseph Chamberlain was more than a match for Beaverbrook, who could only retaliate later in life by saying: "Balfour was a hermaphrodite. No one ever saw him naked".[1]

Beaverbrook and his ministry had more public troubles. These were provoked by Robert Donald, who resented being pushed aside by John Buchan and Arnold Bennett. Moreover, though he had been enthusiastic for Lloyd George in December 1916, he was now drifting into antagonism against the government. This was shown in May 1918, when he appointed General Sir Frederick Maurice, hero or victim of the Maurice debate, as military correspondent of his paper, The Daily Chronicle. At the end of June, Donald severed his connection with the ministry of information, though still with an outward display of friendliness. He then inspired a series of articles against the ministry in The Westminster Gazette, organ of the Asquithian Liberals. The articles, based on Donald's inside knowledge, attacked Beaverbrook's policy of appointing business men as heads of departments. This system of rule by "capitalists", it was alleged, opened the door wide for corruption.

Here was an opportunity for highminded Radical MPs, who hated both Beaverbrook and Lloyd George. An assault was prepared for 5 August. Law, as usual, would not defend Beaverbrook on the ground "that our friendship was so close that his remarks might not seem impartial". Beaverbrook doubted the parliamentary ability of Baldwin, Law's deputy. He has described, in his most brilliant way,[2] how he summoned Healy to his aid. Healy laughed at Beaverbrook's anxiety and refused to look at the documents he had assembled. When the debate came on, Baldwin made an effective speech in Beaverbrook's defence, though he also used a phrase which promised trouble for the future. Baldwin said: "The Minister of Information is a man of very strong personality. Men with strong personalities have this in common, that the magnetism which comes with that personality either attracts or repels". The debate threatened to turn out badly for Beaverbrook. As he remarks, "If a whole discussion turns on one man, more charges are made than can be answered". Then Healy spoke. He switched the debate back to Carson's time and alleged that Carson had staffed the department of information with Irish Unionists. At this, Irish passions blazed, and the ministry of information

---

[1] I asked Beaverbrook whether it was usual to see cabinet ministers naked. He replied "Ah, you are a very clever fellow" and repeated his original remark.
[2] Men and Power, 295–99.

was forgotten. Healy returned to Beaverbrook at the Hyde Park Hotel and said: "Get me some pea-soup and a steak and a bottle of beer, and I will tell you the fun".

There followed an exchange between Baldwin and Beaverbrook, which illustrated the character of both men. Baldwin, having defended Beaverbrook, felt that he was entitled to warn him against future attacks. He heard a rumour that the ministry of information was planning to send a man who had been connected with the Marconi company as its representative in South America. Baldwin knew that Marconi was a name of ill omen in politics. He therefore wrote to Beaverbrook on 7 August:

> I know the House of Commons pretty well, and it would be a fatal error to employ anyone connected however remotely with the Company.
> The House has for the time being swallowed your business men, but they would throw this particular appointment up.
> I know the feelings of the silent men as well as of the vocal.
> My chief concern is that any error of judgement you make reacts on Bonar pretty quickly, and I am sure that any result of that kind would be as unwelcome to you as it would be to me.

Beaverbrook gratefully accepted the advice, but he flared up at the reference to Law. He replied to Baldwin:

> It would be absurd that any action of mine should affect Bonar's position. I did not owe my appointment as Minister to him: when the trouble about newspaper proprietors started immediately afterwards, he wanted me to resign: and he does not support my minutes in the War Cabinet. . . . So I really think it ought to be admitted that I am on my own.

This was no more than the truth. Beaverbrook had not sought or received help from Law throughout his troubles with the foreign office. At last, despairing of Lloyd George, he turned to Law after all. At the end of August he recorded old grievances and new ones for Law's benefit —grievances directed as much against Lloyd George as against the foreign office. This appeal, too, proved fruitless. Law made no reply and took no action. Balfour and the foreign office remained in control of the field.

The prolonged wrangles between the ministry of information and the foreign office showed that Beaverbrook was ill-suited to be a minister except in abnormal circumstances, a fact he fully appreciated himself. He would not be a subordinate unless he could turn his leader into a hero as he did with John F. Stairs, Bonar Law and later Churchill. He had to be the boss, issuing orders without respect for protocol or the rights of others. When this position was denied him, he relapsed into impotent rage and threats of resignation. His behaviour as minister of information in the first world war was a rehearsal for that as minister of aircraft production in the second. Otherwise the story of the ministry has little importance, and it was not accorded the dignity of a volume in the Carnegie Social and Economic History of the war—as for that matter its successor did not attain to an official history in the second. Probably the ministry conducted useful publicity for Great Britain in the United States and Canada, perhaps also some in France and the Scandinavian countries. Beaverbrook might even claim to be the remote progenitor of the British Council, an institution later held in low esteem by the Beaverbrook press. The direct work of his ministry has vanished beyond recall.

Beaverbrook believed that official propaganda should end with the war and himself abandoned it before the war was over. On 21 October he at last succeeded in resigning as minister of information. He gave ill health as his reason and immediately afterwards had an operation for a glandular swelling in his neck. Even one so close to him as Arnold Bennett did not take Beaverbrook's illness very seriously and attributed it more to ministerial frustrations than to any infection. For once, this seems to have been unfair. Early in the following year, Beaverbrook was undoubtedly gravely ill with "an unusual and serious infection known as actinomycosis".

Still in 1918 his illness did not last long. He soon recovered his energy when new opportunities opened to him. The ministry of information, coming on top of his Canadian work, had given him an insatiable appetite for publicity and propaganda, and the malady to which he really succumbed in October 1918 was the ambition to exercise these arts free from the control of governments or parties. Law urged him to stick to politics or, if he must embark on journalism, to run an official Unionist paper. Beaverbrook replied: "No. In politics I am bound—for no man can really be a politician without submitting to the necessary trammels of Party. In the Press, on the contrary, I am free and can work from the outside".[1] He wanted independence and said truthfully: "I never mean to hold a public office again except during a period of war". Beaverbrook still aspired to be a go-between, but no longer as the hidden reconciler of individual politicians. Now he aimed to be a go-between with the public. His instrument lay ready in his control of The Daily Express. The moment of action appeared with the general election which followed the defeat of Germany. As usual, Beaverbrook anticipated only a short commitment—for the election and a little after. This time he was wrong. He had found an activity which enthralled him till his dying day.

[1] Politicians and the Press, 21.

CHAPTER EIGHT

FULLBLOODED JOURNALIST, 1918-21

In later years Beaverbrook presented his turn to journalism as a conscious dedication to the cause of Empire. This was rationalizing after the event. He was originally drawn into the newspaper world more or less by accident—first to please Acland-Hood, then to help Blumenfeld, and of course to protect the money he had invested. The propaganda he sought was purely personal, sometimes for himself, more often for Law. There was no need for him to bother about the imperial cause. Blumenfeld provided plenty of that without encouragement. Nor did Beaverbrook move further in 1918 for the sake of Empire. He was again tempted, this time by Lloyd George.

Lloyd George fully appreciated the power of the press in wartime and knew by now, if he did not know earlier, that a newspaper campaign had been of great assistance to him in December 1916. He was also acutely aware that, as a prime minister with no effective party organization behind him, his hold on the newspaper world was insecure. Most of the Liberal papers were Asquithian or, at best, independent of both factions, and Lloyd George had to rely on his personal contacts with such proprietors as Lord Riddell and Sir Henry Dalziel. If it had rested with him, he would no doubt have employed the minister of information to influence opinion at home as well as abroad. Feeling in the house of commons forbade this. As usual, Lloyd George sought a way round.

He first turned to Beaverbrook in March 1918. He wanted help in regard to The Daily Chronicle. This was a prosperous property, paying $32\frac{1}{2}\%$ on its ordinary shares in 1915 and 1916.[1] It was firmly radical in a Lloyd George spirit. Frank Lloyd, its proprietor, was frail and elderly. He wished to sell out. There was grave danger that the paper would be bought by an Asquithian Liberal such as Lord Cowdray, perhaps with the aid of Liberal party funds. Lloyd George wanted Beaverbrook to capture The Daily Chronicle and turn it into an official organ of Coalition Liberalism. Beaverbrook was willing. But he was a Tory. It would never

[1] Part of this profit came from Lloyd's Weekly News, a Sunday newspaper with a circulation of over one million.

do for him to head a Liberal newspaper, nor would Frank Lloyd sell to him.

A cover-man was needed. Beaverbrook hit on Lord Leverhulme, the oil and soap magnate and a Liberal, who had been made a baron by Lloyd George in 1917. Ostensibly Leverhulme and an unnamed Canadian friend of Beaverbrook's would buy The Daily Chronicle and promise to keep it loyal to Lloyd George for five years. Actually Beaverbrook would put up the money for a commission of £20,000. Later he would sell the shares to the public, he hoped at a considerable profit. It is impossible to tell what Leverhulme hoped. For he was very deaf and, when consulted, said he had never heard of the scheme at all. However this did not matter. Beaverbrook's accountant reported that The Daily Chronicle was worth £595,000. Frank Lloyd killed the scheme by demanding £900,000 which was more than Beaverbrook was prepared to pay.[1]

Beaverbrook's ingenuity was not exhausted. He suggested that Lloyd George's wealthy friends should form a syndicate, headed by Sir Henry Dalziel, and offer £800,000. He himself would contribute £100,000 "irrespective of the financial side"—whatever that may mean. Lloyd George's friends replied that they could not raise the money. Beaverbrook next proposed that he should buy The Sunday Times from the Berry brothers for £200,000, which could then be added to the syndicate for The Daily Chronicle. The Berry brothers agreed. When Beaverbrook met them to complete the deal, they informed him that F. E. Guest, the Coalition Liberal chief whip, had forbidden them to sell their paper to a Tory. Beaverbrook was excluded from all further negotiations. Lloyd George remained anxious to lay hands on The Daily Chronicle, particularly when Robert Donald, its editor, turned against the Coalition. In October 1918 Sir Henry Dalziel and others bought The Daily Chronicle for £1,650,000. Most of the money came from the political fund which Lloyd George's wealthy admirers had contributed for his support—and no doubt for their peerages.

Probably Guest, if not Lloyd George, took fright over Beaverbrook after first planning to work through him. Guest may well have recalled how Sir Max Aitken had gone into The Daily Express as agent for the Unionist party and then carried it off for himself. It would have been a formidable combination if Beaverbrook had merged The Daily Chronicle and The Daily Express, the one prosperous, the other ailing, and then added The Sunday Times unto them. He would have monopolized propaganda for Lloyd George and, as experience showed, he ran propaganda according to his own ideas, not at the direction of others. The Lloyd George group had some excuse for keeping him out.

[1] The complications with Leverhulme come from a memorandum by Donald in the Donald papers, the rest from Beaverbrook's papers.

However they were not content with this. Guest and Dalziel went around, declaring that Beaverbrook was unreliable. Lloyd George added that he was ungrateful. The talk reached Beaverbrook's ears. He wrote a letter to Lloyd George, unfortunately undated, going over The Daily Chronicle affair. He concluded:

> I do not think that in this transaction there can be any suggestion of ingratitude or inconsistency on my side.
>
> ... The only basis for such charges seems to be that I have on occasion compromised my political convictions out of private friendship, and this I shall probably continue to do until the end of the chapter. But ought you to make this particular charge of levity against me?

It seems that Lloyd George, thus challenged, made some sort of apology. For pinned to the draft of Beaverbrook's letter is a slip of paper with the words: "P.M.'s surrender, still with Mr. Needham". Needham had been Beaverbrook's secretary at the ministry of information and had conducted the interminable disputes with the foreign office. He was a very efficient secretary, but in this case his efficiency broke down. Lloyd George's communication did not reach Beaverbrook's archives, and we shall never know the nature of his surrender.

There is however other evidence that a reconciliation took place. The Daily Chronicle had not been the only ground of conflict. The Daily Express also caused trouble. On 29 August 1918 it carried a leader, demanding to know Lloyd George's programme for the coming election:

> What, for instance, is the prime minister's programme on TARIFF REFORM and IMPERIAL PREFERENCE? ...
>
> What would be the IRISH POLICY of the government which hopes to be returned?
>
> Is the WELSH CHURCH to be sacrificed simply because the party of spoilers just tottering to its fall over the Irish crisis of 1914 was saved for the moment by the outbreak of the great war?

In all probability the leader was Blumenfeld's unaided idea. Beaverbrook was too busy with the ministry of information to have time for The Daily Express, and in any case there was nothing he cared for less than the preservation of the Welsh established church.

Lloyd George attributed the leader to Beaverbrook. He wrote at once to Law:

> Have you seen the leader in to-day's Express? That is Max. Having regard to the risks I ran for him and the way I stood up for him when he was attacked by his own party, I regard this as a mean piece of treachery. It explains why no man in any party trusts Max.

Since Lloyd George had given Beaverbrook little support at the ministry of information, the talk of treachery was somewhat far-fetched. As usual Law refused to be involved. Lloyd George therefore sent Churchill to ask whether Beaverbrook admitted responsibility for the leader. Lloyd George said: "If he admits it, he's out". Beaverbrook, who was often not above blaming his editors, was this time defiant. He proudly took full responsibility. Lloyd George trembled and turned the other cheek. He failed to demand the resignation which Beaverbrook in any case was constantly pressing upon him. What was more, he soon sent Churchill again, this time on a more agreeable mission.

Churchill wanted to know whether Beaverbrook would organize press support for Lloyd George at the coming general election. Beaverbrook agreed. He pledged the support of The Daily Express and set out to canvass others. Lloyd George refused to have anything to do with North-cliffe, despite Beaverbrook's urgings. However Beaverbrook brought Rothermere[1] and Edward Hulton[2] to dinner with Lloyd George in Downing Street. Law characteristically refused to attend. Lloyd George promised to make Rothermere a viscount and Hulton a baron. Beaverbrook declared that he wanted nothing for himself except to be dis-peered. All three press lords were thus won over and duly supported Lloyd George at the general election. Afterwards Lloyd George had some trouble in paying their stipulated price. King George V strenuously objected to making Rothermere a viscount and gave way only when Law added his persuasive voice. With Hulton the king would go no further than a baronetcy. Hulton agreed, on condition that there should be special remainder to his son, who had been born out of wedlock. Lloyd George promised that this should be done. When Hulton died, Baldwin was prime minister, and the promise was forgotten.

These were not the only honours distributed on Beaverbrook's prompting. Lesser honours went to many press men, ostensibly for their work in the ministry of information. Beaverbrook was loyal to his flock and continued to press for rewards long after the election. In the summer of 1919 Guest reported to Lloyd George that Beaverbrook was demanding more KBEs for his old associates in exchange for continued press support. Guest commented: "This is very unprincipled of our friend Max, but not an excessive price to pay for his full support". Not all the projected recipients welcomed their honour. When Kipling was offered the CH, he wrote in fury to Law: "How would you like to be waked up on a Sunday morning by a letter from the Acting Secretary of the Clerical Aid Society, informing you that your name was among the list of Bishops that had been recommended to the King?"[3] Wells and Bennett were offered

---

[1] Proprietor of The Daily Mirror.
[2] Proprietor of The Daily Sketch, The Evening Standard, The Illustrated Sunday Herald and many provincial newspapers.
[3] Both Kipling and Shaw later refused the OM on the grounds that Galsworthy was a member of the order.

knighthoods. Bennett said of Wells: "If he does take it, I'll never speak to him again". Both men refused. John Buchan was assiduous in the opposite direction, though without success.

The general election was held in December 1918. The Coalition candidates triumphed, perhaps more so than Lloyd George desired. In the feverish state of national opinion, the triumph needed little support from the press. Nor was this support as wholehearted as it had appeared round the dining table at 10 Downing Street. Soon after that meeting Rothermere wrote to Lloyd George in his blunt way:

Your Administration has been sustained by a Coalition of the Press, a section of the Liberal party, and the Conservative party. It should have been a Coalition of reciprocal understanding and of reciprocal concessions, but has worked out quite otherwise.

Without the aid of the Press, it is a fair thing to say that the present Coalition Government could not have survived the storms of the last eighteen months. Some other Government there would have been, but it would have had a composition quite different from the present one, and many of your associates who now hold high office would have been relegated to the back benches.

It would have been thought that, with the full knowledge of what the Press has done for your Government, some united effort would have been made by the Conservative leaders to put an end to the calumnies uttered at meetings of the Unionist War Committee in regard to your Press friends. I am entitled to mention this matter because I share, with Lords Northcliffe and Beaverbrook, the distinction of having been among the victims. Some two months after my reluctant acceptance of the Secretaryship of the Air Force, a meeting was held to discuss Lord Northcliffe's, Lord Beaverbrook's and my appointments, at which the elegant statement was made that no newspaper proprietor should hold office in any Government because there was quite an obvious risk he might publish for his own profit any secret intelligence which might reach him in his official capacity. . . . The author of this statement received a Peerage in the next Honours list.

Instead of curbing these people, Mr. Bonar Law invited me, on the telephone, to resign the office which I held because he feared the criticisms of Mr. Austen Chamberlain and some others.

It is now expected that I for one shall do what I can to insure the return of the Conservative members for the next House of Commons. I really do not see why I should do anything of the kind. I deeply feel that you have not got, and will no more than the returning soldier get, a square deal from these people. They will baulk and thwart all land legislation, and without land legislation of a most revolutionary character, it will be impossible to save this country from movements which will have a Bolshevist tendency.

Moreover, at every convenient opportunity, these same people will endeavour to subject you to the ignominy of such scandals as the Hayes Fisher one of last week.

As I have promised, I will do all I can to help your candidates but I must reserve for myself the full liberty of telling the readers of my papers what they must expect if they are so foolish as to return an increased number of Conservative members to the next House of Commons.

The Daily Express was more wholehearted in its support of Lloyd George, at any rate during the election. Even so, Beaverbrook gave warning that this support might not last. He said in a speech: "I am a supporter of the Government for this election, but I do not necessarily consider myself bound to the Government. I look upon myself somewhat in the light of an Independent". Churchill resented this on-and-off attitude and complained that Beaverbrook had gone back on his word. Beaverbrook replied on 28 November 1918 with a long letter defending himself and defining the position which he tried to maintain in politics thereafter:

> I take an independent attitude. I am not bound to the Coalition Minis-
> try in any way, since I resigned before the new departure began. Nor do
> I object in any way to the inconvenience caused by the Prime Minister's
> choice of the present moment for a General Election—since I advised him
> myself to dissolve. . . .
> . . . I claim the right to criticize the Coalition leaders in their public
> capacity in the columns of a daily paper. Nobody is bound to me by more
> intimate ties of friendship and affection than Bonar Law. But, at the same
> time, I know that I can disagree with his public policy on occasion without
> forfeiting his friendship or, indeed, doing anything to forfeit it.
> Does not the same argument apply to yourself and the Prime Minister?
> You are a close friend of mine. But surely you do not expect that fact to
> make a vital difference in any public comment I make on your policy in
> affairs of state? One supposes, of course, that we honestly disagreed and
> that the comment was made without malice. Well, that is the case today.

The truth is that Beaverbrook was a bad party man. He had been a Unionist MP. He remained a member of the Conservative party until late in life, and his papers always supported the Conservatives at a general election, though sometimes half-heartedly. But where policies were concerned he took an independent line. Before the war he had regarded with indifference such burning Unionist causes as the preservation of the house of lords or of the Welsh church and worked strenuously to promote Irish Home Rule, which the Unionists opposed. On the personal side, as his letter to Churchill showed, he often supported a political leader and yet felt free to criticize policy. His loyalty to Law did not prevent his continuing to advocate Imperial Preference even when Law abandoned it. In December 1916 he helped to make Lloyd George prime minister, and in December 1918 he supported the coalition because it was led by his two friends, Lloyd George and Law. In neither case did he regard himself as bound to support the policies which followed. For that matter he often encouraged men with whose policies he disagreed if they were his friends—most notably in his encouragement of Churchill before the second world war. During that war he did not always support government policy even when he was a minister. After it, he was still supporting Churchill and opposing the policies of the party which Churchill led. As Churchill said: "Max likes the jockey and dislikes the horse".

Beaverbrook had one steadfast conviction which he put far above party. This was a desire to promote the economic unity of the British Empire. Blumenfeld asserted that Max Aitken was a Free Trader when he arrived in England and had to be taught the rudiments of Tariff Reform by himself and Goulding. This was an exaggeration. What was true in it was that Beaverbrook had no clear idea how to translate economic unity into practical terms. Even odder, he was in his general outlook a disciple of Cobden, as Maurice Woods early remarked, and even thought that a closed imperial system could be reconciled with Cobdenism by calling it Empire Free Trade. Beaverbrook's Empire was an association of free British communities rather than the Indian and colonial Empire of exploitation, though he was sometimes carried away by a Stevensonian response to drum-and-flag patriotism.

Empire apart, Beaverbrook was in economic affairs an old-style Radical. He believed in individual enterprise, free from government control except in wartime. He defended individual freedom and disliked every form of orthodoxy. He added one new element, without appreciating how new this was in British terms. Because of his Canadian and American experience, he grasped that high wages meant high profits, and he was in favour of both. He defined his creed in 1922 when he declared that The Daily Express stood for "More life—more hope—more money—more work—more happiness—the creed which is going to redeem Great Britain from the hard aftermath of war, and set her feet once again on the path which leads to prosperity". Universal prosperity was for Beaverbrook, as it had been for Cobden, the one certain way to social and international peace. It was also next door to godliness, if not the same thing, and he was fond of quoting from the shorter Catechism: "The Eighth Commandment forbiddeth whatsoever doth or may unjustly hinder our own or our neighbour's wealth or outward estate".

Beaverbrook was also a straightforward Cobdenite in his outlook on foreign affairs. He believed that nations, like individuals, served the community best by minding their own business. Though he disliked tyranny and oppression, he had no desire to ride out on a crusade of liberation. He set down this creed, too, at some unknown date:

I Believe that the pursuit of Peace is the highest and the most urgent moral task before civilization.

I Believe that Britain can take the leadership of the world if she sets an example of peaceful purpose to the nations.

I Believe that the only certain way for us to live in peace is by following the policy of Splendid Isolation, which involves a resolution to incur no commitments whatever to fight by the side of foreign nations or in the quarrels of foreign nations.

I Believe that Splendid Isolation offers us the prospect of the unity of the Empire. The policy of alliances and obligations in Europe must bring with it a divergence between Britain and the Dominions which will end in the destruction of the Empire.

I Believe that by taking the path of Isolation we shall escape from the quarrels of Europe and We shall gain in the companionship of the United States in a common outlook, with all the possibilities of a just, lasting and prosperous peace which this association holds.

Beaverbrook had been reluctant to enter the first world war. He was resolutely opposed to entering the second. Once Great Britain was in, he threw all his energy into winning these wars, but he continued to regard them as unnecessary and mistaken. Essentially, despite his blusterous temperament, he remained a conciliator and, in the best sense, an appeaser.

There was the same apparent contradiction in his attitude to politics at home. Though he loved the drama and excitement of political conflict, particularly at election time, behind the scenes he was always trying to bring politicians together. H. G. Wells said wisely:

If Max gets to Heaven he won't last long. He will be chucked out for trying to pull off a merger between Heaven and Hell . . . after having secured a controlling interest in key subsidiary companies in both places, of course.

This was as true of Beaverbrook's behaviour in politics as it was of his financial dealings. He admired both Lloyd George and Bonar Law, both Churchill and Birkenhead, as later he admired both Aneurin Bevan and Brendan Bracken. Of course he expected them to contend in public, but underneath, he supposed, they all wanted much the same as he did— dynamic, creative policies. The politicians he disliked were the staid and cautious, above all the complacent planners who thought they could arrange other people's lives.

This attitude soon landed him in difficulties as regards Lloyd George's Coalition. On the one hand, it was composed of his friends; on the other, it threatened to extend wartime controls into peace. Considering the rapid retreat from the policy of controls, this was perhaps a mistaken view. But it can be argued that the restoration of economic freedom was promoted by the criticism of Beaverbrook and those like him. He set down later his reasons for opposing the continuance of the Coalition:

The Coalition was an attempt to carry over the situation created by one epoch into another, to prolong an old system into a new age. It would have been better to have acknowledged the peace and made a clean cut with the past. . . .

The Coalition set out consciously or unconsciously with an impracticable object. It thought that much of the Government organisation and control which war conditions had brought about could be imposed in perpetuo on the national life and character and be grafted as a living tissue on the body politic. This view was and is a profound mistake. Just because the British are bad bureaucrats, they can never be governed by a bureaucracy. The result was a continued and disastrous extravagance in administration, and a kind of insincerity in the treatment of political principles. Party politics can no more be exorcized out of the blood of this people by a five years war than the extreme individuality of the race could be curbed by five years of necessary subservience to Government departments and to generals. The very success with which these old and imperative instincts had been stifled during the struggle made them rise to life anew with the unparalleled vigour of nature long suppressed. The new Government with all its colossal majority was therefore born dead from the waist down and the bye-elections immediately showed signs of the sweeping reaction.

Whether I was saved by instinct or by reason, the fact remains that I did not fall into this particular error. . . . I began to advocate the abolition of controls, the restoration of private enterprise to freedom, and the practice of a rigid economy. But for these purposes the Coalition with the implied abolition of an effective Parliamentary criticism was no suitable instrument, and for this reason I was opposed to the very idea of the Coalition Government.

No doubt Beaverbrook's rejection of the Coalition developed more slowly and less clearly than he makes out here. The first open breach came over Churchill's policy of intervention against the Bolshevik government in Russia. The Daily Express opposed this crusade and found itself embarrassingly alone with The Daily Herald. Lloyd George tried to quieten Beaverbrook, who sensed, correctly as we now know, that "his heart was not in the business". Sir George Buchanan, the former ambassador to Russia, wrote urging support for Kolchak and Denikin, the White generals, and complained that Beaverbrook had fallen under the influence of Bruce Lockhart. Beaverbrook replied on 4 August 1919:

I came across him when I was a Minister and his view then was for agreement with the Bolshevics. Since however no one in authority would listen to him, he said that the only alternative to peace was *intervention— but only while the war lasted*. I think much the same. I take the exact opposite view to Churchill.

This dispute, though with a friend, did not affect Beaverbrook's relations with the leaders of the government. Further disputes were not so harmless. In the autumn of 1919 the demand for a capital levy on war fortunes took practical form. Beaverbrook spoke in the Lords for the first time since the general election and urged a capital levy "not only on the ground of the national necessity, but also as a measure of fiscal justice". The cabinet appointed a committee, composed of Lloyd George, Austen Chamberlain, Edwin Montagu, and Law. All except one were in favour. Law set his face against it "like a flint" and stirred up opposition among the backbench Unionists. The proposal was killed. Law and Beaverbrook were considerably estranged.

In 1920 finance caused further trouble between Beaverbrook and the government. Austen Chamberlain, chancellor of the exchequer, proposed to raise the excess profits duty from 40% to 60%. Beaverbrook and The Daily Express warmly supported this patriotic proposal.[1] Beaverbrook observed that Lloyd George was less than wholehearted in backing his chancellor. Riddell's organ, The News of the World, reported that Chamberlain was about to resign, and The Daily Express remarked that Riddell had spent the previous weekend with Lloyd George. The Daily Chronicle also opposed Chamberlain's proposal. On 2 July Beaverbrook wrote to Chamberlain:

> May I offer you some advice? It is this. Send for F. Guest and inform him that you will not tolerate the opposition of the Chronicle even if confined to headlines. Insist upon the active support of that newspaper since the Prime Minister is wholly responsible for fixing the EPD at 60% instead of 40%. Inform him I beg of you, that Government by two parties cannot withstand the active or passive opposition of a newspaper which is the property of the Party Chest of one section of the coalition.
>
> Guest will protest that he does not control the policy of the Chronicle— but you needn't bother about his disclaimer.

This was, among other things, Beaverbrook's revenge for being denied The Daily Chronicle earlier. Lloyd George, thus caught out, professed that he had not inspired the campaign against Chamberlain, and Beaverbrook professed to believe him. But the breach between the two men was wide.

These were isolated episodes. Beaverbrook became detached from politics as he often did between elections or when there was no issue on which he felt deeply. He was not in office. He never went to the house of lords except on the one occasion when he made a speech. He saw Law comparatively little and Lloyd George not at all. His detachment increased when he moved his London base from the Hyde Park Hotel to the

---

[1] The gesture, though patriotic, proved mistaken. There was a serious slump in the autumn of 1920. Many businessmen incurred losses instead of making profits and were able by setting off these losses against earlier profits to recover the EPD they had paid in previous years. They could not have done this if EPD had been abolished.

Vineyard in Hurlingham Road, Fulham. The Vineyard was the most delightful of Beaverbrook's main residences, indeed the only one with real character and charm. It was a tiny Tudor house which Beaverbrook rescued from ruin. It had a small sitting-room with chairs for four people at most, a dining-room equipped with a cinema-projector, and two small bedrooms. Here Beaverbrook was safe from "casual callers and long-winded visitors". It was his "sure retreat". He could see his intimate friends and be sure of seeing no one else. Social life on a larger scale was kept for Cherkley at the weekends.

The Vineyard had the further attraction of a tennis court. Beaverbrook much preferred tennis to golf, the other fashionable game of the time, if only because it took up less time. Arnold Bennett was an enthusiastic tennis player at the Vineyard. So were Birkenhead, Law and, more occasionally, Balfour. Lloyd George could not be weaned from golf—another reason for Beaverbrook's neglecting him. Beaverbrook was devoted to exercise and almost obsessed with his physical condition. He fussed over his diet. He recorded each day his temperature, his motions, and his maladies, real or imaginary. Immediately after the armistice he was struck down by a real malady which almost cost him his life, though he managed during its course to run government publicity during a general election, quarrel with Churchill and launch a newspaper. He has left a dramatic account of his illness and its cure:

It started with the tooth-ache.

The year was 1918, the month August, which saw the beginning of the battle of the Hundred Days.

I took my aching jaw to Sir Francis Farmer, a leading dentist of the time. He had no success. The swelling increased. So did the pain.

I decided to change dentists. I went to Victor Smith, a well-known American practitioner. When he had no better luck I consulted Sir George Badgerow, a throat surgeon. He came with me to see Smith.

Eventually Smith laid down his instruments. "I am not prepared to go on," he said. "There is something more than dental trouble in this case. You should see a surgical specialist."

"Do you mean a cancer specialist?" I asked.

Smith said that this was indeed his meaning.

The information profoundly depressed me. Lord Morpeth, who sat with me in the House of Commons, had died just before the war of cancer under similar conditions. I did not want death. I wanted to live long and with comfort. What was the prospect? Very dreary indeed.

So I went with all speed to Sir Wilfrid Trotter, then the specialist on cancer.

After examining me he said that he would be obliged to operate to uncover the cause of the trouble.

News then swept through political circles that I was to be operated on for cancer. Commiserations poured in from all quarters. Mrs. Asquith, writing to express sympathy, said that she now regretted the abuse she had been hurling at me.

The probing operation took place in October. Two or three days later Sir Wilfrid told me the result. I was suffering, he said, from a rare fungoid infection called actinomycosis. It was often fatal. He had known no more than five cases, and in only one of these had the patient survived.

I made up my mind that I would fight all out for life. But I was miserable. The Battle of the Hundred Days ended with a glorious triumph for Britain and her allies. Germany was utterly defeated. But my own joy during the Armistice celebrations was greatly curtailed.

It was not because my jaw was swathed in bandages. The streets were filled with wounded men whose heads were similarly bound. It was not because I was wearing a beard which made me look odd even to myself. It was because I knew that my trouble remained.

Sir Wilfrid decided to operate again. He told me that if he found the throat to be involved the operation would be extensive. I did not fail to grasp the situation. What he meant was "too extensive".

The operation was performed on 15 February 1919. At the end of it the surgeon told me that the entire fungus had been removed.

My delight was short-lived. It was soon apparent that the fungoid growth was again taking a hold.

Reggie Fellowes, another man who had survived the affliction, recommended me to a Portuguese doctor—a man so swarthy that he may have come from Goa, Dr. Gomes.

His treatment was radical. It was heroic. He had 400 drops of iodine poured down my throat everyday. I lay in bed most of the time with my heart pounding, my head bursting, my eyes rolling out tears. A prodigious battle seemed to be taking place within me.

At the end of the treatment Trotter performed another, this time very minor, operation. That clinched matters.

Despite general expectations, despite Mrs. Asquith's remorse, I did not die. It had not been my intention to die.

This savage treatment was successful, though doctors would not use it nowadays. Beaverbrook grew a beard to conceal the scars at his throat. When, thus adorned, he was photographed in the company of a pretty nurse, it was a sign that his recovery was complete.

Beaverbrook often asserted that he ceased to be a financier after the war and became purely a newspaper magnate. Thus he wrote to Grandi in 1955:

Many years ago I used to try and manage a business in Canada. Kipling set me right. He said to me one morning at breakfast—"You cannot live in two continents at one time".

Thereafter, I cleared up my Canadian affairs, put my money into industrial shares, and retired from active life in favour of plenty of work in London.

Certainly he disposed of the Colonial Bank to Barclays and of Royal Securities Corporation to Killam. But he continued to take an active interest in the Canadian financial market and often used Kipling's dictum in the opposite sense, remarking "I live in two continents at once".

In practical terms, Beaverbrook merely transferred his Canadian fortune to two private corporations, W. M. Aitken & Co. and Canadian Assets Realization Company, which were run for him by his brother Allan. For Allan Aitken this brought training in a hard school. Beaverbrook's impatient rebukes rained fast upon him. Thus on 13 February 1924:

> I have now to make a request of you and, although I do not expect fulfilment with that degree of precision and despatch which indicates efficiency in business, I am hoping that in due course you will write to me. Besides I have a certain claim upon my brothers which none of them recognises— they do nothing to support the family to which we all belong, so that since I bear the whole burden of the finance, I should be justified in asking the others to help me with the burden of administration.

On 15 May 1924:

> If you do not attend to this letter, I will find some means of reprisal.

On 17 January 1930:

> I do wish that you would say something that would not leave me suspended between heaven and earth in relation to financial transactions carried out between us.
>
> ... You know of course how far I am committed to politics. It makes a great difference to me if my financial affairs are all nicely smoothed out.
>
> This letter is not a desire on my part to get anything out of you in the way of advantage in selling stocks. It is merely a request, urgently pressed forward, to do for me two things—
> (1) Not to leave me at dead ends;
> (2) Give me answers to my letters.

Finally, on 17 May 1934 a more conciliatory note:

> I emphasise that there is no criticism. There is merely an attempt to get my organisation into shape.
>
> I cannot bear to hurt the feelings of others. I cannot get on swiftly if I have to take them into account.
>
> I am afraid your feelings are too easily hurt. But if we could get to the basis where I would not be likely to upset you, then I could write very freely, and swiftly.

This treatment does not seem to have ruffled Allan Aitken, and he became in time Beaverbrook's indispensable agent in Canada. He also became a very rich man himself.

It is possible to ascertain what Beaverbrook did with some of his Canadian income. $137,000 a year went in annuities—about half to educational institutions and old friends in Newcastle, the rest to members of his family or, as Beaverbrook expressed it, "to descendants of the late Reverend William Aitken". He exclaimed at one point: "How the devil I ever made enough money, in the space of ten years, to pay out so much in annuities, I cannot tell". There was really no mystery. Beaverbrook had backed Canadian expansion and, as Canada prospered, he prospered with it, except during the depression of 1929–33. Even then, being well-endowed with mortgages and bonds, he suffered little diminution of income. He drew $55,000 a year for his own living expenses and emphasized that he did not care whether this came from capital or revenue: "I do not want to leave any money behind me, except sufficient to pay the annuities of my survivors". Beaverbrook sometimes drew on his Canadian capital when he wanted to finance the expansion of his newspapers. These loans from himself to himself were always repaid, but it was no doubt an advantage to have two or three million pounds available at short notice. A good deal of the income of Beaverbrook's Canadian holdings was not paid out and hence was free from British income tax. In this way his fortune steadily accumulated despite all the calls upon it. His expenditure and generosity ran a race with Canadian prosperity which, it seems, they did not win. When Beaverbrook died in 1964, he was richer than he had been in 1910.

Where a man's treasure is, there shall his heart be also. Beaverbrook retained his Canadian domicile all his life and constantly announced his intention of returning "home", though he went to Canada comparatively little in the nineteen-twenties. Being a British subject, as all Canadians then were, he travelled for many years on a British passport, but he took out a Canadian passport as soon as this became possible in 1947 and with it a certificate of Canadian citizenship. However he had many financial interests in England despite his disclaimers. The largest of these was the cinema in which he became interested during the war. After the war he acquired control of the leading cinema chain and as early as 1920 was invited to become president of the cinematograph exhibitors. He refused on the characteristic grounds that he was a shareholder, not a director, but he presided over at least one meeting—a meeting memorable in film history for at it Friese-Green, the cinematograph pioneer, fell dead. Beaverbrook was interested only in exhibiting films, not in making them. He played a considerable part in expanding the industry until 1928 when he sold out at a profit of over one million pounds to the Ostrer brothers. He had chosen his time well: it was just before the storm caused by the coming of the talkies.

Newspapers were Beaverbrook's main activity, especially in the estimate of others. He was a newspaper proprietor of an unusual kind. Other proprietors either put money into their newspapers or took it out. The old-stylers ran their papers at a loss, or very near it, for the sake of the political influence and prestige which this brought. The new ones, of whom Northcliffe and Rothermere were the chief, started poor and grew rich by running their papers at a profit. This profit remained their principal concern, though they naturally enjoyed the influence and prestige as well. Beaverbrook fell into neither class. He was already a rich man before he had anything to do with newspapers and never derived his income from them. On the other hand, as a good businessman, he could not tolerate a concern which made a loss. Even propaganda, he believed, should pay its way, as he had made money for the Canadian government out of his propaganda during the war. Many years later he told the royal commission on the press: "I run my papers purely for propaganda. I am not interested in profits". Afterwards he had second thoughts: "I was wrong to say that I'm not interested in profits. But I was very interested in losses when I first ran The Express". Beaverbrook set out to turn The Daily Express into a profitable enterprise, though once it made profits he ploughed most of them back instead of paying dividends— much to the annoyance of the shareholders.

Beaverbrook gave The Daily Express three things: more money, better management, and brighter presentation. Between 1919 and 1922 he put £200,000 into The Daily Express and took nothing out. Some of this was to cover the losses caused by the high price of newsprint in 1921. Most of it had a more creative purpose: to make a bigger paper with more room for advertisements. Reliance on advertisements as a main source of revenue was Beaverbrook's great innovation as a press lord, and every morning he turned first to the advertisement pages. This was much in character. More than anything else, Beaverbrook was an advertiser, rating publicity above all other virtues. He publicized himself and remarked: "It has always been my habit to print everything about my career, good and bad, pleasing and disagreeable".[1] He believed that it did not matter what people said about you so long as they said something. He publicized others—Law, Lloyd George, Churchill. He even claimed that he had acquired The Daily Express solely in order to publicize Law— a typical exaggeration: he really acquired The Daily Express in order to recover the money he had already sunk in it. Similarly he publicized causes: Empire Free Trade, making more aircraft, the Second Front. Again the causes were no good unless people talked about them.

Advertisements in his papers were a two-way traffic. They helped to pay the bills, and the better the papers the more attractive they were to advertisers. Beaverbrook is said to have sold space personally only once: it was to Gordon Selfridge, the great storekeeper. But he supervised his advertising staff as closely as he supervised the writers. The money did

[1] Beaverbrook, Men and Power, 244.

not go only on increased newsprint. It went also on staff. Beaverbrook recruited young men with ideas who could write, and his papers paid the highest salaries in Fleet Street. Hence he was never troubled by a labour dispute. It was more than money which held the papers together. Beaverbrook secured a personal devotion from all who served him, though his nagging could also provoke irritation or even savage anger. He often took pleasure in deflating the man who was up. He never failed to succour those who were down.

The better management was provided by E. J. Robertson, a young Canadian who ranked second only to Beaverbrook himself in the success of his papers. As earlier with cement or steel, Beaverbrook found the best man for the job and then left the detailed running to him. Unlike Northcliffe, Beaverbrook rarely went to the office, and he had no experience on the technical side. He never supervised his own articles on the stone or set a page. He operated from afar, sometimes stimulating, sometimes criticizing. He knew that he could rely on Robertson, and his faith was abundantly justified. Beaverbrook's newspapers rested on the firm foundation of E. J. Robertson for more than a generation.

Beaverbrook claimed throughout his life that, while he applauded or even determined the general policy of The Daily Express, he was not involved in its daily workings. This was a characteristic evasion. Many ideas and stories can have come from only one source, and the modesty of "the principal shareholder", as Beaverbrook called himself, was no more than a convenient cover. He derived considerable amusement from professing innocence and left rich material for an anthology of apologies. Here are some from his early days. The routine apology (to Ian Macpherson, 8 July 1922):

> I do not see the Daily Express until I go into breakfast in the morning, and I knew nothing of the so-called attack on you.

The lighthearted apology (to Hugo Cunliffe-Owen, 24 May 1919):

> This sort of thing sickens me of the Daily Express and makes me inclined to throw it up in despair. . . . I remember some time ago advising you to buy a newspaper—now I cancel the advice. But if you are inclined to take my first advice and not its cancellation, I suggest you buy the Daily Express.

The indignant apology (to Lord Knutsford, 13 May 1919):

> I am the principal shareholder in the Daily Express but I am not the Editor or the Manager or even a Director of it. I practically never go to the office . . . and I leave the staff to carry on their duties in their own way. Of course in a large and important question of policy I should put my foot down if I thought the Daily Express was going wrong. But attempts to saddle me personally with responsibility for what appears in the newspaper in the ordinary way of journalism are simply ignorant when they are not malicious.

The impudently flattering apology (to Lord Leverhulme, 22 November 1922):

> Let me take this opportunity of informing you that in the Express office, where there is a distinct trace of Communism and a considerable degree of Bolshevism, I find that all capitalists are subject to criticism, save only yourself. It would really astonish you to know how highly you are esteemed by the turbulent troop of pressmen. I believe there is no parallel in the history of industry.

These evasions were not altogether without substance. Blumenfeld was a highly respected journalist of great experience. He was the only editor of Beaverbrook's who could end a telephone conversation by saying "Shut up, Max" or "Go to hell". Wentworth Day, a Beaverbrook journalist who became Lady Houston's political secretary, tells this story. One day Beaverbrook stormed into Blumenfeld's room, shouted: "Where the hell's R.D.B.?" and swept everything off the table on to the carpet. Blumenfeld came in and said quietly: "Who did that?" Beaverbrook: "I did. Now look here I want to talk to you." Blumenfeld: "Then pick these things up and put them back on my desk first, Max. Then I'll talk to you." Beaverbrook's face broke into a swift dawn of impish laughter. His mood vanished like snow in June. "Sure I'll pick 'em up."[1]

Blumenfeld agreed with most of Beaverbrook's policies, particularly over Imperial Preference. Previous proprietors had held him to a strict party line, and he welcomed the greater independence which Beaverbrook thrust upon him. After the financial worries of his earlier years, he welcomed also the increased circulation and, in time, the profitable position which followed on Beaverbrook's money and ideas. In the long run Blumenfeld was not what Beaverbrook needed. Essentially he was too staid and old fashioned in his writings, perhaps also too exclusively political. The real breakthrough came only when Beaverbrook discovered Beverley Baxter, yet another Canadian. Baxter's ambition was to be a musician, not a journalist. On one occasion he took part in a ship's concert, when crossing to Canada. Beaverbrook, who was also on the boat, sent him a note: "I have heard you sing More than ever I advise you to take up journalism". Soon afterwards Baxter took Beaverbrook's advice.

It was Baxter who gave both The Daily Express and The Sunday Express the special stamp which they have retained to this day. Like The Daily Mail they were organs of mass circulation. Baxter added an element of worldly sophistication, a sheen which appealed equally to all classes. Baxter was the only editor in Fleet Street who regularly appeared in the office late at night in tails and a white waistcoat after a visit to the opera or some grand party. Like Beaverbrook himself, Baxter was an

[1] J. Wentworth Day, Lady Houston DBE (1958), 84.

amateur who did not know the technicalities of the trade. Northcliffe once said to Beaverbrook: "Your amateurs will ruin you". Beaverbrook replied: "Some day my amateurs will conquer your kingdom". This story, though perhaps apocryphal, was essentially true.

Beaverbrook's closest associates were outsiders in another sense: none of them was English until Christiansen came along, and even he was partly of Danish stock. Robertson and Baxter were both Canadians, and Beaverbrook once remarked: "I carried The Daily Express to greatness with the aid of a bell-hop and a piano tuner".[1] John Gordon and John Junor, successively editors of The Sunday Express, were both Scotchmen. This choice of outsiders was not fortuitous. Canadians and Scotchmen escaped the conventions and class-prejudices of English life. None of them had been educated at an English public school.

No doubt they would have been less inspired without Beaverbrook, the greatest amateur and outsider of them all. Most newspaper proprietors were dull men apart from their trade. Even Northcliffe was not an interesting man in the ordinary sense despite his powerful personality, and Rothermere was very dull indeed. Beaverbrook was among the most exciting men of his age. He knew every great political figure. He counted writers such as Kipling, Arnold Bennett and H. G. Wells among his intimate friends. He consorted with music-hall artists and the gayer members of society.

Northcliffe had succeeded by providing more news. Beaverbrook also appreciated news, and his papers kept a larger staff of foreign correspondents than any other paper. He once wrote: "I think it is curiosity that builds a newspaper. Wanting to find out about things. Curiosity". Especially he wanted to find out about people. He commented on a financial article about a company promoter:

> We didn't tell that he was married. We didn't tell the data that I gave you; what his furniture is like in the flat in town. We didn't tell anything about the homely, agreeable and yet old fashioned manner in which the flat is furnished.

News was no good for Beaverbrook unless it was also entertaining. He announced in a publicity hand-out:

> *News, Opinion and Advertisement* must all come under the head of Entertainment to a reasonable extent—or they will not be read. *People do not read to be bored. Unless a newspaper can make its material in every department interesting it simply is not read. Be sure that when you read your Daily Express you will not be bored.*

[1] Robertson, while at college, had maintained himself during vacations by working in an hotel, where Beaverbrook first met him. Baxter had been a piano salesman and hoped to become a concert pianist before he turned to journalism.

Robert Aitken (grandfather), Jane and
William Aitken (parents), c. 1870

Rev. William Aitken, 1900

Ancestral home:
Silvermine, 1947

The Manse, Newcastle, N.B.
Rev. William Aitken on
steps, Max Aitken
over his shoulder

Load of mischief, 1893

L. J. Tweedie's
law-office, Chatham

Gladys Drury,
first Lady Beaverbrook

(left)   Montreal pre-war
(below)   London post-war

Bonar Law accepts food
taxes (Sir Max Aitken
on his left), Ashton-
under-Lyne, 1912

At Ashton–under-Lyne,
1912: *(left to right)*
H. S. Heap (Unionist
local chairman), Rudyard
Kipling, Lady Aitken,
Sir Max Aitken

In France, 1916:
(left to right) Lieutenant-Colonel
J. E. B. Seely, Lieutenant-General
Sir Sam Hughes, Lieutenant-
Colonel Sir Max Aitken

With Tim Healy
(Arnold Bennett in background)

Minister of Information, 1918

At the Vineyard, 1922

The Vineyard, Fulham

Deauville, 1925: *(left to right)* Viscount Castlerosse, Max
Aitken, Peter Aitken, Beaverbrook, a friend

With daughter Janet (Hon. Mrs. Ian
mpbell) and grand-daughter, Jean, 1931

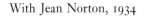

With Jean Norton, 1934

Empire Crusader:
Norwich, 1931

Second Front Now: Birmingham, 1942

Beaverbrook liked fun, and in this he was in tune with the times. The nineteen-twenties were the great fun generation: escaped from the solemnity of the past and not yet faced with the weighty problems of the future. Maybe the Beaverbrook newspapers of the present time have not kept at the top of the circulation lists because they do not conform to the staider taste of today's youth.

Beaverbrook also liked independence and again found readers among those who agreed with him. It was of course independence within safe limits. Beaverbrook, like his readers, could stand above Conservative and Liberal. He could never reconcile himself to the Labour party while it aimed, or so he believed, at the ending of private property and rich men. His unconscious ideal was a Conservative government always in power, with himself attacking it on almost every detailed item in its programme. Many others shared his taste, and this made The Daily Express the most classless of British newspapers—the only one which drew its readers in equal proportions from each social and financial group. Beaverbrook gave an accurate description of his readers:

> It has been said that the Daily Express appeals to the middle class mind. That is not so. It appeals to a particular kind of mind in every class. Having begun in a small way it appeals to those who are not ashamed of small beginnings but who look forward to dealing with the events of life on a larger scale. We appealed to the character and temperament which was bent on moving upwards and outwards and which was not to be trammelled by any doctrinaire conceptions in its view of national needs and opportunities.

The Daily Express was not Beaverbrook's only venture into journalism nor his most original. His appetite for a Sunday newspaper had perhaps been whetted by the abortive bid he made for The Sunday Times just before the war ended. He also claimed that he wanted a further channel of propaganda during the general election, though in fact the election was over before his plans matured. At any rate on 29 December 1918 Lady Diana Manners[1] started the presses for the first issue of The Sunday Express. Beaverbrook had no idea what he was in for. He imagined that The Sunday Express would be merely a seventh day edition of The Daily, produced by the same people working overtime. Blumenfeld assured him that it would cost £20,000 to get the new paper going. The result came near to disaster. The Sunday Express secured only half the circulation of The Daily Express and cost Beaverbrook nearly half a million pounds in its first two years. Altogether he drew nearly two million pounds from his Canadian fortune before the paper turned the corner.

Direction was even more difficult. At first Beaverbrook expected Blumenfeld to act as editor. Then he tried one editor after another, none

---

[1] Later Lady Diana Cooper and one of Beaverbrook's most treasured friends.

with success. He wrote later: "The corpses of Sunday Express editors were spread up and down Fleet Street in every direction". The most disastrous appointment was the fifth, James Douglas, a columnist from The Star. Douglas had no editorial experience, and his first issue provoked a general strike on the part of the editorial staff. Beaverbrook came back from the Riviera in haste. Douglas was deposed, though keeping the title of editor for the five-year term of his contract. Beaverbrook then tried his own hand as editor. He announced that he would hold a staff conference every Tuesday to survey the last issue and a staff dinner every Friday to plan the next one. He would act as editor every Saturday evening, and he established a flat for himself at the top of the building, recalling: "I often went to bed with a load of care in my belly".

After a few exciting weeks Beaverbrook became irregular in his attendance. His absences were longer and more frequent than he ever tolerated in his editors. The Sunday Express was virtually rudderless for years. At one time Baxter was supposed to act as managing editor on top of his duties with The Daily. There was no firm direction until John Gordon was appointed. He became one of the great editors of Fleet Street. He recently told me this characteristic story. In his very early days as editor he had to make a decision of considerable importance. He rang up Beaverbrook. Beaverbrook said: "Can you decide this yourself?" Gordon: "Of course I can but as it is so important and I thought you as the principal proprietor might be the most affected, you might like to be consulted." Beaverbrook answered: "The paper is yours. You make the decision. If it's wrong I'll kick the pants off you. If it's right, I'll probably never mention it again".

Somehow The Sunday Express gradually succeeded from its own momentum. It was unique like its founder, and this in two ways. Most daily papers had no Sunday associate and merely hired their presses to entirely distinct concerns. Even where there was an overlap in ownership, there was none in character. Beaverbrook set his stamp on both his papers despite differences in emphasis. Moreover The Sunday Express was a paper of a new kind as it has remained. The existing Sunday papers still reflected the Victorian market when Sunday newspapers were disapproved of by the respectable church-going classes. There were two sophisticated journals of small circulation for the emancipated few: The Observer and The Sunday Times. There were more journals of large circulation for the rough, irreligious many, with The News of the World and The People predominant. These papers, with a much larger readership than any daily paper, specialized in sensations, scandals, and pornography. Beaverbrook wanted what he called a family newspaper which would yet have a large circulation. After some years of striving, he succeeded.

The Sunday Express gradually achieved a circulation of a popular kind, but it never aped the character of the other popular papers. It managed without pornography, which was a good deal commoner in Sunday newspapers then than it is now. It managed without retailing private scandals, though there was plenty of harmless gossip and public sensation. The Sunday Express was certainly not sophisticated. Indeed it was often Philistine, particularly in the column written by James Douglas. Douglas specialized in indignant morality, a line which reached its highest point in his attack on a harmless lesbian book, The Well of Loneliness. Beaverbrook evidently did not share Douglas's indignation. He wrote to a friend: "You must read the Well of Loneliness. It is a very good book. But of course you must read it in the unexpurgated edition". Beaverbrook liked all the good things of life, and it did not escape comment that Douglas's thunderbolts might have fallen upon him also if he had not been the proprietor of The Sunday Express. Thus in 1921 Douglas denounced Lord Dawson of Penn for championing birth control. Lloyd George wrote to Dawson: "When Beaverbrook holds up hands steeped in the blood of slaughtered commandments to express horror at your speech it beats the record for disgusting hypocracy".

Beaverbrook was not perturbed by this charge. On some subjects he felt strongly and firmly asserted his control. He would not tolerate, for example, attacks on the Empire, advocacy of socialism or of involvement in Europe, or for that matter scandal about an individual's private life in the columns of The Sunday Express. Where he did not feel strongly, he was quite prepared for the paper to reflect the opinions and even the prejudices of its readers. Beaverbrook aimed at winning a wide readership among the respectable, and to his mind therefore Douglas did no harm if he carried respectability to the verge of the ridiculous. After all, Beaverbrook did not propose to take his own morality from The Sunday Express, and there was no reason why others should do so. A further point may be added. The very people who condemned Beaverbrook for giving Douglas a free hand were to be found on other occasions vociferously championing the editor's right to be free from all interference by his proprietor. Evidently their idea of freedom was all one way: freedom only to express the ideas in which they believed. No doubt Douglas's articles were really indefensible; no doubt also they gave a lot of fun to the principal shareholder and to many others.

Beaverbrook contributed more than finance and inspiration to The Sunday Express. Like other Sunday newspapers it offered general articles rather than news, and Beaverbrook became, without premeditation, its principal columnist. With The Sunday Express, and with none other of his papers, he was for many years a journalist in the accepted sense—a man who writes articles for newspapers. His output was impressive even for a fullblooded journalist. It began in November 1920 with three articles. In 1921 he contributed 25 articles; in 1922, 35; in 1923, 23; in 1924, 24; in 1925, 10. Some were large-scale political leaders; some were straight reporting, from Germany for example, or the near East; some were fragments from his stock of contemporary history; many were a form of lay-preaching, as though he were trying to show himself a true son of the manse after all. One series gave advice on careers to young men. Not surprisingly, it warned them against becoming bank clerks. The most ambitious of the lay sermons were brought together in a book entitled Success. This book was dedicated to the worship of mammon and contains the remarkable sentence: "Shelley had genius, but he would not have been a success in Wall Street". In general, Success is a sensible little book, as such books go, built round the proposition that making money is as interesting an art as any other for those who have the tastes and gifts for it. Its moral teaching, though sometimes platitudinous, is often wise and always moral. Anyone who followed Beaverbrook's advice might become rich; he would certainly become honest and a man of impeccable financial rectitude.

The emergence of Beaverbrook as a writer was not really surprising. His letters were packed with vivid phrases, and he had learnt a good deal of literary craft while writing Canada in Flanders. He was always modest about this part of his gifts. Writers from Kipling to Ian Fleming were the only men in whose company he felt humble, and he liked to make out that he was dependent for literary guidance on Maurice Woods. When challenged to demonstrate that Venetia Montagu was a brilliant talker, he replied: "The other day someone said to her: 'Where is Max?', and she answered: 'Oh, he's with Maurice Woods trying to re-assemble his split infinitives' ".

The collaboration between Woods and Beaverbrook was certainly close. Woods was now the chief political leader-writer on The Daily Express and Beaverbrook's private secretary as well. He drafted most of Beaverbrook's longer letters. He assembled the material for Politicians and the War, which was virtually ready for publication in 1919. He wrote a life of Beaverbrook in seventeen chapters, which has not been published, though it is a good deal better than some which have. He also made two drafts of Beaverbrook's autobiography until 1910, and much of this survived unchanged when Beaverbrook wrote My Early Life many years later. Woods also prepared material for a history of pre-war British politics which was never completed. In Beaverbrook's published articles, he provided the more recondite historical allusions and most of the literary references.

Imitating Beaverbrook in either writing or talk became quite a common accomplishment later, and many a man achieved fame as a dinner-table wit by retailing, or fabricating, Beaverbrook's repartees. But, as with Dr.

Johnson, the imitators would have had no success if there had not been an original for them to build on, and the same was true of Maurice Woods. He was the first, though by no means the last, who knew how to speak with his master's voice.

Beaverbrook's own style grew better all the time. In his early articles, the paragraphs were still much too long—a criticism he often levelled later against his editors. But the zest was always there. He believed in making a story work hard for its living and, if it were good enough, would use it again and again. The story of how Tim Healy diverted criticism from the ministry of information in 1918 appeared first in a Sunday Express article, was then used in Politicians and the Press, which was published in 1925, and finally emerged unchanged in Men and Power, which was published in 1956. The anecdote of Bonar Law's "private tap", which was in fact ginger ale, appeared three times in articles before graduating twice into books.

If a story could not find its right place, it was sometimes used in the wrong one. Thus in The Decline and Fall of Lloyd George, Beaverbrook tells that he went down to the Unionist leaders at Wargrave in October 1921 and triumphed over them by recounting how the Irish negotiators would escape from a dilemma which Lloyd George had forced upon them. When asked to reveal his source, he replied: "Barnes's mistress". What was Barnes doing here?[1] He had left the cabinet eighteen months before and had no contacts with Lloyd George. Beaverbrook could not in fact remember what reply he had made to the indignant Unionists and was reluctant to waste one which he had made on another occasion. The true story illustrates how maliciously funny he could be.

> On one occasion Lloyd George sent for me to inquire as to the source of my information. The Daily Express had announced Barnes's retirement from the Ministry—which was true. I accepted George's invitation to lunch. He had summoned Bonar Law from next door—and the party was completed by Miss Stevenson. George tackled me directly and solemnly. Where had The Daily Express got the information? I replied, "Will you promise me not to divulge the source? Will you swear that no one shall be punished for an indiscretion?" Lloyd George took the oath. Then I turned to Bonar Law. "Now Bonar, will you enter into the same engagement?" Bonar Law also swore secrecy. By now the audience was worked up to a pitch of excitement by the promised revelation. "But," I said, "there is Miss Stevenson. She might reveal the secret—she has not said she will not". Miss Stevenson also took the vow of silence. *"Well, I will tell you now—I got it from Barnes' mistress".*

[1] George Barnes, a former leader of the Labour party, succeeded Arthur Henderson as the Labour member of the war cabinet and remained in Lloyd George's government until January 1920. He then left public life.

Mr. Barnes was an admirable and typical Trade Unionist of the old school, who subsequently took a permanent post in the Labour ministry as a civil servant.[1] His morals were above all suspicion and his appearance conformed to type.

Lloyd George never tackled me on this subject again.

In these first years after the war, Beaverbrook worked hard at knowing everything and everybody. In his newspaper articles he was always ready to write about himself and about his finances—never was there a franker public figure. He scored also by being on the spot. Northcliffe was travelling round the world in search of health. Rothermere was usually in the south of France, prophesying universal ruin. Beaverbrook was at the centre of things. He briefed himself on every subject from industrial disputes to international affairs. In October 1920, during the coal strike, he wrote to a friend in New York:

> I saw Smillie and Hodges and spent hours with them trying to understand their point of view. The show down between the extreme labour leaders and Government is yet to come.

A letter to Beaverbrook of a different kind shows the consistency with which he promoted Anglo-Russian relations throughout his life. On 21 March 1921 Krassin, head of the Soviet trade delegation, wrote in his own hand:

> Upon the conclusion of negotiations with the British Government in connection with the signing of the Trade Agreement between Great Britain and Soviet Russia, I place on record with particular appreciation the assistance rendered in this matter by you personally and your paper.

To another friend in Montreal, Sir Andrew Macphail, Beaverbrook sent a general survey of world affairs on 14 June 1921:

> The Greeks will get a bad smash, and the Turks will get to be intolerable. The Poles are extending their Empire from pole to pole and the Russians are getting ready to take over Warsaw when these Nationals have extended their lines sufficiently to make conquest easy. The French want to make a partition of Germany.
>
> All this is the consequence of the war to end wars.
>
> Ireland supplies the press with a lead story each day, and the Jews make us pay for Palestine.

In 1921 The Daily Express conducted its first truly independent political campaign, appropriately over an imperial issue. This was the embargo on the import of Canadian cattle, which had been imposed as a war measure in 1917. The real purpose was to cut down meat imports, but it had been dressed up with the excuse of protecting British herds from disease, though there was in fact none in Canada. A pledge had been

---

[1] This is not correct.

given to remove the embargo after the war. This pledge was not fulfilled, as an indirect device for protecting the home farmer. Attacking the embargo brought popularity for Beaverbrook in Canada—perhaps too blatantly. At any rate, Meighen, Borden's successor as Conservative leader, failed to support the campaign during the imperial conference of 1921. It also brought Beaverbrook into alliance with the meat traders' association and, ironically, with the opponents of dear food, including someone as remote from Beaverbrook as Arthur Henderson.

In February 1921 Griffith-Boscawen, a Unionist and an old acquaintance of Beaverbrook's, had to seek re-election as minister of agriculture. The Daily Express demanded a pledge that he would remove the cattle embargo. Boscawen refused, and The Daily Express then campaigned against him. Boscawen was defeated. There was much Unionist indignation against Beaverbrook, not for the first time, and the general committee of the Carlton Club sent him a letter of rebuke. Beaverbrook drafted a reply, which was insolently marked "*Not* Private":

> The letter appears to me to be tantamount to a claim on the part of the General Committee of the Carlton Club to be the governing body of the Unionist Party.... The Members of the Committee possess no doubt great experience on methods of political attack, but I do not recognize their right to sit in judgement ex cathedra on the arguments I may choose to use in public controversy.

The letter is also marked "not sent". Beaverbrook remained silent. He did not resign from the Carlton Club, but he rarely visited it thereafter.

After this stroke, the government sought a compromise. The Daily Express and the meat traders agreed not to oppose Griffith-Boscawen at a further by-election if a royal commission were appointed to consider the embargo. The commission duly reported that the embargo should be removed. The government, reluctant to the last, left the question to a free vote in both houses. Accusations of bad faith were exchanged, but the embargo was lifted. This was a considerable success for a newspaper campaign. It was also a misleading one. When later Beaverbrook took up the cause of Empire Free Trade, he looked back to the affair of the cattle embargo for inspiration. But it was one thing to change official policy on a single issue where the government's position was indefensible. It was quite another matter to impose an entirely different general policy on a party and a government, as events were to prove.

Beaverbrook now seemed not merely independent of the government, but hostile to it, and it was hard to believe that he had once been the intimate friend of cabinet ministers. Events took an unexpected turn, and Beaverbrook found himself again on the inside. He reappeared, to his own surprise, in his old role as the go-between who could sway the fortunes of ministers and governments.

CHAPTER NINE

REPEAT PERFORMANCE, 1921–23

On 6 November 1920 Law made one of his rare visits to Cherkley. The talk impressed Maurice Woods, who recorded it, as "about the most brilliant conversation I have ever heard". Law sang Lloyd George's praises. He said: "When anyone (myself included) has made a big speech in the House we are full of it—trying to lead the conversation round to it. I never remember L.G. mentioning a past speech". Beaverbrook cried out: "Ah—you are hypnotized by L.G., Bonar—you'll believe anything—even that he has an original mind. I tell you that there are only two forces which lead to success in politics, character and hypocrisy. And now you have a coalition of two men—you character—the P.M. hypocrisy. Of course you beat us every time". Whatever the truth of Beaverbrook's generalization, his conclusion was certainly correct. While Law and Lloyd George stood together, the Coalition government was unshakable. It is not surprising that Beaverbrook had become an independent. He had really no choice if he was to exercise any influence at all.

In March 1921 the political situation changed. Law fell ill. His doctors insisted that he must resign, and on 17 March he did so. Two days later he left Charing Cross[1] for Cannes. No great personage came to see him off—no cabinet minister, not even a representative from the cabinet office. Apart from secretaries and members of the family, Beaverbrook stood alone on the desolate platform. As he watched the departing train,[2] he was sad and forlorn. At the same time, he grasped with excitement that there was a new opening for him in politics. The Coalition was no longer invulnerable. In later life Beaverbrook wavered between insisting that Law's illness was genuine (as it undoubtedly was) and himself taking the credit for it. He even said on occasion: "I had to get Law out of George's government".

[1] Then the station for the continent.
[2] When Beaverbrook came to write an account of this many years later, he checked the weather ("cold with bursts of cheerless sunshine") with the meteorological office and also sent a secretary to Charing Cross in order to ascertain exactly how long he watched before the train went out of sight.

At any rate Law had gone. Austen Chamberlain, his successor as both Unionist leader and lord privy seal, lacked his hold over the Unionist party. He offended the Unionists by his excessive loyalty to Lloyd George and like Asquith—though not, as Beaverbrook remarked, for the same reason—fell asleep in the House after dinner. Birkenhead, the lord chancellor, was on bad terms with Lloyd George and eager to challenge Chamberlain's leadership of the Unionists. Churchill, the colonial secretary, was angry that Horne, and not himself, had been appointed to succeed Chamberlain at the Exchequer. Montagu, the secretary for India, denounced the backing which Lloyd George gave to the Greeks and the Zionists. Here were materials for an explosion, and Beaverbrook prepared to use them. His motive was not simple mischief-making, though of course he enjoyed a political stir. He had always disliked the Coalition and, with Law gone, did not believe that it could endure. Beaverbrook had a clear picture of the alternative: a Conservative government under Law, pledged to Imperial Preference. He refused to accept Law's illness as genuine or at any rate as permanent. Therefore, if there were a crisis and Lloyd George fell, Law would have to return and become prime minister, whatever his reluctance or, in his own word, indolence. Beaverbrook set out to help the necessary crisis on its way.

Law had foreseen something of this and tried to head Beaverbrook off. Before leaving England he wrote to Lloyd George from Dover:

> I think it would be worth your while, if you can do it, to send for Max just to have a talk with him for I think that he could now be easily influenced by you to support you.
>
> He must be doing something but I really believe he has more sympathy with you than with anyone else and the feeling he has had that I prevented him having a free hand (of which I admit there was no sign in his action) perhaps made him more difficult than if I had been out of it altogether.

Lloyd George took this advice and invited Beaverbrook to No. 10 Downing Street.[1] The meeting was not a success. Beaverbrook recorded:

> The conversation, though political in character, was in general terms. I did not then understand the reason for the meeting as he had not been in good relationship to me and held me accountable just then for several displeasing incidents.

It was not only the conflict over the cattle embargo which lay between the two men. Beaverbrook was after other game.

He watched Churchill, Birkenhead and Montagu intently. They repeatedly lunched or dined with him at the Vineyard, and he recorded

---

[1] In The Decline and Fall of Lloyd George, 19, Beaverbrook implies wrongly that no meeting took place.

every sign of their discontent. In his impatience, he constantly urged Law to return. He wrote in late April:

> Come home now. The public is satisfied and you might as well be comfortable. I offer you my little house until you find your new home.... Winston is very-very-very angry. F.E. is as bitter as Winston is angry.

On 30 April Law refused the invitation: "I should not know what to do in London with the House sitting". On 11 May Beaverbrook tried again. He telegraphed: "Please do come home for Whitsuntide. You can arrive in disguise stay at Vineyard and go away again before holidays are over if you wish". Law was unmoved: "I am sure I could not be in London without its being known and I would have to see people and till I see a little more clearly what is going to happen I do not want to do that". So perhaps Law was nibbling after all.

Still, his hesitation was exasperating. On 12 May Beaverbrook wrote to Borden in Canada:

> The Government is passing through difficult times on account of internal differences.... Churchill is the bitter enemy of George. He has just grounds for his hostility....
>
> F. E. Smith means to challenge Chamberlain's leadership of the Tory party. He may not defeat him but he will diminish Chamberlain's authority. Curzon too has pretensions. I am told that Lady Curzon means to give us a son, so that good government is assured for another generation.

Since Law would not come to Beaverbrook, Beaverbrook went to Law. At the end of May Beaverbrook and Goulding visited Law in Paris. Evidently Beaverbrook revealed something of the stroke which he was preparing. Evidently also he had not counted on any counter-offensive by Lloyd George. He soon learnt better. Immediately on his return to England, he telegraphed to Law:

> My plans smashed. Little man made terms with Colonial and made Smith a viscount. The Jew will probably get an O.B.E. I get vicious denunciations scattered broadcast. Wont you come over for weekend.[1]

Law replied coolly on 4 June: "I understand all your telegram except the O.B.E. and the Jew. I told you that you were wasting your energy in going back".

Beaverbrook had despaired too soon. Though Lloyd George strove to win over Birkenhead, he was still resolved to fight Churchill and his other enemies. Lloyd George's first step was to secure his rear against any intervention by Law. On 15 June, Law arrived in London, at Lloyd George's prompting, not at Beaverbrook's. Law told Beaverbrook: "he

---

[1] The little man is Lloyd George. The colonial is Churchill. Smith is Birkenhead. The Jew is presumably Montagu, though the inducement sounds inadequate.

would not return to the battle". He gave much the same answer to Lloyd George: though he would not support the attack upon the government, he would also not return to office. This was enough for Lloyd George, who said defiantly: "I may go out of office, but if I do go it will be because I want to go, and not because I am turned out".

Back at the Vineyard, Law repeated his refusals. He would not join in the attempt to overthrow Lloyd George; he would not attack Chamberlain; he would not consider succeeding Lloyd George even if the government fell without his help. And he made Beaverbrook promise not to mention his name as a possible alternative leader. After this, Law left abruptly for Paris on the afternoon train.[1]

This was a bitter blow for Beaverbrook—"a shattering and unnerving defeat". But he still hoped that Law might come back after all if Lloyd George were overthrown. "The plot", as it was coming to be called, therefore went on. Its immediate target was Dr. Christopher Addison, Lloyd George's devoted adherent among the Coalition Liberals and the man who had done as much as Aitken to make him prime minister in December 1916. As minister of health, Addison had incurred much criticism for his policy of building houses without regard to cost. In March 1921 he had been demoted to the position of minister without portfolio. Now even this was challenged. In order to provoke a crisis, Churchill encouraged Addison to stand firm, while at the same time Beaverbrook, and perhaps Churchill also, briefed the press against him.

Lloyd George was again too much for them. Rothermere, for once, was in England. On 20 June he spent an hour with "the Big Beast". Rothermere did not share Beaverbrook's enthusiasm for Law. On the contrary he blamed Law for the "Squandermania", against which he was running a noisy anti-waste campaign. He was therefore delighted to act as Lloyd George's instrument. On 22 June Rothermere's paper, The Daily Mirror, revealed that there was a Unionist plot to oust Lloyd George and put Law in his place. The article spoke contemptuously of Law: "He left no real gap in our political life. . . . He has no following in the country. . . . He is largely responsible for our present financial plight". The intrigue therefore was "doomed to failure". On 23 June The Manchester Guardian repeated the story more staidly with information derived from Sir William Sutherland, Lloyd George's press agent. As became a Liberal organ, The Manchester Guardian tactfully diverted attention from Churchill and put the guilt on Birkenhead and Beaverbrook.

On the same day, Lloyd George triumphed in the house of commons. He declared that Addison would hold office only until the end of the

---

[1] Beaverbrook left no contemporary account of these conversations with Law, which have to be taken from The Decline and Fall of Lloyd George. In this book, Beaverbrook passes lightly over his part in "the plot".

session. What was more, he proposed that Addison's salary should be cut not only by the £2000 which the critics were demanding, but by an additional £500 as well. Lloyd George certainly knew how to push a former friend overboard when the raft was threatening to sink. The plotters hastily protested their innocence. Birkenhead wrote to Lloyd George that the story was "a tissue of lies from beginning to end" and told the press that it was "a farrago of wild invention". Curzon, who had no doubt held aloof until he saw which way the wind was blowing, announced: "There is not a word of truth in the story. It is quite absurd". Only Churchill remained silent.

Lloyd George determined to make victory sure. He again saw Rothermere, who produced a further article in The Sunday Pictorial of 26 June. This said brusquely: "Deny it how they may, it is true that the attempt was made". The women's vote, he asserted, would be decisive at the next election.

> All the women electors know about Lord Birkenhead and Mr. Bonar Law is that both have been apostles and defenders of Squandermania. They know something about Mr. Lloyd George.
>
> They know he has strength and skill, that he forced the unity of command which brought victory to the Allies, and that while he has been engaged in the tremendous task of winning the peace his spendthrift colleagues have squandered the nation's money and piled up the rates and taxes.
>
> They will not vote for pulling down Mr. Lloyd George in order to elevate Mr. Bonar Law or any other mossgrown politician who has been tried and found wanting.

J. C. C. Davidson, who on Law's retirement had joined Baldwin at the board of trade, sent the article to Beaverbrook with this postscript: "I still think Bonar thinks the Big Beast is an Archangel!". Beaverbrook affected to be unmoved. He replied to Davidson on 29 June 1921:

> I do not think this nonsense is worth taking any notice of. These brothers specialize in vendettas and, in this case, the grievance seems to arise out of assistance received during the crisis at the Air Ministry.[1]

"The plot" had failed, and Beaverbrook cut his losses, as he would have done with a merger which miscarried. His friendly correspondence with Rothermere over newspaper finance and newsprint went on unabated, and later there came a time when Beaverbrook joined in one of Rothermere's vendettas, perhaps unwisely. Even more surprisingly, the failure of the plot was followed by a reconciliation with Lloyd George, indeed by an intense, though shortlived, intimacy. This was not time-serving or subservience on Beaverbrook's part. The approach came from

---

[1] This seems a far-fetched explanation. In 1918 Beaverbrook had drafted Rothermere's innocuous letter of resignation from the air ministry, and Law had given sensible advice in the same spirit. It is hard to see how this could be a grievance.

Lloyd George and was due to his change of policy over Ireland. For eighteen months past the government had tried to restore order and its own authority in Ireland by methods of increasing terrorism. Lloyd George was himself the leader of the hard men in the cabinet. Beaverbrook reported to Law on 13 May:

> At the cabinet yesterday the decision was taken to reject all overtures for a truce during elections[1]—except on condition of surrender of arms. The division of opinion was sharp, all Co-Liberals to the left except Sir A. Mond with Curzon on the Cross Benches. All Unionist opinion with the P.M. including Horne who had taken up an attitude of compromise on the previous day. Horne explained his change of view with disarming frankness— he had enjoyed in the meantime the advantage of a talk with the P.M.

Beaverbrook detested this policy. He had always sympathized with the Irish desire for national freedom and did so the more when his close friend Healy sent him detailed reports of the outrages. Healy wrote of Sir Hamar Greenwood, the Irish chief secretary, on 28 May:

> Out of Bedlam no such councillor of the King as Greenwood could have been selected. His lies alone would set the hearts of the people ablaze. They make no account of the loss, deaths and wounds he has inflicted on them and they will take a vengeance more fearful than any he can decree.

Early in June Healy came to England with further information for Beaverbrook. On his return to Ireland he wrote on 17 June:

> The soul of Ireland is aflame, and killing or jailing a few thousand lads, or burning towns won't mend matters.

Beaverbrook had an additional motive for opposing the government's course over Ireland. In the autumn of 1920, he had spent three months in Canada, with a short visit to New York also. There, in the intervals of financial affairs, he learnt how deeply the outrages in Ireland were offending opinion in both Canada and the United States. Reverting to his former role of propagandist, he addressed a meeting of the leading editors and columnists in New York. He emphasized the British efforts at compromise and urged the opening of negotiations.

Beaverbrook had preached an acceptable compromise since before the war, when he was a good deal more steadfast for it than either Law or Asquith. What he always wanted was what ultimately came about: freedom for the south, and preservation of the Union in the north. It did not trouble him that he was nominally still a member of the Unionist party and, as the outrages mounted, he imposed his outlook on The Daily Express also. Beaverbrook turned to Captain Craig, now prime minister of Northern Ireland, whom he had known when they were both in the house of commons before the war. He asked whether the Ulster

[1] For the two Irish parliaments set up by the Government of Ireland Act, 1920.

Unionists would yield over the rest of Ireland if they got security in the north. Craig answered that they would. Armed with this, Beaverbrook approached de Valera through Tim Healy, and it was thanks to him that Craig and de Valera met. The meeting was barren. But in July, again thanks to information from Healy, The Daily Express had the exclusive news that de Valera and Lloyd George were to meet. The troubles were over, and Beaverbrook played a large part in ending them. Many years later Healy said: "If it had not been for Lord Beaverbrook the Free State would not be in existence today". This was true. There is however no independent evidence for Beaverbrook's further claim that he himself could have been the first governor general of the Free State if he had so wished.

When the Sinn Fein delegates came to London in October, The Daily Express called each day for conciliation and compromise. On this grave matter, Beaverbrook was not afraid to advocate what he thought was right even though the readers of The Daily Express did not want to hear it. Behind the scenes he played an even more decisive part. Healy came also, to the Vineyard, and he and Beaverbrook acted as secret advisers to the Sinn Feiners. On 17 October Lloyd George presented an ultimatum: would the Irish government concede to the British admiralty control of the foreshores and harbours of Ireland? The Sinn Feiners were in dismay. They could not yield this point at the outset. Yet they feared that, if they did not, negotiations would be broken off. On 22 October Healy's ingenuity provided the answer. The Irish need only ask: what is Ireland?, and the dispute over partition would be reopened. Healy's draft has survived in Beaverbrook's papers:

> The Govt is determined to wring a definite answer to the enquiry whether Ireland is ready to take her part in the British Empire or not. The Shins allege that the use of the word "Ireland" is a trap and that the Govt by the 1920 Partition Act split Ireland in twain and that by their legislation no such country now legally exists, and that two fictitious entities have been created known as Northern and Southern Ireland and that until the Govt inform them what their intentions are as to perpetuating the division of the country no question can arise as to their allegiance to the Crown and Empire because the Partition destroyed the status of Irish subjects of His Majesty and they will never consent to be known as Southern Irishmen.

Later on 22 October Beaverbrook went to Goulding's house at Wargrave, where Law, Churchill, and Birkenhead were spending the weekend. They were rejoicing that Lloyd George was about to force a break with the Irish. Beaverbrook was able to tell them that the Irish had escaped from the trap.[1] But the news did not shake them. Churchill insisted that

[1] This was the occasion to which Beaverbrook later transferred the reply as to his source of information: "Barnes's mistress".

repression was the only possible way to preserve a united Empire. Birkenhead worried about the unity of the Tory party, and Law about the lower income tax which a free Ireland would pay.

On 26 October, the situation changed. Lloyd George invited Birkenhead to join the Irish negotiations. Birkenhead would not risk his political life on his own and insisted that Churchill must be brought in also. Both men were flattered at being apparently treated by Lloyd George as equals. Both were won back to Lloyd George's side, Birkenhead more wholeheartedly than Churchill. Birkenhead also brought about a reconciliation between Beaverbrook and Lloyd George. On 27 October Beaverbrook dined with Lloyd George at Birkenhead's house. This was a renewal of old alliances with one exception: Churchill was there, but Lloyd George had ruled out Law. The Irish question stood between them. Lloyd George asked whether the opinions of The Daily Express in regard to Ireland were Beaverbrook's. Answer: Yes. Was Beaverbrook prepared to fight for them? Again: Yes. Even if a settlement with Ireland were defeated in the house of commons and there were a dissolution along with a revolt in the Conservative party? Answer: Yes, even then.

These were bold answers, given on grounds of high principle. Beaverbrook knew that he was running into danger and even risking his association with Law. Law said firmly that he disliked and indeed detested the political line which Beaverbrook had adopted. He warned Beaverbrook that he would lose some of his friends. Beaverbrook held bravely on. While the Irish negotiations were proceeding, Beaverbrook arranged several meetings between Lloyd George and Law, as he had once done between Asquith and Law. His efforts as a mediator were again attended with little success. Law would not be moved from his support of Ulster. In the end, his usual indolence extracted some concession: though he would not approve Lloyd George's actions, he would not actually lead an opposition against them. He may have been calculating that opposition would blow up without him. Others expected the same. Sir Samuel Hoare, who had been advocating a settlement with Ireland for some time, believed that the diehards were about to capture the Unionist party. He wrote to Beaverbrook on 16 November 1921: "I am sure things are going as we both expected, and that 90 p.c. of the Conservative party is drifting Die Hard". Beaverbrook himself wrote to Rothermere on 18 November: "The general impression is that the Conservative Party is hopelessly split. I hold this view".

These expectations were not fulfilled. On 5 December Lloyd George with miraculous skill reached agreement with the Sinn Feiners which satisfied a majority of them for the time being and yet preserved the separate existence of Ulster, or rather of six Ulster counties. Even Law spoke grudgingly in favour of the agreement when it was submitted to the house of commons. His attitude was consistent. Northern Ireland was secured. More than this, Law's first concern was with the unity of the Conservative party, to use its revived name. Previously it had looked as though promoting a settlement with Ireland would split the party. Now most Conservatives acquiesced, and it was opposing the settlement which would cause a split. Nevertheless the coalition was now insecure. The Conservative backbenchers were resentful at having to surrender their old position over Ireland, even though they recognized that this was inevitable. They were again beginning to move against their leaders as they had done in November 1916.

This time Beaverbrook was on the other side. He had promised to support Lloyd George over Ireland, and he kept his promise to the full. He also believed that, with the Conservative party in its present state of confusion, Lloyd George could again win a general election. And the programme? Beaverbrook thought he knew the answer: Empire unity and Imperial Preference. Lloyd George was attracted by the idea of a general election and maybe even by that of Empire. But his associates hesitated. Chamberlain doubted his own hold over the Conservative party, particularly with Law in the background. Churchill was against any infringement of Free Trade and equally against Lloyd George's plan for a reconciliation with Soviet Russia. Birkenhead dared not act without Churchill. The topic was thrashed over again and again. On 20 December there was a dinner party at Birkenhead's house. Salvidge, the Conservative leader in Liverpool, was among those present, and urged that Law must be brought in: otherwise there existed an alternative prime minister to whom discontented Tories could turn. As the party broke up, Beaverbrook grasped Salvidge's arm and remarked: "You've said it. 'Bring Bonar back'. They can't see it, but that was the best thing of the evening".[1]

After Christmas, the great men gathered at Cannes. Once more Beaverbrook urged a general election. He was powerfully supported by Worthington-Evans, the secretary for war. It seemed that the proposal for a general election would carry the day. Then a parrot broke in from its cage nearby: "You bloody fool! You bloody fool!" The meeting broke up in laughter. The general election was forgotten. There were more serious reasons against it. Younger, chairman of the Conservative party, and Chamberlain, the only one of the inner cabinet group not at Cannes, both opposed it. There was a way of overcoming this opposition. If Law were won back to Lloyd George's side, the Conservatives would be reduced to obedience.

Beaverbrook tried to pull off this stroke. He arranged a meeting between Lloyd George and Law in his hotel room at Cannes. Lloyd George

[1] Salvidge of Liverpool, 223.

invited Law to become foreign secretary. Law refused. The idea of a general election faded away. Beaverbrook wrote to Herbert Bruce, a Canadian MP, early in February 1922:

> Last January was the time for a General Election. George knew it but failed to seize the opportunity so that it is clear that he suffers too from the fault of indecision. It is always an early sign of declining powers.

To Macphail Beaverbrook painted a picture of universal gloom on 13 February:

> We are in a dreadful state. There is no prospect of recovery in Europe. At home, unemployment is gaining and Ireland is sinking into a state of anarchy. France is going mad and Germany is going bankrupt. Austria is in a starving state and Russia.

There was also a refusal on Beaverbrook's side to record. Canadian friends wished to run him for the post of high commissioner. He replied on 16 January: "I would rather die and go to Hell at once than have to take up my official residence at the Canadian High Commissioners office".

This was not the first high commissionership which Beaverbrook had refused. According to his account,[1] early in 1921 Lloyd George summoned him one evening from the Criterion, where he was entertaining the Dolly Sisters—a famous variety pair of the day—and offered to make him high commissioner to the General Assembly of the Church of Scotland. Beaverbrook, a son of the manse, was attracted, but he replied firmly that he was not suited to the office. "It was my intention to continue my practice of sitting up late into the night"—particularly with such company as the Dolly Sisters. Lloyd George turned to Law, who was also present, and said: "Geordie gets it". Geordie was the duke of Sutherland. Beaverbrook returned to the Criterion and found the duke of Sutherland dancing with one of the Dolly Sisters.

Beaverbrook could not resist giving fresh advice to Lloyd George, especially when he learnt that Churchill was planning to make a new coalition under the leadership of Austen Chamberlain—principally in order to defend Free Trade. On 13 March Beaverbrook sent a long letter to Lloyd George in Wales. Until a fortnight ago, he wrote, he had favoured a move to the Left, aimed at reuniting the Liberal party. "I think I should have found myself in sympathy with most of the policies which a Liberal Party would undertake under your leadership". Now it was becoming clear that Churchill was moving to the Right: "his principles are becoming more Tory". The answer to Churchill was obvious: bring back Law, always Churchill's enemy. Lloyd George and Law would be far stronger than Churchill and Chamberlain. "But if it is to be done, it

[1] Decline and Fall of Lloyd George, 107–8.

has to be done immediately". Two days later Beaverbrook sent a further
warning against Churchill:

> At the present moment, Winston undoubtedly considers himself heir to all
> the Caesars and, at least, part of their appurtenances. As you know he is
> subject to periods when the intensity of his imagination quite overbalances
> his judgement.

Finally on 19 March Beaverbrook urged Lloyd George to return at once
and demand a vote of confidence from the house of commons:

> I would make one further suggestion. In the course of your speech the
> main object of the attack should be the opposing newspapers. The Press is
> always unpopular with members of the Commons and you would rally a lot
> of sympathy.

This was curious advice to come from a press lord.

Lloyd George took some of Beaverbrook's advice. He returned from
Wales, asserted his authority over Churchill, and secured a vote of
confidence before going to the conference at Genoa. But he made no new
approach to Law, and on the great issue of a general election Beaverbrook
found him "really woolly in outlook, and confused in argument. . . . The
glitter of his supreme office held him in chains". Actually Lloyd George
was hoping that success at Genoa would save him: he would be the man
who won the peace. Beaverbrook reported to Borden early in April after
a gay dinner with Lloyd George and Law:

> The P.M. wants a chance at Genoa to re-make the peace of 1919. Bonar is
> no believer in the Genoa proposals. I am very firmly with George and a
> talkative supporter at that. . . . George will probably succeed at Genoa and
> he will have no difficulty in persuading the House to give him a chance.
>
> As to the future of the George administration. Everything depends on the
> cunning of the Master. The Tories are divided and ready to unite in deter-
> mining that their leader is their devastating and destroying influence. On
> every appearance of such union the Master rolls into their midst a modern
> apple of discord—entitled Genoa, this time—The unity of the Party is for-
> gotten, for the time being, only to be remembered again when the last discord
> on policy is forgotten or solved.
>
> There is a real difficulty in the offing which the Master may find to be
> insurmountable. It is Ireland. If his policy is moderately successful—of
> which there is little hope—he may go further. If Ireland fails and Collins
> fails our last Coalition will collapse and Party government will prosper.
> Personally I believe in George's Irish policy whether the result is peaceful
> Government or revolutionary chaos for "Dark Rosaleen".[1]

[1] Civil war was raging in Ireland between the supporters and opponents of the
Anglo-Irish treaty.

Beaverbrook repeated much the same themes when he wrote to G. G. Foster on 19 April:

> We shall have an election over here shortly. George has lost his opportunity. He did not take his tide at the flood during last January and after the supposed Irish settlement. He may get another chance and next time I hope he will not be so slow but that he will launch his barque on the waters at once.
>
> I cannot tell what is the outlook for Ireland. . . . It seems to me that the situation resembles the position in Mexico, with which we are both so familiar.

Ireland proved less dangerous to Lloyd George than Beaverbrook expected: the civil war ended in victory for the Free State forces. On the other hand, the conference at Genoa was a failure. Lloyd George remained prime minister, apparently supported by a great majority, but with no constructive policy to offer.

Beaverbrook, too, seems to have been at a loss for suggestions. Perhaps also he was busy with The Daily Express, which made its first substantial profit in the year ending 30 June 1922. Moreover, with Northcliffe mortally ill, there were rumours that Beaverbrook was about to buy The Times. In later years Beaverbrook always denied that there was any truth in these rumours, which have certainly left no trace in his correspondence. But of course it is unusual to record enterprises which fail. Beaverbrook kept up his social relations with his friends in the cabinet. On 15 June, for instance, as he wrote to Macphail, when in bed with rheumatism, he had a "very jolly" bedside dinner party with Lloyd George, Churchill, and Birkenhead. Two bottles of Pommery 1906 were drunk, surely a modest ration. However, according to Beaverbrook, there were only three consumers. "Birkenhead doesn't drink in these days. But he was the gayest guest and talked the most". Elsewhere Beaverbrook has recorded that Birkenhead was "like Mr. Bonar Law, a teetotaller".[1]

An unforeseen storm was rising in the east which would destroy the Coalition and drive Lloyd George from power for ever. At the end of the war, when the Ottoman Empire was in ruins, Greece had been given Smyrna and its hinterland in Asia Minor. The three great allies—France, Great Britain, and Italy—took control of Constantinople. By 1922 Greek strength was exhausted. The new nationalist Turkey, under Kemal, had made a remarkable recovery and was preparing to drive the Greek armies into the sea. France and Italy, though still sharing in the occupation of Constantinople, had made their peace with Kemal, and the French were supplying his forces with arms. The Greeks appealed for British aid of

---

[1] Success (1921), 46. Beaverbrook's remark was perhaps made by way of encouragement, or alternatively of provocation. He bet Birkenhead a large sum—reputedly £1,000—that the latter could not remain a teetotaller throughout 1921. Birkenhead held out until the early morning of 6 December, when the excitement of signing the Irish treaty led him to take a glass of brandy. For this, it was worth losing his bet.

the same sort. None was given, though the Greeks were told to fight on. They asked to be allowed to occupy Constantinople in exchange for Smyrna. This, too, was refused. Lloyd George was the only steadfast friend of the Greeks in the cabinet, but the other ministers failed to go against him. If the Turks triumphed over the Greeks, British policy would be in grave disarray.

Beaverbrook's attitude to the Near East was clear and simple: he was opposed to any British commitment there beyond control of the Suez Canal. He wanted to make peace with the Turks. He was against thrusting Jews on to the Arabs of Palestine. He pressed for British withdrawal from Irak. Beaverbrook's imperialism was oceanic, indifferent to both Europe and the Near East. As he wrote many years later:

> Our soldiers from Britain and from the Dominions had died for the sake of Belgium, for the sake of the White Russians, for the subjugation of Ireland. Why should the Empire give yet another generation of youth to enable Greece to seize territory from Turkey?[1]

Until this moment Beaverbrook had been very much on Lloyd George's side, principally because of Ireland, and had been trying to win Law's support for the Coalition. With the approach of the Near Eastern crisis, he gradually swung the other way. He still wanted to bring Law back, but now with the object of overthrowing Lloyd George, not of sustaining him.

In August 1922 Beaverbrook went to Deauville, at that time his favourite resort. There he met the Aga Khan, whom he had often advised on Canadian investments. The Aga, as a leading spokesman of the Moslem world, was anxious to reconcile Great Britain and Turkey. He urged Beaverbrook to visit Turkey and promised to arrange a meeting with Kemal. Beaverbrook agreed to go. Evidently he did not yet appreciate how deeply Lloyd George was committed to the Greek side and was anxious to get some sort of message or commission from the British government. He therefore invited Lloyd George, Churchill, and Birkenhead to Cherkley for the weekend of 26 August. He made no headway. Lloyd George remained confident that the Greeks were the stronger and in any case was only interested in discussing the prospects for a general election. Churchill was violently against the Greeks. Birkenhead, though reluctant to disagree with Lloyd George, went along with Churchill. Lloyd George and Churchill fell into dispute over the failure to hold a general election in the previous January. Lloyd George declared that Churchill had opposed it "because you thought I would win". Churchill did not deny the accusation. The quarrel left Beaverbrook in a dilemma. He agreed with Churchill and disagreed with Lloyd George over the Greeks. On

[1] Decline and Fall of Lloyd George, 150.

general grounds, he preferred Lloyd George, in his opinion a Radical imperialist, to Churchill, the Free Trader. Perhaps it was now he changed his tactical aim. Instead of bringing back Law to sustain Lloyd George against Churchill, he would use Law to sweep Lloyd George and all his associates from office.

Beaverbrook received no commission from the government. When he left for Constantinople on 27 August, he announced only that he was doing so "at the request of the editor of The Sunday Express". The tendering of this "request" by the editor must have been an interesting occasion. By the time Beaverbrook reached Constantinople the situation had changed. The Turks had won. At Smyrna they were driving the Greeks into the sea. Beaverbrook resolved to return home at once, there to play the role of peacemaker between Great Britain and Turkey. On his way back he stopped in Athens and sent a vivid report of the scenes at the Piraeus. It appeared in The Sunday Express on 17 September:

> As each haggard infantryman limped on shore he was deprived of his rifle; but every second man had no rifle left. The docks were a litter of discarded material and accoutrements. . . . The men drifted off into the town with two months' leave (in the middle of a war!) in a hopeless, disorderly stream, with nothing to distinguish them but a dirty uniform and a transportation pass to some distant home.

Beaverbrook arrived in England on 20 September. He found that the decision for war had apparently been taken. Lloyd George had resolved to fight the Turks and, to Beaverbrook's astonishment, Churchill and Birkenhead, once so firm against the Greeks, were now supporting him.

Each day at the Vineyard, Beaverbrook preached peace: Birkenhead to lunch on 21 September, Birkenhead and Churchill on 22 September, Birkenhead and Lloyd George on 23 September. It was all in vain: Lloyd George inveighed against the atrocities which the Turks were said to be committing at Smyrna. On 24 September Beaverbrook published a letter in The Sunday Express instead of his promised article:

> On my return from Constantinople I am unable to furnish you with the article on the Near Eastern situation which I promised you for to-day, because I cannot support in its entirety the policy of His Majesty's Government.
> Neither can I criticise that policy at a moment when the prospects of a peaceful and satisfactory settlement of our differences with Turkey depend on British public opinion showing a united front. . . .
> The great interest of Britain and Turkey alike is peace, and so long as both Governments recognise this fact and are working for its realisation I will make my own humble contribution of silence.

Beaverbrook did not make this humble contribution for long. He became increasingly convinced that the government were set on war, and he was resolved to stop them. On 29 September the government in fact authorized an ultimatum to the Turks, which fortunately their general on the spot did not deliver. On the same day, Beaverbrook published in The Daily Express a long article entitled The Path of Honour, in which he insisted that a conference would reach a secure peace and that no border clashes should be allowed to provoke a war. Two days later, on 1 October, he contributed to The Sunday Express an article on The Fall of Greece. He blamed the British government for Greece's sad state and wrote: "For this folly on the part of our Premier we owe some debt to the Greek people". He therefore urged that British resources of wheat should be used in order to save the Greeks from famine.

Throughout this time Law had remained silent. He was no doubt embarrassed by the fact that he had been a leading member of the government when the pro-Greek policy had been embarked on. Beaverbrook argued with him in vain. On 5 October Beaverbrook said to him: "Lloyd George, Churchill and Birkenhead mean war. . . . You alone can save us from war". Law was stirred and perhaps even more so by the news that Curzon was leading a peace group in the cabinet. If there were to be a revolt, Law did not intend that it should be led by someone else. On the evening of 6 October, Law came to the Vineyard and told Beaverbrook that he had written a letter to The Times. Its vital sentence ran: "We cannot alone act as the policemen of the world". If the French would not cooperate with us against the Turks, "we shall have no alternative except to imitate the Government of the United States and to restrict our attention to the safeguarding of the more immediate interests of the Empire".

Beaverbrook was delighted. On 8 October he wrote triumphantly in The Sunday Express under the heading, The British Empire First:

> Until yesterday no statesman of the first rank had raised the flag of non-interference round which men of any political creed, weary of strife, and seeking prosperity, or at least peace, can rally. . . .
> The only thing that Great Britain can do is to set other nations an example by working hard and minding its own business and limiting its expenditure. Such a policy would do more to restore the prosperity of the world than all the "crusades" of the Coalition Government could achieve in a decade.

Law was however still far from deciding on open conflict with Lloyd George. He hesitated as he had formerly hesitated to go against Asquith. Birkenhead tried to act as mediator. At his suggestion, Beaverbrook invited Lloyd George and Law to lunch at the Vineyard on 9 October. Lloyd George urged Law to rejoin the coalition government. Law refused and declared that the Conservative backbenchers were set on resuming their independence. But it was still not clear that he would lead their revolt.

On 10 October the immediate war-crisis ended. An armistice with the Turks was signed at Mudros. The way was opened for the peace negotiations which reached a successful conclusion later at Lausanne. The political crisis was only beginning. On 11 October the cabinet decided to hold an immediate general election on a coalition ticket. On 11 October Beaverbrook wrote a dramatic survey to Dwight Morrow in New York:

> We are now in the throes of a political crisis. The failure of the Prime Minister's Greek policy has resulted in a complete collapse of his prestige with the Conservatives. Practically the whole Party is anxious to withdraw. Though some of his Ministers remain loyal to him in public, they state frankly in private that they wish he would withdraw and allow them to save their own souls. The immediate future will decide whether the Conservative Party is to remain intact, or whether the Prime Minister is strong enough to split it. It will be a great achievement to have smashed two parties in one short administration. Yet that is what he can claim if he succeeds in destroying the Tories.
>
> Bonar Law is the obvious choice for the Conservative leadership. He alone can lead the quarrelling groups. With extraordinary astuteness and much mental agility, he has offended none of them, and, at the same time yielded nothing.
>
> The only doubt lies in his own personality. At the critical moment a desire to walk humbly before the men of his own generation may destroy his opportunity for a place with posterity.
>
> I have not been so intrigued for a long time. It is like the beginning of the drug-taking habit. . . .

Beaverbrook's estimate of Law was, as usual, somewhat flattering. There was not much astuteness or mental agility in his hesitations, which were still continuing. Beaverbrook was also wrong in supposing that the Conservative ministers wished to be rid of Lloyd George. After some backsliding, particularly on the part of Birkenhead, they had resolved to stand by him to the last.

Austen Chamberlain, technically leader of the party, summoned the Conservative members of parliament to a meeting at the Carlton Club on 19 October. He hoped to browbeat them into continuing the coalition. For the rebels, all turned on the question whether Law would attend and speak on the other side. Law would not make up his mind. Beaverbrook wisely would not make up his mind for him and, when they met, talked on everything except politics. On 18 October Beaverbrook sat all day at the Vineyard. No outgoing calls were made on the telephone so that all lines should be free. At eight in the evening Beaverbrook was at last summoned. By then he had developed a temperature, perhaps due to a cold. Law showed Beaverbrook a letter which he had drafted to the chairman of his constituency organization in Glasgow, stating that he did not intend to stand at the general election. He asked Beaverbrook's opinion. Beaverbrook remembered the incident in 1911, when he had thrown a similar letter of renunciation by Law on the fire, much to Law's anger. He therefore merely replied: "The letter is too long". However, after pleas from Law, he put forward his arguments, "concluding on a high Imperial note". Law said: "I am going to the meeting". Beaverbrook hurried from the room and telephoned the news to the Press Association and The Daily Express. Then he retired to bed with two hot-water bottles and some rum and sugar. Beaverbrook was by no means alone in persuading Law to attend the meeting, but he gave the final push.

Next morning Law rang and said he had had second thoughts. Beaverbrook replied that it was too late: the news of his decision was in all the papers. To make matters doubly sure, Beaverbrook drove round to Law's house, picked him up, and delivered him at the door of the Carlton Club. At the Conservative meeting, Baldwin fired the first shot against coalition. Law finished it off. In Beaverbrook's phrase, "His words were little more than a formal burial service read over the dead body of coalition". By 185 votes to 88 the Conservatives resolved to fight the election as an independent party. There was an ironical twist at the end which Beaverbrook left out of his published account, no doubt saving it for his unwritten Age of Baldwin:

> Bonar Law came down the stairs of the Club alone. He was the man of the hour, the victor today, the Premier tomorrow. His slight figure, with the deepset eyes and the lined features, held everyone's gaze. No one among the onlookers paid much attention to the stocky little man, five feet nine inches in height, with the florid, almost bucolic features, the face still unmarked by care, the gait yet unhindered by twinges of gout, who was following his leader. Not one of those present gave a thought to the possibility that in the guise of this unremarkable figure, this "typical Englishman", destiny was stalking forward. Stanley Baldwin took, that morning, an obscure place on the stairway. But just the same he was the man of the future.

Lloyd George resigned at once. Law became prime minister, after first securing election as leader of the Conservative party. Few of the prominent Conservatives agreed to join him. Birkenhead, Balfour, Austen Chamberlain, and Sir Robert Horne all turned their backs. Churchill did not need to do so. Law invited McKenna to become chancellor of the exchequer. McKenna had no confidence that Law could win the election and therefore refused to join him. Baldwin received the vacant place by default. In this almost accidental way, he became the second man in the government and heir apparent to Law. Beaverbrook remarked: "To the memory of Reginald McKenna he must surely owe a considerable debt of gratitude".

For the second time Beaverbrook had made a prime minister or at least had helped to make one. Many have exaggerated his achievement. In 1922, as in 1916, to use his own favourite phrase, he did not create the opportunity; he took advantage of it. The fundamental cause of

Lloyd George's fall was the discontent of the Conservative backbenchers, as the fundamental cause of Asquith's had been the general dissatisfaction with the conduct of the war. On each occasion Beaverbrook pushed Law forward, but with less effect than he subsequently claimed. Law took his own time. He moved in 1916 only when Asquith refused to compromise. He moved in 1922 only when the Conservative party threatened to split asunder. Beaverbrook's essential contribution in 1922 was to get Law to the Carlton Club meeting, and he would not have succeeded unless Law had himself resolved to go. At most, Beaverbrook imposed resolution upon the irresolute.

There is no indication that Beaverbrook was offered a place in the government, and he would certainly have refused one. This was not from a desire for "power without responsibility"—a charge which the disgruntled coalitionists were already levelling against him. It was from a determination to preserve his independence with all the responsibility which that entailed. He sent Law a declaration of this independence on 21 October:

> I think it would be better if I remained outside, doing everything in my power to secure your election through the columns of the *Express* only.
> In consequence I am not speaking with Hulton or Morden[1] on questions of support. . . . I advise you to send Younger after both. . . .
> I am convinced that you must look after your propaganda. I would advise your propagandists to study the figure of Lincoln—and this is the first and last word of advice that I offer.

This cryptic advice presumably referred to Law's integrity; or, as Lloyd George put it, he was "honest to the verge of simplicity". Beaverbrook may have thought that Law would do better if not associated too closely with a "press lord". But he also had considerable points of difference from Law where he meant to take his own line.

In the account which he wrote many years later,[2] Beaverbrook implied that the greatest difference was over Empire Free Trade. It is true that Law, following the urgent advice of leading Conservatives, gave a pledge against protection and food taxes. This advice was given even by Amery, a most persistent protectionist. It is not clear whether Beaverbrook knew this at the time. He learnt it many years later from Amery's memoirs and, when on top of this he felt that Amery had in general treated Law slightingly, he at once severed relations after a friendly correspondence lasting over twenty years. He noted (1954): "Amery treated Bonar Law very badly. . . . I do not propose to answer him now or in the future", and he stuck to his resolution. None of this was apparent in 1922. Then

---

[1] Sir Edward Hulton and Grant Morden, two leading newspaper proprietors.
[2] Decline and Fall of Lloyd George, 212.

Beaverbrook accepted the renunciation of protection without a word of regret or complaint.

The causes of dispute then were quite other. The first was over the British forces in Mesopotamia and Palestine. Beaverbrook was for clearing out at once, just as he had been for clearing out of Turkey. He wrote to Law on 25 October:

> I think I ought to write and tell you that I really cannot follow you on Mesopotamia and Palestine. I am for the clean cut, as I have always been. . . .
>
> You must not imagine for a moment that this means that I, as [about the only] a rare newspaper proprietor who does not want or wont take anything from you in the way of honours or office, mean to declare hostility to your administration. On the contrary I am going to help you all I can in the circumstances. But I feel so strongly on the Middle Eastern question that I am going to bring public pressure to bear on the Conservative candidates in the Constituencies to pledge themselves to the bag and baggage policy of evacuation in Mesopotamia and Palestine. . . .

Law replied gently on the same day:

> It would indeed be a strange thing if you added to my troubles and worries in the position into which I have fallen and I am sure you will not do that. You yourself said on Sunday that though you wanted a bag and baggage policy you realized that I might find it impossible.
>
> There is nothing more that I can say.

Beaverbrook was not shaken by this appeal. On 5 November he pronounced for bag and baggage in The Sunday Express:

> The most urgent issue of the general election is that we should evacuate Mesopotamia and Palestine bag and baggage *and at once.* . . .
>
> Britain is under no treaty obligation to remain in Mesopotamia. Her mandate has no time limit either to force her out or to compel her to remain. . . .
>
> The British garrison in Palestine is there to support 30,000 Jews against 300,000 Arabs. If the British garrison is not used for this purpose it is useless. The moment it is so used the expense and responsibility becomes unlimited. . . .
>
> I am no Anti-Semite, as everyone who has read my writings knows. I am a friend of British Jews. It is their enemies who want to brand them in this country with the undying unpopularity of forcing the British soldier to fight and die and the British citizen to pay for the national home in Palestine. It is the Zionist who is the most dangerous foe of the patriotic British Jew.

Beaverbrook's advocacy did not prevail. Great Britain remained in Mesopotamia and Palestine for many years. All that he foresaw came to pass. In retrospect it is difficult to resist the conclusion that, as with Ireland, it would have been better for the British name and British fortunes if Beaverbrook's advice had been taken.

Beaverbrook's other difference with Law was over tactics. Law, and the Conservative central office also, had little confidence of victory and proposed to make an electoral pact with Lloyd George's Coalition Liberals, almost as they had done in the "coupon" election of 1918: if Coalition Liberals would withdraw in some constituencies, Conservatives would withdraw in others. Apart from timidity, there was perhaps a sentimental regret towards old associates and, most of all, an unavowed belief that right-thinking men should unite against the "Bolshevistic" Labour party. In that case, why overthrow the Coalition at all? Law seemed to be advocating Coalition under new management, or not even that. Lloyd George's Liberals would return in sufficient numbers to hold the balance, and he would be again master, even if not prime minister.

Beaverbrook would have none of this "saw off" as he called it. He had been against Coalition from the beginning and was not likely to change now. He knew that the Coalition was unpopular throughout the country and therefore held that Law would become stronger the more he assailed, and was assailed by, his former associates. In Beaverbrook's opposition to any continuation of coalition, there was a deeper political purpose, which rested on a clear-cut analysis of the British constitution. In a sentence, he wanted to restore the two-party system. Obviously, he wished to restore the independence of the Conservative party. Equally, though less obviously, he wanted to restore the independence of the Liberal party, and this could be done only by purging it of its Coalition taint. Beaverbrook expounded this outlook in an article on The Opposition which appeared in The Sunday Express on 19 November, immediately after the Coalition Liberals had been discomfited at the general election. He declared his conviction that the Liberal party would revive and that Lloyd George would lead it:

> The ex-Premier is by nature and conviction a Radical. His only Tory leaning has been a tendency to toy with Tariff Reform—and no great importance need be attached to that. . . .
> Now that the Centre Party idea has broken down, as it was always bound to do, he will go back to his temperamental home. Mr. Lloyd George will make himself the leader of the Opposition in the House in the coming years because he is the greatest force on the Liberal and Labour side.

Beaverbrook went on to foretell that Lloyd George would work with the Labour party. He continued:

> For my own part I should welcome such a development. It would recreate the party system on an understandable basis, and while revivifying Liberalism it would be a check on the extremists of Labour. One of the fundamental blunders of the whole argument in favour of the continuance of Coalition was the view it propounded for dealing with the Labour Party.

Labour was to be treated as a kind of political leper—with the inevitable consequence that some day it would be returned single-handed to power embittered and absolutely devoid of any experience of administration or, indeed, of the world as a whole. The consequence must have been a disaster on a first-rate scale. *But a Liberal–Labour administration would not bring with it those risks. It would simply be a strong Radical Government....*

The formation of a strong Opposition is just as necessary as the creation of a strong Government, and for the same reason. Both are essential to the proper working of the British Constitution.

This article wonderfully illuminates Beaverbrook's political attitude, both in its vision and its defects. He was a true independent, wishing to see a clear and healthy conflict between Conservative and Radical—a wish appropriately fulfilled in Canada, though not in Great Britain. On the other hand, he did not understand the motives which divided even the most moderate Labour men from the Liberal party, nor did he grasp how gravely Lloyd George had tarnished his Radical standing by his actions when prime minister. Beaverbrook knew that Law would remain in office only a short time—Law himself had wished to announce that he would serve as prime minister only for one year; and it is tempting to surmise that Beaverbrook, even if only half-consciously, looked forward to a time when he would be again Lloyd George's man. After all, he had always shown a divided loyalty in his relations with Law and Lloyd George: personally with Law and in policy nearer to Lloyd George. Once Law retired, Beaverbrook would like nothing better than a new alliance with Lloyd George, a Radical Imperialist like himself.

These are remote speculations. Beaverbrook's immediate task was to destroy the electoral relics of Coalition. While Law and the Conservative central office were arranging mutual withdrawals with Coalition Liberals, Beaverbrook was doing his best to wreck the deals. Local Conservative associations needed little encouragement to revolt, and it is impossible to tell how much Beaverbrook helped the revolt along. In The Decline and Fall of Lloyd George he claims that he launched a number of Conservative candidates and in some cases paid their expenses. In conversation he even took the credit for all the 56 Conservatives who ran against Coalition Liberals. His records provide no evidence for this general prompting nor for any financial assistance except in one case, which certainly left its mark. This was East Dorset where F. E. Guest, Churchill's cousin and formerly Coalition Liberal chief whip, had reached agreement "satisfactorily and constitutionally" with the local Conservatives. Beaverbrook stirred up Ralph Hall Caine to run as an independent Conservative and promised to pay his election expenses.

Guest, who had dined at the Vineyard only a few days before, was indignant and wrote to Beaverbrook on 5 November 1922:

Guided by my instincts I have now for nearly nine years consistently defended you, in the world in which we both live from misinterpretation and attack.

The world has said that you were an adventurer with a closed past, that you were subtle, ambitious, unscrupulous and unreliable and that the word friendship was unknown to you.

Can it be the world was right in its diagnosis and advice and that I have been wrong in adhering to my belief that you had, a sometimes hidden heart of gold—!

I remember towards the end of the war helping you over the stile into the Govt, so that having once faced the music of public opinion you could lay your foundations in British public life for all time.

Have you forgotten your hesitancy?

Beaverbrook replied on 7 November:

I really do not feel inclined to go into a kind of balance sheet of the past services we may have done each other in politics—except to deny the suggestion that I desired office, or accepted it, at your hands. . . .

Your proposal appears to be that I should withdraw opposition on account of friendship.

This argument did not move me when Churchill insisted on fighting the Russians, and it does not move me now when you and your friends are turned out for trying to fight the Turks. I have been working against the Coalition for weeks—ever since this present crisis began—and I am utterly opposed to the continuance of the alliance between the followers of Lloyd George and Conservatives, either in the constituencies or at Westminster. I cannot put you in a category apart in response to an appeal based on friendship.

Beaverbrook descended on Poole and spoke repeatedly on Hall Caine's behalf. Hall Caine won by a 5,000 majority in a traditionally Liberal seat. In all, 56 coalition Liberals were challenged by Conservatives, and only 2 of them were returned. The other 55 supporters of Lloyd George in the new House crept home only because of the "pact". The Conservatives won 345 seats, a majority of 77 over all parties.

This was for Beaverbrook a moment of triumph. For years past, he had preached Law's superlative merits, and few had shared his judgement. Now apparently the electorate did so despite the taunts of the brilliant men around Lloyd George. Beaverbrook's task was done. With governments, as with mergers, once they were made, he turned to other interests. He still hoped to win Law back to Imperial Preference, but he was content to wait. Law spent Christmas at Cherkley—for the last time. He was oppressed by the conflict between France and Germany over reparations. Beaverbrook encouraged him to keep Great Britain out of the conflict, and Law did so at the beginning of January. Beaverbrook had good reason to be content with the government which he had helped to create.

Beaverbrook had also reason to be content with the outcome of the backing which he had earlier given to Lloyd George over Ireland. In December 1922 the Irish Free State came formally into existence, and Beaverbrook's old friend Tim Healy became the first governor general. On 13 December Beaverbrook gave a dinner in Healy's honour. There were 34 guests, prominent among them H. G. Wells. There were also some refusals, which illustrated the survival of Unionist resentments. Gideon Murray, for example, wrote that he did not wish to criticize Beaverbrook's action in giving the dinner, "because it must be done if we are to collaborate with I. F. State . . . but I positively cannot bring myself to meet the Governor General at dinner".

Beaverbrook's content did not last. Almost without warning, he was drawn into a new dispute which was to have a profound effect on his future. The question at issue was the settlement of the British war debt to the United States. Great Britain was paying interest, as she had contracted to do, at 5%—£46 million a year. This was a heavy sum. It was obviously desirable both to reduce the rate of interest and to fund the debt, so that the principal could be gradually paid off. In Beaverbrook's opinion, the time was not ripe. In another year or two, he believed, easier terms of settlement could be obtained, as indeed proved to be the case when France and Italy, the two other great debtors, negotiated later. On this subject, Beaverbrook spoke with authority, or, as he put it, "when it comes to Finance, I am a tub which stands on its own bottom". He was a] financier of great experience and knew the American situation, both political and financial, at first hand. Any British government would have been wise to take his advice.

Law does not seem to have done so, and Baldwin, perhaps already jealous of Beaverbrook's influence, also ignored him. Lloyd George had promised to negotiate with the Americans, and Law felt that he must keep this promise for the sake of British credit. Baldwin was dispatched to America, in the company of Montagu Norman, governor of the Bank of England. One of the few surviving fragments from The Age of Baldwin tells the story:

> Baldwin had been given precise instructions by Bonar Law. He was to talk but not to commit himself. He was not to give any promise or even indication of Britain's willingness or capacity to settle. . . .
>
> But in Washington Baldwin came under powerful influences. Sir Robert Horne, who was on a private visit to the United States, Sir Auckland Geddes, the British Ambassador, and Paul Cravath, an American business man strongly pro-British in his general attitude, all pressed on him the necessity of a settlement of some sort on the grounds that only thus could lasting good relations and collaboration between the two countries be achieved.
>
> Baldwin went from Washington to New York. There he stayed at the house of J. P. Morgan. He spent much time lying on a sofa in the library, listening to the advice and arguments of his host.

Now Morgan and his friends were all Gold Standard men. Their life's business was international finance. And international finance, they had discovered, could not work smoothly in the absence of the Gold Standard. But an essential prerequisite of the restoration of the Gold Standard was the settlement of Britain's debt to America. . . .

Suddenly Baldwin sent a cable to Bonar Law asking for authorization to settle. . . . The prime minister cabled back: "Come home".

Baldwin returned. On his arrival at Southampton, he gave the proposed terms of settlement to the press and declared that they were the best which could be obtained. Subsequently, according to Beaverbrook, "Baldwin exclaimed penitently that he would rather have bitten his tongue off than given the interview. But the mischief had been done". The Sunday Express violently attacked the settlement the day after Baldwin landed. Law descended on Cherkley and rebuked Beaverbrook "for seeking to prejudge the whole issue before the Cabinet had taken a decision". Beaverbrook was impenitent, the more so as he knew that Law agreed with him. Indeed Law told him that he intended to resign unless the cabinet rejected the settlement. Beaverbrook urged him to fight. The next day, all the cabinet except Philip Lloyd-Greame (later Lord Swinton) favoured acceptance. Law consulted Keynes, who was strongly against the settlement. He also consulted McKenna, who is also said to have advised rejection. A letter which McKenna wrote to Beaverbrook on 18 January 1932 shows that this is not correct:

> I did not think Bonar's case a very good one.
>
> The American claim was based on a series of promises to pay signed by the British representative in Washington—at the time I think Reading—and expressed to be on behalf of the British Government. Lloyd George was then Prime Minister, and Bonar Chancellor of the Exchequer, and they had approved the American terms. . . . Undeniably Bonar had a direct responsibility for the original contracts with the United States.
>
> The Baldwin terms were accepted by the whole of the Cabinet with the exception of Bonar. . . . Bonar, you and I, thought the terms bad and that better could have been obtained, but they were certainly a considerable improvement on the original contract. I felt, and still feel, that if Bonar had resigned on the issue that the terms were not good enough, with his whole Cabinet and public opinion generally, so far as I could see, against him, it might have been regarded as a refusal to honour his own signature although his colleagues and the public were ready to do so. He made his protest—now public property—and I did not think he would be justified in going further.

Law in fact told the cabinet that he would resign if the terms were accepted. His colleagues unanimously implored him to stay, and apparently even Beaverbrook added his voice. The terms were accepted, and Law did not resign. Beaverbrook commented: "you cannot blame the master if the office boy throws his cigarette stump into the waste paper basket and burns down the building".

At the time the controversy seemed to leave no mark. Law and Beaverbrook had made their protest and had been overruled, and that was all. Baldwin gave no outward sign of resentment, even if he distrusted Beaverbrook's intimacy with Law. Later Beaverbrook came to believe that the controversy "marked the beginning of a personal and political antagonism which was to colour many of the political events of the times, and which nothing could for long assuage". He also believed that the debt settlement was the cause of many subsequent evils. He wrote during the second world war:

> The settlement led by an inevitable process to the Gold Standard, and so on to deflation, the General Strike, the dreaded growth of unemployment, the crisis of 1931, and to all that long period of frustration, poverty and uncertainty in Europe which made possible the growth and temporary triumph of the false ideologies we fight today.

In 1923 Beaverbrook was fighting a different battle. The Sunday Express of 4 February carried an article by him entitled Bring Home the Bayonets. This renewed the campaign which he had told Law before the election that he intended to pursue. The message was, as before, clear out: withdraw British troops from Germany, from Constantinople, from Mesopotamia, and from Palestine. "Get back to the peace spirit of work and leave Europe and the East alone". Beaverbrook himself went to Palestine, taking James Douglas with him. There he met a large Arab deputation and promised them the cooperation of Express newspapers "in a common hostility to Zionism". In England the Zionist press accused Beaverbrook of anti-semitism. He was able to answer that he had first been warned against Zionism by a deputation of influential British Jews, who came to him when he was minister of information.

Back in England, Beaverbrook once more extolled Law and his government, despite its failure to withdraw from the Middle East. On 22 April he announced in The Sunday Express: "This is the best Government which the present generation has seen". And of Bonar Law: "His simplicity and courage have been proof against either threat or blandishment. . . . His frankness and honesty are almost unparalleled in the history of our politics". The praise no doubt came from the heart, but it had also a practical purpose. Law was flagging. He had lost his voice. He was low in spirits, and a holiday at Torquay did not restore him. Beaverbrook still supposed that Law's illness was "neurasthenic", as perhaps it had been in 1921 and as Beaverbrook's often were. He sought to inspire Law. He enlisted Rothermere, whose earlier opinion of Law had been almost contemptuous. Thus he wrote to Beaverbrook on 25 October

1922: "Bonar has made a hash of things as usual", and he refused to support the Conservative cause at the election. Now Rothermere was won over. On 26 April 1923 he wrote to Beaverbrook:

> If Bonar places himself in my hands I will hand him down to posterity at the end of three years as one of the most successful Prime Ministers in history, and if there is a general election I will get him returned again. This may sound boastful but I know exactly how it can be done.

This embarrassing offer of help did not restore Law to health. On 1 May he left England on a Mediterranean cruise. Beaverbrook began to accept the prospect that Law might resign, though he had no inkling of anything worse. On 7 May he wrote lightheartedly to R. B. Bennett:

> The political situation here is very uncertain. If the Prime Minister retires, the succession will be stoutly disputed by Baldwin and Curzon. If I am in good form and sufficiently interested, I will certainly start a dark horse in the race. It is quite likely that such a starter might first pass the winning post; but the truth is that I do not care who becomes Prime Minister and my only desire is to have no responsibility for supporting the Administration in the columns of The Daily Express.

On 10 May Beaverbrook further elaborated his views in writing to Borden, and this time he revealed the dark horse:

> Here we have (1) Curzon with his claim supported by the senior members of the Government who are not competing with him, but handicapped by his personal unpopularity (2) Baldwin with the younger members of the Government who are influential, and closer in touch with the machine and the constituencies, and then (3) the possibility of a dark horse winning if Curzon and Baldwin cannot come to terms. The dark horse is Lord Derby— who would bring Austen Chamberlain back to the Government as his contribution.
>
> If Curzon is to succeed, he must come to an accommodation with Baldwin. If Baldwin is to oust Curzon, he must work the Press in his own interest—an art for which apparently he has no inclination or talent. . . . Baldwin is in fact in the position of a man who has a stronger hand than he realises. For Curzon could not be premier if he resigned; while Baldwin could be if Curzon went. Only however in the event of a complete disagreement between these two principals and some sign or fear of a party rupture, would Derby's candidature become a serious possibility.
>
> This is the situation as I see it to-day, and it obviously calls for an honest broker. You may be inclined to ask why I do not undertake the role. My answer is that if you back a man for the Premiership, you are more or less obliged to support him afterwards and I should prefer the chance of regaining a complete independence for my own policies.

The situation developed faster than Beaverbrook expected. On 8 May Law broke off his cruise. He landed at Genoa and went to Aix-les-Bains.

8

J. C. C. Davidson, who was with him, wired urgently that Beaverbrook
should join them.[1] On 15 May Beaverbrook arrived in Aix and, seeing
Law's condition, at once proposed a move to Paris, where Horder could
come over for a consultation. On 17 May Horder examined Law and
then took Beaverbrook for a walk down the Champs-Elysées. He gave
his diagnosis: Law had an incurable cancer of the throat and would be
dead within six months.

Beaverbrook went back to Law and said, with simulated cheerfulness:
"My friend, I encourage you to resign. You have become so determined
to go that you will not recover until you get nervous relief". Law cheered
up at once. He had one remaining worry—whom to recommend as his
successor? Beaverbrook stumbled on a way out. He went round to the
British embassy in order to arrange a game of bridge for Law with Lord
Crewe. While there, he mentioned Law's worry. Crewe replied that there
was no need for Law to recommend anyone. Gladstone had not recommended Rosebery when he resigned in 1894; Campbell-Bannerman had
not recommended Asquith in 1908. The precedents were not quite
exact. Neither Gladstone nor Campbell-Bannerman had been asked for
advice. Law was saying in advance that he did not wish to give it. However
the precedents were near enough to let him out. Law returned to London
with his anxiety removed.

Law's hesitation was not due solely to his illness. He was desperately
puzzled what to do. On this point Beaverbrook gave varying accounts.
He earlier says: "I have no doubt that he intended to nominate Curzon
if he nominated anybody, and that *he wanted* in his heart to nominate
Baldwin". Later, in 1954, he dictated some notes to help Robert Blake
in his biography of Law. Here Beaverbrook said:

> Law said that he could not recommend Baldwin and must recommend
> Curzon. But he felt that Curzon could not hold the Cabinet together. He did
> not want to have the responsibility of recommending a man who could not
> hold the Cabinet together. Just the same, he believed that Baldwin was too
> inexperienced and had no public position, and that Curzon must be the
> recommendation.

This was all that Beaverbrook learnt from Law. On 20 May Beaverbrook
heard Law tell Baldwin that he expected Curzon would be chosen.
Baldwin replied that he would serve under any man who could hold the

---

[1] Beaverbrook later stated that he was summoned to Aix by Kipling, who was also
staying there. This seems unlikely. The telegrams from Davidson survive. There is
no record of any message from Kipling. Beaverbrook suggested that it might have
come by telephone, but there is no other indication that he used the long-distance
telephone at this period. Correspondence between Kipling and Beaverbrook ceased
in 1918, when Kipling took offence at Beaverbrook's enlightened attitude over Ireland.

party together—a remark from which Law derived much pleasure, presumably without appreciating that it was double edged. However George V passed over Curzon and chose Baldwin as prime minister. This decision has been mainly, and rightly, attributed to advice from Balfour, who was after all a former prime minister and whose advice had carried great weight in December 1916 also.

According to evidence which Robert Blake collected,[1] it seems that Law had a hand in the choice after all. Though he himself made no recommendation, his private secretary, Waterhouse, told Stamfordham, the king's secretary, that Law favoured Baldwin. Waterhouse also submitted a memorandum in Baldwin's favour. It had been drafted by J. C. C. Davidson, as he himself told Blake. Stamfordham was left in no doubt that all those round Law shared this estimate of his opinion. Beaverbrook knew nothing of this at the time. When Blake produced the story, he refused to believe it. He said of the memorandum: "It is not in the style of Lord Davidson in the first place, and it is far above the mental attainments of Lord Davidson". Alternatively, "if he wrote that memorandum then Davidson was false to his master". When Beaverbrook was finally convinced that the story was true, it became "a wickedness", "a piece of rascality" on the part of Waterhouse. This is one possible explanation. There is another and more likely one. At the best of times Law had difficulty in reaching a firm decision, and now he was mortally ill. Beaverbrook who often propelled him towards a decision was himself in a quandary as between Curzon and Baldwin—hence his references to a dark horse. To Beaverbrook therefore, Law genuinely gave the impression that he was at a loss what to say. When others pressed Baldwin's claims, he may well have yielded to the temptation of agreeing with them. If he did so, he certainly did not reveal it to Beaverbrook—which would only have provoked another wearisome round of argument.[2]

There was another reason for Beaverbrook's belated anger. He saw that someone else had played the part of kingmaker which he had often

---

[1] Blake, The Unknown Prime Minister, 520-25.
[2] Davidson (Memoirs of a Conservative, 156-60) claims that he wrote the memorandum at Stamfordham's request, "*simply expressing the views of the normal backbencher on the Government side*". It is hard to believe that Stamfordham regarded Law's confidential adviser as a "normal backbencher", and he accepted without question Waterhouse's statement that the memorandum "practically expressed the views of Mr. Bonar Law". So it probably did, and it was in this form that the information reached the king.
Davidson also claims (ibid., 161) that Beaverbrook was backing Curzon in the belief that the "old gang" of Coalition Conservatives would serve under him and not under Baldwin. There is no other evidence for this. Beaverbrook was busy ministering to his sick friend and had no time for political intrigue. In any case, as we have seen, if he had run a candidate, it would have been Derby, not Curzon.

performed himself. At the time, he had no such ambition. His only concern was for Law. He returned to London ahead of Law in order to break the news to the press. He wrote an article for The Daily Express of 21 May which described Law as "the greatest Conservative Prime Minister since Disraeli". The article ended:

> Mr. Bonar Law's magic consists in a cool brain and an honest heart, so that his life has been to a political world not unduly given to simplicity, a pattern which all men might imitate with advantage.

Beaverbrook's admiration for Law was never dimmed. He said towards the end of his life: "I have known one honest politician: Bonar Law. He was without guile". In the few sad months remaining to Law, Beaverbrook proved himself once more the foul-weather friend. He accompanied Law to Brighton and Le Touquet. He kept up an appearance of high spirits and optimism. He brought Law and Lloyd George together for a lunch of reconciliation at the Vineyard. He bought large blocks of shares in which Law was interested so as to announce the cheering news that their price was going up. In October Law returned to London to die. His last words to Beaverbrook were: "You are a curious fellow".

Law died on 30 October. The Daily Express urged that he be buried in Westminster Abbey. Rothermere's papers took up the cry. The press lords were for once successful. Law was buried in the Abbey. Baldwin and Beaverbrook were among the pallbearers.

CHAPTER TEN

THE GAY TWENTIES, 1923–28

An epoch in Beaverbrook's life ended with the death of Bonar Law. He lost his most intimate friend, and the scar seemed to grow deeper as the years went by. Long afterwards, he destroyed a large part of his correspondence for 1923, which is thus the only year between 1903 and 1964 not covered by a bulky general file. He often planned to continue his historical writing into the period after Law's resignation and never managed to do it. A psychological block stood in the way. Law's death also changed Beaverbrook's position in politics. He wrote: "Something was severed for ever in my political associations. I had never cared much for the purely political life, but Bonar Law's charm, his urbanity, his wisdom, his firm and reasonable attitude towards all problems, held me like a silken chain".[1] Beaverbrook was also fond of quoting a remark of Churchill's that he had sat on a three-legged stool: "one leg was myself; the second was my newspapers; the third was my relationship with Bonar Law—now the third leg had gone and Churchill said I could no longer balance myself in politics".

Law's death was more than a personal loss. It completed what the fall of the Lloyd George Coalition had begun and put Beaverbrook on the outside of political life. He had been on the inside almost from the moment when he arrived in England. His friendship with Law had been only the beginning. He was soon almost equally close to Birkenhead and Churchill and, in time, became intimate with Lloyd George also. Few secret conferences on great political matters were held without Beaverbrook's being present. When he helped to make and unmake governments, as he did in December 1916 and again in October 1922, this was by means of his personal contacts, not because of his newspapers, and he would have been just as much a kingmaker if he had not been a newspaper proprietor at all. After the war, Lloyd George, Birkenhead, and Churchill were the great men of the moment, and Beaverbrook threw his net over them. The prime minister himself was sometimes a guest at the Vineyard.

[1] Politicians and the Press, 75.

On occasion, prime minister, lord chancellor, and colonial secretary gathered at Cherkley for vital discussions.

Now all was over. Lloyd George would never be in office again. Birkenhead, though ultimately restored to office, ceased to count in the Conservative party. Churchill seemed to recover more completely, but he remained dangerously isolated and would not risk political intimacy with Beaverbrook, even if they had agreed more. Beaverbrook was only distantly acquainted with the new leaders of the Conservative party, and with the Labour leaders he was not acquainted at all. The backdoor into the political world was closed against him until the strange circumstances of 1940 opened it again. No more lunches at the Vineyard and weekend parties at Cherkley when cabinet ministers discussed their problems or fought out their differences. No more calls for Beaverbrook's services as the invaluable go-between. No prime minister came to Cherkley between 1922 and 1941, and the names of famous public men vanished from the visitors' book. Only Austen Chamberlain's continued to appear, and this friendship, though of long standing, remained always formal. Beaverbrook's visitors had now only private importance: old friends from Canada; writers for his newspapers, such as Maurice Woods, Leslie Hore-Belisha, and Valentine Castlerosse, Beaverbrook's greatest find as a gossip-writer; literary figures, among whom Arnold Bennett was preeminent. It is hardly too much to say that Bennett took Lloyd George's place as the most distinguished figure in Beaverbrook's social circle. There was still plenty of talk about politics, but it was the talk of observers, not of practical politicians, and no doubt all the gayer for that.

Beaverbrook's new remoteness from the inside of the political world was not due only to changes at the top, or in more personal terms from Lloyd George and Law to Baldwin, though Baldwin certainly disliked the Lloyd George–Beaverbrook group and its atmosphere. The larger change was the reversion to party politics and the comparative diminution of independents, including independent newspaper proprietors. Beaverbrook paid the penalty for the revolution in the newspaper world which Northcliffe had begun and which he himself had furthered. Before 1914 editors and owners, other than Northcliffe, were the servants of party, either from conviction or financial dependence, and in return got the reward of being treated as party advisers, on the same loyal level as the whips or the party agents. Balfour consulted Garvin; Grey consulted Spender; Asquith and Lloyd George consulted Scott. Beaverbrook, and Rothermere also, were still ready to advise, but, being financially secure, they advised as independent potentates, not as devoted subordinates, and this was not advice which Baldwin welcomed. Of course Baldwin deliberately built up his hostility to the press lords in order to exploit the general dislike of Lloyd George who had been friendly with them, and when he found in Dawson of The Times an editor suited to his taste was as ready to listen as ever Lloyd George had been. Even the breach between Baldwin and Beaverbrook was not as complete as that between Baldwin and Rothermere. But it was deep enough to push Beaverbrook into becoming primarily a newspaper man for a long time.

Probably the push was not unwelcome to him. In the newspaper world he was becoming more powerful and more successful. In 1922 The Daily Express turned the corner and began to show a good profit. The Sunday Express was no longer losing money. Success brought a somewhat surprising offer. On 18 November 1922 Rothermere asked in a scribbled postscript: "How would you like me to purchase an interest in your newspapers?" Beaverbrook replied at once: "Nothing would give me greater pleasure than to work in co-operation with you and, indeed, with the *Daily Mail*". Rothermere took the hint which came at a propitious moment. Northcliffe had died in August 1922, and Rothermere was engaged in liquidating his brother's estate. He sold The Times, perhaps reluctantly, to J. J. Astor and John Walter, the previous proprietor. He acquired The Daily Mail for himself. At the same time Rothermere and Beaverbrook bought out the minority shareholders in The Daily Express such as Lord Faringdon and Sir John Ellerman, survivors from the days when they had acted as "channels" for the Unionist party.

Northcliffe's 400,000 shares in Associated Newspapers, which owned The Daily Mail, were transferred to a new holding company, the Daily Mail Trust. This trust also bought 49% of Beaverbrook's holding in London Express Newspaper, paying him £200,000 and 80,000 Daily Mail Trust shares. Rothermere himself held nearly one half of the DMT shares in one guise or another.[1] The deal was principally a straight financial partnership. Beaverbrook, like any good investor, wanted to diversify his holdings. Also, being a relative newcomer to newspaper finance, he welcomed association with the greatest master in that field. It was certainly a good bargain for him. Rothermere ran his newspapers primarily for profit, despite amateurish excursions into politics, and the Daily Mail Trust was soon paying 40% on its ordinary shares. Beaverbrook derived his income solely from his large Canadian fortune and ran his papers for fun—or as a public duty. He wrote to a friend in 1929:

> I have never made a penny out of the Daily Express.[2] I am a "remittance man", living on what comes to me from Canada.

---

[1] A note of 25 January 1928 gives the total shares in DMT as 2,014,500, and the principal shareholders, apart from Beaverbrook (120,000) and Rothermere (68,900), as Daily Mirror (533,328), Sunday Pictorial (266,665) and Esmond Harmsworth (100,000). These last three were of course Rothermere's nominees.

[2] This was not quite true. Beaverbrook sometimes lent considerable sums to The Express when it was short of cash and took a reasonable interest on these loans.

When London Express Newspaper began to prosper, Beaverbrook ploughed back most of the profits. He wrote to Rothermere: "I do not regard newspaper holding as a purely commercial business in which every penny of the profit goes to the shareholders". At the time Rothermere raised no objection. Later, when The Daily Express began to challenge the primacy of The Daily Mail, he did not find it at all funny that Beaverbrook should use his income from the Daily Mail Trust to finance The Daily Mail's dangerous, and ultimately successful, rival.

The financial tie-up brought immediate benefits. It enabled the two newspapers to keep down the price of newsprint. Beaverbrook also claimed, in a letter to Time and Tide of 19 October 1928, that the arrangement had been further designed "to secure good relations between the two newspapers". He added: "It proved unworkable from this point of view, and failed. The reason was that the directors of The Daily Express would not conform to the policy". This evokes an agreeable picture of The Express directors gallantly defying Beaverbrook's benevolent wish that they should cooperate with The Daily Mail. One can hear his lament to Rothermere: "Ah, they are hard men. I can do nothing with them".

The association between Beaverbrook and Rothermere soon went further. Sir Edward Hulton, who had a newspaper empire in Manchester and some London interests as well, was a dying man. In 1923 he retired to the south of France and wished to dispose of his newspapers. Many proprietors, including the Berry brothers, were interested. Beaverbrook beat them by his old resource of offering ready money. He rang up McKenna and asked: "Will the Midland Bank honour my cheque for one million pounds?" McKenna said it would. Beaverbrook sent his cheque the same day and agreed to pay some five million more within the week. Before the week was up, he sold the entire Hulton empire to Rothermere for six million pounds, keeping one item for himself as commission. This was The Evening Standard, a somewhat lame evening paper with premises in St. Bride Street, immediately adjacent to those of The Daily Express, which Beaverbrook had long coveted.[1] The Daily Mail Trust took 49% of The Evening Standard, paying Beaverbrook with a further 40,000 DMT shares. The Daily Mail Trust also received an option to buy Beaverbrook's controlling interest in The Evening Standard, if this ever came on the market.

To complete the story of these transactions, in 1924 Rothermere sold the Hulton provincial interests to the Berry brothers, keeping for himself The Daily Sketch (a potential rival to his Daily Mirror) and a few other London newspapers. The following year he decided that The Daily Sketch was no danger and sold it also to the Berrys. He is said to have made £1,800,000 on these deals. The Berrys also made large profits from their

[1] Part of the site is now the Beaverbrook Library, where this book was written.

purchases. Beaverbrook had got for nothing The Evening Standard and 40,000 shares in the Daily Mail Trust. All parties had reason to be satisfied.

Beaverbrook had been concerned to acquire more presses and more office space for The Daily Express and took on The Evening Standard as a more or less accidental bonus. It is true that he now had a well-balanced empire—a morning paper, an evening paper, and a Sunday paper. But The Evening Standard did not fit in with the pattern he had previously created. The two Express papers aimed at a mass readership, and Beaverbrook steadily increased their size with the aim of increasing their circulation. Later, he pushed further into the national market by establishing offices and presses for The Daily Express in Manchester and Glasgow, and then founded The Scottish Daily Express as an independent venture. The Evening Standard, on the other hand, had a circulation limited to the well-to-do of London and the suburbs. It never attempted to rival the mass circulation of Rothermere's Evening News, and news-vendors, it is said, have always known that the man in the bowler hat will ask for The Evening Standard. Experienced observers therefore surmised that Beaverbrook would one day break out with an Evening Express for the masses, and Maurice Woods even foretold this in his draft life of Beaverbrook, presumably with Beaverbrook's approval.

However Beaverbrook never did so, though he took some preliminary steps in 1928. Perhaps he had enough of starting a paper from nothing when he founded The Sunday Express. Perhaps he recognized that an evening paper could not attempt a national circulation. More probably he welcomed The Evening Standard as something different. Those who thought that Beaverbrook could only inspire one kind of newspaper did not grasp the many-sidedness of his nature. He wanted political influence. He wanted mass circulation for some of his papers on the Northcliffe pattern. But he also wanted fun, and The Evening Standard provided an outlet for his eccentric radicalism.

Of course Beaverbrook was determined that The Evening Standard, too, should not run at a loss, and he watched its circulation with the same intensity. When on a motor journey near London, he would often send out his secretary to ask whether the late edition of The Evening Standard was on sale. Writing to Tom Blackburn on 27 March 1962 he alleged that for twenty-five years he had stood around in odd places watching the sales of The Evening Standard—"watching outside Harrods sometimes for an hour on end". No wonder that he added: "It is an exacting occupation, the ownership of newspapers. It is only for the very strong, the very healthy, the very vigorous". How often Beaverbrook kept these vigils is another matter. Advertising, too, was pursued with intensity, and with a difference. The Evening Standard did not merely seek more readers; it sought readers with a higher income. In technical advertising terms, the two Express newspapers aimed at all classes of readers; The Evening Standard was designed for A and B readers only.

The Evening Standard was politically less important than its two stable companions and a great deal more sophisticated. The topics were gayer and more general. Arnold Bennett ran a weekly column, which Beaverbrook claimed, with a little exaggeration, to be the most influential literary feature in London. Dean Inge provided a cultivated nihilism which earned him the title of the Gloomy Dean. Londoner's Diary was edited by such distinguished figures as Harold Nicolson and Bruce Lockhart. Beaverbrook himself contributed many of the most irresponsible paragraphs. It would be an interesting task to identify his contributions, if it were not rendered impossible by the trick others acquired of imitating his style. Many of Beaverbrook's paragraphs must have been bewilderingly incomprehensible to those outside his circle, but he did not mind. The Evening Standard was his house journal, providing fun for himself and for those who shared his tastes.

Beaverbrook's biggest capture for The Evening Standard was David Low, the cartoonist. The Daily Express already had its cartoonist in Strube, inventor of the Little Man, very efficient at expressing in vivid form the prejudices of its readers. Low was an artist of genius and with strong political views as well. He differed from Beaverbrook over almost everything—sceptical about the Empire despite being a New Zealander; enthusiastic for the League of Nations and collective security; to say nothing of being a leftwing Socialist. Beaverbrook never attempted to interfere with him or to censor his work. This was the more remarkable in that Low's scathing pencil did not spare Beaverbrook himself. The Empire Crusader appeared in many an odd corner of Low's cartoons as a diminutive figure breathing mischief. No doubt it pleased Beaverbrook to be shown, however comically, alongside prime ministers, American presidents, and foreign dictators. There was a deeper reason for his tolerance. Those who marvelled at it did not reflect that perhaps Low's version of Beaverbrook was really how he saw himself—the Puck or Robin Goodfellow (some said Badfellow) of the political world. At any rate Low had a free run for the best part of twenty years in The Evening Standard.

Beaverbrook did not long renounce the world of politics despite the death of Bonar Law. For one thing Rothermere, who professed world-weariness and spent most of his time in the south of France, talked of making their partnership political as well as financial. He wrote to Beaverbrook at the time of Law's retirement:

> I don't think that those who were really hard hit during the war have any real zest for affairs. I know I haven't and if I received from my doctor or other source a peremptory order to get out I should really welcome it.

For some weeks I have been cudgelling my brains to devise a scheme by which you could be associated with the political direction of my papers. It must be managed somehow because I am tired of being a galley slave. Moreover my ambition is a life largely of solitude and obscurity. I am now 55 and a poor life at that.

Beaverbrook was not slow to take up this invitation. The moment for action arrived in October 1923 when Baldwin announced without warning that only Protection would cure unemployment and that he must have a general election in order to free himself of Law's pledge not to abandon Free Trade.

This seemed a recipe for disaster. Free Trade sentiment was still strong even within the Conservative party. The powerful phalanx of Lancashire Conservatives was overwhelmingly Free Trade, and Lord Derby, its leader, openly announced his opposition to Baldwin. On top of this, many Liberals who had voted for Law and tranquillity would now presumably revert to their old allegiance. Beaverbrook, as an old Tariff Reformer, might have been expected to go with Baldwin. Instead he denounced the election as unnecessary and "a serious blunder". This was not a mere personal antagonism. Beaverbrook was angry that Law's majority, which he had helped to create, should be wantonly thrown away. More than this, he was an Imperialist, not a Protectionist in the ordinary sense. His cause was Empire Free Trade, which he presented as a policy of expansion, not of restriction. A one-sided protection of the home market would not enable British industry to prosper. Worse still, it would offend industrialists in the Dominions and yet, by excluding food taxes, would not win the Dominion farmer. Beaverbrook even regarded the existing Free Trade system as a lesser evil than home protection—at least it did not raise a barrier against Dominion goods. Thus his concern for Canada, which was what his imperialism amounted to in practice, brought him into alliance with the Lancashire Free Trade Conservatives who had wrecked his plans for Empire Free Trade and food taxes ten years previously. Of course the fact that this alliance would work against Baldwin was not altogether absent from his mind.

Baldwin sought to enlist Beaverbrook's support and invited him to No. 10 Downing Street. Beaverbrook, according to an account which he gave to Peter Howard on 16 June 1962, said: "I won't go along with you unless you incorporate the policy of Imperial Preference". Baldwin answered that he might do so another day but that it would be impossible at that election. Beaverbrook was convinced from this moment that Baldwin had no faith in Empire:

Protection attracted Baldwin for the wrong reason; it was a catch-penny reason. The grandeur of an all-embracing association between the Empire peoples, of fiscal union giving benefit to all and harming none, was something Baldwin did not understand.[1]

Baldwin told Beaverbrook that he wished to enlist Birkenhead and Austen Chamberlain who were supposed to command considerable support— Birkenhead in Lancashire, Chamberlain in Birmingham. He talked of offering them places in the cabinet. Beaverbrook assumed that Baldwin was on the point of surrendering to the Coalition Conservatives whom he had turned out the year before. The moment for revenge had come.

At Beaverbrook's invitation the old Coalition held its last meeting. On 12 November 1923 Lloyd George, Churchill, Birkenhead and Austen Chamberlain met at Cherkley for the weekend—four men who were never to confer together again. Arnold Bennett was also there, so the talk cannot have been entirely political. Or maybe Bennett collected material for a future novel. The old Coalitionists were in high hopes of discomfiting Baldwin. They agreed that Birkenhead and Chamberlain should accept Baldwin's invitation to join his government. Birkenhead would then stump Lancashire on behalf of the Conservative Free Traders. Lloyd George and Churchill would sound the Free Trade call as Liberals. Beaverbrook would contribute by expounding Empire Free Trade, as against Protection, in his newspapers. Austen Chamberlain maintained an embarrassed silence. In his simple-minded way, he could not understand the difference between Empire Free Trade and Protection, and his sense of honour, which had previously bound him to Lloyd George, was now beginning to operate in favour of Baldwin. This was of little moment. Austen Chamberlain had never belonged to the inner circle of the Lloyd George Coalition. The others were in high spirits. Free Trade would win. Conservative Free Traders and Liberal Free Traders would come together in a new Coalition under Lloyd George, and he, according to Beaverbrook's secret expectations, would then promote the imperial cause to the surprise of his supporters. Beaverbrook telegraphed triumphantly to Rothermere: "I think Baldwin will be defeated and George will be strengthened if political tactics adopted".

The plans miscarried. When Arnold Bennett got back to London, he accidentally revealed the story of the Cherkley meeting to a Daily News journalist. Baldwin read the story and took alarm. He went back on the offer of cabinet office which he had made to Birkenhead and Chamberlain. Beaverbrook reported to Borden on 16 November:

> Baldwin has muddled the negotiations as usual. He first of all tried the donkey and carrots game with Birkenhead. When the latter jibbed at coming in without definite office, he fell back on the "I'm an honest man; what I promise I perform later" style. Birkenhead was not cajoled. His reply in

---

[1] Beaverbrook to Stanley Morison, 4 May 1951.

effect was "My stock of oratory is for sale. It is at the top of the market just now. You can buy now in cash, or you can't buy at all". Chamberlain is, in consequence, in a rather difficult position. He is tied to F.E. by bonds of honour, and to backing the policy of his dead father by conviction. The two views are in conflict, and with plentiful incapacity backing both.

Beaverbrook failed to grasp the skill of Baldwin's tactics. Birkenhead had to campaign in Lancashire even without office, if he were to make a come-back. Chamberlain could make his come-back only by keeping clear of Lloyd George and the Cherkley group. Both remained dependent on Baldwin's future favours.

Things went wrong also on the Liberal side. Once Lloyd George took up Free Trade, he had to become the obedient second of Asquith, the official leader. As Beaverbrook put it, "he really had a choice between death and surrender on fairly easy terms". Churchill, sensing Lloyd George's unpopularity among the old faithfuls of the Liberal party, grasped at the succession for himself. To quote further from Beaverbrook's letter to Borden:

> Churchill has definitely separated himself from George—and wishes this to be understood in the inner tabernacles of Liberalism. His idea is that the reversion of Asquith's leadership will thus fall to him, because George has against him certain powerful irreconcilables, who will never trust him as leader again. All this seems to be me to be highly speculative.

This plan of Churchill's, if he really had it, also did not work. He failed to win a seat at the general election and thereafter abandoned the Liberal party.

Beaverbrook had a disappointment of his own. On 14 November he telegraphed to Rothermere:

> Have seen Derby who declares he is against election and opposed to general tariff. Will you let me on your behalf run policy of Hulton Manchester newspapers on Conservative Free Trade lines?

Rothermere was shocked at this suggestion. He replied on 15 November:

> As you know I am a convinced protectionist. Cannot speak with different voices London and Manchester. After meeting Lancashire Conservatives last night and their declaration against general tariff shall be unable to support them. Conservative Free Traders and semi Free Traders are worst enemies of protection. Will advise electors to vote for Liberal candidate if there is no downright tariff candidate instead of candidate who is neither fish, flesh nor fowl.

Beaverbrook refused to contribute to the Conservative election fund. When pressed by Sir George Younger, he finally agreed to pay the entire expenses of "two needy candidates who are sound Imperialists". Younger produced two names, and Beaverbrook paid £1,000 for one and £750 for the other.[1]

The general election fulfilled Beaverbrook's expectations in one way: the Conservatives lost their overall majority. But Labour, not the Liberals, remained the second largest party. It is extraordinary how the plotters of Cherkley had failed to foresee this, and indeed Beaverbrook went on assuming that one day Labour would disappear in favour of a revived Liberal party.[2] He had another blind spot and did not grasp that Lloyd George was discredited for ever as a national leader. Events immediately after the election demonstrated this. Various schemes were aired for keeping Labour from office: a coalition under Balfour or Asquith or McKenna, even under Sir Robert Horne, who, in Beaverbrook's words, "refused the purple". No one thought of suggesting Lloyd George. In any case Asquith put an end to these schemes by using the Liberal vote to put Baldwin out and Labour in—a course which Baldwin himself approved. Ramsay MacDonald became prime minister. Beaverbrook consoled himself by writing to Arthur Brisbane:

> I have formed great expectations of MacDonald's European policy. I think it may bring France to the point of settlement with Germany.

The Labour government had one novel feature: it had no contact with Fleet Street. As Beaverbrook wrote:

> Heretofore no British Government for a hundred years had been without considerable newspaper backing. The Socialists could only claim one organ with a small circulation (the *Daily Herald*), and this newspaper could not be depended on by the new Prime Minister, for it really represented the extreme Left of his own supporters.[3]

This was no doubt a handicap, but it also meant that the newspaper magnates, including Beaverbrook, lost all political influence. They could only criticize from outside. Not that Beaverbrook minded. The future leadership of the Conservative party remained the prime topic for him. Surely, he felt, Baldwin was now doomed. He wrote in The Sunday Express of 17 February 1924:

> Mr. Baldwin is in the descending scales of values. . . . Now that he is stripped of power and *patronage* he must rely on his own capabilities as a

[1] Beaverbrook told Peter Howard in 1962: "I put up twenty-five candidates or rather I financed twenty-five candidates who stood out for Imperial Preference. I think they were pretty nearly all elected". This was a romantic story without foundation.

[2] In another, almost whimsical attempt to show that the Labour party was an alien association of impractical theorists, unsuited to British politics, Beaverbrook always referred to Labour as "the Socialists". He imposed this practice on his papers, which still maintain it.

[3] Politicians and the Press, 83.

parliamentarian in opposition. Here his qualifications have so far proved of second rank—suited to a minor post, adequate for an Under-Secretaryship, but far below the level of a Prime Minister or a Leader of the Opposition.

However nothing happened. Beaverbrook wrote to Sir Archibald Salvidge on 19 February 1924:

> As far as I can make out nearly all Baldwin's ex-colleagues are profoundly dis-satisfied with him. The exceptions are Amery from self-interest and Neville Chamberlain from stupidity. . . . The Party will simply jog along in the bad, mad, sad old way.

Beaverbrook reviewed Baldwin's Conservative rivals in the columns of The Sunday Express and decided that none of them would do. Lloyd George was lost as a national leader by his return to subordination in the Liberal party. Reluctantly, Beaverbrook came round to the view that Churchill, the most discredited of them all, must be the national saviour.

The opportunity came in March 1924 when Churchill presented himself as an Independent Constitutionalist at a by-election in the Abbey division of Westminster. Imperial preference appeared in his programme for the only time in his life, no doubt on Beaverbrook's prompting. The two men differed in their practical aim. Churchill wanted to lead an anti-Socialist coalition. Beaverbrook wanted Churchill to supplant Baldwin as Conservative leader. Many prominent Conservatives, such as Lord Wargrave and Sir Robert Horne, supported Churchill. So at first did Baldwin himself, or so Beaverbrook informed Arthur Brisbane in a letter of 13 March. The local Conservative association, however, perhaps secretly prompted by Baldwin, refused to accept Churchill and ran a nonentity of their own. Baldwin went down to consult Austen Chamberlain who refused to support Churchill "until he repented in sackcloth and ashes for his Liberal past, and joined the Tories openly as a penitent convert". Baldwin then stepped tactfully aside. Churchill failed to defeat the official Conservative by 43 votes. Beaverbrook commented bitterly: "The Ex-Prime Minister is a very well-meaning man, but utterly unfit mentally for high command". In fact Baldwin's tactics had again succeeded, and Beaverbrook's had failed.

Beaverbrook's letter to Brisbane contains other observations which show greater insight:

> Ramsay MacDonald is being hard pressed inside his own party by Wheatley, the Minister for Health, representing the Socialist extremists. The latter is certainly the coming figure, and some people profess to believe that he will overtake MacDonald in the race. But there is very little permanency about these revolutionary figures. He is only dangerous to MacDonald in so far as he is inexperienced and extreme. Let him cease to be so, and he becomes merely another clever subordinate with a good debating

style. And it is difficult to remain violent in politics—for office in England, as you well know, is a great emollient and softener of rough edges. Still, at present, Wheatley plays to MacDonald the part Lloyd George used to play to Asquith in January 1910. . . .

All parties tend to be fissiparous—but the underlying reality is this: England (free of the Irish vote) wants by its nature, and wants now, a Conservative government. It only casts off such a government because of follies and idiocies like those of Baldwin, or simply because in the process of time it gets tired for an interval of a long period of Conservative domination as in 1906. It is only waiting now for a decent Tory leadership, and a reasonable occasion for putting an independent Conservative Government of the Bonar Law type back in power.

This proved to be a correct judgement except of course that the new Bonar Law turned out to be Baldwin.

Beaverbrook now preached the need for a revived Liberal party to provide a more effective Radical alternative than Labour was doing. Wearying of this barren cause, he departed for Canada and returned in September with the news that Canada was a country of unbounded resources. He renewed his advocacy of isolation and Empire in an article of 28 September 1924, entitled Expand and Grow Rich:

If Britain will keep out of the tangle of European diplomacy and the mutual hatreds of those nations it has nothing to fear now from hostile forces on the continent. It has a boundless Empire rich in natural resources, capable of maintaining immense populations which will in time supply it with the markets lost in Europe during the war.

He concluded by commending the words of the Psalmist:

> To any nation never he
>   Such favour did afford;
> For they his judgements have not known,
>   O do ye praise the Lord.

Beaverbrook's voice was drowned by the tumult of a new political crisis. Sir Patrick Hastings, the Labour attorney-general, had instituted proceedings against a Communist journalist, J. R. Campbell, and then, as the result of protests by Labour leftwingers, withdrew them. The Liberals demanded enquiry by a select committee. The Conservatives supported the demand—according to Beaverbrook, a tactic agreed on between Austen Chamberlain and Lloyd George. The government was defeated. MacDonald demanded a general election, which the king accorded him.

Beaverbrook protested that the election was unnecessary and even wicked. "The whole nation is to be thrown into confusion to prove whether Sir Patrick Hastings is a fit person to be Attorney-General".

Beaverbrook did not believe that any decisive result could be achieved: "no Ministry independent of external support would return to Downing-Street". He claimed also that MacDonald was out to destroy the Liberal party. As he wrote to Borden on 20 October 1924:

> MacDonald precipitated the election in order to ruin the Liberal Party. He is taking the long view of his own and his party's future. In politics the long view is usually the wrong view. It is quite certain, however, that he will attain his object. The Liberal Party is like the Spanish army in the Peninsula —quite good until brought into action.[1]

Beaverbrook now wanted an electoral pact between Liberals and Conservatives—the very arrangement which he had resisted in 1922. The pact would preserve Liberalism "as a great political power". It would provide security for social reform and Free Trade. Beaverbrook himself displayed an unusual solicitude for this latter cause. He wrote in The Sunday Express on 26 October:

> As to Protection, Mr. Baldwin was a prisoner in chains to the Die-Hards at the last general election, and after the next one he would be in the custody of the moderate and progressive elements in the Conservative Party.... Liberal voters need not fear that votes given against Socialism would be used to destroy Free Trade.

Beaverbrook appreciated that the prevailing cry of the Red Peril, reinforced as it was at the last moment by the alarm of the Zinoviev letter, would drive panic-stricken Liberals to vote Conservative and would so ruin the Liberal party. He therefore tried to keep the Red Peril out of his newspapers, or so he claimed, and preferred a quietly reasoned campaign against Socialism which would help the Conservatives without damaging the Liberals. When Baldwin however made some harmless academic remarks about Socialism becoming respectable in fifty years' time, Beaverbrook used this as an excuse for refusing to contribute to Conservative election expenses. He wrote to Sir George Younger on 29 October:

> If you can conceive any plan by which I would contribute to the expenses of Conservative candidates, who are definitely and publicly opposed to the Baldwin leadership, I would do my best to fall in with it. They would have to be pledged to work hard to obtain a new leader.

No such Conservatives could be found, and Beaverbrook made no contribution. The moderation of his newspapers was also ineffective. The Red Peril raged in Rothermere's newspapers and had the result which Beaverbrook expected. The Conservatives received an overwhelming majority. The Liberal party was almost destroyed.

[1] The historical allusion in the last sentence was outside Beaverbrook's usual range and was no doubt supplied by Maurice Woods.

Beaverbrook reluctantly admitted that Labour had become the alternative party. He ascribed the Conservative victory to Rothermere and telegraphed to him on 30 October:

> I congratulate you on your magnificent victory. You have made the new Baldwin ministry now control it if you can.

Rothermere replied on 1 November that the Zinoviev letter had altered the situation to the extent of something like 100 seats and added in his lordly way:

> What is to become of our old friend L.G.? Unless you and I can frame up some way of escape, his career as a political star of the first magnitude is definitely closed.

Beaverbrook was not interested in the fate of Lloyd George, with whom indeed he never cooperated again. He was concerned with another old friend, Churchill, who had at last been returned to parliament as an official Conservative. Churchill doubted whether he would be offered office, and as usual Beaverbrook sustained him when he was down. At the Vineyard Churchill declared that he would not accept anything except a first-rate post without consulting Beaverbrook and then departed for the country.

On 5 November Beaverbrook gave a dinner party to Churchill, Birkenhead, and Guest. It happened to be the day on which the major cabinet appointments were made. Churchill arrived first. Beaverbrook asked: "Well, are you in?" Churchill replied: "Oh, yes, I'm in all right". Beaverbrook: "What have you got?" Churchill: "I'm sorry, but I would prefer not to tell you". Birkenhead appeared and at once announced that he was secretary for India—"just what I wanted" (which was far from true). He asked Churchill: "What have you got?" Beaverbrook cut in: "No, Churchill prefers not to disclose that in front of me". Birkenhead turned on Churchill: "You've been consulting with Max for weeks past in the most intimate way—you've been taking his help and advice and support. You were ready enough to appeal to him in your despair and now you neglect him in your hour of triumph". Churchill was abashed and said: "I will tell you". But Beaverbrook was too quick for him: "No, no—if you tell me I will publish it tomorrow in the Daily Express— I won't hear it". Dinner was an unhappy occasion. Churchill kept on trying to tell his news, and Beaverbrook kept on refusing to hear it. Finally Churchill broke out: "I am Chancellor of the Exchequer". Beaverbrook said: "You have told me against my will—and if I hear it from any other source but you tonight I shall publish it".

Soon afterwards, the telephone rang. Another member of the new cabinet (presumably Hoare, Beaverbrook's constant source of leakages) told of his own appointment and then of Churchill's. Beaverbrook returned to his guests and said he could now publish the news, but finally yielded to Churchill's solicitations and refrained. Beaverbrook then teased Churchill by depicting the row which would follow from the passing over of Sir Robert Horne, who had expected the Exchequer for himself. Churchill was again cast down and said: "Do not spoil my hour of triumph". As the party broke up, Birkenhead again upbraided Churchill for his treatment of Beaverbrook. With a flash of intuition, Beaverbrook made a shrewd guess. He said: "I don't believe Churchill is really to blame. He promised somebody he wouldn't tell me before he came—yes—he promised his wife". Churchill replied: "You are right. She drove me to the door of your house".[1]

This was a symbolic happening. Mrs. Churchill had decided that her husband was at last restored to respectability and wanted to cut him off from the disreputable influence of Beaverbrook. Churchill himself was on his best behaviour, if only to be reconciled with the Conservatives. Beaverbrook tried to find consolation by pointing out that Baldwin, by appointing Churchill, Birkenhead, and Austen Chamberlain to high office, had practically restored the great Lloyd George coalition—with one exception. But the exception was the man who had made it great. Readers of Balzac may remember that Louis Philippe similarly restored Napoleon's prefects and generals without bringing back the glories of the Empire. Baldwin's spirit reigned, not Lloyd George's. Beaverbrook wrote to Rothermere on 28 November:

> Baldwin sits silent, except when he announces the next speaker in the Cabinet debates. In fact his real role seems to be rather similar to that of the major-domo at the Lord Mayor's banquet who cries "Pray silence for" etc. In fact, Berry, the door-keeper at Downing Street, sometimes serves in this role at public dinners. I think it might be a good thing to put him in Baldwin's place in view of past experience.

But, as Beaverbrook gloomily acknowledged to Borden on 28 January 1925, Baldwin gave the country what it wanted: "Britain has at last attained Bonar Law's ideal of tranquillity—under Baldwin. So long as the Conservative Government do nothing, they can go on for a very long time".

Beaverbrook was now completely severed from the inside world of politics. Birkenhead, though in the cabinet, was losing political ambition and was wrapped up in a love affair with Mona Dunn, the daughter of Beaverbrook's Canadian friend and fellow-millionaire, Sir James Dunn. Churchill had turned into a respectable Conservative. Beaverbrook wrote to Rothermere on 12 February 1925:

> Winston came to dinner with me the other night. He is a firm supporter of Baldwin and his debt settlement. He criticizes George freely for his wicked

[1] Beaverbrook recorded this story at the time.

Irish treaty and declares that the Coalition Government ought to have continued to prosecute the war against Sinn Fein for another winter. I tried to shame him into acknowledgement of his leading part in making Irish Treaty. It is not easy to succeed.

Churchill's support for the American debt settlement was a foretaste of worse things to come. He resolved to restore the gold standard at the pre-war parity. Beaverbrook, with his expansionist outlook, was wisely and resolutely opposed to this. Churchill, after some argument, accepted the advice of the treasury and the Bank of England.[1] Anticipating Beaverbrook's disapproval, Churchill did not reveal his intentions to Beaverbrook beforehand and alleged that Beaverbrook counted this against him. Beaverbrook replied, that as with the news of Churchill's appointment, he would have refused to listen. It was a bitter moment for Churchill when Beaverbrook enlisted J. M. Keynes to write in The Evening Standard a destructive series of articles on The Economic Consequences of Mr. Churchill. As Beaverbrook remarked, "Churchill resents an assault on his public policy as much as Lloyd George does an attack on his private life".[2] Beaverbrook might have added that this was the most vulnerable spot in both cases. Beaverbrook's own letters ran over with contempt for Churchill's policies. He wrote to H. A. Gwynne on 15 May 1925:

> The trouble with Winston is that he will take no advice when he is "up"— when he is "down" it is another matter—and his judgement being fundamentally bad, he is, when in the "up" frame of mind, sure to land himself and his party in difficulties.

And to Borden on 10 June:

> Churchill is a good judge in every matter which does not concern himself. There, his judgement is hopeless, and he is sure to come to a big crash in time. . . . He is born to trouble for like Jehovah in the hymn—"He plants his footsteps on the deep and rides upon the storm".

[1] Until recently it was believed that Churchill, understanding nothing of finance, tamely accepted the arguments put forward by the advocates of the gold standard. The opening of the official records has shown that he put forward powerful arguments on the other side, and his credit for foresight is now as much up as it was formerly down. This, too, seems to be an exaggeration. D. E. Moggridge, who has studied the subject the most thoroughly (The Return to Gold, 1925), writes of Churchill's memorandum: "It more probably represents an example of Churchill's tactic of evoking all that could be said on the other side of a particular argument. . . . He normally achieved this most effectively when he put the opposing case very strongly or even made accusations of incompetence". In any case, a return to the gold standard had been accepted as the ultimate aim ever since the end of the war, and even Keynes only advocated return at a lower parity. Beaverbrook was almost the only thorough-going inflationist, and this on instinctive grounds. He was against anything which stood in the way of permanent boom.
[2] Politicians and the Press, 108.

When Borden complained of the reporting of Canadian news by The Times, Beaverbrook answered on 16 July with an analysis of the obsession for appeasing the United States shared by The Times and the British government:

> The "Times" has now become simply a great propaganda organ directed, as far as transatlantic affairs are concerned, by Jack Astor, its proprietor, to further some vague idea of Anglo-Saxon union. In effect this makes it a pro-American newspaper, always ready to sacrifice British interests to the States. . . .
>
> The present editor, Geoffrey Dawson, originally one of Milner's young men, is no good. At least he cannot counteract this tendency. His job is to please Astor—which he does remarkably well—on points about which Astor cares such as kow-towing to the United States. . . .
>
> The clue to this mystery is to be found in the fact that British governments have recently given in to The "Times" and Astor policy of surrendering everything that America demands on the ground that the Empire would thus secure complete American sympathy and support. This policy has gone on for years. In the first event we were told that if we gave Southern Ireland practical independence, the Irish-Americans would cease to raise up anti-British sentiment in the United States. We did so. Then came the demand for the instantaneous payment of the American debt. Then came a request for the abolition of the twelve-mile limit off the USA coast. We abolished it. Then Churchill was pressed to return to the gold standard in order to mobilize the useless gold hordes of the United States.
>
> I have no anti-American prejudice, but I cannot see that these successive surrenders have in any way improved our relations with America.

These were the comments of a detached observer. Beaverbrook had virtually lost interest in politics, as he often did when there was no crisis to master and no friend to sustain. Birkenhead encouraged him to keep up his activities. Beaverbrook recorded on 7 August 1925:

> Birkenhead expressed the view that I had a right to pursue my attack on Churchill. The latter had received so much assistance from me in climbing the ladder which led to the Tory loft of the Exchequer, that he was under some sort of obligation to place himself in touch with my views. . . .
>
> I did not suggest that Churchill ought to have seen eye to eye with me on the return to the Gold Standard. Nor did Birkenhead say so—or mean it—yet he meant something very much like it.

However, Beaverbrook did not respond to this unusual encouragement. He had acquired a new recipient for his impressions in Mackenzie King, now Canadian prime minister, and wrote to him on 28 December 1925 of Baldwin's "miraculous success". Beaverbrook added:

> I attribute it to two causes: (1) the great skill of Tom Jones, one of the Premier's secretarial advisers (2) The hostility of the Tory Party to Rother-mere and myself—principally, I fear, myself. The mere fact that we curse a

policy, however wrong and distasteful, makes the rank and file swallow it for fear they should be thought to be supporting us.

This hostility is likely to continue until the election draws nigh. Then, of course, the Conservative Party will want our support very badly—and we shall not hear any more talk about the Platform being able to beat or do without the Popular Press. . . .

Meanwhile he ceased to write political articles in his newspapers or to retail political news to his correspondents. To judge from his writings, he was now interested only in the expansion and prosperity of his newspapers. Beaverbrook never tried to hide anything, or at any rate only his rare failures. Members of his staff, when summoned for an interview, were likely to find him in the bath or sunning himself naked on the verandah. So now he wrote frankly about the early difficulties of The Sunday Express. "The original adventure into the Sunday Express was folly. . . . I sometimes used to go out into my garden and shake myself like a dog. Had my right hand lost its cunning? I always wrote off the very considerable sums I had invested in, or advanced to, the Sunday Express as a potential total loss". Similarly he explained that The Evening Standard derived 40% of its revenue from circulation and 60% from advertisements.

There was one curious feature about these articles. Later in life Beaverbrook claimed that he ran his newspapers for the sole purpose of promoting Empire Free Trade. In this publicity campaign of 1925–27 the cause of Empire Free Trade was not mentioned. The Sunday Express fulfilled "the desire of the ordinary men and women of every walk of life, who require sound news and good views put before them in an attractive manner". The Evening Standard directed its appeal "to the men and women who themselves form opinion in every walk of life". The Daily Express "is an incessant pleader for all who seek to rise. . . . It has always been the prophet of equal opportunity and the unrelenting opponent of that system of preferred chances which gives one man an unfair opportunity over a more competent rival". The first number of the northern edition on 17 March 1927 was introduced by Beaverbrook with a declaration that The Daily Express stood for freedom of opportunity and freedom for the private life and development of the individual. Quoting once again his favourite passage from the shorter catechism, he added:

This means that all our activities to our own advantage are good unless they directly damage other people. Similarly, all our natural enjoyments are not only justifiable, but excellent, so long as they hurt no other person.

Enterprise, energy, freedom, sport, good fun, prosperity, and happiness, these are the gifts The Daily Express would bring in its path.

And he really believed it.

Others did not or, if they did, were the more provoked. It had long been the fashion with delicate-minded writers to number Beaverbrook among the press lords. But every article he wrote showed that he was a press lord of a different kind. The charge against, say, Rothermere and Northcliffe was that they ran their papers for profit, not as a public service, and therefore subordinated everything to increasing circulation. They were further charged with using their papers to acquire political power, instead of following the democratic course. Neither of these charges applied to Beaverbrook, though both continued to be made throughout his life. He did not run his papers for profit. He did not seek political power. On the contrary, he repeatedly tried to avoid it. He was a secular missionary, in rivalry with the other preachers, and, still worse, with a creed which they detested. Where they with one accord wanted sophisticated intellectual activity for the few, he sought increased wellbeing for the many. Beaverbrook's creed was that every man should enjoy himself and that this would bring enjoyment for others. It is not surprising that this creed met with disapproval—except of course from those who were enjoying themselves.

Occasionally Beaverbrook defended himself from these harassments. On 4 March 1927 he sent Rothermere a collection of cuttings from The New Statesman and G. K.'s Weekly and wrote:

> All this stuff emanates from one source.
> I have given an order to the Express Newspapers that neither G. K. Chesterton nor Hilaire Belloc are to appear in the columns of those papers. They spend so much time in writing articles in abuse of me elsewhere, that I feel they have not got time to do good work for the newspapers with which I am connected.
> In the "Evening Standard" Diary there was a perfect passion for mentioning the names of Chesterton and Belloc. I have cut down the space allotted to advertising them. Now their names seldom appear. Besides, their journalism is so dull, and their statements are utterly unreliable.

This instruction of Beaverbrook's was no doubt the origin of the story that his paper kept a black list, forbidding the mention of those who had attacked him. In fact the black list, as with other papers, was of men with a passion for litigation—particularly of course for libel actions. In any case, Chesterton and Belloc were not aggrieved at lack of mention. They were aggrieved at lack of pay. Neither scrupled to take Beaverbrook's money even when they were abusing him.

Usually Beaverbrook was on good terms with writers. Bennett and Wells—both more distinguished writers than Beaverbrook's critics—were among his close friends. He himself joined the company of authors. At the end of 1925 he produced a little book entitled Politicians and the Press as further publicity for his newspapers. At least, this was the explanation which he gave to his friends. In fact the book was his first venture into the writing of contemporary history, a field where he later displayed his greatest and most unusual gifts. Beaverbrook was un-characteristically modest about this and snatched at any excuse for making out that he was not writing history at all. Politicians and the Press has much valuable information presented in a rather jumbled form, some of which Beaverbrook turned to better use in his last published work. It is almost without personal anecdotes and entirely without the reinforcement of original documents which Beaverbrook produced with great advantage later. It is not unfair to suspect that Beaverbrook accepted a draft from Maurice Woods without much revision. This time he managed to get the Empire in, though only in the last sentence. If he were to be debarred from expressing his real views on the needs and future of the race and the Empire, "I would at once quit public life and return to the Canadian village from whence I came"—a threat, or promise, constantly repeated in future years.

Politicians and the Press sold over 100,000 copies, and this sent Beaver-brook back to the material on politics during the first world war which he had prepared much earlier. He had said originally that this could not be published for twenty years or so, but now, with others including Churchill producing books on the first world war, Beaverbrook felt free to go ahead. Relations with Churchill were resumed, if only on the basis of history. Churchill sent his proofs of The World Crisis, volume III; Beaverbrook sent his proofs of Politicians and the War, volume I. Beaver-brook, after reading Churchill's proofs, defended both Law and Lloyd George from Churchill's criticisms; Churchill, after reading Beaver-brook's proofs, defended himself—a contrast that was not surprising. Of Lloyd George Churchill wrote: "He was always wrong. . . . Still there is no doubt he was much better as No. 1 than anybody else. The same may be said of Haig"—a backhanded compliment which Lloyd George would not have appreciated. And of Politicians and the War, "I think it vy valuable and sincere, recalling the earliest Max I knew—when he still had worlds to conquer, and kings to captivate".

Politically, the two men were still far apart, the more so when Churchill threatened Beaverbrook at the most intimate point, his newspapers. This arose during the general strike of May 1926. Beaverbrook had observed the mounting troubles in the coal industry with detached interest. He wrote to Brisbane on 30 November 1925:

> Churchill goes on his amazing course. . . . He seems to arrive at no fixation in his views. It was really his influence which secured the passage of the Coal Subsidy—a measure which was the absolute negation of everything which he had been preaching for six years past—surrender to the very forces which he had been denouncing as the public enemy.

This may not have been true. The coal subsidy was probably Baldwin's own idea. Beaverbrook, as the advocate of high wages and efficient management, sympathized with the miners. But his main concern was to get his papers published. On Saturday, 1 May 1926, with a general strike in the offing, Beaverbrook was summoned to the office of The Sunday Express. The fathers of the chapels were objecting to a government advertisement, appealing for strikebreakers. Beaverbrook rang up Birkenhead, who encouraged him to compromise. Immediately afterwards Churchill rang and gave exactly contrary advice: "Close down; you can afford it". Beaverbrook compromised by removing a few words from the advertisement. The Sunday Express duly appeared with a firm statement in the leader that a general strike would fail.

On Sunday, 2 May, Beaverbrook kept away from the office. Blumenfeld managed to write a leader which the workers were willing to print. At The Daily Mail Marlowe, the editor, provocatively underlined the government appeal in a leader which his technical staff rejected, and the paper did not appear. This provided the excuse with which Baldwin broke off negotiations with the TUC. Beaverbrook still tried to bring out Monday's Evening Standard. In his own words:

> I should have been perfectly prepared to go on publishing at almost any cost . . . even though the actual editing of the Evening Standard was interfered with by the Fathers of the Chapels.

He gave this general instruction at The Evening Standard office, though he noticed that Wilson, the chairman of the company, did not agree with him. After Beaverbrook had left, negotiations with the men broke down. Beaverbrook offered to return and meet the men, "but the directors demurred". In all this, Beaverbrook adopted his usual pose of being simply "the principal shareholder", not a director. He concludes his account: "I had no right to give a direction or an order though I had made my own opinion clear". No doubt he would have made his "opinion" prevail easily enough if there had been any real chance of agreeing with the men. As it was, it pleased him to demonstrate that, if he had had his way, there would have been no strike at all.

Beaverbrook believed that the general strike could have been avoided if Baldwin had taken Birkenhead's conciliatory advice instead of surrendering to the bellicosity of Churchill and others. Nevertheless he fought the strike once it had started, just as later he flung himself into the second world war despite his belief that it was mistaken and unnecessary. He at once lent some key men so that Churchill could bring out an official paper, The British Gazette. He also struggled to keep The Daily Express going, at first only in a rudimentary form. He himself took charge with his family and friends. Lady Beaverbrook ran the canteen. Lady Louis Mountbatten and Mrs. Jean Norton manned the switchboard. Beaverbrook wrote afterwards to Tim Healy:

> I think everybody enjoyed the strike—on both sides—volunteers and strikers alike. It was treated in a holiday spirit; and the pickets outside the "Daily Express" office were quite as amused as the amateurs working the mechanical side of the newspaper within. I am almost inclined to favour the idea of having a General Strike once every year by law.

At the end of the first week, Beaverbrook was ready to bring out a full-sized Daily Express. This did not provoke a conflict with the strikers. The resistance came from Churchill, who wished to keep a monopoly for his British Gazette—now printing three million copies. Churchill was greedy for all the available newsprint. He actually requisitioned The Times stock. When faced with Beaverbrook's competition, Churchill threatened to requisition his newsprint also and to seize The Express premises. This was, as Beaverbrook remarked, "the old Gallipoli spirit . . . one of his fits of vainglory and excessive excitement". Beaverbrook defied Churchill and there was "a terrible scene" between the two men— indeed the worst row they ever had. Meanwhile Beaverbrook out-manoeuvred Churchill behind the scenes. Joynson-Hicks, the home secretary and an old friend of Beaverbrook's, was alone empowered to sign a requisition order. When approached by Churchill to requisition The Express newsprint, he refused to sign the order. The end of the strike enabled Churchill to "abandon an impossible position", but it was also the end of any political cooperation between Beaverbrook and Churchill for years to come.

Afterwards Beaverbrook watched sardonically the praise now heaped on Baldwin for his skilful leadership. He wrote to Brisbane on 24 May 1926:

> The laudations which are being poured upon Baldwin are pure hysteria. I have worked with him intermittently at one time for ten years at a stretch, and he is a man absolutely without a mind or a capacity to make one up.

He noted that Baldwin's popularity was on the wane. He wrote to Borden on 12 July:

> Baldwin is harassed by the personal attacks on his connection with Baldwins Ltd. . . . He foolishly defended himself against the accusations of being a war profiteer, though no one had mentioned the charge. He said he had always refused to sell out of British industry and invest abroad, and had clung to the old firm. Therefore he was a poor man, not a rich one.
> As a matter of fact an effort *was* made to sell the whole of Baldwins en bloc during the post war boom, and simply failed because the vendors overstayed their market.

Baldwin soon recovered his authority if he had ever lost it. During the summer of 1926, as the coal strike dragged on, Churchill, swinging round once more, tried to bully the mineowners into compromise. Beaverbrook reported to Lord Derby on 20 September: "He did promise me that he would not use any threats. Then he showed me what he had said that afternoon—full of threats of course". The mineowners defied Churchill, and the cabinet failed to support him. Beaverbrook would have liked him to resign:

> If he had gone the full length of resignation and suffered shame in this cause, he might have got a rally of moderate opinion round him and emerged at the end with a political halo and a stronger general position.

Churchill however clung to Baldwin's mantle. Beaverbrook concluded to Derby:

> It is curious to reflect that Baldwin, who is undoubtedly a man of peace at heart—if only he had a nature sufficiently violent to impose his will on others —worked with Birkenhead over the General Strike, and with Winston over this business, and made them accessories to a policy of moderation.
>
> Each time the move went wrong. And since Baldwin, as the titular leader of the Conservative party cannot—and rightly so—do wrong, F.E. and Winston in succession have had to take the blame and suffer the rebuff, while Baldwin goes scot-free.

When the miners were finally defeated, the owners made nothing of their opportunity. The coal industry drifted in decline and loss. Beaverbrook was virtually the only man who produced a courageous and practical solution. With his long experience of trust-making in Canada, he advocated the establishment of a coal combine which would rationalize the industry —the course adopted many years later though in the form of nationalization. Beaverbrook wrote and spoke repeatedly on this theme. In his customary frank way, he told how he had made the Canada Cement Company. "I was out to make money and at the same time to sell a sound security which would enhance my reputation...". The government and the owners did not heed Beaverbrook's advice. Nor did anyone take notice of his perfectly honest account of how and why the Canada Cement Company was made. The legend of his misdealing haunts his reputation to the present day.

Advocacy of a coal combine was Beaverbrook's only incursion into politics during the two years after the general strike. An account which presents him only as a politician or even as a newspaper proprietor gives a misleading impression of his activities. Beaverbrook always had time and energy for half a dozen things, and never more so than in this brief age of gold when everyone in England with money was out to enjoy himself. He was a keen tennis player—hence in part his little house in Hurlingham

Road. Every summer, he hired an expensive yacht, in which he cruised impatiently in the Channel or crossed to Deauville. On one occasion, he created a political sensation by penetrating into the Irish Sea and carrying off both the governor general of Ireland and the prime minister for the weekend. But there was no political intent behind this. Beaverbrook merely wanted to see his old friend Tim Healy.

Beaverbrook's life was now taking on the pattern which it maintained until the end. The novelist William Gerhardi knew him well at this time and provides a contemporary description:

> Lord Beaverbrook has the air of being enormously privileged in meeting someone whom no one else has ever met, or even heard of. He made me feel as if I had indeed heard of myself.
>
> . . . .
>
> He has the faculty of giving everybody he meets his "individual" attention. The impression is assisted by his habit of conducting his business while entertaining his guests, as if his friends were his real pre-occupation, and business an agreeable irrelevance. There is something irresistible when, behind all this solid success, behind the solemn outposts of editors, you penetrate to the signal-box and find the man who pulls the strings a youngish little man with the face of a mischievous urchin. You cannot resist the fascination of being there in the signal-box with him. By not going out and so being accessible only in his own house, Lord Beaverbrook has created an impression of something socially and intellectually special going on there.[1]

It is certainly true that Beaverbrook disliked any setting where others occupied the centre of the stage. This was true in a literal sense. He rarely went to the theatre, where others did the talking and he had to sit silent. He wrote to Dorothy Cheston on 24 September 1927, courteously addressing her as Mrs. Arnold Bennett:[2]

> I went last night to a play called "Seventh Heaven". I sat through two acts and registered a solemn vow that I would not enter a theatre again for a long time. All plays are dull. The public is persuaded by the newspapers into believing that they are interesting. Those who cannot read may find the play tolerable.

He instructed his newspapers to give more space to films than to plays— "100,000 people go to the cinema for every 100 who go to the theatre"— and his preference was not due only to the fact that he was the principal shareholder in the largest cinema chain. He himself constantly watched films, usually in his private cinema at Cherkley or the Vineyard, where he could talk all the time while the film was showing.

[1] William Gerhardi, Memoirs of a Polyglot (1931), 239, 245.
[2] Bennett's first wife refused to divorce him, and he and Dorothy Cheston were unable to go through a legal ceremony of marriage.

Beaverbrook had a particular dislike for the opera, mainly from its association with high society. He instructed the editor of The Daily Express:

> Cut down the amount of space given to the Opera. There is not sufficient public interest to justify it.

And to the editor of The Evening Standard:

> If you will read the names of the persons who went to the Opera on Monday night, you will see that they were a lot of "duffers". Most of them are too old to be out in the cold night air.

He professed a greater interest in other music, though it is unlikely that he could tell one note from another. What he liked was background noise. He had quartets down to Cherkley, again giving offence by talking during the performances. Paul Robeson received a more appreciative welcome and came four times in succession, at a fee of £84. 10. for each recital—a large sum for those days. Harriet Cohen was another welcome visitor and expressed her thanks in letters which were more than usually effusive.

Beaverbrook became acquainted with Malcolm Sargent through Michael Wardell—a man of high social connections who entered Beaverbrook's circle and employment in 1926. Beaverbrook guaranteed £1,000 for Sargent's first big concert, when he performed Hiawatha for the Royal Choral Society. On 17 October 1928 Beaverbrook wrote to Sargent:

> I should like to make for myself a small orchestra of four pieces to play me the music I want to hear. I should like the orchestra to be available at any time and to stay as long as I desire. I want the music to go on like a gramophone or a hurdy-gurdy, no matter what I do or where I go.

Sargent reduced this proposal to more sensible terms. He enlisted a quintet of young players who received a retainer of £10 a month each and were available to play at Beaverbrook's houses during the evening. This arrangement lasted until Beaverbrook became engrossed in the Empire Crusade, when the quintet was abandoned and its members found employment with the BBC orchestra.

Some of Beaverbrook's musical ventures were simply publicity for The Daily Express. This was particularly true of the community singing which he promoted in many big halls in the mid-nineteen twenties. In 1925 he announced to Bennett that he proposed to found his own symphony orchestra "as an advertisement for the Daily Express", and Bennett provided a shrewd list of possible conductors, all of whom became famous later. Beaverbrook did not pursue the idea. In 1928 he tried again with Sargent, who replied that he could run an orchestra for £15,000 a year. Again, nothing came of this. A guarantee of £500 for John Goss to give recitals of folk songs in the United States was also publicity of a sort. Much however was pure charity. Thus Beaverbrook, on Bennett's suggestion, gave Eugene Goossens a subsidy of £1,200. The arrangement did not work out well. Goossens was supposed to turn over to Beaverbrook any fees which came in during the year and instead used some of them to pay earlier debts.

Beaverbrook's charity was not of course limited to musicians. He supported old friends in Canada and did not forget his old supporters in Ashton-under-Lyne. G. H. Dyson, who had bought the bowling alley at Calgary from him, was given a job as a canvasser for The Daily Express. When Sir Reginald Brade, Beaverbrook's wartime associate at the war office, died, he left his widow unprovided for. Beaverbrook paid her an annuity which continued until her death in 1952. Two instances of his charity have a wider interest. Asquith, now Lord Oxford, was poorly off in his old age. In 1927 Lord Reading raised an annual endowment for him of £3,500, and Beaverbrook agreed to contribute £1,000 of this. The Liberal press wrote slightingly of the gift. Beaverbrook retorted that he would gladly withdraw if "the Rowntrees and Cadburys" would take over his commitment. They did not do so. Lady Oxford was more appreciative. She wrote on 30 July 1927:

> Acts of generosity such as yours are rare and remarkable. When I think of the behaviour of our Liberal *friends*—men who owe us not only their political reputation but their political salvation and contrast it with what you have done I can only say I am stunned. Bonar Law always said you were the best friend in the world and he was right.

Lord Oxford wrote on 3 August 1927:

> I have been much touched by, and more than grateful for, your kindness to me during the last fortnight. I shall always remember your generosity and your delicate consideration.

Beaverbrook replied to Lord Oxford on 6 August:

> Men who devote themselves to their country's service and suffer in their private fortunes as a consequence, make it possible for others to amass wealth under their aegis.
> I believe that I was fortunate in being included in the list of wealthy men who recognise their duty.

Beaverbrook paid only three instalments of his gift. Lord Oxford died in February 1928. Beaverbrook had a later opportunity to show his appreciation of Asquith. In 1935 Lady Oxford asked for a donation for her Soho slum kitchen and added:

> I feel rather ashamed of asking you a *fresh* favour,—as I know how much you love Mr. L.G., and despise my husband,—but you are a really generous man.

Beaverbrook replied on 14 June 1935:

> You say I despised your husband. That cannot be supported.
> I admired and praised him. Every word I have written about him is praise of him, written by an avowed political opponent.
> It is my view that he was the greatest Parliamentarian of our time.

This was overdoing things a little.

Another act of charity did not work out so well. Charles Masterman had been a Liberal politician with a brilliant promise which was never fulfilled. When he died, Arnold Bennett sought to raise a trust fund of £4,000 for the education of his children. Beaverbrook, who had often worked with Masterman and greatly admired him, at once responded with £1,000. Then he discovered that Bennett meant the idea of a trust literally. The trustees, not Beaverbrook, would decide how the money should be spent. This was not to his taste. He reluctantly paid the money and wrote to Bennett: "It gives me no pleasure". This was typical of him. Although the most generous of men, he liked to decide for himself how his money should be spent. His lesser gifts were earmarked in the same way—for a holiday, for jewellery or a new dress, for a refrigerator or a home movie.

Beaverbrook did not give only money. He was lavish with his praise and assiduous in his friendships. He greeted T. P. O'Connor on his eightieth birthday as "the greatest living journalist"—a touch of flattery which did no harm. When Tim Healy ceased to be governor general of the Irish Free State, Beaverbrook wrote to Maurice Healy, Tim's nephew and a leading barrister: "Invent some work for Tim". Subsequently he paid Tim Healy £1,000 a year to act as legal adviser to The Daily Express. He flattered D. H. Lawrence by asking for a first edition of The Rainbow —"to complete my collection". He wrote to Norman Douglas: "South Wind has been my constant companion. I turn to it over and over, and often in the night".[1] Beaverbrook pushed the sales of the novels of William Gerhardi, another associate of his, and he came near to enlisting Aldous Huxley as a columnist in The Evening Standard. He also developed a shortlived enthusiasm for George Moore and cared for him when he was in a nursing home. This enthusiasm waned when Moore, whose powers were failing, pressed on Beaverbrook an inferior work which The Evening Standard refused to serialize.

Rudyard Kipling quarrelled with Beaverbrook at the time of the Irish treaty and never spoke to him again. His place was taken, and more than taken, by Arnold Bennett, who was Beaverbrook's most intimate friend during the later nineteen-twenties. For Bennett's sake, Beaverbrook forgot his usual dislike of the theatre and helped to back the Lyric Theatre at

---

[1] This remark was accompanied by a request for a copy of How About Europe? "unless it is banned in England"—which it was not.

Hammersmith which Bennett directed. When Bennett gave him a finely-bound prayer book for his birthday, Beaverbrook wrote endearingly: "You know I prefer books to any other possessions and would give up food and drink for them". The two often went abroad together and in 1927 paid a memorable visit to Berlin along with Viscount Castlerosse. A young freelance journalist bought copies of the German magazines for them, and Beaverbrook thus discovered the talents of Sefton Delmer, later one of his most brilliant foreign correspondents.

Beaverbrook made out that he contributed little to Bennett except material gifts: "How I loved my Arnold and how he loved my champagne". In reality Beaverbrook and Bennett had deep ties of mutual love. Tim Healy had been the first to win Beaverbrook's heart. Bennett reigned supreme until his death. Valentine Castlerosse was closest to Beaverbrook during the nineteen-thirties, Stanley Morison after the war, and Michael Foot towards the end. They made a noble company.

Beaverbrook supplied much of the background for one of Bennett's most remarkable novels, Lord Raingo. This is almost a fictionalized version of Politicians and the War, which Bennett read in proof at the time. Beaverbrook also provided the central theme with less happy results. Lord Raingo had a wife in the country and a mistress in town. When the book was published, Birkenhead came to Beaverbrook in anxiety and asked: "Am I Lord Raingo?"[1] Beaverbrook replied innocently that the situation appeared to him drawn from the life of Lord Rhondda. Birkenhead went round, stating that Lord Raingo was Rhondda. Bennett denied this, asserting that Raingo was a fictional character, who had no resemblance to Lord Rhondda except that he had a mistress. There was an unseemly wrangle, from which none of the three involved came out with credit.

There is more of Beaverbrook in Lord Raingo than there is of Rhondda so far as real people are drawn on at all. Lord Raingo was minister of records, which was close enough to Beaverbrook's wartime activities, and had much the same difficulties with Lloyd George's evasiveness. There is also much of Bennett himself, but such speculations do not lead far. Essentially Lord Raingo was a work of fiction. Beaverbrook appeared more avowedly in one of H. G. Wells's novels and then only in a limited sense. Wells wrote to Beaverbrook on 1 November 1929:

> The knowing ones say I have been "putting" you "into" my book, Mr. Parham.[2] Don't you believe it. I wanted a man who had made money fast and had an original mind. You seem to be the only one who answers to that description in London. That doesn't make it you.

[1] Two other cabinet ministers asked Beaverbrook the same question. Until they asked, he had no idea that either of them was leading a double life.
[2] The full title of the book is The Autocracy of Mr. Parham. It does not occupy a high place in the Wellsian canon.

Sir Bussy Woodcock, the character concerned, has some of Beaverbrook's mannerisms and still more of his appearance in the illustrations which Low provided. That is all. Sir Bussy is an expression of Wells's faith that international capitalists would impose peace and good sense on the world. The real Beaverbrook was a good deal nearer to silly romantic Mr. Parham who dreamt of putting the British Empire back as top nation.

Beaverbrook had a wide circle of theatrical friends despite his dislike of the theatre. Among them were Noël Coward, Bea Lillie (whom he addressed as "Delicious Beatrice"), Fay Compton, Gertrude Lawrence, and Sophie Tucker. Though there was a great deal of Darling in his letters to actresses, it seems to have been mainly on paper. "Darling Sophie" for instance was in England for five months, without their managing to meet. His relations with the "Darlings" of society were much the same— more regrets at not meeting than appreciation of times spent together. Not that Beaverbrook was solitary. On the contrary, he was rarely alone. But he was a social hermit who stuck firmly to his own chosen group. He never went to other people's houses or to a public function and rarely to a restaurant. He made out that he could not stand the food and wrote to Arnold Bennett, who was persistent in invitations:

> I never go out to lunch or dinner. It is not because I would not gladly do so, but I am accustomed to my own food and if I go and eat elsewhere, I should get indigestion. I know this is an idiosyncrasy—but there you are! I know perfectly well that it is a nervous condition.

With Bennett, Beaverbrook ultimately yielded and went to tea.

Food was only the excuse, even when Beaverbrook had occasional whims for vegetarianism or even nuts and water. At other people's houses he was one guest among many. At his own table he ran the show. It was not so much that he was an autocrat, rather that he wanted to be in on everything, and he could do this only if he were in control. He always sat at the middle of his dinner table, not at the head. There he could join in three conversations at the same time—to left, to right, and also across. Similarly he did not observe the detestable English custom of sending the ladies out of the room after dinner. When dinner was over, everyone stayed or everyone moved. If the ladies had gone off on their own, Beaverbrook would have missed their society and still more their conversation. He did not believe in missing anything.

Yet there was something he missed, and which was not in his nature to make. He never had a real married life. He loved his wife, and they often had gay times with Cherkley full of distinguished guests. But with her, as with everyone else, he thought himself free to turn the tap on and off at will. When he wanted a social weekend at Cherkley, she was to provide it. When he wanted to be at the Vineyard or at Deauville or visiting

Berlin, she was to remain contentedly at Cherkley, forgetting him as he almost forgot her. He left the three children mainly to her care and, when the two boys went to Westminster, alleged that he would have sent them to Harkins Academy, Newcastle, New Brunswick, if she had not insisted on an English public school. Gladys protested against her isolation at Cherkley, as she had done long ago at Halifax, and Beaverbrook relented. He acquired Stornoway House, St. James's, as he told Arnold Bennett, "to reconcile my wife to country life". She was there a good deal, he less often. Even when he was, their habits did not coincide. She went to bed early. He came in late. She left many pencilled notes by his bedside, regretting that she had fallen asleep before he came in or had gone out before he woke up.

They had disputes usual among married couples. Gladys more than held her own as this little exchange bears witness. It is undated:

> My Lord dear Lord
> I enclose the P.S.S. saying what you desire. I greatly regret that such a mistake entered my head. perhaps I wasnt thinking clearly (or too clearly) what say you.
>
> Till three when we meet.
>   Your sleepy
>   Wifie.

The enclosure reads:

> I Gladys Beaverbrook agree to pay super tax on my private income which is to come in on June 1st
>
> | | Gladys Beaverbrook |
> |-------------|--------------------|
> | 1st witness | Gladys Drury |
> | 2nd   „ | Gladys Aitken |

She sent him this message on his forty-sixth birthday:

> For my Beloved One and may he have 46 more happy birthdays & may we have them all together.

His notes were in a similar tone, though they were usually messages of farewell. Thus:

> Sweet & beautiful
> Dear & only
>   I am off & wishing so much that you were with me.
>   My love to you for Ever & a day
>   M.

Gladys Beaverbrook was a wonderful woman. Birkenhead wrote after her death: "She had a breeding, a beauty, a poise, and a judgement which would have recommended her to any society in Europe at the most critical moment of that society. . . . She made allowances easily and generously". She made many for her husband. She accepted that he spent much of his time in the company of attractive young women. She regarded these affairs as trivial, a mere social champagne. There came a time when one was not trivial. Jean Norton was a star even in the smartest London society. She had one attraction which Gladys could not offer: she had still to be formed. Beaverbrook loved to make people. Once they were created, his interest in them declined. Gladys Beaverbrook did not need to be made. She was perfect in herself. Beaverbrook taught her how to spend money and to live as a rich woman. Her character owed nothing to him. Jean Norton, when Beaverbrook met her, was a tousleheaded Scotch lassie. He transformed her into a woman of the world. Though she often fought him, even these combats helped to shape her character.

Jean Norton had the further advantage that she was a married woman with a family to look after. She could not complain that Beaverbrook neglected her. On the contrary he complained that she was not always available when he wanted her to be, particularly during her children's holidays. Even so she became his constant companion. She, not Gladys, shared the gay evenings with Michael Wardell and Valentine Castlerosse. She, not Gladys, accompanied Beaverbrook to Deauville or on his longer trips abroad. He endowed her with shares in The Daily Express, characteristically making her pay the stamp duty. He entertained her at the Vineyard and brought her down to Cherkley. This was too much for Gladys Beaverbrook. She moved from Cherkley to Stornoway House, more or less permanently. In 1926 she departed with Janet on a trip round the world.

There was, it is clear, considerable estrangement, though not, as some have suggested, to the point of separation. Beaverbrook preserved the letters which Gladys wrote to him from Canada on her way home. Addressed to "My Darling One" or "My Darling Boy", they express her longing to be with him again. While in Canada, she was seriously ill, according to her doctors from physical exhaustion. Back in England, she went with Beaverbrook to Belgium and Le Touquet, and they were happy together for the last time. Gladys Beaverbrook was convinced that she was dying. Beaverbrook was busy with his many concerns and did not realize her condition. The doctors prescribed absolute quiet, and Beaverbrook kept away for fear of exciting her. She went to Brighton in search of rest. Beaverbrook sent her a letter which tells everything of their relations. It was ruthlessly honest and yet skilfully winning at the same time:

> How I wish you well again. There is so much happiness in life for you & me if you will get strong. The time has come when your obligations & duties are lighter & easier. You have brought up a magnificent family. Your daughter

is really a credit to you. At her age I was much more wayward & gave plenty of trouble to those about me. She will be splendid when her responsibilities begin to weigh upon her.

As to Max & Peter. They are taking after you, just as Janet takes after me. And you have a much better personality than I have. So the boys will be easier to deal with than Janet has been.

For myself, I have many faults. But I love you. If the expression of that love is full of faults the defects spring from a wilful & wayward past. But so far as my love is constant & fixed you are the object of it.

In time I will become easier & I hope better to deal with. You must give me now companionship & encouragement.

You must show me how to bring back the happy & joyous days of our youth.

With years & years before us we can live like wise people far from extravagant & foolish habits & pursuits.

You remember how happy we were in Belgium last summer, though my life was full of worry for the moment.

Let us recapture that little interlude in your illness. We can easily do it, I am *sure sure*.

But if you dont get well quickly you know in your heart that I shall get into a state of apprehension & anxiety. And when you are doubtful think of how much Ive improved in such a short time. Heaven knows there was room for it.

And I declare that you are the only permanent love in my bad & wicked life. So come back soon & strong too.

There was no coming back. Gladys Beaverbrook returned to Stornoway House, only to die there on 1 December 1927. Beaverbrook did not see her before she died. He was greatly distressed. Though he had often treated Gladys in an offhand manner, she had been a centre of his life, and he found no real substitute.

Outwardly Beaverbrook soon shook off his grief. He gave up the Vineyard and made Stornoway House his town base until it was gutted during the second world war. This seemed a move back into the world. Stornoway House was at the end of Cleveland Row at the bottom of St. James's Street. It overlooked the courtyard of St. James's Palace on one side and the Green Park on the other. Here history had been made, and Beaverbrook was to make history again in 1940 when Stornoway House provided the first offices for the ministry of aircraft production. Lord Grenville had lived here when he was prime minister in 1806–7 and Beaverbrook was fond of remarking: "Grenville lived at Stornoway House and in 1807 abolished the slave trade. I lived at Stornoway House in 1940 and reestablished the slave trade at the ministry of aircraft production". Later Lord Durham had lived here and wrote his report on Canada in the library.

Stornoway House had historic grandeur, but Beaverbrook somehow transformed it into a modest residence: an elegant dining-room on the ground floor, an impressive library on the first, a few bedrooms and bathrooms, and that was virtually all. Most of the house became offices for Beaverbrook's secretaries, of whom he had many—a chief secretary, a financial secretary, a social secretary, political secretaries, literary secretaries. He was a factory in himself. Stornoway House, despite its position, became almost as effective a retreat for Beaverbrook as the Vineyard had been. Looking out from the library over the Green Park, the centre of London seemed far away, just as Cherkley seemed to be in the Highlands of Scotland, not some twenty miles from London.

Here was a constant element in the character of this extraordinary man: for ever retreating from the world and then girding against his solitude. Beaverbrook always knew where to find others. They rarely knew where to find him. Later he fled further and further afield—to the south of France, the Bahamas and Jamaica. No sooner arrived at his chosen retreat than he was on the telephone to London, cursing the bad connection, or writing letters, imploring friends to join him. I always felt that Beaverbrook was delighted to see me and equally relieved when I went. Such was the man: he wanted to be alone and hated to be alone, sought company and was bored by it. Only the arrival of tomorrow's newspaper never failed to excite him, and then he was usually disappointed when he read it.

For a short time Beaverbrook added yet another house to his stock. He took up the breeding of racehorses and bought a house at Newmarket. This new taste gave him a little thrill of wickedness. He wrote to H. A. Gwynne on 3 July 1929:

> The sun is shining—the racing begins in an hour. Hogarth pictured it as the "road to Ruin". My spiritual leader, Mr. John Knox said: "Fornication, Abomination, Desolation".

He knew that his father would not have approved and changed the name of the house from Bedford Lodge to Calvin House "as a gesture of expiation". His racing acquaintances assumed that Calvin was a Canadian jockey.

Beaverbrook remained faithful to his spiritual leader, at any rate in words. He gave the following extraordinary answers to an enquiry from a Salvation Army journal:

1. Who was the hero of your youth? John Knox.
2. What book has helped you most? Samuel I and II.
3. What is the motto of your life? Do justly, love mercy and walk humbly.
4. What is the chief qualification for a successful career? Judgement, health and industry.

He somewhat modified his motto in an interview he gave to the American journalist, G. S. Viereck.[1] There he said:

> If you will read my book Success, which deals with money-making, you will see that I believe in doing justly. If you will read Politicians and the War, you will see that in my treatment of the incompetent I love mercy, and if you read Politicians and the Press you will see that I do *not* walk humbly.

There is another revealing passage in the interview.

> Viereck: Do you care most for money or for power?
> Beaverbrook: For neither in itself. I like activity, to wrestle with life and to beat it, to dare and win. I made my first million before I was thirty.
> Viereck: But having achieved so much, what keeps you going? Why do you spend yourself, your vitality, in politics and in business?
> Beaverbrook: To escape boredom.

He found this escape difficult. He moved restlessly from one house to another, rarely taking more than one meal in the same place or sleeping more than one night in the same bed. He claimed to take seriously his responsibility towards his sons and used this as yet another excuse for refusing social engagements. Thus in April 1928:

> I ought to explain that I am passing through the critical period in relation to my sons & do not wish to leave them during the holidays on that account.

In practice, this only meant occasional weekends at Cherkley or taking them with him on his visits to Deauville. There the two boys were consigned to bed at ten o'clock in the evening while their father went off to the Casino.

Beaverbrook's relationship with Jean Norton grew ever closer, and she remained the predominant, though not the only, woman in his life until her death in 1945. He then destroyed every scrap of their correspondence, but by some chance there came into his possession her private diaries for the years 1928 to 1931. These record the engagements of a society woman—bridge, the theatre, backgammon, even "washed my hair". They also record her almost daily meetings with Beaverbrook: "Dinner with M at the Vineyard", "To Stornoway, stopped the night", "At Cherkley. Rode with M a.m." Sometimes there is a more personal note: "Row", "Hell of a row", "trouble still continuing", "unsatisfactory talk with M", and then: "M perfectly sweet", "all's well", "blissfully happy", until the pattern was repeated.

---

[1] The interview was given in May 1929. The first passage quoted is however an insertion by Bruce Lockhart, who revised the interview for Beaverbrook in December 1929. The interview, as revised, was published in The New York American in June 1930.

Beaverbrook kept another record in the blotter of his desk. It is headed, in his pencilled scrawl, "By Mrs Norton Undated":

> How should not absence from thy presence change me,
> Since in thy presence all my future is,
> And in thy absence all things do estrange me
> From that, and bind me to past miseries.
> I, like a shadow, when the lighted candle
> Is snuffed, into a little pool of Black,
> Shrink in a second.—But if you rekindle
> Your flame,—Then on the instant I am back.—
> Oh my bright candle,—Since it is your virtue
> And use to shine, Set my shadow moving.
> Shine, well assured that nought in me can hurt you,
> And least my small and ghostly way of loving,
> Ghosts with God's word are laid, but mine with less,
> Who only need for that, my dear man's "Yes".

Let this be her memorial.

CHAPTER ELEVEN

PRELUDE TO THE EMPIRE CRUSADE,
1928–29

The death of Gladys Beaverbrook was not the only break in Beaverbrook's life towards the end of 1927. At exactly the same time, he gave up his rooms at The Daily Express and never entered them again except on one dark night during the second world war, when he brought Churchill to see a Russian film. He even claimed that he had never set eyes on the new Express building in Fleet Street which was put up some years after his departure. Certainly he refused to advise on its design or financing, with the remark: "Lord Beaverbrook says he ain't going to work no more no more".

When Beaverbrook moved his office to Stornoway House every scrap of his dealings—financial, journalistic, political, and personal—was preserved in rows of files, which have weighed heavily upon his biographer. Thus for the year 1929 alone there are 30 boxes of general correspondence, 4 of correspondence with The Express papers, 2 with The Evening Standard, another 10 with Canada, to say nothing of household receipts and stock exchange dealings. His private activities were full of whims. He always paid his bills at once and knocked off 10% discount. Many stores disputed this, claiming that they had already made a reduction, and a bitter correspondence followed. For almost forty years, he never failed to rise to the bait. He checked the details of each bill and queried much. No scrap of expenditure escaped him. He disliked committing himself financially for the future. When asked to pay his subscription to the Other Club by bankers' order, he replied to Freddy Guest: "No Canadian, faithful to his upbringing, could possibly put his name to a bankers' order".

He took advantages, though not money, from his papers. He bought the petrol for his cars, the lawnmower for his garden, and even the motor car which he presented to Mrs. Norton through The Evening Standard, so as to obtain the trade discount. His action in regard to review books and gramophone records sent to his papers was outrageous, at any rate in the eyes of a professional reviewer. He simply claimed the lot: "No review books or gramophone records are to leave The Daily Express office until

Lord Beaverbrook says whether he wants them", and he sent lists two or three times a week. The wretched reviewer had to write his review in the office and then departed without the book which otherwise he would have been able to sell at half price. When St. John Ervine, a very distinguished writer, jibbed, Beaverbrook merely laid down: "The choice between Lord Beaverbrook and Irvine must be made". When a ticker was installed at Stornoway House on election night, he queried the bill for £20, and this time with more reason: "He gives The Express continuous service. Should the paper charge him for acquiring information and results which enable it to get such service". The Express paid.

Each year saw some particular comedy. 1928 was the year of the piano tuning dispute. The music firm offered an annual contract, payable in advance, for four quarterly visits. Beaverbrook wished to pay for each visit individually after it had happened. When defeated on this, he kept careful tally on the tuner's visits, until he was able to announce triumphantly one year that the tuner had called only three times. Even then he lost: the tuner had called only to learn that Lord Beaverbrook was away and Stornoway House closed. 1929 saw the row over the delivery charge which W. H. Smith's made for bringing newspapers to Cherkley. Beaverbrook claimed that there should be a reduction for the days when he became impatient and sent down his chauffeur for the papers at dawn. He obtained no reduction and therefore cancelled his newspaper order. For some time the chauffeur had to collect the papers off the train every morning. In the end Beaverbrook admitted defeat.

A main task of his secretaries was to fend off enquiries with such statements as that Lord Beaverbrook was away in the country, busy racing, or merely that he had withdrawn from all public affairs. He himself dictated most of these statements. He had a fantasy that his life was over. Thus to J. C. C. Davidson on 27 May 1928:

> My aim is to move further and further from Party politics and more and more in the direction of an old age devoted to contemplation and repose.

Beaverbrook was then forty nine and had another thirty six years to live. He was already announcing the retirement to Canada which he never achieved. He wrote to G. L. Berry on 31 August 1929: "I intend to return to Canada and spend the rest of my days in peace". When James Rothschild innocently enquired whether his peerage was the last bestowed on a Canadian, he pretended not to take up the challenge, though he actually did so. He wrote to Rothschild on 5 November 1928:

> I am getting to be an old man, and—I think and hope—a kindly one. In consequence, I do not argue or dispute with anyone.

He then went on to point out that his barony had been given in 1916, that other honours were given to Canadians between 1916 and 1919, and that the practice was stopped in 1919 after a debate in the Canadian parliament where his own peerage was not mentioned.

Beaverbrook claimed, too, that he had lost interest in financial adventures. He wrote to Lord Wargrave: "I always go for the long shot. The quick turnover does not interest me", and to Richard Norton, who aspired to act as his financial adviser: "I hate selling securities. I like to invest the cash I may possess in permanent holdings". He added that his Canadian enterprises were conducted in entire independence by his brother Allan. In fact, as his files show, he directed Allan's every move, and, if he did not speculate for himself, he certainly did so for others, as his intimate friends still often found to their surprise and advantage. A financial writer on one of his papers who slipped up soon learnt that Lord Beaverbrook had studied the London and New York prices that morning more carefully than he had. On any really big deal, finance had its old excitement for him. In November 1928 he sold his cinema interests at a fivefold profit and telegraphed to Lady Diana Cooper this apology for missing her dinner party (which no doubt he would have scraped out of somehow in any case):

> All day yesterday I was involved in the most difficult negotiations for the sale of our cinema interests for a very large sum of money and only received my deposit at the Tivoli cinema at ten o'clock last night. I returned to Stornoway House at half past eleven greatly excited and forgetting everything except the aftermath of financial battle. . . . Men of affairs are unreliable in social appointments and deserve nothing but contempt and derision from the world of society and politics.

Beaverbrook's ostensible withdrawal from active finance had one element of truth in it, though the withdrawal itself surely had financial motives and did not spring from world-weariness. During 1928 and the early part of 1929 Beaverbrook sold a large proportion of his ordinary shares and placed the proceeds in secure bonds. In England, as well as selling his cinema interests, he sold all his shares in the Daily Mail Trust on the open market. In Canada, he sold out almost entirely from the Canada Cement Company and liquidated many of his smaller holdings. Of course share prices were high at this time, and it was reasonable for Beaverbrook to take his profits. It is tempting to suggest that there was a deeper motive—a flash of intuition such as Beaverbrook had often shown before, by which he unconsciously sensed the great depression of 1929–33. Whatever the explanation, this shift in investment policy certainly enabled Beaverbrook to remain a rich man throughout the depression when others were ruined.

At one moment Beaverbrook's withdrawal was on the point of extending to his newspapers. In October 1927 Rothermere revolted against the unequal terms of their partnership. He was paying Beaverbrook large sums from the profits of The Daily Mail. His Daily Mail Trust was receiving very little from its holding in The Daily Express, which instead was being built up as the deadly rival of The Daily Mail. Rothermere therefore insisted, in his usual peremptory manner, that he *must have* Beaverbrook's newspaper interests. He offered "the immense sum" of two and a half million pounds for what "may not prove to be at any time a profitable transaction". Beaverbrook seemed to be on the point of accepting the offer. Rothermere added the condition, which was not unreasonable, that Beaverbrook must undertake not to engage in any new newspaper enterprise. Beaverbrook refused. Rothermere then replied that, without such an undertaking, Beaverbrook's 51% holding was not worth more than one million pounds. Beaverbrook turned smartly round and offered to buy the Daily Mail Trust's 49% at that price. Rothermere refused the offer, and negotiations were broken off. Financially relations between the two men continued to be uneasy, but this does not seem to have affected their personal or political cooperation.

Beaverbrook resumed his modest role as "principal shareholder". Thus, refusing to advise on an article: "I have retired and intend to spend the evetide of my life far from the quarrels of Fleet Street". Refusing to advise on the balance sheet:

> I am just a retired old man but willing to read the newspaper, make comments on it from time to time, submit suggestions, and give my advice on politics.

This was to the financial manager. To Blumenfeld, Beaverbrook put his refusal the other way round: he would advise on finance, but not on "the contents and production of the newspaper":

> To do anything of the kind would involve my living under the same roof with you and your colleagues and being compelled to take hourly decisions. It would be quite impossible for me to live any such life.

Of course no one on his newspapers took these statements seriously. When Robertson, the manager, stated at a staff dinner that Lord Beaverbrook had withdrawn from the conduct of the papers, this statement, he regretted to report, was received with "general laughter".

From afar, Beaverbrook criticized the quality of the ink and the newsprint, the style of the leaders and the judgements of the music critic. He complained that there were no New York stock exchange prices. On 18 May 1928 Beverley Baxter received this rebuke:

> Lord Beaverbrook has not the time to point out the mistakes in the Savage[1] story, and, like the hairs of the head, it is doubtful if they can be numbered.

[1] Presumably the case of Miss Savidge.

Hannen Swaffer, the dramatic critic, was told after one piece: "It tastes like boiled potatoes that were prepared for dinner last night and hashed for breakfast this morning". The Daily Express attacked both the League of Nations and the Olympic Games "at my instigation". His wrath was terrible if a sub-editor changed a single word in any leader which he had dictated.

Beaverbrook rejected any comparison of himself with Northcliffe and stamped on attempts to give him Northcliffe's title of "The Chief". His secretary wrote: "Lord Beaverbrook does not come from the Highlands of Scotland nor is he head of The Daily Express", and on another occasion: "Lord Beaverbrook is nobody's Chief. He springs from the Scottish serfs. The only Chief in his family is his son-in-law".[1] In fact The Daily Mail was his standard of comparison at every moment. When at Newmarket he wanted to know why The Daily Mail's early edition arrived before that of The Daily Express. He chased after a device for telegraphing illustrations and wrote to its American owner on 19 March 1928:

> The two great newspaper groups in England are locked in a death grapple. One or the other must emerge with supremacy. Things will change.
> The Daily Express so far has had to fight an uphill battle. But it looks as if we might get to the mountain top shortly. So you can see that my heart's desires are centred in the Daily Express.

On 30 October 1928 he told Davidson, the Conservative party chairman: "I shall go back to New Brunswick and retire a failure if I don't succeed in killing The Daily Mail". Though Beaverbrook anxiously counted the advertisements and suggested ways of getting new ones, he knew that he could win in the end only by producing a better newspaper. As he wrote to William Mellor, editor of The Daily Herald: "Whoever reads the newspaper must be convinced that its first object is to tell him the news of the day and that its other aims must be subordinate to this".

Beaverbrook was himself always ready to act as a publicity agent for his paper. When the first volume of Politicians and the War was published in the autumn of 1928, Beaverbrook was more concerned to serialize it in The Evening Standard than to see it as a book, and indeed gave all rights in it to The Evening Standard. The paper, not Beaverbrook, made the contract with the publisher. This was an aspect of his general reluctance to make money out of anything except his central financial activities, just as he refused to take a salary, or even expenses, when a minister in both world wars. It reflected, too, his timidity as an author, a timidity which made him explain to his friends, quite wrongly, that the book was a mere diary, not a work of history.

This first volume of Politicians and the War had to compete with

---

[1] Ian Campbell, first husband of Janet Aitken and later duke of Argyll.

Asquith's Memoirs which came out at almost the same time—a more substantial and, it was alleged, a more reliable work. The only favourable reviews were in Beaverbrook's own papers, though the reviewers were by no means satellites of his. Philip Snowden in The Daily Express called it "a work of great historical importance", and A. G. Gardiner in The Sunday Express found, to his surprise, that it was "a real contribution to the resources of the historian". Philip Guedalla, the only historian or near-historian to notice it, dismissed it in The Nation as "a blend of hearsay and random anecdote", and the anonymous reviewer in The New Statesman said: "It is not history, nor even the material of history. . . . A great deal of it is sheer unhistorical nonsense".

The book sold only 9,000 copies, and the publisher did not recover the advance he had given on it. A later generation was readier to accept the realities of life, and Beaverbrook's book was accepted at its true worth. When republished in 1960, it was also a financial success, though perhaps not by his standards. When I remarked to him that he could now live on his royalties if all else failed, he replied: "Not the way I live".

Beaverbrook lived always as a very rich man. He maintained three houses in going order. In 1929 at Cherkley alone he paid tax on 21 male servants. He spent £300,000 on his racehorses before he abandoned racing, more from boredom than because it cost too much. He complained of racing men: "They know nothing of politics or books. They can talk only about horses". He spent large sums on his yachts and later on his private aircraft. All the same Beaverbrook loved the romance of wealth rather than its rewards. When Gerhardi asked him whether he was a multimillionaire, he replied: "No, a Maxi-millionaire", and that was nearer the truth. Though he liked others to imagine that he was fabulously wealthy, he was in fact a millionaire on a fairly modest scale and nothing like so rich as the real tycoons—Lord Cowdray, Sir John Ellerman, or even Lord Rothermere. Once he had enough money to live without anxiety, he did not bother to acquire more, and his reputation for great wealth rested largely on his readiness to give it away.

His day-to-day life was comparatively simple. He gave two or three large parties a year at Stornoway House, with professional singers or players. Otherwise he rarely had more than two guests at lunch and four or at the most six at dinner. The weekend parties at Cherkley were small except on special occasions such as Christmas or his birthday, and Cherkley itself was for a country house on a modest scale. He did not spend much on his clothes, went rarely to the theatre or the opera and provided cigars and champagne more for his guests than for himself. His one luxury was the private cinema, where he watched mainly westerns and the Marx Brothers. Even so most of the films were provided free by the distributors as a "plug" for their wares.

Many people have described Beaverbrook's appearance. Christiansen, who worked with him for thirty years, has a good account of their first meeting:

> Lord Beaverbrook was a mere forty-seven, a tiny figure in a blue serge suit. . . . He had a little "pot" around the middle then, and he has the same little "pot" now. He wore blue serge suits then and he wears them now. . . . He wore black trilby hats and drab black overcoats then and he does so now. He wore buttons on his shirts then, having no patience with cuff-links, and he still wears buttons now. He wore white shirts and still does. He did not care if his collars were frayed then, nor does he now. The knot of his tie was loose and careless then and is now.[1]

Beaverbrook had the appearance of a Presbyterian minister, were it not for his mischievously Puckish face.

There was one odd thing about him. Christiansen writes of his "tiny figure". Everyone spoke of him as "the little man". In fact he was a good medium height, just under five feet nine inches in his socks, and his physique was powerful. Yet the impression of slightness and fragility was inescapable. It was, I think, Beaverbrook's quickness of movement which made people see him as smaller than he was—again a sort of Puckish illusion. He was there one moment and gone the next.

The great difference between Beaverbrook and most rich men was that he worked all the time. Boredom alone would have driven him to this even if he had not had other motives. He followed the stock markets, more in New York than in London, and convinced himself by an occasional speculation that he had not lost his cunning. He exasperated his servants by enquiring into the household economy. Above all, he read every copy of his three papers and usually compared them with their rivals. He counted the "Smalls" in The Evening Standard and noted each exclusive story, achieved or missed, in The Daily Express. He looked over the weekly sales figures and raised queries over the six-monthly accounts. He always carried financial figures in his head and could therefore ask at once: why are we £20,000 down on last year? Or, more critically, why have we so much cash in hand? For Beaverbrook believed sternly that the object of money was to use it. Every day for forty years, except when he was a minister during the second world war, Beaverbrook was a more scrupulous reader of newspapers than anyone else in Great Britain. What had begun as a hobby became a thraldom from which he made only ineffectual attempts to escape.

Though Beaverbrook groaned at the prospect of addressing meetings or attending dinners, he went whenever Robertson told him that it was good for the papers. One such prospect threatened to take him further

[1] A. Christiansen, Headlines All My Life (1961), 47.

afield. Relations between Great Britain and Soviet Russia had been broken off in 1927 after the police raid on Arcos offices. Robertson wrote in March 1928:

> It would be a wonderful thing for The Daily Express if we could be the means of re-opening Trade relations through your personal intervention!

Beaverbrook was tempted and discussed the idea of visiting Russia with E. F. Wise, adviser to the Russian cooperatives. He consulted Churchill who returned a discouraging answer:

> Either you wd speak up for them on yr return, or you wd run them down. If you did the former, you wd probably (unless they have changed vy much) run counter to prevailing opinion here. If the latter, they wd think it rather shabby of you after having lavished, as they no doubt would, their most seductive caresses upon you.

Beaverbrook then got cold feet and wrote to Wise on 6 June 1928:

> I am a ruined man in the world of politics. I cannot take any interest in current events. . . . I tried to put my attitude down to uncertainty and doubt about the future. But it is not so. The real truth is that I am no longer of any use in the world.

Ruined or not, Beaverbrook was drawn back into politics as the general election approached. He had already foreseen its outcome and had charted his own course in a letter to R. B. Bennett of 14 November 1927:

> The Conservative party will be defeated—and pretty badly defeated at that. I would not be surprised if the Labour Party came back as the largest single party in the next house of commons—but with Lloyd George and his Liberals holding the balance of power.
> . . . .
> I suppose I shall have to support the Government and oppose Lloyd George. For I am in favour of a strong Navy and against a form of Land Nationalization in agricultural districts which is Lloyd George's first plank in his programme.
> Thus I shall be reduced willy-nilly to supporting Baldwin, whom I like personally, but regard as perfectly incompetent in the intellectual sphere. He takes no part in Cabinet discussion and is a mere cypher in his own administration.

On 4 August 1928 he wrote to Mackenzie King, another Canadian prime minister with whom he had established friendly relations:

> The Tory party is fundamentally disunited on Protection and the moment the subject is given any prominence the mischief is done.
> Joynson Hicks knows his own strength and the weakness of Churchill. He knows that he is the only possible alternative to or successor to Baldwin. . . . He beat Baldwin on the Prayer Book and probably reflects that he might

beat him again on the next issue. Yet Baldwin always treats him with contempt—and Bonar Law used to do just the same. . . .

Luckily for the Conservatives and for Baldwin, Rothermere, his chief
enemy, has not grasped what is up. He is silent when his Press ought to be
out every day stirring up the mischief by printing articles in favour of
Protection. But Rothermere doesn't understand when to bring his machine
guns into action. It is the old story "Sheridan was twenty miles away".

Beaverbrook himself did not bring his machine guns into action: Empire
Free Trade did not appear in the columns of The Daily Express. As to
the idea that Joynson Hicks might succeed Baldwin, Birkenhead made the
only possible comment: "Never swop donkeys when crossing a stream".

On 1 October 1928 Beaverbrook gave a somewhat unusual survey of
electoral prospects in a letter to Herbert Swope of The New York World.
Swope persuaded him to expand his views in an article which duly
appeared in The New York World on 16 December. After discussing the
weaknesses of Conservatives and Labour, Beaverbrook went on to praise
Lloyd George but argued that his programme of economic reconstruction
was too like Labour's to be a winner. Beaverbrook therefore urged that
the Liberals should run on a ticket of disestablishment, anti-gambling,
and prohibition. He added: "of course such a step would be contrary to
my own convictions. . . . However it sometimes takes an outside observer
to detect new movements in an old country". The Liberals did not take
this advice, which, however much against Beaverbrook's convictions,
betrayed the relics of his puritanical background.

Beaverbrook's letter to Swope also contained an interesting personal
judgement:

> A coming figure in Socialist politics is Sir Oswald Mosley, the Socialist
> baronet. His opponents stigmatize him as an adventurer and declare that as
> a consequence he has no future in politics. I think they are premature and
> ill-informed in this judgement. They do not know the working side of
> Mosley's life. . . . I do not perceive that he is any more of an opportunist
> than a good many other eminent politicians I could name who sit entrenched
> in apparent respectability on Conservative or Liberal front benches.
>
> Sir O. Mosley is the type of recruit to the Socialist ranks which is certain
> to bring quite undeserved yet formidable accessions of strength to that party,
> namely, the young men in search of careers and the other glittering prizes
> of life.

Writing to Borden on 26 December 1928 Beaverbrook was less enthusiastic about Mosley:

> There are no new young men anywhere—except Oswald Mosley who sits
> on the Socialist benches. He is a careerist like Birkenhead and Churchill.
> The type is familiar. Mosley has more character than Birkenhead but less
> personality than Churchill.

Most of Beaverbrook's letter to Borden was occupied, as usual, with Baldwin. Somewhat earlier, on 31 August 1927, Beaverbrook had sent this account of Baldwin to Fred R. Taylor, a friend in New Brunswick:

> He never reads books but digs into them in an occasional way, reading a sentence here and there out loud and asking his associates to admire it. He used to spend much of his time playing an automatic organ. He is fond of his food and when his stomach is full, he pats it appreciatively. He says occasionally shrewd and witty things; but not very often.

Now however Beaverbrook reported to Borden that Baldwin had delivered a brilliant speech at a dinner to celebrate Birkenhead's son's coming of age: "I began to revise all my views of his powers". Beaverbrook also wrote to Birkenhead on this occasion (8 December 1928):

> That boy is going to make a very brilliant man. If I may say so without impertinence (and I admit that the remark trenches on impertinence) after an intimate acquaintance of eighteen years standing—persuade him not to touch all the things with which you and I made too early an acquaintance. I mean by this the pleasures of life. It is really better for a boy on the pure calculation of happiness to be an anchorite.

Birkenhead replied in the same spirit on 10 December:

> As to his own life I am sure you are right. But I am unlikely to help him by example and therefore disqualified from rescuing him by advice. He must dree his own weird. But I think he is steadier by nature than we were.

On the general outlook Beaverbrook remained gloomy. His letter to Borden continued:

> Churchill is plunged in despair. He accepted electoral defeat in advance, but then his judgment on such matters is worse than that of any prominent man I know.
> Birkenhead is out and down—for good I should say ...
> I believe that the Conservatives will be defeated if only by a Liberal-Socialist combination. But the Socialists are within "a hoop and a holler" of a straight win.

Beaverbrook's life had often been shaped by accidents. Now one occurred literally. Just before Christmas 1928 he was involved in a car crash at Surbiton. Though badly shaken, he was not seriously injured and soon recovered. Maurice Woods, who was with him, had two ribs broken and, being already in weak health, succumbed to pneumonia in February 1929. This was a catastrophic loss for Beaverbrook. He never found again a secretary who could reproduce his thoughts and expressions so well or who could write a sustained historical narrative. The loss of Maurice Woods interrupted Beaverbrook's activities as a historian for a quarter of a century. The second volume of Politicians and the War was ready for publication and would have come out in May 1929 if it had not been for the general election. Then the Empire Crusade caused further postponement until 1932. Woods also left a draft of My Early Life, which Beaverbrook apparently intended to publish—at any rate he showed the proofs to Churchill in September 1930. Churchill remarked: "We both had to try very hard when we were young", and Beaverbrook replied: "We both had a big job on when we were young. But we have a bigger one on now that we are old". My Early Life was held up until 1956 and then came out a good deal altered. Woods also left a draft which Beaverbrook used at the end of his life for the later chapters of The Decline and Fall of Lloyd George. Among Beaverbrook's major works, only Men and Power owes nothing to Maurice Woods.

As a thank-offering for his escape, Beaverbrook gave £25,000 to charity. He asked Baldwin to distribute this for him, almost as though Baldwin were the voice of his conscience. Of course it also enabled him to refer begging letters to Baldwin for a long time. Baldwin actually broke his longstanding vow against entering under Beaverbrook's roof and called at Stornoway House. Afterwards Baldwin told Tom Jones about this "extraordinary interview":

> He is an extraordinary mixture and I think that since the death of his wife the better elements of him have been coming to the surface. He had a really narrow escape from death and I found him very earnest about things. . . . He told me that after Bonar's death he had played a low mean game and that he was sorry. Whereupon I said I wished to bear no malice towards any man, and I shook hands with him.

As to the money:

> I asked him did he want to endow a Professorship or to help one or two big objects, like cancer research, or was I to give it away in packets? He replied, "Packets", adding that he had in train a scheme for some foundation for endowment later on.[1]

The conversation showed both Baldwin's complacency and Beaverbrook's tendency to overdo the guile.

News of this gift was made public. Another, of much the same time, has remained shrouded in secrecy. The story sheds a curious light on the claim made for Baldwin that he cleaned up politics and ended the association of honours with gifts to party funds. In the autumn of 1928 Beaverbrook was sorting out his cinema finances, preparatory to making a large profit. One of these subsidiary deals was the acquisition of shares in Standard Film Company from Andrew Holt, son of Sir Herbert Holt, Beaverbrook's old banker-friend in Montreal. Beaverbrook must have

---

[1] Tom Jones, Whitehall Diary, ii, 167. The explanation of the gift, provided by the editor in a footnote, is erroneous.

suggested that he should use the money to buy Andrew Holt a knight-hood. Holt agreed. On 27 November 1928 Beaverbrook received this letter from J. C. C. Davidson, chairman of the Conservative party and confidant first of Law's and then of Baldwin's:

> Please write a letter recommending H either to the P.M. or me preferably to Baldwin. I can't make a definite promise but I think it will be all right.
>
> What is essential is a recommendation in writing however short & the reasons.

Beaverbrook replied the same day:

> Here is the letter for the P.M. I think it is a good case.

The letter praised Holt's work for commercial aviation and concluded:

> I am sure he would be much encouraged if he were recommended to the King for the honour of knighthood.

Baldwin replied at once in his own hand:

> I can never give an undertaking where an honour is concerned but I will give my personal attention to the claims of Mr. Andrew Holt about whom you have written.

Beaverbrook sent three telegrams to Holt:

> I have received message from Davidson to say that my proposals will be accepted.
>
> I have received letter in reply to mine from top man in equally satisfactory terms. January first is proper date.
>
> Position may be summarized as follows. Everything in order & two letters in my possession. Of course you understand there is always the last fence to jump.

On 15 December Beaverbrook wrote to Davidson:

> Here is the ten thousand pounds.

Davidson replied on 17 December:

> Thank you most awfully for the ten thousand pounds for which I am most grateful.
>
> It is a very anxious time for me!

Beaverbrook wrote to Davidson on the same day:

> I am sure you know the source of supply.
>
> I only scribble this note in case you may think that I am the good Samaritan myself. I know you dont think so. But then, you might.

Davidson answered on 18 December:

> I realized what the Source is. It will be all right though a week or two later than normally would be the case.

Beaverbrook's activities were then impeded by his car accident. He did not telegraph Holt until 29 December: "I am confirmed two weeks postponement", and Holt's name did not appear in the New Year list of honours.

The delay was much longer than two weeks. In mid-March Beaverbrook telegraphed to Holt:

> D came to see me on Tuesday. Declares that omission of name due to misfortune on account of illness of another person. I remained very stiff. D says can be remedied in May suggests you come to see him & receive personal assurance supported by his superior.

The illness was presumably that of the king, though this seems an inadequate reason. With May came the general election. The Conservatives lost. Davidson held out new hope for the resignation honours. Beaverbrook telegraphed to Holt on 5 June 1929:

> Davidson has avoided me all day. There is another issue in a few days but I have been swindled so dreadfully that I believe nothing.

Holt's name did not appear in the resignation list. On 12 June Davidson concluded the correspondence:

> You sent me on December 15th 1928 a cheque for £10,000. As I have had no occasion to make use of the money I return it herewith.

Beaverbrook had a fleeting hope of doing a deal with the Labour government. At any rate, he telegraphed to Holt on 13 June: "Have arranged with the new custodian on satisfactory lines". Nothing came of this also, and Andrew Holt never received a knighthood. Instead he received his money from Beaverbrook on 3 August.

This is a mysterious episode. Holt did not receive a knighthood, and therefore no honour was sold. But Davidson clearly knew that money was being paid for this purpose, and it is difficult to believe that Baldwin was kept in ignorance. Did Davidson take the money merely for the pleasure of paying it back as he seems to have done in other cases? This too is unlikely. Maybe he was hoping to secure the support of Beaverbrook's newspapers for the Conservative party until the election was over and so pretended to meet Beaverbrook's wishes. There is no means of knowing. Money was paid. A knighthood was promised. Baldwin's claim to clean hands is hardly redeemed by the fact that the promise was not kept.

Another act of charity by Beaverbrook had no political overtone. He was captivated by Dr. Charles Wilson, later Lord Moran, who urged him to provide a new medical school for St. Mary's Hospital. Beaverbrook decided to survey conditions for himself. He went alone to the outpatients' department and studied the crowded benches. There was a cafeteria serving tea and buns:

> I wondered whether it was a profit-making enterprise. Now I had just breakfasted on orange juice, toast, butter, honey and coffee. While I did not seek food it was my intention to gain information. So I asked the attendant at the counter, an old lady of benign countenance: "How much for a bun and a cup of coffee?" The old lady answered: "A penny for tea and a bun". Certainly the cafeteria was not operating at a profit. I went back to my place on the bench. The old lady then came over to me and whispered: "If you haven't got a penny you can have the bun and tea free". I thanked her and replied with truth: "I'm not hungry".

When Wilson came in and greeted Beaverbrook, the old lady was greatly distressed. She ran after Wilson, whispering: "What shall I do? What shall I do? I've made a terrible mistake. Shall I apologize?" Wilson answered: "Do nothing. You've got us our money". Beaverbrook provided £63,000 for the new building. He also bought trouble later. He backed Wilson against Horder as president of the Royal Society of Physicians, and Horder never forgave him.

In January 1929 Beaverbrook, to recover from his accident, departed with Jean Norton and other friends, on a cruise to the West Indies. The preparations displayed one of his whims. The Cunard Company asked for a deposit of £100. Beaverbrook's secretary replied:

> Lord Beaverbrook never pays a deposit. If he has to cancel his reservations, he pays in full, unless the Company can dispose of them.

The trip seems to have been a success. At any rate Jean Norton, who had to return before Beaverbrook, wired to him: "Dammit I'm bored". When Beaverbrook got back he found the pre-electoral jockeying in full swing. He wrote to J. M. Patterson of New York on 24 March 1929:

> George has got a sudden accession of strength & it appears likely that Rothermere will support him. If George gets consistent support he will win a great many seats & so no doubt hold the balance of power in the next Parliament.
>
> In that case I think he will work with the Conservatives, forming a Government possibly under the leadership of some reputable member of that party, who will leave the parliamentary machine to George's keeping.
>
> The Conservative party stands no chance of coming back with a majority. Baldwin has frittered away his heritage again. He cannot help it. He sits down in the garden with his arms folded and talks about the beauty of it, while the weeds grow all about him.

On 26 March 1929 Beaverbrook wrote to Borden:

> Lloyd George's unemployment scheme is sound and has raised a lot of enthusiasm.

Churchill himself appears to be more defeatist than ever. I dined with him last night and I judge he is certain the Government is going out. The Conservative faith in Baldwin has evaporated.

Churchill has no intention whatever of allying himself with Lloyd George, though rumours to this effect in Conservative circles are doing him a great deal of harm.

A month later, on 30 April 1929, Beaverbrook wrote to Borden again:

Baldwin is promising nothing, and is deriving a certain amount of glamour from this assumed modesty. He is, in fact, cunningly posing as the typical John Bull, and may even get support on this ground.

Ramsay MacDonald is anxious at all costs to appear reasonable and moderate, and his speeches might all be made by Baldwin.

Lloyd George is making the running of the election, and he alone has persuaded the electors that he has a definite scheme for the cure of unemployment, which is the one and only issue.

On the other hand, his past pledges are continually being brought up against him, and are his opponents' chief weapon.

Beaverbrook was always fascinated by political manoeuvring, whether he were taking part in it or not. The electorate was less concerned. Beaverbrook wrote to E. M. Young, an American friend, on 15 May 1929:

The public apathy is astonishing. . . . I have never known anything remotely resembling the indifference of the public on this occasion. Nor can I think of a satisfactory explanation.

Beaverbrook's newspapers did little to disturb the calm. He had no faith in Baldwin and disliked the slogan of Safety First. He recognized that Lloyd George had the only creative policy, but could not bring himself to say so in public. In the last resort, Beaverbrook, despite his vaunted independence, could never shake himself free from the Conservative party. Now, all his papers could think of was to run a campaign for larger railway wagons—hardly an idea to awaken electoral controversy.

The poll on 31 May fulfilled some, though not all, of Beaverbrook's estimates. The Conservatives won 260 seats—exactly the figure he gave as their maximum in a telegram to Rothermere on 12 May. But Labour did better and the Liberals worse than he had expected. Labour won 288 seats and the Liberals only 59. Lloyd George supported Labour, as everyone except Beaverbrook had expected, and Ramsay MacDonald formed his second government. However, Beaverbrook felt justified on his main point: his warnings against Baldwin had proved true. He wrote to Sir E. H. Vestey on 5 June: "In my opinion the Conservative party will have no success in the future unless there is a change of leadership", and to E. M. Young on 17 June:

The Government richly deserved its fate. . . . If the Conservative Party re-forms and divests itself of the banking element, and if the Leader gives up his vendetta against Horne, Birkenhead, etc., the next election will give the Party another chance of office.

There were those who felt that Beaverbrook had his share of responsibility. At a Derby Eve dinner on 5 June Birkenhead put the blame for Conservative defeat on Beaverbrook and Rothermere. Beaverbrook replied with this telegram on 6 June:

That Jemmy Twitcher should peach me I own surprised me.

Arnold Bennett, who had his own reasons for disliking Birkenhead, no doubt supplied this quotation from the Beggar's Opera, which he had himself produced at the Lyric Theatre, Hammersmith. The allusion was both appropriate and offensive, as both Bennett and Birkenhead knew. In 1765 Lord Sandwich, a notorious rake, denounced John Wilkes in the house of lords for his obscene Essay on Woman. That evening Sandwich rashly attended the Beggar's Opera, and at the reference to Jemmy Twitcher the whole house rose in delighted applause. Sandwich was known as Jemmy Twitcher for the rest of his life.

Birkenhead hit back savagely the same day. After recounting Beaverbrook's persistent denigration of Baldwin, he went on:

While during my political career you have often shown me great friendship and very valuable support, you have very often caused me deep mortification and done me great injury. Your Cartoonist over a long period of time published filthy and disgusting cartoons of me which were intended and calculated to do me deep injury.

Anyone who has turned over the albums of Low's cartoons will know what Birkenhead meant. Beaverbrook was unabashed. He replied on 7 June:

I rejoiced in Baldwin's downfall. I wanted the defeat of the Government because I believe it was bad.

If I am right in assuming that you did not regret it, then my Jemmy Twitcher telegram is to the point.

You are out of touch with the times, and I am too old at fifty. The new generation like the Low caricatures. For my part, Low outrages my feelings when he makes me crawl out from under the table or peep through the door. But I hold the view that a caricature cannot give good ground for complaint. Perhaps I am wrong, but I stick to it.

The Conservatives are trying to blame everybody but the right persons, for their failure at the polls. They had better concentrate on their jockey.

It would be wrong to leave the relations between the two old friends on this sad note. The Jemmy Twitcher telegram was soon forgotten, at

any rate in appearance. The next year Birkenhead died. Beaverbrook
wrote a letter of sympathy to Lady Birkenhead on 2 October 1930 and
concluded:

> You may be in some confusion about your plans, if you have given them
> any thought at all. Would you & Freddy & Pam allow me to continue the
> arrangements you & Fred made for their education?

It did not prove necessary for the Birkenhead family to take up this
generous offer, but Beaverbrook settled annuities of £325 on Lady
Eleanor and Lady Pamela Smith for ten years as a tribute to their father.
Further, when the second Lord Birkenhead was preparing to write his
father's life, Beaverbrook wrote to him on 21 September 1934:

> Your father fought hard and clean. He never concealed that he wanted
> the prizes of life. When they came to him he took them with dignity and
> without any illusions about their value. When hard knocks came he met
> them with great high spirits. He bore no man a grudge, and he never struck
> a foul blow.

In his heart, Beaverbrook felt the force of Birkenhead's rebuke, however much he might shrug it off. He had indeed been tepid during the
election and had not attempted to provide any positive lead. He was stung
into action by an article in The Morning Post, which declared that for
Beaverbrook to reproach others for remaining silent about the Empire
was "a bit thick". On 30 June 1929 he returned to active journalism. An
article by him in The Sunday Express asked: Who is for the Empire?
He confessed: "I stand in the dock together with all those I indict". But
now he intended to preach the cause of imperial unity, and he announced:
"The fiscal union of the Empire will only be achieved by a crusade carried
on by those who are animated by the crusading spirit". Such was the
first muttering of the Empire Crusade.

Beaverbrook had laid little stress on the Empire during the five years
of the Conservative government, and it was possible to argue that he took
it up now as a weapon against Baldwin. It was also possible to argue that
he took it up out of boredom. William Gerhardi wrote:

> Whether Empire Free Trade is good for Britain is beside the point: it is
> good for Lord Beaverbrook. It is not that the conditions have produced
> the man. It is rather that here is a man in need of a vocation to complete
> his personality, and so Empire Free Trade had, like Voltaire's god, to be
> invented.[1]

There was some truth in this view, but it was not the whole truth. The
cause of Empire had always been at the back of Beaverbrook's mind. He

---

[1] Gerhardi, Memoirs of a Polyglot, 249.

believed more in it than in any other political cause. Once he took it up, he championed it with all the enthusiasm of a revivalist preacher.

At the outset Beaverbrook intended to win over the Conservative party, not to run an independent campaign. He had evidently discussed this tactic with Rothermere, to whom he wrote on 3 July 1929:

> You will remember that . . . I said I would undertake certain negotiations.
>
> I have now exhausted my efforts and I am bound to say that there is a list of "Untouchables". Both you and I are on this list. There are a number of others.
>
> I therefore give up any prospect of accomplishing anything in that direction . . .
>
> . . . I have seen almost every Conservative ex-Cabinet minister. I do not believe the leader has a single sincere supporter.

Rothermere was a more brutal and arrogant character than Beaverbrook. He replied on 5 July:

> I am very glad matters have had the outcome which you explain in your letter.
>
> You use the expression "Untouchables", there are two or three Conservative ex-Ministers who, from my point of view, are Untouchable, and I will take no part whatsoever in helping them back to office. When I saw Winston, I made it perfectly clear to him that if the Conservative party wants an alliance with the Rothermere Press, the terms will be of a most exemplary character. They will have a direct relationship to policy and personnel.
>
> You and I have the situation entirely in our hands. Without our active support, there is not the remotest chance of the ex-Premier and his group of intimates returning to office.

Thus rebuffed by the Conservative leadership, Beaverbrook had no alternative but to go forward alone. On 7 July in The Sunday Express he called for an Empire Crusade, "independent of all parties". Having gone so far, he at once drew back. To all offers of help or support, he returned the familiar answers that he was too old, his powers were failing, he was about to retire—"I must leave it to others to carry on the work". At this time, he did not contemplate that he would lead a crusade. As usual, he wanted to start something and then stand aside. Also he had rushed into advocating Empire Free Trade without considering what was involved. It was easy enough to propose taxes on the import of foreign food, or perhaps even a total ban, which would give Canadian and Australian farmers a better market in Great Britain. But what were the Dominions to concede in return? The obvious answer was to remove tariffs on British industrial goods, while retaining or increasing those on foreign goods. Beaverbrook even at his most idealistic knew that the Dominions industrialists had no greater affection for British imports than for any other. He therefore proposed that British goods should be admitted only to the extent that they replaced industrial imports from the United States or Germany. He wrote to a Canadian friend on 20 July 1929:

> It is not part of our propaganda to flood the Dominions markets with English manufacture. All that we ask is that British goods should be allowed into the Dominions tax free.

This implied a cartel or quota system of excessive complexity, and Beaverbrook never managed to work it out.

He pleaded as excuse that the summer vacation was at hand. The crusade was laid aside until the autumn. Beaverbrook departed with his friends on a cruise to Russia and the northern capitals. Arnold Bennett and Michael Wardell were the men; Jean Norton, Lady Louis Mountbatten and other socialites, the ladies. They must have occasioned some surprise during their tours of Leningrad and Moscow. This was the first visit to Russia by a British privy councillor and ex-minister since the revolution. It was probably also the most luxurious visit of its kind. But as trade relations had already been resumed by the Labour government, the visit had no political significance, nor does Russia seem to have made much impression on Beaverbrook.

His mind was on other things. He took copies of his papers with him on the voyage and collected others at Oslo and Copenhagen on the way back. Thus equipped and at leisure, he accumulated criticism. In theory he had neither reason nor grounds to do so. On 19 June 1929 he announced that he had transferred his shares in The Express to his elder son Max for whom they would be held in trust until he came to age. In fact he did nothing of the kind. He merely transferred his shares to a private company in which he held all the voting shares and thus remained supreme.[1] During the cruise he dictated no fewer than fourteen letters of detailed criticism. Here is one example:

> Lord Beaverbrook wishes to know who engaged Edith Sitwell to write the leader page story. He says he has stood in the breach for ten years defending the paper against the publicity stunts of the Sitwells. His Lordship is betrayed from time to time, and he would like to know who gave to the Sitwells the keys of the gate. . . . This family group is less than a band of mediocrities.

---

[1] Beaverbrook transferred his shares to the Beaverbrook Co. Ltd. in which he held the voting shares (5,000) and Max Aitken the non-voting shares (35,000). Subsequently Beaverbrook bought the non-voting shares from Max Aitken and thereafter wholly owned the company until it was wound up in 1940, when Beaverbrook resumed direct possession of London Express Newspaper.

A similar arrangement was made in the Aitken (English) Co. Ltd., which was set up for the benefit of Beaverbrook's younger son Peter. Again Beaverbrook owned the 5,000 voting shares and Peter the non-voting capital (35,000). This company still owns 2.2% of the voting shares in Beaverbrook Newspapers.

However Beaverbrook did not always think so lightly of the Sitwells. It was their recommendation which brought Tom Driberg to The Daily Express, bringing in his train "William Hickey".

Beaverbrook's directives ranged over great things and small. Baxter, at The Daily Express, was told not to publish articles glorifying T. E. Lawrence—"a greater effort should be made in the interests of truth". Among a miscellany of other orders:

There is a picture of Foch that is as dead as the great field marshal himself.

The Express has the worst record in relation to talking pictures and the newspaper ought to have the best.

Keep the duchess of Sutherland out of the Social column. She does not want to be mentioned.

Report Sir Patrick Hannon's meeting at Birmingham in full.

Review a book for children by Mrs. John Buchan favourably—"the reviewer must do this for political reasons, and must do it in a big way".

There is no explanation for the last instruction. Perhaps Beaverbrook was hoping to enlist Buchan in the Empire campaign. Gilliat, at The Evening Standard, was told that he ought to have a column of financial advice and must prepare an obituary of D. H. Lawrence. More generally:

If Lord Beaverbrook were in your position he would insist on book reviewers telling the story of the book, play critics giving the story of the play, and cinema critics the story of the picture.

This was a principle on which Beaverbrook always insisted and to which reviewers rarely conformed.

During 1929 Beaverbrook had a much bigger worry over his two Express papers. Their direction had fallen into confusion. Robertson had final authority as general manager. Baxter edited The Daily Express. John Gordon had become managing editor of The Sunday Express in 1928. But Blumenfeld was still theoretically editor-in-chief and, as the only man in the office with an understanding of politics, was expected to provide the political leaders. He could not be on hand seven days a week and was often not to be found when a political decision had to be taken. Sometimes indeed The Sunday Express leaders were written by Castlerosse, the social columnist. There may also have been an underlying difference over policy. Blumenfeld, though keen on Imperial Preference, did not like going against Baldwin, a personal friend as well as being party leader, and acquiesced only because "the paper is Max's—he can do what he likes with it".

Robertson hesitated to act against Blumenfeld, who had once almost owned the paper and had been in control of it long before he had. Also

Baxter and Robertson were busy trying to reform the Glasgow office which was in bad shape. Beaverbrook knew that Blumenfeld ought to go and yet also shrank from action after their long and intimate acquaintance. He therefore harassed Robertson. "Look to the Sunday Express". "Something should be done at once". "Gordon must be given charge. . . . Take drastic steps if necessary". In August 1929 Baxter provoked a crisis by announcing that he had resigned and was joining The Daily Chronicle. Robertson acted firmly at last. Baxter was restored with full powers, and Robertson reported to Beaverbrook concerning The Sunday Express: "Gordon accepts full responsibility".

Blumenfeld, returning from holiday, found that his room had been taken from him. He wrote to Beaverbrook a letter of bitter complaint. Beaverbrook replied with a mixture of evasion and firmness:

> I am not a shareholder in the Daily Express.
> Robertson has the complete confidence of all of us.
> I saved the paper from bankruptcy. I make no claim to credit but I expect no reflection.

After this, Blumenfeld's connection with The Daily Express virtually ended. Perhaps Blumenfeld was not altogether sorry. At any rate, he and Beaverbrook remained friends, and he helped to raise money for the Empire Crusade.

R. D. Blumenfeld was not the only one of the family whose life was altered by Beaverbrook. His son, John Elliot Blumenfeld, was employed on The Evening Standard. One day Beaverbrook sent for him and said: "I intend to make you editor of the Evening Standard one day. In ten years' time there will be another war with Germany, and I cannot have one of my papers edited by a man with a German-sounding name". John Blumenfeld, who had no German background, refused. A year later, Beaverbrook said: "Why haven't you changed your name?" This time R. D. Blumenfeld said to his son: "If Max insists you'll have to do it". The change was made. Shortly afterwards, the young man made an editorial slip, was criticized by Beaverbrook, and left journalism. He had a distinguished career elsewhere as Sir John Elliot.[1]

The reform of the papers was completed by a reconstruction at Glasgow. The office there became autonomous, publishing The Scottish Daily Express "founded by Lord Beaverbrook". Though the news came mainly from London, the features were Scotch,[2] and the paper became a powerful element in Scotch life. It also provided a rich recruiting ground for the London papers. Beaverbrook had a strong preference for Scotchmen on his staff, when he could not get Canadians. They understood

[1] Private information.
[2] I use the English word "Scotch" in defiance of Beaverbrook and other Scotchmen.

his references to the shorter Catechism and the metrical version of the psalms. They did not query his use of "I will" for the first person future indicative. They also demonstrated the superior merits of Scotch education, even though Junor once let him down by admitting ignorance of Trilby. The most striking sign of this Scotch preponderance was The Sunday Express, which has been in the hands of Scotchmen throughout most of its successful career: John Gordon from 1928 to 1952 and John Junor from 1954 to the present day.

Beaverbrook now resumed his Crusade, still without much forethought. On 24 October he published a penny pamphlet, Empire Free Trade, the manifesto of the Empire Crusade. Its two vital sentences read:

> The foodstuffs that we need in this country could all be raised either on our own soil or in the British Dominions, Colonies and Protectorates.
>
> The coal, machinery and textiles that the increasing populations of our new territories overseas demand could be supplied by the mines and factories of Great Britain and its Dominions.

The movement, Beaverbrook wrote, "is political, but it is the property of no political party". Underneath Beaverbrook was not sure whether he was out to wreck or to capture the Conservative party—much as the campaign for nuclear disarmament, a very similar venture thirty years later, ruined itself by being unable to decide whether it was out to wreck or to capture the Labour party.

Publicly, Beaverbrook proclaimed his independence. Tom Clarke of The Daily News, having asked when he would return to the "Tory fold", received the answer: "Never again as far as I am concerned. . . . I do not wish to go back to the Tory caucus. I was there in Bonar Law's time—never again". And on 2 October Beaverbrook wrote to W. R. Hearst about the Conservative party:

> Churchill should be their leader. But the Conservatives will have none of him. He has served too many parties. If Baldwin is dismissed Neville Chamberlain will take his place. He is as bad as Baldwin.

In private Beaverbrook was not so sure. As always, he shrank from a conflict and made threatening noises as a preliminary to a settlement. In finance, he had pursued mergers; in journalism he was as much Rothermere's partner as rival. Now he aimed to capture, rather than to overthrow, Baldwin. His ambition was still to be the man behind the scenes, once more Lord Bunty who pulled the strings.

The opening soon came. Sir Samuel Hoare was Beaverbrook's closest acquaintance other than Baldwin himself among the former Conservative ministers, and on 4 November Hoare, himself a compromiser, brought Beaverbrook and Neville Chamberlain together for the first time. Chamberlain regarded Empire Free Trade as "obsolete, impracticable and mischievous". On the other hand, he was a Protectionist and, in his way, an Imperialist. He offered that the Conservatives would, at any rate, not pledge themselves against food taxes. Beaverbrook replied that "we should incur precisely the same difficulties as if we came all the way at once". However, the next day Beaverbrook rang up Hoare and said that, if the Conservatives meant business, he was prepared "to do a deal". He added: "His personal feelings about S.B. would not stand in the way as he cared more about Empire Free Trade than he did about his vendetta"[1]—the exact words being presumably Chamberlain's, not Beaverbrook's.

There was certainly support for Beaverbrook among the younger members of the Conservative party who were contemplating a breakaway. A memorandum, dated 5 November 1929, describes a meeting between Boothby, Harold Macmillan, Edward Hulton, and Walter Elliot.[2] Elliot, asserting himself to be an ex-Communist, wanted a crusade against Communism. The others were enthusiastic for Empire Free Trade and wanted Beaverbrook to expound it to them. There was a general feeling that "if necessary we must throw S.B. overboard". They were against the other "old men", such as Lloyd George, Birkenhead, or Winston "Who feels himself bound hand and foot for the rest of his days to Free Trade". Among possible recruits for their Young party they counted on Oswald Mosley, Keynes, and Jowitt "who apparently is ready once more to jump".[3]

Meanwhile, Neville Chamberlain had urged Baldwin to meet Beaverbrook. Baldwin responded. On 11 November 1929 he invited Beaverbrook to his house—so much for his repeated assertion that he would never put his feet under the same table as Beaverbrook's. Baldwin wrote:

> I will ask Neville Chamberlain to join us (not as a witness!) because he is a colleague whom I trust implicitly, whose judgement I value, and who knows my mind.
>
> It seems not inappropriate that this letter should be written on Armistice Day.

Beaverbrook replied:

> I will be there at ten a.m. and bareheaded.

The meeting on 12 November was friendly enough. Baldwin was more concerned about his position as party leader than about Empire Free

---

[1] Feiling, Neville Chamberlain, 173. Macleod, Neville Chamberlain, 132–3.
[2] The memorandum is initialled "E.M.". No E.M. was present. Perhaps this was a typist's error for H.M., Harold Macmillan.
[3] Jowitt, returned as Liberal at the general election, had immediately jumped to Labour, in order to become attorney general. Jowitt wrote to Beaverbrook on 13 May 1929, during the election: "When you take up politics again and lead a party I shall join it".

Trade. He wanted to keep up appearances. In particular, it must not seem that he had yielded to dictation from the press lords. He therefore urged Beaverbrook to work through the respectable channel of parliament— no doubt also calculating that on this field he himself was the stronger. Beaverbrook complied. On 19 November he made one of his rare appearances in the house of lords and delivered a speech in favour of Empire Free Trade. Two days later he again called on Baldwin and received approval for his good behaviour.

Baldwin seemed to have made an astute move when he drew Beaverbrook into parliamentary activity. Beaverbrook wrote powerful propagandist articles, or knew how to get them written for him, and he had all the force of a revivalist preacher on the public platform. But he was not a careful reasoner or an experienced debater. The old hands in the house of lords, who had been logic-chopping over Free Trade and Tariff Reform for more than thirty years, had little difficulty in tripping him up. The faded pages of Hansard are still hot with his irritation, and it is easy to hear him muttering under his breath: "Oh, to hell with them". Yet Beaverbrook had what his clever critics had not: a passionate desire to pull Great Britain out of her economic difficulties. Empire Free Trade was a propagandist phrase, and Beaverbrook often put his case too crudely as when he argued that, since it was Free Trade, not Imperial Preference, there would be no rise in food prices. More seriously, Empire Free Trade, with its deliberate sharing out of imperial markets and resources, implied planning for prosperity. It was another version of the programme which Lloyd George had offered at the general election and which Sir Oswald Mosley was now working out, even more creatively, within the Labour government. The party machines defeated Lloyd George, Mosley, and Beaverbrook, to the satisfaction of all right-thinking men. In retrospect, it can hardly be claimed that this brought advantage to the country.

On the immediate tactical level, Baldwin had miscalculated. Beaverbrook was not silenced merely by being outwitted in the house of lords. Rather his impatience urged him back into public propaganda. He was being pulled hard also by Rothermere in this direction. Rothermere had none of Beaverbrook's desire for a compromise. He aspired to dictate to governments as his brother Northcliffe had done before him. He had no underlying tug of loyalty towards the Conservative party, indeed much dislike of it, and he supposed that his papers could impose their will. On the other hand, he was no speaker and shrank from public activities. Beaverbrook became his chosen instrument. The political partnership between the two men was as equivocal as their financial one. Though they both talked "Empire", they meant different things by it. For Beaverbrook the Empire meant Canada and, by extension, the other Dominions. For Rothermere it meant India. Beaverbrook had fierce old-fashioned views about India, which he might have learnt from Kipling or even G. A. Henty. In his eyes, all Indians were Red Indians and deserved no better treatment. But he regarded India as a nuisance or distraction in his own campaign and hardly bothered to include her in Empire Free Trade. His outlook on India is expressed in a letter which he wrote to Arthur Brisbane on 28 May 1930:

> The Viceroy[1] is an earnest and an honest fellow—not quite stupid, but inexperienced in worldly affairs. He is a typical example of a "safeguarded" member of the Conservative party. He was brought up with a silver spoon in his mouth, and he has led a sheltered life. Bad speeches by him are praised as masterpieces of oratory; good speeches are looked upon as unprecedented in history. The Viceroy was continually spoken of during his House of Commons career as of Prime Ministerial timber. But he has never had to face the realities of the world.
>
> Honourable and trustworthy, his word can be relied upon, and his promises are always performed. He leads a splendid private life, with no feminine influences in it, believing in a big God with long boots, praying to Him nightly for guidance. Such a man, if he stumbles on the right course, will do it through God's grace and not on account of any worldly wisdom.
>
> Now as to the other side of the picture.
>
> The day that a policy of repression is decided on will mark the end of the crisis.
>
> There is no sense or reason in comparing the position with the Irish situation, which the Indians quote. In Ireland we were never free to bomb towns, wipe out villages, or turn machine guns on the people. In India we can, and the rebellion can be crushed the moment a decision is taken to do so.
>
> Will we do it? I say "Yes of course we will".
>
> The English are a kindly but determined race, and you understand them better than any other person in America. So I need not tell you that in addition to their justice, their kindliness and their mercy, their critics believe them to be incapable of extreme cruelty when the occasion demands it. It is a mistaken belief.
>
> How much further the trouble will go in India depends on how long we delay repressive decisions.
>
> But, of course, I am not taking a close interest in the present crisis, for all my time is occupied with our campaign for Empire Free Trade.

Beaverbrook was indifferent about India. Rothermere was indifferent, or even worse, about Empire Free Trade. He was an insular Protectionist —exactly the quality Beaverbrook disliked in Baldwin—and had taken over his brother's dislike of "stomach taxes", which Beaverbrook regarded as the essential element in Empire Free Trade. As Beaverbrook remarked to Melchett: "Rothermere never does get over his hostility to food taxes".

---

[1] The Viceroy, then known as Lord Irwin, was later known as Lord Halifax. Beaverbrook's opinion of him did not change.

In addition, Rothermere was a Liberal, according to his own description. Beaverbrook claimed to be acting in the best interests of the Conservative party. Hence, though both struck at Baldwin, they did so with different motives. Rothermere wanted to enforce a die hard policy in India and backed Winston Churchill for Conservative leader so far as he backed anyone. Beaverbrook wanted to inspire the Conservative party with faith in imperial unity and regarded Churchill, Free Trader and man of the gold standard, as the worst of all possible outcomes.

Nevertheless Beaverbrook turned towards Rothermere when his conciliation of Baldwin produced no result. The association gave him the backing of what was still the largest newspaper chain in the country—a publicity asset which he fully appreciated. It also weakened the accusation that the Empire Crusade was a one-man band, and Beaverbrook did not realize at first that it increased instead the suspicion with which respectable Conservatives regarded him. Perhaps also, as he said about someone else during the second world war, "I was driven on by a stronger man". In political matters, Beaverbrook always needed someone with a stronger will than his own, and Rothermere could certainly provide this wooden-headed obstinacy.

At any rate, Beaverbrook took the plunge into independent action. On 10 December 1929 an advertisement in the principal newspapers announced the opening of an Empire Crusade Register. A month later another advertisement invited the enrolment of members and appealed for a campaign fund of £100,000. Beaverbrook himself contributed £25,000. Rothermere followed with £5,000—"to be specially earmarked candidates expenses hope you are taking strong line on India". The Empire Crusade was launched.

CHAPTER TWELVE

THE CRUSADER, 1930-31

The Empire Crusade was Beaverbrook's one venture into independent political leadership. He often took an independent line in his newspapers and often inspired independent political action behind the scenes. But the Crusade was the only occasion when he promoted a policy and fought other politicians with the recognized political weapons. The Crusade was not merely a newspaper campaign, despite the support it received from Beaverbrook's and, less reliably, from Rothermere's papers. The Crusade raised money, enlisted supporters, set up local committees, conducted mass meetings, and finally ran candidates at by-elections. It nearly had a tie, until Doidge, the chief organizer, objected: "No young man would wear one in the Berkeley."

Essentially Beaverbrook was the Crusade. Many leading politicians, including Amery and even Neville Chamberlain, expressed sympathy. None became a Crusader. Beaverbrook's only political associate of any repute was C. A. McCurdy, formerly Lloyd George's chief whip, who managed to be a trustee of both the Lloyd George fund and the Empire Crusade fund—hardly a significant capture. Beaverbrook rewarded McCurdy with a place on The Express board and paid the salary of £1,500 out of his own pocket. Rothermere gave intermittent and erratic support, but did no speaking and played no part in the organization. In any case, he was always trying to bolt the Crusade into sabre-rattling over India, and Beaverbrook complained: "Rothermere came in trampling like a bloody elephant, messing up my campaign by running it in other directions". The only Crusade speakers, apart from Beaverbrook himself, were Sir James Parr, formerly high commissioner for New Zealand and Senator Elliott of Australia—again not voices of any significance.

Some members of parliament, such as J. R. Remer of Macclesfield, gave local support. Sir Hugo Cunliffe-Owen, the tobacco millionaire, ran the appeal for funds, and Sir James Dunn took the hat round the City. Sir William Morris, the motor car manufacturer, was an early recruit, and Beaverbrook wrote to him: "You and I should run the campaign together". But Morris had little time for political activities. Lord Melchett, another great industrialist, was a more useful supporter, but there were obstacles to full cooperation. Melchett was keen on quotas[1] which Beaverbrook did not like. On the other hand, Beaverbrook would not include Palestine in "the Empire"—an exclusion not at all to Melchett's taste. Horatio Bottomley offered to take the crusade to Canada. His letter is minuted: "Robertson advises you to be out of town to Bottomley and have no correspondence with him. Bottomley would blaze his way through Canada, on your name". Other odd supporters (in both senses) were Conan Doyle and Lord Alfred Douglas, Cutcliffe Hyne, St. John Gogarty and Lady Houston—an unpromising team. All received polite letters of thanks. Beaverbrook was left to make his own way.

He did so erratically and impulsively. All memory of the Empire Crusade was washed away by the great depression, and it seems in retrospect a trivial episode hardly worthy of record. Yet it was in its time an astonishing achievement. Beaverbrook had no standing in the Conservative party. He had never been a member of a Conservative government. Yet he came nearer than any other single man has ever done to unhorsing the accepted leader of a great political party. Joseph Chamberlain, a far greater figure, failed to overthrow Balfour. Labour party rebels did not shake Ramsay MacDonald until he chose to go. Beaverbrook's one-man Crusade brought Baldwin to the verge of resignation.

From the first Beaverbrook alone provided the drive and the organization. The chief organizer was found by the simple expedient of moving F. W. Doidge from the financial direction of The Daily Express to the Crusade office. Express journalists, such as Bruce Lockhart, wrote the Crusade pamphlets under Beaverbrook's directions and provided the statistics and other material for his speeches. He now forgot his doctrine that the first duty of a newspaper was to tell the news of the day. Instead it became the duty of his newspapers to tell only the news of the Empire Crusade. Each day he sent instructions to report the speech of some politician who inclined towards Empire Free Trade, often with the final injunction: "the reporter must stay until the end of the meeting". Beaverbrook's own speeches were set beforehand and were accompanied by a flamboyant account of the meeting and of its success. Speeches of opponents were not reported. When Sir William Bull expostulated against this policy of suppression, Beaverbrook replied on 19 December 1929:

> It is impossible to open the columns of the Daily Express to those who are against us. And for this reason—Our space is limited and we need every inch of it for the purpose of putting forward the views of our supporters.
>
> In every campaign in which I have been engaged I have been advised "Open your columns to the opposition". My answer has been "Go to the opposition newspapers".

[1] The system of limiting imports quantitatively.

Beverley Baxter repeatedly complained of the effect which this policy was having on The Daily Express. He wrote on 21 January 1930: "The concentration which I have been forced to give to Empire Crusade matters has undoubtedly injured the paper", and again on 14 February, when Beaverbrook was proposing to found a new party: "Tactically this may be necessary, but we are a Conservative paper, with a million Conservative readers". Baxter now became "that infernal fellow", and Robertson was instructed to give him a stern and solemn warning. This had little effect. Later in the year, The Express failed to report an important speech of Amery's at Glasgow, and Beaverbrook wrote in apology on 1 October 1930:

> It is a terrible thing to have to deal with an Editor who replies "crowded out". This answer practically rules out any means of correcting him. The truth is that an Editor of a newspaper is only useful so long as he works honestly and earnestly in furtherance of the political programme. The moment he shows the slightest tendency to "stall" he can do incredible injury.

The other members of The Express staff cooperated more loyally, but it is doubtful whether their hearts were in it. William Barkley, it is said, was the only Beaverbrook journalist who believed in Empire Free Trade as fervently as did Beaverbrook himself.

Beaverbrook was often accused of running the Empire Crusade purely from political ambition or even out of sheer mischief-making. These accusations are wide of the mark. He got fun out of the Crusade as he did from all his activities, but imperial unity was the strongest and most sincere of all his convictions. At bottom this was pure sentiment—a desire to be British as well as Canadian and a desire also, characteristic of a Canadian, that the British Empire should maintain its independence of the United States. When Beaverbrook tried to translate this sentiment into the practical terms of Empire Free Trade or Imperial Preference, he landed into all the tangles which Joseph Chamberlain and the pre-war Tariff Reformers had encountered before him. This does not alter the fact that Empire Free Trade was for Beaverbrook a genuine ideal, deeply felt.

The political situation favoured Beaverbrook and tempted him forward. Baldwin's leadership had never commanded universal support within the Conservative party and was particularly questioned after the electoral defeat of May 1929. Baldwin was harassed from the one side by the old Tariff Reformers and from the other by the younger generation of Conservative planners. Both groups welcomed the stir which Beaverbrook caused, though they rarely committed themselves to him. In addition, Churchill opposed Baldwin over India. Was Beaverbrook also motivated by personal dislike of Baldwin or jealousy towards him? At the time he claimed to like Baldwin personally and to be irritated only by Baldwin's indecision. Later, after the second world war, he wrote to Peter Howard: "I really disliked Baldwin and truly liked Hoare. Didn't you?"—but this was when he had convinced himself that Baldwin had ruined his Crusade singlehanded. It is fairly clear that he would have cooperated with Baldwin if Baldwin had been willing to cooperate with him. Here was the real unsurmountable obstacle. There is abundant evidence that Baldwin detested Beaverbrook and lumped him in with Lloyd George, Birkenhead, and even Churchill as the clever, irresponsible, immoral men from whom he had redeemed the country. It is curious that Baldwin is generally admired for avowedly pursuing a vendetta against Beaverbrook, while Beaverbrook is condemned for allegedly pursuing one against Baldwin. Baldwin, not Beaverbrook, was the good hater.

As for political ambition, Beaverbrook never wanted to be a minister, still less to be prime minister. He was a missionary, concerned to promote a cause, not to grasp high office. Of course he sometimes feared that power would be thrust upon him. Early in the Crusade, he wrote to his American friend E. M. Young on 23 January 1930:

> I have a very great fear that my present complications may land me at 10, Downing Street. I cannot conceive anything that would be more unpleasant though I am not afraid to take responsibility for carrying out the policy I support if the country is willing to give me the opportunity.

This was a passing fancy. More often, he groaned against the drudgery and wished that it were over. On 24 February 1930, he wrote to Morrison-Bell, who had been in the house of commons with him before the war:

> How I dislike the present strife and worry. I prefer the life of ease and freedom in the old days when we had nothing to do except attack Lloyd George and Charlie Masterman (a man I loved in our middle life).

And to Amery on 24 September 1930:

> The reason why I could never lead a political party, even if any other than the United Empire Party would be willing to take me, is because I cannot be bothered with tosh.

Beaverbrook would have been content with Neville Chamberlain as Conservative leader and wrote to Sir Samuel Hoare on 18 May 1930:

> I have a great affection for Neville Chamberlain based on his resemblance to Bonar Law, which I find quite startling.

This, from Beaverbrook, was tribute indeed. Alternatively he looked to Sir Robert Horne. When these failed, he offered the leadership of the

Crusade to less likely candidates. He wrote to Walter Elliot on 6 June 1930:

> I like the prospect of your leading the Empire Free Trade movement more than I can tell you. . . . Horne won't lead, and Neville Chamberlain won't lead.
>
> . . . While I have tried them both, I would rather have you to lead it than either, so far as I am concerned.

Similarly he wrote to Amery on 24 September 1930:

> I want to put it on record that I am ready to work under you. I would rather have you for leader of the Conservative Party than either Horne or Neville Chamberlain. Not because of your personality but because of your mental process.

But as Elliot wisely replied: "In fact, you are the leader of this show, and the whole of the leader, and rightly and inevitably so".

The Empire Crusade started out as a straight campaign for Empire Free Trade. Beaverbrook gradually modified his original line under the force of argument. He admitted that the Dominions could not be expected to offer more than a measure of Imperial Preference and even spoke of Empire Free Trade as "the ultimate ideal", a phrase which he had earlier condemned when used by the weaker brethren. The Crown Colonies, which Beaverbrook forgot at the beginning, were to have Empire Free Trade thrust upon them, and the display of its delights would soon win the Dominions. The truth is that Beaverbrook knew very little about the Dominions. He never visited any of them except his homeland, Canada. He rarely referred to Australia or New Zealand, and to South Africa not at all. He emphasized his own Canadian origin often enough. When reproached with it, he replied (16 October 1930):

> Canada is my domicile of birth and I cannot possibly give it up. I must return to my own country in due course and I want a handful of New Brunswick soil on my bosom at the end.

This wish was ultimately granted. He even offered to retire to Canada— on condition. He wrote to C. J. Morrissy of Newcastle, New Brunswick on 22 July 1930:

> Lord Hugh Cecil in The Times yesterday morning, advised me to go home to the fold from whence I came. I am seriously thinking of taking his advice, providing that Jack, Waldorf and Nancy Astor[1] will go to the home from whence they came—which is the United States.

[1] Respectively chief proprietor of The Times, proprietor of The Observer, and MP. Beaverbrook's hostility to the Astor family did not prevent his performing a great service for Lady Astor. In 1931 her son by a former marriage was involved in a court case, and Beaverbrook at her request ensured that the story was kept out of all the newspapers.

All the same, Beaverbrook gravely misjudged Canadian politics. He seems to have thought that Empire Free Trade would be complete if Canadian wheat were traded for British anthracite.

Food taxes became the key issue of his Crusade, as they had been for Joseph Chamberlain long before. Privileged access to the British food market was, Beaverbrook claimed, the decisive advantage which would induce the Dominions to open their own markets to British industry. Yet he also claimed that food taxes would not increase the price of food-stuffs to the consumer. "The Dominions can supply all our needs". He preached a high-wage, not a high-cost, economy. He wrote to a Canadian friend on 10 January 1930:

> The object of the policy of Empire Free Trade is, not to keep costs of production up, but to bring them down; and this not by reducing wages, which is a disastrous policy, but by mass-production for a wide protected market. Only so can we bring about a reduction of overhead charges, and so reduce costs, while maintaining, or increasing wages.

Food taxes, according to Beaverbrook, should be imposed unconditionally without previous bargaining with the Dominions. The Dominions were to be shamed or inspired into Empire Free Trade, not bribed into it. As time went on, Beaverbrook talked more about protecting the British farmer and less about winning the Dominions. Beaverbrook addressed many meetings in the course of 1930. He only once ventured into an industrial constituency, at Preston, and even that was to address the local branch of the National Farmers' Union. All his other meetings were either in agricultural constituencies or in London suburbs.

Beaverbrook's enthusiasm for agriculture sprang from much the same emotional basis as his enthusiasm for Canada, and rested on even less knowledge. He wrote to Melchett on 11 November 1930:

> Baldwin and I will have difficulty in coming together. There is a hereditary obstacle. He is the grandson of a blacksmith. I am the grandson of an agricultural labourer. It is an instinct of the blood to protect the offspring of our own kind. Baldwin talks a lot about pigs, but he really means pig-iron. While I talk of pig-iron, I understand pigs.

Beaverbrook made up the Empire Crusade as he went along in both policy and tactics. Though he often spoke of "my colleagues", in fact he made all the decisions himself. It may seem surprising that such an impro-vised affair achieved even the success it did. But Beaverbrook had many advantages, apart from his instruments of publicity. With the great depression and over two million unemployed, the old order was plainly breaking down, and men of all parties looked for new ideas. Many Liberals announced their conversion to Empire Free Trade. The ILP summer school listened to Beaverbrook with much sympathy, and he counted strongly on Sir Oswald Mosley, to whom he wrote on 17 July 1930: "I am ready at any moment to make overtures in your direction in public, if you wish me to do so". Beaverbrook's strongest hope, however, lay with the Conservative party. His own background tied him to it, and he could not help wishing for its success if it came to its senses.

The Empire Crusade was hard work for Beaverbrook and still more for his secretaries. For its sake, he abandoned many distractions. He resigned from most of the golf clubs and yacht clubs to which he belonged. He took few holidays during 1930—five days in Paris in January, another weekend there at Easter, and a fortnight cruising to Normandy in August. This last trip sent Beaverbrook home with chronic diarrhoea. Doctors could find no remedy and suspected that the illness was nervous. Beaverbrook complained that a neurologist had been sent down, "as I am believed to be insane". He noticed that an attack came on every day at precisely four o'clock and therefore went for a strenuous walk from 3.45 until five. Ultimately paratyphoid was diagnosed. Beaverbrook recovered at once. Perhaps the doctors had some miracle drug, or maybe he was cured as soon as his illness was given a name.

Beaverbrook also announced: "I am out of newspapers and racing: one a nuisance and the other a bore. I won't say which is which". The withdrawal from racing was real. Beaverbrook's racehorses were sold— at a loss which he sometimes gave as £120,000, sometimes as £300,000. Calvin House was put up for sale, though it took some time to find a buyer. The withdrawal from newspapers was equally emphatic. "I am no longer a journalist—and for good" (3 April 1930). "My association with the Daily Express is now at an end. I hear nothing of them and I give them no assistance" (20 May 1930). Of course this was the same old pretence as before. Beaverbrook not only pushed his papers into the Empire Crusade. He continued to shower directives and rebukes on subjects great and small. Perhaps they gave him some relief from his crusading labours. The selection which follows can be omitted if pressed, as Baedeker says of Cambridge.

On 20 January 1930, Beaverbrook sent Robertson three pages of criticism from Paris:

> The Leader column is bad. . . . A leader writer needs the crusading spirit or a disposition to instruct or uplift his readers. The present method is quite colourless and can come to no good. . . . As to the leader "What is happiness?" If the leader writer is happy I should have an unhappy fellow to do them in future.

To Robertson, 27 March 1930:

> What fun it would be if we settled on turning out a good paper, well edited, some body overseeing it who really takes part in putting it right at night.

On 1 June 1930: "Use airplane—not aeroplane".[1]

Baxter was rebuked when he complained of overwork (11 June 1930):

> Consider the immense amount of work which is my daily portion. I assure you it is a pleasure to me and nothing in the way of a task. I do not require any praise for it. In fact, if I did not like doing it I would not pursue my duties any further.

Other rebukes followed. On 29 August 1930:

> If His Lordship catches the Daily Express attacking co-education or Board School education or Grammar School education—or failing to attack Public Schools or the segregation of Youth, then—he declares—he will turn the direction of the paper over to Mr. Bottomley.

And on 4 September:

> The Daily Express is not nearly so good as it was. Don't think that this is the view of the public. It is the view of your own old colleague. The energy is gone. The initiative does not exist any more. The originality has disappeared. The exclusive news service has drooped into decay.

John Gordon did not escape. On 14 September 1930:

> I am not in touch with the people at the moment, but I give praise to God that I spring from them, and I know in what I am interested. Neither the people nor I are greatly interested in the Sunday Express or the Daily Express at the present moment.

On 23 November 1930:

> Lord Beaverbrook says—with emphasis impossible to put in writing— that never, never again must the Sunday Express challenge Christianity in its columns.
>
> Failure to observe this direction will result in his Lordship bringing the paper down to a state of bankruptcy, which would mean the disappearance of the Editor and his staff.
>
> The Sunday Express is a Presbyterian organ. Lord Beaverbrook says that with all finality, and he means it seriously. . . . I can tell you he is not joking, and you would be foolish to think he is.

The business manager of The Evening Standard was harassed to the point of resignation. Why was The Evening Standard not on sale at Maidenhead? at Boulogne? at Dover? In each case, sale was not an economic proposition. This answer did not content Beaverbrook when he saw The Evening News on the bookstall. Gilliat, the editor, was told (12 June 1930):

> Many readers hate cricket. Most of them know nothing about it. The cricket public is dwindling every day.

---

[1] This was a campaign which Beaverbrook waged unsuccessfully for years. He did better with "aircraft".

On 23 September 1930:

> The public like to know the fortunes men leave behind them. They like to know what disease men die of—and women too.

On 19 December:

> Lord Beaverbrook reminds you that the Evening Standard is a Capital Punishment paper.

Harold Nicolson received an historical judgement after he had reviewed G. M. Trevelyan's Blenheim:

> Blenheim has been highly praised by the critics. The book is as dull as Marlborough himself was dull. Trevelyan makes pathetic efforts to explain away Macaulay's unfavourable opinion of Marlborough. Yet he could have done it in a sentence. Macaulay did not like the man because he climbed into his position by making his sister the mistress of the king and afterwards selling his sister's master.
>
> Trevelyan, like the Manchester Guardian, is not what it was. Perhaps, too, Trevelyan, like the Manchester Guardian, never was, anyway.

As though this were not enough, Beaverbrook was in hard negotiation with Henry Harrison throughout March and April, when the Empire Crusade was at its height, to buy The Daily Chronicle and its associated papers for one million pounds. Harrison was on the point of agreeing, when, it seems, other shareholders objected. Perhaps, as Free Traders, they would not sell the paper to the Empire Crusader. In May negotiations were broken off. Later in the year The Daily Chronicle was sold to The Daily News, which thus became The News Chronicle for its last thirty years of existence.

On 4 January 1930 Beaverbrook dined with Rothermere and his editors. Rothermere declared that he and Beaverbrook were running on parallel lines and "there is no difficulty in dovetailing his programme to mine". On the following day Ward Price, Rothermere's principal mouthpiece, hailed Beaverbrook in The Sunday Pictorial as the next prime minister. Ten days later Beaverbrook agreed on joint action and a joint appeal. But they were not really in line. On 15 January Rothermere warned him against the Conservatives: "Don't budge one inch otherwise these people will collar your campaign and leave you in the lurch". Even worse was Rothermere's obsession with India. He telegraphed on 24 January: "You should stress India day in day out. This question will definitely cause a change of leadership", and on 4 February: "India is Baldwins Achilles Heel pertinaciously press him on this point and you are inevitable leader".

Beaverbrook did not welcome this prompting. He did not mind being ridiculed by Lloyd George, though he wrote bitterly to E. F. Wise on 31 January 1930:

What a terrible reflection on the House of Commons it is that a buffoon like Lloyd George should dominate it. Bottomley used to have much the same effect on the House when I first entered it.

He was still anxious to keep in with Baldwin, who wrote to him on 29 January 1930:

If you are agreeable I should be glad to see you when I am in a position to tell you my line for next Wednesday's meeting. It is only fair to you, after our conversations, that you should have an early acquaintance with my views.

Beaverbrook duly visited Baldwin on 3 February and afterwards informed Rothermere: "Baldwin will say safeguarding of every industry requiring assistance. He will be vague about Empire. Vigorous attack on expenditure". Rothermere was unimpressed. Beaverbrook was less sure. On 5 February Baldwin addressed a meeting at the Coliseum. He attacked Rothermere and did not mention Beaverbrook, to whom he wrote at once:

After a good deal of deliberation, I decided not to make any allusion to you this morning in my speech.

I am quite sure it will make it easier for both of us if you decide to support my policy. And no harm is done, if you don't!

Beaverbrook swung first one way and then the other. He replied to Baldwin: "I find your speech quite thrilling in parts, if I may be allowed to say so". But to Rothermere: "Baldwin made bad speech. His party is overwhelmed with depression". On the same day the Crusade committee issued a manifesto stating that Baldwin's proposals were inadequate.

The truth is that Beaverbrook could never resist being all things to all men. He was indeed the flatterer, and when he dictated a letter it was to conciliate, to win over. Besides, in this case, he was really feeling his way, uncertain what to do. If he could commit Baldwin to Empire Free Trade, this would be the easier course. If Baldwin proved recalcitrant or evasive, then he needed Rothermere's support for the Crusade. Meanwhile he kept both men in play, as he did with his business affairs, until the bargain was clinched one way or the other.

Beaverbrook was hard-pressed by Rothermere to make up his mind. Rothermere wrote: "No two men ever had the ball more completely at our feet than you and I have today". Beaverbrook still hesitated. He made another attempt to compromise with Baldwin, alleging to Gwynne: "You know I like him. Further I come under the influence of his charm every time I talk to him". Beaverbrook saw Baldwin on 12 February and asked: "Would he object if we put up Empire Free Trade Conservative candidates?" Baldwin: "That would be disastrous". "Would he object if we tried to get Empire Free Trade candidates before the selection committees?" Baldwin: "would not countenance such a course". Would we be entitled to push over the brink into a declaration for Empire Free Trade members of the house of commons sitting on the front bench, and others? Baldwin: "could not tolerate an Empire Free Trade declaration from his colleagues in the late government". Beaverbrook then said that the only course would be to form the United Empire party, and Baldwin "indicated that he considered it the least damaging course from the Conservative Party's standpoint".[1]

Beaverbrook's bluff, if it were bluff, had been called. He had no choice except to go ahead. Besides, as he wrote to Amery on 22 February, "I knew it would bring Rothermere in to support me. I wanted his support more than I can tell you". On 18 February Beaverbrook announced that the Empire Crusade had been transformed into the United Empire party. Rothermere was delighted and telegraphed: "This movement is like a prairie fire. It is bigger than you, me and all the Conservative party put together". Few shared his enthusiasm. The 1900 Club cancelled an invitation it had given to Beaverbrook, and Gretton, its chairman, wrote: "we should be entertaining you as a declared opponent of the Conservative Party". Amery also sent a rebuke: "I am sorry you have done this, as it makes the situation much more difficult for all who were sympathizing with you". Beaverbrook really took this view himself. His aim all along was compromise, and there was nothing he disliked more than to be captured by Rothermere, with all the trumpetings over India which this implied.

On 28 February therefore Lord Elibank, a member of the original Empire Crusade committee, went to Baldwin with an olive branch. Elibank offered agreement on the policy of a free hand to impose food taxes if the Dominions offered adequate concessions in exchange. Baldwin was sympathetic, particularly when Elibank added that "Lord Rothermere was getting out of hand with his press". Baldwin rejected a further proposal that Beaverbrook should be given a voice over appointments to the economic offices in a future Conservative government. "The party would have to trust him", but he agreed that Churchill could not have the Exchequer—hardly a concession when he and Churchill were feuding over India. The opportunity for driving a wedge between Beaverbrook and Rothermere was however too good to miss, and Baldwin said: "He would only be prepared to come to an arrangement with Lord Beaverbrook and would have nothing to do with Lord Rothermere whom he thoroughly distrusted". Elibank replied: "Lord Beaverbrook would have to make himself responsible for Lord Rothermere".

The way for compromise was opening. Baldwin was due to speak to a Conservative gathering at the Hotel Cecil on 4 March. On the morning

---

[1] Beaverbrook to Gwynne, 22 February 1930.

before Beaverbrook, using Gwynne as intermediary, again went to Baldwin. Baldwin proposed two elections. At the first the Conservatives would not mention food taxes. If they won they would negotiate with the Dominions, and if the Dominions gave adequate concessions, would campaign for food taxes at a second general election. Beaverbrook rejected this idea. He wanted to get in a mention of food taxes at once. He therefore proposed that the Conservatives should take up food taxes now, but with an assurance that they would be introduced only after a referendum and of course if the Dominions wanted them. This was the proposal which Balfour had made in 1910, and Beaverbrook had laboured to undo it. Since then the stone had rolled far down hill. Beaverbrook was content if he could get rid of Baldwin's 1924 pledge against food taxes and bring them back even on a conditional basis. Baldwin, who had forgotten Balfour's proposal, was favourably impressed and agreed to consider the idea.

Beaverbrook at once went to Rothermere who said: "You have won the main point. Duties on foreign food must now be a live issue and you have at least recovered the ground lost since 1910. . . . At the next election the country will vote, referendum or no referendum, on the food tax issue". All day long Beaverbrook waited in a mixture of hope and doubt for a call from Baldwin. At 9.30 p.m. the call came. As soon as Beaverbrook appeared, Baldwin said: "I have decided to adopt the Referendum". Baldwin made one condition. The referendum must not be represented as a victory for the United Empire party and there must be no suggestion that it was "a successful attempt to dictate policy through the Press". Beaverbrook at once agreed for his own papers and said he would do his best with Rothermere. This took some time. Rothermere took the line of an independent potentate and wanted a bargain between the Conservative party and the United Empire party as equals. He yielded only at 2.30 a.m., and a satisfactory message reached Baldwin at nine o'clock the next morning.[1]

Baldwin kept his bargain or so it appeared. Generations to come, he declared at the Hotel Cecil, would regard the next election as the moment "when the people of this country finally and ultimately made its choice to be one with its kindred overseas". His actual proposal was less specific. An Imperial Conference "should meet in an atmosphere of perfect freedom, and if . . . there should emerge any form of agreement, arrangement, treaty . . . that does give us great benefits and that demands in return a tax on some articles of food from a foreign country—that whole issue could be put clearly before our people" by means of a referendum. Would the Conservative party in fact campaign for food taxes or would it

[1] Beaverbrook gave an account of these negotiations in The Saturday Review of 2 August 1930 and in a letter to Bechofer Roberts of 13 April 1936.

merely swallow them with a wry face if compelled to do so by the Dominions? This was the very equivocation which Law had played on in 1912. Then Aitken had kicked against it. Now he ignored it. No doubt he hoped to lure Baldwin one way, and Baldwin hoped to lure him the other—or merely to shut him up.

For the moment Beaverbrook was triumphant. His spirits soared. He telephoned Rothermere who agreed that Baldwin's statement was completely satisfactory. Unity with the Conservatives was apparently restored. Everyone was delighted. Churchill burst in while Beaverbrook was still reading Baldwin's speech and said "how happy he was that we should now be able to work together again in a common cause"—an odd statement from an unrepentant Free Trader. Davidson, chairman of the Conservative party, wrote on 5 March 1930:

> Thank God. The ranks are closed. You have done what our party could not. You have made the public think politically. Obviously to get the maximum result there must be complete cooperation in the campaign of education and propaganda.

Baldwin added his word of thanks for the way Beaverbrook had handled his papers and Rothermere's. Writing on 5 March, he addressed Beaverbrook by his Christian name for the first time:

> My Dear Max,
> You have indeed played the game, and believe me I am grateful.
> R. has done more than I could have expected, for I know and can fully appreciate his difficulties.

Beaverbrook went further in conciliation. He withdrew from the United Empire party and returned all the subscriptions which had been sent to him for it. Instead he renewed the Empire Crusade, to work in cooperation with the Conservative party, and invited fresh subscriptions for this, which soon brought in promises of £110,000. But he could not decide whether he had won or had been cheated. His correspondence showed his oscillations. On 6 March to F. B. Edwards:

> My principle is—take a trick while you can and go on with the game. Our policy has gained much from recent events. After being opposed by all three political parties, it has now at least the support of all the members of one of the parties.

This was hardly the line taken by the Conservative papers which opposed food taxes. On 9 March Beaverbrook wrote to Davidson:

> It seems to me that I ought to have taken guarantees from some of the papers friendly to Baldwin that they would not picture me in the light of a man who has surrendered everything for nothing.

Beaverbrook tried to look on the bright side. He wrote to Edward Shanks on 11 March 1930:

> Baldwin has given us the Referendum. So many people think that this is a surrender on our part to Baldwin. So many people will think, a month hence, that Baldwin has given us too much.
>
> The Referendum merely means that we have to take two jumps instead of one. The first jump is the big one. . . . It worked out on the platform in that way in December 1910, and it will work out on the platform in the same way at the next election.

But on the same day to Lord Queenborough:

> I pointed out the bridge to Baldwin. He built it.
>
> Now it remains to be seen if the piles will hold the structure. Many signs point to weaknesses which will destroy the bridge.

The weaknesses soon showed. Lord Salisbury wrote to The Times opposing food taxes. Beaverbrook telegraphed to Rothermere on 25 March:

> My view is he believed referendum would destroy food taxes but when strength of Empire Free Trade section of party was disclosed he adopts new wrecking tactics.

Rothermere replied:

> Am not at all surprised at development. Hope you will put your foot firmly down and insist on implementing of your personal agreement with Baldwin. . . . You should be unsparing in your criticism. Your personal position requires it.

And on 27 March:

> You should have leader prepared calling upon your people to drop referendum and come honestly out on your policy. Information reaching me is that electors especially women regard referendum as a trick.

Rothermere believed that Baldwin was deliberately cheating. Beaverbrook regarded him as "a weak man who has been pulled backwards and forwards", as Beaverbrook himself had been.

Worse things followed. The Conservative central office issued a leaflet giving assurances against food taxes. A by-election was impending at Nottingham, and O'Connor, the prospective Conservative candidate, spoke slightingly of food taxes. Despite this, Baldwin sent him a letter of blessing. Beaverbrook, dining with the big five of the Conservative party (not including Baldwin) on 3 April, said: "The public believe I have been swindled". On 7 April he wrote to Davidson:

> Two days ago Baldwin writes a letter which makes a blow by me at O'Connor appear to be a blow at Baldwin. Why was such a situation allowed

to develop? How can we get on with Empire Free Trade if I am compelled to fight with Baldwin? If I do not shun the fight, at once I rally again to my standard all those who are hostile to him. Does that suit you? Does it suit anybody?

Neville Chamberlain tried to make peace and wrote to Beaverbrook:

> The cause is much too important and vital for us to risk it by any misunderstandings. We are passing through a critical time now but if only we have a little patience we can bring it to success. My confidence in you is unabated even though you do want sometimes to go off the deep end!

Chamberlain was secretly more on Beaverbrook's side than anyone supposed. He wanted to get rid of the referendum and to carry food taxes openly. But he wanted to do this inside the Conservative party and not at Beaverbrook's dictation. Beaverbrook was still clinging, though with waning hope, to the referendum. He wrote to Frank Humphrey, a New York broker, on 9 April:

> Our objective was to force the Conservatives into an acceptance of the policy of a duty on foreign foodstuffs. The nearest we could get to it was the promise of an election on the issue followed by a referendum on taxation of foreign foodstuffs. . . .
> If we had refused the referendum, we should have been obliged to launch an immense programme of work and organization throughout the country. We could not have hoped to realize our policy for many years, and would have involved ourselves in unnecessary effort in the interval.

Beaverbrook was beginning to think that conflict was unavoidable. He descended on Nottingham and delivered a speech in favour of Empire Free Trade, which implicitly condemned O'Connor. Rothermere was delighted. He telegraphed on 13 April 1930:

> Very pleased see you are taking strong line. When you came fresh from your negotiations you told Ward Price Outhwaite and myself that the position was that Baldwin had adopted your programme but that before he introduced food taxes the question would be submitted to a referendum. Baldwin's speeches at Albert Hall and in Manchester in which the whole suggestion is that the party is broad enough to include Free Traders moderate and extreme Tariff Reformers taxers of foodstuffs and antitax-fry of foodstuffs are a complete reversal of that position. As you know throughout the negotiations I repeatedly warned you against betrayal. I said you would be deliberately misled or let down. This has now happened. Your course is clear.

On 16 April Beaverbrook issued a statement that the Conservative leaflet and Baldwin's backing of O'Connor were contrary to the understanding he had reached with Baldwin. Chamberlain wrote to him on 17 April:

> Your letter issued to the press yesterday fills me with despair. . . .

Your one concern ought to be to educate the public on the merits of the policy. Instead of that you spend all your time pointing out to the public how entirely unreliable and untrustworthy is the only instrument available to carry it out.

... To see in the leaflet anything sinister or "contrary to the understanding" seems to me the delusion of a—No, of a good fellow with whom I *will* not quarrel, but whom I hate to see cutting the throat of his own project.

Do you, or do you not care about your policy more than anything in the world? If you do, stop stabbing at those who are trying to help, and have a go at those who are even now preparing a campaign to kill it.

Beaverbrook replied on 20 April:

If Baldwin means to put a tax on foreign foodstuffs by means of a Referendum I am with him. If he is dodging the issue I am against him.

....

Davidson does not believe it possible to carry the next election if he is to be faced by the cry "food taxes by the back door". Therefore he is determined to shelve the policy. I am as anxious to make it impossible for him to do so. If he succeeds the party will be ignominiously defeated, in my firm belief. It is the old story of indecision and apology for the policy. Chamberlain knew all about it, and suffered from it to the full.

Beaverbrook was diverted from Nottingham by another by-election at West Fulham, previously a Labour seat. Sir Cyril Cobb, the Conservative candidate, was a keen Empire Free Trader. The resources of the Empire Crusade were mobilized in his support. Beaverbrook addressed nine large meetings to great effect. Cobb won the seat—though he did less well at West Fulham with Crusade support than O'Connor did at Nottingham without it. Still even Baldwin was impressed or claimed to be. He wrote to Beaverbrook on 7 May 1930:

My dear Max,
You must be nearly dead and I congratulate you on your gallant conduct in the arena once more—it must have brought back happy days at Ashton once again.

Behind the scenes Baldwin was strengthening his position. Many Conservatives who did not support the Empire Crusade criticized Davidson as too negative and unenterprising. At the end of May Baldwin jettisoned Davidson, and after some delay Neville Chamberlain became chairman of the Conservative central office. This was an adroit move. Chamberlain was a strong Protectionist, sympathetic to Beaverbrook's campaign, and the obvious successor as leader of the Conservative party if Baldwin were pushed out. Appointing him chairman might seem a surrender on Baldwin's part. Actually Baldwin had taken Chamberlain prisoner.

Beaverbrook appreciated nothing of this and believed that he was on the winning stretch. He wrote to Paul Cravath on 14 May 1930:

> I will make no progress in co-operation with Stanley Baldwin. He is a useless fellow and I hope he will have to walk the plank, or get the black spot, or anything else you like to call it.

A meeting had been arranged at the Crystal Palace for 24 May, when Baldwin and Beaverbrook were to speak from the same platform. Now Beaverbrook refused to attend. The meeting was called off—a considerable humiliation, it appeared, for Baldwin, leader of the party.

Beaverbrook went instead to Hastings, where he announced that, as the Canadian government had just declared in favour of imperial preference, a referendum was no longer necessary. It was already clear, he claimed, what the Dominions wanted, and it only remained for the mother country to respond. Beaverbrook wrote to Hoare on 15 May 1930:

> The Referendum has failed as an instrument of policy. The Conservative leader has used it as a shield instead of a sword.

Beaverbrook rejected Hoare's suggestion that he should meet Neville Chamberlain:

> I outrage him by the vigour of my views.
> In any case "It's past debating. It's out with all we have".

His one anxiety was that the Labour government might collapse under the weight of unemployment. He wrote to Bowker, editor of The Lancashire Daily Post, on 30 May 1930:

> What a creature of favourable chance is Mr. Stanley Baldwin. If the unemployment figures mounting to two million, put him in Office again, it will be a story fit for Arabian Nights.

Beaverbrook was completely on the offensive. He wrote to some Conservative candidates in Cornwall on 3 June:

> I offered Mr. Baldwin advice in private. I got no response. I then offered him advice in public. I have received no reply. It is now my intention to offer the advice to the electorate—Otherwise there are no difficulties between Mr. Baldwin and myself.

To Sir Rennell Rodd on 6 June:

> I hope you will not be prejudiced about Rothermere. He is a very fine man. I wish I had his good points. It would make the Crusade more popular among the aristocracy—the real enemies in the Conservative Party. . . .
> It is time these people were being swept out of their preferred positions in public life and their sons and grandsons being sent to work like those of other people.
> I am getting very tired of the present situation.

Everybody is saying "Don't go heresy hunting". "Don't raise discordant issues in the House of Lords".

I should like to know where this movement would be at the present moment if such advice had been taken in the past.

And to a Canadian friend on 18 June: "Baldwin wants all the assets of Empire Free Trade without taking on the liabilities".

Baldwin too was now on the offensive. He spoke openly against food taxes: "We have to rule that right out. It would be madness at the present time". He summoned a meeting of Conservative MPs and candidates for 24 June. Beaverbrook was not entitled to attend. In letters to The Morning Post and The Times, he explained why he had turned against the referendum, after having himself proposed it. It had been intended as a means of introducing food taxes. Instead it was being used against them, and he repeated his phrase to Hoare: "Mr. Baldwin has used it as a shield instead of a spear". Beaverbrook concluded by an appeal to the Conservatives "to put all personal matters out of their thoughts. Persons are of no consequence in this".

Baldwin ignored this appeal. His speech on 24 June made no mention of policy and turned instead against the press lords.

> There is nothing more curious in modern evolution than the effect of an enormous fortune rapidly made, and the control of newspapers of your own. ... It goes to the head like wine, and you find in all these cases attempts have been made outside the province of journalism to dictate, to domineer, to blackmail.

Baldwin bracketed Beaverbrook with Hearst and Rothermere. He gave examples of their attempt to dictate. His example of Beaverbrook's attempt was peculiarly crushing and peculiarly dishonest:

> Before I saw Lord Beaverbrook in March for the first time, an emissary of his came to me and told me that his lordship would desire, in the event of our becoming allies, to be consulted as to certain offices in the Government which I might recommend to His Majesty if I came back to power.

No one would suspect from this that Baldwin had had a number of meetings with Beaverbrook before March, or that he had later repeatedly addressed Beaverbrook by his Christian name—never, it may be added, again. Elibank issued a correction. The suggestion about approving ministers had been made on his own behalf, not on Beaverbrook's.

> He disagreed with my having raised the point of key-posts at all with you. Three days afterwards the agreement was reached between Lord Beaverbrook and yourself without this matter being mentioned.

The correction passed unregarded, as such corrections usually do. Baldwin was held to have triumphed.

But when Baldwin asked, in a speech at Wimborne, "What is Empire Free Trade?", Beaverbrook was ready with an answer. He issued a statement to the Press Association on 30 June: "Empire Free Trade is like liberty, something to be striven for. Men strive to be free; they never wholly succeed". The immediate objective was "a 'tariff wall' round the Empire, with duties on foreign foodstuffs". Beaverbrook asked a question in his turn:

> If Mr. Baldwin is not yet sure what our policy is, is it surprising that I should have felt that he was not backing it to the full extent of his power?

Perhaps the confusion was not all on Baldwin's side.

Beaverbrook now had a new opportunity to show the Empire Crusade in action. There was another by-election, this time in North Norfolk, and again the Conservative candidate, R. A. Cook, was an Empire Free Trader. This was an agricultural constituency where Beaverbrook felt thoroughly at home. He arrived with Lord Castlerosse, two secretaries, and three motor cars. He addressed ten large meetings. On the platform at each meeting was a large black box which gave a loud buzz every minute. Beaverbrook would then say: "The country has just spent another thousand pounds on imported food". These tactics, though sensational, did not succeed. Lady Noel-Buxton, the Labour candidate, was the wife of the former member, who had just gone to the house of lords, and had all the appeal of a famous local family. The electors were mostly Radical agricultural labourers, not farmers. Beaverbrook also complained that he was weakened by the abstention of many local Conservatives, including his friend Hoare. Lady Noel-Buxton was returned, with a reduced majority.

Beaverbrook, though saddened, was not dismayed. He recognized that there was much more work to do. He wrote to Amery on 12 July 1930:

> I would like to have the opportunity, in the first place, of contesting a seat against a Conservative Office candidate. This would show whether we were stronger than the Conservatives. Next, I would like to have an opportunity of a constituency with a Conservative Empire Free Trade candidate, thus testing if we were gaining strength in the industrial centres.

Chamberlain was not idle on his side. Using Hoare as intermediary, he met Beaverbrook on 18 July and put forward peace terms. According to his account, these were:

> Beaverbrook must call off his attacks on Baldwin and the Party, cease to include offensive cartoons and paragraphs in the *Evening Standard*, and stop inviting Conservatives to direct subscriptions to him in order that they might be used to run candidates against official Conservatives. In return, Central Office would support any Conservative who accepted

the official policy, even though he expressed personal agreement with Beaverbrook, and tried to persuade his local association to adopt these views.[1]

Beaverbrook's account is rather different. He makes no mention of Chamberlain's demand to censor Low, and indeed it is inconceivable that he would have accepted it. He lists these proposals:

1. By-elections. The policy to be decided by the Conservative Association in each constituency, with the right on my part to state our case.
2. Sitting member may be required by me to accept our policy if the Local Association approves by a majority vote. . . .
3. The procedure . . . to apply to candidates already selected.
4. The Empire Crusade to discontinue applications to Conservatives to divert their party subscriptions.[2]

The discrepancy is considerable. Maybe each man recorded the points which mattered to him, as often happens in this sort of negotiation.

Beaverbrook agreed to consult his friends. His choice was odd. It did not occur to him to consult McCurdy or Elibank, the only prominent figures in the Empire Crusade. Instead he consulted Rothermere, McKenna, and Beatty, president of the Canadian Pacific Railway. Rothermere offered "100 per cent" support to the Conservative party, provided Chamberlain ousted Baldwin and became leader himself—a suggestion which Chamberlain of course rejected. McKenna said: "Operate on these lines, but refuse to make an agreement". The exchange of telegrams with Beatty has not survived. Negotiations broke down over a practical difficulty: yet another by-election, this time at Bromley. Chamberlain feared that Rothermere intended to put forward his son, Esmond, as Conservative candidate and asked Beaverbrook to stop him. Rothermere refused the request. The Bromley Conservatives evaded the dispute by taking E. T. Campbell, who pledged himself to Empire Free Trade, though also declaring his loyalty to Baldwin. Beaverbrook would have been satisfied with this. Rothermere was not and insisted on running a United Empire party candidate, Redwood, whom Beaverbrook repudiated on grounds both personal and political.

Beaverbrook wrote sadly to Chamberlain on 30 July:

I recognise that this decision involves the re-opening of hostilities.
I am sorry that we could not agree, but your difficulties, and also my own troubles, were far too many.

This was a contradictory outcome. Chamberlain and Beaverbrook agreed with each other much more than Chamberlain agreed with Baldwin or

[1] Macleod, Neville Chamberlain, 136.
[2] Beaverbrook to Gogarty, 1 August; to Bowker, 8 August 1930.

Beaverbrook with Rothermere. They were pulled apart by the claims of conflicting loyalties. Chamberlain noted: "It looks as if I might have to go down fighting for S.B. when my own desire is, as it always has been, for the free hand",[1] and Beaverbrook felt much the same about his association with Rothermere. After a few days he recovered his spirits and became convinced that a decisive moment was approaching. He called off his projected visit to Canada and announced this to various Canadian friends in a characteristic phrase:

> I am like the poker player in Kamloops who had to put his spittoon on the table because he dared not turn his back on his companions.

His failure to visit Canada was perhaps a mistake. At all events political developments in Canada bounced back on him, to his considerable discomfiture. A Canadian general election was in process. R. B. Bennett, Beaverbrook's old friend and early patron, led the Conservatives, and Beaverbrook might have been expected to support them as he had always done in the past. He failed to do so now. The estrangement between Bennett and Beaverbrook was in part personal. Bennett had become a millionaire, thanks to Beaverbrook's advice and assistance, but he had wanted more—to become an equal partner. This Beaverbrook would not grant. He often sought colleagues in politics and even in journalism. In finance he was truly self-confident and remained sole boss. He would never admit any partner except his brother Allan, and this equality was more apparent than real. Bennett resented his subordination and often kicked against it. The friendship between the two men became, for the time being, superficial.

Political differences cut deeper. Mackenzie King's Liberals were the traditional party of agriculture and low tariffs. Beaverbrook was hoping to win the Canadian farmers by imposing food taxes in Great Britain. The Canadian Liberal government appealed to him even more when its 1930 budget offered a measure of imperial preference by lowering the tariff on British goods, not by raising it against everyone else—exactly the policy which Beaverbrook himself preached. Bennett, on the other hand, led the party of industry and high tariffs, with at most a half-hearted gesture towards Great Britain by making the increase of tariffs on British goods a little less high than on others. Maybe also Beaverbrook foresaw, wrongly as it turned out, that the Liberals would win. At any rate he did not conceal his sympathy with them. When F. D. L. Smith, a Canadian friend, complained of this, Beaverbrook replied on 17 July 1930:

> The Mackenzie King Budget can be interpreted as an acceptance by a Liberal Prime Minister in the Dominions of the principle of Empire Free Trade. I am appealing for Liberal votes every day. It is only on Liberal

[1] Macleod, Neville Chamberlain, 136.

votes that I can turn the scale in a division like North Norfolk. I would be false to my policy if I failed to avail myself of the opportunity.

He dismissed Bennett's policy as on a level with Irish isolationism or with Baldwin's insular protection of 1923:

I hate this movement in Canada which is taking a Sinn Fein form. It is contrary to the spirit of the Canadian people. (To Page Croft, 19 August 1930.)

Bennett won his election on what is, in effect, a Canadian Sinn Fein policy for their manufacturers. He wishes to carry out a programme of exclusion of manufactured goods made in any country, including Great Britain. (To Lord Bridgeman, 6 September.)

Beaverbrook did not keep these opinions to his private correspondence. He praised the Liberal budget in an interview with The Toronto Globe and spoke indiscreetly to Dafoe, editor of a Winnipeg Liberal paper. Dafoe reported, on his return to Canada, that Beaverbrook "was on the point of turning Bennett's picture to the wall". Bennett was deeply offended and, what was worse, the Conservatives won the Canadian election. Beaverbrook then tried to undo the damage. He explained that the interview with The Globe had been given "several months" (actually some weeks) before the election and that his praise of Mackenzie King had then been quoted out of context. He claimed that Dafoe's remark was surmise, not something he himself had said. Bennett was not appeased. Ketchum, Beaverbrook's reporter in Canada, telegraphed on 14 August after seeing Bennett:

Attitude one of uncompromising bitterness going so far say you formerly regarded friend but henceforth enemy. He finished and you'd know this in six weeks time.

This last threat applied to the Imperial Conference at the end of September which Bennett would be attending. Beaverbrook's friend Sir Andrew Macphail sent a warning early in September:

This coming week he will raise the tariff. He will go to the Imperial Conference and offer a Preference equal to a part of this increase; but he will demand that England put a corresponding duty upon imports from outside the Dominions. England will not agree; he will come back, having given no further preference, and he will put the blame on England.

So indeed it proved.

Thirty years later, when Beaverbrook came to write the story in his life of Bennett,[1] he made out that he had at worst "remained on the fence, through the mistaken desire to be free of any entanglements with the Conservatives if the Liberal Party should be returned". He depicted

[1] Friends (1959), 56.

the estrangement between Bennett and himself as purely personal. By then Beaverbrook had come to believe, or wanted others to believe, that Empire Free Trade was ardently desired by the Dominions and was not achieved solely because of Baldwin's evasions or his own tactical blunders with regard to Bennett. In reality, as Beaverbrook recognized at the time, Empire Free Trade had less support in the Dominions than in Great Britain. The Dominions would rally to the mother country in time of war, as both world wars demonstrated. They would make few economic sacrifices for her in time of peace. The general election in Canada had just shown this. The Conservatives, traditionally the pro-British party, wanted protection solely for Canadian industry. The Liberals, though inclining to Free Trade, cared little about the Empire. Perhaps it needed a Beaverbrook in every Dominion to make Empire Free Trade a reality.

Beaverbrook would not acknowledge this insuperable obstacle. He went on insisting that the Dominions would respond if Great Britain gave a clear lead. Hence even "the free hand", which Chamberlain advocated, was not enough. There must be an unconditional programme of food taxes, which might move the Dominions and would in any case benefit British agriculture. Beaverbrook wrote to Amery on 12 September 1930:

> I think Neville Chamberlain has made an awful mess of things. It is terrible when a man believes in a policy, feels the strength of it, knows the electioneering value of it, and yet allows another to reap the crop.
> There is an old Irish song, the refrain of which is—
>
> > I know who I love;
> > But the dear God knows who I'll marry.
>
> That applies to my political position at the present moment.
> I have got to get Empire Free Trade.

Lord Melchett urged Beaverbrook to accept quotas instead of food taxes. Beaverbrook replied firmly on 22 September: "Nothing will shift us from the advocacy of duties on foreign foodstuffs so far as I can see". This letter to Melchett also shows Beaverbrook's tangle over Bennett:

> The Conservative Government in Canada is pledged to the eastern manufacturer. . . .
> Our only hope is that Bennett may want very much to hold his western representation. In order to do so, he must find markets abroad for Canadian wheat.
> But his simple principle is that a Canadian dollar spent in the West Indies is just as damaging to the Dominion as a dollar spent in the United States. You can be quite sure that he will stick to that principle. . . .
> I wish to do nothing to displease him at present. And never, never, never, if he adopts the principles of Empire Free Trade.

Thus Beaverbrook glossed over his differences with Bennett, in the hope that he could somehow use Bennett against Baldwin.

This appeared clearly when the Imperial Conference met at the end of September. On 8 October Bennett proposed Imperial Preference, by a 10% increase or imposition of tariffs against others. He concluded: "In our opinion Empire Free Trade is neither desirable nor possible, for it would defeat the very purpose we are striving to achieve". This sentence was widely interpreted as a condemnation by Bennett of the Empire Crusade. Beaverbrook shrugged it off as merely a punishment for his bad behaviour during the Canadian election: "Bennett was hitting back and, according to his life-long habit, was hitting hard".[1] Beaverbrook was only concerned with Baldwin's answer, and at first this seemed satisfactory. A statement, drafted by Chamberlain though signed by Baldwin, accepted the principle of Imperial Preference and promised that proposals would be put before the electors "for their definite and final assent". In other words, the referendum was dead, and Chamberlain's "free hand" was achieved. Amery told Beaverbrook that he ought to be satisfied:

> Now Baldwin has come along on the essential point—though still with a certain fluffiness of language—I think it is only fair that those of us who believe in the policy should back him. (11 October 1930.)

Beaverbrook remained sceptical and was soon justified. Baldwin rejected any tariff on foreign wheat. Beaverbrook answered on 16 October:

> Mr. Baldwin still shrinks from the acid test. . . . His successive attempts to find a policy remind me of the chorus of a third-rate review. His evasions reappear in different scenes and in new dresses and every time they dance with renewed and despairing vigour. But it is the same old jig.

This was a declaration of war. Beaverbrook humbly appealed to Bennett for aid. If only Bennett would explain that, in his dismissal of Empire Free Trade, "he was referring to Empire Free Trade in its strictly literal sense and not to that limited partnership which the Crusade has always advocated", the unfortunate effects of his remark would be undone. Bennett did not respond. Beaverbrook then urged Bennett to lead the Empire. He wrote on 18 October: "If we in England refuse to assume the hegemony of the Empire, why not consider taking it for Canada?" Still Bennett did not respond.

Meanwhile Beaverbrook found a more propitious battleground against Baldwin. There was a by-election at South Paddington. The local Conservative association was entirely in the hands of Empire Crusaders. Sir Herbert Lidiard, the Conservative candidate, stated that he was enthusiastically in favour of Empire Free Trade, but could not go into parliament with his hands tied. Under pressure from the Conservative central office he protested his loyalty to Baldwin. The local association, somewhat

[1] Friends, 58.

prodded by Beaverbrook's agents, then revolted and adopted Vice-Admiral Taylor as Empire Crusade candidate. Here was the opportunity Beaverbrook had long wanted: a Crusader running against an official candidate. Once more Beaverbrook descended on the constituency with an array of canvassers and motor cars. He spoke at eight meetings. William Gerhardi describes how, when accused of furthering Empire Free Trade so as to increase the circulation of his newspapers in the ensuing prosperity, Beaverbrook replied: "Yes, I hope it will. But if you think this the real motive behind my policy, I have nothing more to say", thereby, as Gerhardi remarks, throwing the imbecility of the suggestion back on the man who made it.[1]

Of course Beaverbrook was as much concerned to carry on his war with Baldwin as to win votes for Admiral Taylor. On 17 October he asked whether Baldwin would leave it to the Dominions to decide whether British food taxes were an essential part of imperial preference. Baldwin replied by letter on 21 October. There was no more of "My dear Max". The letter began "Dear Lord Beaverbrook" and ended "Yours faithfully". Baldwin pointed out that in February Beaverbrook had promised his support for the policy of "the free hand". This was the policy which Baldwin now intended to put before the electorate. "I would rule nothing out", though he added that he would urge the Dominions to be satisfied with quotas instead of food taxes. Melchett, who was himself keen on quotas, regarded Baldwin's letter as "a great victory for Empire Free Trade ... a complete surrender ... the greatest political triumph of anyone I know in all my political life" (22 October 1930).

Beaverbrook was unmoved. He replied to Melchett on 23 October:

> I have no intention of taking Baldwin's offer. It would be a great mistake it seems to me to let the fellow take only one tablespoonful of castor oil, when at least two is required. I don't think even two tablespoonfuls will do much good.

Beaverbrook's answer to Baldwin expressed the same thought in a politer form:

> Eight months ago, I should have been glad to accept your declaration in favour of the free hand. But in the crisis through which we are passing eight months is a long time. Today the country demands a positive policy. In my opinion only a positive policy will carry the Conservative Party to victory at the next election. But while you have abandoned your own pledge not to impose duties on foreign foodstuffs, you still refrain from advocating them. ...
> My sole concern is for the triumph of the policy which I am convinced is the only policy that will restore prosperity to our stricken industries

[1] Gerhardi, Memoirs of a Polyglot, 248.

and ruined agriculture. For the success of that policy I am willing to make any sacrifice, but until I am convinced that it is going to be prosecuted with the necessary vigour I am not prepared to retire one step from the position I have taken up or to abandon one jot or one tittle of the principles it involves.

For some reason Beaverbrook did not send this letter and contented himself with answering Baldwin at a public meeting:

> Mr. Baldwin is the champion of all backsliders. We believe we have brought him to grace; we lift up our voices in the hymn of rejoicing; and we have hardly got through the first line of it before we see him crawling down the aisle again.

South Paddington polled on 30 October. The Empire Crusaders were out in force. Eleven members of the household staff at Cherkley were among the canvassers. Beaverbrook himself was elsewhere. Seventeen Conservative MPs had called on Baldwin to resign and demanded a party meeting in order to voice their dissatisfaction with his leadership. Baldwin decided to call a meeting himself before one was forced on him. The meeting of Conservative peers, MPs and candidates was held on the morning of 30 October. Chamberlain, as chairman of the party, had assiduously whipped up support and himself drafted the resolution expressing confidence in Baldwin. This resolution was carried by 462 votes to 116. Another resolution in favour of the free hand was carried by all votes except one—Beaverbrook's. Afterwards he wrote an account of the meeting to Brisbane:

> Baldwin secured an immense majority. But there was a terrible minority of 116 votes, representing the real spirit of the Conservative party. That minority is made up of the men of courage and vision.
>
> I surprised the leader by appearing at the meeting myself. . . . I sat quietly in my seat—the centre of attention. I tried to give no sign in my countenance when I was subjected to a violent attack. Baldwin, of course, was intending to put me in the dock in place of himself.
>
> The debate was, however, centred on Baldwin's leadership, and it appeared that differences on policy would not come up for discussion.
>
> But at a dramatic moment, when many present were calling out for a division, a man named Lord Howe, who belongs to the Baldwin group, . . . asked why Beaverbrook had taken no part in the discussion. He evidently intended to make a point against me on that account.
>
> At once I rose slowly to my feet, and with bent shoulders and weary footsteps made my way to the rostrum. The audience screamed with disapproval. However, I got in my few sentences entirely on policy and returned to my place amidst a little ripple of applause from the anti-Baldwin section.
>
> It was a curious experience. I have never seen, at one time, so many faces showing unmistakably the signs of bitterness and hatred.
>
> The pioneer always gets a bad show. I have no doubt that the policy I advocate will be adopted in the long run. I should think it likely that my

great-grandson will unveil a statue to my memory in some obscure Square
in a remote town in the Provinces, or perhaps on the waterfront at Mombasa,
or in the Blue Mountains of Jamaica.

But I have already aroused hostilities in the Conservative Party which
will never die down.

Baldwin claimed that Beaverbrook had come out badly. He wrote to
Davidson on 2 November 1930:

> The Beaver would not have spoken but Francis Curzon [Lord Howe]
> challenged him to speak. He was booed and made a poor speech. He talked
> about the quota which was out of order, and said that he didn't care two-
> pence who was leader as long as his policy was adopted!

Bridgeman, though a close friend of Baldwin's, thought differently and
also wrote to Davidson on 2 November:

> Max really made rather a good show before a very hostile audience.
> Quiet, modest and unaffected by the nasty things which had been said—
> and said it was only policy he cared about and that he was not concerned
> as to leadership. Although at Paddington two days before he had been
> attacking SB's leadership. I feel and always have felt that Max will be
> "all right on the night" and is only waiting to choose the moment to come
> round and say we must all work together and that he has really got all he
> wants.[1]

This latter judgement was probably close to the truth.

Baldwin seemed to have won a great victory. The effect was reversed
the next day when the South Paddington result was declared. Vice-
Admiral Taylor had beaten the official Conservative candidate and was in
by 941 votes. Among the messages of congratulation to Beaverbrook
was one from Duff Cooper. Victory brought another consolation. R. B.
Bennett called at Stornoway House, and it seemed that past estrangements
were forgotten. Beaverbrook later recorded his ups and downs:

> What a life! Excitement (being howled down at the party meeting),
> depression (being heavily defeated by Baldwin), exaltation (being success-
> ful at South Paddington), and restoration, (being forgiven by Bennett)!
> All in the space of a few hours. A day to remember.[2]

The quarrel with Bennett left its mark despite the subsequent reconciliation. Perhaps Beaverbrook was also offended by the way in which the
other Dominion prime ministers had ignored Empire Free Trade during
the Imperial conference. At any rate, he moved gradually away from
imperial preference and put more emphasis on the protection of agriculture at home. If the Dominions would not help him, he would not help

[1] Robert Rhodes James, Memoirs of a Conservative, 352–54.
[2] Friends, 64.

them. British farmers, on the other hand, gave him big audiences, and he was particularly gratified when J. F. Wright of Norwich founded the Agricultural party in order to advocate food taxes. Gradually and imperceptibly Empire Free Trade faded except in name. Protection for British agriculture took its place as the real purpose of the Empire Crusade.

For the moment Beaverbrook was on top of the wave. He believed that victory was in sight. He wrote to Smeaton White of The Montreal Gazette on 12 November 1930:

> I believe the Empire Crusade controls London. And we can, I am sure, dominate the Southern counties of Surrey, Sussex, and Kent, and we will dominate Baldwin too, for he must come to full acceptance of the policy.

Beaverbrook now scored another triumph: he expounded Empire Free Trade on the BBC. This was the end of a long and not unusual battle. Beaverbrook had originally been invited to broadcast on 31 March. Ramsay MacDonald consulted Baldwin, and the two protested to the governors of the BBC that this was a party political broadcast and would have to be followed by talks on the same theme by official spokesmen of the three political parties. The governors forbade Beaverbrook's broadcast. But there were traitors within Broadcasting House. Gladstone Murray, BBC director of public relations, was himself a Canadian and supported Empire Free Trade. Mrs. Philip Snowden was a governor and indignant at government interference, maybe out of hostility to MacDonald. These two briefed Beaverbrook and advised him to try again. Murray arranged a new date for the broadcast on 16 October. This time, Lloyd George added his protest to that of the two other party leaders, using the South Paddington election as an excuse. The broadcast was postponed once more. Finally it was delivered on 27 November. The political parties made no claim to a reply, and the case for Free Trade was academically stated by Sir William Beveridge. This was by no means the last occasion when the BBC showed its reluctance to use Beaverbrook's undoubted talents as a radio, and later as a television, speaker.

Neville Chamberlain, as might be expected, was still looking for a reconciliation. In mid-November he approached Beaverbrook once more for a "lowering of the temperature". The two men met. Chamberlain drafted a letter as from himself to Beaverbrook on 26 November:

> The policy of the Party, as expounded by the Leader in his latest utterances, appears to me to present no material difference from that which you have long advocated with so much eloquence and sincerity. . . .
>
> Can we not forget past differences, and devote ourselves solely to one united and determined assault upon the obstacles that block the way to victory?

Beaverbrook was not convinced. He replied to Chamberlain on 28 November:

> I hold the view that you allow yourselves to be placed on the defensive over the food tax. I believe you must abandon it, or take glory in it. If you try to balance yourself you will come to a bad end.
> . . . .
> I propose to drift for a bit until we see how things are developing.

In private Beaverbrook was more scathing. He wrote to Melchett on 1 December:

> The Conservative Party is not breast high. . . . The Free Hand is no platform at all. It is a bog.
> I would like to support this party, but I will not be involved in another 1923 business.

To make matters worse, Beaverbrook discovered that the Conservative central office was preparing to run H. G. Williams as official candidate at South Paddington against Vice-Admiral Taylor at the general election. At this he broke off negotiations with Chamberlain who returned a soft answer on 10 December:

> If the trouble can be kept local, the damage will not be irreparable, but if it is allowed to develop into general hostilities, it would be extremely dangerous. I will do my best to prevent its spreading, and I hope you will do the same. We must each recognize and make allowance for the other's difficulties, but, with patience and goodwill on both sides, we should be able to achieve the purposes we discussed.

Beaverbrook was in less conciliatory mood. He wrote to Amery on 24 December:

> At the first of the year we open up with propaganda, but for the purpose at present, of putting to the country the difference between the Conservative policy and the Crusade policy. . . . Neville is not measuring up to his job, and should not succeed Baldwin. He has taken the wrong decision over South Paddington on three occasions.

When 1931 arrived, Beaverbrook of course was not content with propaganda. Any full-blooded advocacy of Empire Free Trade was bound to turn into an attack on Baldwin. Beaverbrook wrote lightheartedly to A. J. Cummings on 2 January:

> I cannot tell what steps Mr. Baldwin will take in the New Year. During 1930 he made thirteen moves. John Buchan, the author of the Thirty Nine Steps, has been lecturing him recently. So perhaps he will out do John by going forty steps all told.

To an Empire Crusader, J. H. MacDonald, Beaverbrook repeated the old complaint on 6 January:

> Baldwin does not mean to tax foreign food. He tries to catch the supporter of foreign food duties by suggesting that he is willing to consider them himself, but whenever he comes down to the real issue he dodges it.

Writing to Borden on 7 January, Beaverbrook came nearer the real explanation of Baldwin's hesitations:

> Baldwin is trying to get the best of both worlds. In the South, he is a food taxer; but in the North, he dare not go quite as far as this. So he says there that he will not support food taxes unless we can get a first-rate bargain with the Dominions.

Beaverbrook continued to demand food taxes unconditionally, for the sake of English farmers as much as for the Dominions or even more so. Thus writing to R. F. Lush on 24 January:

> The agriculturists of this country have as much right to consideration as the agriculturists of any Dominion and we therefore demand duties on foreign foodstuffs for the benefit of our own people first and the Dominions second.

Baldwin had other vulnerable points at this time. One was India, where many Conservatives disliked Lord Irwin's conciliatory policy. Brendan Bracken wrote to Beaverbrook on 14 January:

> This wretched Government, with the aid of the Liberals and some eminent Tories, is about to commit us to one of the most fatal decisions in all our history, and there is practically no opposition to their policy.
> Disagreeing, as I did, with much of your Empire Free Trade policy, I could not but admire all the force and resource which you put into your campaign, and I believe that if those great talents were devoted to combating defeatism, it would still be possible to preserve the essentials of British rule in India.

Beaverbrook had certainly no faith in the policy of concession. He wrote to Borden on 7 January:

> The Government is trying to unite Mohammedan and Hindu. It will never succeed. There will be no amalgamation between these two. There is only one way to govern India. And that is the way laid down by the ancient Romans—was it the Gracchi, or was it Romulus, or was it one of the Emperors?—and that is "Divide and Rule".

But he would not be diverted from Empire Free Trade. Moreover Baldwin's principal opponent over India was Churchill, and he, in Beaverbrook's opinion, was a dead force, as well as being of course a Free Trader. Thus to Borden on 7 January:

> Winston Churchill is trying to make a corner for himself in Indian affairs. He is now taking the stand of a veritable Die-Hard. But he does not carry

conviction. He should have done it on the occasion of the Montagu-Chelmsford Bill in Lloyd George's time. He has disclosed too many shifting phases to expect to be regarded as immovable now. His voice lacks that note of sincerity for which the country looks.

And to Brisbane on 13 January:

It is Churchill who is roaring and declaiming and trying to make a corner in Indian affairs. And the majority of the Conservative public shares his point of view. But he himself does not carry conviction. He has gone through too many shifting phases to be regarded with authority now. His voice lacks the proper note of sincerity for which the country listens.

In fact the country is heartily tired of the old voices altogether—George, Churchill, Baldwin, even MacDonald's voice, beautiful as it is, is a toneless echo from the past.

Beaverbrook was the readier to take the offensive when the Conservative central office issued a pamphlet defending Baldwin's settlement of the American debt in 1922. Beaverbrook at once answered by telling in The Daily Express the story of Law's opposition to the settlement. Sir Robert Horne, who had prompted Baldwin at the time, expostulated that Beaverbrook should not attack Baldwin alone and ignore Lloyd George who was equally involved. Beaverbrook answered on 23 January 1931:

Lloyd George cannot do the Crusade, or our policy, the slightest harm. You are wrong about his being our enemy. It is not Lloyd George but Baldwin who is our enemy. Lloyd George is impotent. Baldwin, by virtue of his titular position as head of the Conservative Party, has opportunities to damage us; and he takes them all the time.

Therefore, in order to achieve Empire Free Trade, we have got to defeat Baldwin.

We have already tried the line of making peace with him, and nothing came of it. Now—not peace but a sword.

Beaverbrook had already decided what sword to draw: it would be to fight by-elections. He wrote to Brisbane on 13 January 1931:

I am going out entirely for by-elections this year, and shall exclude all other forms of propaganda. I shall make the by-elections the occasions for my propaganda. It then becomes more human and far less boring to the people.

Rothermere warmly approved. He wrote on 14 January:

My feeling about the Empire Trade Crusade is that it is no use if it is simply going to splutter. If you are going to build up a real organisation with full intentions of fighting all by-elections, go ahead and you will find me with you, but if it is a campaign of occasional episodes I do not see that much could be done.

Beaverbrook described his tactic to Horne in vivid terms:

> Last year, we trampled trumpeting through the jungle like great clumsy elephants—I have never seen an elephant, except in a circus, but I'm told that that is what they do. This year, we will be like a tiger, or rather a tigress, waiting in our lair ready to spring. And the moment to spring will be provided in a by-election.

This policy had obvious attractions. Beaverbrook was in practice the Crusade, and he could not be endlessly stumping the country on an undefined mission. By-elections gave him the opportunity for bursts of activity which was what he liked. Moreover there was a practical purpose —voters to be won—and an immediate result—the Crusader, it was hoped, ahead of the official Conservative candidate. But there was also a great danger. When it came to actually splitting the Conservative vote, even the most devoted Crusader drew back. Horne warned Beaverbrook correctly on 24 January: "As to Baldwin, the attack which you project upon him will only have the effect of riveting him in his seat more firmly than ever".

I learnt the same lesson during the campaign for nuclear disarmament. We had great meetings all over the country, much bigger than any official Labour leader could command. Then came the question: what do we do next? The obvious answer was: run CND candidates. At this the supporters of the Labour party, who made up the bulk of CND, turned tail with one accord, and we ended up with the anti-CND leader of the Labour party stronger than before. Beaverbrook said to me in 1961: "You'll never do any good until you run your own candidates". If I had known as much about the Empire Crusade as I do now, I should have replied that he did not do himself much good when he took his own advice thirty years earlier.

These difficulties appeared in February when a by-election occurred at East Islington. Labour was defending the seat. Miss Cazalet, the official Conservative candidate, was in favour of tariffs, but coupled this with loyalty to Baldwin. The Crusade candidate, much pushed by the Conservative central office, announced his satisfaction with her declaration and withdrew. Another candidate, Brigadier-General Critchley, was hastily discovered. The Crusade, which was well in funds, having spent only £23,000 out of the £109,000 subscribed, paid all his expenses. Beaverbrook spoke at eleven meetings. It was a rough contest. Lord Hailsham, who must have been rifling Sir Robert Horne's desk, said at one meeting:

> Lord Beaverbrook comes to East Islington and is compared to an elephant trumpeting in the jungle or a man-eating tiger. I am inclined to compare him to a mad dog running along the streets and yapping and barking. I would remind his Lordship that the best way to treat a mad dog if you cannot muzzle him is to shoot him.

John Strachey attended one meeting with Aneurin Bevan and wrote to Beaverbrook afterwards that it was a mistake for the stewards to chuck out hecklers. Strachey added: "We were both impressed by your sincerity". Beaverbrook answered with an invitation to dinner, which does not seem to have been accepted, though Bevan later became one of his close friends.

The poll was declared on 19 February. Labour held the seat on a minority vote. Brigadier-General Critchley polled eleven hundred more votes than Miss Cazalet. Beaverbrook professed to be undismayed. He wrote to one supporter on 20 February: "The policy of protection for Agriculture has become the dominant political issue in Great Britain", and to another on 25 February: "As Mr. Baldwin represents the minority, it is clear that any responsibility for splitting the vote must rest with him". The fact remained that the Conservative vote had been split and Labour allowed to slip in. Many Crusaders wrote to Beaverbrook in dismay. Unknown to him, Baldwin's position was in fact shaken. On 25 February 1931, Sir Robert Topping, the chief Conservative agent, wrote to Neville Chamberlain that the party needed a new leader. On 1 March Chamberlain showed this letter to Baldwin and afterwards recorded in his diary: "4.30, S.B. has decided to go at once". The Times prepared a leader entitled "Mr. Baldwin withdraws".[1] At this dramatic moment Baldwin was ironically saved once more by Beaverbrook's intervention.

The occasion was yet another by-election—the last, as it turned out, of the series—at St. George's, Westminster. This was an impregnable Conservative seat, with no danger of letting Labour in on a split vote. Indeed there was neither a Labour nor a Liberal candidate. It was a straight issue of Baldwin's leadership, and the party had difficulty in finding an official candidate. Two prominent Conservatives refused to champion Baldwin. Finally Duff Cooper came forward, although he had actually congratulated Beaverbrook over South Paddington and was married to one of Beaverbrook's closest friends, Lady Diana Cooper. The challenger was Sir Ernest Petter, a west of England industrialist and really more Rothermere's man than Beaverbrook's, keener to fight on India than on food taxes. At the time, Beaverbrook did not mind and remarked cheerfully of Petter: "one of his planks is in line with our policy". Nor did Beaverbrook complain that the contest was over Baldwin's leadership, not over food taxes. He wrote to Brisbane on 3 March—adding an incidental reference to what he thought was the wrong way of doing things:

> The primary issue of the by-election will be the leadership of the Conservative party. . . . If Petter is defeated, we shall not be seriously discouraged. If he wins, Baldwin must go, and Empire Free Trade must become the accepted policy of the Conservative Party. . . .

[1] Feiling, Neville Chamberlain, 186.

Mosley has, in my opinion, done a foolish thing. He should not have detached himself from the Labour Party, he should have stayed inside it and bombarded it from within, as we have done to the Conservatives.[1]

Similarly to Clifford Turner on 14 March:

If we win this fight the Conservatives will select a new leader and take up our policy and we'll all live happily ever after.

The Crusade paid all Petter's expenses. Beaverbrook put forth his greatest effort, speaking at sixteen meetings. He made out of course that the contest was over policy, not personality, writing to L. W. Dent on 8 March:

Lord Beaverbrook regrets to have to confess that Mr. Baldwin is liked by him. No matter how much he muddles up the country and the policy, his Lordship still has a personal regard for him. It would, perhaps, not be a bad thing if he could get rid of it.

Certainly Beaverbrook at no time made reflections on Baldwin's private character or record. Rothermere was not so scrupulous. The Daily Mail sneered: "It is difficult to see how the leader of a party who has lost his own fortune can hope to restore that of anyone else, or of his country". This gave Baldwin his opportunity. Speaking at the Queen's Hall on the eve of poll, he denounced "the proprietorship of these papers"—thus including by implication though not by name Beaverbrook as well as Rothermere—for seeking "power without responsibility—the prerogative of the harlot throughout the ages".

On 19 March Duff Cooper won St. George's by 5,710 votes. Baldwin had triumphed, and there was no more talk of his resignation. Neville Chamberlain's hope for an early succession to the leadership crumbled into dust. Beaverbrook professed to be undismayed. He made out that he had fought on the wrong issues—Baldwin's leadership and concession in India—and so had lost the Labour and Liberal votes in St. George's to Duff Cooper. He wrote to Mrs. Pinckard, wife of the proprietor of The Saturday Review and a keen Crusader:

The defeat is due to my own stupidity. It was wrong to fight on India and the leadership of the Conservative Party. The issue might have been the policy of Empire Free Trade and the cause and cure of unemployment. On that platform we can turn and win Socialist and Liberal votes.

[1] When Sir Oswald Mosley's economic plans were rejected by the Labour government and the annual conference, he left the Labour party along with a few others and founded the New party. Beaverbrook often hankered after an alliance with Mosley, but noted that his programme did not include food taxes and wrote regretfully to Cunliffe-Owen on 6 January: "I do not think that either you or I can make any cash contribution to Mosley's fund".

Maybe these votes were as little likely to be won by the promise of food taxes, and in any case it was mainly Conservatives who rallied to the defence of Baldwin.

Beaverbrook and Chamberlain had both been defeated. The result, surprising only at first sight, was that they came together and redeemed what they could. Though Baldwin could not be dislodged, he might yet be saddled with food taxes. On 23 March Chamberlain wrote to Beaverbrook: "There is now a lull in the storm; is not this a good opportunity to make contact again?" The two met repeatedly, and Chamberlain devised a formula for appeasement. Beaverbrook did not trouble to consult his Empire Crusade colleagues, such as they were. Instead he turned to J. F. Wright, leader of the Agricultural party—a further indication that he was by now more concerned with British agriculture than with the Dominions. He defined his terms to Lord Londonderry thus: "If Mr. Baldwin will say that farming must be made to pay and, for that purpose, he asks for a free hand to put duties on foreign foodstuffs, the fight is at an end". The deal, when actually made, was less clear-cut. The Stornoway Pact, as Beaverbrook liked to call it, was concluded and published on 31 March. It took the form of an exchange of letters between Beaverbrook and Chamberlain, both in fact drafted by the latter with some amendments by the Norfolk group. Beaverbrook wrote:

> May I be assured that the programme of the Conservative party, as it stands to-day, proposes to develop a policy of increasing not only manufacturing production but also of increasing wheat and general agricultural production at home, and that it will seek to achieve this policy by the most efficient and practicable method, that is to say, by quotas, prohibition of, or duties on, foreign foodstuffs?
>
> It is well known that I hold to the opinion that duties on foreign foodstuffs are the most effective method of dealing with the need for increasing production at home. Nevertheless I recognize that the quota system and prohibitions have advantages in relation to increased production of some foodstuffs in Britain.
> . . . .
> The cause is infinitely greater than the quarrel.

Chamberlain replied:

> Mr. Baldwin authorizes me to say that you have correctly stated the present[1] Conservative policy in regard to agriculture. It is his intention to employ for the development of agricultural production all, or any, of the methods you enumerate, as they may best effect the object aimed at, and to ask the electors for a mandate[2] for that purpose.

[1] "present" inserted by Wright in order to imply that Conservative policy had changed.
[2] "mandate" substituted by Wright for "the free hand".

Beaverbrook had got specific mention of agriculture and the substitution of the mandate for the free hand. Otherwise this was an odd document to be presented as victory for the Empire Crusade. Not a word about the Empire; no reference to Empire Free Trade or even to Imperial Preference. Perhaps Beaverbrook thought that, if food taxes could be put over for the sake of British agriculture, they would benefit Empire Free Trade by a side wind. In any case it was far-fetched to claim, as Beaverbrook did, that the agreement committed the Conservative party to the rip-roaring campaign for food taxes which he had always said he would demand as the price of his cooperation. Incidentally there was no personal reconciliation this time between Baldwin and Beaverbrook, and it does not appear that they ever met again.[1]

In later years the Stornoway Pact acquired legendary significance for Beaverbrook. He came to believe that he had captured the Conservative party. The next election would have been fought on food taxes and Empire Free Trade achieved, had it not been for the financial crisis of August 1931 which led to a general election fought on quite other issues. It is true that Beaverbrook never pressed the Empire Crusade with any intensity after the Stornoway Pact, but this was due to the accident of the financial crisis and not to any belief that he had triumphed. As often happens, the Empire Crusade did not reach any decisive conclusion. It trailed away into obscurity, its memories echoing through the nineteen-thirties and even later. But the real political battle ended on 31 March 1931. Baldwin's leadership was not challenged again, and Beaverbrook became once more a figure on the side lines of politics.

[1] When Baldwin unveiled a portrait of Bonar Law at the Constitutional Club in 1932 Beaverbrook courteously stayed away.

CHAPTER THIRTEEN

EPILOGUE TO THE EMPIRE CRUSADE, 1931–33

The Empire Crusade was not wound up at the end of March 1931. It continued to splutter, with Beaverbrook revolving round it in bewilderment. Immediately after the Stornoway Pact Beaverbrook was in two minds, or rather three, about what he had done. Had he won? Had he secured a satisfactory compromise? Or had he lost? Letters written on 31 March 1931 show his changing moods:

(To Springham) I believe the settlement will give us our duties on foreign foodstuffs.

(To Francis Wortley) I look forward to going to the country with the Conservatives on a united programme.... It still remains to be seen how far this agreement will work in practice, and whether the Conservatives intend to stand by the full policy of duties on foreign foodstuffs.

(To Duncan Fitzwilliams) I tell you secretly that I do not think the fight is over.

You will see from the correspondence that there is room for Baldwin to crawl down the aisle again. As you and I will be in the choir on that occasion, Baldwin can get out through the door before we can match him.

Still, we will be in the choir, and we can sing more discordant notes if our penitent bolts again.

The truth was that Beaverbrook had run out of steam, as always happened with him after a big effort. Rothermere sized up the position more or less correctly when he wrote on 28 March:

I am relieved and glad that you have taken this course, because I have felt, with the onerous business obligations which now rest upon you, you would not have sufficient time, health or strength to conduct the kind of campaign that would be necessary to enforce your views on the electorate.

Two days later Rothermere tried to stir Beaverbrook up. He telegraphed from Lisbon:

I do not conceal from myself that Conservative candidate will probably be asked near future if in favour taxing foreign foodstuffs and will say no. This is dilemma I see immediately ahead.

Beaverbrook at once replied:

> If dilemma arises I shall oppose candidate. Chamberlain promised food tax policy.

On 1 April 1931 Beaverbrook telegraphed to Rothermere again:

> Chamberlain pledged himself in conversation with me and Norfolk farmers separately to include duties on foodstuffs. I think he will stick to it.

No doubt Beaverbrook intended to renew the Crusade when he had mustered fresh energy. He wrote to C. F. Crundall on 17 April:

> Chamberlain promised us that the party would adopt duties on foreign foodstuffs, if I would make a satisfactory settlement protecting the Conservative leaders against the appearance of being rolled in the mud.
> I agreed to do so.[1]
> But the Conservative party will not really adopt and advocate our policy unless my friends drive them on with more success than our opponents drive them back.

For the time being, Beaverbrook regarded the Stornoway Pact as the order of release. Immediately it was signed, he went off to Paris for a week. Later in April he spent a fortnight in Germany and Austria. Throughout May he never left Cherkley except on another visit to Paris. He addressed a meeting of the National Farmers' Union at Slough on 24 June. Otherwise he was silent. He wrote no political articles. He met no politicians except occasionally Neville Chamberlain and departed for Canada at the end of July.

Beaverbrook's foreign travels produced some brisk opinions, worth recording, as he told Arthur Brisbane, to see whether they turned out to be "prophecy or preposterous misjudgement". He wrote to Brisbane from Berlin on 23 April 1931:

> The Germans expect the Nationalist parties to prevail at the next election. Hugenberg is the leader of the Conservative section, and Hitler of the Socialist section. This pair find common ground in their Socialistic[2] aspirations. If they find favour with popular opinion they will persuade the Americans to lend large sums of money to Germany. Then they will say: "Interest or Reparations?", and reparations will be sacrificed.

Beaverbrook had enough confidence in his judgement to advise a Halifax friend, McCurdy, to sell American stocks and invest "in the electrical undertakings of the Deutsche Bank". It is not possible to state whether he took his own advice.

---

[1] This does not appear in the Stornoway Pact and seems to be an echo of the agreement concluded between Beaverbrook and Baldwin twelve months before.
[2] This is surely a typist's error for "Nationalistic".

But he continued to hold the same opinion. When the German financial crisis broke, he wrote to Peter Rodd on 21 July 1931:

The end will be an alliance between Germany, England and America, with an isolated France and a very good thing too.

Two other judgements of Beaverbrook's on foreign affairs retain their interest. The News Chronicle denounced him as a warmonger because of his attacks on the League of Nations. He replied on 2 June 1931:

I am a pacifist, and no one more than I abhors the prospect of our sharing in another war. . . .

I dread the peril of war which our European commitments bring in their train.

The treaty obligations into which we entered at Locarno compel us to take one side or the other in any quarrel between France and Germany, no matter what the cause of the quarrel may be. It may be as remote from us, both economically and politically, as Poland. A single shot fired on the borders of that country . . . may send our young men again to the slaughter, and expose our civilian population to terrors of which the last war was but the faintest shadow.

The last sentence was prescient. Less fortunate was a forecast to Brisbane on 23 August:

I hold strongly to the view that Stalin cannot make Russia into an industrial nation. I wish he could.

During his retirement at Cherkley, Beaverbrook threw himself into a final revision of the second volume of Politicians and the War, which had been hanging fire for the last two years. Thornton Butterworth, who published the first volume, complained that the royalties on it had not covered the advance of £2,500. As Beaverbrook, with his usual desire for a mass market, had insisted on publishing at 7/6, a low price even for those days, this failure was not surprising. Thornton Butterworth would now offer an advance of only £1,500, which Beaverbrook refused. Doidge shopped around in the intervals of running the Empire Crusade and got even lower offers from other publishers. Meanwhile Thornton Butterworth had the book set. Early in 1931 they presented a bill of £39 for keeping their presses standing. This provoked Beaverbrook into action. He decided to publish the book himself under the fictitious imprint of The Lane Publications. The book was serialized, this time in The Daily Express. Beaverbrook selected the instalments. He also made some final changes. The most substantial was to cut out a long passage on Baldwin's first elevation to office in 1917. The reason for this cut is not hard to conjecture.

Book publication was fixed for the autumn of 1931. The economic crisis caused a postponement until 1932, which no doubt explains why the book has no date of publication. Someone cut out the wrong year and forgot to put in the right one. However the dedicatory quatrain has the date: January 29, 1932. The quatrain fell out later when the two volumes of Politicians and the War were republished as a single volume. It deserves reprinting:

> Rose leaves, when the rose is dead,
> Are heap'd for the beloved's bed;
> And so thy thoughts, when thou art gone,
> Love itself shall slumber on.

The verses were presumably a last tribute to Bonar Law, though perhaps intended for Gladys Beaverbrook as well. Beaverbrook did not explain.

The original introduction also fell out when the book was republished. Some passages in it also deserve rescue. Beaverbrook answered the criticism that he had failed to establish Law's greatness:

> A politician, granted that he is a man of good character, largely stands and falls by the view he holds of himself. If he is a pushing, ambitious man, with a great belief in his own power, which is justified by his capacity to attain high office, the nation is ready enough to take him at his own valuation. Self-confidence breeds the confidence of others and the valuation arrived at will probably be quite correct.[1]
>
> But Bonar Law was a self-effacing man who underestimated his own talents. He was very willing to let the credit for his own actions go to others. As a consequence his contemporaries took him at his own valuation, which was a wrong one. He was bound to be written down, and posterity is sure to accept the verdict.
>
> . . . .
>
> I know that Bonar Law was the greatest figure on the political stage with which these books deal—that by action, by support, or by withdrawal, he made and unmade every government from 1915 to 1922.

Beaverbrook also answered the criticism, still often made, that he had merely described "the jealousies, the feuds, the personal ambitions of politicians at times of political crisis". He pointed to the underlying fear of a compromise peace or, as it was then called, Peace by Negotiation. He called in aid Lansdowne's memorandum advocating Peace without Victory and concluded:

> Those who revolted in favour of reform were united by one single point only. They believed that the war was being inefficiently and half-heartedly conducted. Some ascribed the defect to the character or political opinions of the men in power. The Liberal rebels thought the Premier was dilatory because he was Asquith. Many of the Tory reformers thought that Asquith

---

[1] This sentence can be applied in reverse to Beaverbrook himself. Lacking self-confidence, he was easily written down as a serious politician.

was inefficient because he was a Liberal. Others again of all parties or none
imputed the blame not to the men but to the machine the men had to work.
They thought Government by Cabinet discussion unsuited to war conditions
and demanded some kind of dictatorship either by an individual or by a
Committee of public safety such as the War Council practically became.
All these currents of thought after many swirls and eddies finally ran together
and, streaming down a single channel, washed the Asquith administration
away.
    . . . [The picture] is certainly not that of a set of self-seeking fellows
quarrelling about their interests. It is a picture of able men, not free in
their humanity from the ordinary faults of mortals, all jealously anxious
to serve their country. They simply differed on the best method to pursue.

The volume passed almost unnoticed. The Beaverbrook newspapers
were busy campaigning for agricultural protection and failed to review it.
Critic commented sourly in The New Statesman: "I expect to see a good
many of Lord Beaverbrook's statements of facts challenged by those who
shared in these incidents"—a remark more applicable to Kingsley
Martin's autobiography. The book sold only 2,700 copies from a total print
of 3,013, and the net profit was £36. It came out at an unpropitious
moment. The political crisis of August 1931 eclipsed the earlier crisis
of December 1916. Men, faced with the economic problems of the present,
were no longer interested in the first world war. The great figures of that
time, such as Lloyd George and Churchill, fell into obscurity, and
Beaverbrook with them. Maybe, too, his campaign against Baldwin discredited his earlier achievements in a similar field, now that Baldwin was
riding high. At any rate Beaverbrook gave up the writing of history for
more than twenty years. When Sir Courtenay Mansell praised the classical
rhetoric of Politicians and the War, evoking parallels with Seneca and
Diderot, Beaverbrook replied:

> So far as I am aware, the book has no merits except those of bare narrative.
> If you are correct in detecting other virtues, they must have found their
> way in by accident.

He claimed to be bored with the book and wrote to A. J. Cummings on
11 May 1932:

> If I had the job to do over again I would gather the documents together
> and try to build a narrative on the basis that "facts speak for themselves".

This was a counsel of imperfection which fortunately he never followed.
    In June 1931 Beaverbrook was himself the subject of a book. F. A.
Mackenzie published the first of many biographies. Mackenzie was a
former Daily Mail journalist, now a dying man. He compiled his biography from press cuttings, and for once Beaverbrook's claim was true—
that he himself had contributed nothing to the book, except a loan of

£400, turned into a gift on Mackenzie's death. Beaverbrook wrote to David Low on 28 January 1931:

> I have dodged reading the manuscript, I have dodged writing a Preface—I have dodged all sorts of things.
> Yet, I am sorry for the poor fellow, because, of course, he is on the way to the graveyard, at a brisk trot. And he knows it.
> I laugh more at your work at the present moment than ever—if possible.

Mackenzie's book still has some value as a public record, particularly on the Empire Crusade. At any rate, it is less inaccurate than some of its successors.

Renewed leisure gave Beaverbrook more time to look at his news-papers, and of course the boredom of foreign travel always forced him to read them. He was satisfied with the two Express papers and sent few comments. They were both showing a profit, and its size did not much interest him. He wrote to Wardell on 21 April 1931:

> There is a very small issue in the hands of the public. I say it shall not go down, and it does not. I say it must not go up, and it does not. . . . Pur-chasers will always get what they paid. Whether more . . . depends upon how soon the Daily Express dominates all other newspapers.

Express ordinary shares in fact remained at 37/6 for many years. Beaver-brook was not really content with Baxter and remarked to Wardell: "I have to hit Baxter on the head every little while". Baxter's coolness to-wards the Empire Crusade was bad enough. His insistence on running features about grand opera was even worse.

Beaverbrook's anxiety was directed towards The Evening Standard which was hardly making a profit—only £8,000 for the whole of 1931. As Beaverbrook explained to Rothermere: "The Evening Standard is a luxury-advertising medium. It is used by all the first-class drapers, and rejected by the popular drapers". It was therefore hard hit by the depression. Beaverbrook considered various remedies. One was that The Daily Express should buy The Evening Standard. Rothermere at first agreed and then wrote that the other directors of the Daily Mail Trust forbade it:

> The Daily Mail Trust have an option, which I did not know they had, to buy the Evening Standard and will not surrender it without some quite substantial consideration.

These hard-headed directors demanded thirty thousand London Express Newspaper shares in exchange for surrendering their option. Evidently Beaverbrook was not the only press lord who was the prisoner of his directors—or perhaps there was some other explanation.

Beaverbrook's next proposal was to transfer control of The Evening Standard to his son Peter. He wrote to the Daily Mail Trust on 4 July 1931:

> I am divesting myself of all my newspaper interests. I am doing so because I am returning home to Canada.

The hard-headed directors of the Daily Mail Trust brandished their option once more, and the transfer was abandoned. Nor was any more heard of Beaverbrook's intention to return home to Canada. Later in 1931 he suggested moving The Standard to the new Express building and transforming it to the size of Rothermere's Evening News. Rothermere advised against both, particularly the second: it would be a great shock to advertisers and would cost £400,000. He had no doubt other objections which he did not mention. Finally Rothermere lost patience and wrote to Beaverbrook on 9 December 1931:

> Go ahead with Evening Standard in whatever way you think its interests are best served. ... You are fully able to decide.

Beaverbrook did nothing.

His messages provide a few points of interest during 1931. On 28 March he wrote to Baxter:

> Success in journalism depends upon that most splendid attribute—simplicity. Others will say that success in journalism depends upon pandering to the public taste. But many a journalist has failed in attempting to pander to the public taste. They all try it, and certainly when they get to their desperate days. Success never depended on pandering to the public taste. It has always been founded on simplicity.

Evidently reiteration was also useful. Beaverbrook gave a slightly different recipe in August, when he dismissed the idea of a school of journalism:

> The secret is—the knowledge of news-values. It is like the art of making money. You might as well establish a Chair to teach men how to make money as to make newspapers.

Beaverbrook always claimed that his contributors had complete freedom of expression. However there were exceptions even with the highly prized David Low. On 23 April 1931 Beaverbrook wrote to Gilliat about Low's cartoons:

> Lord Rothermere objects to being caricatured. Have we a right to cartoon a newspaper proprietor who objects? I think not, for there is a principle, of long standing in journalism, that dog does not bite dog. That does not apply to me, for I do not mind being eaten.

Beaverbrook did not detach himself entirely from politics during this period. His only practical act was to negotiate with Neville Chamberlain over the position of Vice-Admiral Taylor, a trivial and tiresome subject. Taylor wanted the Conservative whip, now that the party and the Empire Crusade were in agreement. The central office would agree only if "the position in South Paddington" were straightened out, by which it meant that Taylor should withdraw in favour of the new official candidate, H. G. Williams. Taylor naturally refused. No solution was reached. Beaverbrook, after fighting hard for Taylor, lost patience and wrote to Chamberlain on 16 June: "The whole situation should be allowed to drift for a bit". The situation in fact drifted until the unexpected general election, when Taylor became the official candidate and remained a loyal Conservative for the rest of his parliamentary career. Apart from this, Beaverbrook's letters merely recorded his fluctuating hopes and fears:

29 May 1931, to Henry Haslam: The enthusiasm of our leaders at the present moment, is no more than a gentle breeze, which may keep the wood smouldering, but will never set it on fire.

3 June 1931, to J. R. Remer: The Conservative campaign is not developing as we were justified in expecting it would. There is still too much pussy-footing.

9 June 1931, to Lord Londonderry: I am getting on very well with Neville Chamberlain and company these days. We all seem to be a very happy family.

12 June 1931, to George Terrell: I am endeavouring from day to day to find some method of pushing the Conservative leader along in the direction of activity. I fear the only weapon I have is the weapon of "revolt". It is a weapon that cannot be used too soon, and must not be wielded too often.

1 July 1931, to Sir Henry Page Croft: If the Conservative Party has taken up the policy I stand for, then my work is finished, and my career in England is coming to a close. I shall return to my own country the moment that there are no more essential tasks in hand in connection with this movement. On the other hand, if the Conservative Party retreats from the policy, I am once more engaged in guerilla warfare.

Beaverbrook made a wiser comment on the idea of returning to Canada when he wrote to a friend in Newcastle, N.B.: "It was very foolish of me to have left the territory. But now it would be quite stupid to go back again".

Beaverbrook watched with interest the fortunes of Mosley's New Party, an enterprise in some ways similar to his own. In May 1931 the New Party ran a candidate in a by-election at Ashton-under-Lyne. The candidate, Allan Young, was not successful, but he polled 4,500 votes. Chamberlain wrote to Beaverbrook on 4 May:

I hope you are pleased with Ashton. I think the result confirmed the view I expressed to you, that Mosley had no chance against the Labour machine.

Beaverbrook replied on 5 May:

> I was not pleased with Ashton. I think the view you expressed was not borne out. Mosley polled an immense vote. Remember, he had no newspapers backing him. I have always had the advantage of newspapers, as well as my own campaign.
>
> I do not write that fellow down. He may peter out, but if he does as well the next time, he will bring the pigs to market.
>
> . . . .
>
> Mosley has arranged with Harold Nicolson to put him up at Brentford and Chiswick. This is folly on Mosley's part. Nicolson is not suited to the constituency. He will not get any number of Conservative votes if the Protectionist issue is advanced. He cannot attract Socialist working-class votes. He will be too "precious" in any case.
>
> This Nicolson escapade may do Tom Mosley an injury.

Chamberlain came back on 6 May with what was perhaps a dig at Beaverbrook:

> I agree with you about Harold Nicolson. That young man has remarkable gifts, but, like so many others, he is not satisfied to use them in the sphere in which he excels; and I expect he will, accordingly, share the fate of others who have tried to do things that they were not suited for.

Nicolson persisted in his folly and in June asked to be released from his contract with The Evening Standard. Beaverbrook tried to dissuade him:

> I think the movement [of the New Party] has petered out. It might be saved by immense amounts of money, and brilliant journalistic support, but of course there is a conspiracy of silence in the newspapers, except for the particular newspaper I am connected with.
>
> If you must burn your fingers in public life, go to a big and bright blaze.

Nicolson was not to be shaken. He became editor of the New Party's journal and then resigned when Mosley turned towards Fascism.

There was one other curious little exchange at this time with a Labour leader. Ramsay MacDonald asked a number of prominent men for gifts of books with which to fill the shelves at No. 10 Downing Street. Beaverbrook sent the collected works of Edmund Burke and with them an accompanying letter on 11 June 1931:

> May I say that my admiration for your direction of the Socialist Party in office, gives me great satisfaction? . . . Bonar Law told me that you were the only possible person who could establish and maintain a Socialist Ministry. I believed him.

Burke's works can have been no great loss to Beaverbrook. His own taste is shown in a short note to Somerset Maugham: "Cakes and Ale is the best book of this generation".

On 29 July 1931 Beaverbrook sailed for Canada. He intended to be away for a couple of months and expected British politics to be unchanged on his return. Once more he would campaign in theory for food taxes and in practice for getting rid of Baldwin. Meanwhile he was immersed in financial affairs, as always happened during his visits to Canada. He spent much time with the leading businessmen of Montreal. In particular he attempted to take over Price Bros., a great paper firm, which was not prospering. The shareholders did not wish to be rescued, at any rate by Beaverbrook, and the deal came to nothing for the time being. Beaverbrook remained certain that the prices of raw materials would soon recover and that Canada would boom again. The bulk of his fortune was still in Canadian stocks, and he did not do badly even during the worst time of the depression. In 1931 after meeting all taxes and payments under covenant, to charities or to members of his family and others, he had £20,000 to spend in England.

During Beaverbrook's absence, the storm suddenly blew in England. There was a run on the pound. The Labour government failed to agree on the cuts in public expenditure which would satisfy the Bank of England and foreign bankers. It fell and was replaced by a National government under Ramsay MacDonald. Beaverbrook had missed a British political crisis for the first time in twenty years. He was in a frenzy to return. He sailed from New York as soon as he could and arrived in London on 31 August. He was convinced that his moment had arrived. As he pointed out, in a perhaps over-simple argument, the country was spending too much abroad, not at home, and the remedy therefore was to stop the import of foreign goods, not to reduce incomes. He at once pressed this argument in public and in private. On 3 September Beaverbrook lunched with MacDonald and he, as Beaverbrook reported to Senator Elliott on 6 September, "gave me reason to hope that he would be willing to support our plan". Of course many people had had reason to hope things from MacDonald without getting them. The same evening Beaverbrook "tried to commit Lord Hailsham and with some success". But Hailsham, though influential, was not in the cabinet. Later that evening Beaverbrook "took on the job with Neville Chamberlain. He could not see the possibility of going to the country at the present time, even on the tariff issue. He thinks the National Government is committed to the carrying out of economies first". Thus Protection was temporarily brushed aside by its principal supporter.

Beaverbrook then decided, as he told Amery, "not to bother any more, but to pursue a different plan". This was to preach tariffs in public. Appeals for Protection poured from his pen. He sent a manifesto to The Daily Express on 4 September 1931 and appealed to MacDonald in The Sunday Express of 6 September. There was another manifesto on 12 September and manifestoes to Empire Crusaders on 15 and 16 September.

All carried the same message: Tariffs were the answer and would make economies unnecessary. Beaverbrook was in fact totally out of line with the outlook of the National government except on a single point: he thought, as they did, that economies would be unpopular and might well lead to defeat at a general election. Beaverbrook wrote to Amery on 11 September 1931:

> The Conservative position is hopeless now, unless Tariffs are introduced and carried forthwith. The disappointment over the Budget will damage every candidate in all the constituencies. The policemen, the postmen, the school teachers, etc., are blaming it on us.
>
> Stanley Baldwin is a very bad boy. . . . For the sake of office or through vain glory, or on account of stupidity, he allows the Conservative party to be dragged at the heels of the City bankers in refusing support to a Socialist Cabinet ready and willing to give us all but 12 millions of the economies, thus ruining the Conservative prospects for the future.
>
> If Bonar Law had been as stupid as Stanley Baldwin he would have insisted on relieving the Liberals of the right and duty to make war in August, 1914.

Amery replied on 14 September:

> I agree that the facts as gradually unfolded make one wonder more than ever why we did not let the Socialists balance their budget with 56 millions of economies. However the blame for that is not Baldwin's but Nevilles' and Sam Hoare's, no doubt pressed in their turn by Peacock and Harvey.[1]

This belief in the unpopularity of economies, though belied by events, was widely held at the time and explains why the Labour party turned so violently against the economies which its own government had been prepared to make.

Beaverbrook, in his hostility to Baldwin, was prepared to regard even MacDonald as the strong man. He wrote to Frank Harrison on 19 September:

> Baldwin is an ineffective fellow. If he gets a huge majority he will muddle it. He does not really believe on strong lines. He always wants to compromise. He is easily got hold of. His counsellors lead him astray.
>
> MacDonald will be much better for our purpose, because a ruthless man must carry tariffs to a complete conclusion.

Beaverbrook's disagreement with the National government was not limited to personalities. He repudiated their programme. He detested the economy cuts. When a school teacher wrote complaining of them, he replied on 16 September:

> How am I to oppose this wretched Government? I really do hate it.
>
> There is no need for the reductions. We ought to go forward in pursuit of our policy of Empire Free Trade. . . . Then we will have plenty of revenue.

[1] Spokesmen of the Bank of England. Amery's account is roughly correct.

Beaverbrook detested even more the defence of the gold standard on which the National government was now engaged. He alleged that "our international financiers have been borrowing from the French and Americans at 2% and lending to the Germans at 8%,"—an allegation that was well-founded. On 2 September he telegraphed to Clarence Dillon in New York:

> Pity us. Our national finances are dominated by Bank of England board drawn from bold brave houses which were salvaging Credit Anstalt three months ago and sabotaging British Empire three weeks ago.

And on 18 September to Arthur Brisbane:

> This Government and its successors will defend Gold standard to extent of our boundless resources. Opposition to Gold Standard confined to Keynes myself and other obscure and ineffectual figures in public life.

Actually the government was forced to abandon the gold standard on the following day. Beaverbrook suspected that they would return to it as soon as they could and wrote impatiently to Robertson on 23 September:

> It is an absurd and silly notion that international credit must be limited to the quantity of gold dug up out of the ground; that if gold runs short the system of international exchange must be curtailed; that if gold comes out of the earth in beautiful quantities the prices of commodities must go up.
> Was there ever such mumbo-jumbo amongst sensible and reasonable men?

Abandonment of the gold standard drove the National government to a general election. Beaverbrook was at first hopeful that the Conservatives would campaign, as according to him they were pledged to do, for the full programme of Empire Free Trade. He telegraphed cheerfully to Brisbane on 26 September:

> Future looks hopeful except that my influence disappears day after polling and my present colleagues free from my contamination will at once strive after gold standard again.

Unfortunately things went wrong. Lord Reading and Sir Herbert Samuel persuaded MacDonald to have pity on the Liberals. Beaverbrook wrote to Sir John Jarvis on 29 September:

> We have had a bad reverse. MacDonald is wavering. He cannot make up his mind. He has gone ill with indecision. He talks about a "Doctor's Mandate". If he goes on in his present course much longer he will get an ultimatum from his own doctor.

Beaverbrook appealed to Lord Brentford (Joynson-Hicks) to lead a Tory revolt, telegraphing to him on 1 October:

> Why don't you call meeting of all Conservative Privy Councillors with a view to safeguarding party's policy at this moment. I would gladly attend

and have no doubt you could rely on Gretton, Churchill and possibly many others. By this means you could set up alternative Tory Shadow Cabinet which is badly needed.

Tory backbenchers in fact held a protest meeting of this character. The National government took no notice. Its leaders promised to consider every remedy "not excluding tariffs", but each party in the coalition was free to campaign for its own policy—or for none. Baldwin even appealed for the withdrawal of Conservative candidates who were opposing Sir Herbert Samuel and other Liberal Free Traders.

Beaverbrook was in a dilemma. He wanted a Conservative victory as the only means of achieving tariffs. He did not want a victory for the free hand which was the official party programme. He therefore decided to run his own campaign. He wrote to Beckles Wilson on 7 October 1931: "I was not able to agree to go to the country without a policy. So I am fighting for the policy which I have advocated for the last two years". He plunged into his most strenuous tour. This time he did not trouble with the agricultural constituencies which were mostly secure and faced instead the challenge of the great cities—Glasgow, Birmingham, Liverpool, Manchester and of course Ashton-under-Lyne. He went also wherever he could challenge a Liberal Free Trader and so implicitly Baldwin—to Darwen against Samuel, to Cornwall against other Liberals. In the fortnight between 13 October and polling day, he addressed eighteen meetings.

Beaverbrook had expected the National government to win 400 seats. Instead it won 521. This was a great victory, but was it a victory for Empire Free Trade and for food taxes? There were many Free Traders, both Liberal and Conservative, among the government's supporters. Moreover the government was now immune from Beaverbrook's crusading tactics. A revolt even by a hundred MPs, unlikely as that was, would not shake it, nor would it be harassed by a split vote at a by-election. Henceforth Beaverbrook would have to rely on vague appeals to public opinion—an ineffective resource. Once more his letters showed his wavering hopes and doubts:

(To J. D. McKenna in New Brunswick, 28 October 1931): Will the new Parliament vote to put duties on foreign foodstuffs? ... We have sufficient new members pledged to this policy to enable us to carry it through to a conclusion. Now we wait only on the courage of our leaders.

(To Toby Jones, 2 November): Some politicians, back in office, have a notion that the swing over was due to fear. They will require to be reminded that the vote was not so much against Socialism as for the Empire.

(To Sir Edmund Ironside, 6 November): We have Neville Chamberlain—that means a great deal. But we also have Samuel and others.

(To Lord Bridgeman, 12 November): I think our Conservatives will miss the opportunity, and Baldwin may have to surrender his leadership to Churchill.

I am hopeful of Churchill's sincerity, but not quite certain of it. I am not afraid of Baldwin's sincerity, although I deplore his procrastination during the last year or two.

The evocation of Churchill is curious. Not long before Beaverbrook had written to Baxter: "I get dragged into playing him up, only to find that he is tearing me down. He has done it again and again".

Meanwhile Beaverbrook was invited to celebrate victory. On 26 November 1931 Lord Winterton and Sir Henry Page Croft organized a dinner in his honour, at 5/- a head, "in recognition of his great services at the election and on behalf of the Imperial cause". Beaverbrook acknowledged this "as the greatest tribute I have received in a long life of work and worry". With his characteristic charity, he did not forget his own tributes to the vanquished. He wrote to Christopher Addison: "If you had had good colleagues, I know you would have been the greatest Agricultural Minister in history"—a judgement which later events have confirmed. When George Lansbury was elected leader of the Labour remnant, Beaverbrook congratulated him and added: "I admire your courage, devotion to your cause and your high optimism and good temper". Lansbury replied: "It is a tough rough old Row to hoe. Always, George Lansbury". Beaverbrook also wrote to Maxton:

> Your policy doesn't suit me. But as we must have an opposition, I'm sure you won't mind if I rejoice that you are the real leader of it. I look forward to the new Parliament with a mixture of hope and fear.

Maxton did not reply.

One other Socialist received his approval. The young Jennie Lee had lost her seat at the general election and now wished to visit the United States. Beaverbrook gave her letters of introduction to his friends. One read:

> Jenny is a great young woman. She follows Maxton; quarrels with the Labour Party; hates MacDonald; loathes Snowden; loves Russia—and may go to gaol.

And another:

> She is pretty. She has brains. She very nearly became a first-rate figure in the House of Commons. It wasn't surprising with that wonderful name of hers, which to my mind surpasses all others. She is Maxton's darling. I mean his political darling, for Jim Maxton has no darlings in the sexual sense, poor fellow.

When parliament met, Beaverbrook's disappointment was deep. He was now firmly against quotas and wrote to Addison on 2 December: "I am like Snowden. I say it may be useful for the Dominions, but practically valueless here. But I come to my conclusion for opposite reasons". On 6 December he poured out to Brisbane his troubles and also his views on foreign affairs:

> The National Government is getting into deep water. That is due to two things. Its failure to protect iron and steel; and its failure to protect agriculture. . . . Yet they are the principal industries of the land, cotton excepted.
> Churchill is, in the meantime, opposing everything he can find. He has joined the tariff movement, and is now a most ardent Empire Free Trader. There is, of course, one difficulty about him, so far as I am concerned.
> I feel certain our horse will win the race—unless we put up Churchill as jockey. If we do, he is certain to "pull" the horse just after rounding Tattenham Corner.
> The French are on top in Europe now. There is only one way to get clear of their hegemony, and that is the demonetization of gold, or the remonetization of silver.
> The Germans, I am quite convinced, will pay their short-term money to Britain and America by-and-by. I cannot see that the legal right of the French to their annuities, under the Young plan, will help them in practice.
> . . . .
> I am told by a film star, who came to see me yesterday, that Hitler is about to become the master of Germany. There you are—that is how I get my reliable information. If I listened to a man named Bernsdorff of the German Embassy here, he would tell me a lot of nonsense. It is from the film stars that one gets the truth.
> I had a call from Hitler's man, who came here to find out if the success of the Conservative-Liberal and petty-Labour Coalition should be attempted in Germany.
> I advised him that a strong policy is damaged by coalition. Plainly, he had already come to that conclusion; and got the advice he was seeking. He went off to telegraph to his master.
> He is a strong anti-Semite, is Hitler's representative, and like many another man who is opposed to the Jews, he has their racial marks upon him.
> I think you will have no peace in Europe for a long time. I think the French will have to be smashed by God or by man before tranquillity comes again.

A letter to Roy Howard on 8 December 1931 struck much the same note:

> We have got a first-rate head of the Foreign Office in Sir John Simon. If his character equalled his cleverness, he would be bigger than God.
> Sir John is in favour of a compromise with France. Runciman, another Liberal minister, is against it. The Tories are divided. Sir Austen Chamberlain said, when he was Foreign Secretary, that he loved France like a mistress. Poor Sir Austen doesn't know anything about mistresses.
> On balance I think the Government will stand up to France. . . . It will do the French so much good.

The Government had enough trouble in resolving to adopt Protection. Winterton reported that MacDonald might demand a dissolution if the present coalition proved *unworkable*. Beaverbrook replied on 14 December:

> Ramsay MacDonald could not possibly get a dissolution. This House of Commons was elected to carry out a policy, and it is entitled to see it through.
>
> These stories are being put about by our fainthearts who want to temporize. They say we must not lose Ramsay MacDonald—it is imperative we should keep Runciman—Philip Snowden is such a good chap and did so much to win the Election that he must not be unreasonably embarrassed—it is better to keep Samuel; after all, many Conservatives got Liberal votes and must think of their Liberal constituents.
>
> The real father of all this is Stanley Baldwin, and it is permeating other Members of the Cabinet.

On Christmas Day 1931, Beaverbrook wrote to his old friend, Heber Vroom:

> The new Goverment is a great disappointment to me. We anticipated great things, but they are far from being realized. We are given a taste of our policy here, and a taste there; but the essence—Agricultural Protection—is withheld from us.

Beaverbrook threatened to "open up an aggressive campaign" in the new year. Little came of this. It was difficult to fight until it was known what the government intended to do, and at the beginning of 1932 the government did not itself know. Neville Chamberlain was demanding Protection; Samuel and Snowden were opposing it. In the end a way of escape was found—an agreement to differ, with cabinet ministers free to attack the government's own proposals. In February Chamberlain introduced a general tariff, with lachrymose references to the belated triumph of his father's policy. Beaverbrook was not impressed. He had no interest in the protection of industry except in exchange for food taxes, and these were still not achieved. Beaverbrook played some part over one issue. The government originally intended to apply the tariff to goods from the Dominions, with a promise that these might be removed if an Imperial Conference produced adequate concessions from the Dominions for British goods. Beaverbrook stirred up Bennett to protest, and the government gave way. There were to be no tariffs on Dominion goods until it was seen what an Imperial Conference could offer. Beaverbrook took the credit for this. He wrote to J. D. McKenna on 8 February 1932:

> A week ago we were in danger of a Government proposal to put duties on Dominion imports. We only escaped making this terrible blunder through the influence of Mr. Bennett whose intervention was decisive. . . . The Empire policy is of course a New Brunswick policy. It was advocated by

Bonar Law of Richibucto and its leader in the Empire is Mr. Bennet—from Hopewell Cape.

Whether Bennett's protest made so much difference is however doubtful.

All now depended on the Imperial Conference, and again there was little to do in the way of campaigning before it met. It assembled at Ottawa in August—the only such conference to be held outside London. Bennett presided, and Beaverbrook longed to be summoned as his adviser. No call came. Bennett proved more anxious to protect Canadian industry than to promote Empire Free Trade. The British ministers held out against taxes on foreign meat, though they accepted control of wheat imports. Beaverbrook commented bitterly on 1 September (to James V. Rank): "When the rabbits are brought out of the hat, I think it will be seen that Ottawa has produced nothing for us". So it proved. Ottawa did little to stimulate imperial settlement.

Once more Beaverbrook built up a legend later about how the Empire Crusade had been within sight of success. When some twenty years afterwards (1959) he wrote Bennett's life, he made out that Bennett was keen on Empire Free Trade. If only he had been there himself, he would have guided Bennett in the right path and given warning of the dangers. As it was, Baldwin issued the command: "Go for Bennett". Baldwin discredited Bennett, turned Chamberlain against him, enlisted J. H. Thomas to condemn food taxes. This was a far-fetched argument. Bennett defended Canadian interests and cared little for imperial unity. The Ottawa conference showed clearly that Beaverbrook had been "a pedlar of dreams", as Howard Spring called him.

Beaverbrook still hoped to provoke a new stir. He wrote to Borden on 14 August 1932:

> You can rely on it—If there is no tax on bacon, there will be plenty of attacks on Ministers. In fact, I think there will be a recourse to the by-election incidents of 1931.
> You cannot lead Baldwin. You can only drive him to it. He is like the cow, that used to be in the manse glebe at Newcastle, New Brunswick, he is always on the far side of the meadow. So there is always a lot of driving to do.
> . . . .
> Ramsay MacDonald is trying to ride two horses. He is trying to appear a strong, virile fellow, who is justified in the eyes of the public, in running after the great ladies in society. In short, a reincarnation of Palmerston.
> The other horse is the ailing, sick, weary Titan, carrying the world on his shoulders. A brave, courageous creature, indomitable in his will-power in the face of all the afflictions God has visited on him—somewhat in spite of God.
> The truth is, he is an old humbug.

Once more, there was little stir. The Ottawa conference had excited little enthusiasm for the Empire in Great Britain. Control of wheat imports satisfied Norfolk, home of the Agricultural party, and taxation of foreign meat appealed only to the cattle-raising areas of Scotland. Beaverbrook campaigned there during the autumn of 1932, with a compound of meat taxes and support for Scottish Nationalism. Early in 1933 he actually intervened in a by-election at East Fife and encouraged an unofficial Conservative meat-taxer to run against the official government candidate, who was a National Liberal. This was a carpet-bagging expedition with little local support. Beaverbrook often arrived at a village hall for a meeting to find it empty and in darkness. The farmers showed little zest for meat taxes, and the ploughmen still less. Beaverbrook's candidate was defeated.

Beaverbrook resolved that he would act again only if there were a local demand, and no demand came. East Fife was the last of his by-election forays. It also marked the virtual end of the Empire Crusade. Though Empire Crusade clubs remained in existence for some years, the Crusade itself was more or less wound up. Doidge found that his post on the Express had been filled and returned home to champion the cause of Empire in New Zealand, ending his career as high commissioner for New Zealand in London. What happened to the Crusade fund is obscure. Some ten thousand pounds had been spent on meetings, another ten on running the office, and about five thousand pounds had gone towards the expenses of approved parliamentary candidates at by-elections and at the general election of 1931. But £25,000 remained in the fund when Doidge gave up.[1] Beaverbrook spent some of this on his later meetings, both in favour of Empire Free Trade and against European entanglements such as Locarno, and apparently Doidge received a retainer of £1,000 a year for some time after he had returned to New Zealand.

In 1935 there was still £13,500 left. No candidate received assistance in the British general election of 1935. Maybe Doidge had something for his election expenses in New Zealand, and perhaps Senator Elliott in Australia also. At any rate, a further £4,000 had been spent by 1938. Cunliffe-Owen, one of the trustees, then complained that the fund was "in a mess", since it had been subscribed for a specific purpose and this was not being pursued. Beaverbrook replied that it was better to have a surplus than a deficit. The remaining money was consumed somehow. On 12 September 1949, a payment of £448. 9. 10 was made to Doidge— "the amount still standing to the credit of the Empire Crusade Fund". The following day Beaverbrook wrote to James Kilpatrick, member of a

---

[1] Though £109,000 had been promised, only £56,000 was actually paid. Beaverbrook himself, though promising £25,000, paid not much over £10,000.

firm of chartered accountants, who had latterly acted as a trustee of the fund. He thanked Kilpatrick for his services and added:

> Now the account is wound up, your task is completed, and the role of the Empire Crusade is brought to an end.
>
> . . . .
>
> The Crusade has had a partial success. But still a success.[1]

Beaverbrook rarely claimed even a partial success. Usually he insisted that the Empire Crusade had failed. He blamed himself—"the cause was greater than the man". He blamed accidents, such as the financial crisis of August 1931 which eclipsed the Stornoway pact, or his estrangement from Bennett, which helped to cause the lost opportunities at Ottawa. Most often he settled for Baldwin's relentless and ruthless opposition. Certainly Baldwin was a skilful tactician, though probably more concerned to preserve the unity of the Conservative party and his own position as leader than to defeat Empire Free Trade. But the Empire Crusade was defeated more by its own contradictions than by Baldwin's devices.

The Crusade did not altogether fail, at any rate in the nineteen-thirties. Protection and even Imperial Preference were actually applied—an achievement beyond Joseph Chamberlain. There were taxes on some foreign foodstuffs, though not on all, and the prosperity of agriculture alongside that of industry became a major object of policy. Of course these things were much in the spirit of the times, and Neville Chamberlain, to say nothing of other Conservatives such as Walter Elliot, did more for them than Beaverbrook did. Nevertheless the Empire Crusade helped them along, and maybe Beaverbrook's attacks on Baldwin also contributed to the discredit into which Baldwin finally fell. The real failure came later. The second world war produced a display of imperial unity in both the military and the financial sphere. Yet imperial sentiment and action perished when the war was over. Empire Free Trade has gone beyond recall. Beaverbrook may sometimes have stood on the heights of Pisgah. He never entered the promised land.

---

[1] Even this was not in fact the end. On 15 September 1953 Robertson informed Beaverbrook that there was £2,334. 13. 7 in The Empire Crusade Fund. How this money got there when the Fund had been dissolved or what happened to it I have not been able to find out. Presumably it was another example of the way in which Beaverbrook often shuffled money from one account to another without knowing that he was doing so. In 1957 there was £2,100 in the Fund. Indeed the Fund still exists. Some of it was spent on the campaign against the European Common Market in 1963.

CHAPTER FOURTEEN

POLITICAL HOBGOBLIN, 1932–36

On 20 October 1932 Beaverbrook sent a political survey to Arthur Brisbane in New York. The National government, he reported, was divided on three great issues. The first in Beaverbrook's mind was obviously the question of agricultural protection. Here he had nothing new to report, only the old story of Baldwin's evasions:

> We made him give in, to keep his leadership. But he did not really give in. He only went through the form of doing so, in order to hold his place and do us down. He is the most dangerous enemy we have, because he is nominally on our side.

The second issue was India. Beaverbrook alleged that Sir Samuel Hoare, secretary for India, "represented the real heart and strength of the Conservative party: the policy of suppression in India". This was quite wrong.[1] Beaverbrook's character sketch of Hoare however had its insight:

> He has all the materials that go to the making of a leader of the Conservative party. He is not stupid, but he is very dull. He is not eloquent, but he talks well. He is not honest (politically), but he is most evangelical, a great leader in the Church of England.
>
> He has a little money, but not too much. He always conforms to the party policy. He knows not Ishmael, but he is well acquainted with the life-story of Jacob.

Beaverbrook made no mistake when he pointed to the leader of the "Treat 'em with kindness" school. It was Edward Wood, Lord Irwin (later Lord Halifax):

> He was once the white hope of the Tories—their young Dempsey but, as distinct from Hoare, he always appears a sort of Jesus in long boots. The long boots are needed because he has had to wade through the mud. But he was not responsible for the mud, oh, dear no! Edward Wood could never make anything so dirty as mud, and the last thing he would think of, would be to throw it at others.

---

[1] Hoare's most considerable political achievement was to carry the Government of India Bill through the house of commons. Beaverbrook's misjudgement is the odder in that he had been on friendly terms with Hoare for many years.

Beaverbrook added correctly:

> The weakness in this Indian issue is, that Winston Churchill is making it his ladder for the moment. Churchill has the habit of breaking the rungs of any ladder he puts his foot on.[1]

The third dividing issue was economy:

> There Neville Chamberlain is the leader of the economists. He wants reduced expenditure and taxation, so that the money may fructify in the pockets of the taxpayers. Against him is the National Labour group, who have got to go out for public expenditure.[2]
>
> A hobgoblin-like element in the Conservative Party is pressing Conservative members into the National Labour camp on the economy issue.
>
> Needless to say, I am the leader of the hobgoblins. I stand for agricultural protection, and for public expenditure on great works, such as reclamation of the land, and re-equipment of the railways, etc.
>
> On one policy I have all the Tory Diehards with me. On the other, all the Tory Diehards are against me. It is not always fun to be a hobgoblin.

The last sentence was perhaps not meant seriously.

At any rate, Beaverbrook was a political hobgoblin during the period of MacDonald's National government. This was a new stage in his career. In the nineteen-twenties, though he produced much journalism, he was an observer, not a propagandist, and many of his articles were moralizing in the manner of Samuel Smiles. Between 1929 and 1931 he concentrated solely on the Empire Crusade. Thereafter, though he sometimes insisted in private that imperial unity was still his deepest concern, he took up other causes which he described as corollaries of this—Higher Wages, Scottish Home Rule, attacks on the cooperative societies, and finally Isolationism. He promoted these causes by articles in his newspapers and occasional public speeches, but not with an organized movement, interventions in by-elections, or negotiations with the political leaders. He was resolved never to plunge into party politics again. He wrote on 19 March, 1935, when the next general election was approaching (to Peter Rennell Rodd):

> If I had not taken promises from Neville Chamberlain and others in 1931, the Economic Empire would be in existence now.
>
> But I did not want to break the Conservative Party. I did not want to be a leader. I did not even want to be a political figure.

[1] Churchill was conducting a one-man campaign against constitutional concession to India. This made him unpopular in the Conservative party and also, as Beaverbrook suggests, actually made the policy of concession easier.

[2] This does too much honour to the National Labour group, which was in no position to "go out" for anything—except out of office.

Again on 6 June 1935, to D. Wightwick, an impatient Crusader:

> I have played my role. What history will say or what the judgement of my contemporaries may be is not a matter of interest to me.

The contrast between Beaverbrook in the nineteen-twenties and a decade later is best shown by the articles he wrote for his newspapers. Typical for 1924 were A Young Man's Chance To-day, the Russian Treaty, and The Greatest Figure in History (King David). Typical for 1934 were Buy!, The Co-operative Menace, and The Menace of War. In 1922 Beaverbrook wrote 2 articles of moralizing; 8 on finance; 2 on recent history; and 8 on political prospects. He did not write a single one putting forward any specific policy. In 1933 he wrote 40 articles advocating high wages and 8 preaching No More War. The Empire Crusade had no doubt given him a taste for crusading on other issues. Moreover he was impelled forward by events. With the Great Depression the hopes of returning to the old world before 1914 were shattered. Nations followed uncharted courses. Laissez faire was in ruins, and collective security was soon to be ruined also. This seemed to be Beaverbrook's opportunity.

Beaverbrook had a firm devotion to democracy and the parliamentary system, but in his readiness to advocate unorthodox policies he belonged to the same political generation as Hitler or F. D. Roosevelt. Like them, he improvised without any ordered body of thought and drew ideas from the inexhaustible fertility of his untutored, but highly original, mind. In the storm of the world the hobgoblin often gave a better light than that provided by more conventional beacons. The later student of the policies which Beaverbrook advocated in these years is impressed not only by their wide-ranging character and zest, but by their wisdom. The Establishment, both Left and Right, disliked him as much for his challenging good sense as for his alleged irresponsibility.

Beaverbrook was often accused of endangering the democratic system by the strident propaganda of his newspapers. He answered that propaganda was needed in order to make democracy effective: "If we are to have democratic government we must have not only free expression of opinion by the public but full expression of it, too" (to Fabian Poole, 8 October 1935). Unlike Rothermere, who subsidized and applauded Mosley, Beaverbrook was never tempted by Fascism. He wrote in 1933 (to Edgar Middleton, 10 July):

> I am not a Fascist. I believe in Parliamentary institutions. I am quite certain that we are not going to solve our problem by altering our political structure.

And in 1934 (to Glover, 7 September):

> The Fascists attack Parliament and mean to destroy it if they get to power. I am a Parliament man. An alliance with Fascism would be an unholy alliance.

Beaverbrook remained personally on good terms with Mosley, as he did with politicians of all persuasions. Evidently he tried to win Mosley back to the democratic course. Mosley replied on 9 September 1932:

> The democratic politics of the last decade cannot interest the executive mind. On public grounds, I do very deeply believe in the constructive conception of Fascism which I am preaching, and am indifferent to the fact that this course probably means "political suicide".
>
> If the normal political system continues there are many men capable of conducting it and I can seek other occupations which I should prefer. On the other hand, if by any chance the normal political system does not endure, it is perhaps better from the nation's point of view that Fascism be built by me than by some worse kind of lunatic.

Beaverbrook foresaw only failure for Mosley and commented in 1934: "When Hitler shot Roehm in Munich, he also shot Mosley's hopes in England to ribbons".

Beaverbrook welcomed controversy even with Mosley. When Mosley attacked him in The Daily Mail, he wrote to Rothermere on 7 May 1934:

> I read his article on me. There is nothing in it objectionable to me.
>
> I was a Canadian Company Promoter. And the best ever. No failures, except Price Brothers after 25 years.
>
> I am quick jumping, like Tom [Mosley] himself. Unlike him, I speak badly.
>
> My policy is an adaptation of the political faith of Joe Chamberlain, and inspired by his campaign.
>
> And I don't mind how much or how often Mosley dresses me down.
>
> You and I have sent too many arrows forth, to complain of the selfsame shafts.

Rothermere wished to discipline Mosley. He replied on 7 May:

> I intend to tell Mosley that if he attacks you I shall drop his Blackshirts.
> You are my greatest friend and this is the least I can do.

Beaverbrook answered on 9 May:

> About Tom Mosley. I hope he will not give up his attacks on me. I would not like him to feel that he should be restrained in this respect. And politics thrive on personalities.

Beaverbrook did not apply his own doctrine. He fought more on policies than on personalities, at least in public. He worked hard at his newspapers, probably harder than at any other time of his life. His instructions to the staffs of his papers reflect this. Where previously he had emphasized liveliness and sense of news, he now stressed industry. Thus to Wardell in March 1933:

> Journalism is not a six-day-week business.
> Only those who believe in working more days than God did, should be in this line of endeavour.

And to Robertson at the same time:

> Lord Beaverbrook believes that all editors should beware of the lunch table and be on their guard at the dinner table. All good journalists dine at Lyons Corner House.

Beaverbrook himself became a social hermit, though not at the Corner House. He had long refused all invitations to lunch, with the excuse: "I have formed the habit of always lunching in the same place and cannot break myself of it". He now refused invitations to dinner also, pleading that this was when he was needed by his newspapers. He described his way of life and that of his staff to a Canadian friend who had recommended her sister as a secretary (to Mrs. Herbert Bruce, 19 December 1934):

> My own office is even worse than the Express. The secretaries have to work from fifteen minutes to nine in the morning until I go into dinner. Sometimes I do not disappear until after nine o'clock at night. And never before that hour. Most of the secretaries have to work "on window-sills", in trains, motor cars and airplanes, sharing typewriters and telephones— suffering constant interruptions.

Beaverbrook did not wait for the second world war to proclaim a state of emergency. For him one existed every day.

As well as his newspapers and his policies, Beaverbrook was still active financially, with an investment of between fifteen and twenty million dollars in Canada and another five million or so in the United States. During the mid-thirties he seems also to have resumed his interest in British cinemas and perhaps in other British concerns as well. Most of the return on his overseas investments remained with his Canadian corporation—it is impossible to ascertain the amount. Part of this income went to Beaverbrook's Canadian charities such as the University of New Brunswick. The rest was reinvested, so that his Canadian fortune grew steadily, except when he thought that it was too large and gave a capital sum to some charity.

In Great Britain Beaverbrook made a return to the tax authorities throughout the 'thirties of between £65,000 and £80,000 a year. About £20,000 a year went on taxes. Another £30,000 went on annuities to British dependants, ranging from retired newspaper men to distant Aitken relatives, and to British charities such as St. Mary's Hospital. Beaverbrook always entered on these commitments for seven years, thus escaping income tax. For, though he was meticulous in his tax returns, he was equally precise in taking any advantages which the law offered him. Nevertheless every year from 1929, when his detailed accounts begin, until 1964, the year of his death, he spent more on others than himself. Not that he was badly off. His own personal expenditure was about £25,000 a year—some of it also casual gifts. In 1933–34, for the only time, he spent rather more than his income, presumably because the yield from his English investments was then at its lowest.

The newspapers always came first though Beaverbrook's control is hardest to document in this period. He no longer made prolonged cruises or foreign visits and so did not have the leisure to dictate detailed criticism. He had not yet discovered the delights of the Soundscriber and relied mainly on telephone conversations which went unrecorded. It seems clear however that, apart from his signed articles, he dictated many of the leaders in The Daily Express and often provided the entire Diary in The Evening Standard. The papers in turn recognized their obligation and throughout the nineteen thirties paid him sums ranging from £3,500 to £4,500 a year as their share of his secretarial and travelling expenses.

In some ways, the papers gave less cause for worry than they had done. All were now making a profit. At The Evening Standard Wardell overcame the previous difficulties by efficient management and hard canvassing for advertisements. Wardell's success was so great that he could devote most of his time to The Farmers' Weekly, a joint Beaverbrook-Rothermere venture, which never prospered as it was expected to do. John Gordon at The Sunday Express had a virtually free hand, earning two contradictory rebukes—one for writing too little, the other for writing too much. In 1932:

> The whole of the Leader page emanates from Leatherhead. It is too much. You will find yourself using Cherkley as a crutch, if you go too far.

In 1934, when Gordon had ventured to write a leader himself:

> The editor must sit on the watch-tower. He should not join in the fray.

The only remaining problem was at The Daily Express, where Baxter kicked against the battery of propaganda most of which he disagreed with. Moreover, Baxter was interested in the contents of the paper, not in its appearance. Beaverbrook had discovered a young genius of presentation in Arthur Christiansen, whose only interest was in lay-out. Christiansen revolutionized the front page, focussing attention on a single important item, and all British newspapers at the present day owe their appearance to him. Baxter saw that he was being superseded and in September 1933 resigned. Christiansen and Beaverbrook made a happy combination, and Christiansen survived as editor for almost a quarter of a century, until 1956. In his own words: "The policies were Lord Beaverbrook's job, the presentation mine".[1]

Beaverbrook himself inspired one non-political feature, which has now found a place in every British newspaper. This was a column on

[1] Christiansen, Headlines All My Life, 144.

personalities, entitled These Names Make News and supposedly modelled on the American magazine Time. Tom Driberg, the original "William Hickey", has described how Beaverbrook hammered and nagged each day until the desired effect was achieved.[1] The records do not show who thought of calling on the ghost of the eighteenth-century diarist—probably Driberg, for Beaverbrook was no great reader of old-fashioned books. Driberg, to his regret, failed to patent the name, and there are said to have been over one hundred Hickeys since his day. But the stamp of Beaverbrook is still there. This was not achieved without much pain. On 7 January 1934 Beaverbrook wrote to Baxter, now an aloof critic:

> These Names Make News is a constant source of grief and woe. I always think that the pattern is emerging. I never see it in a satisfactory form for any length of time.
> I don't mind if the circulation of the paper goes down, providing the tone of the paper goes up.

This last was a somewhat extreme boast. The early nineteen-thirties saw the battle for circulation at its height. The running was made by Elias, proprietor of The Daily Herald, a man who understood nothing about the contents of newspapers and therefore relied on gift schemes and other non-journalistic devices for promoting sales. Beaverbrook deplored this and constantly tried to organize a self-denying ordinance among the newspaper proprietors. Every time Elias broke away.

Beaverbrook, despite his disclaimers, enjoyed the fight. Though he claimed to be fighting only The Daily Herald, he was challenging The Daily Mail as well, and it became increasingly anomalous that he should conduct this fight partly with Daily Mail Trust money. Rothermere did not actually complain, at any rate on paper, but Beaverbrook resolved to break the connection. During the winter of 1932–33 he bought for cash the 80,000 shares which the Daily Mail Trust held in The Express. He paid something over £550,000—less than half what he had offered five years before. As he had then sold his Daily Mail Trust shares for a much higher figure, his partnership with Rothermere turned out a very profitable venture.

It was even more urgent for Beaverbrook to shake off the option which gave the Daily Mail Trust a veto over the future of The Evening Standard. In February 1933 he asked for an option on The Evening Standard shares which the Trust held and gave an assurance that he would gradually dispose of them. The Trust answered that it wanted a firm purchase and demanded £324,405. Beaverbrook would offer only £282,030. The Trust refused this offer, but also revealed that it was short of ready money.

Driberg, Beaverbrook, 218.

Beaverbrook was content to wait. His patience was rewarded. On 17 May 1933 the Daily Mail Trust accepted £275,483. 8s. od. for all its shares in The Evening Standard. Beaverbrook was now master in his own house. He was free to hold down the dividend and could thus pay off all the prior obligations, leaving London Express Newspaper without mortgages or debentures. He could also transfer The Evening Standard to the ownership of The Express.

As well, he could now wage open war against The Daily Mail without any twinge of conscience. He remarked with a chuckle to Baumann (17 July 1933): "Rothermere used to be my brother. But he has no more brotherly love now that The Express has passed The Mail". He also watched with amusement The Daily Mail's attempt to recover by serializing Dickens' Life of Christ. This was reputed to have cost £60,000 and to have yielded results worth only £30,000. Beaverbrook commented to Baxter (10 March 1934): "You always disputed my view of Dickens. You will come to it if you read his Life of Christ".

With this concentration on newspaper affairs, Beaverbrook was now remote from politicians, though not from politics. Between 1932 and 1935 he hardly met a single cabinet or even ex-cabinet minister, a striking contrast with the days when he had all the inner ring of Lloyd George's cabinet at Cherkley or bargained with Neville Chamberlain over Conservative policy. In a sense, too, he was without even non-political friends. Tim Healy and Arnold Bennett had been real intimates. Both died early in 1931, and Beaverbrook never replaced them. Castlerosse and Wardell were now his most constant companions, but both were employees as well as friends, and this made some difference. In the last resort neither would stand up to him.

Two younger men provided Beaverbrook with most fun and stimulation during the nineteen-thirties: Brendan Bracken and Aneurin Bevan, an apparently ill-assorted pair. Bracken was as extremely Right as Bevan was extremely Left. But both enjoyed lively argument and they dined with Beaverbrook two or three times a week, disputing violently with his impartial encouragement. Beaverbrook and Bracken were close in other ways. Bracken, too, was a financial adventurer, deeply involved in journalistic affairs, and usually agreed with Beaverbrook's political outlook. Their friendship knew only one short period of estrangement. Bracken, an aggressive British patriot, liked to make a mystery of his origin. At the time of the general election of 1935 Beaverbrook revealed in The Evening Standard that Bracken came of an Irish Roman Catholic family. This was the kind of harmless prank that Beaverbrook liked to play on his friends. Bracken, however, was deeply offended until reconciled by the mediation of Sir James Dunn. Beaverbrook and Bracken never quarrelled again.

First appearance as minister
of aircraft production

Last appearance
as a cabinet minister

On the Prince of Wales with Churchill, 1941

Off to Moscow:
(left to right) Eden,
Beaverbrook, Bevin, Churchill

Return from Moscow: *(left to right)* Sir William
(later Lord) Rootes, Captain Harold Macmillan,
Beaverbrook, Sir John Anderson

Ambassador Gusev presents Order of Suvorov, 1944

With Churchill,
Downing Street, 1944

With Max Aitken, 1945

With Brendan Bracken and Albert (valet), 1946

"Who is in charge of this clattering train?"

With much affection
to the greatest journalist
of us all.

Arthur Christiansen

November 19...

With Arthur Christiansen, 1945

With E. J. Robertson, 1949

With grand-daughter
Jean (Lady Jean
Campbell),
Montreal, 1950

At Cap d'Ail, 1955

With Beatrice Lillie
(Lady Peel), Jamaica, 1951

Farm inspection, Somerset, 1957

Aneurin Bevan shared Beaverbrook's radical outlook on social affairs. As a high-principled Socialist he was also embarrassed by their intimacy. He wrote to Beaverbrook on 11 March 1932:

> As one who hates the power you hold, and the order of life which enables you to wield it, and furthermore, because I know I shall never seek that power for myself, I feel emboldened to tell you that I hold you in the most affectionate regard, and confess to a great admiration for those qualities of heart and mind which, unfortunately, do not appear to inspire your public policy.

Later, after Bevan had married Jennie Lee, Beaverbrook offered them a country cottage at Cherkley. Bevan replied on 14 May 1935:

> As you know Jennie springs from the same Covenanter stock as yourself, only she has sprung further, or not quite as far, according to the point of view. She takes the view, for which there is of course much to be said, that it would be improper for us to live within the shadow of your castle walls. Like Lobengula, you cast a long shadow, and it is difficult to grow under it.
>
> In plain English, we think it would be politically indiscreet for us to take the cottage on your estate.

However Bevan relished Beaverbrook's company and his champagne— hence Bracken nicknamed Bevan the Bollinger Bolshevik. There is also a tradition that Beaverbrook once sent Bevan a substantial cheque which was returned the next day. No trace of this is to be found in Beaverbrook's bank ledger. Besides, he had given up making money presents to his men friends, even in the guise of stock exchange profits. He endowed members of his family and old associates in Newcastle. He helped Express men to buy a house or educate their children and repeatedly rescued Castlerosse and Bruce Lockhart very substantially from the hands of moneylenders. Both men promised to mend their ways and neither did so. Beaverbrook joined with Lloyd George and two others in providing an annuity of £2,000 for Philip Snowden, onetime Labour chancellor of the exchequer and wrongheaded champion of economy in 1931. Apart from this, only one man in public life received money from Beaverbrook. The sums were large and the individual surprising, as will appear in due course.

With his women friends Beaverbrook formed the habit of giving each of them £100 for Christmas and another £100 on his birthday. In the nineteen-thirties the list was not much more than half a dozen: Lady Sibell Lygon, Lady Weymouth, Mrs. Montagu, Lady Diana Cooper, Lady Inverclyde, and Lady Victor Paget. Gradually new names were added without the older ones being struck off, until by the nineteen-fifties it was costing Beaverbrook £2,500 to celebrate Christmas and another £2,500 to celebrate his birthday. Of course Beaverbrook always liked giving pleasure—in its most concrete form. But the habit reflected also his inner uncertainty. Though he was in fact the most captivating of men, inspiring love in the most differing characters, he could not believe that people liked him for himself. The presents of money and other things were a way of making sure. Also they were a compensation for the way he switched his friendships on and off. He often failed to see his dearest friends for months on end, and the regular cheques were a reminder that he loved them all the same. Jean Norton was not included in this system. She saw Beaverbrook nearly all the time and received £6,000 a year, occasionally interrupted when they quarrelled.

Beaverbrook did not altogether lose touch with his older friends. Lloyd George was busy writing his War Memoirs, and this naturally aroused Beaverbrook's enthusiasm. Besides, as he wrote to Borden: "Though I have no sympathy with his politics, I have a great affection for the man". Beaverbrook drifted further away from Churchill, partly because he had no interest in the Life of Marlborough, which Churchill was then writing. More than this, Beaverbrook believed that Churchill was finished politically—"a busted flush", as he expressed it to one of his editors. His letters ran over with the same judgement in more moderate terms. He wrote to Dr. Cox, his old headmaster, on 27 December 1932:

Winston Churchill is now almost out of public life. I would not be a bit surprised if he retired from Parliament at the next election.

A year later, again to Dr. Cox:

Winston Churchill has the best of the rhetoric over India, but the worst of the battle. The Tories forgave him for ratting to the Liberals long ago, but they cannot forgive him for returning to the Tory fold.

Similarly to Borden, on 7 January 1934:

I think Winston Churchill will retire from Parliament. It is really the best thing for him to do. In any case, if he continued on his present course, I would not be surprised if Baldwin put a veto on him in his constituency. And believe me, Baldwin can do it.

Again to Borden on 28 March 1934:

Churchill, now that he seems to have reconciled himself to the part of a farewell tour of politics, speaks better than for years past. He has cut the rhetoric and gained in dignity.

But he can do nothing with the India issue.

Baldwin can deal with that situation.

Finally to Theodor Fink on 19 November 1934:

The supporters of the policy of setting up a federal rule in India are led by Baldwin, who is at heart a Diehard. The Diehards are led by Winston Churchill, who gave Home Rule to Ireland.

The result is that Baldwin does not feel happy about his policy, and the Diehards are not happy about their leader.

However this was not Beaverbrook's last word on "Churchill down". On 12 June 1935 he wrote to Maisky, the Soviet ambassador, concerning Churchill:

> In character he is without a rival in British politics. I know all about his prejudices. But a man of character who tells the truth is worth much to the nation.

Beaverbrook's estrangement from Churchill was in part an estrangement over policies. Beaverbrook had no interest in Churchill's campaign on behalf of the Indian princes. His own concern, equally futile, was to bring India within the imperial tariff system. Though originally a diehard in Indian matters, he came to believe that federal concessions would do no harm and made the surprising confession to Lord Hailsham (5 December 1934): "I do not disagree with Mr. Baldwin over the India issue". Beaverbrook's own campaigns offended Churchill, challenging as they did most of what Churchill had done as chancellor of the exchequer. Over both war debts and the gold standard, Beaverbrook was able to say: "I told you so", and said so often, usually evoking the shade of Bonar Law as additional satisfaction. Of course he blamed Baldwin as well. He wrote to Roy Howard on 31 January 1932:

> I should be surprised if our Mr. Baldwin does not continue to "look the dollar in the face". But he does not suffer. He lives in a fine house supplied by the state. He eats at the public trough. He has done so for many years. The rest of us pay the price.

Beaverbrook did not believe that payment of the American war debt helped British relations with the United States. On the contrary, these would be much better once war debts were out of the way. He concluded his letter to Roy Howard: "The English can be relied upon to back up the Americans if the nation gets into trouble or difficulty with any foreign country". Howard asked Beaverbrook to endorse Stimson's doctrine of non-recognition in the Far East. Beaverbrook replied on 29 February 1932:

> British public opinion expects America to equip itself with navy big enough to dominate the Pacific.
> Such decision will make our taxpayers shiver and our old ladies sleep soundly.

Beaverbrook had no sympathy with the League of Nations's attempt to play a part in the dispute between China and Japan. When the Lytton commission of enquiry was set up, he wrote to Baxter on 29 May 1932:

> Who pays for Lord Lytton's journey to Manchuria? If any portion of it is being paid by England you ought to raise a row. It is a great waste of money.

Lord Lytton has been given official status to stick his nose into something which does not concern us. He might embroil us.

This message was not welcomed by Baxter, a supporter of the League of Nations.

Beaverbrook's first big campaign of his own devising after the establishment of the National government was for higher wages. He opposed the policy of reducing wages advocated by most economists and government spokesmen. He demanded the restoration of the cuts imposed during the financial crisis of 1931. In his view, the way to recovery was to increase purchasing power by giving it to the wage-earning and salaried classes. "If we do that, the benefits will radiate through the whole structure of industry and commerce". He did not believe that capitalists were entitled to reduce wages in order to maintain their profits:

> Capitalists, who invest money in an undertaking are under an obligation to give an economic reward to those they employ. In good times they are permitted to make good profits. In bad times they must be willing to stand the loss.

Naturally Beaverbrook attacked the control over the supply of money exercised by the banks, and particularly by the Bank of England. He attributed the economic ills of the country to Montagu Norman, "a good man with a bad policy", and wrote in The Sunday Express on 1 May 1932:

> I want to deprive the Bank of England of its power to regulate money and the price of it, to determine credit and the amount of it.
> I want to place that power and the responsibility for the use of it in the hand of the Government, subject to scrutiny of Parliament.
> . . . .
> The powers of the bankers must be wiped out. They have used their powers so badly that they have shown that they are not safe custodians of the money and credit of the country.

Such doctrines now seem deceptively simple, though by no means everyone is converted to the obvious truth that a country is prosperous when the mass of its people is prosperous. In the nineteen-thirties Beaverbrook was unusual in holding them, at any rate among Conservatives. There was of course an expansionist school, including such different characters as Keynes, Harold Macmillan and Sir Oswald Mosley. But the straight doctrine of high wages was regarded as heretical even by most of the Labour party. Beaverbrook was peculiarly challenging even among the heretics.

He applied his own doctrine. He never reduced salaries on his newspapers. He increased his personal expenditure and boasted of this. The boast had an impish background. At New Year 1932 Lord Londonderry complained of paragraphs in The Daily Express about the gay doings at Londonderry House. Beaverbrook answered that the social column had every right to report Londonderry's New Year party. Londonderry then explained that he had cancelled the usual festivities at his country seats and did not want his retainers to know how he had been enjoying himself in London. He also asked why The Express did not report Beaverbrook's parties. Beaverbrook answered maliciously: "I now understand why you did not want your party reported" and added about himself:

I am not in Society. I spring from the working class and belong to them. I don't go to parties. I never dine outside my own house or go to a restaurant. So there is not much use in printing news about me in the Society columns.

However the following Sunday Beaverbrook printed news about himself, though in a leader, not in the society columns. In The Sunday Express of 10 January 1932, he referred to "a man distinguished in our public life", who had resented an account of his New Year celebrations because they were said to have been on a generous scale. Beaverbrook continued:

I cannot understand why he should be so resentful.
My own Christmas celebrations have never cost so much as they did this winter. At New Year I was even more extravagant.
In 1931 I spent more money than ever before in my life. . . .
In 1932—if I have the cash—it is my intention to spend more money than in 1931.
I am employing more servants than I used to. I am employing more secretaries. I am working harder than ever I did, and life is more pleasant for me in consequence.
. . . .
Why should you and I stint ourselves of the pleasures we used to enjoy? Let us go to the cinema and the theatre when we have a mind to it! Why should there be empty seats if the entertainment is good?
Why should we not buy a new suit of clothes and another car? The price of fresh air and lovely scenery remains the same as ever, and clothes and cars have never been so cheap. As for money—it is just as scarce as we make it!

Once started on his line, Beaverbrook pursued it nearly every Sunday. He sang the praises of inflation. In one delightful article, he imagined the annual excursion of the employees of The Sunday Express, not surprisingly to Leatherhead. They arrive at Waterloo Station and ask for return tickets. They are told:

Oh, we are very sorry, but we are afraid that it is quite impossible. We have got the locomotives all right. We have got enough carriages. The line is in good order. There are engine drivers and guards and signalmen. *But we've got no more tickets and so you can't go!*

The article continued:

> It sounds grotesque. But that is exactly what Mr. Montagu Norman is saying to-day.
> He sits in his ticket office in Threadneedle Street and he won't give us the necessary tickets for the conduct of commerce and industry.

In an article on 3 July 1932 he exclaimed:

> Look with hatred and contempt on those rich men who cut down their private expenditure and their public benefactions. Cover those wealthy niggards with ridicule! Pour scorn on the stingy!
>
> . . . .
>
> This is the policy I advocate—the policy of cheap and plentiful money, of expansion and optimisim, of courageous construction, of increased output, and greater consuming power.

The article about there being no tickets to Leatherhead had a curious sequel. Fred Henderson, a veteran Socialist writer, complained that the argument had been lifted from one of his pamphlets. Beaverbrook, after some delay, answered that the illustration had been used many times, beginning with Major Douglas's Social Credit, which was published in 1924. Beaverbrook concluded: "It seems, indeed, that you and I have each in our turn, given a fresh span of life to an old fable". The letter also revealed that the illustration had in fact been provided by Frank Owen and thus gave one of the few pointers to Beaverbrook's ghosts. From occasional hints, it seems that, after Maurice Woods's death, Bruce Lockhart took on the main task. The Express office of course supplied the Empire Crusade material. Frank Owen, who had been a young Radical MP between 1929 and 1931, lost his seat in 1931 and then became the ghost for all articles on economic policy. George Malcolm Thomson succeeded to the shadowy post when Beaverbrook shifted to foreign affairs and continued so to function until the end of the second world war.

However this is only one side of the story. Beaverbrook ghosted for others even more than others ghosted for him. He wrote many of the leaders in The Daily Express. He often wrote the entire Cross Bencher column of political gossip in The Sunday Express. He contributed Diary entries to The Evening Standard practically every day. Even when his own articles were ghost-written he supplied the ideas. Was Cross Bencher Beaverbrook's ghost or was Beaverbrook his? The answer must be: both and neither. Many men acquired the trick of writing in Beaverbrook's tone, but they were successful echoes only because there was a great original.

When 1933 arrived, Beaverbrook decided to give his campaign a more practical form. His newspapers printed a coupon, modelled on those accepting a gift scheme: "I am ready to do all in my power to assist in the campaign to defend the wage levels of Britain and restore the cuts made in 1931". The appeal did not evoke much response—at least there was no triumphant announcement in The Express newspapers that thousands of signed coupons had been returned. There was however response of a less favourable nature. City opinion was offended and showed this in a peculiarly offensive way. In July 1932 Lord Waring, Beaverbrook's old friend, proposed to put up young Max Aitken for the Goldsmiths' Company and enlisted the aid of Sir Henry Goschen, a prominent City figure. At the last minute, Goschen reported that the motion would be opposed. He therefore suggested that it should be withdrawn. Waring attributed the opposition to others, but on further enquiry decided that it sprang from Goschen himself. Max Aitken wrote to Waring on 16 July 1932:

> I am sorry the motion was withdrawn for I would much rather have been rejected.
> During my short life my father has bestowed upon me untold benefits so now I am glad that the obloquy aimed at him should fall on me.
> I enjoy being shot at on his account.

This was the spirit which made Max Aitken a devoted son and a famous fighter-pilot. Beaverbrook himself wrote to Waring:

> I suppose you know I have a great deal of trouble in my life. It grows apace every day. Of course, I am not unaccustomed to trouble, and when it hits me I do not seem to mind it. But this is the first time that one of my children has come up against it.
> I am bound to say that Max is a great comfort at the moment, and in the circumstances.

Max Aitken was not always a comfort to his father during the nineteen-thirties. It is not my intention to write a chronicle of the Aitken family, though its tenor was of a piece with the rest of Beaverbrook's life. As a father he was inordinately generous and inordinately tyrannical. He endowed his children richly and then complained savagely when they did not manage their money affairs well or failed to give him precise accounts of their expenditure. Peter was never drawn seriously into the newspapers. He served in the army during the second world war and was drowned in 1947 while yachting in Swedish waters. Janet's marriage with Ian Campbell, later duke of Argyll, was dissolved. Lady Jean Campbell, their only daughter, later became Beaverbrook's favourite. Janet then married the Hon. Drogo Montagu, a son of the earl of Sandwich, who was killed during the second world war. After it she found lasting happiness with a Canadian husband Edward Kidd. Max Aitken often jibbed against the newspapers during the nineteen-thirties and for a time left them altogether. The second world war brought father and son together for good.

Somewhat strangely, Beaverbrook's campaign for higher wages was greeted with hostility by the trade unions who might have been expected to welcome it. He was accused of hypocrisy, to which he himself made the best reply, when Norman Angell voiced the same accusation. Beaverbrook wrote to Beverley Nichols on 5 March 1933:

> He says I am a hypocrite; therefore I say he is a fool. For why? Because of my many vices, hypocrisy is not in the list. Anybody but a fool must be aware of that fact.

Labour leaders would not believe that a rich man genuinely favoured high wages. They declared that he had opposed the general strike in 1926 and had supported the National government in 1931. Therefore his conversion to high wages was a belated sham, designed only to promote the sales of his newspapers.

Beaverbrook answered by pointing to his record: "From 1920 to the present day, I have been a high wages man". Though he had opposed the general strike, he had also opposed any reduction of miners' wages. In 1931 there was nothing to choose between the two sides. The entire Labour cabinet had accepted all the proposed cuts except that in unemployment relief, and the majority of the cabinet had accepted all the cuts without exception. He explained patiently that he did not run his papers in order to make money and that, far from devising policies in order to push up circulation, he pushed up circulation solely so that he could promote the policies in which he believed. He wrote to Ernest Bevin, who had attacked him (17 March 1933):

> I have always advocated high wages. I have advocated the restoration of the Cuts since 1931.
> What is your object in trying to discredit my movement? What is in your mind? We are supposed to be fighting in a common cause, and you attack me.

It was no use. Labour leaders demanded higher wages as a moral right and were outraged at Beaverbrook's claim that high wages were actually good for capitalism. This seemed to them mockery. If true, they would almost sooner reject high wages and welfare, as of course some extreme Socialists did. Both Tories and Socialists thought in terms of a crude class war: the workers wanted to push wages up, the rich wanted to force them down. Hence men of Beaverbrook's own class regarded him as a traitor, and Labour leaders dismissed him as a fraud, in short a hobgoblin.

Beaverbrook's real fault was to be ahead of his time. He had an outlook obvious enough to a later generation, and beyond the grasp of his contemporaries. He held that there was plenty for all and that the class war was unnecessary. High wages meant also high profits, though in his view profits were less important than general prosperity. Socialists were right in fearing that Beaverbrook's doctrine, if applied, would save capitalism from revolution or collapse, and so it has proved throughout Europe and North America since the second world war. Many a Socialist thinker has achieved fame in recent times by discovering in portentous volumes the simple truths which Beaverbrook displayed in his newspaper articles long before. The less learned did not take so long to be convinced. Even in the nineteen-thirties Beaverbrook won the unconscious agreement of ordinary men, despite unanimous condemnation from the pundits both left and right. The British people pulled themselves out of the Depression by spending when they were told to save. They thus avowed their unconscious agreement with Beaverbrook's economic doctrines, much as the Russian soldiers, according to Lenin, voted against the war in 1917 with their feet—by running away.

Beaverbrook's advocacy of high wages ran throughout 1932 and 1933. Thereafter it tailed off as he moved to foreign policy and No More War. In this he reflected the spirit of the decade which began with economic crisis and ended in European war. When that war came, Beaverbrook's policy was dismissed with contempt. He was accused of preaching complacency. His papers, it was alleged, were constantly announcing "There will be no war in Europe" and thus remained blind to events. It is true that The Daily Express, with its invariable habit of looking on the bright side, sometimes announced "There will be no war in Europe", just as it usually foretold fine weather for the following day or general prosperity just round the corner. But the phrase, though perhaps psychologically misleading, really applied to the situation of the moment, as is bound to happen in any newspaper. It meant: there will be no war over German rearmament or over Abyssinia or over the German reoccupation of the Rhineland. These judgements, however deplorable to some, were correct.

When Beaverbrook applied himself seriously to foreign affairs, he often said that a European war was possible and even likely. What he insisted on was that Great Britain need not be involved in this war, provided she kept clear of European alliances and built up her armaments. It was the two provisos, not the general prophecy, to which he attached importance. Beaverbrook was not ignorant of European affairs. He was not a timid appeaser. He was emphatically not a sympathizer with Fascism. He was preaching Isolationism and Great Armaments, not prophesying smooth things. He remained a voice crying in the wilderness. In the end he was vindicated by events, though even now few people appreciate this.

All the policies which Beaverbrook opposed were tried in vain. Collective security was tried, even if half heartedly. It failed. Active appeasement of Germany was tried. It failed. Alliance with European countries, France and Poland, was tried. It not only failed to avert war. It brought Great Britain to the brink of disaster. In June 1940 Beaverbrook's policy of isolation and great armaments was forced on Great Britain by events under most unfavourable circumstances. This policy enabled Great Britain to survive and to get through the second world war with far fewer casualties than in the first. Yet Beaverbrook received little acknowledgement. As in economic affairs, he suffered from being more clear-sighted than others, once more a hobgoblin who went against established outlooks, both Right and Left.

The articles which Beaverbrook wrote on foreign policy between 1933 and 1936 were his most original and alert achievement in political thinking. With Empire Free Trade, he was content to repeat the same argument again and again. With foreign affairs, he developed new arguments, though not of course a new basis of policy, as the situation changed. The underlying problem in these years was simple. It was Germany. With the establishment of Hitler and his Nazi dictatorship, Germany was clearly on the way to recovery as a great power. She would no longer tolerate the peace settlement imposed upon her after her defeat in 1919. She had already shaken off reparations. Soon she would begin to rearm. She would somehow end the demilitarization of the Rhineland. She would demand, and if necessary enforce, a revision of her frontiers, using the plea of self determination, once granted to others and denied to Germans. Thus restored to her former greatness, she would advance, peacefully or otherwise, until she overshadowed the entire European continent, west of Soviet Russia. Beaverbrook foresaw all this from the outset. He wrote to a friend in Vancouver on 22 January 1934:

> I don't think the conflict will come between Germany and France in the first place. I expect the Poles will be attacked if they don't settle with the Germans.
> Next to the Poles, come the Czechs.
> France, in my opinion, is a pacifist country at the present time. You cannot make the Frenchman fight.

This forecast was not right in every detail. The Poles concluded a non-aggression pact with Germany in 1934, and their turn came therefore after the Czechs, instead of before it. Beaverbrook was however right on the essential point. Whereas most English people still regarded France as a great military power, he grasped that the French, though anxious to maintain their supremacy in Europe, would not fight effectively in order to do so.

What attitude was Great Britain to adopt in face of the new Germany? Most English people sympathized with the German grievances, however much they disliked the Nazi system. They held that these grievances should be redressed by peaceful means—an impossible hope. They had fantasy that other countries would acquiesce in the German demands an

that the grateful Germans would then take no advantage of the concessions made to them. Beyond this, the majority of British people placed
their faith in "collective security" and the League of Nations. This
involved a vague universal guarantee to all countries everywhere and
therefore obviously increased British commitments. Yet paradoxically
the more a man advocated collective security, the more he opposed any
measure of British rearmament—a contradiction particularly marked in
the Labour party.

Beaverbrook cut through all these confusions and contradictions. To a
simple problem he gave a simple answer: Isolation. Great Britain should
rely on her Empire and turn her back on Europe. This had always been
his policy. He had done much to prevent war against Turkey in 1922 and
was fond of quoting what Law had written then: "We cannot alone act
as the policemen of the world". He had opposed the treaty of Locarno
when it was made. He raised his solitary voice against the League of
Nations. To borrow a phrase from an American historian, he rejected
"perpetual war for the sake of perpetual peace". He even argued, in true
Radical spirit, that Great Britain had gone to war in 1914 because of
secret promises made to France by Lansdowne and Grey and not because
any British interest was involved. He wrote in The Sunday Express on
2 September 1934:

> Are the present generation of boys and girls now rising into manhood
> and womanhood to be trapped in the same futile, purposeless, insensate
> engagements as Lord Lansdowne and Lord Grey made with the French?
> Are they to suffer from all the bloodshed and strife and sorrow which the
> policy of the entente brought upon our generation?

This was good Radical doctrine. Every word which Beaverbrook wrote
would have been endorsed by Cobden and Bright. Like him, they rejected
"that foul idol", the balance of power. Like him, they held that Great
Britain's duty was to seek peace and pursue it, not to wage war for "the
liberties of Europe". As Bright said in 1855: "It is not my duty to make
this country the knight-errant of the human race". It might have been
expected that the Radicals of the nineteen-thirties, themselves campaigning against war, would have welcomed alliance with Beaverbrook. They
did not do so. In general, they could not believe that a rich man and a
newspaper proprietor, calling himself a Conservative, was genuinely on
the Radical side. They were further estranged in that Beaverbrook, with
superior logic, coupled isolation with British rearmament. Most Radicals
regarded all armaments as wicked, however defensively intended. As well,
Radicals were offended by Beaverbrook's advocacy of Empire, which
had now become for them a word of shame. In Beaverbrook's view,
isolation and Empire went together. The Empire gave Great Britain the

resources with which to stand alone, and imperial unity could be maintained only by isolation. He pointed out that the Dominions were not parties to the treaty of Locarno and that therefore Great Britain might find herself at war, while the Dominions remained neutral. Beyond imperial unity was a wider dream: only isolation would make possible a close partnership between Great Britain and the United States.

Beaverbrook first took up foreign affairs when the coming problems still seemed theoretical. In the autumn of 1933, Baldwin endorsed Locarno as contributing to British security. Beaverbrook answered in The Daily Express on 9 October:

> The greater the menace of war, the nearer our boundaries are to the belligerents, the more need there is for us to withdraw from Europe.

And on 11 October:

> Who is prepared to join with the French in driving the Germans back beyond Cologne?
> Nobody, nobody, nobody.
> What advantage would it be to Britain and the Empire?

Beaverbrook ingeniously suggested that Empire Crusade funds could be used for a campaign against Locarno, because, as he wrote to Cunliffe-Owen on 21 October, "if we go to war with Germany on account of the mobilizing of troops in the demilitarized zone, the Dominions will walk out on us". Cunliffe-Owen agreed, and the Empire Crusade paid for Beaverbrook's meetings. At this time he believed that he was knocking at an open door. Everyone, he thought, would soon agree with him that "Alliances with foreign powers are bound to weaken us. They would give us friends on whom we could not rely, and they would certainly multiply the occasions of war for us" (to H. F. Piper, 9 February 1934).

The fortunes of the National government were certainly in a bad shape. In October 1933 its candidate lost to Labour at East Fulham, allegedly because of anti-war feeling. In the following March, Labour won the LCC elections. A strong factor was the demand for an immediate restoration of the cuts in teachers' pay, imposed in 1931—a demand which Beaverbrook did much to promote. The leaders of the National government attempted to win Beaverbrook's support. J. H. Thomas, secretary for the Dominions, approached him and enquired whether they could make a new version of the Stornoway pact. Beaverbrook answered by demanding a complete economic union with the Crown Colonies. Thomas professed sympathy and passed Beaverbrook's demand to Neville Chamberlain, who after a long delay produced a series of objections from treasury officials. Beaverbrook tried again and then, after further objections, lost patience. The negotiations ran to nothing. Beaverbrook announced in The Daily Express:

> The Daily Herald declares that I am hostile to the MacDonald-Baldwin Coalition. That's right.

He wrote privately to Kingsley Wood on 25 October 1934:

> I hope it will not be long before you are Prime Minister . . . I have lost all hope of Neville Chamberlain. He is strange. He might have erected a magnificent tombstone to the memory of that great man Joseph Chamberlain.

It was not only the denial of Empire Free Trade which held Beaverbrook against the government. Foreign dangers were now the overriding factor with him. He returned to the attack in the summer of 1934. He wrote in The Sunday Express on 15 July 1934:

> The powers of darkness are gathering in every direction. The web is being woven more and more securely round us.
>
> . . . .
> Interference in Europe means war for certain.
> There must be war in Europe. The reason is plain: the territorial clauses of the treaty of Versailles cannot stand. Millions of men feel themselves under unbearable injustice because of the treaty. These millions will fight sooner or later.
> If we stand out of European commitments, we are given the hope and expectation that there will be no war for Britain, that we will not be compelled to fight on one side or the other in a dispute about territorial clauses which are no concern of ours.
> Interference in Europe divides us from the Dominions. It is a policy which means the break-up of the British Empire. . . .
> There is another nation whose interests, like our own, lie outside the European embroglio. It is the United States. . . .
> I am ready to take any steps, to develop any plan, that will enable us to bring the era of interference to an end.

A fortnight later, on 29 July 1934, Beaverbrook wrote:

> We are pledged to fight for Austrian independence.
> We are pledged to defend the frontiers of Belgium against all comers.
>
> . . . .
> What consideration do we get in return for undertaking such momentous liabilities?
> Nothing! Nothing! Nothing but toil and trouble, sorrow and disaster.
>
> . . . .
> We must join in the gang-war raging in the streets for fear the gangsters unite to attack us in our house.
> Oh! The folly of it!
> The British Empire minding its own business is safe.

The British Empire meddling in the concerns of the Balkans and Central Europe is sure to be embroiled in war, pestilence and famine.

....

I want no office. I seek no place. I will take no power.

My sole object is to bring our people together in our own dwelling house. When the struggle is over and the victory won, I will go home.

And on 1 August 1934 Beaverbrook telephoned to The Daily Express:

Mr. Baldwin advises us to undertake European entanglements.

He says isolationists suffer from distempered imaginations.

....

That man's counsel has brought us disaster in the past.

He lost us our money.

If we accept his advice now he will lose us our Empire.

Though Beaverbrook took the danger of war seriously, he did not believe that it would be necessary for him to lead a new campaign. He wrote to Gordon on 18 October 1934:

It was a different thing when we dealt with Empire Free Trade. There I was willing to make great sacrifices.

Isolation will come about any way. So that we need not put ourselves to so much trouble. We need merely wait.

Besides, he now remembered his old campaign with bitterness. He wrote to Herbert Dunnico on 19 December:

I gave up my orchestra, my drink, my friends, my time. In return, I got cheated and swindled and betrayed.

However, Beaverbrook welcomed the chance of broadcasting on isolation for the BBC—a broadcast again attended with obstacles and repeatedly postponed from April until October. When finally delivered, it had a great impact and produced a large post-bag. Approval came from Pemberton Billing, Sidney Bernstein, D. W. Griffith, and F. J. Marquis (later Lord Woolton). This last wrote: "Even if I had not agreed with your views, I think I should have been converted". About one in five of the correspondents disagreed, and their stumbling block was always the same: if Germany attacked France, Great Britain must go to France's assistance. Otherwise she herself would be attacked next.

Beaverbrook answered by drawing a lesson from the last war—a practice he condemned in others. He wrote to E. L. Fleming, MP, on 22 November 1934:

If we had pursued the policy of Splendid Isolation in 1914 there would have been one certain result, in my opinion—we should not have been involved in the war between France and Germany. We should have been a million British lives to the good, when the weary combatants laid down their arms.

And if the victor had contemplated making an attack on us, we should have been strong and he would have been weak. We should have been rich and he would have been impoverished.

Beaverbrook expected the same thing to happen next time. Every answer he gave, and he gave many, was a variation on the theme: "After a modern war is over, there can be no fight left even in a victor country, for generations. . . . Even if Germany defeats France she would emerge from the war too weak to attack us." Events in 1940 seemed to prove Beaverbrook wrong. Even so, Germany failed to invade Great Britain, and Great Britain would have been a good deal more secure if she had not just lost all her military equipment at Dunkirk, after a futile gesture of aid to France.

Beaverbrook also argued that alliance with France was likely to provoke a German attack rather than to avert it. Thus to J. E. Perceval on 2 November 1934:

> It is a fallacy to think that by alliance with France we can prevent Germany from attacking France. This failed in 1914. It would fail again. Great Britain would be more secure if she stood alone.

He wrote to Mrs. Marriott on 3 November:

> It is not the width of the Channel that determines our relation to war in Europe. The deciding factor is the extent to which we permit ourselves to become parties to Continental politics and jealousies.

Beaverbrook also argued that the development of air power, far from destroying British isolation, had removed the one factor favouring continental entanglements. To F. C. Davies, 20 September 1934:

> The airplane has destroyed the only argument there ever was for taking part in the quarrels of Europe. A modern airplane can fly across Belgium in twenty minutes. Belgium is no longer of any interest to us.
>
> By intervention we embrace the possibility of war. By isolation, we flee from it.

Every man's vision has its limits, and Beaverbrook, usually so alive to the implications of technical advance, did not at this time debate what air strategy was most suited to isolationism. The Royal Air Force, thanks to Trenchard's influence, was entirely dedicated to bombing. Its leaders believed with Baldwin that the bomber would always get through and that the only defence lay in the threat of massive retaliation. A. S. Cunningham-Reid, a Conservative MP, suggested that what he called interceptor-fighters would be a more effective defence than bombers and would strengthen the isolationist argument. Beaverbrook was not impressed. He replied to Cunningham-Reid on 22 May 1935:

> Maybe, as you say, interceptor-fighters will put an end to the menace of Europe and that, in consequence, we will be able to adopt the policy of isolation.
> But there is nothing in your speech in favour of isolation.
> I am out for the policy of isolation.

Thus men fail to foresee their destiny. Only five years later Beaverbrook had his greatest moment when he provided the fighters which won the Battle of Britain and so proved the invincible strength of isolation.

All Beaverbrook's critics in October 1934 used the argument of national security. Not one mentioned the League of Nations. In November 1934 the League however suddenly came into the forefront when the League of Nations Union organized a plebiscite of public opinion. This was called the Peace Ballot and has often been treated by historians as a demonstration of pacifist feelings. Beaverbrook was almost alone in realizing that its real purpose was to elicit support for collective security. He alone named it the Ballot of Blood. He wrote in The Daily Express on 25 October:

> The plebiscite will drag you and your children into a war on behalf of the League of Nations, a moribund institution which is a convenient instrument of ambitious and unscrupulous powers in Europe.

And on 17 November:

> The League of Nations is now a greater danger to peace than the armament makers. And I do not deny that they are a danger.
> Tear up the ballot paper. Throw the pieces in the waste-paper basket.
> Turn away from Europe. Stand by the Empire and Splendid Isolation.

It was this mixture of isolation and Empire which made even Socialists who opposed the League of Nations, as I did in a humble way, regard Beaverbrook with distrust. Now I think that his combination of isolation, rearmament, and Empire was more sensible than anything we offered.

Despite Beaverbrook's hostility to the peace or blood ballot, he did not appreciate how strongly enthusiasm for the League of Nations and collective security had gripped public opinion, or at any rate its more moral exponents. When 1935 opened, he was still entirely engaged in opposing alliance with France and others against Germany. He denounced the Stresa Pact with France and Italy as a Bad Bargain. He declared that, in supporting Locarno and the League, the Socialists Mean War. European war, he wrote, was inevitable. The Germans would redress their national wrongs, but it was no concern of Great Britain's. On 28 March 1935, he wrote to W. J. Brown, the rogue left-winger who had now become a close friend of his:

> I believe that Germany is looking eastward this time. Assuming that to be so and Germany does attack Russia or Lithuania, I agree that France might march against the Germans. But in that event, do you think that opinion in this country would rise up to demand intervention on the side of France? I do not.

On 6 April he wrote to Brown again:

> You think that if Britain continues to take part in the affairs of Europe we can keep the Germans from fighting. I say that the Germans mean to fight in any case, sooner or later, and if we stay in Europe we shall only get drawn into the war.
>
> The present strength of Germany is due to the sense of injustice that the Peace Treaties have left. There is not a chance of our being able to put these injustices right if we interfere in Europe. On the other hand if we fight to maintain the status quo we fight for something which the people of this country believe to be unrighteous.
>
> . . . .
>
> You regard the antagonism of Germany and Britain as inevitable. Assume that to be true. It is also true that the conflict is a remote contingency. And which would you rather have—war with Germany accompanied by a French alliance and neutral Dominions, or war with Germany in which the Dominions fight by our side?
>
> Believe me, you cannot have both, for the Dominions will not follow us into a war where we fight because of continental alliances.

On 29 April 1935 Beaverbrook wrote to J. M. Patterson in New York:

> The great struggle we must make in Britain is to keep us out of a French alliance. Immense pressure is being exerted to bring this alliance into being. Mr. MacDonald, the prime minister has just made it clear that he means to enter it if Germany continues with her re-arming programme. The foreign office which is controlled by Sir Robert Vansittart is warmly espousing the alliance.

Beaverbrook was getting pretty deep into a campaign despite his reluctance to lead. The Daily Express organized an exhibition of No More War photographs at Dorland House. Volunteers were recruited to distribute ten million leaflets in favour of isolation and an American alliance from door to door. Beaverbrook also asked D. W. Griffith for a good band made up of Americans who took part in the last war to march from county to county, carrying the message of Anglo-Saxon unity. Unfortunately Griffith failed to provide one. Beaverbrook himself addressed a number of meetings and even talked of again intervening in by-elections.

It was another sign of his preoccupation with international affairs that he now sought out the leading foreign ambassadors in London—not a society he had previously cared for. Dino Grandi, the Italian ambassador, became the most intimate. The two men had much in common. Both disliked the League of Nations; both wanted Anglo-Italian friendship and deplored Mussolini's moves towards Hitler. They worked much together during the Abyssinian crisis, though without leaving anything on paper. Their friendship was actually renewed after the second world war, when Beaverbrook wrote to "Dino" on 6 June 1955: "We might continue the conversation we carried on at Stornoway House fifteen years ago". Thereafter Grandi often visited Beaverbrook in the south of France until old age made both of them immobile.

Beaverbrook also had some dealings with Ribbentrop, Hitler's roving representative. In November 1935 he visited Berlin on Ribbentrop's invitation and met Hitler who sang his usual song about the need for friendly relations between England and Germany.[1] In August 1936 when Ribbentrop became German ambassador in London, Beaverbrook wrote to him:

> Never, never, never was any appointment to an Ambassadorial post in London as well received as your own.
> You have praise from the press and from the people.
> You may save the peace of Europe, I truly believe, by your conduct here.

The two however met only once during Ribbentrop's time in London. This did not prevent Beaverbrook's congratulating Ribbentrop in 1938 on his appointment as foreign minister. He wrote:

> It is with real pleasure that I hear today of your appointment to the highest office in the gift of your leader.
> I know full well that you will take full advantage of your great authority and immense power to develop still further the policy of peace and tranquillity. And you will have the loyal support of my newspapers in this pursuit.

This was not a letter which Beaverbrook was subsequently proud of, and it was not provided for Ribbentrop's defence at Nuremberg.

Beaverbrook's relations with Maisky, the Soviet ambassador, were very different. Aneurin Bevan first brought them together as Maisky has written,[2] and thereafter they met constantly. Maisky supplied Beaverbrook with Soviet films for his private cinema, and he and his wife often visited Beaverbrook at Cherkley. Undoubtedly they talked politics together a great deal but none of this has crept into their correspondence

---

[1] In 1941 Beaverbrook told Hess that he had met Hitler three times. If so, it can only have been during this visit. Beaverbrook did not meet Hitler when he went to Berlin for the Olympic games in 1936.

[2] Maisky, Who Helped Hitler (1964), 56–57.

which, apart from social arrangements, was mainly about Beaverbrook's bronchitis and Mme. Maisky's sinus trouble. I have found only one political remark. On 2 July 1939 Beaverbrook wrote to Maisky:

> In 1919 and 1920 The Express fought Mr. Churchill so long, and so hard, that it is fun now, for the proprietor of The Daily Express, to see Mr. Churchill being hugged by the Bear.

There was more such fun to come during the second world war, though Churchill did not always appreciate it.

It would be wrong to give the impression that Beaverbrook's time was entirely devoted to international affairs. 1935 might be the year of the first great crisis leading up to the second world war. For Beaverbrook it was also memorable as the year in which he discovered the delights of air travel. He first flew (to Paris) in 1934. This flight converted him. Henceforward he visited Europe in a chartered airplane. This satisfied his impatience and sense of drama. It was a new way of making business for his secretaries. An airplane had to be chartered after prolonged balancing between the air companies. A skilled pilot had to be chosen. The ambassador or ministry of every country to be visited had to be informed and asked for special facilities. On arrival at the foreign capital, there was a government representative at the airport and a fleet of official cars to sweep Beaverbrook and party to their hotel. There were interviews with high dignitaries or even the head of state, Mussolini, Hitler, Schuschnigg, and others. After a couple of days, Beaverbrook was off again. Within ten days, he was back at Cherkley. There was no time for boredom, no hanging about at railway stations, no staring through the carriage window as the train lumbered across the country. Beaverbrook made three such sweeps in 1935: to France and Spain in April, to Italy and across most of central Europe in July, to Paris and Berlin in November.

Another episode of a non-political kind is worthy of record. Like most events in Beaverbrook's life it did not pass over without trouble. Sir James Dunn commissioned Sickert to paint Beaverbrook's portrait. Sickert, in his usual way, painted it from a snapshot of Beaverbrook which had appeared in The Daily Express.[1] In April 1935, when Sickert submitted the portrait to the Royal Academy, he was asked to withdraw it because it was *the only one on a colossal scale*. On top of this Dunn at first refused to accept it. Sickert wrote to Beaverbrook on 2 May 1935: "My portrait is and remains a political portrait in the grand manner by a painter who appreciates and admires your policy.... It will certainly rank as one of my best and most important works". Beaverbrook made peace between Dunn and Sickert and praised the portrait as "a brilliant

---

[1] Sickert took the background from St. Peter's, Thanet, where he then lived and where Beaverbrook had never been.

piece of work". In reality he did not care for it. The portrait was consigned to the Manchester office of The Daily Express, from which it was snatched later to become the principal adornment of the Beaverbrook library.

At home politics were being transformed. In June Baldwin at last superseded MacDonald as prime minister. Hoare became foreign secretary, much to Beaverbrook's pleasure—the elevation of an old friend who also, he believed, agreed with him over foreign policy. Eden, the apostle of collective security, became minister for League of Nations affairs, "and that is bad". Beaverbrook acknowledged that the political weather was changing in the government's favour. He wrote to Dr. Cox on 4 June 1935:

> Hitler, by making Britain weak in the air, has made the Conservative party strong in the country.
>
> Lloyd George will stump the country with his "New Deal". I do not think he will have a success. He may stump, but the government will not stump up. Any way the day for a New Deal has passed. We have a New Deal in operation in this country. A big housing boom. It gives a great deal of employment. It improves the social condition of the country.

Beaverbrook was still hammering away against collective security and British commitments in Europe. He did not yet foresee the ingenious use Baldwin would make of these causes.

There was, it is true, a conflict blowing up between Italy and Abyssinia. Beaverbrook feared rightly that Eden was trying to pacify Mussolini by suggesting that Abyssinia should be induced to make concessions to Italy and receive part of British Somaliland. Beaverbrook denounced this as "a monstrous and shameful transaction". He would never relinquish one square inch of British territory. Mandates were a different matter. They were exposed to interference from the League of Nations and, still worse in Beaverbrook's eyes, could not be included in an imperial customs union. Germany could have them back, so far as Beaverbrook was concerned, and the sooner the better.

Mussolini rejected Eden's offer. This was not the end. On 28 June 1935 the results of the Peace or Blood Ballot were announced. More than ten million votes were in favour of economic sanctions; nearly seven million favoured even military sanctions, that is, war against an aggressor. Here was Baldwin's opportunity: he could redeem his standing with British opinion by seeming to support collective security and the League of Nations. Beaverbrook was almost alone in divining what would happen. Perhaps he had a private line of information, like most successful prophets. Hoare had often kept Beaverbrook in touch with cabinet proceedings—maybe from vanity, maybe for some other reason—and, as foreign secretary, might well be inclined to boast of the stroke he was planning

At any rate, Beaverbrook wrote to Doidge, now back in New Zealand, on 25 July 1935:

> The Government will make some show of intervention at Geneva in order to please the pacifists.
>
> They will push the League like a worn-out nag into the bull-ring. The bull will rip up the nag and then the Government will claim credit for a determined effort to kill the bull. But they will not put any matador into the ring.
>
> The Isolation movement, which ought to be strengthened by these European troubles is not making the progress it should.

On 11 August he wrote to J. M. Patterson:

> We can rely on the French to put an end to the League imposture. They are certain to make it impossible for the League to interfere between Italy and Abyssinia.
>
> . . . .
>
> If the war between Italy and Abyssinia breaks out, the Government will promise at the Election to keep Britain out of the war.
>
> If war between Italy and Abyssinia is averted, the Government will say at the Election that they saved us from conflict in Africa.

Beaverbrook foresaw a general election in November and expected the government to win a great majority, though Labour—"the Socialists"— might hold two hundred seats.

As the crisis deepened, Beaverbrook recognized that the government were using it to silence both Empire Free Trade and Isolation. He wrote to J. H. Fletcher, a Crusader, on 17 September 1935:

> The international situation is completely occupying the mind of men and the attention of Ministers. We must wait until the international situation clears up. If, on the other hand, war comes from the international crisis, there will be no time for domestic issues.

On 23 September 1935 he wrote to J. D. McKenna in Halifax:

> As for isolation, the difficulty about that campaign is that it cannot be pursued in such a way as to give comfort to foreigners in a moment of difficulty. But, on the other hand, we must not let the cause go by default.

Beaverbrook did not long follow his own counsel of restraint, just as he had burst out during the Chanak crisis. On 27 September, when it seemed clear that the League would impose sanctions on Italy, he repeated in The Daily Express: "we cannot, we will not, we must not police the world alone". On 30 September he wrote in The Daily Express against sanctions:

> War cannot stamp out war. War breeds war.
>
> Do not be led into warlike courses by hatred of dictators. . . . Let the people who are misgoverned rid themselves of their autocrats.

His own mind was fixed. On 1 October he wrote to H. K. Hales:

> I do not care in the least whether the Italians beat the Abyssinians or the other way round.
>
> It is true that the Italians are white and the Abyssinians are black. But, on the other hand, I hate dictatorships. If there were one fewer in Europe, I should not be downcast.

He summed up the situation to Paul Block in New York on 1 October:

> The pacifists want war for the sake of peace. The Socialists want to fight Italy because they hate Fascism. The big navy people want a war because it strengthens their argument for more naval expenditure. Some of the imperialists want to defend our possessions in the Mediterranean and the road to India.
>
> There is an odd mixture of tents pitched on the field.
>
> But the mixture in the next field is just as queer. Super-pacifists who won't fight, even for peace. Socialists who won't fight because the League of Nations is an imperialist racket. Isolationists who won't fight because the League of Nations is an anti-imperialist racket. Imperialists who don't see why the other fellow shouldn't have an Empire too. . . . The Labour party want to fight but their leader[1] wants to pray.

On 3 October Italian armies invaded Abyssinia. The League at once prepared to impose sanctions in Italy. Beaverbrook remained sceptical. He telegraphed to Cunliffe-Owen on 4 October 1935:

> We will not be involved beyond mild economic sanctions. Government is now ratting on pacifists who wish to make war.

Nevertheless, the state of public opinion was alarming. A. J. Cummings, a prominent journalist, who was a warm friend of Beaverbrook's despite being the principal columnist of The News Chronicle, wrote to him on 18 October:

> Are you really prepared to see Great Britain climb down, disperse her Mediterranean fleet and have her tail twisted by every hobo in every continent?

These were curiously patriotic sentiments for a professed internationalist. Beaverbrook replied on 21 October:

> I believe that the policy on which the fleet was sent to the Mediterranean a profoundly mistaken one. Naturally I want that policy to be reversed. If it can be done—as I think it can—without any danger to our prestige so much the better. But if our prestige must suffer, that, in my view is only what is to be expected when we meddle in affairs which are no concern of ours.

On 18 October Beaverbrook faced the moralists head on. He stated in The Daily Express that he had sent eighty thousand letters to professional

---

[1] George Lansbury. This was a correct description.

men, inviting their opinion on the Isolationist cause. 30,000 clergymen were for the League by six to one, and the majority of them were in favour of war. 10,000 solicitors were for the League by a majority of six to four. 40,000 doctors split fifty-fifty: maybe they knew war was war even when it was called military sanctions. Beaverbrook then answered the moral case. The League was not a universal association; it was an alliance of France and her satellites. As to the cry: Am I my brother's keeper?:

> Well, of course. We have a responsibility.
> But here God has given us a special duty, a particular task.
> In our charge there are the countless races of the British Empire. That is where our immediate duty lies. That is a burden which we must bear, and we alone.

He added a moral issue of his own:

> By our conduct we must not impose terrible misfortunes on countless people who have no responsibility for the present situation.
> Of course we should pity the Abyssinians. But we must not on that account inflict sorrow and grief and death on those who live far outside the zone of war.

Political developments were now playing into Baldwin's hands. The Labour party was rent asunder: the majority favouring even military sanctions, a strenuous left-wing minority opposing sanctions of any kind. Lansbury, the leader, was driven to resign and was succeeded by the apparently insignificant Attlee. Beaverbrook commented (11 October): "We are about in the same position as in the days of the Zinoviev letter in 1924 when Mr. Baldwin escaped". On 25 October Baldwin launched a general election with the plausible cry: "All sanctions short of war". Labour did not know what to answer. Beaverbrook held to his sceptical line: "After the election we shall hear much of the failure of Geneva and little of the need to make it a success".

Beaverbrook kept aloof throughout the election. He addressed only one meeting (for Lennox-Boyd at Biggleswade) and in The Daily Express advised electors to put Isolationist questions to the candidates. Beaverbrook's one interest was to defeat the National Liberal and National Labour candidates, just as he had opposed Lloyd George's followers in 1922. He wrote to S. Samuel on 2 November 1935:

> I am not going on the platform. I am not in sympathy with the National Government. I hate the elements in it, drafted from the Socialists and Liberals.
> I am against the policy of "collective security" and the League of Nations. I am entirely in favour of Isolation.
> I am opposed to the Government's fiscal policy. I want Empire Free Trade, and cannot get it. I can only get bits of it—just enough to swindle me out of the promises they made me in 1931.

On 6 November 1935 he wrote to J. H. Fletcher in Bassetlaw:

> Unless Malcolm MacDonald answers satisfactorily on Isolation, do what you can to defeat him and do it quite openly.
> Do not be deterred by the fear that you will be thought to be supporting the Socialist. The important thing is to make an end of the insincerity in politics which has already disgusted many of our people in the course of this election. Let us get back to honest politics and men who stand up and fight for the things they believe in.

Beaverbrook acknowledged Baldwin's tactical skill (2 November): "I place him along with Lord Liverpool and W. H. Smith. He is a bigger man. He is an incorruptible Walpole". On 14 November Baldwin duly triumphed: 492 supporters of the National government and only 154 Labour men were returned. Beaverbrook sent only one letter of congratulation—to an Independent Liberal, Sir Hugh Seely—and it was a backhanded compliment:

> How I wish that we might have fifty or a hundred Liberals in the House. It would do a great deal of good. And your opposition to Protection would drive the Government into an adequate defence of it.

On 25 November Beaverbrook expounded the election to Doidge:

> Isolation was not an issue at the polls. Baldwin went after the Liberal vote. It was League, collective security and economic sanctions all the way. One has to give the man credit for that—he had a great election triumph.
> But we have not finished with Isolation. Not by a long way.... As the sky darkens, the hopes of the Isolationists must rise.

The time had indeed arrived for the other side of Baldwin's strategy: abandonment of collective security once the election was over. The League had already authorized Great Britain and France to seek a way out of the conflict. At the foreign office, Sir Robert Vansittart, the permanent under-secretary, dug out the offer which Eden had made to Mussolini in June and made it still more favourable to Italy. Hoare showed the proposal to Baldwin, who approved it. On 6 December Beaverbrook and Vansittart went to Paris by the boat train. Hoare followed the next day. That evening, while Hoare negotiated with Laval, the French foreign minister, Beaverbrook dined with Jean Prouvost, proprietor of Paris Soir, with whom he had at this time a close journalistic alliance. He also met Pertinax, most influential of diplomatic commentators. Beaverbrook left no account of his activities, but it is unlikely that he went to Paris at this precise moment by chance or that he confined his talks with Prouvost and Pertinax to social gossip. Obviously he and Prouvost were preparing a joint press campaign in support of the Anglo-French plan.

On 8 December Hoare and Laval reached agreement. Abyssinia was to surrender the fertile plains to Italy. The Emperor would retain his mountain kingdom and would receive a corridor through British Somaliland, linking Abyssinia with the sea. Everything, it seemed, was going well. The war would be ended; the prestige of the League would be enhanced; the Stresa front of the three western powers against Germany would be restored. Beaverbrook and Vansittart returned together to London. Hoare went to Switzerland for a holiday, recommending the British cabinet to accept the plan, which it did on 9 December. News of the plan appeared, perhaps prematurely, in the French press. British morality was outraged. The storm blew against Baldwin. He retreated into obscurity and declared that his lips were sealed.

Beaverbrook had no sympathy with the outcry and was ready to go against it. This was an unpopular line. He wrote retrospectively to Eden on 24 November 1942:

> Strange as it may seem, I am listed among your admirers.
> This is in spite of the fact that I looked on your League of Nations policy with horror; your rejection of the Italian deal with consternation. And that I regretted that you did not part at that time with Baldwin who was on my side at first and then went over to the other side, leaving me almost alone. In fact I had no company at all, except for Sam Hoare and Lady Maud [Hoare] and Vansittart.

Hoare was summoned to return from Switzerland. Beaverbrook never failed a friend in trouble. He wrote to Hoare on 14 December:

> My desire is to back you up, to support and sustain you in the present difficulty.
> . . . .
> It is my intention to stand unswervingly in support of you in this present crisis.

On 17 December Hoare dined alone with Beaverbrook. Beaverbrook urged him to stand firm. The next morning Beaverbrook went to Hoare's house. Hoare had seen Neville Chamberlain and had told him that he meant to defend the plan as the best settlement obtainable, short of war. Chamberlain agreed. Baldwin had also called on Hoare and had said: "We all stand together". With Beaverbrook's aid, Hoare then drafted the speech which he intended to deliver.

In the afternoon Beaverbrook saw Hoare again. The situation had changed. Chamberlain had been round with a different message: the cabinet insisted that the plan must be repudiated. This burnt offering to morality, we now know, was imposed by Lord Halifax.[1] Hoare refused to recant. Chamberlain offered a compromise. If Hoare resigned without

[1] Macleod, Neville Chamberlain, 189.

compromising Baldwin or the government in any way, Baldwin promised that he should be brought back into the government at the earliest possible moment. Hoare accepted. While Beaverbrook and Hoare were chewing over this, Vansittart arrived. He declared that he would also resign, as he had had an equal part in making the Hoare-Laval agreement. Beaverbrook dissuaded him: "There would soon be no public service if public servants resigned on issues of policy".[1]

On 19 December Hoare duly made his sacrifice. While defending the plan in the house of commons he took all the blame on himself and failed to remark that the cabinet had approved it. Baldwin, in his usual manner, confessed his mistakes and talked solemnly about the deepest feelings of his countrymen. Baldwin, according to Beaverbrook, had covered himself in another way. Sir Austen Chamberlain had led the outcry against the Hoare-Laval plan and might have been expected to attack the government. Beaverbrook reported to Lord Derby later (21 February 1936):

> Baldwin had given Austen to understand when the Hoare issue arose that Austen would be the next Foreign Secretary. He allowed Austen to pilot the Government barque through stormy water in the House in the belief that he was about to take office.

Austen Chamberlain defended the government. But he did not receive his reward. Eden became foreign secretary.[2]

Beaverbrook gave Hoare what consolation he could. He saw Hoare on 21 December and again on 22 December, when Hoare showed him a letter from Baldwin promising to bring him back into the government. Hoare then returned to Switzerland. Beaverbrook also sent Vansittart a letter of encouragement which has not survived in his papers. Vansittart, acknowledging it, wrote on 20 December 1935:

> You have been the soul of kindness throughout this trouble—when so many others have failed—and I most truly appreciate it, and shall not forget it. You know what my aims have been, and I have followed them disregarding the cost to myself. I shall not desist from them myself; but there are many who want to stop me. But I shall remember what you say, and stick it as long as it is made possible.

Beaverbrook loyally defended his two friends publicly in The Daily Express. On 20 December his paper asserted:

> The Peace plan was sound and should have been pressed as a basis for negotiation.
> The Government should never have given way and never allowed Sir Samuel Hoare to be sacrificed.

[1] Vansittart, The Mist Procession, 542.
[2] Hoare's story is in Nine Troubled Years, 163–200. Beaverbrook wrote a short account of the affair in 1960.

Mr. Baldwin must go.

The rest of the Cabinet who are tarred with the same brush should follow him, and make way for men who know how to make wise decisions and abide firmly by their acts.

The article went on to observe that Eden had been closely associated with the plan and yet had gained high office because of its rejection. Eden's fixed idea was the League of Nations, "But in the recent crisis he also showed himself to be a man without sufficient resolution to adhere to his fixed idea".

Hoare displayed little loyalty in return. Beaverbrook was also in Switzerland for Christmas. Hoare wrote to him on 25 December 1935:

If I come and lunch with you, it will be in every paper and my former colleagues will see the red light. As we neither of us have any wish to excite suspicions, I feel sure that it would be wise not to run this risk.

Beaverbrook acquiesced. He replied on 27 December:

It would be a mistake for you to come near me at the present moment. And I am quite convinced that I should not go to see you.

Of course it was no great loss: Hoare was not a gay companion. From afar, Beaverbrook continued to sustain him. On 15 January 1936 Beaverbrook advised Hoare to seize the first chance of supporting the government—perhaps over the oil sanction, perhaps over some Indian issue. Beaverbrook concluded:

You have the best political judgment of any man in public life today. It is true that you were mistaken in public opinion over the Abyssinian war. But no one supposed you would be assassinated on that account. Baldwin might have been assassinated by Bonar Law over his mistake in making the American Debt Settlement.

Hoare took Beaverbrook's advice. Indeed he carried it too far. He returned to London and championed the government in a debate on defence. This was too blatant a bid. Inskip, not Hoare, became minister for the coordination of defence. But Hoare did not have to wait long. On 5 June 1936 he became first lord of the admiralty. Beaverbrook's account of the affair ends with this comment:

Hoare, like Juliet, had taken a potion to simulate the effects of death. But, unlike Juliet, he did not waken to find that his simulation had been too successful and that he had lost his reward.

The Hoare affair was characteristic of Beaverbrook. Though he did not wholly agree with Hoare and Vansittart—for instance in their desire to resuscitate the Stresa front—he sustained them as soon as they ran into trouble. He even advised Hoare how to get back into office when he would have preferred that Hoare should go into opposition. Friendship came ahead of policy, as often happened with Beaverbrook. Not that he was altogether dissatisfied with the political outcome. He wrote to J. J. Berger on 15 January 1936:

> I predict that there will be no oil sanction. The French will not have it. ... Oil sanctions or no oil sanctions, there will be no war between Britain and Italy.

On the other hand, Baldwin had not been dislodged. Beaverbrook wrote to Paul Block on 4 February 1936:

> The Government suffered a serious blow over the Hoare-Laval agreement. They were humiliated as few Governments have been in history.
> But is the damage to their prestige of a permanent character? ...
> It seems that the Government is so strong, it cannot even commit suicide.

Beaverbrook's final comments on the Abyssinian affair were made in June 1936 when Italy had conquered Abyssinia and the emperor was an exile in England. Beaverbrook wrote to W. H. Dennis of Halifax on 13 June 1936:

> There have been two victims: (1) The Emperor of Abyssinia. He was sacrificed by Baldwin to the Italians. (2) Sir Samuel Hoare. He was sacrificed by Baldwin to the anti-Italians. Now Hoare is back in the Cabinet. ... The other victim is not back on the throne. Baldwin cannot salve more than one half of his conscience. But he need not suffer too severely on account of the emperor. That black potentate lives in great comfort. He has a fine house here. He has plenty of gold in the Bank. And he spends his days agreeably acknowledging the curtseys of the ladies of the League of Nations Union.

Beaverbrook welcomed the abandonment of sanctions as a victory for isolationism. He even brought himself to urge support for the government in a backhanded way (Daily Express, 22 June 1936):

> Don't be put off just now on account of Mr. Baldwin's speeches.
> When he asked us on Saturday to be patient with Mr. Eden he was only intending to shift the blame for our misfortunes during the past six months.
> He is like the general manager of a business that goes wrong asking the angry shareholders to forgive the office boy for the collapse of the concern.
> Pay no attention to these futile explanations.

Beaverbrook had never attached much importance to the Abyssinian affair. He rightly divined that this was an exercise in moral principle, not in power, so far as British policy was concerned, and it had the admirable outcome, in his view, that it killed the League of Nations. His real cause of anxiety still lay in British commitments to France under the treaty of Locarno. He continued to think that these would not lead to war. When it came to the crunch, British opinion and policy would back away—as indeed happened. His letter to Paul Block on 4 February 1936 continued:

In international affairs the new development seems to be the big part Russia is playing in the world. The Russians have become very respectable. They wear high hats at the funeral of King George V, and they please the high Tory newspapers.

The truth is, that if we are to continue to take part in the European game we need Russia. We are united by fear of Germany.

Beaverbrook did not share this fear. He wrote to E. R. Wood on 7 February 1936: "I predict that there will be no war. For one thing, Germany is not ready. And it is not certain that she will fight when she is ready". Beaverbrook looked forward to an alliance with America, "If there is a threat to the United States in the Pacific resulting in a deal between the United States and ourselves by which the British fleet gives protection to their Atlantic seaboard, leaving them free to concentrate their warships in the Pacific". This dream did not come true until the changed circumstances of December 1941.

The shadow of war with Germany however was raised almost at once. On 7 March 1936 German forces occupied the demilitarized Rhineland. The obligations of Locarno were invoked. Beaverbrook retained his confidence. He telegraphed to J. J. Berger on 9 March 1936:

No war and no sanctions against Germany but turbulent interval of international politics.

So it proved. The British government refused to act against Germany. Instead they offered to France a guarantee for the future. Beaverbrook resumed his journalistic opposition. On 15 March he pointed out in The Sunday Express that his criticism of Locarno had been justified by events. Now the government were repeating the same mistake or worse:

The bond to fight for France which we gave at Locarno was bad, but the new bond would be worse. It would simply postpone the day of payment.

And it would do so by engaging us to fight for France in years to come against a Germany which will have strengthened her position in the Rhineland enormously.

A week later he repeated his warnings in stronger terms:

If we make this alliance, we must fight to maintain the integrity of Czechoslovakia, an ally of France, an ally of Russia, a country with a German population of over three millions.

We must fight for Poland if the Polish corridor, which the Germans regard as an intolerable grievance, becomes the cause of war. For why? Because Poland is allied to France.

. . . .

If we make this alliance we commit ourselves to a war—a war near or remote, but nevertheless inevitable.

Beaverbrook spent the early part of April in Cannes. On 8 April 1936 Brendan Bracken telegraphed to him:

> Mr. Baldwin's political life is passing unpeacefully to its close.

Beaverbrook replied:

> I have ordered my top hat with mourning coat & black gloves. So please see I am not disappointed.

Beaverbrook also attempted to speed up this happy event. On 21 April he speculated in The Daily Express as to who could overthrow Baldwin as Law had overthrown Lloyd George in 1922. Hoare could do it, but he had refused "to carry out the frontal attack on his old leader and former colleagues". Austen Chamberlain could do it, but "as he associates himself with the present foreign policy of the Government, it is fairly obvious that he is not the leader who will strike down the men who have made such grievous errors". There remained that old white hope, Sir Robert Horne. But "he has turned away from responsibility again and again. He has retired from the field over and over even when he knew that victory was perched upon his banners". Surely there was a saviour somewhere, when men holding high positions "seem determined to play the game of Idiot's Delight once more".

Beaverbrook himself could not give a lead. Early in the year he was stricken with asthma and never shook it off. He wrote to Viscount Chaplin on 25 March 1936: "I never had it in my life before. And it is as difficult to get rid of as the treaty of Locarno". Beaverbrook's trouble was no doubt psychological in origin, but its outbreak at this moment remains difficult to explain.[1] Perhaps he was worn down by his prolonged period of excitement, both in journalism and politics. Perhaps it was a reaction from success. He had got Protection. The economy was prospering again. The League of Nations was dead, and Locarno had followed it to the grave. The newspaper war ended in 1936, and The Daily Express alone held its circulation at well over two million, far ahead of its rivals. Boredom was always Beaverbrook's deadliest enemy. He suffered from it now. His journalistic writing dwindled. His outlook can be followed only in his private letters. He wrote to J. M. Patterson on 8 August 1936:

> We have no foreign policy. . . . Mr. Duff Cooper wants to make an alliance with France. . . . But the trouble is that the pro-French lot are neutralized by a pro-German party. There are many important personages in this sect. The most important being the editor of The Times newspaper.
>
> The strange thing is that both these groups are actuated by the same motive. They are both afraid of Germany.
>
> . . . .

[1] Later he alleged that he contracted it by speaking on a wet night during the East Fife election. This does not seem to be the case.

Neville Chamberlain will probably be the new Prime Minister. He lives on an inflated version of his Father's reputation, or a diluted measure of his Father's policy.

He has not Baldwin's talent for hypocrisy. This will be a weakness in the leader of a "National Government", who must satisfy the Tories by pretending that by adopting half their policy he is adopting the whole; and at the same time placate the Liberals by pretending that half a Tory policy is not a Tory policy at all.

Isolation has made considerable progress with the public. I suppose that seventy per cent are with us. We still have no strength among the politicians. But that will come.

On 14 August 1936 Beaverbrook wrote to Patterson again:

I do not believe that war is at hand. I do not think that Germany means to fight at the present time at all. I believe that Germany is intent upon assembling all Germans under the Reich banner. My view is that this purpose will be accomplished without resorting to war.

Later on, the Germans may fight. But Europe has had a bellyful of wars, and European dictators will not readily engage in military operations. The outlook is too uncertain. And the results of victory are too small. The French have discovered that victory does not perch for long on the boughs of their trees.

Here was the old mixture of wisdom and error: a correct realization that Germany would establish her domination over eastern Europe without war and a failure, common to men of all outlooks, to foresee that France herself might be totally defeated.

On 8 September 1936 Beaverbrook sent a cheerful survey to F. Odlum:

The feeling between the employers and the Trade Unions is excellent. It is quite natural that this should be so because the Unions are just as much a pillar of capitalist society as the masters are.

... When everybody is arming, war is not necessarily brought nearer. Relative strengths remain much the same as before. War remains just as great a gamble as ever.

. . . .

There is another reason for confidence—one great mischief-making agency has been put out of action. The League of Nations counts for little or nothing now.

On 18 September 1936 Beaverbrook risked an even wider prophecy. He wrote to James V. Rank:

I still hold to the view that the French are strong enough by land and sea to beat the Germans in a war in Europe. I do not believe the Germans can be ready for battle in a great many years. Besides, if they do try to fight now, the Russians will be on top of them and certainly the French and the Russians together can beat the Germans.

Pitt, writing once to Lord Liverpool[1] about the conquest of the St. Lawrence and Wolfe's victory at the Plains of Abraham, described the French as a "too much dreaded and altogether over-valued nation". That is what I think about the Germans. I do not think there will be any war in Europe for many years.

This letter will condemn me if I happen to be wrong in my prophecy.

It would be entirely wrong to conclude from this that Beaverbrook trusted Hitler or was in any sense pro-Fascist. When Lloyd George visited Hitler and sang praises of the Nazi system in The Daily Express, Beaverbrook wrote to him on 6 October 1936:

I have been very interested in your German experiences, and the viewpoints that you brought back from that country. I went there too. But I hated so much the regimentation of opinion that I could not bear it.

On home affairs, Beaverbrook added:

I think Baldwin will retire soon. And when Chamberlain comes to form his Government he will demote Duff Cooper, who has been a dreadful failure at the War Office. He made a muddle of his recruiting for the Army.

. . .

Hoare will, I suppose, be Chancellor of the Exchequer. And that man has some of Baldwin's qualities and defects. He will not forget his enemies.

These personal prophecies also were not fulfilled.

Like many British people, Beaverbrook refused to take sides in the Spanish civil war. He wrote to E. H. Dennis on 27 October 1936:

It is a mistake to regard the struggle between Fascism and Communism as the only thing of importance in the European situation. . . . For one thing there is no united Fascist front in Europe. . . . For another, the Fascist and Communist faiths are not in reality violently opposed to one another. They have the same origin—in Socialism. And they have the same characteristics of dictatorship, regimentation and militarism.

. . . Sir Oswald Mosley, the Fascist leader is a man of character and ability. . . . I have a respect for him, but none whatever for his policy. And I am convinced that the path he has taken can never lead him anywhere.

Beaverbrook passed two other judgements on individuals. On 5 November 1936 he telegraphed to J. M. Patterson: "Roosevelt appears to me the foremost figure thrown up in many generations perhaps in countless years". And to Maisky, the Soviet ambassador, he wrote on 12 November: "I have a high regard and esteem for yourself. . . . As to your leader [Stalin], I admire and praise his conduct of government".

Beaverbrook believed that, with the virtual repudiation of Locarno, the crisis was over and the danger of war removed. The French system

[1] This should be the duke of Newcastle. What ghost inspired it? Maurice Woods would not have made this mistake.

had collapsed. Germany was free to revise the settlement of eastern Europe. There would be no war. He wrote triumphantly in The Daily Express on 6 November 1936:

> The whole responsibility for our mistaken concern with French and German affairs rests on the shoulders of the financiers in the City.
> ... These banking interests led us into collective security and all that sort of thing. Their projects have come to ruin. Their plans have been frustrated. And their plots have been exposed.
> The path is clear now. Collective security has been smashed and broken. Locarno is at an end. All our engagements in Europe have come to nothing. And the commitments that involved us so deeply have passed away.

He called for some younger man who would lead Great Britain into the promised land of Isolation and Empire Free Trade. For himself, he was finished. On 14 November 1936 he sailed in the Bremen for New York. He announced in The Daily Express that he would soon be ten thousand miles away:

> I am going away. I am going away for a long time .. back again to see once more the forests and rivers of New Brunswick, colonized by our Scottish ancestors.

He wrote of his asthma. He looked forward to an even greater circulation for The Daily Express. But it would be the work of others. Beaverbrook imagined that his own public life was over. He was leaving England for many months. There was no task remaining for him to perform.

13

CHAPTER FIFTEEN

ON THE WAY TO RETIREMENT, 1936-39

Beaverbrook's expectation of a prolonged absence from England was not fulfilled. No sooner had he arrived in New York than he turned round and went back again at the urgent request of King Edward VIII. This was certainly a new departure. Beaverbrook was by no means a king's man. He did not move in court circles. He had never been invited to Buckingham Palace. He had a slight acquaintance with the prince of Wales, whom he had once entertained at Stornoway House, but the prince was little more to him than a friend of Michael Wardell's. When George V died, Beaverbrook felt a faint twinge of romance at the prospect of a glamorous and fairly young king. He struggled into his privy councillor's uniform, which he had worn only once before, and attended the accession council of Edward VIII at St. James's Palace. Thereafter Beaverbrook saw the king no more and did not give him another thought.

Of course Beaverbrook knew of the king's friendship with Mrs. Wallis Simpson, an American lady now married to an Englishman and living in London. He knew the stories circulating in the American press about the king and Mrs. Simpson. These stories were kept out of British newspapers, without any sort of instruction from above or agreement between the proprietors. In the autumn of 1936 Mrs. Simpson sought a divorce, and her case was set down at the Ipswich assizes for 27 October. The editor of The Evening Standard enquired of Beaverbrook whether he should publish this piece of news. Beaverbrook, who believed that suppression usually caused more scandal than it avoided, said: Publish. However he obviously had some doubt and therefore spoke to Goddard, Mrs. Simpson's solicitor, who was an old friend of his. Goddard sought privacy for his client. Beaverbrook refused. At this the king telephoned and asked Beaverbrook to come to Buckingham Palace. Beaverbrook, having first satisfied himself from Mr. Simpson that the divorce case was genuine, went to the king on 16 October. The king explained that Mrs. Simpson was distressed at the prospect of publicity which would be due only to her friendship with himself, and that he felt a duty to protect her. Beaverbrook agreed to use his influence with the press. He saw Esmond

Harmsworth[1] and Sir Walter Layton.[2] He wrote to newspaper friends in Dublin and Paris. As the result, Mrs. Simpson's divorce received only brief, formal reports and went through almost unnoticed by the public. The king had given no hint that he intended to marry Mrs. Simpson. Goddard declared that he had no such intention. Beaverbrook repeated this assurance to the newspaper proprietors. "And I believed it." He wrote to Jean Prouvost: "The sole purpose of the application to you is to escape, as far as possible, the publication of unjustifiable gossip concerning the King".

Edward expressed a wish to see Beaverbrook again, but was dilatory in fixing another meeting. Beaverbrook assumed that he would be asked to influence the American press. He sailed for New York on 14 November without seeing the king again and was relieved to have escaped a task "both tedious and difficult, and quite likely to end in failure". The king pursued him with telegrams and, on his arrival at New York, with telephone calls. Beaverbrook now learnt, presumably from Wardell, that the king intended to marry Mrs. Simpson. He was told that his advice was needed on wider issues than the handling of the press. Castlerosse, who was with Beaverbrook, said: "Go on to Arizona. He's not worth it". But Beaverbrook could not resist the king's appeals. Announcing that the Atlantic crossing had been good for his asthma and that he wished to repeat it, he returned to England on the Bremen.

Beaverbrook himself wrote the story of the part he played in "the King's Affair",[3] and it is unnecessary to repeat his detailed narrative. In truth there was little he could do. The battle had already been lost before he arrived back in London. As Beaverbrook realized, the king was in a strong position so long as he remained silent. It took six months in those days for a divorce decree to become absolute, and it would have been embarrassing, if not impossible, for Baldwin or anyone else to ask about the king's intentions in some remote future. But Edward VIII could not wait. He was captivated by the idea of a morganatic marriage, with Mrs. Simpson becoming his wife without becoming queen, and pressed this idea on the government. By so doing, he put himself at Baldwin's mercy. The government had only to reply that a morganatic marriage was impossible, and the king must either abandon Mrs. Simpson, which he was determined not to do, or abdicate.

Beaverbrook at his first meeting with the king advised him to withdraw the plan for a morganatic marriage at once. The king appeared to be convinced, but later in the evening telephoned Beaverbrook that Mrs. Simpson preferred the morganatic marriage to any other solution and

[1] Then in charge of The Daily Mail.
[2] Director of The News Chronicle.
[3] The Abdication of King Edward VIII (1966).

that therefore he intended to go on with it. Beaverbrook then tried another tack. He persuaded Mrs. Simpson to leave England for the south of France, and from there she announced her willingness to withdraw from the marriage. Edward VIII refused to be shaken. He resolved to abdicate, and when Churchill wished to continue the struggle, Beaverbrook said to him: "Our cock won't fight". Though Beaverbrook allowed his newspapers to campaign for the morganatic marriage until the last moment, he knew there was no chance. The king refused to see him, and he himself washed his hands of the affair.

As so often happened with Beaverbrook, his activities were given an unfavourable interpretation by his enemies and even by some who claimed to be his friends. He was supposed to have intervened in order to overthrow Baldwin or to demonstrate his powers as an intriguer. But Beaverbrook tried to keep out of the affair while he was in England and ran away from it to New York. He returned solely because the king implored him to do so. He could never resist an appeal from someone in trouble, and he aided the king in 1936, just as he had stood by Hoare and Vansittart in the previous year and was to restore Churchill's flagging spirits the year after. Beaverbrook did not need to agree with those whom he aided. In the king's case, there was a measure of agreement. Beaverbrook had a deep hostility, part Presbyterian part Radical, against those who regarded marriage as a sacrament or saw something sinful in divorce. Also, though caring little for the monarchy himself, he feared that a dispute involving the king might weaken the Empire.

Of course the tactics of the affair fascinated Beaverbrook. Despite his combative talk, he was always a fixer when it came to the point, and what he wanted now was not a knock-out blow inflicted on Baldwin, but a compromise: the king secure on his throne and the question of marriage with Mrs. Simpson postponed to a time when men had got used to the idea—or the king had lost interest. If Beaverbrook's advice had been followed there would have been no crisis: no abdication and also no threat to Baldwin's position. This is the decisive answer to those who see in Beaverbrook a calculating and unscrupulous schemer. The accusations against him rest on little more than late-night gossip by Randolph Churchill, not the most reliable of authorities. Beaverbrook was for Edward VIII a foul-weather friend, as he had been for many others including the first earl of Birkenhead.

Beaverbrook left some contemporary statements of his views on the affair, which are at any rate better evidence than speculations made later. While the crisis raged, he wrote three letters to friends overseas. The first was to Roy Howard in New York on 8 December 1936:

> The opposition to the King's project of marriage to Mrs. Simpson i essentially religious in character. He is lay head of the Church of England

and the chief priests and the Sanhedrin say, in effect, that he may live in sin with her, but must not marry a woman who has been married twice before.

Now, of course everybody does not take that view. The divorced and the free thinkers, for example, might be expected to line up on the King's side. But the trouble about these two elements is this—the divorced are all hard at work trying to become respectable. And the free thinkers don't care much about the monarchy anyway.

. . . .

But there is a large body of opinion in the country—respectable opinion—which believes that this King has built up for himself a position with the people, that gives strength and stability to the whole political structure. This sort of opinion does not much like the marriage with Mrs. Simpson, but it is willing to make concessions in order to keep the King.

On 11 December, to Howard Robinson in New Brunswick, when the abdication had taken place:

I am numbered among those, who hoped for another solution. For abdication is a very grave course. While it may close one set of problems, it opens another. For instance, it is an object lesson in the quick disposal of a monarch, who got at cross purposes with the executive. And later on, other and different executives may profit by the lesson. For the fact is, that much of the stability of the throne is derived from the fact that it has been stable.

Then the departing King must necessarily carry with him some measure of public sympathy. This may well grow, as time passes. It will be felt by many that he has been a martyr to his principles. That he has made a sacrifice in acting according to his lights.

And the effect of this may well be that the new King will not be able to command to a complete degree the loyalty and devotion of his people.

There is another point. With the existing King we knew where we were. We knew his defects and limitations. But with a new King we have to start all over again. And maybe we will find ourselves up against a new lot of defects of a different kind.

These were some of the motives which actuated me in urging reflection and calm on the public, and a reasoned consideration of the morganatic marriage project.

. . . . Anyhow it all belongs to the past now. We have our new King, and we must make the best of him.

Finally to R. D. Elliott on 15 December 1936:

I believe that King Edward need never have gone. I took—and still hold—the view that if he had had sympathetic handling from the Government, coupled with a strong determination to delay the issue by every possible means, we stood a good chance of avoiding a marriage fatal to his position on the Throne. . . . As things turned out, the publicity broke in the press, and when that occurred the situation changed. It was no longer probable that a decision could be avoided, and the Government evidently took the view that the sooner the thing was settled, the better. . . .

The King's case was not well handled. And, indeed, it seemed that he was often undecided and wavering in his attitude.

Beaverbrook's apprehensions turned out to be unfounded, as he himself admitted twenty years later in his account of the affair. He wrote in the preface: "During the reign of George VI, the monarchy withstood the blow". Still, they were reasonable apprehensions to feel at the time. They were not Beaverbrook's only motives. He was fond of saying: "I never had so much fun in my life", and this explanation, too, had a good deal of truth in it. With Beaverbrook, love of fun and excitement was never far from the surface. During the affair, Beaverbrook and Churchill were drawn closer, though they acted from rather different impulses. Churchill's attachment to the king was more personal and romantic, and his hostility towards Baldwin was at any rate a good deal more open. Some years later, Churchill and Beaverbrook recalled the many conflicts they had waged against each other. Churchill said one or other had certainly been right or wrong, as they had always differed. Except once, said Beaverbrook, mentioning the abdication. Churchill replied: "Perhaps we were both wrong that time".

Beaverbrook made a couple of political comments while he was in England. On 11 December 1936 he wrote to Guy Ross, who had urged that Churchill, like Lloyd George, should meet Hitler:

> With Churchill, the man's whole political faith—as he sees it—is bound up in running the anti-German line coupled with a demand for more arms. He has had some success with this already. Indeed he has emerged as the leader of a big armaments, anti-German movement in politics, hostile to the Government, which is believed to be in fact sympathetic to Germany, or at any rate willing to pay her something as good conduct money.

And his letter of 8 December to Roy Howard continued:

> With the strengthening of Britain, the big developments that are going on in the French Air Force and Navy, and with the emergence of Russia as a military power of immense importance it looks as if we might have peace in Europe. For nobody is going to strike until he is sure of swift and over-whelming victory. And who can count on that today?

Edward VIII's appeal caused only a short interruption in Beaverbrook's plans for leaving England. As soon as the abdication crisis was over, he set off once more for New York. He did not visit the New Brunswick home of his Scottish forebears and had probably never intended to do so. He bought a Lockheed airplane and flew to Arizona where the dry air was supposed to be good for his asthma. It proved altogether too dry. Beaverbrook ran into continual duststorms and took refuge at Miami. This was the beginning of a new pattern in his life. Previously his foreign holidays, apart from business trips to Canada, had been occasional weeks in Paris and even more occasional weeks in an hotel at Cannes. Now he discovered the pleasures of spending the winter months in a warm climate and swimming in a warm sea. He soon came to believe that this was the only way of holding his asthma in check. He returned to Miami in the two succeeding winters. As a nearer refuge, he also bought La Cappocina, a house at Cap d'Ail near Monte Carlo, from Captain Molyneux, the dress designer, though it was not ready for his occupancy before the second world war. That war interrupted Beaverbrook's plans for leaving England during the winter. After it he never spent a winter in England until forced to do so by illness at the end of his life.

Beaverbrook soon broke his resolution of not returning to England for many months. The coronation of George VI on 12 May 1937 gave him a convenient excuse, and Baldwin's impending retirement perhaps a more serious one. Not that he had political ambitions or even interests. When A. J. Cummings reported a rumour that Neville Chamberlain would make him colonial secretary, he replied (27 March 1937): "Lord Beaverbrook is done with governments. He will never be in any governments any more". His attitude to the coronation was equally detached. He wrote to William Mathews in Arizona on 15 May 1937:

We are now going to lose Mr. Baldwin from the Premiership. In the Coronation procession on Wednesday he had a great reception from the crowds. He had been given a closed carriage to ride in, but he leaned out of the window and generally conducted himself so as to win the public applause. And this he got in immense measure.

. . . .

Mr. Baldwin will go to the House of Lords. Mr. Ramsay MacDonald who is also leaving us will not go there fortunately. I use the word "fortunately" on purpose. For Mr. MacDonald was responsible for the seating arrangements in Westminster Abbey for the Coronation service. And there is furious indignation among the peerage about the poor seats they were given. But Mr. MacDonald and Mr. Baldwin had just about the best seats in the house. And so, if he went to the Lords, he would get a hot reception there!

There are seven hundred and forty seven peers, and seven hundred and forty six of them were at the Abbey on Wednesday. One was absent. It was your friend.

Baldwin's retirement gave Beaverbrook opportunity for the only political article which he wrote in 1937. Entitled Mr. Baldwin is Always Right, it appeared in The Daily Express on 29 May 1937, and Beaverbrook intended to use it again as the tail-piece for his Age of Baldwin which was never written. It begins:

Mr. Baldwin makes his bow. He takes farewell of the political stage. Let the audience not stint its applause. This has been a remarkable performance.

The turn has lasted for just fourteen years. . . . And in those fourteen years the chief actor has given us our money's worth—not in statesmanship, not in solid gain to the public welfare, but in variety, in interest and bewilderment.

Beaverbrook then recounted Baldwin's changes of policy:

In 1923, before his Premiership, Mr. Baldwin made the American Debt Settlement. In 1934, before his last Premiership, he repudiated that Settlement.

In 1925 he put this country on the Gold Standard. In the autumn of 1931 he took it off the Gold Standard.

. . . In 1930 he boasted that there would never be food taxes in the country so long as he was leader of the Conservative Party. Two years later he voted in the House of Commons to impose those taxes. He was still leader of the Conservative Party.

Was Mr. Baldwin wrong in making the Debt Settlement and wrong in returning to the Gold Standard? Were his later reversals of policy admissions of error? That is not what Mr. Baldwin would claim. For the biggest paradox about Mr. Baldwin is that he claims to be right when he does a thing, and claims also to be right when he undoes it. The truth is that Mr. Baldwin is always right when he contradicts himself.

. . . .

Mr. Baldwin, who had championed the black warriors of Abyssinia against Mussolini, did nothing to champion the white militiamen of Spain against that same Mussolini.

. . . .

In April 1935 his government made a solemn declaration, along with the French and the Italians, against German rearmament in defiance of the Treaty of Versailles. But in June of that same year Mr. Baldwin made a naval treaty with Germany in defiance of the Treaty of Versailles.

. . . .

What will the historian make of a record as baffling as Mr. Baldwin's? He will look for a man embarrassed by the inconsistencies of his policy and the contradiction of his statements. But he will not find that man. For Mr. Baldwin has been, all through, remarkable for the calm sense of rectitude with which he has pursued its opposite. The Flying Scotsman is no less splendid a sight when it travels north to Edinburgh than when it travels south to London. Mr. Baldwin denouncing sanctions was as dignified as Mr. Baldwin imposing them.

At times it seemed that there were two Mr. Baldwins on the stage, a prudent Mr. Baldwin, who scented the danger in foolish projects, and a reckless Mr. Baldwin, who plunged into them head down, eyes shut.

But there was, in fact, only one Mr. Baldwin, a well-meaning man of indifferent judgement, who, whether he did right or wrong, was always sustained by a belief that he was acting for the best.

This verdict does not leave much room for improvement.

Beaverbrook now ceased to concern himself with politics or to worry about foreign affairs. He believed that the corner had been turned. In this he was not alone. On 15 September 1937 a contributor wrote in The Evening Standard: "I declare my belief that a major war is not imminent, and I still believe there is a good chance of no major war taking place in our time". This cannot be dismissed as the work of a Beaverbrook journalist, faithfully echoing his master's voice. The writer was in fact Winston Churchill. Nowadays it is too easily believed that there was a steady slide towards war from 1931 to 1939. This is not so. There were two quite distinct periods of tension. In the first Germany shook off the restraints of the so-called Versailles system. The fear then was that France might attack Germany in order to uphold the system, not that Germany might attack France in order to overthrow it. That period ended when Germany reoccupied the demilitarized Rhineland without war. There was then a calm stretch when it was supposed that a new balance of power was coming into existence. Fresh alarms arose when Germany began to exploit the freedom she had won in eastern Europe—or when it was feared that she would do so. This was not until the summer of 1938 or perhaps even the spring of 1939.

There was as yet no irremediable breach with the dictators. Churchill himself praised them in The Evening Standard. Thus he wrote of Hitler on 17 September 1937: "If our country were defeated, I hope we should find a champion as indomitable to restore our courage and lead us back to our place among the nations", and of Mussolini in October: "It would be a dangerous folly for the British people to underrate the enduring position in world history which Mussolini will hold; or the amazing qualities of courage, comprehension, self-control and perseverance which he exemplifies". Churchill felt that his own opportunity had passed, particularly with the unpopularity which followed his stand over the abdication. Meeting Beaverbrook in Paris, he said that his political career was over and that the time had come for him to retire. Beaverbrook answered: "What nonsense! A man in your position may be in the depths of despair one day and the next find himself raised to the heights and appointed Prime Minister". Beaverbrook adds: "It was only by chance that he was a member of parliament when war broke out". It was not only by chance. It was also due to the encouragement and inspiration which Beaverbrook, while disagreeing with Churchill's policies, gave to him as an individual.

With little else to fight for, Beaverbrook returned to the campaign for a greater circulation of The Daily Express. Having outstripped all rivals, he now wanted to outstrip himself. His aim was a sale of two and a half million copies which he achieved and then of three million which before the war he did not. He wrote over a dozen articles on this theme between

September 1937 and September 1939. In each article he explained that he did not run The Daily Express in order to make money—"I have plenty"—nor to further political ambitions—"I have none. I would not take office again". His sole aim was to promote the unity and security of the British Empire. The emphasis had changed from a few years previously. Tariffs and economic unity were hardly mentioned. Isolation and cooperation with the United States had taken their place. Beaverbrook also harked back to the early days when he had propounded a philosophy of material well being. Thus, on 5 November 1937:

> The Daily Express is the first newspaper to serve every class in the community, rich and poor, high and low, barbarian, Scythian, bond and free.

On 8 March 1938:

> Our policy demands for each of us social equality and equal opportunity. ... Equal educational facilities, the same opportunities, and a fair start for all together.
> And the joy of living must not be restrained, limited or confined by any measures whatsoever. The Express is allied to the group of human beings who like to have a good time.

On 6 January 1939:

> This paper adheres to the philosophy of constant advance. It believes in the necessity of progressive increases in the power to buy and to consume.

Similarly he wrote to Robertson (20 August 1937):

> The progress of the British people, must be the story of the rise of our newspaper. If it is not the story of the rise of our newspaper, then we may become big, but we will never become great.

Beaverbrook claimed to take little money from Express newspapers except for his expenses, and this was correct. His control rested on an ingenious financial structure. There were only 25,000 voting shares, most of them in his hands. He originally owned about three-quarters of the non-voting shares, some of which he passed to friends and relatives, or sold to members of the staff and on the open market. When later one of his financial editors criticized non-voting shares, Beaverbrook replied sharply: "What's wrong with non-voting shares? People don't have to buy them". The bulk of the capital, one and a half million pounds, was in 7% preference shares, which had no vote so long as they received their dividend, which they always did. Much of the profits went to "secret reserves", but of course the real backing was a millionaire proprietor, who could come to the rescue from his own resources if things went wrong. This is what Beaverbrook had done originally. He had advanced over two million pounds to his newspapers on mortgage. When he boasted that there were now no mortgages, debentures or bonds, he meant that he had got his money back.

It was sometimes said that the staffs of Beaverbrook's newspapers did not agree with his policies. This is an exaggeration. Nearly all shared his love of excitement and success. Nearly all believed in permanent boom both for the papers and the country. Nearly all were rebels in one way or another. In May 1938 Christiansen held a poll of the editorial and reporting staff on The Daily Express. There were 28 Conservatives, 10 Socialists, 2 Liberals, 5 Communists (though only one returned strictly: "I am a member of the Communist Party of Great Britain"), and 48 Independents. Christiansen reported of himself: "At the last election I was living in the City and so did not vote. I voted for Sir Ernest Petter at the Westminster by-election and for the Socialist candidate at St. John's Wood so as to help him save his deposit".

There was one curious feature in Beaverbrook's journalistic concerns at this time. All his interest was centred on The Daily Express. The Evening Standard and The Sunday Express went their own way unharassed. Their circulations were not driven remorselessly upwards. There was no war with competitors and therefore presumably no fun. Beaverbrook sometimes spoke slightingly of The Evening Standard. He wrote to Herbert Bruce on 10 March 1938: "The Daily Express is the largest, most active, and most nervous paper in the world. . . . The Evening Standard is the most sluggish, leisurely and conservative newspaper in the world". At other time he said, more truly, that The Evening Standard was the most independent of newspapers, publishing articles by men of all parties and of none. The divergence was particularly marked over foreign policy. The Daily Express was held firmly by Beaverbrook to the line of isolation and "Britain will not be involved in war". John Gordon of The Sunday Express was an oldfashioned patriot who detested Hitler and would have no truck with a soft line. Frank Owen, who edited The Evening Standard, was a passionate Radical who preached the popular front and a grand alliance against the Fascist powers. Beaverbrook occasionally tried to restrain him. There is a note made some time in June 1938:

> Frank, be careful of your attacks on Ribbentrop. If you get making attacks on Ribbentrop, you are going to disturb the immense efforts that are now being made for an accommodation with Germany.
> And we want it for the sake of our people, and we can't put any impediment in the way of it, no matter how much we may feel like doing it. . . . We have got to give over criticism of those foreign powers for the time being. It is a great misfortune, a terrible deprivation that we face but at the same time we must be big enough to do it for ourselves, by ourselves, and for the benefit of our people.

Frank Owen took no notice.

Those who condemn Beaverbrook for the slogan, "Britain will not be involved in a European war this year, or next year either", should remember that he was also the man who stood by David Low against all comers, even indeed against the combined expostulations of Neville Chamberlain, the prime minister, and Lord Halifax, the foreign secretary. The divergence between his newspapers may have been partly reinsurance. It was also that Beaverbrook could not bring himself to restrain a hard-hitting journalist, except of course over the Empire, when it came to the point. Nor did Beaverbrook follow as simple a line as was later alleged. His dislike of the dictators was second only to his dislike of war. His insistence on the need for armaments was as strong as his insistence on isolation. Paradoxically this demand for armaments actually served to discredit Beaverbrook. During the Czech crisis of 1938, for example, his newspapers were by no means alone in supporting Chamberlain's policy of appeasement, and at the end every national newspaper except Reynolds News agreed that the Munich settlement was better than war. Yet Beaverbrook was more condemned than any other press leader except possibly Geoffrey Dawson of The Times. It was felt, quite wrongly, that there was something peculiarly perverse in advocating great armaments and at the same time rejecting all European commitments, and Beaverbrook was represented almost as a bully who ran away when it came to the crunch. In fact of course armaments and isolation were logical companions.

Beaverbrook kept a sharp eye on his newspapers even when he was out of England. Quentin Reynolds met him in Miami in the early days of 1938 and heard some rather distorted fragments of his autobiography. "I was selling papers when I was six and now I'm sixty I'm still selling them. . . . I acquired the Express solely in order to back Bonar Law". Then, looking at the latest Daily Express: "Two turn-overs today, that's bad. If there were three, I'd be on the phone to London. If there were four I'd be on my way home". Beaverbrook sang to Reynolds his usual song of peace:

> Talk of a major war is absurd. We won't have one for a long time. Germany isn't ready for a war. France is a pacifist country. Russia can't afford a war. Italy can't stand up a month against any first-rate army or navy. . . . No, there won't be a war.

Beaverbrook returned to England early in March 1938 when Eden had resigned as foreign secretary and Hitler was on the point of taking over Austria. Beaverbrook wrote to Governor Cox in Ohio on 7 March 1938:

> Eden decided to get out of the Foreign Office. He got out because he could not get on. All the harvest he could reap from that field had been gathered in. . . .

The great new factor in British politics is the rise of Chamberlain. He has become very active at the age of 69. He is doing more work than any Prime Minister in our time, and has become very strong and determined in his decisions. . . . His decisions are honest, and his conclusions are wise.

. . . He has a bigger position than Baldwin ever had in the Government and in Parliament, though he has not got Baldwin's popularity in the country.

. . . .

If he succeeds in separating Italy from Germany—which is easy—he will be a big man. If he is triumphant in his plan for an understanding with Germany, then he can be Prime Minister for life if he wants to.

Two days later to R. B. Bennett:

Neville Chamberlain is the best P.M. we've had in half a century, excluding A.B.L. who never got a chance.

And also on 9 March to H. B. Swope:

We are now trying to reach an accommodation with Germany. That is a difficult business. Germany has not the same reasons as Italy for coming to terms, and many influences are at work here against a settlement.

There are twenty thousand German Jews in England, in the professions, pursuing research, in chemical operations, etc. These all work against such an accommodation.

The Italians use their influence to disturb relations between Britain and Germany. So do the French.

Against these embattled foes, Lady Astor stands almost alone with Lord Lothian and Geoffrey Dawson as her standard-bearers.

Lord Halifax is a considerable improvement on Eden at the Foreign Office. But I do not think that he has the respect of Hitler, who calls him "Christ's brother".

On 10 March Beaverbrook himself championed Chamberlain, or what he thought Chamberlain was doing, in The Daily Express. He remarked that a British pledge had been given to maintain the independence of Austria. When it came to the point, this pledge could not be fulfilled. "And it would have been better for Britain's reputation if it had never been given". From this, it was easy to argue against any new pledge to Czechoslovakia. "What concern is it of ours whether the Germans in Czecho-Slovakia are governed from Prague or have their home rule?" Beaverbrook went on to dismiss the idea of war with Germany:

Let no one be deceived. Germany is not as strong as Britain.

The Germans are not likely to make war on us. They have no money. They cannot feed their people from German soil. They are short of many of the raw materials which are essential to modern warfare. . . .

Even if you assume that the German Air Force is capable of delivering a blow against us, what effect would that have if the air attack was not backed up by military and naval strength?

. . . .

Although the modern airplane is a terrible and terrifying weapon, modern wars are not short. That is the lesson of Spain and China.

Beaverbrook then urged that Great Britain should reach a friendly agreement with Germany over her former colonies, to which, as mandates, he attached no value. The article concluded:

The Isolation which we favour is friendly and generous and considerate towards all. It is not an Isolation of bitter gestures and snarling words.

Beaverbrook's emphasis on German weakness seemed to be exposed two years later as a disastrous misjudgement. It was not perhaps as mistaken a judgement as that of those who thought Germany equipped for a prolonged war, and in 1940 Beaverbrook himself helped to prove that his faith in the strength of isolation was not a misjudgement at all. For as always, in his mind, armaments went along with isolation. On 13 March 1938 he asserted this side of his policy, for once in The Sunday Express. He demanded a new defence of the realm act, which would enable the government to control production as far as necessary in order to produce as many airplanes as the exigencies of the situation required:

The consequences of that decision will be very serious. The financial structure of Britain must be impaired. The balance of trade against us must be ignored. The price of living will go up and wages levels will change.

. . . .

This is a clamant and an urgent need. It imposes a duty on all of us. A readiness to make sacrifices. A willingness to bear heavy burdens for the sake of our national security.

. . . On this subject I would like to speak words so harsh, words so strong, words so vivid as to awaken our people to the need for essential sacrifices in the nation's cause.

These were hardly the words of one prepared to prophesy smooth things for the sake of increasing the circulation of his newspapers.

This article, and others like it, gave the decisive answer to those who complained that Beaverbrook ignored the cost of isolation. On the contrary he was already advocating in 1938 the emergency measures which were introduced only in the summer of 1940. Beaverbrook's critics were themselves on weak ground. They advocated collective security, in other words a British guarantee to every country in the world or at any rate in Europe, and yet most of them opposed increased expenditure on armaments. They seemed to think that collective security or alliances with European powers increased Great Britain's security rather than added to her liabilities. They were wrong. The guarantees later distributed by

Great Britain were impossible to fulfil and lured the guaranteed countries to disaster. Isolation was the more honourable course as well as the one more likely to lead to safety.

Beaverbrook constantly repeated these two points: "We must limit our liabilities in foreign affairs to the defence of our own interests" and "We must continue with increasing vigour to make Britain strong in arms". His persistent prophesy of peace had a wise proviso:

> Given this strength, I make bold to predict that there will be no European war involving this country for years to come.

A. J. Cummings wanted Beaverbrook to push Churchill into the government. Beaverbrook replied on 16 March 1938:

> Unhappily he would bring pressure upon the Government forthwith to give a guarantee to Czecho-Slovakia that we will fight in defence of that artificial nation, brought into existence by Messrs. George, Clemenceau and Wilson.
>
> And I want the soldiers to stay at home and guard the frontiers of Britain, and protect the Empire, and keep watch on our outposts.

On the other hand, when Lady Maxwell Scott urged him to support Franco, he replied on 25 March 1938:

> It is my desire to avoid intervention in Spain, but my sympathies are with the Spanish Government, because I am opposed to every form of Fascism. And I like liberty.

Beaverbrook had no doubt that a crisis was approaching over Czecho-slovakia. He wrote to Governor Cox on 28 April 1938:

> I will venture to predict that trouble over Czecho-Slovakia is on the way. We shall have it in all probability before the summer is over.
>
> . . . .
>
> The Czech Government is in retreat. They have made concessions. No doubt they will make more. But they still refuse to go the whole way, abandoning their treaties with France and Russia, and entering into the German orbit as a vassal state. . . .
>
> The French are worried about it. They never know when the Czechs may call on France to implement her treaty and march to their aid. . . .
>
> Yet I do not think the French will fight for Czecho-Slovakia. The French people don't want war. . . .
>
> And how can the French help the Czechs anyway? Just as the French frontier is protected against the Germans by the Maginot Line of fortifications, so is the German frontier protected against France by a similar line.
>
> The question then arises, will the Czechs fight for themselves? I do not think so. They will take what terms from Germany they can get and pray for

better days. No doubt they would be willing in the end to hand their Germans over to Hitler, detaching that part of the country altogether. . . .

Your friend Mr. Chamberlain has ridden cock horse to Dublin. The Irish Treaty has given him splendid credit. Added to his Italian triumph, he now appears to be a mighty man—even to his opponents. The Manchester Guardian has taken to praising him occasionally.

Beaverbrook's forecasts in regard to France and Czechoslovakia were to prove correct.

In mid-May there was an alarm that the Germans were mobilizing, and the Czechs mobilized in answer. The alarm was in fact without foundation, as Beaverbrook divined. He wrote to Dr. Cox in New Brunswick on 1 June 1938:

Some people still think we have had a narrow escape from a war. But there is not a shadow of evidence that Germany contemplated anything of the kind. And certainly Chamberlain did not. He was acting as a mediator and nothing else. . . . If he is seeking peace in Europe, he is also intent on keeping peace for Britain.

As for the succession to his throne. Hoare has the lead at present. He has something like first claim to the crown. Inskip comes next. But the position may alter before Chamberlain gives up.

On 14 June 1938 Beaverbrook gave Governor Cox a more light-hearted account of another possible challenger to Chamberlain:

Baldwin made a speech at a dinner on Friday night. . . . On arriving at the dinner, he laid on the table three pipes and a packet of American "Lucky Strike" tobacco.

In the course of his speech, he attacked Russia and declared against an alliance with that country.

He attacked Lloyd George and Churchill.

He gave an erroneous and misleading account of Chanak and the general strike.

He then attacked the "Daily Mirror" newspaper and said that journalism of this pornographic type might bring him back into public life to denounce and destroy it.

. . . .

And he said not a word of praise of Neville Chamberlain from first to last.

He never referred to America, and never touched on the Empire.

So you see we have three dangerous old men in public life instead of two. For long we have had to put up with Lloyd George and Churchill, but it was believed Baldwin was really in retirement. Not so, however. He is at it too.

If only those old men would confine their attacks to each other, we would rejoice. But rest assured they will all turn on Chamberlain one day. Two will attack openly, and one will attack with subtlety.

Baldwin, who claims to be the plain, blunt country gentleman, interested in pigs and books, will, needless to say develop the subtlety.

Eden is, of course, also in the field. He is attempting to establish himself as leader of the Left Wing of the Conservative Party, in favour of the League of Nations, and anxious to restore in Britain the old Whig policy of the Balance of Power, based on the simple expedient of backing the losing horse and making it the winning beast!

Beaverbrook made few pronouncements on foreign policy during the summer of 1938. As often happened with him, he was torn between his attachment to individual statesmen and what he himself believed. He liked Neville Chamberlain, the prime minister, as he had never liked Baldwin, and had considerable faith in Hoare, who was now one of Chamberlain's intimate advisers. At heart he did not agree with them. Chamberlain and his group hoped to avert war by actively promoting the appeasement of Germany. Beaverbrook believed that the right course was to stand aloof. For this reason he deplored the sending of Lord Runciman to Prague as a mediator, this inevitably making Great Britain a party to the dispute. He wrote after the Czech crisis was over (Daily Express, 8 October): "Chamberlain put pussy in the well. It is quite true that we owe him gratitude for pulling pussy out again. But the original mistake should never have been made".

Still Chamberlain remained in Beaverbrook's eyes better than anyone else, certainly better than those who wanted to resist Germany. When Sir Edward Grigg tried to stir Beaverbrook into opposition, he replied on 20 June 1938:

> As we have Isolation in fact, although not in name, I have not much to complain about.
> Later on, if the Government tries to change its policy, then I must try to do something.
> If you are for the Churchill policy, then of all alternatives offered to us, that is the worst.

At the beginning of September Beaverbrook came out against talk of war. He announced in The Daily Express on 1 September: "There will be no European war". He asserted that, if the Czechs failed to make concessions, France and Russia would not support them, and that, if they made concessions, Hitler would shrink from war with France and Russia. Even if Hitler himself wanted war, his generals would not allow it. Similarly he wrote on 7 September to Frank Gannett, whom he had just tipped as the next president of the United States:

> The preparations which have been going on are not, in my judgement, preparations for war, but preparations for negotiation.
> Germany is, certainly, not strong enough to take on France and Russia, as well as Czechoslovakia. Later on, it may be that she will build up her

position to the point where such an enterprise would be possible. But at present the balance of strength lies with the other side.

... Hitler's high card is not German might, but French unwillingness to risk a challenge to combat.

When the crisis deepened and Chamberlain flew to Munich, Beaverbrook urged on him and Halifax that they should strengthen their relations with the press. He wrote to Halifax on 16 September 1938:

Newspapers are all anxious to help the Prime Minister and to help you. But they are greatly in need of guidance.

A Minister should be authorized to have direct contact with the newspaper proprietors.

He was told in reply that Sir Samuel Hoare would undertake this task. As Hoare had been revealing cabinet secrets to Beaverbrook since before the abdication, this nomination cannot have surprised him.

Beaverbrook made only one short public statement during the critical fortnight. On 22 September he wrote in The Daily Express:

Britain never gave any pledge to protect the frontiers of Czechoslovakia. ... No moral obligation rests on us.

His private correspondence turned on a different subject. H. A. Gwynne, the former editor of The Morning Post now in retirement, asked him to meet Frank Buchman, leader of the Oxford Movement. Beaverbrook replied:

I do not presume to criticize the movement of which he is the founder. But, temperamentally, I find myself unattracted by it. . . .

I was brought up in the Presbyterian faith. And that faith still seems to me the creed making the strongest appeal to logical minds.

On 30 September, with the news of the agreement reached at Munich, The Daily Express printed its notorious streamer—despite popular myth to the contrary for the first and last time:[1] "Britain will not be involved in a European war this year, or next year either". The first part of the sentence was a correct statement of fact. The last four words were added by Beaverbrook himself: "We must nail our colours *high* to the mast". The streamer only expressed the general opinion of the moment, even if in a provocative way. Nearly everyone believed that peace had been secured, though many regretted the price that had been paid and looked forward gloomily to a German domination of eastern Europe.[2]

[1] The phrase "There will be no European war" sometimes appeared in a leading article but not otherwise in a headline.

[2] To indulge in autobiography, my own view after Munich was that Germany would proceed to attack Soviet Russia with either the support or the benevolent neutrality of Great Britain and France.

Beaverbrook also congratulated Chamberlain privately, writing to him on 28 September:

My dear Neville,

My faith is very great, but not so immense as my joy and delight over your reward.

Dont answer

Yours ever
Max[1]

For Chamberlain replied on 2 October 1938: "Your note gave me *great* pleasure. Thank you". As was to be expected, Beaverbrook attacked the guarantee given to the truncated Czechoslovakia. He wrote in The Daily Express on 14 October 1938:

Remember always that the British Empire is a Treasure House.

Do not ask foreigners to protect your possessions.

And do not get caught up in quarrels over foreign boundaries that do not concern you.

Beaverbrook still professed to be cheerful about the future. When James Agate argued that Great Britain was now in danger of attack by Germany, Beaverbrook replied on 5 October 1938:

Defence is much stronger than attack. If Britain is thrown on her own resources against an aggressive war by Germany, she can hold out indefinitely, providing we keep command of the seas, and equip ourselves adequately against attack from the air.

On 6 October he wrote with equal confidence to R. D. Elliott:

The Germans will not move westwards again for some time. They are deeply committed to Eastern operations. . . .

The prospects of a more effective handling of our armament programme have been improved by the resignation of Mr. Duff Cooper. He was not a satisfactory Minister.

Beaverbrook preserved in his records a reminiscence of Duff Cooper's resignation, which Wardell received from Duff Cooper himself:

Chamberlain called a Cabinet meeting on his return to England after his first meeting with Hitler. A group of ministers that included Oliver Stanley had discussed their critical attitude to Chamberlain's policy of appeasement before the meeting. They had talked of a threat of resignation. At the meeting Duff had been the articulate voice of the group, and he alone had threatened to resign.

When Chamberlain returned from Munich with "Peace in our time" his colleagues, including Duff, were unanimous in the expressions of joy and gladness. Duff stayed behind at the end of the meeting at Chamberlain's

---

[1] A copy of this handwritten letter was kindly supplied to me by the library of Birmingham University.

request. Duff was quite conciliatory and said he supposed his threat of resignation would be forgotten. Chamberlain refused, saying: "I am afraid that at this stage that is impossible". Duff was out.

Beaverbrook always held a low opinion of Duff Cooper's administrative abilities, though he did not say so in public. When one of his journalists wished to criticize Duff Cooper, Beaverbrook said to him: "Do you love your wife? Well, I love Duff Cooper's wife, so lay off him". Beaverbrook treated another member of Chamberlain's cabinet very differently. On 4 December 1938 Lady Maud Hoare wrote to him:

> We grow poorer every year & that is worrying all enjoyment of life out of Sam. . . . What is he to do? If he is not to retire at this election, he must be relieved of financial anxiety. The double burden is too heavy. If he goes, I believe it will be a great loss to the country. Do you share this view?

Beaverbrook talked to Hoare and then wrote to him on 22 November:

> My long experience in public life has given me a very brilliant picture of the misfortunes of the man who takes office.
>
> . . . .
>
> It is on this account that I send you out of a full pocket a very small sum which I would like you to put into your empty purse.
>
> And this time next year and for the rest of this Parliament and for the next Parliament, if you still cling to decide to stay in office and if I still have the necessary money, I will send you another dribble of the same size.

The dribble was £2,000. The payment was duly repeated in November 1939. Hoare also received £2,000 on 2 September 1939—presumably as a sort of bonus for his efforts to avert war.

Throughout the winter of 1938–39 Beaverbrook continued to profess in public his confidence that there would be no war. He assured American newspapers of this on 12 December 1938, so long as Great Britain followed a policy of isolation:

> If we join either side, we simply add sufficient strength to encourage our allies to go to war. For it is always from strength that war is launched.

Similarly he wrote in The Daily Express on 18 January 1939:

> Neither Germany nor Italy will invade France or seize French territory Such an enterprise would be madness. . . .
>
> Britain has nothing to fear at home or abroad, although our security depends upon increasing our strength by land and sea and in the air.

Privately Beaverbrook was not so sure, and his letters provide striking evidence how the climate of opinion was changing. He wrote to W. R Mathews on 10 November 1938:

> Churchill is not an important factor in government in Great Britain This man of brilliant talent, splendid abilities, magnificent power of speech and fine stylist has ceased to influence the British public. . . .

Our future here is not too bright. We must fight one day when, perhaps, our resources are sufficient to justify us in joining battle. But for the present we are in the same position as the United States. We have not got the war equipment necessary to meet and destroy European enemies.

"But still the heart is strong, the blood is Highland".

On 9 December 1938 he wrote to Frank Gannett:

Neville Chamberlain has lost one chance after another of holding a successful election. . . . His policy of appeasement has been killed by British increased armaments, which upset the Germans, and by German persecution of the Jews which upset everybody.

The Jews have got a big position in the press here. I estimate that one-third of the circulation of the Daily Telegraph is Jewish. The Daily Mirror may be owned by Jews. The Daily Herald is owned by Jews. And the News-Chronicle should really be the Jews Chronicle. Not because of ownership but because of sympathy.

The Times, the Daily Mail and the Express are the only papers left. And I am not sure about the Mail.

I have been, for years, a prophet of no war. But at last I am shaken. The Jews may drive us into war. I do not mean with any conscious purpose of doing so. They do not mean to do it. But unconsciously they are drawing us into war. Their political influence is moving us in that direction.

This was a deplorable letter, which shows how little Beaverbrook really understood the British people. What turned the British people against Nazi Germany was Hitler's treatment of the Jews, not propaganda by Jews or anyone else in British newspapers. The facts made the propaganda by themselves.

In any case this letter was no more than a passing aberration. Beaverbrook had no sympathy with anti-semitism. Many years later there was criticism when a Jew was appointed to a high post on one of his papers. He reacted sharply:

It would be intolerable if prejudice existed against Scots in England. And certainly much worse for that race if Canadians should object to them. And what is the difference between Scots and Jews.

It may be claimed that the prejudice is unreasoning and nothing can be said to account for it. Certainly that is true. But it is the duty of newspaper editors to refuse to be moved by any such survival of ignorance and prejudice.

Beaverbrook would have been on stronger ground in 1939 if he had argued that Hitler's tyranny had destroyed the British sense of judgement. People no longer asked: What can we do? They asked: What ought we to do? If they had been told that the price of overthrowing Hitler would be twenty-five million dead, they might have hesitated. They might even have hesitated, as some did, if they had been told that the price of destroying Germany would be Soviet domination of eastern Europe. The question of peace or war was never put on this practical basis. It was considered solely in terms of moral obligation and emotion, and Beaverbrook himself, by asserting German weakness and championing British strength, helped to make war appear relatively easy.

Beaverbrook became a little more cheerful in the new year. He wrote to R. D. Elliott on 2 January 1939:

> Neville Chamberlain suits us in foreign policy. For, of course, he is running an isolationist policy all the time. His whole purpose in foreign affairs is to isolate the Empire from the quarrels of Europe.

On 25 January he wrote to Dr. Cox:

> Hitler and Mussolini will pitch their requests just below the point where we must refuse.
> Even so, there is always the danger that the public will reject the demand, whatever it may be. There is an increasing demand to yield no more to Germany. The argument is that if we give something up, it becomes only an encouragement to further demands. . . .
> The public does not reason on this issue. And it may be swept away by feeling.

On the same day he composed a long "forecast of the days to come" for J. M. Patterson in New York:

> Germany and Italy are apparently going to put the heat on. In my view they will go no further than an intention to keep the peace will permit. But, of course, there is always the danger that the temper of the British and France may result in a resistance so violent in type that defence will become aggression.
> . . . The Germans will want a return of their colonies. There will be immense opposition in Britain. The Jews to a man and woman, the Die-hard Tories, the Labour Party and the Communists, will all be against the surrender. The importance of the Communists is, that they will hold the Labour Party up to it.
> . . . .
> Although the whole situation looks insoluble, I believe that a way out will be found. We will go through 1939 without war. As for the succeeding years, that depends on preparations in Britain and elsewhere, including the United States.
> . . . .
> I am not to be numbered among those who think that America can, or should, defend London. That is the job of the British people, and cannot be delegated to any other country.

The fortitude and endurance of this race will settle that issue. And I believe implicitly in the fortitude and endurance of the British race.

Here and now the English fear war, and show their anxieties in every direction. But that disposition is not at all inconsistent with the highest degree of sacrifice and heroism in the day of battle.

As the winter passed, Beaverbrook grew still more cheerful. He wrote to Herbert Swope on 21 February 1939:

The British people is growing in confidence about the prospects of peace. We do not see why there should be a war. And in the growing strength of our armed forces, especially in the air, we find some good reason why this should not come.

On 23 February 1939 he assured J. M. Patterson that his forecasts still stood:

There is immense confidence in the future here. We are becoming strong. The production of airplanes is very big. As a result we feel safe.

. . . .

Chamberlain sticks to appeasement. That dog will not leave that bone. . . .

In the decision to go on with appeasement, Chamberlain will carry the country with him. His Government is very strong now. . . . Indeed, if the Government decided to go to the country now, they would have a big electoral victory.

Meanwhile, I think you can discern some temporary infirmity of purpose in the policy of the totalitarian states. They do not seem to make up their minds in which direction to move. It is now east now west with them. . . .

One thing must be troubling the Dictators. Their own people do not want any more adventures, and do not want war at all, at all. They are making that quite plain. And, of course, dictators are just like other types of government. They rule within the limits which the population permits.

. . . .

If you come over here . . . you will see some reasons why nobody will feel inclined to make war on us. You will see a great many fast airplanes in the skies. And more and more uniforms in the streets.

Beaverbrook was not alone in these misjudgements. On 10 March Hoare announced that a new Golden Age was approaching. The same day Beaverbrook wrote to Herbert Bruce:

The result of a war would be just like last time. The United States will come in at the end, and win it for us in a few weeks.

. . . The recruiting speeches will be just the same too.

On 15 March 1939 a new period of crisis began. Rump Czechoslovakia fell to pieces, and Hitler turned Bohemia into a German protectorate. The high hopes of Munich were shattered. Beaverbrook of course had never shown any faith in Czechoslovakia. He wrote to E. M. Macdonnell on 15 March:

> Our Government could never have defended Czechoslovakia, and that combination of races could never have worked together, in their common defence, against Germany.
>
> The structure was bound to fall as soon as the weight of reality was imposed upon it.

The following day Beaverbrook received a long survey of the political situation from Brendan Bracken. Bracken was almost Churchill's only supporter in the house of commons and a relentless opponent of appeasement. His opinions might therefore be expected to diverge widely from Beaverbrook's. Bracken began by describing the discredit to Neville Chamberlain whom he called "the Coroner", in reference to the Ballad of Reading Gaol:

> One of the Coroner's principal colleagues declared to me to-day that a National Government was inevitable, and that an effort should be made to retain Chamberlain's services by offering him the Lord Presidency of the Council!

Bracken then turned to the general situation:

> War talk is beginning again, and will probably deepen the slump that has been with us since 1938. In my humble judgment, the fear of war is negligible if we push on with our rearmament programme and avoid internal political quarrels. My optimism is not solely based on our strength. The real hope for peace lies in the fact that the Nazi gangsters in Germany are all so conscious of their own weakness in the event of a war in which first class powers are engaged. The Nazi bosses now live on the fat of the land. If war broke out the grim German General Staff would take command, and some of the blood and thunder Nazi bosses would be drafted into the front line trenches. The leaders of the Nazi Party have an unappeasable appetite for blackmail, but I am sure that they will stop short of war.
>
> The other great hope for peace is, of course, that Germany is without any of the financial, raw material and industrial resources necessary for a nation which launches a European war. She has collected a good deal of booty in Czechoslovakia, but that country contains none of the metals necessary for a sustained conflict.

Thus Bracken, the most stalwart of Churchillians, echoed almost word for word Beaverbrook's estimate of the future. For him as for Beaverbrook, Britain would not be involved in a European war.

With appeasement thus apparently shattered, Beaverbrook once more rallied a friend in trouble. Sir Samuel Hoare recorded:

> I felt that my part in the Government was finished, and that I had better retire from public life. A sudden attack of influenza made my depression

even blacker. Beaverbrook, once again a faithful friend as in the days of the Abyssinian crisis, came to see me. He, like me, had set his heart on peace. None the less, his advice was against my leaving the Government, although he fully realized the magnitude of the change that had come over the political scene. After all, war had not started, and there was still a chance of preventing it. It might well be that when we had become militarily stronger, we should be able to resume our efforts for a peaceful settlement with a better chance of success.

I accepted his advice. . . .[1]

Beaverbrook was in fact a great deal less confident than he claimed to be. He wrote to R. H. Murray of Halifax on 21 March 1939:

Certainly we are now faced with a challenge from the Germans of a character we cannot mistake. And that challenge will have to be met sooner or later. One or the other, the British Empire or the German Reich, must be destroyed.

But I do not think that the final clash is imminent. And, in the meantime, factors may intervene making war unnecessary.

Similarly he wrote to Quentin Reynolds a month or so later, on 26 April 1939:

We believe that we are all living on a great keg of gunpowder, with some burning fuses about. And we do not know when the gunpowder will blow up.

By the time this letter was written, the situation had changed fundamentally. On 31 March the British government guaranteed Poland against German aggression. The Daily Express was almost alone among British newspapers in opposing this guarantee. Beaverbrook himself wrote: "This was a pledge that should not have been made, that could not be honoured, and which defied the bounds of practical reality when it was entered into". He was especially indignant because the guarantee had been given without consulting the Dominions. Like Churchill and Lloyd George, Beaverbrook at once appreciated that the guarantee to Poland could be made effective only by an alliance with Soviet Russia, and his papers preached this alliance strongly right up to the outbreak of war. Here was a foretaste of the line which Beaverbrook took during the war itself: the best thing for Great Britain was to keep clear of European affairs, but if she insisted on becoming involved it must be in wholehearted alliance with Soviet Russia. No more war was best of all, but in case of war Great Britain must see to it that Russia won and Germany lost.

However as the summer wore on, Beaverbrook reverted to his belief that war could be avoided. He saw much of Hoare, whom he advised on the setting up of a ministry of information, and he got a clear impression

[1] Templewood, Nine Troubled Years, 329.

that Hoare, and Chamberlain too, were still hoping to pull off a stroke of appeasement—of course at Poland's expense. We now know from the records that this was indeed the case. In 1943 Beaverbrook wrote a defence of the policy which he and his newspapers had followed before the war. He quoted a statement which Chamberlain had sent to Baxter on 12 June 1939: "Generally speaking I should say that Italy is more pacifist than Germany. But neither does Germany want to go to war unless she is obliged". Beaverbrook continued:

> The newspapers controlled by me never ceased to carry on a campaign in favour of arms. They pursued a vigorous and continuing propaganda. All of them were completely determined in their efforts to see the country made strong. . . .
> At the same time the Daily Express was declaring from time to time that there would be no war. The newspaper was invited by the Government itself to make these declarations, the purpose being to influence opinion favourably so that there might be delay and time for consideration.
> My newspapers and I supported the Government completely and entirely throughout the months of crisis that preceded the war. And I now record my belief that the course taken by me was not only in accordance with the Government's policy, but also sound and wise.

Beaverbrook sent this statement to Hoare in Madrid. Hoare replied on 15 February 1943:

> I was constantly trying to push Neville into more resolute action and, particularly, if you remember, to take you into the Government. The evil influences on the other side were too strong and, rightly or wrongly, I was not prepared to go to the point of breaking with him over it. Undoubtedly, his two worst advisers were Horace Wilson and David Margesson, both of them determined to keep everything in their own hands. . . .
> I hope you will bring out the influence of the atmosphere in which we were all working. It was an atmosphere of peace at almost any price; the peace ballot, the Labour opposition against Service estimates and con-scription, the pressure of business and industry against war. Neville was not the man to fight this opposition, for at the bottom of his heart he sym-pathized with it. Nor, I believe, would Churchill have fought it if he had not been in opposition.

There is no other evidence that Beaverbrook ever contemplated taking office under Chamberlain. Probably war itself was needed to overcome his reluctance. But no reader of The Daily Express in 1939 could doubt that war was possible, though not inevitable. Beaverbrook himself issued statements, describing the preparations being made to ensure that the papers would continue to circulate in wartime even under air attack.

Otherwise he gave little public lead. There were no more forecasts in his private correspondence. Only two scraps merit quotation. One was a personal judgement. On 13 June 1939 he wrote to Sir Warren Fisher, himself a civil servant of great eminence:

> Of all the Civil Servants in my experience, the one least suited to the job has been selected for the highest place—Sir John Anderson.

The other solves a little riddle which has puzzled historians: how did the press learn that Hudson, secretary of the department of overseas trade, had offered the Germans a loan of a thousand million pounds if they would keep the peace? Beaverbrook wrote to Rothermere on 29 July 1939:

> Strange to say Hudson was trying to place the story in various papers before publication took place. He did not seem to realize the nature of the political dynamite he was trying to throw hither and thither.

In this time of high crisis, Beaverbrook's mind was largely taken up with other things. Castlerosse was gravely ill, and Beaverbrook cared for him. Lord Ashfield forwarded to Beaverbrook a letter which Castlerosse had written to him on 27 March:

> My word tho' fate has been playing queer tricks with us. I never thought I would pull thro' & I am perfectly sure I never should have but for Max.
> I cannot tell you what he did for me, he had the room next door & sat up night & day, just fighting & battling, determined that everything possible should be done. Do you know Albert that if you have a man like that struggling for you, you cannot lie down & die. There is something about Max which makes him different from other men, when he is really set on something.

Beaverbrook was also engaged, or so he imagined, in getting rid of his newspapers. He had long spoken of himself as an old man whose active life was finished. He was obsessed with his birthdays, particularly when they marked a decade. Fifty, sixty, these struck the notes of the passing bell. His fiftieth birthday in 1929 had provoked him into supposedly handing over control of his newspapers to his sons. This arrangement was never made. On 25 May 1939 Beaverbrook was sixty. Once more he resolved to make an end. This time he proposed to sell his papers to the members of their staffs. Michael Wardell was to be chairman for seven years. The staff would buy Beaverbrook out for three million pounds, with payments spread over fifteen years. They would be entitled gradually to sell the non-voting shares to the public, though in such a way that no individual possessed more than a 7% holding.

This venture into ostensibly cooperative ownership was an appalling project. Even the initial payment of £200,000 was beyond the resources of the twenty or so journalists concerned. They would have to shoulder, as amateurs, a crushing burden of underwriting and would be remorse-lessly shackled to The Express newspapers for years to come. Nor would they enjoy any real liberty of action. It was as certain as anything could be that, whether Beaverbrook theoretically disposed of his financial control or not, every member of the staff would continue to jump at his slightest bark. Yet, such was Beaverbrook's personal ascendancy, the staff took the proposal seriously. Agreement was formally drawn up and apparently went through. On 18 July 1939 Beaverbrook wrote to his accountant, T. M. Till:

> I am now returning to Canada.
> I sail on the Empress of Britain on the fifth of August, and I shall not be back again, except as a visitor.
> I have agreed to sell my various holdings in London Express Newspaper Limited to members of the staff of that company for three million pounds.

Before leaving, Beaverbrook tried to make certain that he was no longer needed. He saw Hoare who assured him that the temperature had been lowered and that he could safely leave for Canada. Looking back, Beaverbrook lamented, "Had I been here I might have been able to strengthen the hands of Chamberlain and Hoare".[1]

His migration was a characteristically improvised affair. Beaverbrook merely walked out of Cherkley and Stornoway House as though he were off on a week's holiday. There is no indication where he proposed to live in Canada. He had left Newcastle nearly forty years before and now had few acquaintances there. He had not yet established any strong links with the University of New Brunswick at Fredericton. His visits to Canada were usually spent in hotels at Montreal and Toronto. Was he now proposing to settle in Montreal where his few friends were retired financiers? Or in some remote estate in New Brunswick? He was bored enough at Cherkley, only twenty-five miles out of London. It is difficult to believe he would have lasted a week in the home of his Scottish forebears. The fantasy could occur only in a romantic novel.

On 7 August 1939 The Daily Express published estimates of the international situation from its principal European correspondents. Ten out of twelve reported: "There will be no war this year". On 11 August The Daily Express asserted, for the eighth and last time in 1939: "Britain will not be involved in a European war". This was no longer Beaverbrook's doing. On 5 August 1939 he had duly sailed for Canada. His life as a newspaper proprietor and as a force in British politics was, he believed, over.

[1] Beaverbrook to Peter Howard, 14 May 1962.

CHAPTER SIXTEEN

THE PHONEY WAR, 1939–40

Beaverbrook arrived in Quebec on 11 August 1939. When asked about the likelihood of a European war, he replied: "I would not be here if I did believe that war was imminent". Three days later he flew to Halifax, Nova Scotia, "the most beautiful of all journeys". The Halifax newspapers treated him as a transient, though welcome, visitor, and he gave no hint that he had come "home" for good. Perhaps a week or so in Canada taught him the emptiness of this dream. Nor did he relax his control over the London newspapers which he was supposed to have sold. Each day he spoke to Robertson on the transatlantic telephone, receiving news and issuing instructions. On 23 August, with the signing of the Nazi-Soviet pact, Robertson told him that war was coming and that he should return to England. Beaverbrook grumbled: "You are bringing me back on a fool's errand".

Beaverbrook was back in England on 31 August. On the following morning he was confronted with the news that German troops had invaded Poland. Despite this, he held to his old line. Beaverbrook saw Hoare twice during the day and said to him: "Poland is no friend of ours". Hoare may well have told him of the government's plan to keep out of war by a new Munich-type conference. At any rate, Beaverbrook remained hopeful to the last. On 2 September he telegraphed to Lowell Thomas in America:

> I hope we are going to escape a European war, and in that case I am going back to America at once.

That evening the house of commons revolted and forced war on a reluctant government. At 11 a.m. on 3 September 1939 Great Britain declared war on Germany. Churchill entered the war cabinet as first lord of the admiralty. According to David Farrer, who became one of Beaverbrook's secretaries a little later, Beaverbrook advised Churchill not to join the government, but to wait for a call to supreme office when Chamberlain ran into difficulties.[1] The advice was in character, but it is difficult to see

---

[1] David Farrer, G—for God Almighty, 31.

when it was given. Beaverbrook only saw Churchill on 1 September, and at that time he still thought that war could be averted.

At all events, Churchill was in. Beaverbrook remained out. He had notoriously opposed going to war until the last moment, and his appointment to office would have been unpopular with all parties, the Conservatives perhaps even more than Labour or Liberals. Besides, what office could be offered to him? Unlike such recruits from the business world as Sir Andrew Duncan or Lord Woolton, he had no experience of routine administration, at any rate since the remote days of the Montreal Trust Company and the Colonial Bank. Maybe he secretly hoped to become minister of information again. But he was not wanted. A ministry of information had already been set up under Lord Macmillan, and its spirit was far removed from that which the ministry of the first world war had shown. The revived ministry of information was bureaucratic, cautious, and seemingly intent only on preaching a supine confidence to the British public. There was neither room nor desire for the bustling, brawling improvisations of 1918.[1]

Beaverbrook was left only with the direction of his newspapers. His scheme for selling them to the staff was never heard of again. The one thing he had to offer was his knowledge of American and Canadian opinion and his ability to influence it. He hastily invented a mission for himself or perhaps one was invented to get him out of the country. He was sent to find out what President Roosevelt really thought about the war. His discoveries, though curious, were of little significance. The real importance of his mission came later. He was a man after Roosevelt's own heart, a New Dealer by nature. He won Roosevelt's confidence and established intimate relations which were to prove invaluable. Beaverbrook had exactly the qualities of zest and unconventional resource which Roosevelt liked in those around him. As a Canadian, Beaverbrook could use American terms and yet speak for the British Empire. He became an intermediary at once independent and effective. Moreover Beaverbrook knew how to win the hearts of men and women—this was his most insidious gift. He now won the heart of F. D. Roosevelt.

Beaverbrook divined Roosevelt's enthusiasm for first editions and historical records, and thereafter played on this interest, as he cajoled other men with money or flattery. After this first visit, Beaverbrook sent Roosevelt two coloured prints: General Wolfe, and the Fashionables of Fredericton. At Christmas 1941 he sent autograph letters of Pitt and

---

[1] There was also a basic difference of purpose despite the similarity of name. The first ministry of information was solely concerned with propaganda in neutral and allied countries. The second ministry was solely concerned with opinion at home, and its activities covered genuine information, i.e. news, as well as the direct influencing of public opinion. Beaverbrook does not seem to have appreciated this.

Wolfe, the original of the poem which Kipling wrote for the opening of Cherkley,[1] and—most precious of all—the original letter of vindication which Churchill wrote to Law, at Aitken's prompting, on 21 May 1915. In 1942 there followed first editions of Browning, Tennyson, Swinburne, the Brontës, and George Borrow; in 1943 first Indian editions of Kipling. On receiving these last, Roosevelt wrote:

> After this show is over I have visions of a visit to Hollywood by Beaverbrook and Roosevelt, joint producers of Mrs. Hawksby, Mrs. Gadsby and the Brushwood Boy. We might then catch a live Viceroy to take that part. Perhaps Winston will select one!

It was not surprising that Roosevelt soon numbered "Max" among his intimates and counted on him for "the kind of real relaxation and fun which comes too rarely these days". Beaverbrook had stored up a fund of good will on which he was to draw profitably.

The report which Beaverbrook brought back in October revealed little except the strange workings of Roosevelt's mind. Beaverbrook wrote to Halifax on 4 November:

> 1. President Roosevelt has the idea of settling dispossessed populations from Central European countries, in a huge area of Central Africa (e.g. Angola).
> 2. Boundaries, in his view, do not count in this war. The issue is not and should not be, boundaries and people, but security and employment.
> 3. The U.S. does not want, while it is under his authority either Bermuda or the Bahamas.

To Roosevelt himself, Beaverbrook was naturally more forthcoming. He also provided a survey of the war and prophecy, as usual a mixture of right and wrong, about the future. Beaverbrook wrote to Roosevelt on 31 October 1939:

> I have come to the conclusion that, if you decide to launch the plan you mentioned, you will get the support you require from the British Government. You will get it, in my judgment, even if it involves, as you so clearly put it, the breaking of the Thin Red Line.
>
> The war in the air goes well for Britain. All the threats of ruin that were directed against us come to nothing. The bombers are driven back on every occasion.
>
> The submarine is not so certain. The Navy has had a bad time, and the reputation of that service has declined. . . .

[1] When Time/Life serialized Churchill's memoirs, it borrowed the Churchill correspondence in the Roosevelt archive for purposes of illustration. The Kipling poem was found attached to this material and was returned to Beaverbrook. He noted that he would one day explain the circumstances of the poem's curious reappearance, but he never did so.

The political situation in some respects resembles the conditions in the last war. . . .

The prophets will say that, if Chamberlain falls, Churchill will succeed him, forming a Coalition Government with Socialists and Liberals, including, of course, Sir Archibald Sinclair.

But Churchill will not have the support of his colleagues in the present War Cabinet. Rightly or wrongly, most of them oppose him.

Such estimates were typical of the phoney war. Beaverbrook confidently expected a prolonged deadlock. He wrote to A. H. Sulzberger on 26 October 1939:

The bomber is a disappointment in war. It cannot stand up against the fighter, and it is beaten by the anti-aircraft gun. . . .

The war will certainly be a long-range war. I think it will be mainly a sea war.

The whole British race is fortified by the knowledge and belief that we are fighting for decent conditions, in which men can go about their daily occupations in security.

And to Roy Howard on 9 November:

I hold the view that German councils are divided and cannot be reconciled. Some favour invasion of Holland, others oppose it. The Germans dare not use their army on the Western Front on account of Russian anxieties. Bombers are at the mercy of fighters everywhere. Everybody is in favour of peace and nobody knows how to get it.

Beaverbrook anxiously watched Churchill's progress. He agreed with Hoare, who had written to him while he was in America: "Certainly in the country he has a very big position. I should say that at the moment he is the one popular figure in the Cabinet". But Beaverbrook always liked to build up alternative candidates. Now his sights were set on Kingsley Wood, the secretary for air. He wrote to the publicity officer at the air ministry on 6 November:

Churchill is already a central figure. But we should have Sir Kingsley also.
The work should be done by the newspapers in close touch with Sir Kingsley, and holding his confidence.

Wood, however, who had been Chamberlain's satellite, preferred to pin his fortunes to Churchill's. He courted the coming leader and so survived in the great National government as chancellor of the exchequer. Beaverbrook commented bitterly: "it was an office beyond his rank and station".

Meanwhile no office came to Beaverbrook, and to judge from his newspapers he deserved none. The Daily Express became the channel for every sort of grumble and grievance. It campaigned against rationing, against the blackout, against increasing the army, even against buying airplanes from America. "American planes are not good enough for fighting. . . . We should buy no more from that country". Chamberlain seems to have given some hint that Beaverbrook might have the ministry of information after all, and certainly he had a poor opinion of its present activities. He wrote to Gladstone Murray on 7 November 1939:

> Campbell Stuart is carrying on something which is called Enemy Propaganda. It appears to be directed to Attlee, Greenwood, Miss Ellen Wilkinson, any member of the Cabinet, and any Newspaper Proprietor who is prepared to lunch or dine with Campbell.

Chamberlain's hint was perhaps not meant very seriously. At any rate, Beaverbrook turned it down in a letter to Hoare, which shows how much he would have liked the job. He wrote on 30 October:

> I really do not want to be Minister of Information.
> The Ministry has now been stripped of its function and appears to me to be nothing more than a minor department, and a discredited one at that.
> I would have been the best man for the job at the outset. I have the experience in journalism and propaganda. And in character I am just the type to have made a success and a real success at that.
> This is not a boast on my part nor is it written in praise of my character. I know my own weaknesses and these are certainly strength where propaganda is concerned.
> I was just the man to send after the German Ministry of Propaganda. My knowledge of America equips me for that job.
> I cannot be accused of seeking the Ministry as this letter stands in the way of my taking it anyway.

Unbeknown to Beaverbrook, Churchill was also urging that he be brought into the government and put in charge of food. Churchill wrote to Chamberlain on 14 November 1939:

> The more I think of it, the more I feel you would be wise to bring Max in. When I talk to him I have a feeling of knowledge, force, experience, which I do not find—at my age—with most I meet. We need this kind of thing.
> He has always been very much of your point of view about food—and the way the ordinary household thinks.
> We are in such a struggle that I think we ought to have the strongest forces massed. I dread the foolish regulation of national life in small domestic details before it is needed. You could get all you want in the food sphere by persuasion if propaganda is managed right.
> I do not think the other Press Lords would make a fuss, and in all the Press you have never had so consistent a supporter.
> But it is of the future I am thinking. In U.S. and in Northern Ireland I am sure he could work a helpful propaganda. Take then this *Food-Rationing—Grow-More* problem: with such a man handling the machinery

of public opinion you could persuade the people to eat or not to eat whatever suited national interests best. People are longing to help; if they are
only told what to do. This man knows all and, after all, the proof of the
pudding is in the eating.

Here are faithful counsels.[1]

Churchill of course shared Beaverbrook's dislike of rationing. Chamberlain took a different view and did not reply to the letter. But the opinions
Churchill expressed in it go far to explain why he turned to Beaverbrook
when he himself became prime minister.

Beaverbrook remained unemployed. He succumbed to asthma and,
failing Miami, departed to the south of France. There he supervised the
furnishing of the house at Cap d'Ail which he had recently bought and
grumbled about the feebleness of the British government. He himself
provided one bright idea. Soviet Russia had recently attacked Finland,
and the Finns had put up a surprisingly successful resistance. Beaverbrook now proposed that the British government should stir up the
Scandinavians of the United States to support the Finns. Others—
Czechs, Poles, even Canadians—would join in, and thus the United States
would be swept into financing the cause of freedom or maybe even into
entering the war. Beaverbrook pushed this idea on Hoare, on Churchill,
and on Hore-Belisha, the secretary for war. He wrote to Hore-Belisha:
"If the United States decides to support Finland help to Great Britain
may not be far off", and to Churchill (13 December 1939):

> The demonstrations should take the form of processions through the
> principal thoroughfares of big centres of population, with collections of
> money for the assistance of the Scandinavian defence forces.
>
> . . . .
>
> It will be said that this is only Barnum and Bailey. Most great enter-
> prises are Barnum and Bailey.

When members of the war cabinet were proposing to go to war against
Soviet Russia for the sake of Finland, Beaverbrook may be pardoned for
being almost as crazy. Maybe the idea looked sensible in the south of
France.

Beaverbrook returned to Cherkley for Christmas. Early in the new
year he announced that he was closing Cherkley for the duration of the
war. The contents of the library and even the visitors' books would be
presented to the University of New Brunswick. He himself would live
in a small cottage adjoining the Cherkley estate. He explained that it was
too much trouble keeping so many servants, particularly with rationing.
Alternatively he blamed the restrictions on petrol which made it difficult
for him and his staff and The Express dispatch-riders to be constantly
on the move between Cherkley and London. There is another possible

[1] This letter was kindly communicated to me by Martin Gilbert.

explanation. Some twenty secondary-school children from London had been billeted on Cherkley, and Beaverbrook, after welcoming them enthusiastically at first, took to worrying over the damage they might cause to his furniture, china, cinema, or swimming bath. Closing the house was the only way of getting them out, and most of them were glad at being pushed back to London.

Some of the books at Cherkley were sent to Canada now or later. The visitors' books remained undisturbed until they found their way to the Beaverbrook Library where they now are. Beaverbrook paid a few visits to his small house at Wellbottom. By the end of February he was going down to Cherkley for lunch. In April he was once more living there at weekends and sometimes during the week as well. When he became a minister, he found that it was possible to maintain a large staff at Cherkley and to keep his stream of cars running after all. The house at Wellbottom was not used by him again.

Early in 1940 Beaverbrook once more championed a victim of political misfortune. When Hore-Belisha was driven from the war office in order to please the generals, The Daily Express wrote: "If Belisha must go, do all the other members of the Government deserve to stay?" Beaverbrook tried to enlist Churchill on Belisha's behalf, an intervention which Churchill took in ill part. Beaverbrook also wrote privately to Frank Gannett (17 January 1940): "I have seen many a Minister in the hour of downfall. Belisha was the most admirable in his conduct. . . . Chamberlain may never recover". More generally, Beaverbrook swung between impatience and optimism. He told Bruce Lockhart: "This is not a real war. Production is bad. A phoney war may land us in a phoney peace. If there's a real war, I'll be in it".

He doubted however whether there would be a real war, or maybe was misled by his own wishes. His judgements were again a mixture of true and false. The absence of bombing raids was in part deliberate policy on Hitler's part, but Beaverbrook was right in believing that daylight raids would prove impossibly costly. Like others, however, he overrated the strength of the Western Front. Hence he foresaw a prolonged deadlock with serious war waged only at sea. This was the theme which he now renewed in articles in The Daily Express. He also repeated it in private. Thus he wrote to Paul Block on 17 January 1940:

> Hitler will not attack the Low Countries. Sweden is in much greater danger. If Scandinavia goes, well it is a nuisance, but not a major disaster.

On 27 January 1940 he sketched a somewhat eccentric programme to Roy Howard:

> I am convinced that Britain can stand for ever. It is only necessary for us to produce at home for our requirements. To give up coffee and drink

beer. To smoke our own tobacco. To build airplanes. To train men and to love the neutrals.

To Lowell Thomas on 5 March 1940:

My first prophecy is that Hitler will not go into Holland or Belgium. He would, by so doing, gain nothing of such decisive importance that it would make up for throwing nearly a million Dutch and Belgian soldiers into the struggle against him.

Nor will he go into Sweden. . . . An offensive in the South East of Europe is equally unlikely. . . .

During this spring and summer, the Germans are going to conduct the war over and under the seas. The land they will ignore. By U-boat and airplane attack they will endeavour to destroy our commerce and break our economic stranglehold.

. . . The real question is, will England attack? To this I will answer, "I think not now but soon".

Beaverbrook believed that this view was shared by the leading members of the cabinet. He wrote to David Stern on 2 March:

There is a noticeable difference of opinion between those who believe that we should go on fighting a war of patience and those who are impatient for results. Chamberlain is of course the leader of the first school of thought and has what may be to you the surprising support of Churchill. . . .

More important is the question whether the ships taking ore to Germany are to be intercepted in Norwegian territorial waters. Halifax is said to be strongly against this.

Beaverbrook continued to maintain his scepticism in regard to bombing. Thus to Frank Gannett on 28 March 1940:

If mass bombing attacks were made on London the attacking force would be fatally damaged before they could achieve any real success.

In my opinion, in fact, air power will not decide the issue in this war. . . . Economic strength and, above all, sea power will bring the final victory.

Similarly to Eugene Meyer on 1 April 1940:

The bomber has been overestimated. . . . Any precision at night is impossible.

The second reason is wastage. . . . If the issue were really joined the wastage would be more than any nation at war could stand. . . . Blockade and money will win this war.

It is seemingly ironic that this sceptic should later win his greatest fame as minister of aircraft production. Yet even then Beaverbrook held to his former beliefs. He provided fighters with which to defeat the bombers and thus demonstrated that a defensive strategy, not retaliation, was an effective answer to the bombing threat. Moreover he remained stalwart in his conviction that British bombing would not win the war against

Germany and, though right, earned much unpopularity for maintaining this belief.

In home affairs Beaverbrook was still running wrongheadedly in favour of free enterprise and against controls. He rejected Keynes's financial plans and wrote to Keynes on 4 March: "I believe in extending buying power and imposing the costs of the war upon a growing volume of taxable profits"—a fine Cobdenite line no doubt, but in the circumstances a recipe for disaster. Was this all that Beaverbrook did during the phoney war? Did he attempt to promote a peace, phoney or otherwise? Ostensibly his record was clear. When an Australian journalist raised the rumour that Beaverbrook and Rothermere were about to launch a tremendous campaign for peace by negotiation, Beaverbrook replied on 1 March 1940:

> You are entirely misinformed about my views.
> I support the Prime Minister. His views represent entirely the opinions that I hold to.

Similarly when the marquess of Tavistock reported to Beaverbrook peace feelers which the German government had made to him through their legation in Dublin, Beaverbrook replied on 8 March 1940:

> I have never felt any anxiety in regard to the wisdom and the certainty of continuing the war.
> I am a supporter of Mr. Chamberlain, and I believe in his war policy. If peace becomes a possibility, I feel sure he will do everything in his power to promote it.

However this was not the whole story. Richard Stokes, a Labour MP, published a pamphlet advocating Peace by Negotiation. Beaverbrook wrote to him on 24 January 1940:

> I have been much impressed by the vigorous manner in which you put forward your views.
> I hope you will not consider it an impertinence on my part to write you my congratulations.

In March Stokes projected a public meeting in London in favour of a negotiated peace and wrote on 20 March 1940:

> What is wanted is a bold pronouncement in favour of supporting a negotiated peace now before even this becomes unnecessary in the eyes of the Germans, a situation which would completely destroy the prestige of the allies.

Beaverbrook answered on 29 March:

> I am glad you are holding a meeting in London. I take the view that discussion on this subject of peace, by intellectual persons is most desirable.
> . . . .
> You know that I differ from you. I am a Tariff man. You hold to Free Trade. I am an Isolationist. I fear that you would concern yourself with

Continental affairs. I hope that the Empire will set up a policy of Isolation after this war is over. You would not like it. You would like to negotiate yourself into Europe. And I would like to negotiate myself out of Europe. You don't like Chamberlain. I do like that man.

So that appears to complete all our points of difference.

There is one measure of agreement. And that is that you are [a] patriotic public-spirited, reliable servant of the state.

This parade of antitheses suggests that Beaverbrook wanted to support Stokes without actually saying so. Beaverbrook also enquired whether Stokes would be speaking at the conference of the Labour party in May. If so, The Express would be told to report him fully—"That I wish to do very much". By the time the Labour conference met, it had other things to discuss than peace by negotiation.

Beaverbrook always inclined to encourage men of strong views, whether he agreed with them or not. On this occasion, maybe, he hoped that advocacy of a negotiated peace would stir up those who wanted a real war, just as he had wanted Liberal Free Traders in the house of commons in 1935, so as to provoke the Protectionists. Or maybe he hoped that Stokes would succeed. There would have been nothing inconsistent in this. Beaverbrook never hid the fact that he had been against going to war. He did not believe Great Britain could do anything to aid Poland, in which he was correct. He did not believe that a strongly-armed Great Britain was in danger from Germany, which was also a defensible proposition. British opinion had insisted on war, and it was not improper for Beaverbrook to favour peace if this opinion could be persuaded to change.

A further flirtation with aspiring peacemakers caused trouble for Beaverbrook later. He had always held a high opinion of the ILP and often praised Maxton, its leader. He wrote to David Stern on 2 March 1940:

We have our various peace movements here, none of them amounting to much. Only in Glasgow and the Clydeside generally have they any real hold. This is the stronghold of the ILP, whose leaders, McGovern, Maxton and Campbell Stephen, are men of force and integrity, as well as being pacifists.

On 5 March 1940 Maxton, McGovern and perhaps Campbell Stephen came to dinner at Stornoway House.[1] Beaverbrook has left no record of

[1] G. M. Thomson composed an account of the meeting for Beaverbrook in June 1941 when the storm blew. McGovern's account is in his book Neither Fear nor Favour (1960), 133–45. Beaverbrook claimed that the ILPers asked to see him in order to discuss the Tavistock peace proposals. McGovern says Beaverbrook approached them through W. J. Brown. This is the more likely version. For some reason Beaverbrook asserted that Campbell Stephen had been unable to come. McGovern disputes this.

the conversation and merely implies that they spent a gay evening, drinking two bottles of champagne.[1] McGovern attributes this statement to Beaverbrook:

> He could not see any alternative at that time but to negotiate an honourable settlement, retire behind our Empire frontiers, arm ourselves to the teeth, leave the Continent to work out its own destiny and defend the Empire with all our strength.

This has the ring of truth. McGovern also says that Beaverbrook offered to give the ILP a minimum of £500 for every by-election they fought— "That I will personally accept as my pledge and responsibility". This is less plausible. Beaverbrook often sang a siren's song and talked of the great things he would do if certain conditions were fulfilled. He took a long time to come out with a firm offer. Probably Beaverbrook suggested that he might help the ILP financially if they could show that they deserved it.

This is confirmed by what followed. There was a by-election in East Renfrewshire with Maxton's sister as ILP candidate. The ILP did not seek or receive financial assistance from Beaverbrook as they surely would have done if he had really made the firm promise alleged. On 9 May 1940 McGovern wrote to Beaverbrook:

> Maxton & I would like to know if you are still of the same mind, as expressed during our recent meeting with you at your home. East Renfrew is over, and we are of opinion that a fairly decent show was put up by Miss Maxton.[2]

This letter certainly indicates that Beaverbrook had not given any binding commitment.

Times had changed. Beaverbrook was now minister of aircraft production and wholeheartedly at war. He replied to McGovern on 17 May 1940:

> Things are not what they were when last we talked. They are not what they were in the world.
> The whole of civilisation has changed since that time. And what has been destroyed can never be reconstructed in our time.
> By the time this letter reaches you immense events may have driven us to new conclusions.[3]

---

[1] Even this is disputed. Two bottles of Pommery 1911 were entered in the Stornoway House cellar book. Beaverbrook says he was teetotal at the time, which sounds improbable. McGovern says the ILPers did not drink alcohol.
[2] McGovern does not give this letter. Instead he implies that he and his colleagues never contemplated taking Beaverbrook's money.
[3] McGovern does not give this letter.

On 12 June Maxton and McGovern lunched with Beaverbrook. According to McGovern, he told them that he had been asked to join the government and felt that, in view of the grave danger, he must accept. Since Beaverbrook had already been a minister for a month, this is obvious nonsense and suggests that McGovern was not an accurate witness.[1]

This was not the end of the affair. On 25 May 1941[2] McGovern told the story of Beaverbrook's alleged offer at a meeting in Glasgow. The Communists, who were then opposing the war, took up the story. This was awkward for Beaverbrook at a moment when he was pressing for increased production of tanks, and he attempted to cover up. A question was asked in the house of commons on 25 June 1941. Churchill, briefed by Beaverbrook, answered by quoting his letter to Tavistock as defining his real position. Churchill also said that any statement of McGovern's should be treated with extreme distrust. McGovern did not like being called a liar. He and Maxton went to see Beaverbrook, who did not dispute the truth of McGovern's version—or so McGovern says. Pressed by Maxton, Beaverbrook replied: "All right, Jimmy, I admit that I was the agitator; I have always been a bloody agitator". Beaverbrook pleaded that publication of the truth would ruin him. Also, with Hitler's attack on Russia, the Communists were supporting the war, and there was no more capital to be made out of the affair. McGovern therefore contented himself with a letter from Beaverbrook of 29 July 1941:

> You and I are engaged in a controversy that neither of us sought.
> You have given an account of a conversation with me sixteen months ago.
> It is not the same account of the conversation that I should give myself.
> But if I do not accept your recollections, I do not doubt your integrity.

Beaverbrook commented in private: "I did not give McGovern's party any money, although I admit the champagne". This was his way of playing down the affair. It was perfectly consistent for Beaverbrook to be against the war in March 1940 and to support it from May 1940 onwards. But it was a consistency difficult to explain in public.

In the spring of 1940 Beaverbrook felt irremediably detached from affairs. He wrote to Lloyd-Jones of Toronto on 17 April 1940:

> I am too old a man to take more than a small part in the war. The main burden must be borne by the younger generation.

But the storm was now about to blow and to involve Beaverbrook even more than others. On 8 April the Germans invaded Norway. The British sent forces to aid the Norwegians, with much trumpeting from Churchill

---

[1] McGovern also says that Beaverbrook had just returned from meeting the French ministers at Tours. This meeting took place on 13 June.
[2] McGovern asserts wrongly that he made this revelation some weeks after his meeting with Beaverbrook on 12 June 1940.

about the might of British sea power. The British intervention was a humiliating failure. Public opinion was aroused. On 3 May 1940, Lord Davies, once as David Davies a supporter of Lloyd George's, wrote to Beaverbrook:

Dear Kingmaker,

Why have you given up your job? You did the trick in 1916 and, by getting rid of old Squiff at the right moment, you enabled us to win the war which we should probably have lost if he had remained in office. Now, even more than in 1916, we are up against it, and if the present Prime Minister is allowed to drag us from one disaster to another, we shall end up in queer street.

... Therefore I humbly suggest that you should plump for Winston. He has drive, energy, determination and vision. He can rouse the country. On the other hand, cold fish can only produce cold feet!

... My dear Kingmaker, come forth from your tent and put an end to the drifting, muddle and tom foolery of the present crowd.

Beaverbrook doubted whether the decisive moment had come. He wrote to Castlerosse in Ireland on 6 May:

The crisis is now upon us. I don't think that Chamberlain will be turned out this time.

But he remains in office with such an immense volume of disapproval in his own Party, that he had better retire.

Beaverbrook also emphasized the need for a Conservative revolt in the reply which he sent to Lord Davies on 7 May:

You can't break every Government the same way.

Those who brought down the first Asquith Government seized upon the differences between Fisher and Churchill at the Admiralty and upon the support they knew existed for Fisher in the Cabinet.

Asquith's Coalition Government fell to pieces when the linchpin Bonar Law was pulled out.

Lloyd George was brought down in 1922 by his enemies exploiting the peace party within the Government.

You will note that in every case the revolt that broke the Government came from within. The same applies this time. Those who try to do it from without are simply wasting their ammunition.

But there are things that can be done and I am ready to tell you what they are. ... What I should tell you would simply be common sense.

Beaverbrook did more than stand aside. He came to the assistance of the government. On 6 May he published an article, What is the Damage?, in The Daily Express—the last article by him, as it proved, for more than five years. He dismissed the Norwegian failure as a minor affair, damaging only to British prestige. Against it he recited the reasons for confidence: no bombing, and "we may hope, with some confidence, that London and

other densely populated areas of Britain will not be bombed at all";
defeat of the U-boats; immense financial resources; impregnable Maginot
Line, attack on which would be "the last throw of a desperate enemy".

So do not despair over accounts in this war of incompetence, of stupidity,
of misunderstanding and even of wilful neglect. Such vices and weaknesses
are inseparable from war.

Neville Chamberlain wrote at once to express his pleasure at this "splendid
article":

When so many are sounding the defeatist note over a minor setback, it
is a relief to read such a courageous and inspiriting summons to a saner view.

Others however were unaffected by Beaverbrook's advocacy. On 7 May
a two-day debate on the Norwegian campaign opened in the house of
commons. On 8 May Beaverbrook wrote a letter to Chamberlain, encouraging him to challenge a division:

In the month of November 1916 Bonar Law faced a truculent House when
Sir Edward Carson called him a liar.
The Party on the division was in favour of the Government by a few
votes. That night Bonar Law considered resignation.
Many favoured that course. Some opposed it. Bonar Law decided to go on.
On May 9th 1918 Lloyd George was confronted by a hostile Liberal
Party. A bitter debate was followed by a division—293 for the Government
and 106 for the opposition.
I recall the discussion in Bonar Law's room in the House of Commons.
Much stress was laid on the abstentions.

What was the purpose of this letter—to sustain Chamberlain, to lure him
to his doom, or simply to force a decision one way or the other? The last
explanation seems the most in line with Beaverbrook's character. He
himself had reached no clear decision. If Chamberlain fell, Halifax seemed
the likely successor, and Beaverbrook certainly preferred Chamberlain
to Halifax. Nor is it clear that he preferred Churchill to Chamberlain.
He doubted whether the bulk of the Conservative party would support
Churchill. Maybe too he was disturbed by Churchill's "harebrained"
strategy in Norway. At any rate, he is reported to have said to one of his
associates: "Churchill? He's the man who let the Germans into Norway"—a judgement slightly less unfair than Lloyd George's description
of Churchill during the first world war as "the man who brought Turkey
into the war against us".
On 8 May a division was forced in the house of commons—though by
the Labour opposition, not by Chamberlain. 41 supporters of the government voted against it, and some 60 more abstained. The revolt from
within had arrived. The future of the government was at stake, much as

in December 1916. Beaverbrook was again active. He has left an undated pencil note:

> I saw Churchill in the morning of May 9th 1940.
>
> I asked—do you intend to serve under Halifax. He answered—I will serve under any Minister capable of prosecuting the War.
>
> It was a disappointment for I had hoped that C. would lead us. Indeed I believed necessary to safety of the Kingdom—that the country wanted him. Any other choice would be a shock.
>
> The choice of Halifax would simply mean the continuance of the present Administration.

Did this conversation ever take place? Beaverbrook's engagement book does not record any meeting with Churchill on 9 May, but of course his secretaries did not know everything he was doing.

In any event, Beaverbrook had not persuaded Churchill to claim the supreme power. He himself believed that Bracken's influence was more effective. Beaverbrook's pencil note continues:

> Brendan Bracken intervened. He asked C. to remain silent and after much argument C. agreed.

It appears however from another note of Beaverbrook's that he had left before Bracken arrived. His evidence is therefore hearsay or conjecture. According to other accounts, also secondhand, Bracken reported that the Labour leaders, though preferring Halifax, would serve under Churchill.[1]

This was not Beaverbrook's only activity on 9 May. Another of his notes records:

> I had Sam Hoare for lunch and I had him at 7.45 in the evening that day. He hoped very much to avoid the collapse of Chamberlain and was discussing ways and means of protecting him against his enemies.

These meetings are confirmed by Beaverbrook's engagement book. Perhaps therefore he was still exploring the ground. Or maybe he was playing things both ways.

What he said and did was no great matter. The decision was taken at the top. At 4.15 p.m. Chamberlain conferred with Churchill, Halifax, and Margesson, the Conservative chief whip. Twenty years later (on 25

---

[1] Eden gives the credit for Churchill's silence to Kingsley Wood. On 9 May Churchill and Wood lunched alone with Eden. According to Eden's diary, Wood "thought that W. should succeed, and urged that he should make this plain". Eden adds, apparently from recollection not from his diary: "I was surprised to find Kingsley Wood there giving a warning that Chamberlain would want Halifax to succeed him and would want Churchill to agree. Wood advised: 'Don't agree, and don't say anything' ". The diary entry is of course an authentic record. The recollection may be an unconscious transference of credit from Bracken to Wood. Avon, The Reckoning, 96–97.

May 1960, Beaverbrook's birthday) Margesson gave Beaverbrook this
account:

> Margesson told Chamberlain that his own Party could no longer be
> relied upon to support him, and that he should resign.
>
> Chamberlain asked who Margesson considered should succeed to the
> Premiership. Margesson answered that the House of Commons would prefer
> Halifax.

Beaverbrook pieced together the rest of the story from accounts left by
Churchill and Halifax:

> Chamberlain asked Churchill for his view. Churchill remained silent.
> There was a long pause.
>
> When it became clear that Churchill would not speak, Halifax said that
> he felt that his Peerage would make it impossible for him properly to carry
> out the function of Prime Minister.
>
> Chamberlain then went off to keep another appointment, while Churchill
> and Halifax took tea in the garden of 10 Downing Street.

This is probably very near the truth. Later still Beaverbrook dramatized
the situation even more. His last summary was made in 1963:

> Chamberlain wanted Halifax. Labour wanted Halifax. Sinclair wanted
> Halifax. The Lords wanted Halifax. The King wanted Halifax. And Halifax
> wanted Halifax.

Chamberlain was in fact not yet convinced that he must resign. After
leaving Churchill and Halifax, he consulted Attlee and Greenwood, the
Labour leaders, who failed to give a clear answer. During the night of
9–10 May German armies invaded Holland and Belgium. Chamberlain
believed that he was saved. This is confirmed in a letter which he wrote
to Beaverbrook that morning:

> I had fully made up my mind as to the course I should pursue and had
> fully agreed it with Winston and Halifax.
>
> But as I expected Hitler has seized the occasion of our divisions to strike
> the great blow and we cannot consider changes in the Government while we
> are in the throes of battle.

This view was endorsed in a public statement by Sir Archibald Sinclair,
leader of the independent Liberals. Others thought differently. Kingsley
Wood led a revolt against Chamberlain within the cabinet. The Labour
leaders refused to serve under him. In the afternoon of 10 May Chamberlain resigned, and Churchill became prime minister.

Beaverbrook at once established himself as Churchill's intimate adviser.
The two lunched alone together on 10 May and dined alone together. On
11 May they again lunched alone together. On 12 May Beaverbrook spent
the afternoon with Churchill and stayed to dinner. Beaverbrook's immediate task was to advise on appointments. Churchill had been an isolated

figure in politics for many years past. Beaverbrook knew everyone from extreme Tories to the ILP, though his judgement of men was not always sound. Moreover Churchill regarded him, whether correctly or not, as an authority on public opinion. A letter which he wrote to Churchill on 12 May indicates their discussions:

> The list goes well because you carry everything before you now with the British public.
> I remember a train load of Blue Jackets at Victoria Station cheering you wildly after you were dismissed from the admiralty in 1915.
> Your popularity has reached the same high again.
> Maybe you might think it worth while to show me your names for other offices before you issue your list.
> I might have useful ideas on the publicity side.

Hankey, a member of the outgoing war cabinet, gave a more jaundiced account of Churchill's activities:

> I found complete chaos this morning. No one was gripping the war in its crisis. The Dictator, instead of dictating, was engaged in a sordid wrangle with the politicians of the left about the secondary offices. N.C. was in a state of despair about it all.
> The only hope lies in the solid core of Churchill, Chamberlain and Halifax, but whether the wise old elephants will ever be able to hold the Rogue Elephant, I doubt.[1]

There was of course far more between Churchill and Beaverbrook than discussion about offices. They had been intimate friends for nearly thirty years, even though they had occasionally drifted apart. Indeed Beaverbrook was now Churchill's only personal friend in political circles. Birkenhead was dead. Lloyd George, as it proved, was worn out. No one else remained. The political leaders, such as Halifax and Attlee, were Churchill's official associates, not his friends. With Ernest Bevin he later established relations of mutual esteem, but not of intimacy. All the rest were admiring juniors, with Anthony Eden as the favourite son. Only Beaverbrook and Churchill were truly Max and Winston.

Bevin, who hated Beaverbrook, said of Churchill's relationship with him: "He's like a man who's married a whore: he knows she's a whore, but he loves her just the same".[2] The saying had some truth in it. Beaverbrook's personality—his fun, even his irresponsibility—helped to keep Churchill going. But Churchill did not value Beaverbrook solely as an entertainer. Despite his indomitable spirit, he sometimes needed to be

[1] Hankey to Hoare, 12 May 1940. Hoare dropped the letter from his pocket when he came to take leave of Beaverbrook on 12 May, and it was placed in the Hoare file where it still is.
[2] Bullock, Life and Times of Ernest Bevin, ii, 178.

sustained, and in a crisis he relied on Beaverbrook, as Lloyd George had relied on Bonar Law. It was no accident that Churchill called on Beaverbrook to accompany him when he had to make great decisions in regard to France or the United States, and no accident that he sent Beaverbrook to break the ice with Stalin. Similarly he turned to Beaverbrook when threatened, as he supposed, by political revolt. In public affairs, as in private, Beaverbrook remained Churchill's foul-weather friend.

Beaverbrook on his side had been without a master, a hero, ever since Law's death. Now he had found one. Despite what some have said, Beaverbrook did not want political power or advancement for himself. He wanted excitement and activity. At last he was once more at the centre of affairs. He had no illusion about his position. He described himself as "court favourite", even as "court jester". He knew that with Churchill as with Lloyd George there was in the last resort no friendship at the top. Beaverbrook had often drawn the contrast between Churchill Up and Churchill Down. Now Churchill was Up in the sense of being prime minister, but Down in the sense of being faced with overwhelming difficulties. While he remained Down he needed Beaverbrook. Beaverbrook did not doubt that if ever Churchill were truly Up he himself might be thrown aside. From the first he expected to be "betrayed".

Beaverbrook did not feel for Churchill the singlehearted devotion which he had felt for Law, although phrases of fulsome admiration came easily to him. Law had been Beaverbrook's senior in every way. Beaverbrook and Churchill were much of an age. Moreover Beaverbrook now had behind him many years of success, at any rate as a newspaper proprietor. Churchill's was a long record of failure, and Beaverbrook had been among the first to emphasize his mistakes. Nor did he expect Churchill to acquire unbroken wisdom with supreme power. Certainly he remarked how Churchill had become good-tempered and tolerant now that he was "on the stretch". The association of the two was perfect while the crisis lasted. But, as with many other things accepted "for the duration", there were reserves on both sides. Essentially Beaverbrook's devotion was to Churchill the war leader not to Churchill the man, and, as often happened with him, he came to care for the man only later when Churchill was in physical distress.

Beaverbrook clearly intended to be the man behind the scenes, an expert adviser perhaps only on publicity. Churchill had other ideas. Before the war he had often railed against the slowness in producing aircraft, and production was still slow. He believed that an independent ministry of aircraft production was the answer, just as the ministry of munitions had been carved out of the war office in order to overcome the shell shortage in the first world war. This was the post which Churchill now pressed on Beaverbrook. Beaverbrook hesitated. He had no experience of executive government. He was being asked to undertake a task which had needed a Lloyd George in the first war. He would have to fight the air ministry and other departments. He was over sixty and harassed by asthma.

Beaverbrook always went on like this before making a great decision. In 1910 he had insisted that he would not run for Ashton-under-Lyne up to the very moment when he arrived at the Midland Hotel, Manchester. Now he told his secretaries "with increasing vehemence that he would not take office".[1] Yet on 11 May he was already discussing the needs of the RAF with Sir Archibald Sinclair, the new secretary for air, and he spent most of 12 May interviewing the businessmen and air officers whom he proposed to enlist in the ministry of aircraft production. At 7.30 p.m. on 12 May, according to his own note, he told Churchill that he would undertake the job, though his secretaries were still drafting letters of refusal for him throughout 13 May.

Of course it was impossible for Beaverbrook to refuse. His old friend needed him. The job would be exciting and dramatic. But these were not the decisive reasons. Underneath the cynical exterior, Beaverbrook was still the romantic boy who had read Scott and Stevenson. Simple patriotism overwhelmed him, as in the dark days of 1940 it overwhelmed many others. On 14 May 1940 Beaverbrook became minister of aircraft production. Though this was a post of great responsibility, its vital importance could not yet be appreciated. With the land battle raging in France, aircraft seemed to be an auxiliary, not the decisive weapon of war. Hardly anyone then foresaw the turn of events which was to place Beaverbrook among the immortal few who won the Battle of Britain.

[1] David Farrer, The Sky's the Limit, 7.

CHAPTER SEVENTEEN

HIS HOUR, 1940

This was a time of great upheavals. France was struck down. Germany dominated the continent. Great Britain stood alone and, as it seemed, almost helpless. As with nations, so with men. For years past Churchill had been a solitary figure, admired and disregarded. Overnight he attained a position which was to bring him enduring fame as the saviour of his country. The transformation in Beaverbrook's destiny was even more startling. Churchill would have left a considerable mark on British history even if he had died in 1939. If Beaverbrook had died before May 1940, he would have been almost forgotten except as a newspaper proprietor.

Hitherto Beaverbrook had been on the margin of events, observing and sometimes trying to manipulate them. He was an extraordinary character, irresistibly captivating to some, immeasurably wicked to others. No one outside his "entourage" took him seriously as a political figure, and he was too shrewd a judge to be serious about himself. He had plenty of fun and excitement. Everything he did was "drama"—with a short "a". It was drama when he helped to raise up Lloyd George. But a foray from Stornoway House to Cherkley for lunch involved almost as much turmoil. The Empire Crusade was a barnstorming operation in more senses than one, on a level with Martin-Harvey's touring theatrical company. Edward VIII and Mrs. Simpson had given Beaverbrook the code name "Tornado". This was a Tornado which could blow up any day and often for the most trivial reason.

In May 1940 the drama invaded real life. Events took hold of Beaverbrook and swept him to a position of supreme responsibility second only to Churchill's. At the moment of unparalleled danger, it was Beaverbrook who made survival and victory possible. Later there arose disgruntled critics who belittled Beaverbrook's achievement or asserted that it could have been done without his dramatic methods. They are answered by the verdict of the man best qualified to know: Air Chief Marshal Sir Hugh Dowding (later Lord Dowding), head of fighter command throughout the Battle of Britain. Dowding wrote in his official report:

I saw my resources slipping away like sand in an hour glass. . . . The effect of Lord Beaverbrook's appointment can only be described as magical and thereafter the supply situation improved to such a degree that the heavy aircraft wastage which was later incurred during the Battle of Britain ceased to be the primary danger.

On 1 June 1945 Dowding wrote in The Times:

We had the organisation, we had the men, and we had the spirit which could bring us victory in the air, but we had not the supply of machines necessary to withstand the drain of continuous battle. Lord Beaverbrook gave us those machines, and I do not believe that I exaggerate when I say that no other man in England could have done so.

Similarly Dowding told Lord Templewood (formerly Sir Samuel Hoare):[1]

The country owes as much to Beaverbrook for the Battle of Britain as it does to me. Without his drive behind me I could not have carried on during the battle.

If another voice is needed, it can be that of Sir Archibald Rowlands, chief civil servant at the ministry of aircraft production and, as such, not originally enthusiastic for Beaverbrook's methods:

The Royal Air Force won the Battle of Britain. . . . It would never have had the chance to do so but for the activities of one man—and that man was Lord Beaverbrook.

In this new world of government Beaverbrook remained what he had always been. He did not run the ministry as a trained administrator or a politician would have done. He ran it as he ran his newspapers, as he had run his financial undertakings, and as he ran his private life. He ran it as drama, working through individuals, not through committees, and ready to fight every rival. He remarked to Citrine: "I have no Production Council. I have no aptitude for Councils or Boards. I am a cat that walks alone". Certainly he had a minister's council, though he was never precise who should be called to it. But there was no discussion. It was exactly like the conferences which he had held in the early days of The Sunday Express. Each member reported the most urgent problems, and Beaverbrook snapped out orders that the difficulties must be overcome.

A production branch of the air ministry was already operating, tucked away in the seclusion of Harrogate. Beaverbrook ordered its return to London and then forgot about it. He deliberately started from scratch as Lloyd George had done with the ministry of munitions. The precedent was much in Beaverbrook's mind. Indeed, Sir Walter Layton, a survivor from the ministry of munitions, was among the first of those whom

---

[1] Templewood to Beaverbrook, 15 May 1945.

Beaverbrook consulted on 11 May. Beaverbrook remembered how Lloyd George had fought the war office and had torn the production of munitions from it, ultimately securing the suspension of the ordnance board for the duration. He also no doubt remembered his own ineffectual fight as minister of information to tear the control of intelligence from the foreign office. Now he intended to fight the air ministry as Lloyd George had fought the war office and incidentally to avenge on Sir Archibald Sinclair, the secretary of state for air, the defeat which he had suffered twenty years before at the hands of Balfour, the foreign secretary.

The analogy between Lloyd George's position and Beaverbrook's was not on all fours. The war office had made no preparations before 1914 to supply an army of millions. The air ministry had long been preparing to produce an air force second to none, and its plans, following a government decision on the outbreak of war, were carefully designed to mature in 1942. Any sudden acceleration or emphasis on some particular type, such as fighters, would disrupt these plans and, according to "the bloody Air Marshals",[1] ultimately leave the RAF weaker than it would otherwise have been. Beaverbrook was not interested in 1942 and never operated long-term plans. His aim was to produce more aircraft at once, and he did not mind the accusation that he was sacrificing the future for the sake of the present. The present was all that mattered to him, and unless that were secured there would be no future to sacrifice. He was confident, too, that the problems of the future could be solved by the same improvising methods which he applied to those of the present.

Beaverbrook listened to one air chief marshal: Sir Hugh Dowding, head of fighter command. No two men could be more opposite in temperament: Dowding as silent and reserved as Beaverbrook was exuberant and talkative. But they established strong bonds of sympathy and outlook. David Farrer has recorded:

> When their talks were finished, Beaverbrook would get up from his chair, accompany Dowding to the front entrance of the Ministry two floors below, and show him to his car. To no one else except Churchill did he pay a similar attention.[2]

This association plunged Beaverbrook headlong into controversy with the air ministry. The doctrine held there by all except Dowding was that the bomber would always get through. There was no defence except retaliation. Hence the air ministry wanted the production of bombers and little else. Dowding believed that he could beat off the bombers if he had enough fighters, and Beaverbrook accepted his belief.

[1] This, writes marshal of the Royal Air Force Sir John Slessor primly (The Central Blue, 308), was "a generic term applied by Lord Beaverbrook to the senior officers of His Majesty's Air Force".
[2] Farrer, The Sky's the Limit, 26.

The controversy went further into high policy. Dowding, like Beaver-brook, was an Isolationist by virtue of his position, caring only for the defence of Great Britain and regarding allies as an embarrassment. On the fall of France, he said to Halifax: "Thank God we are now alone".[1] Hence he defied Churchill and refused to waste fighter squadrons in useless assistance to the French. Unlike Beaverbrook, he attached no importance to dramatic gestures. He would not operate offensive sweeps over the Channel. During the Battle of Britain, he rejected the tactic of "the big wing", as favoured by the air staff. For once Beaverbrook took the undramatic side—coached by his son Max Aitken, himself a fighter pilot, and restrained also by his own grasp of realities which often pulled him up in mid course. Dowding paid the penalty for having been right and was thrown on the scrap heap as soon as the Battle of Britain was won. Beaverbrook also paid a penalty and earned the unrelenting hostility of the air marshals.

Unlike the ministry of munitions in the first world war, the ministry of aircraft production became directly involved in the disputes over strategy. Lloyd George, as minister of munitions, did not much concern himself with new types of weapons apart from the Stokes mortar. Even the development of the tank owed little to him. He simply produced in far greater quantity the weapons which the war office was producing already—shells, guns, machine guns, and rifles. Far from cutting across strategy, Lloyd George actually made it easier for the war office and the generals to conduct their existing strategy of mass onslaught—a strategy of which he much disapproved. Types of aircraft were not stabilized in the same way. The air ministry was as much concerned with development as with production. New types were coming along all the time, and the choice between them affected the strategy of the air war for years to come. It was not merely the choice between fighters and bombers. There was also the problem whether to push on with the production of existing types or to develop new types even at some cost to current production. Then what about trainer aircraft, dive bombers for the army, aircraft for the fleet air arm? Every decision taken by the minister of aircraft production was a strategical decision.

The air ministry had a simple solution. The minister of aircraft production should make no decisions. He should merely fulfil the orders for such numbers and types of aircraft as the air ministry specified. Beaverbrook rejected this solution violently. He was not prepared to be anyone's handmaiden. In any case, the air ministry's proposal was unworkable. It was useless for the air ministry to specify what it wanted. Only the ministry of aircraft production knew what numbers and types could be produced. Beaverbrook carried the day by his persistence and with

[1] Wright, Dowding and the Battle of Britain, 129.

Churchill's backing. But he also carried the day because he had the whip hand. He alone could judge which orders the factories could fulfil. With this, relations between the two ministries were turned upsidedown. The air ministry had no say until Beaverbrook's ministry delivered the aircraft to the operational squadrons. Beaverbrook decided what types of aircraft were produced and in what numbers. It was small consolation to the air marshals that the decision was usually made according to what was possible and not on any long-term strategical doctrine. The air ministry had been pushed aside. It merely appointed the commanders and operated such strategy as Beaverbrook permitted.

Beaverbrook's encroachments went further. The air ministry had worked out a balanced programme—so many aircraft in reserve, so many allotted to training fresh pilots, stocks of engines accumulated for future use, spare parts stored on every operational airfield. Beaverbrook claimed control of the aircraft storage units, and his agents went round putting MAP padlocks on the hangar doors long before the air ministry had conceded defeat. Henceforth when the air ministry wanted aircraft for training or to send overseas, a prolonged wrangle would follow. Beaverbrook even decided which airfields the new aircraft were to go to. Each evening during the Battle of Britain, he rang Air Vice-Marshal Park, commander of No. 11 Group, which bore the brunt of the fighting, and asked how many Spitfires and Hurricanes were required the next day. The air ministry was neither consulted nor informed.

Beaverbrook took over the stocks of engines and put them to immediate use. He sent his agents round the airfields, where they surveyed the spare parts and raided the cupboards at will—finding "pots of gold", Beaverbrook called it. He told his successor Moore-Brabazon: "Better a stringency in spares and a bountiful supply of aircraft than a surplus of spares and a shortage of aircraft". Repair had languished under the air ministry. Beaverbrook demanded control for his own man, Trevor Westbrook. The air ministry once more resisted and after a fierce contest gave way. Westbrook did not repair aircraft. He "cannibalized" them, making one serviceable aircraft out of two or three damaged ones. This was a shocking departure from established practice. But it worked. Before the battle of Britain ended, as many cannibalized aircraft as new ones were serving in the front line.

Any minister of aircraft production would have had difficulties with the air ministry in 1940. It was Beaverbrook's nature to push these difficulties to extremes. He enjoyed such fights and was surprised when others did not enjoy them too. Significantly one of his first recruits was Raymond Needham, the man who had conducted the battle with the foreign office for Beaverbrook in 1918. But Beaverbrook remained also the skilful tactician and conciliator he had been in the world of finance and newspapers. After a sharp exchange of letters, he would then quietly fix things with Sinclair, the man at the top, just as he used to settle his newspaper disputes directly with Rothermere or Southwood. Harold Balfour, the under-secretary at the air ministry, recorded indignantly:

> The two Ministers would confer—usually by telephone. An offer would be made to withdraw the paper if the Air Ministry would agree to such and such. . . . The claim would be dropped in order to establish a position on something whereby MAP could more easily obtain agreement on something previously rejected by us, or something still in Lord Beaverbrook's mind and yet to come to our ears.

Beaverbrook knew how to write soft letters as well as hard ones. Thus he wrote to Sir Cyril Newall, chief of the air staff, on 10 July, when dispute over the aircraft storage units was raging:

> You have, of course, many problems on hand and I am sure you try as hard to discharge them as I do to dispose of the obligations that fall upon me.
> Next let me say to you that your problems of shortage of aircraft are being solved by this Ministry and by no other agency.
> I should think that this service might be recognized by placing at our disposal all those portions of the Air Ministry now engaged in the production of aircraft.
> That is all I ask. And I cannot understand why it is not given to me at once.

MAP got the aircraft storage units.

This was a strange ministry, disregarding all the rules. It was strange in its base, operating for some weeks from Stornoway House, as though it were a new province of Beaverbrook's private empire. Indeed it bore little resemblance to a government department. Beaverbrook himself never drew a salary at any time during the war. He used his own cars, paid for his own petrol, and even reimbursed the wages of a driver if he had to take one occasionally from the RAF pool. During the Blitz he bought his own armoured car (for £695) and afterwards perversely presented it to the war office, where it ended its days being used by General Dempsey during the invasion of France.

Beaverbrook also largely provided his own staff. When on his departure the treasury put the ministry on a regular footing, it found that more than half the typists were still being paid by The Daily Express. J. B. Wilson, the publicity officer of the ministry, had been news editor of The Daily Express, from which he continued to draw his salary. Other Express men were taken off their journalistic work at a moment's notice to produce "data"—again with a short "a"—or to write appeals for higher production. The civil service provided two secretaries for Beaverbrook, Edmund Compton and Eaton Griffiths. But he had also two "political" secretaries of his own, David Farrer and George Malcolm Thomson; and the four did the work indiscriminately. Only two of the senior officials were career men: Sir Archibald Rowlands, the permanent secretary who came from the treasury, and Sir Wilfred Freeman, who had been director of development and production at the air ministry. Rowlands refused to be trampled on and was prevented from resigning only by a case of champagne and another of spirits "from a bad Minister to a fine secretary".[1] Freeman had production taken from him and found little to develop. With unselfish generosity he acknowledged that Beaverbrook's methods were right in the circumstances of 1940 and thus, though an air marshal, became a traitor to the air ministry. Beaverbrook himself acknowledged this. In November 1940 Freeman reluctantly left MAP to become deputy chief of the air staff. Some time later he sent over photographs of the results of bombing and added lightheartedly: "Lord Beaverbrook may remember me". Beaverbrook's secretary replied:

> Lord Beaverbrook remembers you quite well. You probably met at school. Although it could not have been a Public School.

From Beaverbrook there could be no finer accolade.

These regulars were eclipsed by the men Beaverbrook recruited from industry: Patrick Hennessy, from Fords, Sir Charles Craven, who came from Vickers via the admiralty, and of course Trevor Westbrook. Associated with them were a host of others allotted to particular tasks. Some of them understood the aircraft industry; some were remote from it. Beaverbrook explained: "They are all captains of industry, and industry is like theology. If you know the rudiments of one faith you can grasp the meaning of another. For my part I would not hesitate to appoint the Moderator of the General Assembly of the Presbyterian Church to take over the duties of the Pope of Rome". Beaverbrook even appointed air officers when they had his sort of drive. Group Captain Grahame Dawson was his great discovery, and Beaverbrook shot him up the ladder of promotion against the protests of the air ministry. The air officers of course were paid. Most of the industrialists followed Beaverbrook's example and worked for nothing. By the end of the year the ministry had 39 "unpaid" senior officials. This was a simple way of escaping treasury control.

An industrialist who failed could easily be got rid of. Air officers were more difficult, and there were many rows when Beaverbrook turned against one of them. The gravest of these rows came when Beaverbrook proposed to put cannon instead of machine guns into fighter aircraft. Dowding favoured the proposal. The manufacturers reported that it

---

[1] Rowlands at first refused to receive the gift and then declared highmindedly that he would drink none of it until after the war. He did not keep his resolve.

could be done. The group captain concerned with this at MAP opposed it. He wrote primly:

> Judgement of aircraft designers on their own projects is not always sound. To try out every scheme, even if independent operational and technical opinions consider it unsound, would mean wasted effort and delays.

A junior member of the group captain's department reported to Beaverbrook that the change should be made at once. The group captain rebuked him:

> It is Air Staff who must decide which is the best armament for aircraft.
> Please avoid in future any expression of opinion on production or operational matters to the Minister.

Beaverbrook at once asked Sinclair to recall the group captain to the air ministry.

Beaverbrook displayed on the walls of his room two notices: COMMITTEES TAKE THE PUNCH OUT OF WAR and ORGANISATION IS THE ENEMY OF IMPROVISATION. He applied these rules. There were no regular committees and no clearly allotted functions. Hennessy and Craven were supposed to divide responsibilities. In fact they did each other's work as need dictated. Charts appended to the official history of Administration of War Production[1] show how Beaverbrook disrupted bureaucratic technique. The first—Appendix IIIA—of May 1940, presumably drawn up by Rowlands, has the permanent secretary in solitary glory immediately below the minister, with posts below him divided according to function. The second of August 1940 has merely a row of individual names under the minister—Rowlands's being one of them. Hierarchy had disappeared. The official history remarks (p. 296): "The very essence of Lord Beaverbrook's administration was its lack of definition of function".

Not all Beaverbrook's appointments were equally inspired. He always tended to call in old friends, not so much from favouritism as because he could rely upon them. Senator Elliott, of Crusading days, somehow turned up from Australia and was put on to the miscellaneous tasks which were too embarrassing for anyone else to handle, such as allocating secure quarters for government departments. This job was given to Beaverbrook by Churchill at the height of the air battle—again no doubt in the calculation that Beaverbrook was the one minister who would not mind offending his colleagues. Elliott was not altogether incompetent. It was different with R. B. Bennett, created Viscount Bennett in 1941, whom Beaverbrook also recruited. Bennett was retired, elderly, and slothful, after being no

[1] By J. D. Scott and Richard Hughes, 1955.

great success as prime minister of Canada. No doubt it pleased Beaverbrook to patronize his old friend who had for a time risen above him. Bennett was sent round the factories to practise his rotund oratory.

Ultimately Bennett failed Beaverbrook. There was in England a refugee Jew named Loewy, who was the only designer of extrusion presses. During the general panic Loewy and all his staff were interned. Beaverbrook pulled them out again to the indignation of the security services. Beaverbrook had a brilliant idea. The former prime minister of Canada should be called in to arbitrate. The urgent need for extrusion presses of aluminium was explained to Bennett. In vain. He reported that Loewy and his staff should be sent back into internment. Beaverbrook disregarded Bennett's recommendation. Bennett expostulated: "But I am the referee". Beaverbrook replied: "I always dispute the referee's verdict". This ended Bennett's connection with the ministry of aircraft production and for a time disturbed his friendship with Beaverbrook.

Another example of Beaverbrook's care for his friends was even stranger and more embarrassing. Rothermere was elderly and a sick man. Since he could no longer live in the south of France, he proposed very sensibly to go to the New World. Beaverbrook encouraged him and, to give him a feeling of being useful, asked him to survey the Canadian capacity for producing aircraft—a topic on which Beaverbrook was already fully informed by knowledgeable Canadian friends. Rothermere went round a few factories and sent some harmless reports. He also talked indiscreetly about British weakness. Halifax, the foreign secretary, grew alarmed and asked Beaverbrook to recall or silence Rothermere—especially to stop his going to the United States. Beaverbrook replied:

> I do not know where Rothermere is.
> I think he is already in the United States.
> In any case he is an old man.

This was true. Rothermere went on to Bermuda, where he died in November, leaving a few hundred thousand pounds of the millions which he had once possessed. The episode had no importance except as a reminder that Beaverbrook was never too busy to show human kindness.

Bennett had protested against Beaverbrook's "disregard of protocol". This characterized all the ministry's work. It left few written records. Beaverbrook's ministry, like his newspapers, was run by telephone. He issued orders to the factories by telephone, and his colleagues soon imitated him. Some time after the ministry had been formed, the forgotten branch at Harrogate reported that production at Castle Bromwich, under Lord Nuffield, was unsatisfactory. MAP replied that Castle Bromwich had been taken out of Nuffield's hands three weeks before and its equipment removed elsewhere. No written record or order had been made. The transfer provoked one of Beaverbrook's first battles. Nuffield stormed in to Stornoway House and threatened to have Beaverbrook sacked. Beaverbrook replied that there was nothing he would like better. Nuffield appealed to Churchill, with dark talk of the sums he had contributed to Conservative party funds. Churchill answered: "I cannot interfere with the manufacture of aircraft".

On another occasion, Freeman was about to leave on a tour of inspection when his aircraft was grounded. He was told that enemy aircraft were approaching and would be over the airfield at any moment. He said: "Oh, my God, is that all? I thought it was a telephone call from Lord Beaverbrook". Often the calls were more benevolent. A manufacturer, however humble, who had exceeded his target, would be called up late at night and told: "Well done. I expect even better next week". There was one incoming call expected every evening, which kept Beaverbrook on edge till it came. It was the call from Max Aitken to say that he had survived the day. Father and son drew closer and established a mutual devotion which thereafter never waned. Beaverbrook wrote to Harold Balfour, under secretary at the air ministry, on 30 May:

> Max Aitken is nerveless. He should be given some Squadron at once. His promotion is long overdue. And he can carry any burden.

This was a testimonial which owed nothing to family favouritism. Max Aitken's name stands high among the Few.

Beaverbrook abandoned the normal method of turning out aircraft only when the production line was flowing smoothly from start to finish. He set things moving at once and waited for a bottleneck to develop. The entire energies of MAP were then flung against the obstacle. A senior official would descend or some businessman be specially commissioned. The bottleneck was cleared. Production moved further downstream and then stuck again. Once more there was drama and swift action. This was exactly the technique which Beaverbrook had developed with his newspapers. He scanned the circulation figures and asked: "Why are we not selling more at Reading?" At this the circulation managers moved into Reading for a month. So now, he put his finger on some factory which was lagging and ordered action next day. In Beaverbrook's time, the production line never worked smoothly. He remarked: "Everything's wrong with the Ministry except production—and that's fine". And he recalled Newman's dying words: "It's true these have been years of strife, but after all there's the Cardinal's Hat".

I recently had an account of Beaverbrook at work from Mr. T. C. Usher, son of Sir George Usher, one of Beaverbrook's recruits from industry. Mr. Usher, then a second lieutenant in an anti-aircraft battery, had been summoned to report on the new Z type rocket guns. He writes:

> Lord Beaverbrook and I discussed the possibility of having these manu-
> factured in garages which was certainly quite feasible all over England.
> He was, during the interview I had with him, talking to the Hamilton Air
> Screw Company of Hamilton, Ohio, proposing payment for propellers for
> aircraft at a time when gold resources were totally exhausted. At the same
> time he was carrying on another conversation, on another telephone, with
> the secretary to Sir Geoffrey De Havilland of De Havilland Aircraft in
> Hatfield and raising hell because Sir Geoffrey was out to lunch for two
> hours. . . . There were at least six other people lined up with memoranda to
> discuss with him whilst my father and I sat in front of his desk.

Some of the stories about Beaverbrook's methods, though apocryphal,
are worth recording. According to Herbert Morrison, for instance, the
war cabinet allotted to the ministry of supply some machine tools being
brought back from France. When the ministry's agent arrived at Southampton docks, he found that the machine tools had already been removed
in MAP lorries. Beaverbrook had been in the cabinet anteroom. He had
heard the promise through the door and left at once to telephone instructions for action. This story does not seem to be true. Beaverbrook himself
spread the story that he had proposed to requisition Broadcasting House
and to conceal aircraft in Winchester Cathedral. He said modestly: "I
asked very much in order to get very little".

Beaverbrook ran his ministry in a blaze of publicity or, as his critics
called it, ballyhoo. Urgency was in his temperament. He always worked
seven days a week and now expected others to do the same. Thus George
Malcolm Thomson, after working twelve hours a day without a break for
90 days, took a morning off. When he returned, he found a message from
Beaverbrook on his desk: "Tell Thomson that Hitler will be here if he
doesn't look out". The urgency was of course also designed as a deliberate
operation to inspire the entire industry. Not all his gestures were well
chosen. To give a trivial example, he instructed his chauffeurs to ignore
the traffic lights. When one of them was pulled up, Beaverbrook replied
impudently to Sir Philip Game, the commissioner of police, on 14 July:

> I did give my chauffeur instructions to ignore the traffic lights. And I am
> in the habit of doing this.
>
> Only today I had to go urgently to Slough to investigate the result of
> a bomb falling on one of my works. I passed through many traffic lights
> on the way. Now what is the position?
>
> Should my chauffeur and I be summoned?
>
> Such a course would at least clear the position. And I would take any
> punishment coming to me.

Evidently Beaverbrook had second thoughts. The letter is marked:
"Not sent".

Then there was the appeal, suggested by J. B. Wilson: "Send me your pots and pans, send me your aluminium". Housewives sacrificed their cooking utensils, only to notice with irritation that there were plenty more in the shops. A note of 21 January 1941 records the result:

We got—
(1) from refining secondary aluminium about 10,000 tons.
(2) from salvage   2,100 tons.
(3) from pots and pans   800 tons.

The Spitfire Fund was more successful. This began as a spontaneous gesture by The Jamaica Gleaner which raised money in the island to buy a fighter. Beaverbrook and Wilson seized on the idea and pushed it hard. Every considerable contribution got a personal acknowledgement from the minister. Of course the fund was an irrelevancy, as the treasury observed. The shortage was in productive capacity, not in money, and even £13,000,000, the sum finally raised, was not a serious stroke against inflation. But the publicity effect was great. Everyone who contributed came to share Beaverbrook's urgency and spread it to others.

For the most part, Beaverbrook directed his drive straight to the factories, both to the employers and to the men. Most factories got a visit from Senator Elliott or some other speaker. The most important got Beaverbrook himself, repeating his revivalist oratory of Empire Crusade days. His message was always: seven days a week and disregard of all labour regulations. This brought him into conflict with Bevin, the minister of labour, who is reputed to have threatened legal action against MAP. Beaverbrook answered in his usual flattering vein on 26 September:

I have been your faithful and admiring colleague from the day I met you in Conference.
I have faith in you, belief in your leadership, confidence in your judgment and complete trust in your character.
So if I commit any errors in working with your department you must know that I am always willing to amend my ways.
You will never get a Minister in Government more willing to work under your Labour leadership.

This flattery had little effect. Beaverbrook and Bevin did not become Max and Ernie until June 1941, and even then Bevin often forgot.

Beaverbrook persisted in beating off all attempts to reduce hours in the factories or to set a bad example. Thus, when it was proposed to close the factories during a national day of prayer, he wrote to Churchill on 27 August:

We have already many interruptions to contend with. Usually, these come from Mr. Bevin, from the air raids and from the air raid warnings.
I hope very much that these troubles will not be reinforced by providence.

A proposal by Sir Horace Wilson that civil servants should be given one day off in four provoked this protest on 27 September:

> But I can show that God worked six days and rested only on the seventh. I could wish that in this respect Sir Horace was influenced by God's law.
>
> If these civil servants are given one day's rest in four, the factories will want to be treated in the same way. There will be one advantage from this: we will have no aircraft to ship abroad. Furthermore, if we adopt Sir Horace's methods, he will be meeting Hitler once again. And this time the Fuhrer will not treat him nearly as well as he did at Godesberg.

There can be no doubt that Beaverbrook was entirely wrong in thus insisting on long hours seven days a week. This might produce better results over a short period. Maybe also the exhortations gave a psychological boost to the workers in the factories. In the long run, as all experience proved, tired men, working long hours, produced less than fit men working fewer. As always, Beaverbrook judged policy from a publicity angle. "Work without stopping" was an exciting slogan, and Beaverbrook refused to consider its practical effect. He never took time off himself and expected this to be successful with everyone else. In this controversy, though not in some others, Bevin was right.

Beaverbrook took much the same line when the Germans began to bomb aircraft factories. Under the rules drafted before the war, work stopped practically all over the country as soon as German raiders crossed the coast. Beaverbrook wanted the factories to go on working unless they were being actually bombed, or maybe even then. He himself set the example. From the first he ignored the cabinet order that work in government offices should stop at the sound of the warning siren. He remained in his room and expected his staff to remain at their desks. This was only done by a supreme effort of will. Beaverbrook had none of Max Aitken's or for that matter Churchill's natural courage. David Farrer writes: "Beaverbrook is a man of nervous temperament. He was thoroughly scared by the noise of a falling bomb. But his sense of urgency prevailed over his fears".[1] He also felt that in this way he was defying Hitler. One day, Thomson and Farrer ducked under the table. They were just back at their big desk, when Beaverbrook burst in and, seeing them at work, cried: "Good boys. That's the way to show them".[2]

To quote Farrer further, "His shouts of protest almost drowned the noise of the sirens".[3] Instead of sirens, he campaigned for visible signs that his factories were being protected. His demands went to the air ministry, the war ministry, the ministry of supply, and to Churchill. We

[1] Farrer, The Sky's the Limit, 65.
[2] Farrer, G—for God Almighty, 63.
[3] Farrer, The Sky's the Limit, 63.

want smoke. We want barrage balloons. We want AA guns. We want fighter protection. We want detachments of soldiers at every factory as guards against parachutists. If Beaverbrook had had his way, fighter command, anti-aircraft command, and most of the British army would have been solely occupied during the autumn of 1940 in protecting aircraft factories. These factories were all-important to him. Therefore they must be all-important to everyone else. He did not trouble to consider whether these measures of protection would be effective. Like everything with him, they were instruments of propaganda. Farrer writes:

It was the appearance, not the reality of safety he was after. The measures of factory protection which he organized were designed less in order to safeguard the lives of the aircraft workers than to persuade them to go on working. He was fully prepared to risk lives in order to produce more aircraft.[1]

The last sentence is unfair. Beaverbrook was a general in wartime and had to risk lives. But he visited every big factory that was bombed and came back haggard with misery.

Producing aircraft at such desperate cost, Beaverbrook naturally opposed any proposal to divert them from the defence of Great Britain. The air ministry wanted to hand over to Canada the aircraft being manufactured in the United States which passed to Great Britain on the fall of France. Beaverbrook wrote to Churchill:

If the decision is taken in favour of the Canadians to give them these first rate fighters, bombers and engines, it will be a crime against the British Empire.

Dispatch of aircraft to South Africa brought the cry: "Is there to be nothing left for the poor wretches who pay taxes in Great Britain?" And later talk of selling aircraft to Sweden was repudiated with the remark: "I would as soon give Presbyterian ministers to cannibals". Beaverbrook also resisted the air ministry's plans for establishing training schools for pilots overseas. This again would mean sending aircraft out of the country. He wrote: "The trainer aircraft are our last reserve. In the last and decisive hour of the battle, they might be decisive indeed". If German raiders occasionally interfered with training, this would be a useful experience for the pupils. And he added an argument subtly tuned for Churchill: "Sending these aircraft would cause a revival of the false rumours concerning evacuation to Canada". On 24 September 1940 he defended his policy to the war cabinet:

If the Germans fail to attack Great Britain, that is a victory. If the Germans attack and are hurled back, that is a decisive victory. If we can prevail

[1] Farrer, The Sky's the Limit, 65.

until the winter months, the Americans will come into the war and the issue will be decided in our favour.

For these reasons, I oppose any diversion of any resources whatsoever other than the defence of Britain.

And I hold that all our resources should be used forthwith, even at the expense of our programme in the future.

Instead of sending aircraft overseas, Beaverbrook wanted to buy aircraft in America and bring them to England. American resources, he believed, were limitless, and he was determined to mobilize them. Disregarding the British purchasing commission in the United States and without waiting for authority from the British government, Beaverbrook appointed his own buying agent, Morris Wilson, president of the Royal Bank of Canada. Wilson, backed by Beaverbrook, pledged British money without reserve. When Henry Ford refused to manufacture Rolls-Royce Merlin engines on the ground that he would not produce weapons for any belligerent, Beaverbrook approached Packard, a smaller firm, and promised them the money with which to extend their plant. The Rolls-Royce agent reported later: "This is the biggest, the best and most profitable job even undertaken by the British government". Beaverbrook was the first to inject into American industry the sense of urgency he was preaching at home, and it was partly thanks to him that the United States were able to switch over so fast to all-out war production at the end of 1941. In this way Beaverbrook helped to win the war for the United States as well as for Great Britain.

Another part of aircraft supply from America was the trans-Atlantic ferry service (Atfero) which Beaverbrook instituted, again without war cabinet approval. The air ministry said that it was impractical to fly aircraft across the Atlantic. Beaverbrook persisted. The scheme, as well as being dramatic, had the further attraction that it was a one-way traffic: there would be no excuse for sending other aircraft back. Once more he called in a Canadian friend, J. P. Bickell, of International Nickel, who was already directing the ferrying of aircraft from the factories to the squadrons. During the winter of 1940-41 some 160 aircraft were ferried across the Atlantic with only one loss. Beaverbrook regarded Atfero as one of his great contributions to the provision of aircraft. The air ministry discontinued it as soon as Beaverbrook left MAP.

Though Beaverbrook disregarded the rules, he was furious when anyone else did so. One episode was characteristic. When Harold Balfour, under secretary for air, was in the United States during the summer of 1940, he ordered three Boeing Clippers for the run to West Africa. He knew that he was acting without authorization, but hoped that the urgency of the need would excuse him. On his return to England, the storm blew. Beaverbrook refused to see him. Kingsley Wood, the chancellor of the exchequer, rebuked him. Churchill wrote sternly: "I really do not see how the government could be carried on if such unauthorized commitments were to be countenanced". An apology satisfied Churchill. He wrote again: "It is my duty to carry on the government in a regular way. Pray dismiss the matter from your mind". Beaverbrook continued to insist that the order should be cancelled. Sinclair for once fought back. The Clippers or flying boats were delivered and put into service. In January 1942 Churchill and Beaverbrook returned from Bermuda in one of them. They were converted. Churchill, meeting Balfour in the house of commons, said to him: "They are fine ships. You apologized to me. It is rather I who should apologize to you". Beaverbrook telephoned to Balfour that the prime minister had given him "hell" for having opposed the purchase. Further Beaverbrook wrote on 16 February 1942:

> I gave you a rough ride about the "Balfour Boeings".
> But I had a difficult job cutting my Ministry out of the ribs of the Air Ministry. I had to defend my position at every step. I was surrounded by those who would betray me and leave me impotent.
> Failure to retain authority would have been failure to do the job.
> Injustice was done to you by me in the pursuit of efficiency.

Thereafter Balfour was Beaverbrook's devoted friend. The gift for frank withdrawal after a row often endeared Beaverbrook even to those whom he most offended.

The occasions for withdrawal were rare during the high summer of 1940. Beaverbrook knew that at this time Churchill would always support him. When the air ministry tried to defend their stock of spares, Churchill wrote sharply to Sinclair:

> I earnestly trust you will see Lord Beaverbrook's wishes are met fully and immediately in the matter of these spares. I really could not endure another bickering over this, considering the gravity of the situation.

Later even Churchill's patience grew thin. When Beaverbrook tried to requisition premises all over the country in defiance of other departments, Churchill wrote to him on 1 February 1941:

> It cannot be admitted that any one Department can peg out claims for itself all over the country, even if it most obligingly hands over the premises and waives its rights whenever a case is shown.
> I think it would be a great pity to bring this before the Cabinet. I could not support you, and everyone else would vote against your having a privilege or monopoly. I do not see how it can be any satisfaction to you to put yourself and me in this position. On the merits I cannot feel you are right, and with anyone else but you I should long ago have settled it by a stroke of the pen.

Beaverbrook kept a score of his disputes with the air ministry. At the end of January 1941 he recorded that Sinclair had said No 28 times and

Yes 14 times. Of Beaverbrook's requests to promote air officers serving in MAP 5 had been rejected and 3 approved. Against this MAP had said No to the air ministry 4 times and Yes 9 times. These were no doubt slanted figures devised for propaganda purposes. In every great issue Beaverbrook won. He made the ministry of aircraft production a truly independent department which was what after all it was intended to be. What use did Beaverbrook make of the powers which he thus attained? This is the decisive question on which he must be judged. There can be no dispute that the production of aircraft greatly increased under his direction. Between January and April 1940 the production branch of the air ministry produced 2,729 aircraft of which 638 were fighters. Between May and August MAP produced 4,576 aircraft, including 1,875 fighters, and repaired 1,872. Later figures for repairs give 703 between September 1939 and 25 May 1940; 5,275 between 25 May 1940 and the end of January 1941.[1]

On 2 September 1940 Beaverbrook reported to Churchill:

> On May 15th last there were 884 aircraft available for operations in the Squadrons—excluding Lysanders.
>
> Now there are 1,325, excluding Lysanders.
>
> There is an increase of about 450.
>
> There is another increase of between 450 to 500 in operational aircraft in operational training units.
>
> So it will be seen that the R.A.F. has drawn from the Aircraft Ministry nearly a thousand operational machines since your Government was formed, for the purpose of strengthening units.
>
> In addition all casualties had to be replaced.
>
> And 720 aircraft were shipped abroad.
>
> "Nobody knows the trouble I've seen".

Churchill minuted: "I do".

A few weeks earlier Churchill showed the weekly graphs of aircraft production to Crozier, the editor of The Manchester Guardian. Churchill said: "Beaverbrook has done astonishing things these last few weeks. He's done miracles", and Crozier noted: "The rise since Beaverbrook began the sprint was very striking, and the comparison with the bad weeks in the spring was enormous".[2]

The air ministry claimed that aircraft could not be stamped out of the ground and that the increased production was possible only because of the plans and preparations which it had made before Beaverbrook took over. This of course was true, and it is impossible to answer the hypothetical question what would have happened if the air ministry had

[1] There were fewer air engagements and therefore fewer damaged aircraft between September 1939 and May 1940.
[2] This note of 26 July and some later ones quoted are from unpublished records of interviews, now in the Beaverbrook Library, which Crozier made during the war.

remained in charge of production. Two things seem likely. There would have been less urgency, and there would have been less emphasis on the production of fighters. These two things might well have lost the battle of Britain. The champions of the air ministry do not contest this. They complain however that Beaverbrook's achievement was made at an excessive cost. Thus Air Chief Marshal Sir Philip Joubert writes:

> In fact Lord Beaverbrook, to put it bluntly, played hell with the war policy of the R.A.F. But he most certainly produced the aircraft that won the Battle of Britain. What he did in the summer of 1940 set back the winning of the air war over Germany by many months. The bomber production programme was disrupted to allow of high-speed production of fighters. And who can say that he was very wrong?[1]

Beaverbrook was certainly ready to sacrifice the future for the present, as he often announced himself. But the complaint about the subsequent shortage of heavy bombers has been overdone. In May 1940 MAP gave complete priority to the production of two fighters (Spitfires and Hurricanes) and three bombers (Wellington, Whitley and Hampden), with precedence for fighters. The development of new types was arrested, and this hit especially hard the heavy bombers which were still in the development stage. But this priority decision lasted only for two months. In July development was resumed, and the tardy production of heavy bombers, which continued for over three years, was little affected by the short interruption. German bombing in the winter of 1940–41 set back the production programme far more. But the major cause of delay must be found in "teething" troubles. Heavy bombers set technical problems which were not solved for a long time and then more by American than by British industry. The complaint of "the air marshals" against Beaverbrook was thus mainly a red herring to justify their general disgruntlement at his success.

There is one point to be made on the other side. Beaverbrook believed in a defensive strategy. He wanted Great Britain to survive until the United States were drawn into the war. Hence his enthusiasm for the production of fighters. He had no faith that independent, or as it was called, strategical bombing could win the war by itself. This faith was uncritically held at the air ministry, and it provided the underlying reason for the ceaseless carping which flowed from the air marshals. If Beaverbrook had shared their enthusiasm for heavy bombers, he would have got production moving despite the overriding need for fighters. As always, technical decisions could not be divorced from strategy.

Beaverbrook found productive resources easily enough when he wanted to please the other services—much to the indignation of the air ministry.

[1] Joubert, The Third Service, 136.

He pushed up aircraft supplies for the fleet air arm and even favoured transferring control of coastal command to the admiralty—a sacrilegious proposal which brought a bellow of rage from the formidable Lord Trenchard. By some strange chance, the transfer was also advocated by The Evening Standard, though Beaverbrook declared innocently: "The Evening Standard is not controlled by me". Beaverbrook was of course not unaware that in pleasing the admiralty, he was pleasing A. V. Alexander, the first lord. In this way he won the support of one service minister, Alexander, against another, Sinclair, and of one Labour minister, Alexander, against another, Bevin.

Beaverbrook also wished to meet the needs of the army. In July 1940 he placed a large order for dive bombers in Canada and the United States. Eden, then secretary for war, was enthusiastic. The air ministry protested and refused to supply or train pilots. In February 1941 Sinclair persuaded Margesson, who had become secretary for war, to drop any further order for dive bombers. Complaints about the lack of dive bombers came from the armies fighting in North Africa. Beaverbrook was blamed for the deficiency. After he left office, he wished to tell the true story in his own defence. Churchill forbade it. He wrote to Beaverbrook on 29 May 1942:

> For one man to go and give his own account of what happens in these secret conversations would be very hardly judged by the public and would also be prejudicial to the whole conduct of the war.

Thus the case against Beaverbrook was permitted to prevail.

Another of Beaverbrook's favoured projects was the Whittle jet which he pushed on from an early stage. He believed that this would revolutionize air warfare, and later events proved him right. When asked to demonstrate it to the American General Arnold, he replied:

> We have not shown it to a soul yet. Indeed we have even flown it on a cloudy day so that the angels should not see it.
> But what is forbidden to the angels shall be permitted to the General.

Again the air marshals were unimpressed. Development of the jet was neglected after Beaverbrook left MAP, and by the end of the war he noted with alarm that the Germans were using their jets to recover supremacy in the air. One other voice may be quoted on Beaverbrook's behalf. Sir Barnes Wallis said recently: "I always knew if I went to see him about what seemed to be some outsize or absurd idea at least *he* would be responsive and push it". Barnes Wallis added that the manufacture of the ten-ton bomb and the Dam-buster bomb was due to Beaverbrook's backing.

Trouble did not only come to Beaverbrook from the air marshals. Many people were ready to snipe at him or to tax him with indiscretions.

He had hardly taken office when Halifax accused him of revealing British weakness in the air to Maisky, the Soviet ambassador—a weakness known to every reader of the newspapers. Beaverbrook replied on 22 May 1940:

I have not seen Maisky, nor have I talked with Maisky since my appointment.

It is very bad that these stories should be circulated and I should like to do what I can to stamp them out.

There are many bad people in the world and they are not all in Germany.

Next, Beaverbrook held a press conference with the industrial correspondents and was alleged to have made slighting remarks about Bevin. The industrial correspondent of The Daily Express secured signed statements from every person present that no such remarks had been made. Maybe the journalists were showing professional solidarity.

Somewhat later, the representative of the air ministry in Canada reported that Beaverbrook's hostility to training pilots overseas was causing general anger among Canadians, including even Mackenzie King, the prime minister. Beaverbrook extracted a repudiation of this story from Mackenzie King and demanded the dismissal of both the air officer and the British high commissioner who had endorsed the story. Then he dropped the affair, perhaps because he had lost interest or maybe because the story was not all that far from the truth. On another occasion however Beaverbrook was able to score a triumph of innocence. When Churchill met the editors of British newspapers, at his instigation, a complaint came, this time from a member of the cabinet office, that only selected editors had been invited. Churchill minuted sternly: "I hope this is not true. Please let me know the facts". Beaverbrook was able to show that every editor of a London paper had been present and that only the northern papers were represented by their London editors. He concluded:

"Demetrius hath good report of all men, and of the truth itself".
Note from Shorter Catechism.

Of course Beaverbrook was not always as innocent as he claimed to be. He could never resist indiscretions in conversation and, immediately after writing a letter of wholehearted devotion to "Winston", would refer critically to "that fellow Churchill" at the dinner table. Such remarks are hard to recapture, but a note from Harcourt Johnstone of 14 November 1940 gives an indication of what dining with Beaverbrook was like. "Crinks" was an old friend of Beaverbrook's, but also a political supporter of Sinclair's and indeed one of the two principal paymasters of the Liberal party throughout the nineteen-thirties. He wrote:

I hate rows, and as your guest I shouldn't dream of making one in front of your staff, but I don't want you to think that I don't deeply disapprove of the way you spoke at dinner last night about Archie [Sinclair]. What you think decent to say in front of your officials is your own affair, but Archie is my friend and, more than that, I have every reason to believe that he is a loyal, hard-working and efficient Secretary of State for Air.

Beaverbrook did not reply to this letter.

Beaverbrook in short remained Beaverbrook even when he was providing the aircraft which won the battle of Britain. It was not in his nature to become a purely departmental minister, intent on a single task. He still watched the currents of politics, estimated the changing reputations of individual ministers and even speculated on future combinations. The flow of gossipy letters about politics to friends overseas did not cease for more than a couple of weeks, though it also no doubt had the serious intention of impressing Americans with the unanimous determination in Great Britain to go on with the war. He even kept one eye on his newspapers. These indeed gave him least trouble. They were in the hands of well-tried men, who could divine Beaverbrook's outlook by instinct. Robertson remained in supreme control, consulting Beaverbrook regularly only on questions of financial policy. Wardell gave up the management of The Evening Standard to go into the army and was replaced by Tom (now Sir Thomas) Blackburn, who was already an old hand. Otherwise nothing changed. John Gordon continued to edit The Sunday Express, and Arthur Christiansen The Daily Express, throughout the war. Frank Owen edited The Evening Standard until 1942. None of them needed directives, though their telephones were by no means silent.

Beaverbrook, as he once confessed, could never remain wholly serious for long, and he got much fun from explaining to his colleagues, including Churchill, how improper it would be for him to interfere with his newspapers, while he was at the same time encouraging his editors in their pugnacity and criticism. When Churchill complained that Low, the cartoonist of The Evening Standard, was "a Communist of the Trotsky variety", Beaverbrook answered on 14 December 1940:

> On the one hand, you are constantly annoyed by the charge that I am interfering with the newspapers and that I should not do so.
> On the other hand, it is said by my colleagues in the Cabinet that I don't interfere with the newspapers and that I should do so.
> . . . .
> I do not quite know how to deal with this situation.
> I do not agree with Low. I have rarely done so. I do not interfere with Low. I have never done so.

Another complaint of Churchill's against John Gordon brought a similar answer on 12 May 1941:

> I would like to control The Sunday Express. It would take little time and involve a small amount of effort.

But unless I do control the newspaper, it is impossible to control the policy of its editor.

One may guess that, immediately after this letter was written, John Gordon received a telephone call saying: "A very fine article".

The Evening Standard continued to give Beaverbrook most pleasure and amusement. Frank Owen was an erratic Radical, as was Peter Howard, one of the principal leader-writers. Michael Foot, the other, was a left-wing Socialist, formerly an adherent of Cripps and now of Aneurin Bevan. On one occasion, when Foot was allegedly restrained from some especially strong outburst, Beaverbrook boasted of this to Sinclair and added: "Michael is my man as Dingle[1] is yours". Michael was much more than that: already Beaverbrook's favourite son and later the last of his intimate friends, the two men bound together by a deep and enduring mutual love. Owen, Foot and Howard had collaborated in writing Guilty Men, the famous pamphlet which attacked the old gang of Chamberlain, Halifax and the rest. Inspiration from Beaverbrook himself had not been lacking. When Halifax said condescendingly: "You must find it hard to live on £5,000 a year"—unaware that Beaverbrook was not drawing his salary—Beaverbrook replied: "Ah! But I've always got my royalties from Guilty Men". This was the kind of remark which did not endear Beaverbrook to respectable circles.

There seems only one clear instance where Beaverbrook interfered with his newspapers while he was a minister, and for a characteristic reason. In the autumn of 1940 he told his editors, and Low also, "to lay off Franco". A request for this had come from Halifax, and it was no doubt common sense to avoid offending Franco when it seemed likely that the Germans would march through Spain and attack Gibraltar. However Beaverbrook would not have restrained the anti-Fascists of The Evening Standard merely in order to please Lord Halifax. The real explanation for the order lay elsewhere. Sir Samuel Hoare was now ambassador at Madrid and was having a hard time, upholding the British cause. He was one of Beaverbrook's oldest political friends, and Beaverbrook was anxious to help him. The call of friendship prevailed, where high policy would have carried no weight.

Most of Beaverbrook's energies went into the ministry of aircraft production for the first few weeks after it was created. From the start he was also involved in the making of policy. On 15 May 1940 he went with Sinclair, the secretary of state for air, Newall, chief of the air staff, and Dowding, chief of fighter command, to meet Churchill. Churchill wanted to send more fighter squadrons to France. Dowding replied that he had none to spare. Beaverbrook often recounted the dramatic scene when

[1] Dingle Foot, Michael's brother, and at this time a Liberal MP.

Dowding, having shown his graph of fighter wastage, answered Churchill's rhetoric by silently laying his pencil on the table. Dowding, as might be expected from his character, denied that the scene was as dramatic as Beaverbrook made out: "I may have thrown down my pencil in exasperation, though I have no recollection of doing so".[1] Beaverbrook also told how Dowding advanced on Churchill with a paper in his hands. The onlookers believed that it was a letter of resignation. In fact it was simply the graph of fighter wastage so that Churchill should judge for himself.

According to Beaverbrook, Sinclair sat silent, and Newall gave Dowding little support. At any rate Churchill was not convinced. More fighter squadrons were sent to France. Newall however had been won over. He insisted that Sinclair should appeal to the war cabinet, and Sinclair did so on 16 May. He repeated Dowding's figures. The war cabinet supported Sinclair's stand. No more fighter squadrons were sent to France. Beaverbrook was not directly involved.[2] Quite apart from his dislike of discussing questions in a committee, even if the committee were called the cabinet, he needed Churchill's support in his own affairs and therefore kept out of other people's quarrels. Nevertheless he had been clearly on Dowding's side, and this hinted at a fundamental cleavage of outlook between himself and Churchill.

For years past Churchill had placed his faith in the alliance with France. Even when France fell, he still cared deeply for Europe and the balance of power. His mind ranged into the future except during the most desperate days of the struggle for survival. Beaverbrook never considered future policy. He looked no further than tomorrow. Europe and high policy meant nothing to him. His sole concern, like Dowding's, was the security of Great Britain, and he regarded allies as an encumbrance. The cleavage took a long time to work out. In the end it drove Churchill and Beaverbrook apart.

Beaverbrook's first real involvement in grand policy came nearly a month later. On 11 June 1940 he wrote to Hoare:

> Winston is standing up to the strain very well. He is like Atlas with two worlds to carry. With one hand he bears up the British Empire, with the other he sustains the French Republic. And the French Republic takes a bit of supporting, let me tell you.

[1] Wright, Dowding and the Battle of Britain, 105.
[2] The discussion of 15 May, described above, took place before the cabinet met at 11 a.m. Sinclair, Newall and Dowding attended the subsequent cabinet meeting. Beaverbrook did not. The question of sending fighter squadrons to France was not discussed. Sinclair and Newall attended the cabinet meeting of 16 May. Dowding and Beaverbrook did not. Newall referred to "the figures laid before us by Air Chief Marshal Dowding yesterday"—though no figures had been laid before the cabinet itself. On 18 May Beaverbrook attended the war cabinet, but this meeting discussed questions relating to aircraft production, such as storage and repair.

This was the task in which Churchill enlisted Beaverbrook's aid. On 13 June Churchill flew to Tours for what proved to be the last meeting of the supreme war council. He took with him Halifax and Beaverbrook. The inclusion of Halifax is easy to understand. He was foreign secretary and, with Chamberlain failing in health, perhaps the second man in the government. But why Beaverbrook? Why did Churchill not take Attlee, leader of the Labour party, as he had done on a previous visit, or Eden, the secretary for war? Was it merely because, as Churchill wrote of Beaverbrook:[1] "In trouble he is always buoyant"? Or did Churchill obscurely sense that Beaverbrook alone could restrain him if he were carried away by his pro-French emotion? At any rate this is what happened. Reynaud, the French premier, asked whether Great Britain would permit France to make a separate peace. Churchill stalled by suggesting an appeal to President Roosevelt. Reynaud renewed his question. Churchill asked to be allowed to consult with his colleagues. The British representatives went out into the garden of the Prefecture.

It had been raining. Churchill and his companions walked in the mud, with water dripping from the trees. None of them seemed to know what to say. Churchill asked some vague questions about the chances of Reynaud continuing the war in North Africa. Spears, Churchill's personal representative with Reynaud, has described what happened next:

> Then suddenly Beaverbrook spoke. His dynamism was immediately felt. "There is nothing to do but to repeat what you have already said, Winston. Telegraph to Roosevelt and await his answer. Tell Reynaud that we have nothing to say or discuss until Roosevelt's answer is received. Don't commit yourself to anything. We shall gain a little time and see how those Frenchmen sort themselves out. We are doing no good here. In fact, listening to these declarations of Reynaud's only does harm. Let's get along home". It was as simple as that, but it was what everyone felt to be the voice of common sense.[2]

The little group rejoined the French. Churchill spoke as Beaverbrook suggested. The question of a separate peace was not mentioned. The British representatives returned to England. Churchill was gloomy and despondent. All his heart was bound up with the French alliance, and he knew that this was all but shattered. Beaverbrook, on the other hand, was radiant. He burst into Stornoway House and announced triumphantly: "We are all Splendid Isolationists now".

There was a similar confrontation some three weeks later when France had signed an armistice with Germany and had fallen out of the war. This time Beaverbrook himself has recorded the story. On the night of

[1] Churchill, Finest Hour, 178.
[2] Spears, Assignment to Catastrophe, ii, 215.

2 July he was summoned to the cabinet room. He found Churchill with A. V. Alexander and Sir Dudley Pound, the first sea lord. The question: what was to be done about the French fleet which had taken refuge at Oran? It must not fall into German hands. Pound was for bombarding it, unless the French admiral agreed to hand over his ships or move them to an American port. Alexander reluctantly agreed with Pound. Churchill was horrified at the proposal. He turned to Beaverbrook. Beaverbrook answered without hesitation: the French fleet must be attacked. He said: "The Germans will force the French fleet to join the Italians, thus taking command of the Mediterranean. The Germans will force this by threatening to burn Bordeaux the first day the French refuse, the next day Marseilles, and the third day Paris". Once more it was the voice of common sense. Churchill yielded and gave the order for attack. Then he seized Beaverbrook's arm and rushed into the garden. Beaverbrook's account concludes:

> There was a high wind blowing. He raced along. I had trouble keeping up with him. And I began to have an attack of asthma. Churchill declared that there was no other decision possible. Then he wept.

Again the friend of France had been overborne by the Isolationist.

Beaverbrook showed the same spirit over another topic of naval policy which arose at this time. Again Spears has recorded the story. He wrote to Beaverbrook on 4 January 1961:

> I had called in to look at telegrams at No. 10 and was in the Secretaries' Room when Winston, who was in the Cabinet Room, called out to ask if I was there. I went in and sat down opposite him. He was sitting with his back to the fireplace. He threw across to me a signal from Roosevelt and as far as I remember this asked that if the situation deteriorated our fleet should sail for North America. I am fairly certain that no mention was made of a German invasion of Britain. I am confident on this point because of my reaction. My point was that even to consider the proposal would be disastrous because things at a distance always seem much worse than they are on the spot and if we showed that we were considering sending the fleet over our situation would seem to them to be far more desperate than it actually was. . . . At this point you walked in and Winston said to me, "Show that signal to Max", which I did and I have always admired and often quoted your answer. You read it quickly and without a moment's hesitation said, "Winston, you can't do that".

Spears, like Beaverbrook, always presented events in dramatic terms. The exchanges between Roosevelt and Churchill over the future of the Royal Navy were less sensational and were prolonged over some weeks. Nor does Churchill seem to have hesitated as to what his answer should be. However there is no reason to doubt that Beaverbrook gave him a push towards asserting British independence.

Here too was a difference of attitude between the two men. Churchill, easily moved to sentiment, tended to believe that the Americans were sentimentally attached to Great Britain and that President Roosevelt especially felt towards Great Britain as he himself had felt towards France. Beaverbrook knew America better and did not share Churchill's belief. In his opinion, the Americans were supporting Great Britain for the sake of their own security, and he was convinced that they would carry off the British Empire as the price of their support if they were allowed to do so. Though quite willing to use sentimental appeals as instruments of propaganda, essentially he wanted a business relationship in which Great Britain asserted herself as an equal partner and a great power. He was in the war for Great Britain and her Empire, not for America or for any idealistic cause.

The first paper which Beaverbrook drafted on 27 June 1940 concerning relations with the United States began with the words: "My view is— give no secrets to America, except for money value received". On reflection he put the sentence in a positive and less aggressive form: "It is my considered opinion that we should give the Americans all our secrets, receiving in exchange money or money's worth. . . . And of course we would be delighted to take the money out in the form of American destroyers or aircraft or artillery". The business spirit was still clear. Later Beaverbrook made it much clearer. On 26 December 1940 he wrote to Churchill:

> It would appear that the United States are demanding our South African gold and proposing to collect it and carry it away.
>
> That is a decision which I would resist very strongly and seek to destroy with every means in my power.
>
> Our financial relations with the Americans have been so loosely handled that it is necessary, now and forthwith, to take up a firm policy and to pursue it in the face of obstacles and even to the extent of a rupture.
>
> . . . .
>
> The present position is this:
>
> They have conceded nothing. They have exacted payment to the uttermost for all they have done for us. They have taken our bases without valuable consideration. They have taken our gold. They have been given our secrets and offered us a thoroughly inadequate service in return.
>
> . . . .
>
> We are told over and over again that we get such wonderful results from the Purvis Mission, but in fact he has nothing to his credit except a kindly disposition on the part of Mr. Morgenthau, and that is easily bought at such a price.
>
> Therefore I declare that the time has come for a complete understanding with the United States.
>
> It should be made amply clear that we are not prepared to relinquish any

more gold here or in South Africa and that we must retain any interest we
may possess in gold in the Dominions.

. . . .

The American government on the other hand is asking for the moon and
appears unwilling to pay sixpence.

On 20 February 1941 Beaverbrook recited grievances accumulated
over twenty years:

We were told that if we agreed to the twelve-mile limit off the American
coast, all would be well. We did agree. But all was not well.

We were told that if we stopped the export of drink from the Empire
to the United States, there would be a wonderful improvement in our
relations with America. There was not.

If we made peace with Ireland, we were to enjoy for ever and ever the
favour of America. We did as we were told. But it brought us no comfort
in Ireland and little credit in America.

If only we settled the war debt, even at five cents in the dollar, we should
have the complete approval of the United States. We settled, and earned
ruin in England and abuse in America.

We were incited by the Americans to break the alliance with Japan.
We did so. And look where it has taken us! The Japanese are our relentless
enemies. And the Americans are our unrelenting creditors.

Now we are told by Roosevelt and Willkie that if only we stand up to
Germany, all will be well. We are doing so. But we would stand up better
if we knew that there would be something left to provide sustenance for our
people in the day of hardship.

If we give everything away, we gain little or no advantage over our present
situation.

Stand up to the Democrats!

As previously with France, Beaverbrook pushed Churchill into asserting
British independence in regard to the United States, and Churchill was
not always grateful for the push.

In the early days of their association however it was Churchill who
pointed to the path of duty and Beaverbrook who attempted to stray from
it. Within a month of becoming minister of aircraft production, Beaverbrook was already proposing to resign, and thereafter letters of resignation
came thick and fast. His secretaries counted fourteen, and there were
others which he wrote in his own hand or cancelled before they were sent.
Some were provoked by exasperation when he failed to get his way against
the air marshals or was unjustly criticized in the house of commons.
Some were tactical devices for winning a particular battle. He told
Churchill on 17 March 1942 after his final resignation that the earlier
threats were "a deliberate act of promotion. The object was 'urgency and
speed'. . . . I was always under the impression that, in your support for

my methods, you wished me to stay on in office, to storm, to threaten resignation and to withdraw again".

There was also a more rational ground. Beaverbrook understood his own nature. He was the man for an emergency, breaking the log jams and getting men to work seven days a week. His methods were unnecessary or even harmful when the production line was flowing smoothly. He excelled in the unexpected, and this lost its force when it was repeated. As Mr. Milestone asked in Peacock's Headlong Hall, when told that unexpectedness was a striking feature of the romantic garden: "By what name do you distinguish this character, when a person walks round the grounds for the second time?" An industrialist was excited when Beaverbrook telephoned to congratulate him in the middle of the night. He became increasingly irritated when the calls were renewed. Beaverbrook had originally assumed that he would hold office only for a few weeks, speeding up aircraft production and then handing over to a more orderly successor. He stayed longer than he had intended, as new emergencies followed the first one—the battle of Britain and then the winter blitz. But he always meant to go when aircraft production settled down, and his critics, who condemned him for going, also approved of his making way for someone else.

However this was not all. Beaverbrook never stuck at anything for long. Though he was angry if one of his journalists threatened to resign and did not weary of quoting Healy's words, "Never resign. Wait until you're sacked", he did not apply Healy's doctrine to himself. In business, he acquired a concern, expanded it, and then sold it off. In politics he never fought a controversy through to a finish. He was constantly announcing that he had given up the direction of his newspapers. At the dinner table he often lost interest in the middle of a conversation and fell asleep or appeared to do so. Even when composing his works of history—the thing he cared for most—he sometimes said: "Aw, to hell with it" and laid aside his dictation for the day or for a couple of months. Here too he understood himself. He said: "I am always excited at the beginning of a journey and bored after the first few miles". In time he became bored with the ministry of aircraft production.

There was a total difference here between Churchill and Beaverbrook. Churchill had sat in cabinet off and on for more than thirty years. He loved office. All his life had been a preparation for the supreme responsibility which now lay on him, and he would have liked to keep it for ever. Also he enjoyed the routine—the ceaseless arrival of boxes, the stickers of "Action This Day", the rotundity of official phrases. Beaverbrook in contrast had no experience of working with colleagues. In all his undertakings, financial or journalistic, he had been the unchallenged boss, issuing orders and knowing that they would be carried out without further discussion. Now he trampled on other departments. He did not conciliate them.

Moreover the roughness which Beaverbrook often showed and his quickness of decision concealed an essential timidity. At heart he doubted himself just as he trembled when German bombs fell, and he had to conquer his inner fears every day. As his responsibilities increased, his asthma increased also, until in the end he lost his battle against his own nature. His offers of resignation were always made in writing. Clearly he could not face either the cajoling or the indignation which they would provoke if offered in intimate conversation. Also many of the letters were never sent. Fear first drove him to resign, and then he feared to do so.

The exchanges between Churchill and Beaverbrook began on 16 June 1940 when Beaverbrook sent a long letter of complaint against the air ministry. He wrote: "I find myself frustrated and obstructed, and I need your help". He demanded control of stores, control of ferry pilots, control of bomb production. The letter ended:

> I began my Ministry with a quarrel with the Secretary of State for Air over a refusal on my part to send Merlin engines to Canada. I appear to be ending it with a quarrel with the Secretary of State regarding his refusal to let me bring Merlin engines back from France.
>
> I cannot take responsibility unless the requisite authority is given to me now.

This letter is marked "cancelled". Presumably it was not sent. Two days later, on 18 June 1940, Beaverbrook sent his first report to the war cabinet:

> Production of new aircraft has risen from 245 a week to 363 a week. Production of engines has risen from 411 a week to 620 a week.
>
> Repair of aircraft has risen from 22 a week to 93. And repair of engines has risen from 65 a week to 226.
>
> . . . .
>
> The supply of aircraft is now in excess of the available pilots. The present output can be sustained and increased.

Some final paragraphs were deleted before the report was sent. They read:

> It is my firm view that a man of different qualities will now manage the Ministry on lines more satisfactory from the standpoint of the Air Ministry. I therefore propose to hand over my completed task.
>
> If my special qualities are of value in any department of the Ministry of Supply, I am prepared to take a difficult post under Mr. Herbert Morrison, provided that he wishes to make use of my services.

Another fortnight passed. Once more Beaverbrook determined to resign and this time sent the letter. He wrote to Churchill on 30 June:

> Production has been immensely increased and a sufficient supply of trainer aircraft put at the disposal of the Air Ministry.

It is now imperative that the Ministry of Aircraft Production should pass into the keeping of a man in touch and sympathy with the Air Ministry and the Air Marshals.

I should be relieved of my duties after my successor has been informed of all our projects. In particular, the new Minister should be informed of my plans for carrying out a vigorous programme of development of new types of aircraft and engines.

My decision to retire is based on my firm conviction that I am not suited to working with the Air Ministry or the Air Marshals.

I am convinced that my work is finished and my task is over. I am certain that another man could take up the responsibilities with hope and expectation of that measure of support and sympathy which has been denied to me.

In handing you this resignation I wish to thank all of my colleagues for the assistance I have received and the courtesy that has been given me.

In particular, I wish to give you a grateful acknowledgment of the inspiring experience of working under your leadership in war.

I am in complete agreement with your policy and the execution of it.

This letter received a brusque answer from Churchill. He wrote on 1 July:

I have received your letter of June 30, and hasten to say that at a moment like this when an invasion is reported to be imminent there can be no question of any Ministerial resignations being accepted. I require you therefore to dismiss this matter from your mind, and to continue the magnificent work you are doing on which to a large extent our safety depends. Meanwhile I am patiently studying how to meet your needs in respect of control of the over-lapping parts of your Department and that of the Air Ministry, and also to assuage the unfortunate differences which have arisen.

In face of this letter Beaverbrook retreated. He was also swayed by a conversation with Dowding, in which he learnt the severity of the battle which was approaching and the need there was for more fighter aircraft. In answer he struck a new blow at the air marshals and kept open his determination to resign. Beaverbrook wrote to Churchill on 1 July 1940:

I will certainly not neglect my duties here in the face of invasion. But it is imperative—and all the more so because of this threat of armed attack upon our shores—that the process of turning over this Ministry should take place as soon as possible.

I cannot get information which I require about supplies or equipment. I cannot get permission to carry out operations essential to strengthening our reserves to the uttermost in readiness for the day of invasion.

It is not possible for me to go on because a breach has taken place in the last five weeks through the pressure I have been compelled to put upon reluctant officers.

In my rush and hurry to achieve substantial results in a period of crisis, I have thought only of our needs in aircraft and of equipping myself with the means and the knowledge to supply these needs.

The breach which has thus been made between the Air Ministry and myself cannot be healed, although I have made many efforts.

It is obvious that another man must be called upon who can work with the Air Ministry and the Air Marshals. He must take up where I lay down.

And, rest assured, I will not lay down until the new Minister reaches my offices, and then only when he has been properly informed of everything that is in hand.

With this the first round ended. Thereafter Beaverbrook was too absorbed in meeting Dowding's needs to have time for thoughts of resignation or of anything else. The battle of Britain began. For Beaverbrook, as for others, this was his finest hour. The next proposals for a change came from Churchill, not from Beaverbrook. Churchill fully appreciated Beaverbrook's great achievement at MAP—as he telegraphed on 21 July: "Results magnificent especially operational"—and now wished to saddle Beaverbrook with even greater responsibilities. The need was clear, the solution less clear. Churchill grasped the supreme direction of strategy as Lloyd George had never done during the first world war. Creating himself minister of defence, he dealt directly with the chiefs of staff's committee. The three service ministers were hardly consulted except on administrative questions, and the defence committee (operations) of the war cabinet, though nominally the constitutional authority, did little more than endorse Churchill's direction. This system began to operate as soon as Churchill became prime minister and worked without change throughout the war.

There was no such supreme direction on the civil side. The defence committee (supply) was ineffective, and the three production ministries— the ministry of aircraft production, the ministry of supply for the army, and the admiralty—grabbed at resources haphazard.[1] Beaverbrook secured A1 priority for his ministry, but even he admitted that this could not be permanent. The obvious solution was to create a civil dictator, as all-powerful as Churchill was over strategy. This solution was impossible. Churchill was too busy to undertake the task himself, and no one else was acceptable either to him or to others. Quite apart from the fact that the production ministries were determined not to surrender their autonomy, war production could not be separated from civilian affairs as strategy could be. Hence a supreme minister would have to dictate also to the ministry of labour and the board of trade, and here there was an insuperable

---

[1] The independence of the three production ministries is shown even in the official History of War Production, which is really three separate accounts, one of them (admiralty) actually written by a different author.

obstacle in the person of Ernest Bevin, minister of labour. Bevin would stomach no authority except Churchill's and often not even that. Churchill therefore devised a way round: an arbiter between the departments who could appeal to the war cabinet in case of difficulties.

Churchill wanted Beaverbrook to undertake this task. He had a high opinion of Beaverbrook's business ability and ruthless will. Perhaps also he recognized that Beaverbrook, an isolated individual, was the only person who could become the second man in the kingdom without threatening Churchill's own supremacy. This was a tremendous opportunity. But it demanded that Beaverbrook should change his nature. He would have to preside over committees, reconcile conflicting claims, and issue directions patiently without giving offence to anyone. These were not things which Beaverbrook could do. Churchill would not relinquish the idea. For the next year and a half he pursued Beaverbrook again and again. Beaverbrook as constantly evaded or put forward the only conditions on which he could do the work—conditions which Churchill had to reject as impossible. It was a battle of wills, with Beaverbrook understanding his own nature better than Churchill did.

The first move came at the end of July, when Churchill proposed that Beaverbrook should enter the war cabinet with general powers of supervision over production. Beaverbrook used the overriding needs of the RAF as his excuse for refusing. He wrote on 29 July:

I am convinced that no change should take place at this Ministry. Here is the most important production centre and here we should concentrate our plans for a limited production during the invasion by land or by air.

In one sense, no doubt, my job is done. So far as meeting the immediate requirements of the Royal Air Force is concerned, the task is at an end.

But there remains the continuing responsibility for production during the invasion. I am completely committed to it.

I cannot lay the job down without doing real damage to the project.

I am only too willing to serve in the War Cabinet if required to do so, but not at the expense of abandoning my plans here.

If, therefore, there is to be a change in the War Cabinet situation, I suggest that Morrison [the minister of supply] and I be drafted in, while retaining our present offices.

We should be asked to attend when specially required by you to do so, and not expected to sit in on routine subjects.

I am fully conscious of the honour which you do me in giving me the invitation. And I wish you to understand that my objections are the result of a deep consideration and a careful review of my present responsibilities.

The idea that Morrison and Beaverbrook should transfer their bickerings to the war cabinet was not a good one, even though the two were personally on good terms. Churchill rejected it. On 2 August Beaverbrook alone became a member of the war cabinet and on 24 August of the defence

BEAVERBROOK

committee (operations) also, without ceasing to be minister of aircraft production. Thereafter, in his own words, he led a terrible life. He left this record:

> I was driven all through the day at the Aircraft Ministry with the need for more production. I was harassed by the fear that our Air Force would go short of supplies. I was required to attend innumerable Cabinet meetings, and if I absented myself the Prime Minister would send for me.
>
> At night-time I was summoned to the "protected" Cabinet room, where I would sit at the Defence Committee until sometimes very late at night. Thereafter, Churchill would require me to attend at his sitting-room for further discussion.
>
> The burden was too heavy.
>
> Churchill was always on the stretch. He had the advantage, however, of sleeping for one or two hours every afternoon.

Attlee was the third member of the defence committee, and Beaverbrook recollected that he never made any contribution to the discussion except to say after Churchill's discourses: "I agree". Here is a neglected factor in wartime politics. It is well-known that Beaverbrook and Bevin fought hard and strenuously, but Beaverbrook had the highest opinion of Bevin's capacity. His opinion of Attlee was very different. General Sir Frederick Pile has recorded one of their early encounters. On 19 August 1940 Dowding and Pile lunched with Beaverbrook. Pile writes:

> It was the first time I had met him, and I was much impressed by his forcefulness. Mr. Attlee was there too, and, with his less flamboyant qualities, did not shine in comparison. Half-way through lunch he was taken badly to task by Beaverbrook because he had not taken a firm line in some matter which he (Attlee) knew was right. Beaverbrook kept saying: "Well, why did you not put it right? Why did you not do something?" To which bullying Mr. Attlee had nothing to reply.[1]

Attlee reciprocated this hostility in his quiet way. A note in Beaverbrook's papers records an address which Attlee gave to the junior Labour ministers in June 1945:

> I am a very diffident man. I find it hard to carry on conversation. But if any of you wish to come and see me, I will welcome you. I will receive you and I will discuss your problems with you.
>
> But there are many other people to whom it will be easy to talk. Chief among these is Beaverbrook. He is a magnet to all young men, and I warn you that if you talk to him no good will come of it.
>
> Beware of flattery.

[1] Sir Frederick Pile, Ack-Ack, 141. Pile inscribed the book "To Max Beaverbrook One of the four 'Greatest Men' I met and a very helpful friend".

And he advised the under-secretaries to refuse dinner invitations from Beaverbrook.[1] Here was a potent source of harassment to Beaverbrook in the future.

On 14 August Beaverbrook wrote to Hoare about his promotion:

> It is indeed a strange turn of the wheel. It would have been difficult to believe a few months ago that my addition to the Cabinet would be looked on as a popular move, bringing strength to the Government on that account.
>
> But there it is. And if I am wise, I will remember that the sudden sunshine of public favour may swiftly fade.

Hoare had expressed his appreciation of Halifax as foreign secretary and hoped that Eden would not take his place—"As a result of the civil war, Anthony is regarded as a friend of the Reds and an enemy of Franco's". Beaverbrook therefore added:

> It is easy to understand that Halifax meets with approval in Madrid, although why they should dislike poor Eden I do not quite see. After all, he never did them any harm. What he might have liked to do is another matter.
>
> While Halifax is thoroughly acceptable in Madrid, he may not be so popular in Moscow. It is quite a pity we cannot have two Foreign Secretaries at once. After all, we have often had two foreign policies at once.

On 30 August 1940 Beaverbrook wrote to Hoare again. This letter shows his immediate activities and also hints of troubles to come:

> The German air offensive is at present the thing that occupies the public's mind to the exclusion of almost everything. Yet looked upon as a serious military operation its effect is small. Production in the aircraft factories is affected more by the sirens than by the bombs and not much by either. This, of course, is a piece of good fortune which may not long continue.
>
> The long night raids over London have affected the sleep of the middle classes and the labours of the working classes. It is only the latter that trouble me. I don't care if the middle classes lie sleepless in their beds, so long as the workers stay active at their benches. And it is one of my chief concerns at the moment to encourage them to do so.
>
> . . . .
>
> You will be astonished to hear that we are now having all the old trouble which we remember so well from the last war. The old squabble between the Eastern and the Western schools.
>
> This time, of course, it takes a slightly different form. The Western School wants to devote our resources to the defence of our island base. The easterners want to reinforce the Egyptian front so as to be sure of holding Suez and the Nile.

[1] The story was told to Beaverbrook by Hector McNeil, an under-secretary and one of Beaverbrook's men.

It is a quarrel between professionals and amateurs. The professionals belong to the Eastern school. The amateurs uphold the banner of the West.

I am, as usual, an amateur. But it is fair to say that some amateurs have had a longer experience of war than many professionals.

Beaverbrook soon found that elevation to the war cabinet had not improved his position. He now had to fight in the cabinet as well as against the air marshals. With the battle of Britain still raging, he hesitated to threaten resignation directly. Instead, somewhat strangely, he appealed to Halifax on 4 September 1940:

I am distressed by the situation in which I find myself at the Cabinet. My colleagues and I are not working well together.

. . . .

It seems to me that when you have a good Minister of Aircraft Production, you should treat him as such, trusting his judgement in matters which concern his own Ministry.

In fact, it is my view that I should have complete authority over aircraft and that I should not be obstructed in my business, either by debates in the Cabinet or by difficulties from the Air Ministry.

. . . .

There is nothing new in this situation of the Air Ministry. I have had a long succession of refusals from that quarter. But I will not trouble you with it. For it is not my purpose to make you the repository of my grievances.

This, rather, is the point I wish to make: I am a particular type, a well-known type often demonstrated in life. I have some virtues and also the defects of these virtues. This has to be taken into account.

I am opposed on this subject and on that. I am exasperated by ignorant discussions. All this is becoming very tedious.

And I have reached the conclusion that the Prime Minister should find a Minister who will get on more agreeably with his colleagues.

As you are the senior member of the Cabinet, I write to you before taking any further action.

This letter may not have been sent. At any rate, there was no reply from Halifax.

On 15 September Beaverbrook telephoned Peter Howard. He said: "Peter, do you keep a diary?" Howard replied that he was too busy writing for The Evening Standard. Beaverbrook then said: "Well, if you had a diary, I would tell you to record in it that this day our country has won a victory that will be recorded in the annals of history in the same terms as Trafalgar or Waterloo are recorded".[1] The story may not be true. Neither Beaverbrook nor Dowding appreciated for another couple of weeks that the battle of Britain was over. But the remark was true, whether made or not. The pilots of fighter command, directed by Dowding

1 Howard, Beaverbrook, 134–35.

and equipped by Beaverbrook, had won a victory, comparable only to Trafalgar in British annals. Great Britain was secured against invasion for the duration of the second world war. Hitler, having failed to invade Great Britain, was driven to desperate courses elsewhere. The battle of Britain sealed his doom. The architects of victory were soon disregarded. Once the battle was over, Dowding was sacrificed to the jealousy of the air marshals and passed into oblivion. Beaverbrook in time was also over-borne. But nothing can dim the glory of those summer months. As Churchill wrote of Beaverbrook many years later: "He did not fail. This was his hour".[1]

[1] Churchill, Second World War, ii, 286–87.

CHAPTER EIGHTEEN

UNWILLING OVERLORD, 1940-41

The early months at MAP had been the high point of Beaverbrook's career, the period when he set his mark on world events. One of his associates wrote to me recently: "I wish I could recapture for you the drama, the fun, the tension. We thought we really were making history and I suppose we were". Beaverbrook himself always put MAP first in his recollections. After the war those who had served with him at MAP formed the 1940 Club. When Beaverbrook died, he left his watches, clocks and other jewellery to be distributed among its members. In a lighter vein, memories of MAP helped to make Destry Rides Again Beaverbrook's favourite film. The staff of MAP became for him "The boys in the back room", and when Dietrich jumped on to the bar of The Last Chance, Beaverbrook would roar, "Come on, the boys in the backroom", at which everyone had to join in. Beaverbrook announced: "Marlene Dietrich singing the Boys in the Backroom is a greater work of art than the Mona Lisa", an artistic judgement which was not meant to be altogether humorous.

Excitement and triumph brought also a heavy penalty. Even Beaverbrook could not work twenty-four hours a day at such tension for ever. Asthma was the danger signal and wracked him savagely for the next eighteen months. Underlying this was a loss of judgement and self-control. Between October 1940 and February 1942 when he finally resigned, Beaverbrook was a man driven by the furies of his own distracted temperament. His torment was the greater in that he had also rational grounds for his outbreaks. He often disagreed over policy. He was pushed into positions of great responsibility and denied the powers which he thought necessary.

The disputes began before September was over. With the battle of Britain won, A1 priority for aircraft production became out-of-date. The production of tanks for North Africa was just as urgent. Here was a new reason for making Beaverbrook general overlord of war production. No doubt there was also a tactical motive: Churchill appreciated that the only way of taking A1 priority from MAP without a terrible row was to take MAP away from Beaverbrook.

There were other grounds for a reshuffle of offices. Neville Chamberlain was dying and had resigned. When he became lord president of the council, it had been intended that he would head a cabinet committee directing civilian production. The task had been beyond him. Now a new head of this committee was needed. At the same time a replacement was needed for Sir John Anderson as home secretary in charge of home security. Beaverbrook had now revised his opinion of Anderson. He wrote to W. J. Brown on 20 September 1940: "You are wrong about Anderson. He is a very able man. He has immense capacity and plenty of courage". But Anderson did not inspire confidence in the east-enders who were being bombed. According to Hannen Swaffer, two east-end clergymen came to Beaverbrook and told him that there would soon be Communist-inspired "Stop the War" marches in the east-end unless a change was made at the home office. The east-enders must be given a man of their own kind.[1] Herbert Morrison, minister of supply, was the obvious answer. Beaverbrook at once proposed this to Churchill, who agreed. Here was the opening for Churchill: he in turn proposed that Beaverbrook should combine the two posts of supply and aircraft production.

Beaverbrook refused. He wrote to Churchill on 30 September:

I gathered from our conversation tonight that you expect me to undertake more responsibility.

But my asthma drives me to the unhappy conclusion that the cold weather and sharp winds bring my labours to nothing.

I have tried many devices, but nights pass in procession without any sleep for me. If I live through the war I shall give you thanks for winning it, even though you may die now.

For the example you gave the nation in the last four months and the leadership in the dark days of the flight from France, decided the battle in our favour.

Asthma was a genuine excuse. But more lay behind. On 30 September Beaverbrook drafted a longer letter to Churchill which he did not send. In this he not only offered his resignation. He also indicated for the first time the dilemma which haunted him: he disagreed with Churchill's strategy and yet was reluctant to oppose it. The letter read:

I have had an opportunity to reflect, with the knowledge that I cannot take any fresh responsibility at present.

Things get a little out of focus with me. No man who is awake all night can give good judgments or sound opinions in the morning light.

If I thought I could carry the burden, I would gladly undertake it. But it is entirely beyond my physical powers.

[1] Alan Wood, Beaverbrook, 267-68.

I had made up my mind to ask for a release from my present duties. A letter was written a few days before Dakar.[1] I only delayed sending it on that account.

Now that re-organization seems to be inevitable, I think I should be dropped at this time.

And here let me say that, while I have the isolationist point of view, while I hold that everything depends on the defence of this island, I give unswerving support to all you do.

There is no doubt about it; you saved us from a disastrous and overwhelming defeat last May. You reconstructed our defences. You uplifted our spirits. You organized our resistance.

All we have and all we are, we owe to you.

Other Prime Ministers may follow, but you alone must have the credit for all that has gone before in the defence during the last four months, and for everything that comes after.

Even if we are defeated, which I do not believe, you will have saved us from the utter destruction that faced us when France collapsed.

Churchill persisted. Beaverbrook recorded:

When Morrison was shifted from the Supply Ministry Churchill proposed to make me Minister of Supply as well as Minister of Aircraft Production. I refused. He called in Kingsley Wood and Bracken. Both put pressure on me when I persisted in rejecting the offer, declaring it was beyond my physical powers.

Beaverbrook provided an alternative solution. Anderson became lord president and in time made his committee a decisive force in directing civilian affairs. Morrison became home secretary, and a businessman, Sir Andrew Duncan, became minister of supply. There was no fear that Beaverbrook and Duncan would quarrel. Like other businessmen in politics, Duncan would do whatever Beaverbrook told him.

The need for Beaverbrook as minister of aircraft production was in fact far from over. It was fortunate indeed that at this time he did not become an overlord. The German night raids struck heavily at the aircraft factories. Defence against them proved for long ineffective. Beaverbrook hit on the answer the very day that the raids started. It was dispersal. The aircraft plants should be scattered all over the country. Once more the improvisers of MAP, led this time by Sir Charles Bruce-Gardner, moved into action. Factories were split up, plant and labour moved into different parts of the country. One big aircraft factory went to 48 different premises, another to 38, another to 30. The aircraft in the storage units were moved also—to garages, sheds, and even barns. There were not enough vacant premises to go round. Other ministries had been earmarking premises since the outbreak of the war. MAP had been operating only

[1] This letter, if written, has not survived.

since May 1940. Beaverbrook issued the order that premises of other departments should be seized where they were not actually being used. This piracy, as David Farrer remarks,[1] "secured him aircraft for the duration and enemies for life". Beaverbrook trampled on all opposition. When Henry Lamb the painter joined the local bishop in opposing a Spitfire factory at Salisbury, Beaverbrook replied on 3 November 1940:

> If I allowed myself to be influenced by objectors there would not be any Spitfire factories anywhere.
> And without Spitfires the objectors' fears would be multiplied a thousand-fold.

Dispersal temporarily slowed production, but it blunted the edge of the blitz. As Beaverbrook told the house of lords: "You may occasionally have heard on the German wireless of our immense losses in aircraft capacity; but they have turned out in fact to be nothing, because our aircraft production had gone away. We were out of the bombed areas altogether". Dispersal brought other gains. Fresh supplies of labour could be tapped in the districts to which the factories moved. Moreover, when the force of the German attack declined, the original factories came back into production, and there was thus a vast increase in capacity, which was soon shown in increased production. Beaverbrook rightly counted dispersal as one of the three decisive contributions which he made to winning the war.[2]

Dispersal was not Beaverbrook's only weapon against the blitz. He continued to rail against the siren and the stoppage of work during the air-raid warnings. He wrote to Arthur Greenwood on 14 December 1940:

> The decline in production is due to (1) the air raid warnings (2) the bombing (3) misplaced confidence in the future. Now how to cure the problem. (1) Stop the sirens (2) Beat the bombers (3) Muzzle optimistic Ministers, including me.

[1] Farrer, The Sky's the Limit, 61.
[2] The production of fighters during the battle of Britain was of course the first. All-out aid to Russia, to be discussed later, was the third.
Beaverbrook wrote to Templewood on 19 May 1945:

"Each of us has made our contributions to public life. But to my way of thinking mine number only three. First, the increase of production of Spitfires and Hurricanes could have been achieved only by my methods. Secondly, dispersal saved the aircraft industry in the blitz. Thirdly I insisted, against the Socialists and others, on backing the Russians in 1941 to the fullest extent."

Beaverbrook could have counted the inspiration he brought to American production after Pearl Harbor as a fourth contribution. He wrote to an American friend in 1946: "I have always looked upon those weeks I spent in Washington in December 1941 and January 1942 as the most eventful and, perhaps, the most useful in my life".

His more serious answer was the emergency services organization, set up as part of MAP. Members of this at once went to any town which had been bombed. They directed the repair of one factory, the removal of others. Thanks to them, production was often resumed within twenty-four hours. After the worst raids Beaverbrook appeared himself. When Coventry was bombed on the night of 13 November, Beaverbrook was there before noon the next day. He told a meeting of leading officials:

> The roots of the air force are planted in Coventry. If Coventry's output is destroyed the tree will languish. But if the city rises again from the ashes, then the tree will continue to burgeon, putting forth fresh leaves and branches.

Birmingham and Southampton received similar visits and similar rhetoric. The inhabitants of the bombed towns were perhaps inspired. Other departments of state that saw priority in reconstruction accorded to aircraft factories, were not so enthusiastic.

Beaverbrook was once again living for the moment: promoting dispersal, hurrying to the bombed towns, a whirlwind of activity. Perversely perhaps he also chose this time to peer into the future. This was a defiance of his critics. They had said that he was incapable of planning. In answer he produced a plan to eclipse all others. In October 1940 Patrick Hennessy was instructed to project production into the future. The Hennessy programme was a typical Beaverbrook enterprise. It did not attempt to estimate what future production was likely to be. It laid down what production could be under perfect conditions. Assuming that there were no bombing, no shortage of labour or materials, no bottlenecks or other hindrances, and that everyone worked to the limit of capacity, then here were the figures of the aircraft which could be produced. Beaverbrook did not claim that the programme could be fulfilled, and in fact it never was. It was, as he called it, a "carrot" programme, something to strive for and never attainable. Subsequently the Hennessy programme was repeatedly scaled down. More "realistic" programmes took its place. They, too, were never fulfilled. The "carrot" programme was maybe not good planning, as the civil service saw it. But it was Beaverbrook all over. He believed that you were more likely to get to Heaven if you said the sky's the limit.

Beaverbrook never drove himself harder than in the autumn of 1940, even harder than during the battle of Britain. His asthma grew worse, his conditions of life more difficult. The railings at Stornoway House had been among the first to go for scrap. Beaverbrook welcomed this, in contrast to some others who clung desperately to their railings, for want perhaps of any better support. This was almost the last he saw of his old house. It was hit by German bombs and made totally uninhabitable.

Beaverbrook moved into a flat on the first floor of The Evening Standard where he spent many sleepless nights.

Most days and every evening he saw Churchill and brought enlivenment. One of their talks was of great importance for Churchill's future. When Chamberlain resigned, a new leader of the Conservative party was needed. Should Churchill claim the position? He told Beaverbrook that his family and close friends thought that it would be better for him to remain above party and the national leader. Beaverbrook never overlooked what he called "the loaves and fishes". He records:

> I took a very strong line indeed. I pointed out to him the dangers of the leadership in the hands of another. No matter how loyal a colleague might be, he would be sure to listen to arguments from back-benchers complaining of the conduct of their Prime Minister. He would have conflicts over appointments and promotions. He would be once removed from the Chief Whip of the Conservative Party.
>
> The opportunity to succeed Chamberlain afforded him a benefit and advantage which should not be neglected.
>
> Churchill decided to accept the offer. He became leader of the party.

With such responsibilities, it is not surprising that Beaverbrook's offers of resignation were soon renewed. He wrote to Churchill on 3 November 1940:

> I must now resign from my Ministry and your Government.
>
> Continuing ill health interferes with my duties.
>
> This decision will not come to you as a surprise.
>
> And in some respects it may be a relief, as my very direct methods, though suited to a desperate situation, are not pleasing when men lull themselves into a state of imagined security.
>
> It has been a glorious experience to serve under your flag through six months of such events.

Churchill apparently did not even answer this letter. Perhaps he never received it.

Churchill would have done well however to heed another note which Beaverbrook sent on 6 November:

> It was a disappointment to me to learn yesterday that the Air Ministry knew nothing about airfields in Crete.
>
> It seems that there should be a close investigation of our Air Force dispositions in the whole of the Middle East, for it is probable that inquiry will disclose a similar lack of information in other directions.

It was said later that no one foresaw the need to strengthen the air defences of Crete. This letter shows that one man at least did so.

On 2 December 1940 there came another letter of resignation, provoked this time by the rows over dispersal. Beaverbrook wrote:

> This bold policy means much interference with other Ministries, on account of the need for suitable premises already earmarked for other services.
>
> I am not now the man for the job. I will not get the necessary support.
>
> In fact, when the reservoir was empty, I was a genius. Now that the reservoir has some water in it, I am an inspired brigand. If the water ever slops over, I will be a bloody anarchist.

Once more Churchill refused. He wrote on 3 December:

> There is no question of my accepting your resignation. As I told you, you are in the galleys and will have to row on to the end. If, however, you wish for a month's rest, that I have no doubt could be arranged. Meanwhile I will certainly support you in carrying out your dispersal policy, which seems imperative under the heavy attacks to which we are subjected.
>
> I am so sorry that your asthma returned yesterday, because it always brings great depression in its train. You know how often you have advised me not to let trifles vex and distract me. Now let me repay the service by begging you to remember only the greatness of the work you have achieved, the vital need of its continuance, and the goodwill of
>
> Your old and faithful friend,

A few days later, Beaverbrook suggested a new way out for himself. On 12 December 1940 Lord Lothian, the British ambassador at Washington, died suddenly. Beaverbrook at once hinted that he should take over the vacant place. He asked Churchill: "Don't you think that I could serve you much better outside the administration?" This was a very foolish suggestion. Beaverbrook would have disliked the routine of an embassy even more than that of a ministry. But maybe it would have been easier to resign from Washington than it was in London. Churchill would not consider the idea. He replied by praising Beaverbrook's "magnificent achievement in the teeth of the bombing" and added:

> I am definitely of opinion that it is more in the public interest that there should be sharp criticism and counter-criticism between the two Departments, than that they should be handing each other ceremonious bouquets. One must therefore accept the stimulating but disagreeable conditions of warfare.

However Beaverbrook became involved in the question of Lothian's successor all the same. Churchill instructed him to offer the post to Lloyd George. It is easy to surmise why Churchill did not approach Lloyd George direct. He was still in awe of his old chief despite the reversal of their fortunes. He had invited Lloyd George to join his government at the outset and was angered, as he always was by a refusal, when

Lloyd George turned down the invitation. Moreover he suspected Lloyd George of favouring a negotiated peace with Hitler. It seems odd in that case that he should contemplate sending Lloyd George to Washington. Maybe Churchill wanted to get Lloyd George out of the way. Or maybe he merely wanted to show that he had made the offer.

Beaverbrook was less suspicious. He had written to Hoare on 14 August 1940:

> Lloyd George has done nothing recently to make his inclusion in the Government less likely. But unfortunately the public are divided into two camps over that statesman. There are the people who think that Winston should bring him in and other people who think Hitler will put him in. This latter point of view is a great piece of injustice to the old fellow.

Of course the idea of a negotiated peace was not so shocking to Beaverbrook as it was to Churchill. Beaverbrook never closed his mind to any possibility. He did not however regard negotiated peace as a possibility at this time. He wrote to his American friend Herbert Swope on 27 October 1940, adding incidentally a remarkable judgement on one of his colleagues:

> There is no peace movement in Britain, either among the politicians or the people. There is no idea whatever of giving up the fight or accepting any compromise peace. That is a point of view which simply does not exist here.
>
> . . . .
> Bevin is an immense figure in the country. A man of great ability and force of character. And he plays a very important part in public life. He is the strongest figure in the trade union movement, which is one of the keys to our war effort.

Later, on 10 January 1941, he wrote to Lowell Thomas:

> I am a Canadian. I have often criticized the English. . . .
> But today they are showing themselves so strong in adversity, so determined, capable of such brilliant acts of heroism and self-sacrifice, that I count it the greatest privilege of my life to be allowed to serve under their banner.

Maybe there was no deep calculation in the idea of sending Lloyd George to Washington, only the recollection of his past achievements and a failure to realize how his powers had declined with age. At any rate Beaverbrook called at Churt on his way back from inspecting air-raid damage at Portsmouth and made the offer. Lloyd George did not want the job. He had more hopes of a negotiated peace and of himself making it than either Beaverbrook or Churchill suspected. This was mere fantasy. Lloyd George was too old and hated to confess it. Lord Dawson of Penn, his doctor, told him that it would be dangerous for him to go to Washington. This was, Beaverbrook thought, "the answer he wanted anyway".

On 17 December Churchill and Beaverbrook looked round for another candidate. The answer was Lord Halifax, the foreign secretary. Once more Beaverbrook was given the task of making the offer or at any rate of taking soundings. This, too, may seem surprising. Churchill and Halifax were colleagues in the war cabinet, meeting every day. It would surely have been easy for Churchill to make the offer himself. There was a simple explanation. Halifax had been the alternative choice as prime minister in May 1940. Many disgruntled Conservatives still looked to him as a possible refuge, and Halifax was not averse to the role. Besides, it was obvious that Churchill wanted to get Halifax out of the foreign office so as to put in his own brighteyed boy Anthony Eden. In short, Churchill hesitated to tell his rival near the throne that he should go into exile at Washington, just as Neville Chamberlain had hesitated to tell Baldwin in March 1931 that he should resign as party leader because he himself was certain to be Baldwin's successor.

There was nothing Beaverbrook liked better in politics than moving men about from one office to another or in speculating how to do it. He had been Lloyd George's errand boy in such affairs during the first world war and was delighted to be Churchill's during the second. He never reflected that in shouldering these tasks he acquired a reputation, largely undeserved, as an intriguer. Now he went happily off to Halifax. That evening Beaverbrook gave a broadcast and on the way back from Broadcasting House called on Halifax. According to Beaverbrook, Halifax said at once: "Yes, he would like it". Halifax himself however merely noted: "Whether his feeling was due to genuine conviction about Washington or a desire to get me out of the Foreign Office I am not sure".[1]

Churchill and Beaverbrook had reckoned without Lady Halifax. Two days later she appeared at No. 10 Downing Street with her husband and argued against his taking the post. In Halifax's version she marshalled political arguments: Churchill might strike a bad patch when he would need Halifax's support and so on.[2] Beaverbrook's account is different:

> Lady Halifax took charge. She said she did not want to go to Washington. She asked what the financial situation would be. They then bargained for plenty of money. When they had been promised plenty of money, all was well.

Lord Halifax went to Washington, and Anthony Eden became foreign secretary.

Another emissary to the United States caused Beaverbrook more trouble. The air ministry were anxious to be rid of Sir Hugh Dowding

[1] Birkenhead, Life of Lord Halifax, 467.
[2] Ibid., 469.

as chief of fighter command. His aloofness offended the air marshals, and they were also angered by his refusal to operate the tactic of the "big wing". Beaverbrook greatly admired Dowding, but with so many quarrels of his own this was not one in which he could intervene. Characteristically he suggested that Dowding should fall soft, being sent to invigorate aircraft production in the United States. Sinclair acquiesced[1] and, when Dowding proved reluctant, Churchill pressed the idea on him also. According to Dowding, Churchill expressed his surprise that Dowding was being replaced at fighter command "in the moment of victory".[2] This may have been so, but it was an odd surprise on the part of the minister of defence, who usually determined every important military appointment. At any rate, Dowding departed to the United States, believing that Beaverbrook was his only friend. This was true. However Beaverbrook also took care to stand well with Dowding's successor. He wrote to Sholto Douglas on 22 November 1940:

> Your predecessor relied on my cooperation and he got it to the limit of my capacity in all things. You may be sure I will back you up to the same extent.

Dowding had been sent to America in order to get him out of the way. His mission was as empty as poor Rothermere's had been. But Dowding was not a dying man. He expressed his opinions freely, and these did not accord at all with those of Sir John Slessor, the air ministry's official representative. Complaints flowed back to London. Churchill indignantly demanded that Dowding be recalled. Beaverbrook attempted to defend Dowding and pleaded that this was merely a quarrel between two air marshals. Tactfully he arranged for Dowding to move on to Canada, where there were no air marshals to quarrel with. Dowding lingered in Canada until May 1941 when he returned home, as the air ministry hoped, a forgotten man.

There was a further occasion when Beaverbrook carried another's troubles. In November 1940 Sir Wilfred Freeman left his post as director of development at MAP in order to become deputy chief of the air staff. Beaverbrook gloomily contemplated the appointment of another air marshal and then learnt that the air ministry would be satisfied with Sir Henry Tizard, who had played a great part in the development of aircraft and even more of radar before the war. Tizard was a scientific adviser of the highest distinction, but he was easily harassed by opposition and as

---

[1] Dowding stated (Wright, Dowding and the Battle of Britain, 241) that Sinclair dismissed him by telephone. A minute by Sinclair, in the Beaverbrook papers, shows that the conversation took place at the air ministry. Dowding at first supposed that he was genuinely needed in the United States and assumed that he would return to fighter command when he came back. Only then did Sinclair tell him that Sholto Douglas had already been appointed to take his place.

[2] Ibid., 256.

highly-strung as Beaverbrook himself. Nor was the opposition which he encountered always imaginary. Professor Lindemann was his enemy, and when Churchill became prime minister, "the Prof." became Churchill's intimate adviser. Churchill might write to Beaverbrook: "The subject of Sir Henry Tizard has never been discussed between me and Professor Lindemann". The fact was that when Lindemann came in, Tizard went out. Now Beaverbrook brought him back. Beaverbrook, too, looked on Lindemann with some suspicion, perhaps with jealousy as a competitor for his own place as "court favourite". He described Lindemann as "an uneasy and far from popular figure without any settled office or portfolio, whose entry into other Ministers' offices was seldom solicited and whose departure was invariably welcomed"[1]—a description which others might have often given of Beaverbrook himself.

Tizard and Beaverbrook got on well. Tizard, who had regarded politics as "an evil-smelling bog", developed the highest admiration for Beaverbrook's ability. But he could not rid his mind of the persecutors, particularly Lindemann, whom he saw lurking round every corner. In February 1941 he fell ill with a nervous complaint and on 23 February wrote to Beaverbrook:

> It seems to me wise, from all points of view, that I should sever my connection with the Department at once. The work that I have been trying to do is too important to be left undone, even for a few weeks, in these critical times. What is more, as I have said before, it should be done by someone who enjoys not only your own confidence, but that of the Air Ministry, and of the Prime Minister. It has been made very clear that that does not apply to me.

It was now Beaverbrook's turn to administer consolation. He wrote on 25 February 1941:

> I have not the slightest intention of accepting your resignation.
> You must be patient and wait until complete health is given to you once more. And when you come back, you will be welcomed with enthusiasm.
> . . . .
> And it is preposterous to say that you have not the confidence of all those who are concerned with the higher direction of the war. This would be entirely wrong.
> You are greatly valued. And certainly your opinions are esteemed and trusted by me as essential to the development department.

Tizard was not to be comforted. He wrote on 5 March:

> At present I feel little confidence in myself. It is bad enough not to have the full confidence of others; but when one loses confidence in oneself it is time to pack up!

---

[1] Birkenhead, The Prof. in Two Worlds, 215.

Once more Beaverbrook sent encouragement:

> You must not allow yourself to be discouraged or irritated because the mending process is slow and trying to a man of energetic temperament.
>
> I assure you, too, that the feeling of despondency which you are experiencing is a passing phase in the recovery.
>
> You must not pay any heed to it. You must look on yourself as your colleagues look upon you, that is with complete and absolute confidence.

Here was much the same correspondence as between Churchill and Beaverbrook but with the roles reversed. Evidently Beaverbrook was better at ministering to another's sorrows than to his own.

This was the moment chosen by Professor A. V. Hill, a scientist who was also a member of parliament, to attack Beaverbrook for his failure to promote development and research at MAP. Austin Hopkinson, another MP, alleged that Tizard had "found it quite impossible to work at the Ministry of Aircraft Production". Tizard wrote to Hill, denying the allegations—a denial which Hill refused to accept. Tizard also wrote to Beaverbrook on 12 March:

> I must say that the talk about my "resignation" affords me some sarcastic amusement! I could not "resign", because I have nothing to resign. All I have done is to advise you that it would be better, in all the circumstances, to make a normal appointment of someone else in my stead. You say you want me to come back, and are prepared to wait. In that case I shall certainly come back, as the thing that interests me is to do the best work I can for the war, whatever the difficulties.
>
> I appreciate very much your kind remarks, and see no reason why I should not work happily with you as my Minister.

This proved to be the case during the short period when Beaverbrook remained at MAP.

Beaverbrook's regard for Tizard did not last. Maybe Tizard did not support him strongly enough against the air marshals. Beaverbrook wrote to me in 1961:

> Tizard was a tiresome fellow. Much more difficult than Lindemann. His spear did not know any brother. He had all the disagreeable qualities of the Highland Scot.
>
> Lindemann did not knife his friends.
>
> Tizard had many jobs during the war. In 1940 he went to Washington in charge of British secrets under the authority of the Ministry of Aircraft Production when I was head of it.
>
> In 1941 under my Ministerial responsibility he became director of development at that Ministry.
>
> He gave too much to the Americans and he contributed too little to the development of aircraft.

The air marshals all praised Tizard because he was on their side. They all damned Lindemann because he prodded them. They needed prodding more than praise.

The Tizard affair was a minor worry. The main one remained Churchill's determination to turn Beaverbrook into the overlord of production. At the beginning of 1941 Churchill came up with a new variant. In the first days of his government half a dozen cabinet committees had been created. They talked in the void, and Beaverbrook never went near them. Churchill now proposed that two of these committees—that on economic policy and the production council—should be replaced by production and import executives, with power to issue orders to the departments. Of course nothing was really changed. The three supply ministers would wrangle as before, sustained only by the hope that, if ever they agreed, they could then issue orders to themselves. Churchill foresaw that the disputes would be even fiercer if Beaverbrook were made chairman of the production executive. He therefore proposed to appoint Bevin as the impartial arbiter, which was to Beaverbrook an added indignity. Beaverbrook was to be consoled by becoming chairman of the import executive. Here again Churchill gave offence by suggesting that, if Beaverbrook found the double role too arduous, Colonel Llewellin, the parliamentary secretary, could run MAP.

Churchill told a sad tale of the burdens which fell upon him and from which Beaverbrook was to relieve him. He wrote on 2 January 1941:

> I want to point out to you that I am placing my entire confidence, and to a large extent the life of the State, upon your shoulders. If, for any reason, this effort should not succeed, or the mechanism which I have devised should be found unwholly suited in your opinion or by the test of events to the business in hand, I have only one resource left, namely to take the burden on my own shoulders, and to preside at a daily meeting of the Import Executive. This would not be the best arrangement, as it is bound to distract my thoughts from the military side of our affairs. I mention this to you because I know how earnestly you wish to help me, and there is no way in which you can help me so much as in making a happy solution of our Import, Shipping and Transport problems.

Beaverbrook was not impressed. Being used to telling sad tales about himself, he was unmoved by Churchill's. Moreover he was angered by the suggestion that Llewellin could do the work at MAP as well as he could and seized on this as another excuse for resigning. Beaverbrook replied to Churchill on 3 January:

> It is with deep regret that I am compelled to refuse to undertake the Chairmanship of the Import Executive.
> I have spent the night in meditation like the good men in days gone by and I have spent it alone.

The reason for my refusal is that I will make a failure under the conditions you are compelled to impose.

I am not a committee man. I am the cat that walks alone.

For some time I have been most uncomfortable and I have asked for my release on that account.

It is now imperative that I should go out.

The reason I will give to the newspapers is ill-health.

Colonel Llewellin is your choice for this Ministry and, if I may be allowed to say so, the best choice. I will inform him this morning and turn over to him in the next few days, completing the process on Sunday night.

I go at a moment when your administration has brought light out of darkness and confidence out of dejection. Under your direction the prospects of the country have been transformed in the most brilliant and dramatic manner.

Now the world waits on you. And everything depends upon you and your leadership.

I have had the joy of serving you through the dark days. Now I will watch with praise and exultations as you go forward to the final triumph. This letter does not need any answer. I will find my own way about.

The letter angered Churchill, the more perhaps because its sentences were so skilfully designed. He answered at once with a mixture of high rhetoric and self-pity:

Your resignation would be quite unjustified and would be regarded as desertion. It would in one day destroy all the reputation you have gained, and turn the gratitude and goodwill of millions of people to anger. It is a step you would regret all your life. No Minister has ever received the support which I have given you, and you know well the burden which will be added to my others by your refusal to undertake the great commission with which I have sought to entrust you. It is not possible in this country, nor would I agree to it even if it were, to entrust any one Minister with dictatorial powers over the vast area covered by the Import and Production programmes. But the arrangement which I have made would give you effective power to render a very great service to the British nation in its days of trial.

If I am to accept as final your refusal to take the Chairmanship of the Imports Executive which all its members wish to accord you, I will myself take your place and will return to London tomorrow for the purpose of holding the first meeting.

If in addition to refusing these urgent duties you propose to give up the Ministry of Aircraft Production and retire from the War Cabinet, that will be an additional offence from which I am sure you will not escape without grievous public censure. I can only hope that your better nature will prevail and that you will once again rise to the height of the great events in which you have played so honourable a part.

Churchill, it need hardly be added, did not in fact take the chair at the import executive.

16

Beaverbrook maintained his old position: a committee could not perform executive functions, and he was no longer needed at MAP. The answer which he sent on 6 January was not without impudence:

> I am very grateful for your letter and have never been so conscious of your kindly forbearing disposition.
>
> But there is one point on which I think you have given expression to public opinion and not to your own opinion.
>
> I am sure that you do not think I wish to be entrusted with dictatorial powers over ships and transport.
>
> Nothing is further from your mind, I am quite confident. For my record with you in this connection is clear.
>
> I did not want to join the Government. The place in the Cabinet was undesired and was, indeed, resisted by me. The offer of the Chairmanship of the Production Council was not accepted. I would not take over the Supply Ministry when Morrison went to the Home Office.
>
> I do not want the Chairmanship of this Committee now because the job requires executive decisions *which cannot be taken by a committee*.[1]
>
> If I had been called on to run this Aircraft Ministry with a committee I would not have got the results.
>
> When your Government came in, Kingsley Wood had left you one Hurricane ready and not many more Spitfires. You would still be in that position if you depended on committee government, in my opinion.
>
> Now may I make once more the briefest explanation of why I am going.
>
> It is because my usefulness has come to an end. I have done my job. The Ministry of Aircraft Production is better off without me.
>
> I can do more good to your Government outside than inside. There is no need for me to enlarge on the reasons. You know them.
>
> And let me take this opportunity to say that I am very conscious of having received from you understanding and consideration and support in a measure that has been more than generous.
>
> My gratitude for all those favours and all that friendship is added to the admiration which I feel for your unparalleled services to a nation in deadly peril.
>
> On personal grounds, I hope you will permit me to see you sometimes and to talk with you occasionally on the old terms.

Churchill evidently felt that he had pressed Beaverbrook too hard. He dropped the affair of the import executive and wrote at midnight a note in his own hand, designed to keep Beaverbrook at MAP:

> You must not forget in the face of petty vexations the vast scale of events & the brightly-lighted stage of history upon wh we stand.
>
> I understand all you have done for us; and perhaps I shall live to tell the tale. "Danton no weakness".

Silence again fell over the question of Beaverbrook's resignation.

---

[1] Handwritten addition by Beaverbrook.

It seems strange that these two men, busied with great affairs, should have time for such prolonged correspondence where neither surely can have hoped to convince the other. The truth is that they both enjoyed it, and of course neither found the writing, or usually the dictating, of letters laborious. Churchill, who in any case did not understand much about other people, went obstinately on trying to change Beaverbrook's nature. Beaverbrook liked parading his troubles and liked still more winding up with a display of emotional attachment which for the moment, while he was dictating the letter, he really felt. The letter of refusal or resignation to Churchill was for Beaverbrook partly a way of releasing his contradictory emotions, with enthusiasm and exasperation mixed together. He spoke the truth when he said that he did not want to be economic dictator. On the other hand, he believed that a dictator for production and imports was the only effective solution and half-feared, half-hoped that the task would fall on him. His desire to leave MAP was more genuine. He was not the right man for the job once the ministry was firmly established.

What was more, he was now bored with a ministry which ran smoothly. He began to interfere in the work of other departments. He advised Churchill on agricultural policy and fell into a dispute with the ministry of agriculture. The ministry wanted to decrease the number of livestock; Beaverbrook wanted to increase it. He wrote:

> The Prime Minister will have to decide upon the policy of optimism with increasing output by every possible means or the policy of deflation with reduced stock based on false arguments and mistaken promises.

On 12 April 1941 he sent a characteristic letter to R. S. Hudson, the minister of agriculture:

> Very many thanks for your letter of 10th April and for your interesting and lively paper.
> I like asperity in public life.
> It was kind of you to suggest that we should meet. I have plenty of time and will be glad of any occasion suitable to you to discuss your views and to conform to them as far as possible, so that agricultural production may have the benefit of our joint efforts.
> But my policy is inflationist and your policy is deflationist. That is the difference.
> It is clear that you are under the impression that my views are formed from the Eastern counties. Equally it is clear that I am under the impression that your views are formed from the permanent officials at the Ministry of Agriculture.
> If only I knew as much about carburettors as I know about potato bugs, then I should make a more useful Minister of Aircraft Production.

On this question of livestock Beaverbrook, according to the experts, seems to have been entirely wrong. Of course most of the experts were champions of the opposite policy.

Beaverbrook also concerned himself with the ministry of information, on the one hand sustaining it against other departments, on the other criticizing the ineffectiveness of its work in the United States. And on 30 April he found time to write a lighthearted letter to Sir Walter Monckton, who had proposed to employ Augustus John in painting the portraits of cabinet ministers:

> Do you know that in the last war the Canadian War Exhibition was run by me?
> Do you know that John then served under me? I made him a Captain, or something?
> Do you know that I saved him at a Court-Martial for hitting a man named Peter Wright?
> I cannot tell you what benefits I did not bestow on him.
> And do you know what work I got out of John—Not a damned thing.

When April came, Beaverbrook once more resolved to leave MAP. He wrote to Sir Charles Wilson on 19 April 1941:

> It is not possible for me to continue in office.
> Even if I were willing to stay, I would be of no value to the Prime Minister. He does not ask my advice, nor does he need it.
> We now have more aircraft than the air ministry can use.

Beaverbrook prepared two long papers in which he answered the criticisms and complaints of the air ministry for the last time. His case could be summed up in two sentences. In the preceding summer everything had to be subordinated to the production of fighters. Now production could not be switched over to bombers at short notice. Fundamentally this was the old dispute between Beaverbrook with his faith in fighters and the air ministry with its enthusiasm for bombers. But Beaverbrook could also appeal to the practical limits of production and answered the air ministry's complaints with the evidence of his success. Thus:

> We were told that we were stripping the cupboard and that we could not sustain our production.

> > "O Time! whose verdicts mock our own
> > The only righteous judge art thou!"

> The fear was expressed that we were going to be short of heavy bombers. But, ever since, there have been more bombers than there is need for bombers.
> If I have to take my lessons in production from the Air Ministry, then the Ministry of Aircraft Production had better go back to that institution,

with its inglorious record of plenty of money, plenty of factories, plenty of opportunities but inadequate production.

It would be better if the Air Ministry devoted more time to operations and less attention to the affairs of the Ministry of Aircraft Production, which seems to have served their needs so far.

Never yet have we fallen down on our obligations to the Royal Air Force. We may do so in the future. And all our activities are subject to two over-riding factors—what the enemy may do to our production in the months to come, and what the Air Ministry have failed to do for our production in days gone by.

This twelve-page onslaught concluded with the inappropriate words: "For my part, I am not in an essay war. I am not going to employ my officers writing documents of a contentious character".

This was the last blast of the MAP trumpet. Beaverbrook was this time really resolved to resign, though even now he could not decide whether to go out altogether or to accept the vague overlordship which Churchill was constantly pressing upon him. On 29 April he seemed acquiescent and wrote to Churchill:

> Will you allow me to look after all priorities. I will undertake to deal justly and to escape absolutely from any and all conflicts between Ministries, thus giving you peace on that front.
>
> It will be necessary for me to retire from Aircraft Production. And in any case my health necessitates my taking this decision.
>
> You will observe that this is not an unwillingness on my part to take and keep the burdens of office. It is just a request for an easy job for a time.

The next day he had changed his mind again:

> I have taken the decision to retire from the Government. The only explanation I will offer is ill health.
>
> You will know that I was rushed this morning and given no opportunity to discuss my objections, or resolve my difficulties. Dont think I make any complaint on that account. Far from it. Your life cannot be impeded by minor considerations.
>
> Too many idols are being thrown down and too many hearthstones are being torn up. And you are the only guardian of mankind.
>
> It is with devotion and with affection that I bring my official association to a close.
>
> Leave me still the personal relations.

Evidently Churchill had not listened with much patience to Beaverbrook's recitation of the problems involved in the allotment of priorities. By 1 May Beaverbrook was even more convinced that the plan would not work, throwing in the additional grievance that Leathers, as minister of war shipping, had been given the dictatorial powers over imports which earlier he had declared that he himself did not want. Beaverbrook wrote to Churchill:

> I see on reflection that my doubts of last night are certainties.
>
> There is no use in adding my name to the list of "Ministers without Portfolio".
>
> You will just have to let me go.
>
> On retiring from the Government, I am ready to take a journey to Egypt or any war zone. The only request I make is "real authority".
>
> I know the difficulties. But the tasks are "real". And those who fear my methods cannot object to giving me the power if I am shorn of my political authority.
>
> You are now appointing Leathers to the post that these same critics refused to allow me to take nearly six months ago. But why should you be compelled in wartime to resort to expedients?
>
> I despair of these weak brethren who will be worried sheep in the day of trial.
>
> So please let me have M.B.[1] here and turn over this day. The big job on hand requires much drive and many inventions. It can only be carried through (if at all) by Ministerial action.

After all this fuss Beaverbrook suddenly gave way as he had often done before. He received the empty consolation that he was not to be a mere minister without portfolio. Churchill invented a new title for him, one never used before though often since: minister of state. Beaverbrook regarded this title with amusement. He told Churchill: "I'm ready to be minister of church as well". The same thought was expressed in a leader for The Evening Standard which he and Michael Foot wrote together at Cherkley one evening:

> The King has been pleased to appoint Lord Beaverbrook Minister of State. What that means is anybody's guess. We have our own private explanation. It is to distinguish him from his father, who was a Minister of the Gospel.

The leader went on to enquire what Beaverbrook's functions were to be:

> Is he promoted or is he demoted? Is he climbing the ladder or has he started down the drain? ... *What have you done with our proprietor? Is he coming back to flay us or is he going to flay somebody else.*[2]

Beaverbrook himself did not know the answers to these questions. He moved into No. 12 Downing Street, two doors from the prime minister. He was to be a general overlord of production, supervising and stimulating the three supply ministries. Churchill appointed him deputy chairman of

---

[1] Moore Brabazon who succeeded Beaverbrook as minister of aircraft production.
[2] The leader was not used. Michael Foot kindly gave me a copy.

the defence committee (supply) and added: "The Minister of State will also from time to time conduct inquiries, on behalf of the Prime Minister, into supply matters of special importance; and will act as Referee in priority questions". Beaverbrook did not believe that the arrangement would work. The three supply ministries would resent his criticism and interference even more than they had done when he was one of themselves. Beaverbrook telegraphed on 13 May 1941 to Harry Hopkins, who stood in much the relationship to Roosevelt as he himself did to Churchill:

> I am now the Deputy Chairman of the Defence Committee (Supply) and Referee in Priorities. I cannot imagine a more unpopular job and if you find that the new Ministry of Aircraft Production the old Minister of Supply along with the fifth Sea Lord combine together to send me back to Newcastle New Brunswick there will be at any rate one compensation as I can always visit you for weekends and sing that very fine old spiritual I Aint Goin to Study War no More.

Beaverbrook was also apprehensive that Churchill would constantly interfere and deprive him of all independent authority. He wrote to Hoare on 14 May 1941:

> I do not know whether this new job will work or not. It will, in large measure, depend on how much authority the Prime Minister is prepared to delegate.
>
> His idea is that he will delegate a very great deal. But he is inclined to think in terms of Bridges and Seal[1] and so on. I do not say this in criticism of Winston. It is part of the man's character, just one of the aspects of his temperament which must be accepted. And, indeed, it is a comment that has sometimes been made about me.

Of course Beaverbrook still believed that Churchill was the indispensable man. He wrote to Lord Wolmer on 12 May:

> So far as I can see we have only one bold man in the Government, and that is the boss.
>
> If we did not have him, God knows where we would be.

And his letter of 14 May to Hoare concluded:

> In the House of Commons' debate the other day, Winston at once brought the whole House under his control. If democracy means the sort of Parliament that he is handling, then in making war, there is no evil in democracy. But, in truth, it is only a sham of a Parliament.
>
> The front bench is part of the sham. There Attlee and Greenwood, a sparrow and a jackdaw, are perched on either side of the glittering bird of paradise.

[1] Bridges was secretary to the cabinet, Seal Churchill's principal private secretary. Their task was to see to the execution of Churchill's orders.

A further difficulty lay concealed beneath the surface. Beaverbrook did not agree with the Mediterranean strategy which Churchill was pursuing. He wrote to Paul Block on 30 May: "The vital issues in this war remain the actual defence of these islands and the maintenance of the sea routes across the Atlantic". When in addition the Mediterranean strategy led to disaster, Beaverbrook could not refrain from comment. He drew attention in the war cabinet to the lack of air support in Crete—a point he, and he alone, had raised earlier—and this provoked an angry retort from Portal, chief of the air staff. Beaverbrook wrote to Churchill on 1 June 1941:

> The Air Chief Marshal surprises me.
> I hope the C.A.S. is not upset by the criticism I made in Cabinet about air support in Crete. And, of course, the same criticism has equal force in relation to the operations in Greece.
>
> . . . .
>
> I am confused. When a plan of campaign is launched, I consider myself justified in opposing it, consistent with my loyalty to your administration. That was the basis on which I opposed the Greek campaign.
> But when operations are launched, then my confidence in your judgement is absolute. But I must be free to criticize errors in execution when these are disclosed.
> It is obvious that the best interests of the Government will be served if I make no further criticism of air power in relation to Greece and Crete.

Churchill replied:

> You are perfectly entitled to criticize the air support of the campaign in Crete, and I do not think any ill will come of free discussion on the subject.

It is unlikely that either Churchill or the air staff really welcomed this criticism. Beaverbrook, for his part, remained convinced to the end of his life that the Greek campaign was a Churchillian blunder of the same sort as Gallipoli or Norway, and there are now many who agree with him. Beaverbrook made his criticism at the time.

The difficulties foreseen by Beaverbrook came to pass. Whenever Churchill instructed him to investigate a shortage in weapons or other equipment, he could only report the negligence and lethargy of the department concerned. Churchill wrote to him irritably: "You are telling me nothing new in either of these minutes. What I should like to know is what you advise should be done about them". What could Beaverbrook advise? If he had been at one of the supply ministries, he would have overcome the particular shortage by emergency action. As it was, the supply ministers resented his interference and would not take orders from him. He could only appeal to Churchill: "If I raise the point, there may be increased resistance. So you may be willing to raise it".

Churchill recognized that the arrangement was not working. Whatever Beaverbrook's great qualities, that of a detached adviser was not among them. Churchill therefore suggested that Beaverbrook should become minister of food. Beaverbrook at once refused. He wrote on 2 June 1941:

> I do not know anything about food, and cannot grasp the problem in a short time.
> Experience is needed. I have none.
> It is not even a production job.
> I have energy and a sense of urgency.
> These are at your disposal if you can use them in face of hostility from all those elements doing little and delaying much.

Beaverbrook hoped that his difficulties might be overcome if Churchill gave him real power. Instead Churchill, by constantly interfering, had deprived him of such authority as he had hoped to possess. On 3 June he prepared a statement of his grievances, for once as long as some of Churchill's own papers:

> My sphere of influence has been narrowed, and maybe it is necessary for political reasons that it should be narrowed.
> You appointed me Deputy Chairman of the Defence Committee (Supply) and I expected to exercise power and responsibility through that appointment.
> I get neither, and for many reasons. In my appointment as Deputy Chairman, I do not even possess the power of an Under-secretary.
> Here are some examples of the limitations placed on my activities:
> (1) The war calls for speed. Urgency is a state of mind difficult to attain and we have not reached that condition, although it should have been possible after one year of good government.
> We are confronted by an energetic and ruthless enemy. Regular ways are our method. Theirs are unexpected and often take us by surprise. We hold to ordinary devices. The enemy avoids them.
> Because I believe in speed and urgency, I am convinced that serviceability is the secret of victory. You call on me to provide serviceability in the Middle East.
> I make arrangements for Dawson to go. There is a delay of 5 or 6 days. Boswell has not gone yet, although 10 days have passed. As for personnel, I was told I was to send ten or fifteen. Nothing is done and I have no means of expediting that programme.
> (2) You tell me I am to fix the Haining terms of reference[1] and select a civilian colleague for him. I do both, when unexpectedly the whole negotiation is taken out of my hands by you.
> The Minute is prepared by you, far better than I could have done it. The nature of the organisation is settled by you.

---

[1] General Haining was being sent to the Middle East as Intendant-General.

And all those about me who should be relying on my decision ignore me altogether. Some of them even complain if I show any disposition to take action.

(3) You called on me to preside over the next Tank Parliament in the presence of all the members. For the two following meetings you took the chair. You are a better man for the post than I am. But by that act you ruin my situation in relation to tanks and leave me somewhat in the position of a secretary carrying out your instructions with no executive power, or responsibility. Yet I believe the tank programme to be a failure.

(4) I am given the job of settling 30 Blenheims for the Army Co-operation Command. The C.A.S. does not like my note and I am asked to withdraw the last two paragraphs, although I am *sure* you agree there is nothing wrong with them. The C.A.S. will in future take a similar course.

(5) I point out to you that all the Halifax aircraft are on the ground. I declare to you my belief that I can pick them up. But, in effect, you say that I must not interfere with the Ministry of Aircraft Production. I had thought that my appointment brought that Ministry under my control, subject to you.

(6) You instruct me to carry out an enquiry into anti-tank weapons and ammunition. I find that a shocking condition of shortages exists. On applying to Sir Andrew Duncan, I am told that these weapons and ammunition are sufficient for army requirements and that any stimulation in production in the nature of a spurt will damage the lines in future. He opposes it.

That answer made it impossible for me to do anything. I could perhaps have got on with Duncan, but it is not worth trying when I am handicapped in practically every other direction.

The deficiencies existing in anti-tank weapons and ammunition also prevail in many other directions. Some I have pointed out to you.

(7) The Tanks. I have offered on many occasions to give you the result of my enquiries, which lead me to the conclusion that the programme is utterly inefficient and improperly developed and directed. But I have never been able to bring the issue to a head.

(8) I raised with you the question of a coal shortage. I told you that I feared that gas and electricity supplies might fail next winter. Although coal falls within the orbit of Mr. Attlee, it is nevertheless a supply matter. But I got no encouragement from you.

(9) Agriculture is also within Mr. Attlee's sphere, according to the political organisation. But it, too, is assuredly a question of supply. Agriculture is not developed to the limit of our resources. Far, far short of it.

(10) U.P. weapons[1] are referred to me, with the direction to confer with the Minister of Supply. I am unable to make any progress with the Minister in discussing the issue.

(11) As long ago as May 19th, I informed you that it was necessary to make an enquiry into the time-lag between the output of pilots from the Empire Air Training Scheme and their arrival at the squadrons. I got no answer.

[1] Unrotating projectiles, i.e. rockets.

(12) In an effort to find some outlet for my energies I suggested that I should go to the United States for the purpose of stimulating production there, since the field here seems to be closed to me. You welcomed the suggestion and, indeed, you approved of it. I have heard nothing since, except through outside channels. From those, I gather that I am not expected to go.

(13) Mr. Bevin's Production Executive goes on without any modification or change, although I was present when the Minister himself asked you if my appointment would bring the Production Executive to an end.

(14) It appeared to me that I should remain on the Import Executive, since shipping would certainly be a matter of interest to the defence Committee on Supply. Without my knowledge, without any consultation with me, my name was removed from the Executive.

(15) Airfields. I sent you a note about airfields and the failure of the Air Ministry to achieve their programme of construction. One airfield in particular I am anxious to see completed, that of Sollum Voe in the Shetlands. My interest in this unfinished project springs from the importance it would have as a fighter station from which Fokker Wulfs could be harried.

(16) I have tried to be of use on operational matters. But I did not know we would be fighting in Crete without air cover, until the battle had been joined. I have not yet seen Air Marshal Tedder's telegrams.

There are many other items which I will not mention, in order to limit your burdens. But the position comes down to this:

(1) I may have lost the qualities which made me a valuable Minister a year ago. If so, I should be informed of it.

(2) You should give me the power and the responsibility, allowing me to take decisions on my own account within my own sphere and dismissing me if I plunge you into political difficulties.

(3) Or I should recognise the existence of a difficult situation in which I am no longer necessary to your defence schemes.

This was a powerful letter. Churchill was shaken. He suggested that Beaverbrook might take over the ministry of fuel, power and light—a suggestion which he knew Beaverbrook would refuse. Alternatively Beaverbrook must reconcile himself to an advisory role. Churchill went on to give Beaverbrook a constitutional lesson:

There are two functions in war-time Government. The Executive and the Supervisory. The Parliamentary and Press mood stresses very strongly the need for men with no Executive office but a broad, instructed and reflective outlook on the war. It is not possible to combine this with vehement executive action in this or that particular topic or particular Department without destroying the responsibility of the Ministerial chiefs of that Department. The Prime Minister, whoever he may be, is indeed accorded a certain right of incursion and as Minister of Defence I have wide powers. The Services and Departments will take from a Prime Minister what they will not take from anyone else. I am in full agreement with you that the present arrangement is not working well. The alternative therefore is that you should either take an Executive Department while remaining a member of the War Cabinet or reconcile yourself to the higher but more indirect forms of responsibility appropriate to a member of the War Cabinet without Departmental duties.

You know that you will always find me ready, so long as I have any life left in my carcase, to try to meet your wishes and harness your drive and force of nature to our heavily-laden wagon.

Churchill must have thought on reflection that Beaverbrook would not be persuaded to change his nature even by the conciliatory tone of the last paragraph. It was Churchill's turn for once to compose a letter and not send it.[1]

All went on as before. Beaverbrook reported on the shortage of anti-aircraft and anti-tank weapons. He defended the Atlantic ferry organization against the attacks of the air ministry. He criticized the large number of aircraft held in the storage units—"Aircraft in A.S.U.'s are like cash in the bank in the old days when running a business to make money—wasted assets". He opposed any reduction in the production of fighters. He beat off a criticism of journalists by J. A. Spender: "I do not think the difficulty is with the young members of the press. The trouble is with some of the old dogs who are cynical, and relieved of the toils and sacrifices of war". He complained that visiting American journalists were not being treated with adequate generosity. All this was routine stuff and no proper use of Beaverbrook's abilities.

All unknown, release was approaching. A new emergency, and with it a new call for Beaverbrook, was in the offing. On 22 June 1941 Hitler attacked Soviet Russia. According to one story,[2] Beaverbrook overslept and only learnt the news from his secretary at 10 a.m. According to another, he was awakened by the Internationale, which Michael Foot was playing loudly on the gramophone. At all events, Beaverbrook hastened to Chequers as soon as he was dressed. Churchill, foreseeing the German attack, seems to have decided on his own response well in advance. Beaverbrook however claimed to have contributed to the decision. Here is his story of the day's events:[3]

Two men were summoned to Mr. Churchill's side at Chequers soon after the news had been received. Lord Beaverbrook, at that time a member of

---

[1] The letter, which was kindly communicated to me by Martin Gilbert, is merely dated "June 1941" and is marked in Churchill's handwriting "hold".

[2] David Farrer, G—for God Almighty, 25. Farrer is wrong in stating that Beaverbrook became minister of supply "towards the end of May", i.e. before the German attack on Russia.

[3] This is from a long narrative entitled The Second Front, which Beaverbrook and Farrer prepared shortly after the end of the war.

the War Cabinet and of the Defence Committee, and Sir Stafford Cripps, on leave from his post as Ambassador in Moscow.

It was a case of the optimist and the pessimist side by side. For by temperament Beaverbrook was ebullient, impatient of difficulties or delay, refusing to see obstacles, rejecting counsels of caution, the maker of many mistakes but the breaker time and again of the pessimist front; while Cripps was clear in his reasoning, restrained in his predictions, looking on the dark side— and on this Russian issue too pessimistic in his prophecies.

For while both advocated to Mr. Churchill support for Russia, Beaverbrook expressed as well faith in Russia's strength and power to resist, but Cripps, with first-hand knowledge, took a different view, dwelling on the handicaps which Russia would face in striving to deal with the type of blitzkrieg which had laid the great French army low within a single month.

Mr. Churchill listened, questioned, considered, all through the day. Occasionally he sat in the garden in the hot sunshine. Then again he would stride to his office, restless to a degree. But though he was restless he had in fact early made up his mind. He would broadcast that night his determination that Russia should be given all the aid in Britain's power.

It was a decision taken without calling his Cabinet together. There was no time to summon his colleagues. It was a decision taken in the likelihood that it would arouse a measure of hostility, albeit unspoken, among sections of his own Party. Nor could he have any guarantee either of the attitude of the British newspapers. . . .

It was a decision, in fact, not without its risks. But one great risk Mr. Churchill knew was hardly a risk at all. Mr. Winant, the American ambassador, had just returned from America, bearing a message from the President of the United States. This message told that Mr. Roosevelt would back Mr. Churchill to the full if he pledged support for Russia. . . .[1]

And so it came about that . . . this man who had been a lifelong opponent of Communism in all its manifestations, affirmed on the wireless at nine o'clock that night, his determination that henceforth Britain and Russia should march together against the country that had proved itself the enemy of all mankind.

Here was Beaverbrook's opportunity. He would now produce tanks and munitions for Russia as in the previous year he had produced aircraft for fighter command. Once more there would be emergency, improvisation, drama. This time there was also a political calculation. The response to Churchill's decision was less than wholehearted. To quote Beaverbrook again:

There were many in Britain who, though they had welcomed Mr. Churchill's broadcast, took a very different view when it came to implementing the promise of help he had made. This section of opinion maintained that

[1] Colville, writing to Beaverbrook on 5 August 1960, gave a rather different account from his diary. According to this, Winant thought that the invasion was a put-up job between the Germans and the Russians. Dill, the CIGS, who was also present thought that the Russians would be finished in six weeks.

it would be folly to denude our still slender resources to aid an ally whose armies, though not in actual disarray, were none the less in retreat. . . . The most that Russia could afford us was a breathing space in which to build up our own armaments to the furthest extent.

Not thus however did the ordinary man—and particularly the workers in the factories—argue. Resolutions in favour of aid to Russia began to reach Downing Street in an increasing flow. At factory meetings the call to sustain Russia was echoed again and again.

Not thus, either, did Beaverbrook argue. It would have been strange if he had. For he had always been in favour of close relations with Russia. He had followed that policy ever since the Bolshevist revolution. Now he took up the Russian cause from the very day of the German invasion, bringing to its advocacy all his powers of persuasion and enthusiasm. Those newspapers which, until he became a member of the government, had been under his control, were quick to seize on his attitude. The Daily and Sunday Express, and the Evening Standard, became the leading and most vigorous exponents of aid to Russia.

The line taken by these newspapers, no doubt entirely on their own impulse, was certainly a remarkable coincidence.

All-out aid to Russia would place Beaverbrook again on the high peak of reputation which he had possessed the year before. This time he foresaw also a great political advantage. Hitherto, though on good terms with Herbert Morrison, A. V. Alexander, and Hugh Dalton, he could make no headway with the really powerful Labour chiefs, Attlee and Bevin, both members of the war cabinet. Bevin resented his demand for the direction of labour and, as chairman of the production executive, constantly obstructed him. But at least Beaverbrook thought that Bevin was "a big man". Attlee exasperated Beaverbrook far more by his cold criticism and depreciation. Now both men shared Cripps's doubts about Russia. Neither could shake off the suspicions against Communism which had been nurtured by twenty years of bitter experience. They welcomed the Soviet alliance grudgingly and halfheartedly. The weapon was placed in Beaverbrook's hands. He could appeal directly to the factory workers, leapfrog the Labour leaders and become himself the leader of the Left. On 22 June 1941 he left Chequers comforted by the knowledge that he was to become minister of supply. He would be again the worker of miracles and, what was more, this time the avowed champion of the new radicalism which was sweeping the country. Soviet Russia's victory would be Great Britain's victory—and particularly victory for Beaverbrook.

CHAPTER NINETEEN

INTERNATIONAL GO-BETWEEN, 1941–42

The ministry of supply opened a great new opportunity to Beaver-brook. Characteristically he did not grasp it without a preliminary tangle. In his usual way, he had criticized Duncan, the existing minister, to Churchill as "complacent" and "inclined to be too easily satisfied". Churchill passed the criticism on to Duncan when explaining the change of offices. Beaverbrook then insisted that he would not take the ministry of supply unless Duncan approved. He wrote to Churchill on 27 June 1941:

I am ready to undertake the Ministry of Supply.

I would like to make it clear, however, that I have been standing down since the beginning of June, and that I certainly will not lift it out of Sir Andrew Duncan's hands unless he is a party to my doing so.

He believes in orderly advance. I am given over to immediate methods. Many persons believe that the Duncan method is sounder and better.

Now I have praised Sir Andrew Duncan more than any other man has praised him. I ask you to bear witness that I have always spoken to you in the highest terms of his performance.

Duncan must be satisfied of this fact if he is to hand over to me.

Beaverbrook also wrote to Duncan: "I am not going to take this job unless you are a party to it". He added unconvincingly: "I am most willing to take coal". Duncan evidently understood Beaverbrook and returned a soft answer:

My sole concern in life today is—as is yours—that we win this war. I deem it a clear duty to accept the Prime Minister's judgment and decision, and I do it without the slightest reservation. I am therefore indeed a willing party.

There is no difference between you and me as to the target, but only as to methods of approach. I yield to none in regard and admiration for your wonderful genius for stimulation, and I can very honestly say that no one could more earnestly wish for, or rejoice in, continued success to your efforts.

With this Beaverbrook had to be satisfied. But he was determined this time to avoid the conflicts which had harassed him at MAP. He therefore sent a second letter to Churchill on 27 June laying down his conditions in advance:

(1) It is my arrangement with you that, if I take office, I am to drive up production as hard as I can over the next several months and that I am to retire on January 1.

(2) That I am to be allowed to retain the occupation of my present offices, as I mean to conduct my business somewhat differently from my last experience, and, I hope, more agreeably to those who do not appear to me to travel as fast as I do myself.

(3) That I am to exploit my own claim of "urgency" to the uttermost.

Churchill would not accept dictation even from Beaverbrook. He replied brusquely on 28 June:

I really cannot interfere in your relations with Duncan. I merely reported to you that he had obtained the impression that you thought he was "Complacent". Certainly you have repeatedly told me that all was not well with the Ministry of Supply, and that you thought he was inclined to be too easily satisfied. That at least is the impression I have sustained. There was nothing wrong in your saying this to me in view of our personal relations and the public interest.

I do not know what you mean by saying that you "have been standing down since the beginning of June". You insisted on leaving the Ministry of Aircraft Production, and ever since then I have been trying to find work for you of the kind that would be most agreeable to you and give the best results to the public. This I feel sure is the executive sphere and I hope that as Minister of Supply you will recapture the immense measure of public acclamation which attended your handling of M.A.P. in the crisis of last year.

No-one I am sure has ever taken more trouble to meet the wishes and suit the bent of a colleague than I have with you on account of my admiration for your qualities and our personal friendship.

With regard to your second note, I hope you will do your utmost to drive up production and that you will regard your work as urgent. This might have gone without saying in time of war. I always try to support all Ministers in their tasks, especially those who undertake the most hard and difficult tasks, and I do not read your letter in the sense of any exceptional or special conditions being required by you, other than those of good will and good friendship. You are quite welcome to stay in No. 12 Downing Street and I am glad it is a convenience to you.

With regard to your wish to retire on January 1, that of course is a matter which rests with you, but I should think it would be better to judge when we see what the state of the war and the state of your health are at that date.

Beaverbrook had obtained precisely nothing except permission to stay at No. 12 Downing Street. Nevertheless he accepted office and at once moved from Downing Street to the headquarters of the ministry of supply at Shell Mex House. This was a sulky gesture.

When minister of state, Beaverbrook had impotently charted the deficiencies in the output of the ministry of supply. Now he was free to remedy them. A letter to Churchill on 17 July 1941 showed his old spirit at work:

> The sense of urgency must be in all we do. It must be raised to a degree of tension greater than anything that has gone before. It must become a passion in the minds of men everywhere, so that energy in the factories does no more than reflect a universal consciousness that emergency is upon us.
>
> . . . .
>
> Providence has been bountiful to the Ministry of Supply. Providence has heaped many gifts upon it. For if there had been heavy fighting during the past year, much abuse would have been directed against this Ministry.
>
> . . . .
>
> In my judgment the sense of urgency can be captured and held without doing any damage at all to the Government. But urgency we must have. And the debate in Parliament will not be satisfactory if the result is to dissipate the unrest in the country.
>
> We thrive on unrest. And I want to take advantage from it for the production programmes during the months that lie ahead.

The parliamentary debate, which took place on 29 July, was intended to promote a ministry of war production. Churchill beat off this demand, and Beaverbrook agreed with him, though not for Churchill's reasons. Beaverbrook wrote to W. P. Crozier of The Manchester Guardian on 25 July 1941:

> A real Production Ministry involves control of labour and the time is not yet ready for that move. By January next perhaps Bevin will have improved his position with the middle classes upwards. He might take the Production Ministry.
>
> But, in any case, I would not, and could not, take the job.

Beaverbrook's impact on the ministry of supply was less sensational than his activities at MAP had been. The ministry was already fully staffed. There was less room, and perhaps less need, to recruit businessmen, and there were few left to recruit. The ministry had a first-rate director in Sir Walter Layton, who had once worked with Lloyd George and knew how to temper Beaverbrook's impulses. The chart of administrative duties at the ministry remained in fact unchanged except for one addition in the margin: "Personal assistants to the minister: R. D. Elliott. Viscount Bennett"—hardly impressive auxiliaries. All that Beaverbrook could do was to put a few fireworks under the chairs of the civil servants, as when he demanded that the weekly production figures should be delivered to him on a Sunday morning. Moreover, the war office had long accepted the ministry of supply, and Beaverbrook did not need to quarrel with it as he had done with the air ministry. Indeed he carried his cooperation to extreme lengths, as a letter of 4 August to Margesson, the secretary for war, shows:

> You have been asking for 250,000 pikes.[1] ... What about bows and arrows? In this event we must lay in a supply of string. String is very short, too.
> ... There is also a plentiful supply of flint at Cherkley, which we could turn into flintlocks.
> Would these be any use?

This letter was not wholly serious.

In any case, Beaverbrook was soon distracted from his new ministry. The urgent need now was to supply Russia and especially to coordinate the flow of supplies from Great Britain and the United States. Beaverbrook could marshal all the figures of British and American production. He was already on friendly terms with Roosevelt and Hopkins; with his new enthusiasm for Soviet Russia, he was likely soon to be on friendly terms with Stalin. He, and no other British minister, was clearly pre-destined for the position of international go-between, and he was suited to it by nature. The first call came to him in August. Churchill had arranged to meet President Roosevelt at Placentia Bay in Newfoundland. His main purpose was to define a joint Anglo-American policy against Japan. The question of supplies for Russia would also be discussed. Churchill therefore ordered that while he went by sea Beaverbrook should fly later to join him.

Beaverbrook arrived on the second day of the meeting, 12 August. The Americans refused to commit themselves against Japan. Instead they demanded a declaration of high principles. One of these, in the American draft, laid down that there must be "the enjoyment by all peoples of access, without discrimination and on equal terms, to the markets and to the raw materials of the world". According to Beaverbrook, Churchill and the British cabinet had agreed to this clause. Beaverbrook at once protested. He said: "Oh, no! That wipes out Imperial preference". He insisted that the Ottawa agreements must be preserved, and Churchill inserted the words: "with due respect for their existing obligations". Sumner Welles, the American under-secretary of state, again according to Beaverbrook, continued to press the American demand, but "Roosevelt wanted his lunch and gave way".

This story, if true, shows Beaverbrook once more defending imperial interests against both Churchill and the Americans. Unfortunately it does not seem to be true. According to Churchill,[2] the American clause was

---

[1] Pikes were a pet idea of Churchill's for the Home Guard.
[2] Churchill, Second World War, iii, 426–50.

discussed on 11 August, and Churchill, though himself willing to accept it, argued that it needed the consent of the Dominions which could not be obtained in time. Roosevelt, pressed by Hopkins, agreed to Churchill's insertion that afternoon, and the British cabinet sent a telegram supporting it during the night. The draft, as amended on the afternoon of 11 August, was approved without further discussion on the morning of 12 August, and the lunch was a celebration, not an occasion for more argument. Churchill's account is fully confirmed in that given by Sumner Welles.[1] The only conflicting evidence comes from Robert Sherwood's biography of Harry Hopkins, which states: "It was he [Beaverbrook] who insisted that the qualifying term be included".[2] But Sherwood derived much of his information from Beaverbrook and worked closely with him while writing Hopkins's biography. Moreover he makes Beaverbrook arrive on 11 August, which is certainly wrong. Undoubtedly Beaverbrook would have leapt to the defence of the Ottawa agreements had this been necessary, and maybe applauded Churchill's stand. But the episode swelled in Beaverbrook's imagination over the years, and this was not the only occasion when, like George IV, he claimed to have been present at the battle of Waterloo.

Beaverbrook's real task was to talk supply, and he did this with great effect. When the Atlantic meeting ended, he went on to Washington and learnt there that Purvis, head of the British buying commission, had been killed in an air crash. Beaverbrook's responsibility was therefore all the greater, and he became the principal spokesman for supply on the British side. He had detailed discussions with the Americans in charge of war production. His methods were attuned to theirs, and they responded to his sense of urgency. One of his impulses was particularly noteworthy. Beaverbrook told President Roosevelt that American industry should be immediately stirred up to produce landing craft on a large scale. Here already was his first attempt to translate the Second Front into practical action, and Beaverbrook at any rate cannot be accused of advocating the Second Front without preparing the instruments for it. This was for the future. The present need was to supply Russia. Agreement was reached on a joint mission to Moscow. Since Hopkins was ill, Harriman was to lead on the American side, and Beaverbrook was clearly the British choice. Back in London, Beaverbrook had his usual doubts. He wrote to Churchill on 29 August 1941:

> I see the importance of the mission leaving by September 30th.
> But I shall have nothing to give or promise the Russians.
> And so it seems to me that Eden should lead it. For he will be able to make speeches and to encourage the martial and national spirit of the Russians.

[1] Sumner Welles, Where are we Heading?, 9–14.
[2] Sherwood, White House Papers, i, 361–62.

But it would be a mistake to send Eden without Harry Hopkins.

If we separate ourselves from the Americans, the whole burden of acknowledging our own deficiencies in supplies will fall on us alone, instead of on both of us together.

Besides our own shortage in supplies is largely due to the failure of American deliveries under British contracts.

Churchill ignored these doubts. He replied to Beaverbrook on 30 August 1941:

I wish you to go to Moscow with Mr. Harriman in order to arrange the long-term supply of the Russian armies. This can only be achieved almost entirely from American resources, though we have rubber, boots, etc. . . . It is our duty and our interest to give the utmost possible aid to the Russians, even at serious sacrifices by ourselves. However, no large flow can begin till the middle or end of 1942, and the main planning will relate to 1943. Your function will be not only to aid in the forming of the plans to help Russia, but to make sure we are not bled white in the process, and even if you find yourself affected by the Russian atmosphere, I shall be quite stiff about it here. I am sure, however, you are the man for the job, and the public instinct has endorsed this.

The decision to send Harriman means that Hopkins does not feel well enough himself to go. There is no point in sending Eden at the present time.

Beaverbrook apparently tried another avenue of escape. He remarked to Churchill that Halifax had no influence with the American government and suggested that he himself should go to Washington as ambassador. According to Beaverbrook, Churchill approved, and Beaverbrook telegraphed to Hopkins on 9 September that he was coming. There is no trace of this in the records, and nothing happened. It was probably another let-out which Beaverbrook conjured up for himself during his sleepless nights.

In any case he was enjoying his role as the leader of pro-Soviet enthusiasm. He drafted an appeal for a Tanks for Russia week, and sent it to Churchill with a covering note:

I hope very much you will approve of it. For I am convinced that it will incite the workers to give us a large measure of overtime, and greatly increased production.

You will see that they are urged to further efforts, not on account of Russia, but because the Russian front line is where the battle for freedom is being fought.

This innocent description was not borne out by the text. Its central sentences read:

The bravery of the Russians, their fortitude and courage, the endurance they have shown, stir us all to admiration and praise.

Now we must show the Russian soldiers that we are inspired by their example, and uplifted by their sacrifice.

Beaverbrook's main concern was to increase production, and he was right in supposing that the cry of tanks for Russia would meet with a warm response in the factories. But he was also taking care to raise the cry himself, thus securing his place as principal champion of the Russian cause. Churchill did not like the two sentences, and they were cut out—another sign, however trivial, of the growing disagreement between the two men over an issue which in time threatened to divide the nation.

There was a further hint of this on 14 September, when Beaverbrook sent Churchill a paper advocating a landing in northern France. By prescience or accident it pointed to the exact spot where the Second Front was actually opened almost two years later:

> Plans should be made forthwith for a raid of a major nature on one of the Ports of northern France.
> Such a raid is feasible at any time before the end of October. The nights are long enough for the expedition to cross the Channel undetected to any point on the French coast east of Cherbourg. And the weather conditions are sufficiently stable for plans to be made in advance.
> Cherbourg is the most important of these ports. And there are good landing beaches for disembarcation and evacuation on the shores of the Cherbourg Peninsula which is itself easily defensible, if necessary, against counter-attack.
> . . . .
> This raid would have effects of great importance. It would surprise the enemy and encourage our friends. It would be evidence to the Russians of our good faith and to the world of our growing strength. And it might well force the Germans to withdraw first class troops from the Eastern Front in anticipation of further more extensive operations.

The landing was thus to be a publicity operation, designed to ensure a favourable welcome for Beaverbrook in Moscow. And something more. As a member of the war cabinet and the defence committee (operations), Beaverbrook must have known that the chiefs of staff had already ruled out a landing in France in view of British commitments in the Middle East. He foresaw, was indeed already experiencing, the controversy that was to come: the established classes, including Churchill himself, on one side; the factory workers, led by Beaverbrook, on the other. His paper of 14 September was a sighting shot for the future campaign.

Beaverbrook made one other preparation for his visit to Russia. It was a surprising one. He had a long interview with Rudolf Hess on 8 September. Hess, Hitler's deputy as Fuehrer, had arrived alone and unannounced in May. He had flown to Scotland and, when taken captive, had sought an interview with the duke of Hamilton. His purpose was to promote a peace between Great Britain and Germany by some undefined means. He was held as a prisoner of war and was seen by, among others, Lord Simon, the lord chancellor. Beaverbrook presumably hoped to extract from Hess some information that might be helpful to the Russians, or maybe he wanted to assure them that there was nothing serious in the Hess affair. The text of the long interview provides no clear explanation. It shows however the dangerous readiness with which Beaverbrook, in order to make things go smoothly, gave the impression of agreeing with whoever he was talking to. Here are a few of the more coherent passages:[1]

Dr. L.   I was very much against the war.

J.   Me too; I know it.

Dr. L.   You too yes, very sorry to see it come about, very sorry indeed; I regretted it greatly. I did my best to escape, hoping greatly that we wouldn't be involved in this terrible world affair. Now it's become terribly complicated. . . . It's not a situation that I can contemplate at all with any understanding or any grasp of vision.

J.   And it is very, very dangerous to play what England plays these days with Bolshevism.

Dr. L.   Very dangerous to play with Bolshevism?

J.   Very dangerous.

Dr. L.   Yes. I can't see myself why the Germans attacked Russia.

J.   Because we knew that one day the Russians will attack us.

Dr. L.   What sort of arms did they have? What sort of war plant did they put up? Good?

J.   Before we attacked Russia we didn't know anything. It had been quite silent.

Dr. L.   Now with what purpose would Russia attack Germany? What would be the object?

J.   To make revolution—world revolution.

Dr. L.   They care enough about it for that? . . . The French would never have attacked you.

J.   Oh, yes, if there had been no Siegfried Line, they had attacked us.

Dr. L.   Would they?

J.   Oh, yes, surely.

Dr. L.   It seems rather degenerating, rather a little bit, the conversation. . . .

I used to go to Germany quite often before Hitler came to power. My newspapers always gave him a good hearing.

J.   I know you had seen with Hitler together a film concerning the last war and the Fuehrer told me you had been very impressed and he himself just, a germ of ending by a good understanding.

Dr. L.   I saw him three times all told.

J.   Oh, I know he likes you very much. He is very sorry we must fight one against the other, very sorry.

Dr. L.   The whole thing is bloody . . .

What does Ribbentrop do? Is he of great importance?

---

[1] For some security reason, Beaverbrook was designated as Dr. Livingstone, and Hess as Jonathan. Hess insisted on speaking English without an interpreter.

J. Yes, quite surely.
Dr. L. He was wrong, I think so, yes, here in England. He was a bit un-compromising. I admired him in many respects. He was a vital fellow.
J. Yes, surely.
Dr. L. I don't see how to go about anything at all really. I go seeking, seeking all the time trying to find some way to penetrate the mists, and I can't manage to see through the gloom at all. . . . The Russian campaign has gone on much longer than I expected.
J. Yes; as we expected too. . . . Even if we defeat them—in a few years they will be stronger than ever.
Dr. L. They fight well because the spirit of the people has been uplifted.
J. I am sure one day they will be a very great danger for your colonies—India for example.
Dr. L. Hm.

Beaverbrook promised to visit Hess again. He did not do so, and this was hardly surprising after their one conversation.

Hess had also drafted a long memorandum in which he argued that Great Britain should support Germany against Russia—a proposal he did not raise in conversation.[1] It seems likely that it was this memorandum, and not the transcript of the conversation, which Beaverbrook subsequently gave to Stalin. Beaverbrook preserved this note in his papers:

> I took a transcript of the conversation to Russia. When Stalin asked: "Do you intend to make a Peace?" I enquired his reason for such a question.
> He said he concluded we meant to make Peace because we kept Hess in our hands instead of shooting him. It was plain that Hess was the line of communication.
> I replied that we could not shoot Hess without a trial.
> He then asked why Hess had come to England.
> I replied: "To persuade Britain to join Germany in making an attack on Russia".
> I produced the transcript.
> Thereafter we got on well.

If the Russians indeed read the transcript, they were no doubt as bewildered by Hess's conversation as Beaverbrook had been.

This was no more than a comic interlude. Beaverbrook's serious task was to ascertain how much he could offer Russia. In particular, any American aid meant a diminution of supplies to Great Britain. The

---

[1] It is often said that Hess came to Great Britain in order to enlist British support against Russia. When he came the German attack on Russia had not started, and it is unlikely that Hess was informed of Hitler's plans. He simply wanted to end the war between Great Britain and Germany. It is conceivable that Hitler knew of Hess's intention. If he did, it fitted in well with his plans, but there is no reason to suppose that Hess understood this.

chiefs of staff resisted this strenuously. Beaverbrook has recorded something of the final meeting:

> It started at 6.30 p.m. Two hours later agreement was still beyond the horizon. . . . Wearily and with some acerbity Mr. Churchill decreed a two-hour adjournment for dinner to be eaten.
> He and Beaverbrook dined together. And over dinner they made a bargain on how much the Russians could be offered. As so often two men succeeded where many men had been failing. And once he had made up his own mind Mr. Churchill abandoned the role of impartial chairman. He knew that he could lead the adjourned meeting to agreed conclusions. And so in fact it happened.

Perhaps Beaverbrook really talked Churchill round. Or maybe Churchill appreciated that, once Beaverbrook had been selected to go to Russia, he must be given his head. At any rate, Beaverbrook went off resolved to give the Russians whatever they asked.

Most wartime missions departed in a cloud of secrecy. Not so Beaverbrook's. Everyone must know that he was on his way to aid Russia. Before he embarked for Archangel he sent a message to the factories:

> I leave you, each one of you, responsible for production during my absence. So send me a message on September 30th, telling me what you have done. And let me tell the Russians then, that in the last days of September you devoted yourselves to their needs, and that you built more tanks than ever before in the history of our country.

Beaverbrook adds:

> There were those who applauded this showmanship. But there were also angry comments, both from the Right and from Left Leaders.[1] Why should the workers be asked to work harder for Russia than for their own country? The effect, however, was just what Beaverbrook had hoped. The output of tanks in the last week in September was easily a record.

Beaverbrook greeted the news of this success with another telegram from Moscow:

> Boys! Oh, Boys! You have raised the roof and lifted the lid and beaten the band. Now let us show them that we can do the same and better for a tanks for Britain week.

The other members of the British mission were Harold Balfour, parliamentary under-secretary for air—now high in Beaverbrook's favour; General Macready, assistant chief of the imperial general staff; and General Ismay, chief of staff to Churchill as minister of defence.

---

[1] Beaverbrook originally wrote simply "the Left". The change was made in order to suggest that, while the Labour leaders were critical of aid to Russia, the rank and file were for it.

Evidently Beaverbrook needed no assistant for his own side of the job, apart from some secretaries, and it looks as though the others went in the hope of discussing strategy. In that case they were disappointed. Presumably also the absence of a naval representative implies that no naval cooperation with the Russians was regarded as possible.

On the voyage Beaverbrook laid down his plan of campaign. Everything must be done in a characteristic rush: "If you stay more than six days in a place you lose your authority". Nor must there be any bargaining. "They were not going to Moscow to bargain but to give. . . . The Mission must not only offer supplies. It must offer them in such measure that the Russian leaders would be satisfied and encouraged. The great danger of the enterprise . . . was that the Russians might be disappointed and cast down and even destroyed by neglect to give ample assurances of help and support. In which case the mission would have done better to stay away altogether". Ismay doubted the wisdom of this policy. He was converted by the results and, on their return, wrote to Beaverbrook:

> It is sometimes satisfactory to be able to say—"I told you so" if an affair goes wrong. It is much less satisfactory to have to admit that one was hopelessly wrong, if an affair goes right. In this instance I confess that I was apprehensive of your plan of action—while greatly admiring its daring. If I had been playing the hand, I should have advised a more cautious, and methodical and stereotyped line of approach. In the event your plan led to a glorious success; mine would have utterly failed. We would still be there—or perhaps trekking eastwards!

In Moscow, Beaverbrook's plan came in for renewed criticism from Sir Stafford Cripps and the other members of the British embassy. They had been exasperated beyond endurance by the Russian passion for secrecy. They wanted to break it down by hard bargaining, "trading supplies against detailed information about Russian production and resources". Beaverbrook was unmoved:

> The one way to break down the suspicious attitude which had given rise to Russian secrecy was to make clear beyond a doubt the British and American intention to satisfy Russian needs to the utmost in their power, whether the Russians gave anything or not. It was to be a Christmas-tree party, and there must be no excuse for the Russians thinking they were not getting a fair share of the gifts on the tree.

Beaverbrook applied this principle without reserve. Whenever the technical committees reached deadlock, Beaverbrook and Harriman saw Stalin on their own and met his demands. Time and again, Beaverbrook gave up Great Britain's share of American supplies so that it could be allotted to Russia. As the list rolled on, Litvinov, who was interpreting, bounded from his seat and cried: "Now we shall win the war". Stalin, though less demonstrative, was also impressed.

Beaverbrook knew how to keep off topics which Stalin did not welcome. He had been instructed to discuss strategy. However he soon realized that Stalin did not want to reveal details of Russian strength, and Ismay was only allowed ten minutes' conversation with the Russian chiefs of staff. Beaverbrook's own airing of strategical problems did no more than ask Stalin for guidance. He mentioned the British forces in Persia, which might go to the Caucasus. Stalin answered: "There is no war in the Caucasus but there is in the Ukraine". Harriman adds a little more:

> Beaverbrook asked Stalin if he thought Britain could invade France. Stalin said he didn't know enough about the situation, but had confidence in Churchill's judgment, but why not send a force to Archangel or the Ukraine? Beaverbrook then concentrated the discussion on Archangel and said: "Churchill was for sending an army there once. Perhaps he will be again". This led to some laughing comments about the incidents of the last war.

Beaverbrook was equally tactful over questions of general policy. He seconded Harriman's appeal that Stalin should be conciliatory on the religious question for the sake of American opinion. But, despite prompting from Cripps, he refused to negotiate with General Anders, the Polish leader in Russia, or to earmark supplies for the Polish army which Anders was raising. On the other hand he listened sympathetically to Stalin's demand that Great Britain should recognize Russia's frontiers as they existed in 1941—incorporating, that is, the Baltic states and the territory of former Poland which Russia occupied in 1939. Here no doubt he saw further material for the pro-Russian campaign which he would conduct on his return.

The formal record of the meetings was kept by Harriman, who himself knew shorthand. Beaverbrook, as in all his business dealings, did not bother with formal notes. Once set on an affair, he could carry all the details in his head. On each item—whether weapons or raw materials—he could say at once how much Great Britain could supply or was prepared to sacrifice from her share of American resources. Afterwards he dictated from memory the agreement which had been reached, and his figures were never wrong. He even divined the topics which Stalin was likely to raise and had ready prepared answers in Russian which he could hand to Stalin as each topic arose. His own notes were personal jottings, with the sort of odd observations he made on anyone he was dining with and remarks which struck him as amusing or interesting:

> Stalin eats heartily. He promotes toasts when drinking. He urged Molotov to do more of it, making him a sort of toastmaster. He talks occasionally during the English speeches and quite often when the Russians are making their orations.
>
> His curiosity about Churchill was insatiable.

His hatred of Hitler appears to be real.

His power I should have thought was absolute and the bottleneck the most effective in history.

I described to him the criticism of Baldwin and Chamberlain in Great Britain, who were charged with failure to make preparations for war, and asked if any similar situation existed in Russia.

Stalin replied that many persons believed that if money spent in beautifying Moscow and Leningrad and other great cities had been used for arms and guns and airplanes, better results might be obtained.

I gathered from his conversation that he took the view that he had refused to go as far as the Germans desired on account of his belief that Germany would have to be curbed, but that the duty and responsibility rested on Great Britain and America and not on the Russians.

He said that many mistakes had been made by Great Britain when dealing with Russia and if I had gone further he would have referred to Chamberlain's hostility and the refusal to send ministerial representatives when discussions were planned.

Stalin then asked me about Lady Astor. He said that her ladyship had told him when she visited the Kremlin that Churchill was done. Stalin had replied to her that when the Conservatives were involved in military operations, they would certainly send for the old war-horse.

He said that statesmen talked too much in England and that they paid too much attention to the newspapers.

All this time, Stalin, who had taken two glasses of Kummel specially served to him, was drinking a great deal of red Caucasian wine, which he poured into a glass the size of a sherry glass. He constantly refilled the glass out of the bottle and on the whole drank much of it.

At this time I decided to try his red wine to see if it differed in quality from our own.

So I grabbed the bottle and poured out a glass for myself, but it appeared to be just the same.

Throughout the dinner he kept one glass over the mouth of his bottle of champagne. This interfered with my trying his champagne, too, as I hardly liked to take the glass off to give the impression I had mistaken his bottle for my own.

So I thought possibly that he had kept his bottle with the glass in order to guard himself against poison and I asked him for an explanation. He said he kept the glass on the neck of the bottle in order to preserve the gases in the champagne. I did not think it a very good reason.

I asked him if Kalinin had a mistress, as I had been told that he had an actress friend. Stalin said "He is too old. Do you?"

Stalin said to me, you can produce arms. You are a manufacturing race. You will have a big output before long. Too many arms perhaps in 2 or 4 years. But it is not enough to turn out arms from your factories. You must also sustain and develop the spirit which enables a people to bear arms.

Stalin asked me about Maisky. He received from me a most enthusiastic account of the Ambassador and his work tempered with a declaration that he was not entirely satisfactory to Great Britain because he subjected us to too much pressure and occasionally represented the interests of his country too vigorously and too firmly to be comfortable.

I then asked him about Cripps. Stalin gave what I thought was a negative shrug and said: "Oh he's all right" without enthusiasm. I said: "He's a bore?" and Stalin said "Like Maisky?" I said, "No, like Mme. Maisky". Stalin enjoyed the joke immensely.

Harriman concluded his report with these words:

Beaverbrook has been a great salesman. His personal sincerity was convincing. His genius never worked more effectively.

Certainly Beaverbrook won Stalin's confidence as far as it was possible for any man to do so. The British and Americans had met the Russian demands far more than had been expected. The practical results of the mission are less easy to assess. The Russians stated their requirements without any real knowledge of their own resources. Tanks and aircraft were supposed to be the decisive weapons of this new sort of war, and therefore the Russians asked for them in vast numbers. Later it turned out that the Russians were themselves producing more tanks than they could use, and their pilots were never enough to man all their aircraft. The vast supplies sent to Russia at a terrible cost in men and ships were largely of the wrong sort, through nobody's fault. Only in 1943 did the Russians realize that what they wanted from the West was mobility, and it was American jeeps and troop-carrying vehicles, rather than tanks and aircraft, which enabled Soviet Russia to win the war.

Beaverbrook himself had another object in mind. The mission, in his view, was a publicity operation directed towards the Russian, as well as to the British, people. He wrote in his later account:

Many voices were raised in Russia in those days of crisis against the "do or die" policy of the Kremlin. There were whispers of mutiny and treason. It was Russia's darkest hour. And then—Stalin announcing the vital, the unexpected, the triumphant news that assistance from the West had been promised and would swiftly be forthcoming.

The psychological effect was vast. And it was the tonic to Russian morale, far more than the nature and amount of the help offered, that was decisive. The Russians had endured three months and more of unrelieved reverses. So often they had heard their "friends" in the West praising their valour and lamenting their inability to do more to help. They wanted something more than praise and laments. And now, at the eleventh hour, they got it.

This was a newspaperman's fantasy. Most Russians outside the Kremlin knew nothing of the Anglo-American mission, and the few who did attached little importance to it. But this was Beaverbrook all over. As a former minister of information as well as a newspaperman, events only became important for him when they made news.

There were others who did not share Beaverbrook's satisfaction, prominent among them Sir Stafford Cripps. Beaverbrook got his blow in as soon as he returned to England. He reported to Churchill on 8 October:

Eight important points of difference between Sir Stafford Cripps and me were revealed during the Moscow Conference. I detail them now so that you may be aware of them when Cripps raises them.

1. Cripps was in favour of a "League of Nations" manner of conducting the Conference. He wanted complete disclosure of information by all three countries followed by a general shareout. He wanted me to force the Russians to "come clean".

2. He wished to decide by negotiation the place of utilization. The inquiry would involve the disclosure of plans of campaign. "In this respect the Russian plan is known, to continue fighting the Germans defensively or offensively in every way possible along the whole of the front".

3. Cripps pressed me to take him to the Kremlin for my interviews with Stalin.

4. He objected also to my refusal to take the Embassy interpreter with me on these occasions.

5. He pressed strongly for discussions on Strategy. He was anxious to arrange an interview with the Russian Staff for me with Ismay as my colleague for that purpose.

6. Sir Stafford wished to trade goods for information, and to insist on performance by the Russians.

7. He urged most earnestly a discussion on the supply of the Polish Army. I agreed to meet the Ambassador and the Generals but declined to enter into any details.

It would be right to say that I refused to be caught up in the Polish negotiations at any time.

8. Sir Stafford asked that the Conference should discuss and determine joint action in supplies for China. He also mentioned Turkey. It was his plan to take these supplies from the available resources of the three countries. I was not willing to agree to these negotiations.

Sure enough, complaints from Cripps were not long in coming. Beaverbrook had safely ensured against them. He hoped also that, in presenting himself instead of Cripps as the friend of Russia, he had established yet another claim to leadership of the Left.

Cripps was, for a time, the least of Beaverbrook's antagonists. The successful mission to Russia gave Beaverbrook a confidence which he had never possessed before. He really believed that he now enjoyed a popularity which would enable him to become the second man in the kingdom—or perhaps even the first. Here is one of the great riddles in Beaverbrook's career. Given the need for an overlord of production, it made sense for Beaverbrook to build up his popularity with the shop-stewards in order to override the opposition from Labour members of the cabinet. Did he go further? Did he contemplate striding to supreme power as Lloyd George had done in the first world war? Others attributed this aim to him, some in apprehension, others with hope. Beaverbrook himself always denied it and insisted that his loyalty to Churchill never wavered. But he was surrounded by sycophants; nervous tension and asthma impaired his judgement and he may have had such fantasies in the dark watches of the night.

More probably Beaverbrook drove ahead without any defined purpose. He had always been a missionary. He rejoiced in his new-found success as a demagogue. He was delighted at the thought of eclipsing Attlee and Bevin. In his romantic schoolboy way, he saw himself as leader of the Radical Left, the hero of the masses. This, rather than the office of prime minister, was what he coveted. He had some reason for believing that he could be successful. Shortly after Beaverbrook's death, William Gallacher, the Communist MP, told[1] how in the autumn of 1941 Bevin was shouted down in the City Hall at Glasgow. Then it was announced that Beaverbrook was coming, fresh from his visit to Moscow. Gallacher arranged with the local shop stewards to make the meeting a demonstration of solidarity with Soviet Russia. Beaverbrook had a phenomenal success. The following week Bevin met Gallacher in a corridor of the house of commons and snarled at him: "You're a bloody fine man". Gallacher said: "For God's sake, what have I done now?". Bevin answered: "You went up to Glasgow to get a reception for that renegade Beaverbrook, after what you did for me". This story would have given Beaverbrook great pleasure if he had known of it.

He did not understand that this success was ephemeral and misjudged his position as he had done in the days of the Empire Crusade. He could stir great audiences. He had admiring friends—Tariff Reformers in the old days, now left-wingers like Aneurin Bevan and Michael Foot. He never acquired solid support. He took up a cause at a moment's notice and imagined that everyone would switch on the new light as abruptly as he did. He was wrong. With the Empire Crusade, he could claim that he had always been a Conservative, even if an erratic one. Shop stewards and factory workers would not swallow a millionaire newspaper proprietor as their leader. The built-in Socialist feeling against rich men was too strong, especially when Beaverbrook flaunted and even exaggerated his riches. In the United States his fate might have been different. There the workers had no Socialist outlook, and Beaverbrook would have been as much at home with the New Deal as was Roosevelt himself.

The difference between the United States and Great Britain raised a more practical obstacle. In the United States improvisation still ruled. American war production, like the New Deal before it, was built up by

[1] Daily Worker, 15 June 1964.

guess, and its leaders had little idea what was coming until it happened. This had also been true in England during the first world war—hence Lloyd George's success. It was no longer true in the second. The war machine had been systematically prepared for years before war broke out. No one moved without a long background of planning. The ministry of aircraft production had been a freak, the one exception. Beaverbrook had been able to start afresh, though even so he found many stumbling-blocks in the way. Elsewhere the resistance of the civil servants and the military planners was too strong. It was an added weakness for Beaverbrook that Churchill, despite his natural impulsiveness, accepted the orderly machine and worked through it. Beaverbrook could not decide whether to number Churchill among his opponents. In the end he yielded rather than fight. Personal affection counted for something. Basic lack of confidence probably counted for more. At any rate, for whatever reason, Beaverbrook did not become the Lloyd George of the second world war.

In October 1941 he was eager to fight. Immediately on his return the service departments renewed their objections against diverting supplies from the Middle East to Russia. Beaverbrook recorded:

> My insistence on supplies going forward tried the Service Ministers to such an extent that I lost all personal relations with them. Even with Margesson [secretary for war] was there such ill-feeling caused that there could be no good terms between us until we had both left the government.[1]

Beaverbrook wrote angrily to Macready:

> The C.I.G.S. shows a complete disregard of this Ministry and its functions in relations to Russia, which disappoints me greatly.

On this issue Churchill supported Beaverbrook, and supplies went forward. It was different when greater questions were raised.

Beaverbrook's urgings in the autumn of 1941 fell under two heads. Crudely put, they were Second Front and a ministry of production. Though seemingly distinct—the one a matter of strategy and foreign policy, the other of economic organization at home—they were really tied together. Each reinforced the other, and both were essential to Beaverbrook's outlook. Advocacy of a Second Front, and of course of friendship to Russia in other ways, strengthened Beaverbrook against Attlee and Bevin, and enabled him to appeal to the shop stewards. But this appeal would be effective, and the Second Front possible, only if there were a unified direction of war production—including the direction of labour, which had hitherto been the stumbling block. After all, Beaverbrook could have combined the ministry of supply, which served the army, and that

---

[1] Margesson, who was shown this paper, queried this sentence, and it was given the more innocuous form: "Ill-feeling was aroused and disputes occurred in relation to the quantities and types and supplies of parts".

of aircraft production long ago if he had been willing; and he rarely attached importance to trespassing on the independence of the admiralty. He had hesitated to challenge the autonomy of the Labour ministry and even now was prepared to suggest that someone other than himself should have the united control. But one way or another, Labour was the nub of the affair.

Beaverbrook's campaigns were never systematic. He had bouts of energy and enthusiasm, and emphasized an idea when he ran up against a particular obstacle. Having always been a man with half a dozen different interests at once, he could not be expected now to develop a coherent political strategy. His outbursts were still improvised and often blew over. Nevertheless the pattern was there, imposed by the march of events. Broadly, it seems, Beaverbrook fought mainly over the control of labour in the first few weeks after his return from Russia. Aid to Russia and the Second Front gradually came to dominate his mind. Once more he found a cause and became a missionary, willing even to leave office so that he could preach his new gospel. For Beaverbrook had one great asset as a propagandist. His first convert was always himself, and he propounded a cause with such emphasis because—for the time being—he genuinely believed in it.

The promptings to action did not only come from within. Those around Beaverbrook urged him forward, and not all of them were political mavericks. One of Beaverbrook's strongest backers was Harold Macmillan, parliamentary secretary to the ministry of supply, a man already of high political standing. On 13 October 1941 Macmillan wrote to Beaverbrook:

> The political system is bad.
> The House of Commons is very restive.
> The Press is hostile.
> The reasons are:
> 1. Our impotence to help Russia by direct military effort causes us to search our hearts again.
> 2. A sense of lack of grip by the Government on internal questions—labour supply, production policy, etc.
> 3. The "old gang" are unpopular. (Halifax, Simon, Kingsley-Wood, E. Brown).
> The "new gang" are largely regarded as failures. (Greenwood, Attlee, Duff Cooper).
> The Bureaucratic method of Whitehall is becoming known in wider circles: Government by Committee; the Lord President's elephantine slowness; the difficulty of getting decisions.
> 4. All the symptoms are developing which marked the end of the *Asquith* coalition (a coalition of parties) and the formation of the *Lloyd George* coalition (a coalition of personalities).

But in this case, the second coalition must be under the same leadership.

The Prime Minister's personal position is as high as ever. But he is thought to be let down by his loyalties.

5. The War Front and the Home Front should be divided. We want a leader for all that comes under the Home Front. This must *include* Labour, which with Raw Materials and Machine Capacity forms the Trinity of Production.

6. The leader of the Home Front must in effect be second-in-command to the Prime Minister.

He must be a man of vision and energy.

His "political" alignments are *not* considered important by the Public.

There is only one possible choice.

7. If the Prime Minister does nothing, he will ride the immediate storm, but the Government will not last beyond the end of this year or the early part of next.

Here was a call to action. Beaverbrook responded. On 19 October he submitted a memorandum to the war cabinet, which he also characteristically sent to Harry Hopkins. It was called Assistance to Russia:

> Since the start of the German campaign against Russia our military leaders have shown themselves consistently averse to taking any offensive action.
>
> . . . .
>
> Our strategy is still based on a long-term view of the war which is blind to the urgencies and opportunities of the moment. There has been no attempt to take into account the new factor introduced by Russian resistance.
>
> There is today only one military problem—how to help Russia. Yet on that issue the Chiefs of Staff content themselves with saying that nothing can be done. They point out the difficulties but make no suggestions for overcoming them.
>
> It is nonsense to say that we can do nothing for Russia. We can, as soon as we decide to sacrifice long-term projects, and a general view of the war which, though still cherished, became completely obsolete on the day when Russia was attacked.
>
> Russian resistance has given us new opportunities. It has probably denuded Western Europe of German troops and prevented for the time being offensive action by the Axis in other theatres of possible operations. It has created a quasi-revolutionary situation in every occupied country and opened 2,000 miles of coastline to a descent by British forces.
>
> . . . .
>
> The Chiefs of Staff would have us wait until the last button has been sewn on the last gaiter before we launch an attack. They ignore the present opportunity.
>
> But they forget that the attack on Russia has brought us a new peril as well as a new opportunity. If we do not help them now the Russians may collapse. And, freed at last from anxiety about the East, Hitler will concentrate all his forces against us in the West.

17

The Germans will not wait then till we are ready. And it is folly for us to wait now. We must strike before it is too late.

This memorandum defined the disputes concerning the Second Front which were to be fought over for the next two years. It was considered by the defence committee on 20 October. Beaverbrook said that he found himself in disagreement with his colleagues on the Russian issue. He wished to take advantage of the rising temper in the country for helping Russia. Others didn't. He wanted to make a supreme effort to raise production so as to help Russia. Others didn't. The line of cleavage between himself and his colleagues and the chiefs of staff was complete. Churchill answered that this was an attack on himself. The discussion rambled off on to the impossibility of invading Norway. Both Churchill and Eden thought greater results could be achieved in the Mediterranean. These conclusions must have been much what Beaverbrook expected.

He was already making a direct approach to the factories, as is shown in a note to Churchill on 21 October. Churchill had enquired, presumably in conversation, what part the shop stewards were playing and why Beaverbrook was meeting them instead of trade union officials. Beaverbrook replied with a long explanation which concluded:

> The Shop Stewards should not be abandoned to Communist influence. They should be given to understand that there is fair dealing and justice for them, and the opportunity to state their grievances.

Beaverbrook's correspondence with Brendan Bracken, now minister of information, gives a more lighthearted illustration of his attitude. Bracken wanted some leading industrialist to state the case against the Second Front for the Australian press. He asked: would Mr. (later Lord) Rootes do it? Beaverbrook replied on 22 October 1941:

> Mr. Rootes refuses. He says he is entirely in favour of aid to Russia, like all other Conservatives and the leading Communists. The only dissenting voice he knows is Mr. Bevin's, who disagrees because he says that Stalin does not answer Mr. Churchill's letters.

It is unlikely that Rootes was consulted on this answer.

Beaverbrook now judged that the time had come to renew his threats of resignation. On 23 October he drafted a letter to Churchill in his own hand:

> You know that I am the victim of the furies. That is the sort of thing that makes me get the job done, so I cannot complain too much of my affliction.
>
> But the rage against committees and against placid & tranquil Ministers who never realize the failure of their own departments as they glibly interfere with the vital affairs of other Ministries is too much altogether.

This rage stands in the way of my being a good Minister in Cabinet & Committee.

So I propose that you allow me to stay at the Ministry of Supply, retiring from the Cabinet and the Defence Committee.

Then I cannot have the furies any more save when my own narrow interest is concerned.

But if in these circumstances you would not wish me to remain in the Ministry of Supply then it would be entirely agreeable to me to go altogether.

In case of my retiring from the Cabinet & the Defence Committee I will say "too much work". If I have to go altogether, it will be "asthma".

In any event there will be no departure by me from the path of complete & unswerving support for you.

This letter was not sent. Did Beaverbrook think it was too violent? He seems to have sent a different letter, which has not survived, referring only to his asthma. This was followed on 25 October by yet another letter, raising again the question of the Second Front:

This is not a complaint. It is not a grievance.

It is, I believe, an important communication.

Two things have been made manifest to the enemy:

(1) Our intention not to attack in the West.

(2) Our intention to attack in Libya.

Now whatever may be the policy of the Government, mayn't we have uncertainty, doubt, anxiety and concern in the hearts of the enemy.

Nothing would be involved save only secrecy, duplicity, deceit and camouflage.

Here let me say that nothing will ever separate me from your policy. Right or wrong, I follow you. But I am the victim of the furies.

On the rockbound coast of New Brunswick, the waves beat incessantly. Every now and then comes a particularly dangerous wave that breaks viciously on the rocks. It is called the "Rage".

That's me.

This is how Beaverbrook liked to see himself, though this very letter showed the real softness of his nature.

Churchill replied on 26 October that a policy of deceit was being followed:

I am surprised you have not realized the enormous extent and elaboration of the deceptive measures which are being taken to make the enemy believe we are going to do an AJAX.[1]

I was not aware that our intention to attack in CRUSADER[2] had been made manifest to the enemy. There have been a good many articles in the papers suggesting this, but I cannot help it. Everything in my power is

[1] An early code name for operations in northern Europe.
[2] Code name for an offensive in North Africa.

done to conceal CRUSADER and to let AJAX become manifest. This is I gather what you wish.

2. I am very sorry to read what you say about your asthma, and of course there is no need for you to attend the night meetings of the Defence Committee during these winter months. I could not however view your retirement from the Defence Committee at this juncture as anything but a mark of want of confidence in me. It would certainly become public, and lead to recriminations of a character fatal to any form of collaboration between us.

P.S. I hope that the rock of our friendship will remain after the "Rage" has passed.

Beaverbrook tried to explain his view that, while he disagreed with Churchill over the Second Front, he was not disloyal:

I can offer an illustration of my attitude which appears to be trifling but defines the position. Bonar Law and I were Food Taxers. He gave up the Tax, for party reasons. I continued to sustain it. But we never separated on that account.

Beaverbrook must then have reflected that no love had been lost between Law and Churchill and that evoking Law's name was not a good line of argument. The letter was not sent. Instead Beaverbrook now turned from the Second Front to the control of labour. Renewed encouragement came from Harold Macmillan, who wrote on 28 October 1941:

I am heart & soul with you.
A Production Ministry (to include Labour) is absolutely necessary.
1. It is a political necessity. Dark days lie before us; the house of commons & the nation are dissatisfied with the present production arrangements.
2. It is a practical necessity.
I have now watched for 18 months (and taken part in) all sorts of plans and subterfuges to evade the straight issue. All our troubles flow from trying to substitute interdepartmental committees for a head.
When we have a head, all the other parts of the body will work harmoniously together. That's the whole story—except to add that there is only one man in the country who will be accepted for a moment as head—yourself.

On 29 October Beaverbrook launched an attack to Churchill against the proposal to leave the direction of labour under the production executive— "That is to say, any dispute with Mr. Bevin is to be referred to Mr. Bevin. This is a continuation of Mr. Bevin's movement for "one big union"." Apparently Beaverbrook added yet another letter of resignation on grounds of ill health. Churchill replied in a letter written on 31 October at 3.45 a.m.:

Yr mission to Moscow, so well discharged, & yr speeches about it, have made you an International figure. You ought not to have put out yr rumours about retiring on grounds of ill health (wh the public wd not accept) without considering this large, grave aspect. You must not let petty departmental squabbles vex you unduly. You know that in all that is essential to the success of your Supply you can count on me to see you get fair play. I feel sure of yr friendship & loyalty wh I have always reciprocated. I am vy sorry indeed for yr asthma. But you are knocking things about now in a good many directions at the same time and this reacts heavily upon me. There is no question of a cabal by yr colleagues against you, & I shd not allow it if there were. You ought not to wear yrself out by yr furies. You need all yr strength, & I need all mine, to beat the only enemy who matters—Hitler.

As you know I am not afraid of any crisis Parliamentary or other because I am only doing my duty without thought of self. My trouble is to restrain my combative instincts, amid the gad-flies of criticism. Try to be as good an adviser to yrself as you are so often to me.

This letter was designed to touch Beaverbrook's heart and perhaps did so. His resignation, as usual, was again forgotten. His disputes with Bevin continued. A letter to Bevin from Harold Macmillan on 10 November 1941 gives a typical illustration:

Lord Beaverbrook does not attend the Production Executive because he says at two meetings you shouted him down.

He suffers from asthma and, in a shouting contest, he is bound to come off worst.

A much later letter from Beaverbrook (to Irvin Ross on 1 February 1964) gave a lighthearted account of the way in which he used to exasperate Bevin:

When the War Cabinet was discussing the exemption of ministers of religion from military service, I listened to the opinion of the late Mr. Ernest Bevin for a long time, and then, on being asked to express my opinion, replied: "I cannot answer just now. I don't know my beliefs on this complicated question. But I will apply to the Moderator of the General Assembly of the Presbyterian Church in Canada, and he will let me know where I stand". The comment was received favourably by everybody but Bevin.[1]

I asked Beaverbrook why he had quarrelled with Bevin so fiercely. He replied: "I was pushed on by a stronger man"—meaning Brendan Bracken—and added that Bracken would wait outside the committee room door "in order to ginger me up before I went in". There was probably some truth in this. Bracken liked fighting. Beaverbrook did not, whatever he might claim. He was at bottom a fixer, and his quarrels were meant to secure a deal, though one of course advantageous to himself. He did not succeed in making a deal with Ernest Bevin.

[1] The Moderator was evidently much in Beaverbrook's mind in 1964. When asked by Hugh Massingham: "Lord Beaverbrook, do you pray?", he replied: "No, I leave that to the Moderator of the General Assembly of the Church of Scotland in Canada". Beaverbrook always made a joke work hard for its living.

Beaverbrook aimed to convince Churchill that the dispute was over the control of labour, and not personal at all. On 10 November he put forward to Churchill a transparently guileful solution:

> The creation of a Production Ministry with Mr. Bevin at the head, and the subordination to his authority of the various Ministries involved.
>
> Certainly I would willingly serve under him for the present and as a means of enabling him to establish his authority, if that were the desire of you and my colleagues.
>
> . . . .
>
> It may be thought that the proposal I put forward involves big sacrifices on my part. Not so. My health makes it impossible for me to undertake added labours. I could not be a candidate for the Production Ministry.

Churchill did not respond to this suggestion. A week later Beaverbrook tried again. He wrote to Churchill on 17 November:

> The relations between Mr. Bevin and me do not hinder nor injure the supply of labour to the factories.
>
> My labour difficulties have been the cause of Mr. Bevin's relations with me.
>
> . . . .
>
> But I am hampered in my demands by the suggestion from you that my complaints arise through disagreement with a member of your Government.
>
> I have done everything possible to persuade you that my conduct in relation to Mr. Bevin is entirely correct. His complaints against me are founded on pressure for labour which I have directed against him.
>
> The trouble began on July 25th last. It will be over when I get my necessary supply of labour.

Beaverbrook added two postscripts:

> In the Production Executive Mr. Bevin is getting so much authority that he overlays the Production Ministries and asserts control. I am not yielding to that movement.
>
> If I were an agreeable fellow, conforming to my colleagues' idiosyncrasies, you would have another chart like the Aircraft Ministry.

For Beaverbrook claimed that the output of MAP had gone down ever since he left it. Again Churchill did not reply. He did not however remain unaffected. On 20 November he told Crozier that while in his opinion, a ministry of production was unnecessary, Beaverbrook could have the post if he wanted. Churchill added:

> When he is all right he can take on anything, but when he has asthma he is miserable, and he wants to get out of things—And, mind you, I need him; I need him. He is stimulating and, believe me, he is a big man.[1]

---

[1] Crozier note of interview.

Beaverbrook now tried a direct approach to Bevin. He wrote on 22 November 1941:

> Can we make a platform for you where I can stand at your side? I am sure you can do so if you determine to build it.
>
> With your leadership of men and women in the industrial centres supported by the principal Supply Minister the war effort can be increased.

Beaverbrook evidently had in mind that he and Bevin should agree on a programme which they could preach together at factory meetings. Bevin, who in any case did not choose to share his platform with anyone, interpreted Beaverbrook's letter as an attempt to build up a private partnership against Churchill. He therefore replied to "Dear Max" on 24 November 1941:

> I welcome what you say and do not think there is any instrument in the Government machine offering greater scope for this mutual effort between all of us responsible for the different factors of production than does the Production Executive.
>
> Your reference to making a platform for me puzzles me a little and I am not sure that I follow what is in your mind. I have no policy or platform except that of the Government as a whole, arrived at through the War Cabinet, and came into the Government not for any personal position but solely to contribute what I could to our common effort under the leadership of the Prime Minister.

The next day Beaverbrook tried again:

> I am so sorry that I failed to make my meaning clear, even if the misunderstanding is not an important one.
>
> It is my hope to persuade you to lead all the people to hard work. It is my belief that you can do more in that direction than anyone else.
>
> And there is a desire on my part to serve you in such a movement in any capacity you wish. It is my resolve to support and sustain you to the full in that leadership.
>
> If you ask me for the Platform—my view is No conscription for women —and Women for Industry only.

There was no response.

Once more Beaverbrook contemplated giving up. On 4 December 1941 he wrote to Sir John Anderson:

> It is my intention in any event to give up my office on January 1st next.
>
> By that date I shall have completed the work with which I was entrusted. My critics will say that I have skimmed the cream off the milk. The public will say—what a big jug of cream.

To Churchill also Beaverbrook repeated the magic date: 1 January, though Churchill had in fact rejected any such condition when Beaverbrook had tried to lay it down six months before. A plausible way out appeared. American supply was falling into confusion. Deliveries to Russia were in arrears. The Americans were keeping for themselves supplies they had promised to Canada and Great Britain. Beaverbrook suggested that he should go to Washington and sort things out. This would be an excuse for leaving the ministry of supply: "I could not go and leave a deputy at the Ministry. It would be a case of the girl I left behind me". However this was precisely what Churchill wanted. He wrote on 4 December:

> There is no reason why you should not go to the United States as you propose. You should go as Minister of Supply and a member of the War Cabinet. In your absence the Under-Secretary would act as your Deputy. This would make no new appointment necessary.

Beaverbrook was on the point of agreeing, when the Japanese attacked the American fleet at Pearl Harbor on 7 December.

All was changed. The United States were now in the war, and, whatever the immediate prospects of disaster in the Far East, the promise of ultimate victory seemed sure. On 14 December Churchill set off to Washington for the first great Anglo-American discussions on strategy. Beaverbrook was the only member of the war cabinet, indeed the only civilian, in the party, and while Churchill had the three chiefs of staff[1] to sustain him, Beaverbrook needed no adviser other than his personal staff. Events were truly making Beaverbrook the second man in the kingdom or so it seemed. He was now as much in charge of all supply problems as Churchill himself was supreme director of strategy and high policy. Most of the discussions on the voyage across the Atlantic were on future strategy, and Beaverbrook took little part. But he found time to renew his complaints against the production executive and the proliferation of committees. Churchill pleaded that the functions of the production executive were being cut down. Beaverbrook replied that there would still be two ministers of supply "with only one output". His statement concluded:

> Voltaire always commenced his letter with the sentence: "Crush the infamous thing".
> I ask your approval for my closing sentence: "Committees take the punch out of war".

Once at Washington, Churchill and the chiefs of staff discussed strategy with Roosevelt and his generals. Beaverbrook handled supply all on his own. He was in a strong position. Churchill was a suppliant. British prestige was low. Two great battleships, the Prince of Wales and the

---

[1] Pound, the first sea lord, and Portal, CAS. The third, Sir John Dill, had just ceased to be CIGS and was destined to remain in Washington as British representative on the combined chiefs of staff's committee.

Repulse, had been sunk by the Japanese. Hongkong had been lost. Malaya was crumbling. The British were in desperate need of assistance which the Americans could not in fact provide. Beaverbrook's reputation in contrast stood high. He had shown triumphant urgency in producing aircraft and tanks. He had laid down the Anglo-American programme of supply to Russia. He knew the right words with which to inspire Harry Hopkins and Donald M. Nelson, who was now in charge of American war production.

Beaverbrook had his figures ready and used them with devastating effect. His first paper of 27 December 1941 began:

> The production of weapons in the United States, Britain and Canada is entirely inadequate.

He went on to estimate that, if existing schedules were followed, there would be a deficit during 1942 of 10,500 tanks, 26,730 aircraft, 22,600 guns, and 1,600,000 rifles. American production plans, he insisted, could be drastically increased. He wrote to Hopkins on 29 December 1941:

> I have been 18 months on the job of stirring men up to do more production.
> If Britain had not taken the task seriously in the summer of 1940, the war would have ended.
> France fell for the want of adequate supplies of tanks and aircraft.
> American cannot stand on the programmes of 1942.

This was language which Roosevelt and Hopkins liked to hear. With Roosevelt himself, Beaverbrook used the argument that American output should be fifteen times that of Canada, "taking into account the national incomes of the two countries". He went on: "In fact, the resources of the manufacturing community in the United States far exceeds fifteen times the Canadian resources". And he concluded with a confession designed to win Roosevelt's heart:

> These arguments, I regret to say, are based on calculations which can be torn to pieces by all those who are experienced in production.
> None the less these arguments in support of increased production here should be considered.

Here was the spirit of the New Deal come alive once more: a deliberate flouting of the cautious experts. Beaverbrook recited his own achievements in England and said to Roosevelt: "Anything I can do, you can do better". Roosevelt was convinced. When he announced his victory programme to Congress on 7 January 1942, he arbitrarily increased by 50% the figures which his experts had prepared. The immediate result was not always successful. For instance, the original American programme was for 30,000 tanks in 1942. Thanks to Beaverbrook, Roosevelt raised it to 45,000. The actual number of tanks produced was 25,000.

Beaverbrook did not mind. He had given the Americans the biggest of all his carrot programmes. They accepted it and, unlike other carrot programmes, in time it was achieved. Beaverbrook, and none other, gave the original inspiration for the flood of American equipment which carried the Grand Alliance to victory.[1]

Churchill was well pleased. He telegraphed to London: "Max has been magnificent and Hopkins a godsend". But Churchill was also jealous. While he had been wrangling with the American generals, Beaverbrook had been firing the directors of production with his own enthusiasm and telling them what to do. Moreover Beaverbrook was at home in the Roosevelt court. He was on intimate terms with Hopkins. He laughed and gossiped with Roosevelt as he did with everyone else. Churchill wanted to talk interminably about the war. Roosevelt soon grew bored with this and took Beaverbrook into another room to show off his stamp collection. On one occasion, Churchill summoned Beaverbrook to rejoin him. Beaverbrook replied that the president had ordered him to stay. A row was bound to come.

It came on 11 January when Beaverbrook and his American counterparts reported on the supply agreements which they had reached. Churchill was angry that Beaverbrook had accepted cuts in American supplies to Great Britain for the sake of keeping the promises made to Russia. Churchill criticized Beaverbrook in front of Roosevelt and the other Americans. Beaverbrook was angry in his turn. Instead of attempting to defend himself, he went straight back to his hotel and sent Churchill a letter of resignation. Churchill replied on 12 January 1942:

> I refuse to accept your resignation, which would be deeply detrimental to the Allied cause, and would undo much of the splendid work you have done over here.

[1] The extent of Beaverbrook's achievement is endorsed by the official American history, Industrial Mobilization for War, Volume I, Program and Administration, 277:

The need for boldness had been dramatically impressed upon Nelson [the director of American war production] by Beaverbrook at a meeting on 29 December. . . . What happened is best portrayed in Nelson's own words:

Lord Beaverbrook emphasised the fact that we must set our production sites [? sights] much higher than we have for the year 1942, in order that we might cope with a resourceful and determined enemy. He pointed out that we had yet no experience in the losses of matériel incidental to a war of the kind we were now fighting. He also felt that we had very little conception of the productive facilities of the Axis powers. . . . He emphasised over and over again the fact that we should set our sites higher in planning for production of the necessary war matériel. For instance, he thinks we should plan for a production of 45,000 tanks in 1942 against Mr. Knudsen's estimate of 30,000.

. . . .

The ferment Lord Beaverbrook was instilling in the mind of Nelson he was also imparting to the president.

I am sorry if you were vexed at the line I took in our talk this evening. I really could not allow the Americans to go away with the impression that we could easily manage on an import of 28 million tons when all my instructions to Salter and others have been to fight for 33 million tons of imports, and when 31 is absolutely necessary. As things are shaping, it will be only with a struggle that we shall get the shipping for that. Neither did I understand the reasons which prompted you to refuse the 100 thousand tons of rubber which the Americans were prepared to offer. Perhaps, however, I did not fully understand what you had in your mind.

Of course, if you want a few weeks' rest in the South I cannot deny it to you, but I had hoped you would share our homeward voyage and resume your duties at the Ministry of Supply which were never more urgent and onerous than now.

Beaverbrook withdrew his resignation. He also showed however that Churchill's complaints were entirely wrong. They could not insist on 31 million tons of imports when the Americans knew that Great Britain had 3 million tons of reserve stocks—a typical example incidentally of the way in which Beaverbrook sacrificed the future for the sake of the present. Nor was there any American offer of 100,000 tons of rubber. This was an overall figure which would be fulfilled during the next two years. The important thing was to secure a pooling of resources—"You gain by it". Churchill was mollified. The row was forgotten. But it had been a new sort of row. This time Beaverbrook was not complaining because Churchill had failed to back him up against others. He was complaining that Churchill himself had criticized his work and had done so unjustifiably.

On 14 January 1942 Churchill and Beaverbrook left Washington. They returned from Bermuda in the Boeing flying boat which Harold Balfour had acquired so irregularly and were delighted with it. Churchill was coming back to face new disasters: defeat in the western desert, Singapore on the point of being lost, two German cruisers passing through the Channel, apparently unscathed. Beaverbrook was returning in triumph. He had inspired British war production. He had organized supply to Russia. He had inspired American war production and coordinated Anglo-American supply for the future. In one way or another, it seemed, he was bound to become the civilian head of the British war effort. His moment of supreme power had arrived. It proved a short one.

CHAPTER TWENTY

BRIEF TRIUMPH, 1942

February 1942 was the crisis of Beaverbrook's public life in the second world war. When the month opened, he was riding high, with all his ambitions seemingly about to be fulfilled. Before the month ended, he had lost power for ever. When he returned to office later, it was in his old role as an adviser and man behind the scenes. He was never to wield real political authority again. What led him finally to carry out his repeated threats of resignation? The reason announced to the public was ill health, his asthma. Beaverbrook soon regretted that this explanation had been given. It weakened him in the political campaign which he still meant to fight. At the other extreme, Beaverbrook's critics alleged that he was leaving the sinking ship or even preparing to supplant Churchill as national leader.

It is true that Churchill was in difficulties for much of the year. As the tale of failure mounted—Singapore lost, the British armies defeated in the western desert, nothing done to aid Russia—the underground mutterings against Churchill swelled also. He had to fight for survival. Immediately on his return from Washington in January 1942, he demanded a vote of confidence from the house of commons. On his next return from Washington in July, he had to face a vote of no confidence—a gesture never attempted against Lloyd George during the first world war. On both occasions he triumphed. The vote of confidence in January was carried by 464 votes to 1.[1] The vote of no confidence in July was defeated by 476 votes to 25. But Churchill was not secure until the victory at El Alamein in October and the Anglo-American landings in French North Africa in November. Beaverbrook never doubted Churchill's hold over the house of commons. He wrote to Harry Hopkins on 2 February 1942:

> Churchill has had many experiences in a life full of colour but came up against a new situation on his return from Washington. Some ten or fifteen

[1] Two members of the ILP acted as tellers against the government and one voted against it.

of his followers set themselves up as authorities on the Far East and on Singapore in particular. They had two or three good days of popularity and then they were required to present their case to public opinion. A most extraordinary reaction set in and by the week-end Churchill had been established in authority and power exceeding all that had gone before.

And he told Churchill: "Pitt was attacked more heavily than you. Chatham had a worse time. Even Lloyd George in the last war".

Beaverbrook would not ride out against Churchill, though he might speculate on what would happen if Churchill fell. The real impact of Churchill's difficulties lay elsewhere. With his own position endangered, he could not sustain Beaverbrook against others as he had done in the past. In the great battle to become the overlord of production, Beaverbrook had to fight on his own. This was the meaning of his later complaints that Churchill had betrayed him, and the complaints were not unjustified. Beaverbrook's position suffered at this time another blow. Sir Stafford Cripps returned, without authorization, from his post as ambassador to Russia and was at once hailed as the new saviour of the country. He enjoyed wide esteem, altogether undeserved, as the creator of the Anglo-Soviet alliance. He had a high, indeed excessive, confidence in his own powers. What was worse from Beaverbrook's point of view, he supplanted Beaverbrook as the hero of the Left. During the autumn of 1941 the shop stewards and factory workers who were enthusiastic for the Second Front accepted Beaverbrook as their champion for want of anyone better. But they did not forget their old suspicions. Beaverbrook was still written down, however unjustly, as the man who had preached isolation and had announced that there would be no war in Europe. Cripps, on the other hand, was sustained by his prewar record. He, it was supposed, had staked his career on the cause of a great popular front against the dictators. For this he had been expelled from the Labour party. Now it redounded to his credit. Beaverbrook wrote:

> And so it came about that Sir Stafford's return from Russia was greeted with almost as much excitement and anticipation as was Napoleon's return from Elba. He marched on Parliament as triumphantly as Napoleon marched on Paris.

No one recalled that Cripps had opposed all measures of British re-armament, while Beaverbrook was demanding their increase. Nor did the public know that Cripps had now changed his tune about Soviet Russia. His experiences in Russia had converted him. He distrusted Stalin and doubted the chances of Soviet victory. He wished to supply Russia only after harsh and ungenerous bargaining. He supported the cause of the exiled Polish government and refused to recognize Russia's 1941 frontiers. Cripps's new outlook, which would have disqualified him in the eyes of the shop stewards, made him acceptable to the established Labour leaders, and especially to Attlee. Of course the Labour leaders would rather have brought in no popular hero, but, if needs must, they preferred Cripps to Beaverbrook. They knew their Stafford. Essentially he was one of themselves. He and Attlee had been close colleagues in the 1931 parliament. Even when a rebel, he had conducted his rebellion in decorous and considerate form. He was now a decoy duck for the popular discontent. Thus Beaverbrook lost his Red Flag to the man who was in fact a standard bearer against the Second Front.

At first Beaverbrook did not appreciate this. He imagined that he could enlist Cripps as an ally and welcomed Churchill's suggestion to make Cripps minister of supply. As later events showed, Cripps was more suited to be an administrator than a popular leader, and this was a wise suggestion. As usually happened, Beaverbrook acted as intermediary. On 26 January he saw Cripps. "I told him, in effect, that he could write his own ticket".[1] This was misleading. Beaverbrook had already decided to become overlord of production, and Cripps's ticket was sharply circumscribed. Cripps was not deceived. On 29 January he turned down the offer. Instead he wrote his own ticket as Beaverbrook had told him to do. The minister of supply must have a seat in the war cabinet and must control priorities and raw materials; Beaverbrook must be shunted off to coordinate Anglo-American supplies in Washington. Beaverbrook at once saw Cripps again. Cripps repeated his demand for a seat in the war cabinet. Churchill had now won his vote of confidence and was therefore less anxious about his own position. He rejected Cripps's demand out of hand.

Beaverbrook now prepared to define his powers as minister of production. He was urged on by Harold Macmillan who wished the minister of production to become a dictator. The four supply ministers (the ministers of supply, aircraft production, shipbuilding, and works and buildings) must become his subordinates. Macmillan wrote: "they would owe an allegiance to the Minister of Production only and abide by his decisions". The minister of production would also control all the factors of production—materials, tools, and labour—and would allocate them to his subordinates. Beaverbrook replied to Macmillan on 31 January 1942: "If the job comes to me and if I take it which are two contingencies not yet settled, it must be a Ministry of policy and not of administration". Beaverbrook did not act on his own disclaimer. His staff had already prepared some forty files, surveying the deficiencies in every conceivable article from Bofors guns to medical supplies, and if he had ever settled into

---

[1] Beaverbrook wrote a detailed account of his negotiations on 28 February, immediately after leaving office. This, though naturally slanted in Beaverbrook's favour, is the only contemporary account of the affair.

office, he would have attacked these deficiencies with the same improvising zest which he had shown as minister of aircraft production.

On 2 February 1942 Beaverbrook produced a document defining his powers. This gave him everything. Thus:

1. All common services will be subject to general direction by the Minister of Production. . . .
2. The labour requirements of the production Ministries will be dealt with by a labour officer under the authority of the Minister of Production. . . .
3. Allocation of industrial capacity, machine tools, iron and steel and all raw materials will be under the direct authority of the Ministry of Production.

. . . .

7. Production policy will be determined by the Minister of Production under the instructions of the Minister of Defence and the War Cabinet.

Uproar followed. Bevin at once objected. He declared that Beaverbrook "had spoken to him more roughly in the past than any man had ever done. He was not prepared to take that treatment". Churchill climbed down. Control over labour was struck out from the powers of the minister of production. Next, Sir Andrew Duncan objected, when offered the ministry of supply. This time Beaverbrook climbed down: the minister of production was to have access to the controllers "only with the consent of the Ministers concerned".

Shipbuilding caused even more dispute. Beaverbrook regarded it, rightly, as "the most pressing task in the war at this time". He wrote:

I had hoped to make a great success of it. I had even begun to plan the methods and the manner of speeding up production in Britain.
. . . Shipbuilding was the foundation of the policy of the Minister of Production, with aircraft as next in importance.
Supply seemed to me quite safe, and needed no stimulation at all.

Alexander, the first lord of the admiralty, was adamant. "He would consult his Sea Lords. And I could be sure they would resign rather than give shipbuilding away". Beaverbrook appealed to Churchill, who cancelled Alexander's meeting with the sea lords and instead summoned Beaverbrook and Alexander before him. Once more Churchill gave way. The admiralty retained control of shipbuilding, and all that remained to Beaverbrook was "the right to determine the types of ships to be built".

It was not surprising that Beaverbrook had now become sceptical about the whole business. He wrote to Hoare on 6 February 1942:

You will have seen that there have been some small changes in the government. They were achieved after some trouble, as you can imagine. And now that they have been made, the question arises, were they worth all the bother?

The public probably does not think they were. But the truth is that people do not very much care who sits in the Cabinet room so long as success presides over the battlefield. And the real popular complaint against the government is the unjust one that it is denied military victories.

The Carthaginians put the blame for failure on the Generals and crucified them. The British do not expect the generals to succeed. But they write leading articles against the Ministers.

Now of course I am very interested in the new ministerial dispositions. It is my hope that they will bring more leisure into my life. If they fail in this respect then I will look upon them with detachment and even disapproval. I still do not know whether I approve.

Beaverbrook was whistling to keep his courage up. Even so, his energies were not exhausted by these disputes. The more he was harassed in his own field, the more readily did he thrust himself into the affairs of others. On 7 February he made two such incursions. The first denounced the policy of bombing Germany:

The events of the past eight months have shown that the achievements of our powerful and growing bomber force have been in no way commensurate with its potentialities, with the man-hours and materials expended on its expansion, nor with the losses it has sustained.

Our raids over Germany and enemy occupied territories have, it is clear from our Intelligence reports, caused only minor damage to German industry.

. . . .

The aircraft employed in these operations could have been performing vital service in other theatres of war.

. . . .

The policy of bombing Germany, which in any event can yield no decisive results within any measurable period of time, should no longer be regarded as of primary importance. Bomber squadrons should be flown forthwith to the Middle and Far East. The temporary loss of efficiency entailed in this decision should be accepted without hesitation. . . . And no difficulties or prejudices should be allowed to stand in the way of its implementation.

These criticisms, though well founded, were disregarded.

Beaverbrook's second document won more attention, though not of a favourable kind. It supported Stalin's request for recognition of Russia's 1941 frontiers. Beaverbrook wrote:

These frontiers fall short of the frontiers Russia possessed in Tsarist times.

At the moment we entered into alliance with Russia, the past was all forgotten. No basis for a confident collaboration was possible, except that which recognised Russian territories as they stood at the moment when the German onslaught made the Russians our Allies.

The Baltic states are the Ireland of Russia. Their strategic control by Moscow is as essential to the Russians as the possession of the Irish bases would be valuable to us.

As for Russia's claims on Finland and Rumania, these two countries have, by throwing in their lot with Germany, forfeited all right to our consideration.

The paper provoked an angry discussion in the war cabinet.

Churchill said that the question should be deferred. Beaverbrook answered that, since no decision had been taken, his newspapers should be allowed to campaign in favour of meeting Stalin's wishes. "This plan was resented by Mr. Bevin and denounced by the Prime Minister". Attlee said he would resign rather than leave the domination of the Baltic states to Russia. Beaverbrook replied that he would leave the government if Stalin's claim were not acknowledged. Estrangement between Attlee and Beaverbrook was complete. Beaverbrook added this private reflection which goes far to explain his resignation a fortnight later:

> Attlee's resignation when in the wrong would have been more important than mine when in the right. For Attlee has a party, I have none. Attlee has political friends, I stand alone.[1]

After this interlude, Beaverbrook returned to the affairs of the ministry of production. Churchill had now drafted a white paper, which deprived the ministry of virtually all power. On 9 February Beaverbrook conferred with Churchill. He gives this account:

> I began to argue that it would be wiser to throw over the White Paper and start afresh.
> I was altogether too tough.
> The discussion became acrimonious.
> The Prime Minister handed the document to Sir Edward Bridges, saying that there was to be no change in it, and that all resignations would be received by 11 o'clock next morning. I told him he could have mine there and then.
> The Prime Minister said, "If we part now, we part for ever".
> Beaverbrook: "If so, it must be so".

The next morning Bridges came round with the proof of the white paper. He brought also a letter from Churchill to Beaverbrook:

> I send you a proof of the White Paper which I have undertaken to give to Parliament in a few hours from now. So far as I am concerned, it is in its final form. I have lavished my time and strength during the last week in trying to make arrangements which are satisfactory to you and to the public interest and to allay the anxieties of the departments with whom you will be brought in contact. I can do no more.
> I am sure it is your duty to undertake this work and try your best to make a success of it, and that you have ample powers for the purpose. I think there is great force in Leather's argument about the Ministry of War

---

[1] The account of this dispute comes from a paper, called Controversy over Russia, which Beaverbrook wrote on 3 March 1942 and from a letter to Eden of the same date.

Transport having an effective say in the types of merchant vessels, as they are the only authorities on the subject who have the knowledge.[1] If, after all else has been settled, you break on this point, or indeed on any other in connection with the great office I have shaped for you, I feel bound to say that you will be harshly judged by the nation and in the United States having regard to the extreme emergency in which we stand and the immense scale of the interests which are involved. I, therefore, hope that you will not fall below the high level of events and strike so wounding a blow at your country, at your friend, and above all at your reputation.

This was an ultimatum such as Churchill had often delivered before. On every previous occasion Beaverbrook had climbed down and withdrawn his resignation. This time the situation was different. Beaverbrook's former appeals had been for aid against others. Now Churchill himself was seeking to impose an arrangement which Beaverbrook regarded as unsatisfactory. Beaverbrook still hesitated and tried to put the responsibility for decision on someone else. He called G. M. Thomson into the room and recited the defects of the white paper. "It would involve me in all the abuses for failures without giving me the opportunity to achieve success. As for the paragraphs about the Admiralty, these meant nothing". Thomson agreed with Beaverbrook but observed that it was too late to reject the White Paper. Beaverbrook gave way. "I then accepted the white paper as laid down by the Prime Minister". The white paper was duly laid before parliament. Two days later Churchill expounded it to the house of commons, and Beaverbrook, whose speech had been approved by Churchill, expounded it to the house of lords. Beaverbrook adds: "There was a considerable difference in the statements made by the Prime Minister in the Commons and by me in the Lords".

All seemed well. Churchill and Beaverbrook dined together that evening. "We got on most splendidly together and with every intention of working to the limit to make the White Paper Plan go". However another storm was already brewing. That same afternoon, after speaking in the Lords, Beaverbrook presided over the defence committee (supply). This was the day on which the two German cruisers, Scharnhorst and Gneisenau, escaped from Brest and passed through the English Channel. Beaverbrook, as he records, was horrified to see A. V. Alexander and Admiral Lyster (the first lord and the fifth sea lord) at the meeting "although there were one and a half hours of daylight ahead of us, with the battle in progress in the Channel". Beaverbrook adds: "I began in my mind to criticise Alexander and I knew that my criticism was tied up with his refusal to let me have control of the merchant shipbuilding programme". Beaverbrook's mind leapt ahead. The British public, he realized, would

---

[1] This was hardly an answer to Beaverbrook's complaint that the admiralty retained control of shipbuilding.

share his indignation at the failure to sink the two German ships. The government's standing would be shaken and must be restored. Thereafter Beaverbrook wrote a note to Churchill, urging that Cripps must be brought into the government. On 15 February Churchill telephoned to Beaverbrook that he agreed. Singapore had just fallen, and desperate remedies were needed.

By 17 February Beaverbrook had again changed his mind. He had now formed the impression that Cripps's popularity in the country was waning. He derived this impression from the response to an article by Frank Owen, no doubt inspired by Beaverbrook, in The Evening Standard. This explains two letters which Beaverbrook wrote that day. The first was to Sir Samuel Hoare:

> We are in the midst of a political crisis. The newspapers made it. But the Prime Minister keeps it alive.
> Already it has passed through several phases. There was the production phase, when it appeared that nothing would satisfy the people but the setting up of a full-fledged Production Ministry. The Ministry was set up. It had not many feathers, but the public have got used to the ugly duckling. They may think that it will grow up to be a swan. The ugly duckling does not think this at all.
> The next phase was the Cripps phase. Cripps must be given a place in the government and indeed in the War Cabinet. Cripps was necessary to the effective conduct of the war.
> I am a Crippsite. So is the Prime Minister. We are for Cripps. We want him to lead the House. Mr. Attlee has imposed his veto. Having excommunicated Cripps in the peace, he is not going to make him assistant pope in the war.
> So Cripps is still out of the Government. He is also, I believe, beginning to sink out of the public mind.
> The latest cry is that there should be a Minister of Defence. The Prime Minister's critics are solicitous for his health. They think that he is carrying too many burdens. And they propose that he should appoint some other minister to guide our strategy. The trouble about this suggestion is that either the new Minister of Defence will disagree with the Prime Minister and get the sack, or agree with the Prime Minister, in which case he will be superfluous.
> So it appears probable that this phase in the crisis will pass away. What the next one will be I know not. But I am bound to say that there is no sign of the agitation coming to an end.

To Churchill Beaverbrook wrote:

> The people have lost confidence in themselves and they turn to the Government, looking for a restoration of that confidence. It is the task of the Government to supply it.
> Now what can be done, by means of changes in the structure of the administration, to give the people what they want?

(1) The addition of Sir Stafford Cripps to the government? But the desire of the public for Cripps is a fleeting passion. Already it is on the wane.

(2) The appointment of a Minister of Defence or, perhaps, a Deputy Minister of Defence? But no one can be found for this post who will at once give satisfaction to the public and to you, under whom he would serve.

It might be possible to appoint some one who, like Cripps, would satisfy the public in its present mood. But Cripps would not be satisfactory to you.

(3) The setting up of a War Cabinet composed of a few Ministers each of whom would preside over groups of departments and would be free from departmental duties? This plan should be adopted.

The War cabinet should consist of Bevin, the strongest man in the present Cabinet; Eden, the most popular member of the Cabinet; and Attlee, the leader of the Socialist party.

The other members of the Cabinet should be wiped out. They are valiant men, more honourable than the thirty, but they attain not to the first three.

(4) Lastly, some members of the Government, especially Lord Moyne, are looked on by the public as unsatisfactory ministers. Their names are well known to you.

One at any rate of the Defence Ministers is in trouble with the public. Maybe two of them.

That is of course, a personal letter with no intention on my part to help or give countenance to any public agitation.[1]

Churchill was angered by this letter and upbraided Beaverbrook for changing his views. Maybe too Churchill did not like the side-swipe at A. V. Alexander, a loyal subordinate, and therefore high in favour.

On the night of 18 February Beaverbrook was summoned to the annexe, where Churchill spent his evenings. Churchill had taken Beaverbrook's advice and had decided to reconstruct the government. He produced two suggested lists for the war cabinet. One had five names, the other seven or eight. Attlee was to be deputy prime minister. Cripps was to lead the house of commons. Beaverbrook was included as minister of production. But in the first list both he and Bevin were excluded from the war cabinet. Beaverbrook said to Churchill: "Take the five and leave me out. I want to retire. Anthony [Eden] should lead the House, not Cripps. And Attlee should not be Deputy Prime Minister. His abilities do not warrant that

---

[1] Lord Moyne was colonial secretary. He left office on 22 February 1942. The defence minister "in trouble with the public" was Margesson, secretary for war. He also left office on 22 February. The other defence minister "maybe" also in trouble was Alexander, the first lord of the admiralty, who was mainly in trouble with Beaverbrook. He did not leave office on 22 February. One other change of minister was indirectly due to Beaverbrook. During the discussions over the ministry of production, Beaverbrook asserted that Moore-Brabazon would not allow him to interfere in MAP. He therefore asked that Llewellin, his old parliamentary secretary, should take Moore-Brabazon's place. Churchill refused, but on 22 February made the change all the same. Beaverbrook later wrote to Moore-Brabazon that he had not been consulted on the government changes. This, though true, was disingenuous.

position. There would be no need for a Leader if this Lord Privy Seal [Attlee] could make a good case for the Government. His contribution towards fighting the war has been nothing, save only as a leader of a party; who is always seeking honours and place for his followers. That is no reason for him to hold high place. We want tougher fellows at a time like this. Fighting men".

Beaverbrook's longstanding grievances had now all focused against Attlee, and for a simple reason: Attlee had become in Beaverbrook's eyes the symbol of opposition to a policy of friendship with Soviet Russia. His objections were in vain. Churchill for once was not backward in political tactics, and balancing Attlee against Cripps was the essential part of his manoeuvre. On Attlee's side, Cripps was preferable to Beaverbrook as the lightning-conductor against popular discontent. Cripps was a threat to Attlee's position, but he was equally a threat to Churchill's, and it was therefore certain that Churchill would not use him against Attlee. With Beaverbrook, on the other hand, Churchill might be tempted to form an alliance against Attlee and even against Bevin. Moreover Cripps would be content with the trappings of power as leader of the house of commons. Beaverbrook, if he stayed, would demand real power as minister of production. In the last resort, Cripps could be manoeuvred; Beaverbrook could not.

If Beaverbrook had to go, Churchill naturally preferred that it should be as the result of a quarrel with Attlee and not with himself. At all events, Beaverbrook and Churchill went into the next room, where they found Attlee, Eden, Bracken, and James Stuart—the Conservative chief whip. Churchill more or less dared Beaverbrook to repeat what he had just said. Beaverbrook did not hang back. He said: "Cripps is being appointed Leader because he has made a successful speech in a Committee Room of the House today. But as Attlee has made a very bad speech to the Labour party, this criterion provides an additional reason why he should not be Deputy Prime Minister".

Attlee: What have I done to you that you treat me in this way?
Beaverbrook: Why should I not talk frankly? You criticize me and I make no objection.
Attlee: I never did.
Beaverbrook: How about the Dalton episode?

This allusion, now incomprehensible,[1] produced general anger, and Churchill silenced Beaverbrook "very roughly". This prevented him from voicing a further grievance, according to which Attlee and Bevin

[1] Possibly it was a reference to the occasion in 1941 when Beaverbrook was called in to arbitrate between the claims of the foreign office (Eden) and the ministry of economic warfare (Dalton) to control foreign propaganda. Beaverbrook backed Dalton —in vain.

were running the story that he was trying to take control of labour out of Bevin's hands. "Now Attlee knew that this was false but he never contradicted it". Beaverbrook contented himself with saying that he did not want to join the new government with Attlee as deputy prime minister. He concluded by reviving his other great grievance: "You can't defend the White Paper anyway. It will be a continuous row. It will be used as a cockshy to knock down the Prime Minister. And I will be the unhappy cause of trouble for him". At this Beaverbrook walked out of the annexe with Bracken and had a quarrel with him also on the way home.

Beaverbrook does not seem to have realized that he had taken the decisive step. It was one thing to offer his resignation privately to Churchill as he had done so often and quite another to stake his position against Attlee's in the presence of others. Churchill could not afford to go against Attlee at this moment of crisis and perhaps did not want to. However, Beaverbrook, back home, offered a way out of a sort. He wrote to Churchill:

> Do you think, in the circumstances, that I might be given four months' leave of absence so that I may deal with the papers in the interest of your direction of the war?
>
> And, while I am your man out and out, your humble servant for the duration of the war, I must say there are certain circumstances in which I would not be prepared to sit in the Cabinet.
>
> But, outside the Cabinet, I am ready to hold office.

Here were Beaverbrook's old convictions both that he could influence the newspapers and that the newspapers could influence public opinion. Evidently he did not appreciate that such activities on his part would have little appeal at this moment.

Churchill did not allude to the suggestion when they met the next morning. He showed Beaverbrook a cabinet list which included Oliver Lyttelton in charge of production. Churchill asked whether Beaverbrook would go to Washington—presumably as ambassador—or become lord privy seal. Beaverbrook said no. Churchill then said that Beaverbrook could be given charge of all foreign supplies including Washington and Russia. Beaverbrook again said no. Churchill then proposed to state: Beaverbrook had been offered a place in the war cabinet but retires on account of ill-health. Beaverbrook agreed. A day or two later Bracken, who had now taken Beaverbrook's place as the go-between, called to ask whether Beaverbrook's decision to retire was irrevocable. Beaverbrook said it was.

Churchill lamented this outcome. He wanted to keep Beaverbrook and, if he had been in a similar position, would have grasped at almost any office in order to stay. But Churchill would not pay Beaverbrook's price and indeed could not understand why he insisted on it. On 20 February Churchill told Crozier:

> He needn't have gone. He could have had anyone of three or four offices if he had liked to stop. He could have gone back to the ministry of aircraft production if he had chosen. I didn't want him to go. He was good for me! Any number of times, if things were going badly, he would encourage me saying, "Look at all the things on your side. Look what you've accomplished. Be of good courage!" and he put courage and pep into me.[1]

Churchill and Beaverbrook met for dinner on 24 February. According to Beaverbrook's written account made at the time, Churchill again asked whether Beaverbrook would go to Washington. Beaverbrook said that he would, but as Churchill's personal representative and not to interfere with the organizations there. Churchill then said: "I did not want you to leave the Government. Come back if you want to". Beaverbrook: "Let us leave things as they are". Churchill went on that neither Attlee nor Bevin wanted to exclude Beaverbrook: "I have assured them that you will not attack them". Nor had Cripps raised any objections to Beaverbrook. Beaverbrook remained stubborn. On parting Churchill said: "We will gain in tranquillity but we will lose in activity".

We have another account of this meeting which Beaverbrook gave to G. M. Thomson immediately afterwards.[2] According to this, Churchill said: "You told Harold Macmillan 'It is either the Premiership or nothing now'.... You will be Prime Minister. Nothing can stop it. Events will make you Prime Minister.... Many of the Ministers will refuse to serve under you.... But I, Churchill, will serve under you". Did this conversation ever take place? Or was it a product of Beaverbrook's day dreams? Churchill's final remark has a more plausible ring: "You made a bad job over the Production Ministry. If you had lain low for a month, you would have got all you wanted". This was not likely to mollify Beaverbrook.

He remained firm. On 26 February he wrote a final letter of resignation in his own hand:

> I am leaving this office today and going to my own place.
> And now I must tell you about twenty-one months of high adventure, the like of which has never been known before.
> All the time, everything that has been done by me has been due to your holding me up.
> You took a great chance in putting me in and you stood to be shot at by a section of members for keeping me here.
> It was little enough I gave you compared with what you gave me.

[1] Crozier note of interview.
[2] G. M. Thomson, Vote of Censure, 135.

I owe my reputation to you. The confidence of the public really comes from you. And my courage was sustained by you.

These benefits give me a right to a place in your list of lieutenants who served you when you brought salvation to our people in the hour of disaster.

In leaving then, I send this [expression of thanks and friendship along with the admiration for you which I hold in common with all my fellow countrymen] letter of gratitude and devotion to the leader of the nation; the saviour of our people and the symbol of resistance in the free world.

Churchill was deeply moved by this letter and told his doctor, Sir Charles Wilson (later Lord Moran): "I like him very much". On 27 February Churchill replied, also in his own hand:

Thank you for all you say in yr splendid letter wh is a vy gt comfort & encouragement to me.

We have lived & fought side by side through terrible days, & I am sure our comradeship & public work will undergo no break. All I want you to do now is to recover yr strength & poise, so as to be able to come to my aid when I shall vy greatly need you.

Yr work during the crisis at M.A.P. in 1940 played a decisive part in our salvation. You shaped the Russian policy upon munitions wh is all we can do for them. The figures of the Ministry of Supplies speak for themselves. You are one of our few fighting men of genius.

I am always yr affecte friend.

Such was the end of Beaverbrook's career at the top. Writing immediately afterwards on 28 February, Beaverbrook set down three reasons for his resignation:

(1) Asthma. Certainly.

(2) Attlee as Deputy Prime Minister. This appointment was damaging to the administration, and could be torn to pieces at any time.

(3) Cripps as Leader of the House instead of Eden. This was a mistake from the Prime Minister's standpoint.

Writing to Eden three days later, Beaverbrook put his three reasons a little differently: (a) Asthma; (b) Attlee's anti-Russian policy; (c) Responsibility without power as minister of production. There is no doubt that increasing exasperation over the ministry of production counted for a good deal. Beaverbrook felt especially angry about the refusal to let him control shipbuilding:

Shipbuilding was the need of the nation, the foundation of our survival. Yet it would not be given to me, although I was the best man to tackle it on both sides of the Atlantic. Against my bad manners I thought the Prime Minister should set my capacity to get the ships.

More generally, as he wrote to Mrs. Inge on 3 March 1942:

Baldwin once said that I was a man of power without responsibility. As Minister of Production I was carrying on my shoulders a great deal of responsibility without sufficient power.

Similarly to David Brown, a leading industrialist, on 5 March:

> I am quite sure that the best results will be got by combining the Production Ministries in one hand, with full power to coordinate and to develop a common effort. But the Government will not carry any such project through.
> There is too much opposition from vested interests.
> The war has become an organisation. And you cannot make amalgamations without taking into consideration the vested rights of those who are now in control.

Here was the old wizard of mergers speaking from experience.

As a matter of historical interest, later events were to confirm Beaverbrook's arguments for a unified control. Lyttelton indeed, as minister of production, only acted as a coordinator, and the anarchy of three supply ministers, with the minister of labour equally absolute, continued as before. A change imperceptibly followed. Sir John Anderson, the lord president, exercised a general supervision through the cabinet committee over which he presided. As raw materials and labour became short, Anderson's supervision turned into direction. When Anderson drew up a manpower budget, Bevin's autonomy was at an end. Without a title and almost without acknowledgement, Anderson became dictator of production, so much so that Churchill nominated Anderson as prime minister in case he himself and Eden were killed. No one else took this suggestion seriously. Anderson acquired the powers denied to Beaverbrook, because he had more tact, knew civil service methods, and above all was no rival to the political chiefs.

Harold Macmillan, who was of course close to Beaverbrook at this time, holds that his resignation was solely the result of a complete breakdown in his health. Macmillan writes:

> Beaverbrook had undergone tremendous strain for twenty arduous months. His exertions at the Ministry of Aircraft Production were almost superhuman. His recent journeys to Moscow and Washington under the harsh conditions of travelling in war-time, had affected him severely. His asthma had grown daily worse. The frame had become too weak to sustain the flame of his spirit.[1]

This is undoubtedly true. But Beaverbrook might not have succumbed to physical weakness if he had not been so deeply committed to the causes of a real ministry of production and the Second Front.

Yet there was no reason why disappointment over the ministry of production should have provoked Beaverbrook's resignation at that particular moment. He had accepted the limitations imposed by the white paper. Data were being accumulated. Even if he could not raid shipbuilding, there were plenty of battles to be fought with the ministries

---

[1] Macmillan, The Blast of War, 144.

of supply and aircraft production—as his complaints against Moore-Brabazon showed. Nor were his relations with Bevin markedly worse than they had been before. Careful examination of the timetable suggests the most likely explanation. When Beaverbrook went to the annexe on 18 February, he did not realize that a wholesale reconstruction of the government was being prepared. He was presented with the prospect of Attlee as deputy prime minister and exploded. He gave entirely personal reasons. Attlee was not fit for the job—according to one account, "a miserable little man who can't even control his own party".[1] Maybe he saw Attlee, not altogether unjustly, as another Baldwin.

This was a cloak for Beaverbrook's real objection. He picked on Attlee as the leader of the anti-Russian party, though on this matter there was little to choose between Attlee and Churchill. Beaverbrook had always insisted that he would never break with Churchill over a matter of policy. As he wrote in his contemporary account: "I was completely dissatisfied with one phase of the war. Yet nothing would bring me to the point of resigning on a policy issue". Attlee's appointment as deputy prime minister gave Beaverbrook a way out. He could declare, "it is impossible for me to serve under Attlee" without giving his reasons, except privately to Eden. He could still profess undiminished devotion to Churchill and even feel it. As he wrote to Eden: "If the Socialist leaders deserted him I would gladly rejoin his Government". Nevertheless support for Soviet Russia was the real cause of his resignation. Recognition of her 1941 frontiers was the immediate issue. The Second Front was soon to overshadow it. Beaverbrook was dedicated to this new crusade. He left the government for its sake. He was to fight for it with increasing force, even against Churchill, during the following months. His days of power were over. Influence had always been more congenial to him, and he now sought to wield it.

NOTE

Baldwin's Gates. This is a topic not worth discussing in the text. Passing it over altogether might imply that there was something in the story or something to hide. According to the story, Beaverbrook was personally responsible for requisitioning Baldwin's iron gates and railings at Astley Hall. There is no reference to any such personal intervention in the Beaverbrook papers, nor indeed to any other aspect of requisitioning, general or particular, except to the requisitioning of Beaverbrook's own railings—a course which he urged. The story is intrinsically improbable. The original requisitioning order was issued before Beaverbrook became minister of supply. In any case its execution was in the hands of the ministry of works and public buildings. It is unlikely that

[1] Alan Wood, Beaverbrook, 280.

Sir John Reith, the minister concerned, would be a party to Beaverbrook's alleged vendetta. Baldwin appealed against the order. When the appeal reached London (again to the ministry of works and public buildings, not to the ministry of supply), Beaverbrook had ceased to be minister of supply and become minister of production. It is again very unlikely that, in this office, he had either time or opportunity to interfere in the affair of Baldwin's gates. When Baldwin's appeal was rejected, Beaverbrook had ceased to be a minister altogether. It is hard to understand why other ministers, who cared little for Beaverbrook, should carry out his orders when he was no longer in office or even in the country.

When the story was first circulated, it was alleged that the gates which were removed had sentimental importance for Baldwin and his family. Sure enough, the visitor to Astley Hall finds that the gates are not there. Further enquiry reveals that the gates were given to a nearby recreation ground by Baldwin himself after the war and are still in existence. The railings actually removed had no personal association with Baldwin or with any other member of his family. Whoever ordered their removal did Baldwin a great service. There would have been considerable outcry if Baldwin of all people had been allowed to keep his railings at the height of the war when all other owners were surrendering theirs eagerly. Those who care for Baldwin's reputation would be well advised to keep quiet about his complainings.

CHAPTER TWENTY-ONE

SECOND FRONT NOW, 1942-43

"With me this is a final curtain". So Beaverbrook wrote on 24 February to General Macready, who had regretted his resignation and hoped he would return to office. Beaverbrook received other letters of regret. Those who wrote, and also those who did not write, make interesting lists. A. V. Alexander wrote—an act of some charity, considering that Beaverbrook had latterly been gunning more against Alexander than against anyone else:

> I would like to tell you how much I appreciate the good fellowship you have so kindly shown me (even when you sometimes took a different view from mine) during all these hard and difficult and driving days.

Sir John Anderson sent a message of regret in his own hand. Anthony Eden wrote:

> We have been through some tough times under Winston's leadership these last two years. I know how much your help has meant to him. He will miss you sadly.
>
> I too, in my less important sphere have counted on you much, especially in our Russian affairs. And whenever I asked for help you always gave it. It will be a bad business without you.

Herbert Morrison wrote:

> I am *very* sorry indeed (even tho' I know you're not) that you're out of the team. It's been nice to work with you & to have your kindly interest in my work.

Attlee, Bevin and Cripps did not write.

Beaverbrook was still anxious to play his part as international go-between. The topic of Russia's 1941 frontiers now filled his mind. On 3 March 1942 Churchill made the surprising proposal that Beaverbrook should go with him and meet Stalin at Teheran. Beaverbrook agreed. Later Churchill decided that he could not leave the country at present and therefore urged Beaverbrook to go to Washington first. Beaverbrook again agreed and wrote to Churchill on 12 March: "It is my understanding that I will act in America as a line of communication from you to the President. I will not be expected to take any part in the organisation and machinery of the Washington agencies of the British Government". But Beaverbrook was determined to show that he now had his own policy and meant to pursue it. He wrote to Churchill on 17 March 1942:

> For twenty-one months that I was a member of your Government I made a practice of submitting my resignation. It became a deliberate act of promotion. The object was "urgency and speed".
>
> It was in storm over delays, protests on account of procrastinations, hostility and opposition to government by committee, fortified and strengthened by threats of resignation, that I tried to accomplish all the many tasks that you entrusted to me.
>
> . . . .
>
> But the time came when I reached the conclusion that I would be more effective as an outsider because I had exhausted all my methods within the Government.
>
> However, I never submitted on any occasion any resignation or even complaint on policy issues. I conformed entirely to the decisions taken by you because you were the leader of our people. This decision, I am thankful to say, was never departed from.
>
> . . . .
>
> My refusal to do or say anything that might embarrass you over policy issues should not, however, interfere with my continuing to press these questions on your attention.
>
> I do so, of course, as a private citizen.
>
> And the gravity of the issues and the acuteness of the differences that arose between some of my colleagues and me make it imperative that I should press the points to the furthest extent within my power and subject to the limitations that I have imposed on my conduct.
>
> What is it that I seek to persuade your Government? To:
>
> (1) Make a decision to recognize the 1941 Russian frontiers including that with Finland but excluding that with Poland, irrespective of the decision of the United States.
>
> (2) The increase in shipments to Russia of 500 tanks and 500 aircraft for which I first asked on 3rd December. Further, the shipment forthwith of the necessary aircraft spares which must be supplied if the Hurricanes are to fight in Russia in the spring.
>
> (3) An expedition into Europe on the lines of your Antwerp attack, a strategy which you have brilliantly defended in volume I of the "World Crisis". The exact form of this expedition is, of course, a matter for the soldiers to determine. I used to urge an attack on Trondhjem or on Brest. But another sector would have to be selected now.
>
> This three-fold issue stands between us and a complete understanding with Stalin. But there is one other matter I should mention.

Stalin has suffered many vexations. Numerous trials of temper are probably not within your knowledge. Some are certainly outside our influence. Unhappily, other incidents making serious friction have arisen in our ranks.
. . . .

Here, in embryo, was the crusade for the Second Front.

Beaverbrook had not quite finished with his past conflicts. Before he left for America, he fired his last shots as the former minister of production. He wrote again to Churchill on 17 March:

I am sending you too many letters, but this one might be called "The Last Will and Testament".

Shipbuilding is the end of the story.

If there is failure now, the consequences will be fatal.

There is no reason why ship-building in Britain cannot be increased by 100 per cent.—doubled.

That is a proposition I am prepared to demonstrate at any time by argument. I am ready also to disclose the ways and means.

The plan will involve us in dealing with labour agreeable or otherwise. But it is my view that the shop stewards can be persuaded to carry the day for us if they are dealt with in the right way.

It is necessary to get some additional labour. This should be taken from the Supply Ministry. Also we have got to deal with ship-plates and power plants.

The output of the United States in February was not more than 200,000 tons gross. Production for the year will, as things are going, fall very short of the President's projects.

It is necessary for you to take drastic action now.

Beaverbrook repeated this warning on 20 March when he was already on his way to the United States:

On leaving for America, I want to give warning as an ex-production minister about the shipbuilding situation.

The American programme falls short of expectation. There is no prospect of getting eight million tons deadweight during 1942.

The British output can be doubled.

Shipbuilding is a crisis this war.

These were not the only messages Beaverbrook sent before his departure. On 19 March he telegraphed to Stalin: "I am leaving for Washington in the morning for the purpose of discussing the 1941 boundaries with the President".

Beaverbrook's journey to the United States produced the flurry and confusion which often attended his movements. He revealed his intention one evening to Hore-Belisha, who thereupon asked a question in the house of commons, and Attlee, when replying, stated that Beaverbrook would act under Oliver Lyttelton's general direction. This was not correct, and Beaverbrook was furious. In his eyes, Lyttelton was still his subordinate and not the other way round. He declared that he would cancel his plans and was not mollified even by Brendan Bracken: "I won't go. God damn it, I've been insulted, why should I?" He was finally calmed by an official statement from Churchill:

His Majesty's Government attach high importance to the visit of Lord Beaverbrook to the United States, where he will renew those contacts in the production sphere which have been so valuable in the past, and will advise the War Cabinet upon the permanent shape which our organisation in Washington should take on the production side.

Besides this, Lord Beaverbrook will discuss other matters of importance in regard to which he has received special instructions.

This harmless second paragraph referred of course to Russia's 1941 frontiers. Churchill also telegraphed to Hopkins: "I should be grateful if you would impress upon the President that though he is for the time being out of office at his own wish, we remain close friends and intimate political associates".

The journey across the Atlantic was not to Beaverbrook's taste. He flew by way of Portugal and Gambia. The flying boat to Lisbon was crowded. He had to spend a day there with the British ambassador and another with the governor at Bathurst. Beaverbrook expostulated: "Why should I spend the day with some God damn Ambassador?" The journey had been arranged by Beaverbrook's faithful disciple, Senator Elliott, who accompanied the party. Retribution was not slow in coming. As soon as they arrived at Washington, the senator was told to find his own way back to England, and the sun of Beaverbrook's favour did not smile on him again.

At the White House the problems of supply were never mentioned. Beaverbrook, in his own words, "Did not concern himself with them at all".[1] He soon abandoned also the question of Russia's frontiers which he had come to raise. For he discovered that Roosevelt, far from being more amenable than Attlee and the rest, was firmly set against determining any frontiers until the end of the war. He discovered something else. "The President had come to the conclusion that an Anglo-American invasion of Western Europe should become the strategy of 1942, and that the invasion should take place as quickly as might be. He learned too that the American military leaders shared the same view. With that view of course Beaverbrook was in the most complete agreement". And no wonder. Here was the Second Front, a far grander cause to campaign for than Russia's 1941 frontiers. Backed by Roosevelt and the American military, Beaverbrook could ride out against the war cabinet and the

[1] These and subsequent quotations are from Beaverbrook's own narrative, The Second Front.

British chiefs of staff, and even against Churchill himself. He would recapture the admiration of the shop stewards and become again the leader of the left.

There was more in this than political tactics. Beaverbrook believed sincerely in the Second Front. Given his favourite motto, "urgency and speed", it was the quickest way of ending the war and therefore the right thing to do. Later critics have argued that the Second Front was impossible before 1944, and they may be correct within their own terms of reference. Certainly an early Second Front was impossible if its needs were put below those of the strategic bombing offensive against Germany and the campaign in the Middle East. Landing craft would have to wait a long time so long as British and American production concentrated on strategic bombers and desert tanks. This is only to say that, if the Second Front were put at the bottom of the list, it would come out at the bottom of the list. Beaverbrook would have turned production plans upsidedown, but there were few to follow him. An early Second Front in short might have been possible only if the entire war had been run as Beaverbrook ran the ministry of aircraft production in the summer of 1940.

This is not merely wisdom after the event. C. P. Snow, now Lord Snow, who was well placed in 1942 as a scientific observer, recently made this statement:

> Beaverbrook's advocacy of a Second Front wasn't as wishy-washy as that of some of the wild Reds and pro-Reds running round London at the time. He had talked it out with experts. His idea was that all other campaigns except the single purpose of invading France and hitting the Germans there should be abandoned. Out with the sideshows like Africa and the Balkans. But of course what he was advocating was a complete change of policy. Instead of building bombers we would have had to change to building landing craft. The big bomber was already taking up an awful lot of our industrial resources and those of the United States, but at that time the change might have been made—and certainly there were plenty of people in America who were all for it. General George Marshall, for instance. His judgement was ultimately better than Churchill's and far ahead of General Brooke, the Chief of the Imperial General Staff, whose judgement, particularly about Russia, was abysmal. Beaverbrook found a ready market for his advocacy of a Second Front among the Americans. They wanted to go in quickly too. Unfortunately, they were out-argued by Churchill.

Snow adds:

> It is important to stress that, with the best will in the world, and granted that production had been shifted from bombers to tank landing craft, there could not have been an invasion until the summer of 1943. This might have shortened the war by nine months to a year.[1]

[1] Leonard Mosley, Backs to the Wall, 244–45.

Head of Beaverbrook by Graham Sutherland

In the Beaverbrook Art Gallery
(portrait by Graham Sutherland
in background), 1959

Birthplace: Maple
Ontario, 1955

Return from the New World, 1959

With President Mackay and Senator John Kennedy,
University of New Brunswick, 1957

With Churchill
at Cap d'Ail, 1958

With Alfred Hecht *(left)* and
David Carritt

After the show

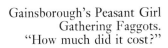

Gainsborough's Peasant Girl
Gathering Faggots.
"How much did it cost?"

AY IN THE BEAVERBROOK
ART GALLERY

Convocation, University of New Brunswick, 1961:
(left to right) Krishna Menon, Beaverbrook, John Johnson,
Sir John Rothenstein, Wilbret Howard, A. J. P. Taylor

At Arlington House (soundscriber on desk), 1962

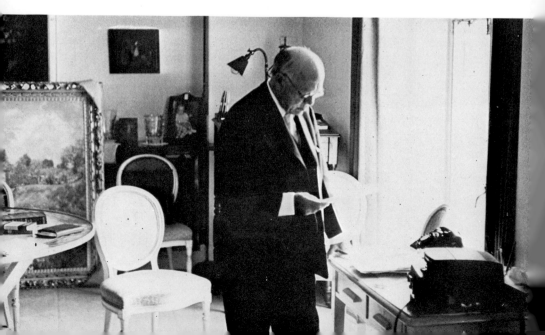

Cherkley, 1962

Churchill, Beaverbrook, Macmillan, 1962

85 years young, 1964

With Michael Foot,
Cap d'Ail, 1964

The controversy can never be resolved. But it is worthy of record that, in the opinion of this highly-qualified judge, Beaverbrook was wiser than Churchill and all the British generals and air marshals put together. Beaverbrook did not champion the Second Front from a desire to make mischief or to become prime minister. He championed it as the quickest and most effective way to win the war and was justified in doing so.

Now inspired by Roosevelt, Beaverbrook retired to Miami. He wanted to shake off his asthma. He had also a more serious purpose: to compose a great speech calling for the Second Front. He and Farrer sat in the sunshine, accumulating arguments and figures. Beaverbrook's thoughts were on Churchill.

"He won't like it, will he?"
"No, sir, I don't think he will".
"You think I oughtn't to make it, is that it?"
"Oh, no, sir. I think you *ought* to make it".
"The President will like it, though".
"Yes, sir, I'm sure he will".
"Alright. Now give me those figures".

Beaverbrook, Farrer writes, "was very like a naughty schoolboy preparing for an escapade which he knows will earn him a caning from the Head".[1] A few days later Beaverbrook was summoned to Washington. Roosevelt said that he was sending Harry Hopkins and General Marshall, the American chief of staff, to London in order to make plans for an early Second Front. Roosevelt wanted Beaverbrook to accompany them. Beaverbrook agreed. He returned to Miami where he received this message from Roosevelt on 3 April:

Harry and George Marshall are in the process of leaving this morning. We talked of the great benefit it would have been if you could have been there too, but I had to make a personal decision and I put my foot down for the very good reason that I want you here.

As you know, there is no one else I can talk to when we get word in the course of the next few days.

Beaverbrook suspected that this was not the real reason. His suspicions were later confirmed. In July 1942 Hopkins told him that when Roosevelt put the idea of sending Beaverbrook over to Churchill, "the Prime Minister had expressed entire opposition to the proposal".

On 21 April Beaverbrook returned to Washington. He lunched with Roosevelt and showed the speech which he proposed to deliver two days later in New York. Roosevelt approved it. On 23 April Beaverbrook spoke at a newspaper dinner in New York—a speech which was broadcast throughout America on a coast-to-coast hook-up. Beaverbrook began

[1] Farrer, G—for God Almighty, 92.

18

the dinner in a bad temper. He had expected to be the principal speaker and now learnt that he would come only at the tail-end. He did not need to worry. Though he rose to speak at ten o'clock, he carried his audience away. His was the most enthusiastically pro-Soviet speech ever delivered in the United States:

> Communism under Stalin has won the applause and admiration of all the western nations.
> Communism under Stalin has provided us with examples of patriotism equal to the finest in the annals of history.
> Communism under Stalin has produced the best generals in the world.
> Persecution of Christianity? Not so. There is no religious persecution. The church doors are open. . . .
> Racial persecution? Not at all. Jews live like other men. There are many races in the Soviet Union and not even a colour bar.
> Political purges? Of course. But it is now clear that the men who were shot would have betrayed Russia to her German enemies.

And so to his message:

> Strike out to help Russia. Strike out violently. Strike even recklessly. How admirably Britain is equipped in weapons of war for directing an attack on Germany I well know. Britain should imitate Russia's spirit of attack by establishing somewhere along the two thousand miles of occupied coastline a Second Front.

American opinion was roused and delighted. In Beaverbrook's words, "Here was no amateur strategist ignorant of the true facts of the situation, here was no military correspondent mingling his imagination with historical analogies from the past. Here instead was a man hot-foot from the White House; a man who till two months previously had been in the innermost circles of the British Government; who even now was on a semi-official Mission; who was known to be on the most intimate terms with the British Prime Minister". Reactions in Great Britain were more mixed. Only the radicals were pleased. Michael Foot, who had just become editor of The Evening Standard, wrote to Beaverbrook on 24 April:

> The speech was stupendous. It caused a great sensation here.
> . . . .
> We are resolved to maintain the stalwart conservative line of the Standard, and outbursts of Communist fervour from whichever side of the Atlantic they may appear are viewed by us with grave concern. We feel that this kind of political output has some psychological or pathological affinity with asthma. I hope the asthma is getting better.

A speech which won this tribute from Michael Foot met with less approval in conservative circles and of course also in The Daily Herald, Bevin's organ. There were questions in the house of commons. Attlee explained that Beaverbrook was free to say what he liked. "He does not hold a definite appointment. He is undertaking a special mission of an informal kind".

Beaverbrook assumed an innocent air. While in Washington, he had talked to Hopkins, just back from London, and Hopkins had assured him that a Second Front for 1942 had been definitely agreed to by the British government. Hence "Beaverbrook had no reason to suppose that his speech would raise hopes destined to be falsified". The succeeding sentences in his narrative are not so innocent. "Did he none the less suspect that it was only with reluctance that the British military chiefs had given their agreement? And was he trying so to stir up public opinion that retreat from the idea of a Second Front would be impossible? The answer is that he did, and that he was".

Beaverbrook liked to make out that he was sustaining a bellicose Churchill against the reluctant chiefs of staff. Privately he was not so sure. His first words to Farrer after making his speech were, "I wonder what that fellow Churchill will say". He did not need to wonder long. The following morning Churchill telephoned and offered to put Beaverbrook in charge of all the British wartime missions in Washington. Beaverbrook suspected that this was a move to silence him. He would be shunted from policy to production. So he did not say yes and he did not say no. Instead he proposed to return to England and talk it over. Churchill agreed. On the way back, Beaverbrook stopped in Washington and spoke to Halifax. Halifax replied that Beaverbrook must have all or nothing. There was no room for both of them in Washington.

Beaverbrook arrived in England on 5 May and at once saw Churchill. He reported what Halifax had said. Churchill answered: "Alright, take everything, the Embassy as well". Eden, when consulted, was reluctant to have Halifax back in England, but ultimately agreed also. On 12 May Churchill telegraphed to Hopkins, asking whether Roosevelt would like Beaverbrook as British ambassador. On 16 May Hopkins replied that "the idea of Max coming is of course agreeable". Then nothing happened. For Beaverbrook had said that there were "certain circumstances" in which he would become ambassador, and these certain circumstances were "the promise of a definite strategic decision in favour of the Second Front". Churchill refused to give this promise. The conflict between Churchill and Beaverbrook was forced into the open.

Beaverbrook remained a freelance. At his instruction, The Daily Express launched a new crusade. Mass meetings were held under the auspices of an imaginary organization, the Centre of Public Opinion. Subject: the Second Front, the most important issue of the day. Prominent Leftwing speakers were enlisted, and other political mavericks as well. Anyone prepared to advocate the Second Front Now was sure of a large and enthusiastic audience. Beaverbrook, as he boasted, "was the acknowledged leader of a popular cause". He also complained disingenuously, "he had to endure the praise of Mr. Churchill's enemies and the condemnation of Mr. Churchill's friends".

Clearly Beaverbrook was agitating against Churchill's policy or at best seeking to impose a policy upon him. Was Beaverbrook also seeking to overthrow Churchill, perhaps even aspiring to take his place? The evidence for this is naturally not much more than hearsay. According to Farrer, Beaverbrook invited Sir Arthur Salter to Cherkley and asked whether he would join him in forming an anti-Churchill party. Salter answered, no.[1] According to Alan Bullock, Beaverbrook asked Ernest Bevin to go and see him. "Beaverbrook expressed the opinion that Churchill was on the way out and started to sound Bevin on the formation of an alternative Government". Bevin thought that Beaverbrook "was proposing an alliance in which he would do for Bevin what he had done for Lloyd George in the earlier war". Bevin said that he would at once go to Churchill and tell him the whole story. Beaverbrook laughed and said Churchill would never believe him. This proved to be true.[2]

According to G. M. Thomson, prompting came the other way round. Aneurin Bevan urged Beaverbrook to assume the leadership of a movement against Churchill. Beaverbrook answered: No. Also according to Thomson, Lloyd George wrote to Beaverbrook:

> Say nothing. Then in two months' time let your newspapers start a demand for a Government of Youth. Form it![3]

None of this can be confirmed from Beaverbrook's records. His engagement book does not show any meeting with Salter, nor any visit by Salter to Cherkley. There is no record of any meeting with Bevin, and Beaverbrook disclaimed any recollection of the alleged conversation, when interviewed by Alan Bullock in 1961, though he described Bevin as "a powerful beast".[4] There is one authentic remark by Bevin. On 27 October 1942 he

[1] Salter told this to Farrer in conversation. Farrer, G—for God Almighty, 83.

[2] This was an account "which Bevin gave to his staff on his return and repeated to others subsequently". Bullock, Life and Times of Ernest Bevin, ii, 177.

[3] G. M. Thomson, Vote of Censure, 138, 168.

[4] The timing of the alleged meetings with Salter and Bevin is also very tight. That with Salter is supposed to have taken place "shortly after Beaverbrook's resignation". At this time Beaverbrook was still on intimate terms with Churchill and was preparing to go on a mission to either Moscow or Washington. It is difficult to believe that he was also contemplating the formation of an anti-Churchill party. The interview with Bevin is supposed to have taken place "in the week following Tobruk". On this occasion Beaverbrook may conceivably have thought at first that Churchill would fall. Within little more than a week he had decided to support Churchill in the house of lords. It would have taken some days after Tobruk for Beaverbrook to invite Bevin, Bevin to refuse, and Beaverbrook to insist. The only possible date for a meeting is Friday, 26 June, and on that day, according to Bullock, Bevin was in Liverpool.

met Christiansen and Michael Foot at a football match and said to them:
"I like Beaverbrook in many ways. He has never got over bringing down
a Government in the last war. It went to his head, and he has been trying
to repeat his success ever since. He's brilliant, a brilliant fellow, but too
unstable". This is a long way from accusing Beaverbrook of conspiracy.
According to the records, Sir John Anderson was the only minister whom
Beaverbrook saw constantly at this time, and this was certainly not for
the purposes of intrigue. Anderson valued Beaverbrook as an authority
on production, and Beaverbrook, son of the manse, had a strange respect
for Anderson, as he had for that other dour Scotchman, Sir John Reith.
Finally, no such letter from Lloyd George has survived.

Undoubtedly Beaverbrook saw much of Bevan at this time, as he had
done for years past. Bevan was at Cherkley on 10 May when a fire damaged
the house and was most anxious that his name should be kept out of the
papers. Not perhaps without reason. The party had been assembled at
Cherkley for a dinner in honour of W. J. Brown, who had just been
elected as a rebel Independent at Rugby, and association with Brown
would have done Bevan no good in the Labour party, even though he
was a rebel himself. W. J. Brown arrived when the fire was already blazing
and said to Trevor Evans: "It was nice of Max to give me such a warm
reception on my victory, but a little ostentatious, don't you think?"[1]

Beaverbrook got fun out of Bevan, as he did from other Leftwingers,
especially Michael Foot and Frank Owen. Their relationship is best
illustrated by an exchange which took place just after the fire at Cherkley.
On 12 May Bevan wrote to Beaverbrook:

> I see you have a paragraph in this morning's Daily Express. I don't know
> whether you think it will do Mr. Morrison any good—it is very doubtful—
> but I am certain it won't do the Daily Express any good because it is wholly
> opposed to the universal opinion of Fleet Street. To describe Mr. Herbert
> Morrison as liberally minded after the Daily Worker and Daily Mirror
> episodes[2] is too funny, not to say too blatant, and merely has the effect of
> encouraging Morrison in his bad ways. I see that the Evening Standard
> prints an attack on Bevin and Attlee which compares with the friendly
> reference to Herbert Morrison.
>
> You know that as far as I am concerned your politics are things in which
> I have not the slightest desire to interfere and I write this note to you merely
> as a close personal friend. I don't believe that the use of your papers will
> have any other than the most harmful effects on your political reputation.
> They will give rise to the unwholesome impression that a straight political

---

[1] Later Brown asked Trevor Evans not to print his remark: "It may indicate my wit
but on consideration I think in the circumstances it reflects on my good taste".

[2] Morrison, as home secretary, had suppressed The Daily Worker and warned
The Daily Mirror. As a matter of fact, Churchill had wanted to suppress The Mirror,
and Beaverbrook encouraged Morrison to let the paper off with a warning.

line is not being followed but rather a series of unpleasant intrigues are being set on foot. I should like to have an early opportunity of a talk with you.

Yours affectionately,
Aneurin.

P.S. I do hope that the damage to Cherkley is less than you feared and that on examination it will be possible for you to restore it to a livable condition.

Beaverbrook replied on 14 May 1942:

I see you have a paragraph in today's "Tribune". I don't know whether you think it will do Mr. Morrison any good—it is very doubtful—but I am certain it won't do the "Tribune" any good because it is wholly opposed to the universal opinion of Fleet Street. To describe Mr. Herbert Morrison's speech as "sane and plucky", after the injustices he has inflicted on the "Daily Worker" and "Daily Mirror" is really too funny, not to say too blatant, and merely has the effect of encouraging Morrison in his bad ways. I see that the "Tribune" prints an attack on Bevin and Attlee (page 7, column 1) which compares with the friendly references to Herbert Morrison (page 4, column 3).

You know that as far as I am concerned your politics are things in which I have not the slightest desire to interfere, and I write this note to you merely as a close personal friend. I don't believe that this use of your paper will have any other than the most harmful effects on your political reputation. They will give rise to the unwholesome impression that a straight political line is not being followed but rather a series of unpleasant personal intrigues are being set on foot. I should like to have an early opportunity of a talk with you.

Yours affectionately,
Beaverbrook.

P.S. I do rejoice that the damage to Cherkley is less than I feared, and I do thank you for the immense part you took in saving the contents.

Beaverbrook's records contain two fragments which might come under the head of political intrigue. The first was advice given to Henderson Stewart, an MP discontented with the conduct of the war. Beaverbrook wrote to him on 19 March 1942:

You ask what you can do. You can, for one thing, become the leader of the opposition. . . . It would be a real strengthening, in my judgment, of the war-time structure of the country.

This was no new line. Beaverbrook often encouraged opposition to a government he supported or even to his own policy. In his view controversy was the best form of publicity. The other fragment is the only open prompting to Beaverbrook that he should head a new government. This came in June from Morgan Phillips, then an obscure member of the Labour party, though he subsequently became its general secretary. Phillips proposed that Beaverbrook should become prime minister, Churchill be sent to Washington and Shinwell be made leader of the house of commons. Beaverbrook replied briefly: "I am supporting Churchill of course" and, in regard to strategy, "The shortest way to Germany is the best road for us to travel".

This, though a fair definition of his policy, was not the whole story. Beaverbrook always talked indiscreetly in private. He was for ever foretelling the fall of old leaders and anticipating the rise of new ones, many of them non-starters. Almost his first question when he came to England had been: "What will happen when that fellow Balfour goes?" Almost the last before his death, zestfully pursued, was: "What will happen when that fellow Macmillan goes?" It is a safe guess that he often asked in 1942: "What will happen when that fellow Churchill goes?". Such speculations were no doubt encouraged by Aneurin Bevan, as they were also by W. J. Brown, another constant guest at Cherkley. Beaverbrook's serious purpose was to promote the Second Front, not to overthrow Churchill. But he was not alone in sometimes doubting whether Churchill would survive.[1]

Beaverbrook was not laggardly also in parading his grievances, even though he had resigned at his own request. One evening in July 1942 he invited Kingsley Martin, editor of The New Statesman, to the Savoy and recounted how Stafford Cripps and Ernie Bevin had driven him from office to the great detriment of the war effort. The sequel is interesting. Martin, according to his own account,[2] wrote a paragraph in his New Statesman diary, saying that though Beaverbrook had been invaluable in 1940, it was now of great importance that he should not again be a member of the cabinet. Some years later Martin was a candidate for the parish council of Little Easton, the Essex village where he lived. He received 80 votes. To his astonishment, this news appeared in The Daily Express together with the comment that while Martin might persuade some gullible people to listen to what he had to say in his paper, those who knew him well rated him at his true worthlessness. "Though he has called into play all the resources of modern electioneering, he has been unable to persuade more than eighty people to vote for him". This item of news was kept in cold storage and repeated, according to Martin, at least five

---

[1] Belief in Beaverbrook as the predestined saviour is to be found in some surprising quarters. In the summer of 1942 E. H. Carr, then the principal leader-writer on The Times, wrote to Barrington-Ward, the editor: "Strong leadership must come from outside. There was no serious candidate except perhaps Beaverbrook" (Barrington-Ward underlined "serious" and minuted NO). Donald MacLachlan, In the Chair, 236.

[2] Kingsley Martin, Editor (1968), 129.

times in one Beaverbrook paper or another. Years afterwards Martin asked Christiansen why the paragraph had appeared so often and told the story of his diary entry in 1942. "Ah", said Christiansen, "that would certainly be enough to explain those paragraphs".

Here we have a clear incontrovertible case of how Beaverbrook pursued a vendetta down the years for a most trivial reason. Or so it seems until we examine the evidence. The actual diary entry in The New Statesman of 18 July 1942 is not so blunt a repudiation of Beaverbrook as Martin claims. It mentions the rumour, in fact unfounded, that Churchill had recently offered Beaverbrook the ministry of defence and continues: "I doubt if anyone favours Lord Beaverbrook's return to the Government except Mr. Churchill himself, who, I well believe, finds Lord Beaverbrook a good companion. Labour and the 1922 Committee unite in distrusting Lord Beaverbrook". Beaverbrook might have written this paragraph himself and often said as much to his friends. And now for the election at Little Easton. On 22 February 1951 Christiansen reported to Beaverbrook, then in Jamaica, that Martin had recently attacked the British press in a speech at the Cambridge Union and that The Daily Express had told the story of his 80 voters in lighthearted retaliation. Thus Beaverbrook had nothing to do with the story, and Christiansen, in blaming Beaverbrook, was covering up for himself. It is possible that Beaverbrook had the story repeated later, though I have no evidence for this. If he did, this was a sign of Beaverbrook's favour. He printed funny stories—and the story was very funny—only about people he liked. Besides, the story did Martin honour. It put him in the same class as Blanqui, Marx, Bakunin and Lenin, great champions of the people who never managed to get elected to the humblest parish council in any free election.

A contemporary exchange between Beaverbrook and Martin was gayer, though irrelevant to this narrative. In November 1942 Martin, being shortstaffed, asked whether Michael Foot might be allowed to write occasional articles for The New Statesman. Beaverbrook replied on 18 November:

> If the newspapers opened that door, it would swing very wide.
> The newspaper pays Foot nearly £4,000 a year. If he were to do similar work for another paper, the directors would ask "Is Beaverbrook losing his punch? Is he going down into the valley where all the newspapermen before him have gone?".
> And they might be right.

Beaverbrook's shifting estimates are shown in the letters which he wrote at this time to his newspaper friends overseas. On 16 May 1942 he wrote to Frank Gannett:

> Complete co-operation and joint planning with Russia, both now and after the war, are demanded by nearly every section of opinion. This desire

is by no means confined to the "left". Indeed it is strongest with those who have no ideological predilections. . . .

It is my belief that on these issues of the Second Front and co-operation with Russia the people are ahead of the Government.

And to Henry Luce on 21 May:

As the battle increases on the Eastern Front so will the demand for immediate action to sustain the Russians grow in volume and intensity. And certainly the people will no longer be satisfied with the despatch of supplies and the bombing of German cities.

The Government will be judged by the speed with which it acts. And should it fail in urgency, not even the prestige of Churchill will save it from condemnation.

On 22 May Beaverbrook brushed aside a suggestion from Harold Nicolson that Russia might make a separate peace:

Of course Stalin is pledged to us. We have every right to respect his word. He's never broken any promise he has given us so far.

Then again the Russian dead stand in the way. You don't cross over that great graveyard with ease.

A few days later the Anglo-Soviet treaty of alliance was signed. It ignored the question of Russia's 1941 frontiers, and Beaverbrook therefore refused to attend the lunch given in its honour.

This was the time of Molotov's visit to London and Washington. An Anglo-Soviet communiqué announced that full agreement had been reached "with regard to the urgent tasks of creating a Second Front in Europe in 1942". Beaverbrook later professed that he had not been taken in. This is not so clear from his comment at the time. He wrote to Damon Runyon on 12 June 1942:

In the dark days after Singapore there was criticism and perhaps a waning confidence in the Government. But now all that has changed. Though individual Ministers are condemned, the mantle of the Prime Minister shelters them all. Churchill's prestige in the country is immense. He is the unchallenged leader without a rival to his place.

. . . There is intense satisfaction that the decision to open a Second Front this year has been irrevocably adopted. The public believe in the future of Anglo-Russian co-operation; and they give high praise to Anthony Eden for his success in negotiating the alliance. He stands today next to Churchill in the country's esteem.

The anniversary of Russia's entry into the war was approaching. Meetings in favour of the Second Front were arranged all over the country. Beaverbrook was to address the largest of them in the square outside Birmingham City Hall. There was a crowd of 50,000 people.

"It seemed the apotheosis of the cause". Just before he went out to speak, Beaverbrook's secretary whispered to him that Tobruk had fallen. A glazed look came into his eyes. He delivered his rousing speech, but he knew that the cause was lost, at any rate for the time being. Public opinion would demand the restoration of British power in the Middle East. Moreover Churchill was now in Washington, debating the Second Front with Roosevelt. With the fall of Tobruk, he would insist more than ever that the Middle East must come first. Beaverbrook concludes: "On the morning of June 21st the Second Front was a near certainty, by the evening the odds were 100 to 1 against".

Churchill returned to England and faced a vote of no confidence in the house of commons. Beaverbrook might have been expected to support the critics. Churchill suspected that he was doing so. Tom Driberg, long-time "William Hickey", ran as an Independent at Maldon. It was rumoured, wrongly, that Frank Owen, who had just been called up, would follow his example. Churchill wrote to Beaverbrook on 14 June:

> The fact that Mr. Driberg and Mr. Frank Owen are standing as Independent candidates in two by-elections will of course be taken by everyone as indicating that you are running election candidates against the Government. This would be a great pity from many points of view.

Beaverbrook did not take Driberg's candidature seriously and warned him that he would lose his deposit. Instead the fall of Tobruk carried Driberg to victory. Beaverbrook himself did not attempt to exploit the popular discontent, though he may have feared its results. Once Churchill was in danger, Beaverbrook was again the foul-weather friend and rallied to his defence. This was not solely personal loyalty. The critics railed against the inadequacy of the supplies sent to the Middle East, and this criticism fell indirectly on Beaverbrook when he had been in office. At last he could vindicate himself.

On the first day of the debate in the house of commons, Beaverbrook spoke in the house of lords. He knew the figures of production better than any man in the country and used them with irresistible effect. "We had more guns and tanks in Libya than the Germans and Italians put together". British guns were better than German. He revealed how, as minister of aircraft production, he had insisted on manufacturing dive bombers against the resistance of the air ministry and the hesitation of the war office. With his experience of two wars, he showed that the prime minister must have final responsibility for strategy, whether he were defence minister or not. The next day Churchill triumphed in the house of commons by 476 votes—among them Tom Driberg's—to 25.

Beaverbrook announced Churchill's victory to his friends overseas. He wrote to Herbert Swope on 8 July 1942:

Churchill's prestige stands as high as two years ago. His critics in the House of Commons do not at all represent the feeling of the people. Everywhere there is a complete acceptance of his leadership. . . .

He has no rival. The position of Cripps has deteriorated. No longer is he regarded as the alternative.

And to Frank Gannett on 24 July:

That Churchill should remain Prime Minister is the unanimous verdict of the country. His position is unassailable, and certainly it was strengthened by the censure Motion. . . . For in the sponsors and supporters of that Motion neither the public nor Parliament could find the qualities of an alternative Administration.

Nevertheless Beaverbrook did not give up all hope of the Second Front, or at any rate his advocacy of it. He wrote to Lord Davies on 10 July 1942:

I haven't abandoned my belief in the Second Front.

If you read the newspapers controlled by me, you will see a great deal in support of this policy, which I think will be carried through by the Government.

Beaverbrook was in a difficult position. He could not go openly against Churchill immediately after defending him. Nor did he like his principal allies, the Communists. He recorded: "Beaverbrook would never consent to speak from a Communist platform".

At the end of July the blow fell. Hopkins and Marshall again came over to reach a final decision on strategy. When Churchill held out against the Second Front, Roosevelt ordered them to agree to a campaign in North Africa. Churchill pledged Hopkins not to reveal these discussions to Beaverbrook—a pledge which Beaverbrook learnt from Hopkins himself. But of course Beaverbrook surmised what had been decided. Immediately after this Churchill resolved to go to Moscow and break the news to Stalin. On the eve of his departure he invited Beaverbrook to lunch and asked whether Beaverbrook would like to go with him. Beaverbrook responded with enthusiasm. "But after lunch Churchill left his guest for half an hour. He paced up and down the garden in conversation with Anthony Eden. When he returned he did not repeat the invitation". Beaverbrook confessed: "Perhaps it was as well". If he had gone to Moscow, he would have harassed Churchill all the way with arguments for the Second Front. "Would Beaverbrook have succeeded in persuading Mr. Churchill to his way of thinking? Almost certainly not. But it is even more certain that all the way to Moscow, and in Moscow too, he would have tried. And if his efforts had failed his position at the Kremlin would have been equivocal in the extreme". Churchill went to Moscow alone.

On 19 August another blow fell. There was a landing at Dieppe, which the Germans easily repulsed. There were heavy casualties, which fell particularly on the Canadian troops involved. Beaverbrook was gravely distressed. He believed that the raid had been deliberately arranged in order to discredit the Second Front. Secretly he felt that his crusade had led to the useless sacrifice of Canadian lives. He writes contritely: "He allowed his bitterness to outrun his discretion to the extent of launching an ill-tempered attack on the chief of combined operations, Lord Louis Mountbatten. The occasion was a private gathering at which Lord Louis was present. Beaverbrook accused him in unmeasured terms of faulty planning leading to the needless sacrifice of human lives. Lord Louis replied that the plans were his, but that in execution they were not carried out. The general sympathy of the gathering was certainly with the defence". It is said that from this moment Beaverbrook pursued a vendetta against Mountbatten. That is an exaggeration. Beaverbrook's relations with Mountbatten, as with other men, went up and down. Privately his view hardened over the years that Dieppe had been a deliberate massacre of his beloved Canadians. More detached historians are inclined to believe that Dieppe was a demonstration of incompetence.

At all events, Beaverbrook abandoned the Second Front for the time being. He relapsed into the indifference of an observer, glad to be out of things. He wrote to Joe Patterson on 18 August 1942:

I have no intention of going back into the Government. I have got rid of the Ball and Chain, and I don't mean to put them on again. When in the Government I had to lift my hat to everyone who passed by. Now I find they lift it to me.

He was sure that Churchill was again firmly in power. He wrote to Paul Patterson on 29 September 1942:

Churchill remains predominant. He has no rivals. And his critics serve only, in the main, to fortify him in the affection of the public. For when the people compare the critics with the object of their criticism they have no doubt which they prefer.

It was no doubt also a pleasure to add a comment on Cripps:

His stock in Parliament has fallen. He gains no praise as leader of the House of Commons. He is reaping the disadvantages of the political freelance. For a man not in Office, lack of Party affiliation may be an advantage. It gives him added freedom in debate. But in office it is a grave handicap.

On 15 September 1942 Beaverbrook entertained Roosevelt with a survey of the political scene:

A new man has taken for himself the post of the Prime Minister's most violent opponent. Formerly this position was held by Shinwell. But now

Aneurin Bevan is far outstripping his rival in vituperation and criticism. Last week he attacked not only Churchill's conduct of the war but even his manner of dress. He takes exception to the wearing of a siren suit in public. And this is the more strange since Bevan himself is for the most part an untidy man. His hair is seldom brushed, he has no waistcoat and his belly is beginning to run over his breeches. He likes Champagne.

It is the general view that Bevan will do Churchill no harm. And certainly at the moment though he is trying to achieve the parliamentary style of Winston when he wished to demolish an opponent, he is attaining only the platform style of Randolph. But just the same, it would be unwise to underrate his effect on the House of Commons. It is the first time that the Prime Minister has been so violently assailed.

There was nothing Beaverbrook liked more than to make fun of a friend—and most of his friends appreciated it.

A comment on William Temple, Archbishop of Canterbury, was also clearly written for the fun of it (to Frank Gannett, 14 November 1942):

> He is by no means an ascetic man to look upon, having a round face and well-nourished body. He needs a hair shirt and bread-and-water diet if he is to conform to the established conception of the leader of a crusade. Such a way of life would not suit me, but it would be good for him.

In this period of withdrawal, Beaverbrook apparently took up again the writing of history. On 8 October he sent a copy of Politicians and the War to A. J. Cummings, an admirer and close friend, despite being the principal columnist on The New Chronicle. Beaverbrook wrote:

> It is a continuation of this work that I am now preparing for publication. "The Years Between" is a subsidiary title; the main title is "Politicians and the War".

This was presumably the germ of the unwritten book which Beaverbrook later called The Age of Baldwin. There is other evidence that Beaverbrook's thoughts had gone back to old battles. His secretaries worked over the press of 1938 and reported that all the newspapers excepting Reynolds News had applauded the Munich settlement. Another list set out the occasions on which The Daily Express had announced "Great Britain will not be involved in a European war" or, more rarely, "There will be no war in Europe". Beaverbrook was unrepentant over his prewar attitude. A little later (in February 1943) he sent for Hoare's approval a statement showing that Chamberlain had asserted his determination to remain at peace until the last moment.

However these researches did not go far. Instead Beaverbrook set Farrer to the task of writing an account of his achievements at the ministry of aircraft production. The outcome was The Sky's the Limit, a book which, despite its concentration on Beaverbrook, has not been seriously challenged as a record of what he accomplished at the height of Great Britain's crisis. There was in the book a curious reversal of roles. Previously Beaverbrook employed a ghost and took the credit as author—justifiably. On this occasion Beaverbrook was the ghost, and Farrer got the credit of authorship partly for tempering his inspiration.

Autumn 1942 saw what Churchill called "the end of the beginning". Montgomery won the battle of El Alamein and began his long march to Tunis. British and American forces landed in French North Africa. Victory was in the air, and the atmosphere of political crisis cleared. Cripps, once the popular hero, left the war cabinet and ceased to lead the house of commons. Beaverbrook expected him to leave office altogether. He wrote to Hoare on 30 November 1942:

> He wants to be a Messiah, and the only Messiah we knew who was a Cabinet Minister was Joe Chamberlain. He did not entirely succeed in breaking up the Government until he left the Cabinet room.

However, Cripps was content to become minister of aircraft production, where he often paraded his bureaucratic superiority to the first holder of that office. Eden became leader of the house of commons and, as Beaverbrook reported to Paul Patterson on 11 November, "the heir to Churchill's throne. . . . He is the most popular of the Ministers, after Churchill. And it must be said that he comes a long way after Churchill".

In the first excitement of the victories in North Africa, men expected an early end to the war, and Beaverbrook's mind turned to postwar policy. He wrote to Joseph Kennedy on 9 November 1942:

> The real clash of opinion in Britain is not between those who believe that the capital structure must be preserved and those who want to destroy it. It is between those who differ in their judgment of the speed and the method by which capitalism should be adjusted to modern conditions.
>
> There is therefore an opportunity for a liberal-minded Conservatism acting with non-doctrinaire Labour men.

Beaverbrook drafted a ten point programme for a group of Conservative MPs. One point declared: "We must protect and defend the profit motive". But an earlier point laid down: "Labour of every type attaching to a factory becomes a charge on it and must take precedence over every other form of charge". On 28 December Beaverbrook wrote in explanation and defence of this to Erskine Hill:

> A charge should be laid on industry to look after the workers before it looks after the shareholders. The claim of the shareholders against industry should rank after the claim of the workers.
>
> Can industry bear this burden and still provide a due incentive to capital under the profit motive?
>
> Yes. I think so.

For the programme lays a charge on the state to provide orders at times when industry is idle.

This had always been Beaverbrook's outlook. It was now a remarkable anticipation of the full employment to which all parties subscribed after the war.

Beaverbrook had now found a new hero, Herbert Morrison, to whom he wrote on 23 November 1942:

> Churchill apart, you are today by far the biggest figure in the country. . . .
> I hope to live under you as Prime Minister. But not to serve under you. For I would not serve again myself, even under you.

On 13 January 1943 Beaverbrook wrote to Paul Patterson:

> Among the members of the War Cabinet, Herbert Morrison commands at present the greatest interest and attention. . . . Were anything to happen to Churchill, his claim to the Premiership could not be neglected.

And to Guy Eden on 19 March:

> Herbert Morrison is far and away the biggest figure in the Socialist Party today. He has gained the confidence and respect, not only of his colleagues in the Government, but in the country as well. He is as fine a Minister as this country has had for a long while.

It may be safely surmised that Beaverbrook was not sorry to see Attlee eclipsed. Beaverbrook's speculations went further. Conflict over the Beveridge report led him to believe that the existing coalition was about to break up. He wrote to Hoare on 5 March 1943:

> The Conservatives have been for a week-end to Brighton. But the Socialists decided that they want to leave home altogether. The Tories have been flirting. But the Labour men were more serious, for their action was determined by a resolution of the Party. They were seeking a divorce.
> In 1916 the Nigerian debate threatened grave danger to Asquith's coalition. Beveridge has done equal damage to the solidarity of the present Government. It was saved in the recent debate by Herbert Morrison's speech only. Morrison now far outstrips Bevin in the country's esteem. But you will find that both will stick by Churchill when he forms his National Government, which will not be long now.

On 20 March Beaverbrook wrote to Arthur Sulzberger:

> The rank and file of the Labour party want to end the Coalition. . . . In my view this development will shortly take place. But not all the Labour leaders will follow their followers. Two or three at least will choose to follow Churchill instead. They will remain in the Government, and the Labour movement will be split again, as Ramsay MacDonald split it in 1931.

This was not a correct guess, though in the mood of the time an excusable one. As Bevin had remarked, Beaverbrook was always on the point of believing that the events of 1916 were about to repeat themselves.

In January 1943 Churchill and Roosevelt met at Casablanca. This time Beaverbrook was not present. But he was not long in learning that the Second Front had been again postponed. Probably Hopkins, who was as eager for the Second Front as Beaverbrook, passed the news to him. Beaverbrook resolved to revive his crusade. The Centres of Public Opinion again went into action. Beaverbrook's own platform this time was the house of lords. He remarked to Hoare: "I am having the time of my life. I have ignored the House of Lords for the last 25 years. But now I have found it, I am absolutely devoted to it". On 23 February he preached friendship with Soviet Russia and demanded an invasion of northern France in the near future. Simon, the lord chancellor, rebuked Beaverbrook for stirring up "ill-founded clamour", and dismissed the Second Front as a "catchpenny phrase". Trenchard, champion of strategic bombing, urged the government not to reply to Beaverbrook's speech at all. Beaverbrook struck back with violence. He called Simon a "master of distortion", and said of Trenchard:

> Long ago he was proved wrong. Before the war he gloried in our air arm, and that was at a time when, as he knows, we did not possess an air arm. . . . He advises the Government to bomb Germany from the air and deplores suggestions to the Government to bomb Germany from the land. He has two programmes, has the noble Lord; one is to bomb Germany from the air, and the other is to get after the Admirals.

Good relations with Soviet Russia now dominated Beaverbrook's mind. He wrote to Sir William Bradshaw on 10 February:

> It is my conviction that in a firm alliance, carried through without any reservations, with Russia, lies the best and possibly only hope of a stable peace after a complete victory.

And to the archbishop of York on 23 March:

> I am giving some thought just now to the question of our relations with the Russians. To me it seems of such paramount importance to gain and keep their confidence. If only we can keep in touch with them so much that is doubtful and difficult in post-war conditions will become easier.

These were wise words. At this moment a new opportunity offered itself. On 24 March Roosevelt invited Beaverbrook to pay another visit to the United States. Roosevelt wrote:

> The war goes on and on—and while I think we are gaining, it is difficult for you and me to curb our impatience, especially when our Naval and Military friends keep saying that this cannot be done and that cannot be done, and their time schedules seem so everlastingly slow to us.

Beaverbrook was delighted. Here was a more or less open invitation to assist Roosevelt in imposing the Second Front on the chiefs of staff— and on Churchill.

Others were less pleased. Beaverbrook showed Roosevelt's letter to Bracken. Bracken was Beaverbrook's friend, but he was Churchill's man. He reported in alarm to Churchill on 12 April: "Max is very anxious to go to America at once". On 13 April Churchill had Beaverbrook to dinner. They went over the old ground. Beaverbrook's sole interest was to defeat Germany: hence he believed that everything should be subordinated to the Second Front. Churchill of course also wanted to defeat Germany, but he had other things on his mind as well: not, as is sometimes claimed, the saving of eastern Europe from Communism, but the protection of British interests in the Mediterranean and Middle East. He would acquiesce in the Second Front only when this was accomplished. On the other hand he could not instruct Beaverbrook to refuse the president's invitation. Reluctantly Churchill agreed that Beaverbrook should go.

Beaverbrook resolved to fire one more shot before he left. He set down another motion for the Second Front on the order paper of the house of lords for 20 April. Once more Bracken acted. On 19 April he came to Beaverbrook with a message from Churchill: the question of a Second Front was now a matter of urgent consideration. Would Beaverbrook please withdraw his motion? Reluctantly Beaverbrook agreed. He received a reward of a sort. Churchill invited him to rejoin the government as lord privy seal and leader of the house of lords. Again Beaverbrook did not say yes and he did not say no. He asked: "Was there, definitely and without possibility of later alteration, to be an early Second Front?". He received no answer. Instead he was told that he could leave for America on 4 May.

The prospect of Roosevelt and Beaverbrook caballing together for the Second Front continued to alarm Churchill. Since he could not stop Beaverbrook from going, there was only one way out: Churchill must go also. Roosevelt had intended to play Beaverbrook against Churchill. Now Churchill was playing himself against both Beaverbrook and Roosevelt. On 30 April Beaverbrook was told that Churchill was going to Washington to discuss future strategy with Roosevelt and that Beaverbrook should accompany him. Beaverbrook divined Churchill's purpose: he was to be kept under lock and key, overawed from advocating the Second Front by Churchill's presence. Beaverbrook foresaw the brawls which would follow. He refused to go to Washington. Churchill insisted. Beaverbrook yielded against his better judgement. Thus it was that he and David Farrer found themselves crossing the Atlantic in the comparative luxury of the Queen Mary. During the voyage all went well. Beaverbrook was in his gayest mood. Good news poured in daily, almost hourly.

Beaverbrook even had an influence on policy. He drafted for Churchill a message to Stalin, repudiating the Polish complaints about the massacre at Katyn.[1] However it is significant that Churchill in his book on the second world war nowhere mentions that Beaverbrook was in the party.

In Washington trouble at once arose. Beaverbrook escaped to an hotel, but was constantly summoned to the White House. Roosevelt sought both his advice and his company. Churchill showed increasing displeasure. Roosevelt wanted a Second Front in the autumn. Churchill would not be diverted from Sicily and Italy. And Beaverbrook was on Roosevelt's side. Finally there was an open quarrel. Roosevelt invited Beaverbrook and Churchill to spend the weekend at Shangri-La, his country retreat. Beaverbrook told Churchill he would go only if Churchill wished it. Churchill replied that he had no objection so long as Beaverbrook kept out of any discussion of military plans. Beaverbrook therefore rang up Hopkins and asked to be excused. Hopkins replied: "The President is not accustomed to have his invitations refused". Beaverbrook went to Shangri-La. That night the storm broke. Churchill accused Beaverbrook of siding with the Americans against his own country. Beaverbrook answered heatedly that in pressing for the Second Front the Americans were acting in Britain's interest. Churchill declared that Beaverbrook had no business to interest himself in strategic projects. They parted in mutual anger.

Beaverbrook recognized that he could do no more. The cause of the Second Front was lost. He withdrew to New York and remained there until Churchill left the United States. Thereafter he visited Shangri-La again, this time in happier circumstances. Roosevelt revealed that he had congratulated Chamberlain over the Munich agreement: "the year's delay had resulted in progress and preparation in the United States which would not otherwise have been possible". Then Roosevelt pulled out a portfolio, which Beaverbrook feared might lead to a discussion of war aims or the Polish problem. Instead Roosevelt said: "Now that Winston has gone, I can get down to my stamp album again". While in Washington, Beaverbrook canvassed American opinion on many subjects, especially on the chances of Roosevelt's re-election as president in the following year. He no longer preached the Second Front.

Back in England, Beaverbrook tendered Churchill "some unasked advice". He wrote to Churchill on 19 July 1943:

> The American Presidential election depends largely on the good opinion there of Britain.

---

[1] The message is reproduced in Stalin's Correspondence with Churchill, Attlee, Roosevelt and Truman, No. 159. Churchill does not print the message in his book. The original message drafted by Beaverbrook was markedly more critical of the Polish government than that finally sent.

Lord Halifax is incapable in disposition of bringing any influence to bear on the American newspapers.

Brendan Bracken would have an immediate and immense success. His influence would be widespread and his efforts would help greatly in promoting our cause with the newspaper publishers.

Churchill did not take this advice. Instead he asked Beaverbrook to rejoin the government. Beaverbrook refused. He became a steadfast critic of the government on agricultural policy, milk marketing, rural housing— on everything in fact except the Second Front. He renewed his observations on the political scene. Thus he wrote to Wendell Willkie on 1 July 1943:

The cleavage between the Trade Unionists and the younger Socialist politicians is indeed already deep and is widening. It may well lead to the break up of the present Labour party and to the formation of a new movement much further to the left. And this, of course, would be to the advantage of the Tories who would obtain power for many years on the split vote of their opponents.

However Beaverbrook was not always confident about Tory prospects. He wrote to Jesse Jones on 27 August 1943:

If the Tories insist on selecting their standard bearers from the class who manage the war instead of from the ranks of those who fight it, they will learn before long the bitterness of defeat.

The Socialists will break from the Coalition as soon as the opportunity comes their way. They will be led by Herbert Morrison who will exalt radicalism and denounce communism.

In August 1943 Churchill crossed the Atlantic once more, this time for a conference with Roosevelt at Quebec. Beaverbrook feared that the Second Front had been again postponed. He resolved to take up its cause anew. He set down a motion in the house of lords for 23 September. He prepared his speech. This ended with his favourite cry for urgency and speed: "There is an old proverb that was told me once by a General who was speaking of himself and his own successful campaign—'Time and I against any two' ". On the evening before the debate in the lords, Churchill summoned Beaverbrook. He gave a firm assurance that attack across the Channel had been decided for the spring of 1944. Churchill asked Beaverbrook to withdraw his motion. Beaverbrook agreed. His dramatic speech was never delivered. Evidently a motion in the house of lords was a more potent weapon than Beaverbrook's old threats of resignation. He had got his way, though sadly late.

Churchill also asked—would Beaverbrook now rejoin the government? Beaverbrook had no longer any excuse for refusing. He had gone out on a question of principle and, with that principle conceded, he had to come back. He became lord privy seal. He did not rejoin the war cabinet, and no member of it commented on his return. Protest came only from Sir Stafford Cripps, now minister of aircraft production. He wrote to Churchill on 1 October 1943:

> You may recollect that some time ago, while I was a member of the War Cabinet, I made certain observations to you as to the rumoured entry of Lord Beaverbrook into the Cabinet. Those observations would reflect upon the recent change which you have made in the Government.
>
> ... Now that I have ceased to be a member of the War Cabinet, I feel, despite my still strong views on the undesirability of your new appointment, that I should continue with my present administrative job.

Churchill replied sharply the same day:

> It is not usual for a Prime Minister to consult all his colleagues—even War Cabinet colleagues—on the advice which he tenders to the Crown in respect of His Majesty's servants. For good or ill in our system in this country, he must bear the responsibility himself.
>
> ... I am sure you will find Lord Beaverbrook most anxious to work on the friendliest terms with you in any contacts which may be necessary.[1]

Harry Hopkins, who understood such things, remarked that Beaverbrook, though not in the war cabinet, was in the real cabinet "of the men who saw Churchill after midnight". There was no longer a conflict of policy between Beaverbrook and Churchill, and Beaverbrook concluded his account of the Second Front: "He could give again, without reservation, the full support he had always wanted to give to the Prime Minister who was also the object of his abiding affection and admiration". And yet their relations had changed. When previously in office, Beaverbrook himself had been a man of great achievements and great power, despite the difficulties which he encountered. What he did mattered vitally for the fortunes of the country and of Churchill. Now he was back in the old position he had held under Lloyd George or Bonar Law—court favourite and confidential adviser, another Davidson or George Wigg. He enjoyed this position, but the glamour and romance had departed.

Beaverbrook must have recognized this himself. Immediately after agreeing to accept office, he drafted a letter to Churchill:

> Not until Thursday do I renounce the garb of the adventurer for the Uniform of your Army of Out riders.
>
> So I can say just what I like now without committing any crime of disrespect, or neglect of the dignity of your high Office.
>
> In the darkest days, I got more encouragement from your confidence in my conduct than in any public praise or credit even though it was the moment of my brief era of popularity.

[1] Letters kindly communicated to me by Martin Gilbert.

Now in returning again I care far more for the opportunity to serve you than for the place & the ceremony.

It is thus that I conceive my duty to this Empire. And it is on these lines that I wish to discharge it.

The letter was not sent and has survived only in a pencil scrawl. Evidently Beaverbrook judged that its high tone was no longer appropriate. And, though friendship was renewed, Beaverbrook also did not forget the occasions when Churchill had failed to stand by him.

CHAPTER TWENTY-TWO

COURT FAVOURITE AGAIN, 1943-45

The twenty-one months which Beaverbrook spent as lord privy seal were the most agreeable of his political life. He was once more on the inside. He knew everything that was going on in war, international affairs and home politics. But the storms which blew around others did not reach him. He wrote to Herbert Morrison soon after resuming office: "I mean to help all applecarts down every road. In fact I now agree with everybody". He saw the war cabinet papers without the harassment of attending its meetings. He was again intimate with Churchill, providing advice and entertainment in full measure.

Beaverbrook had accepted power reluctantly but resolutely when there was desperate need for his urgency and speed. He was relieved to be needed no longer. Production was running smoothly under Anderson's direction. The Second Front had been determined and was duly launched in June 1944. Relations with both Soviet Russia and the United States seemed to be cordial. Occasionally an alarm stirred Beaverbrook into action, as over the flying bombs and, at the end of the war, the prospect of German superiority in jet aircraft. For the most part he could be a contented observer.

Asthma, the product of his many anxieties, vanished overnight and did not return until after the war. Beaverbrook wrote to Randolph Churchill on 11 April 1944: "The Lord Privy Seal is not willing to change the office held by Lord Beaverbrook. . . . It is peaceful and unadventurous. It is in fact like marriage descending upon the prodigal bachelor and lapping him in its comforts and privileges"—an echo of Mrs. Patrick Campbell's famous dictum which Randolph no doubt appreciated. Beaverbrook had still plenty of leisure. When old friends in Canada wrote that their sons were serving in England, he tracked down each boy and sent an invitation to Cherkley for the weekend. Any of them who were wounded received gifts of fruit and flowers and, where necessary, special medical attention.

In 1943 Beaverbrook acquired a new interest. He was receiving large sums in sterling as compensation for the dollar funds which he had surrendered to the treasury, and he used these sums to buy dairy farms at Cricket Malherbie and other places in Somerset. This was oddly enough the first time that Beaverbrook, the great champion of agriculture, had any practical experience of its problems. The investment was run as a powerful contribution to home production of food. The farms had other uses. The honey which they produced was often distributed to Beaverbrook's friends, and even Attlee was mollified by the jars of honey which flowed to Mrs. Attlee. Cricket Malherbie had also an old manor house, where Beaverbrook could give his friends country holidays without the bother of entertaining them personally. Sir Walter and Lady Citrine were among those who enjoyed prolonged stays at Cricket Malherbie. One old opponent remained implacable. Ernest Bevin fell ill in September 1944. Beaverbrook wrote to express his sympathy and added:

> Although we have been in difficulties occasionally and even when you found it difficult to get on with me I have never ceased to admire your flair for public life and I have always acknowledged the immense part you have taken in winning the war.

This letter received no answer.

Beaverbrook suffered two great losses from among his most intimate circle. Castlerosse had retired to Ireland early in the war when he succeeded as Earl of Kenmare, and devoted his last years to the laying out of an unmatched golf course. He died in September 1943. Beaverbrook described him as "my most intimate friend through a quarter of a century" and added:

> On the surface, no two men could be more utterly different than Castlerosse and me. I had a talent for hard work and in consequence I made money. Castlerosse had a supernatural talent for getting rid of it.
>
> He was an enchanting and warm-hearted companion. We are told no man is a hero to his valet. Perhaps the best epitaph for Castlerosse would be to say that he remained a hero to his valet even when the valet had been not paid for weeks.

During the war Beaverbrook saw comparatively little of Jean Norton. He was busy on his onerous public duties. She worked full-time first in a mobile canteen and then in a shell factory. In January 1945 Beaverbrook wrote, congratulating her on her son's military career. She replied:

> I value *your* appreciation of my children above all others. Perhaps because of the love I have and always shall have for you come what may—I can say no more but that I am and always shall be your ever loving Jeannie.

It was her last letter. A few days later she died suddenly. Beaverbrook was attending a meeting of the war cabinet when news of her illness reached him and passed a note to Churchill: "Jean is dying". Churchill said: "The cabinet can do no more business today" and adjourned the meeting. Jean Norton's death brought greater grief to Beaverbrook than anything since the death of Gladys Beaverbrook in 1927.

Beaverbrook also lost some of his young Leftwing associates. Frank Owen was far away, editing a forces' newspaper in India. Tom Driberg continued to write the William Hickey column for some time, despite his activities as an Independent MP. In the summer of 1943 he alleged in a public speech at Braintree that Sir Andrew Duncan was unpatriotically leaving the ministry of supply in order to return to big business. Driberg had received this information from Trevor Evans, the industrial correspondent of The Daily Express, and was therefore accused of betraying a confidence. He was dismissed. The real reason of course was that Beaverbrook did not wish to offend Duncan, who regretfully had to remain in office. Three weeks later Driberg was offered his job back. Having fixed up with another newspaper, he refused and never returned to The Daily Express. As he had omitted to establish his rights in "William Hickey", he lost his name also.[1]

One other loss was less permanent. As the end of the war approached, Beaverbrook looked forward with pleasure to a renewal of party strife, and it became increasingly difficult for him to maintain The Evening Standard as a Leftwing paper. Michael Foot ceased to be its editor, being succeeded by a safe man Herbert Gunn. For some time Foot continued to write leaders, until in June 1944 he wrote a letter which does honour to both writer and recipient:

Your views and mine are bound to become more and more irreconcilable. As far as this Socialist business is concerned my views are unshakable. For me it is the Klondyke or bust, and at the moment I am doubtful whether I am going the right way to Klondyke. There does not seem to be much sense in my continuing to write leaders for a newspaper group whose opinions I do not share and some of whose opinions I strongly dissent from. I know you never ask me to write views with which I disagree. But as this works out it is good business neither for you or for me. The leaders which I now write are hardly worth writing since they are non-committal and from my point of view I am associated with a newspaper group against whose policies (but not against the proprietor) I am resolved to wage perpetual war. Somehow things were different before. The compromise worked and certainly greatly to my advantage. But I do not see how it could work very much longer. The business of maintaining allegiance to my own political ideas and to a newspaper which fundamentally must be opposed to them is too difficult.

. . . .

It seems foolish to raise a personal matter like this at a time when much bigger things are happening. But it would also be foolish to disguise the

[1] Information from Driberg, confirmed by a letter which Beaverbrook wrote to Duncan on 4 August 1950.

fact that my feeling is I am wasting my time and there is so much I want to do and accomplish. Your kindness to me has given me great advantages in this world. I do not forget them. But I am sure it is right for me to make a change and I dearly hope you will understand my reasons.

Foot left The Evening Standard. In 1945 he became a Labour MP. During the brief period when it seemed that the Labour government might really put socialist principles into practice, he and Beaverbrook were not on close terms. Later Foot found himself almost as much out of step in the Labour party as he had been on Beaverbrook's newspapers, and before the end he and Beaverbrook were happily agreeing that they were the last true radicals left in England.

Beaverbrook's closest intimate at this time was Brendan Bracken, whose letters were as entertaining as those of Beaverbrook himself. The two men combined a radical impatience towards the traditional governing classes with an enthusiasm for private enterprise. Even so Beaverbrook was not above playing a prank on his friend. In July 1944 The Evening Standard revealed that forty years before Bracken's father had been refused a gun licence in Ireland as a dangerous Nationalist. Beaverbrook professed ignorance of the story and described its publication as "a desperate thing to do". He was not however pleased when Bracken used his power as minister of information and attempted to have the story suppressed.

A more surprising addition to Beaverbrook's inner circle was Herbert Morrison, whom Beaverbrook insisted on hailing as a future prime minister. Of course Morrison's great attraction for Beaverbrook was that Attlee and Bevin both disliked him—decisive considerations in Beaverbrook's eyes.

In December 1943 Morrison, largely on Beaverbrook's prompting, released Sir Oswald Mosley from his internment under Regulation 18B. This was really an incontrovertible decision. Internment was a measure of security, not a punishment, and it was impossible to maintain that Mosley was still a security risk in 1943—if he ever had been. There was however an outcry that Morrison was compounding with Fascism. Beaverbrook derived amusement from the affair and wrote of it to Hoare on 8 December 1943:

> We have been staging a small political comedy here. The title was "Gaol Delivery" and the roles of hero and villian were both filled by Herbert Morrison.
> He played them with equal vigour and aplomb, being cheered as hero from the stalls and hooted as villain from the gallery.
> It is true that the comedy nearly turned into drama. This was because another, and quite unauthorized, set of producers took a hand. Citrine mistook the T.U.C. for the Committee of Public Safety. And the Communist

Party with its genius for crowd scenes brought a series of well-disciplined processions into Whitehall. One is passing my window at this moment. I am sure that the mobs in Madrid, who are under different management, are a more formidable spectacle.

I would err however, if I were to give the impression that the piece had an unqualified success with the critics. Conservatives felt that Morrison was right in releasing Mosley but wrong in the method by which he announced the release.

The Left was divided. Some felt that the principle of release was right but the man released was wrong. Others did not want to release anybody at all. Not under 18B at least. In some quarters, that regulation appears to have become a sort of amendment to the Constitution.

These domestic issues for a time diverted our attention from the war.

Their longer-term effect is that Morrison's position with his own people is badly shaken and that the old feud between the Unions and the Labour Party has been given a new venom. How long this aftermath will be an active influence in politics it is impossible to say.

Beaverbrook himself, though at ease, was by no means idle. He found two principal outlets for his energies, one a campaign which he waged until the end of the war, the other one which he continued to wage until the end of his life. The first campaign was in preparation for the conflict between the political parties which he expected to follow the war. The other was the defence of British independence against American encroachments. Politically Beaverbrook always tended to stay on the side lines until the approach of a general election and then rushed into the fray as much for the fun of the thing as for anything else. He had also convictions at stake. Though a lifelong believer in high wages and full employment, he believed just as strongly in private enterprise and took the socialist threats of the Labour party seriously. He distrusted almost as much the projects of the younger Conservatives and championed the Conservative party more out of loyalty to Churchill than for any other reason. After all, he had taken the same line with Lloyd George and, to some extent, even with Law.

Beaverbrook watched the approach of political conflict with his usual pleasure. He wrote to James A. Farley on 18 November 1943:

In the debates and decisions on postwar reconstruction, which now lie ahead, many battles will inevitably be fought in Parliament, and the will to compromise will be absent.

The Socialist party, unlike the Tories, is controlled by a caucus. Its policy is determined by vote and decisions taken by the party members outside the debates in the House of Commons. And this caucus has complete control of the party funds.

It might even come to pass that the Socialist members of the Government were pulled out of office by this caucus in spite of their own desires. But I think not. For their belief in Churchill as a war leader is complete, and so long as the war lasts this will transcend all party ties.

The same faith in Churchill was expressed in a letter which Beaverbrook wrote to Bickell on 18 November 1943:

> The Socialists have been the recipients of many a Tory kiss. But now they proclaim that those kisses came all the time from Judas.
>
> The Tories can rest more securely in the knowledge that they hold the ace of trumps.
>
> And that ace, of course, is the Prime Minister.

Soon after this the ace was endangered. Churchill fell ill in North Africa on his way back from the meeting of the Big Three at Tehran. After a period of alarm, he began to recover and flew to Marrakesh for convalescence. There Beaverbrook joined him on 28 December. Beaverbrook's main task, as ever, was to provide gay companionship, but he also attended the military conferences which resolved on the landing at Anzio and finally determined the date of the Second Front. This was a brief return to Beaverbrook's old days of glory and the last time that he attended such a high-level meeting.

Back in England, Beaverbrook became active as Churchill's political adviser. On 19 January 1944 he complained that the virtues of one particular Tory candidate "consisted entirely of what happened in the past":

> His early struggles belong to the past. His early achievements belong to the past. The local dignities he has later attained are likewise a portion of the past, although some of them survive into the present.
>
> If we attempt to hold the present chained to the past, we shall find we have lost the future.

On 4 February 1944 Beaverbrook sent Churchill a long paper, discussing —against his own convictions—how the coalition might be continued into peacetime:

> It is my view that if the Prime Minister's programme of "Food, work and houses for all" could be implemented on lines which the Labour Party could agree, then either the Socialists would be prepared to go to the country as a united party in defence of the Coalition, or the Party would be split into two factions.
>
> As to food. . . . It might be possible to frame an agricultural policy which the Labour Party could accept as the fulfilment of the pledge of food for all. This policy would involve the production in this country of all our foodstuffs except cereals, of which an adequate supply would be secured by long-term import agreements. But an unavoidable consequence would be a programme of equitable food distribution, which would involve the major concession of the continuance of food rationing as well as of the present policy of food subsidies.

Homes. ... Here there is little difficulty in the way of an arrangement between the two parties.

Now comes the first terrible issue—nationalisation of the banks. A way out might be found if a plan could be evolved whereby money and credit became instruments of Government. This might provide common ground for holding on to the existing system of joint stock banks. But there would be difficulty in persuading the Conservatives to agree to this solution.

Next—nationalisation of the coalmines. Here the Conservatives would have to give way. There has been so much propaganda on this issue that there can now be no escape. ...

Transportation. ... Here the Labour Party will press for full nationalisation as registering what they will claim is in the main already an accomplished fact.

The Labour Party in fact will seek a programme of work for all which will enable it to say that the four most important industries—coal, agriculture, transportation and the building industry—have been placed under the influence of the Government. They would then claim that they were in a position at any time to limit unemployment by cutting down the working hours of those four industries. This is tough doctrine, but after all it is only a talking point.

. . . .

It is realized that there would be very great difficulty in getting Conservative acceptance and backing for these policies. For they would certainly open the door to other demands—particularly the claim for the public ownership of land—when another election fell due.

Lastly there is the need for "international" propaganda. But here the Atlantic Charter provides all the ammunition required.

It is interesting however to speculate on the inherent weakness of the Socialists and on the extent of their fear of the Communist Party.

That fear could, in my view, be so played on that the Labour Party would be willing to accept an increase of not more than 25 seats in their Parliamentary representation. Certainly that representation could be restricted to not more than 200 members.

Nor would it be difficult to lay hands on 25 seats at present held on a minority vote by Conservative members who mean to retire in any case.

Beaverbrook's friend Herbert Morrison could have said with Sir William Robertson: "I've 'eard different".

Beaverbrook himself was convinced that the Conservatives would win an election. He was therefore set against coalition. He wrote to Sulzberger on 9 February 1942:

The Labour caucus is increasingly nervous both at the development of the new Commonwealth Party, which preaches a form of Christian Communism, and at the threat at the polls from the real Communists. There are many in the Labour movement who complain that their case is going by default.

But whether when the time for an election comes, the prospect of a full dose of socialism will commend itself to the electorate is altogether another matter. In my view the demands of the people will be simple but fundamental. Churchill has summed them up as "Food, homes and work for all".

Beaverbrook urged that Conservative propaganda should become more aggressive. "The appeal should be positive throughout. . . . The Tory party has need, not of a Maginot line, but of a Second Front". Beaverbrook wanted a Conservative committee to prepare plans for postwar reconstruction. But he would not join it: "For though I am a Conservative, I am not of the Conservative Party".

He was equally indifferent about stories, much circulated at this time, that he was about to succeed Grigg as secretary for war or Eden as foreign secretary. Nothing would shift him from his present ease. He wrote to Randolph Churchill about Eden on 11 April 1944:

Perhaps the news has filtered through to your mountain fastnesses[1] that Anthony Eden is going to give up the Foreign Office. . . . The truth is that Anthony wants to go and that, so far, only Lord Cranborne wants to succeed him. The position is one of the plums of public life—one of the sour plums perhaps. But Cecils like even sour plumbs.

Of course Beaverbrook concerned himself with foreign affairs. He made a strong comment on relations with Soviet Russia, when he wrote to Joseph Kennedy on 11 April 1944:

Those who uphold the Poles—and they include Conservatives as well as Socialists—do not attempt to answer the question whether they would be prepared to fight to restore Poland's 1939 frontiers. And the position they take, that compensatory transfer to Poland of German territory, would be an infringement of the Atlantic Charter—does additional injury to the Poles, whose champions they claim to be.

Relations with the United States occupied most of Beaverbrook's attention, and more than any other man he fought for British independence. This was always his line from his first days in Nova Scotia until the end of his life: friendship between the two great Anglo-Saxon powers but friendship between equals. He wrote to Churchill on 21 February 1944:

That we should pursue friendship and collaboration with the United States is an unchallengeable principle. But in seeking that friendship we should aim, with an equal consistency, at maintaining and strengthening our own position as a world power.

The two objectives are not irreconcilable. Indeed, we shall approach the nearer to a sound and lasting relationship with the United States in so far as we are able to build up our own prestige and safeguard our own inherited interests in the economic as well as the political and military spheres.

[1] Randolph Churchill was serving with Tito's army in Yugoslavia.

In this great dispute, Beaverbrook fought almost alone. Churchill always overrated American generosity and imagined that if he opened his arms wide the Americans would do the same. Beaverbrook understood the Americans better. He expected them to drive a hard bargain and knew that they would respect Great Britain more if the British did the same. Perhaps he misjudged British strength at this time. But those who went about proclaiming British weakness did much to cause it.

The American attack was on three fronts. They sought to reimpose a virtual gold standard and with it free trade and the ending of imperial preference. They demanded postwar agreements on oil resources and civil aviation, which would have opened all the world, especially the British Empire, to them, while keeping the United States closed to others. Beaverbrook fought them on all three counts. In financial and economic policy, he could only raise a solitary voice as one adviser among many. In a note to Churchill on 10 March, he asserted that "tariffs often serve as the guardians of a high-standard economy against the competition of a low-standard economy", and he put forward "a more hopeful method" than free trade:

> If the nations bind themselves together in an agreement to pursue policies providing high wages with high employment within their own boundaries, we shall achieve the active and expansive individual economies out of which an active and expansive world economy will emerge.

The same day he wrote to J. M. Keynes, who had now been converted to the gold standard and free trade:

> I would not be prepared to support a proposition that destroyed imperial preference and sacrificed agriculture on account of compensations which appear to be both dubious and inadequate. . . . I believe that it is possible to secure expansion within the Imperial ambit. Indeed, we shall build a firmer foundation if we do so.
>
> . . . American leadership is not a development which we should welcome.
>
> On the contrary, we are likely to have more than our fill of it before we are finished.

On 3 May 1944 Beaverbrook wrote again to Churchill:

> The assumption is that the United States is the dominating factor in export trade and that agreement with the United States will enable us to expand our sales.
>
> Not so.
>
> World trade is dependent on the United Kingdom, the British Empire, the three Scandinavian countries, Holland, Belgium and France (with their colonies).
>
> These countries take 60% of the export of United Kingdom goods (two-thirds of this percentage goes to the British Empire).

On this issue, Beaverbrook lost. Keynes won. And the industrialized world has been trying to escape the consequences ever since.

On oil and civil aviation Beaverbrook played a more direct part and was himself the principal British negotiator. He had unrivalled skill in this kind of dealing and now bargained with the Americans as he had once done with other financiers or as he did with newspaper proprietors over newsprint. He was always conciliatory in conversation, holding out the prospect of enticing concessions if he could carry his main point. He flattered A. A. Berle, the American negotiator on civil aviation, with first editions of Cardinal Newman's works—apparently a subject in which Berle was interested. He even proposed to buy Berle a cardinal's hat. In July he went to Washington for conferences on both subjects. This was incidentally the first occasion when a cabinet minister flew to Washington direct without coming down on the way—another instance of Beaverbrook's urgency and speed. The flight to Washington took 19 hours 44 minutes, and the return 17 hours 37 minutes—times which seem now as remote as the horse-and-buggy age.

The two conferences took much time, and the material concerning them now occupies much space on the shelves. It is all dead stuff, never to be stirred again except perhaps by some researcher desperate for a subject. Great Britain and the United States imagined that they would run the postwar world as autocratically as they conducted the war against Hitler: some concessions to Soviet Russia, but otherwise a "carve up". When oil and civil aviation came to be discussed after the war, it turned out that many other parties had to be considered, and the agreements made in 1944 were superseded. This is what Beaverbrook had always wanted over oil. His sole purpose was to evade the American attempts to restrict or to control British oil resources in the Middle East. In this he succeeded. Over civil aviation, he struck a bargain: world bases were to be open to British and American air lines and to no other. None of this came to fruition.

These affairs did not exhaust Beaverbrook's activities. He early sounded the alarm over flying bombs and rockets. Later he recorded the discussions which followed:

Duncan Sandys strongly supported the view that Peenemunde was building V1s and V2s.

Cherwell opposed the notion that rockets could fall in Britain. He said they would ricochet back to France; that they would fall in the Channel; that the Germans would not waste an engine in such a venture; that they would rather send an airplane that could bring the engine back again.

When Sandys's forebodings proved true and flying bombs began to fall on London, Beaverbrook again heard the call of emergency and suggested that he should be put in charge of plans for dispersal and defence—a suggestion not welcomed by Cripps or by Duncan Sandys, the two ministers whom he would have displaced.

Beaverbrook had also time for fun. Bracken, shocked to discover that Beaverbrook owned some church livings, wrote on 22 June 1944:

> Mr. Bracken thinks there is now a good case for dis-establishing the Church of England. He considers it the ripest of scandals that a bigoted Presbyterian should become a patron of church livings. Were it not for the flying bomb, the weather and the reading of Mr. Lyttelton's speeches he would have reported this matter to the Archbishop of Canterbury.

Beaverbrook had his own back when he discovered that the ministry of information had commissioned busts of Bevin, Maisky, and General Cunningham. He complained: "As a tax-payer, laying down 19/6 in the £, I find it difficult to countenance this expenditure". Bracken replied with mock formality on 18 April 1945:

> Dear Lord Privy Seal,
> The Minister of Information is honoured by your letter of 7th April about busts. He is generally responsible for the doings of the War Artists' Advisory Committee. But he is not obliged to approve or veto the subjects which the Committee may choose. In January 1942 at the height of pro-Russian feeling in Britain they commissioned Jacob Epstein to deliver a replica of the bust he had already made of the Russian Ambassador to England. In May 1942 the Committee also commissioned Epstein to deliver a modelled head of the General who had conquered East Africa. Bevin's head was commissioned in March this year, just in time to avoid political controversy.

Beaverbrook and Bracken provided fun for Churchill. On 24 January 1945 they addressed him a joint letter:

> Our attention has been called to the lament of Mr. Attlee in his Paper L.P. (45) 17 that Ministers do not attend his Committee.
> We now offer to fill two of the vacant places.
> We are moved to this offer by the sad plight of the Lord President [Attlee]:
> "Alone, alone, all all alone,
>   Alone on the wide wide sea",
>
> Yours ever,
B.
B.B.
>
> P.S. Our offer depends of course on the approval of the Lord President.

Churchill replied from the Crimea:

> All the Bs.
> Wait till I return please.

On another occasion Churchill complained against the use of "tensed" by The Evening Standard. Beaverbrook replied:

> The just indignation of the Prime Minister should be addressed to the Minister of Labour, who has deprived newspapers of staffs of compositors and proof-readers, adequate to prevent such outrages.
> In manning the defences of England, Mr. Bevin has weakened the defences of the English language.

In October 1944 Churchill recommended Beaverbrook to Stalin for the order of Suvorov. Beaverbrook was greatly pleased and wrote to Churchill: "The only honour I liked as much was my knighthood and that was in 1911". The Soviet embassy informed Beaverbrook of the privileges which the order of Suvorov brought with it:

> Irrespective of your earnings, you are entitled to an annuity of 20 roubles a month (just under £1).
> You are granted free travel once a year all over the USSR by rail or sea transport.
> You are entitled to travel "personally" in trams, buses and local transport, in all cities in the USSR.
> You are exempted from income tax or other types of civil or military obligations and/or the worker peasant Red army levy.
> Your descendants inherit your privileges on your death.
> In your free travel by rail or ship you are entitled to priority in reservations of sleeping berths and cabins, to free use of soft plush seats in trains and cabins, and to ride on all passenger trains.
> You are expected to set an example as a law abiding citizen by carrying out all duties, etc., laid down by the USSR.

Beaverbrook had well deserved the honour and the privileges which went with it. Quite apart from his organization of supplies to Russia and his advocacy of the Second Front, no man preached Anglo-Soviet friendship more fervently or more sincerely. He wrote to Eden on 26 August 1944, when the Soviet armies failed to assist the Polish rising in Warsaw:

> I am disturbed by the present state of our relations with Russia.
> So I write this letter, not in any way as a complaint, but as an attempt at argument, for I am responsible for the situation along with the others who take decisions.
> (1) The Poles have always been unsatisfactory. They seized Teschen at the time of Munich, etc. I need not make the case.
> (2) The Polish war effort has been consistently overvalued in the press.
> (3) The Polish newspapers have been a constant source of worry. They have excited anti-Semitism in a virulent form. Their political attitude was a major factor in the break of Soviet-Polish relations.

(4) Our hope for days to come, so far as relations with the United States are concerned, depends on a close measure of friendship with Moscow. I need not argue this point.

(5) We have given the Russians many opportunities for suspicion. We delayed too long in taking decisions.

Now the issue of Poland rises between us.

For my part I believe the story of the Red Army officer as related in Clark Kerr's telegram no. 2219. If it is true that the Polish underground made no attempt to interfere with the movements of the German armoured divisions towards the Warsaw front then any support we give to the Poles in the present controversy would be paralleled if the Germans had occupied Dublin and an uprising by the I.R.A. interfering with our plans for recapturing the city became the subject for similar controversy with Moscow.

Of course the truth of the Warsaw tragedy is that the Russians met with an unexpected and serious reverse almost at the gates of the city, due to the arrival of those armoured divisions which, they say, the Poles allowed to pass. The Russians got so near that it needed no exhortation from Moscow or London to make the citizens rise.

But whatever the cause of the tragedy the friendship of Russia is far more important to us than the future of Anglo-Polish relations.

The grasp of reality shown in this letter was unfortunately not shared by other western statesmen. Beaverbrook expressed the same outlook more directly when he wrote to Bernard Baruch on 27 September 1944:

I continue to pursue my simple policy in relation to Britain, the United States and Russia. It is, in fact, too simple to be appreciated by any but a very simple man. That policy is to be one of a mutual admiration society of three.

In the autumn of 1944 final victory seemed to be near, and Beaverbrook turned his attention increasingly to politics. He wrote to A. A. Berle on 31 August 1944:

Collaboration between the two parties is growing increasingly difficult. As victory draws near, the urge for a return to party warfare grows stronger and the strains and stresses in the structure of the Coalition become harder to withstand.

Personally, I am not in favour of a long continuance of the Coalition. In my view, a state of hostility between parties brings, except in times of extreme emergency, a more healthy and invigorating atmosphere to political life than conditions of armistice. I would welcome an early return to party strife. But it must be added for my part, I shall take no share in it. My place will be on the sidelines.

A few days later, on 9 September, he set down his political forecasts for John S. Knight, an editor in Ohio:

The movement of opinion during the war has been to the left. But that is not to say it has been towards the present Labour Party. In my view that

Party will never poll an effective majority of the Country's votes, while it is dominated by the Trade Union interests. For the electorate will prefer the straight conservatism of the Tory Party to the disguised conservatism of the Trade Union bosses.

So it is my prophecy that Churchill will lead his Party to victory at the polls. His immense prestige will be worth, of course, very many votes. The weakness and divided counsels of his opponents may prove an even more valuable asset.

These expectations had a convincing plausibility except that they turned out to be entirely wrong.

Curiously at this time Beaverbrook noted that Churchill was losing heart, as though his great days were over. Perhaps Beaverbrook lost heart himself. He wrote to Harry Hopkins on 23 October 1944:

Here in Britain we are passing through a strange phase in public life. For the first time, the English are not sure of themselves. They are anxious about their future. And this is in some measure due to the extent to which they have had to rely on outside assistance in the war.

However Beaverbrook hastened to add a consolation: regarding Bevin and Morrison, "that is a quarrel beyond the wit of man to heal".

Though Beaverbrook expected political conflict to break out soon, he endowed others with his own good sense and did not think that there would be any differences over foreign affairs. He wrote to J. P. Bickell on 30 November 1944:

In the sphere of foreign policy there is and will for long remain all-Party unanimity.... No Government could deviate from the path or friendship with America and alliance with the Soviet. No amount of propaganda from Polish sources can wean the public from the deep conviction that only by co-operating with the Russians can peace in Europe be preserved.

And similarly to Frank Gannett on 7 December:

It would be altogether a mistake to suppose that there is any real cleavage of opinion on foreign issues.... There may be differences over the manner in which policy is pursued, but unanimity will remain about its objects, a stable Europe based on the Anglo-Soviet alliance and the closest collaboration throughout the world with the United States.

A conflict over foreign policy in fact arose when British forces intervened in Greece against the Communists. This was opposed by the entire Left as well as by The Times and The Manchester Guardian. Beaverbrook supported Churchill, though against his own conviction. He had no doubt that Churchill would carry the day, as indeed he did. Beaverbrook commented to Frank Gannett:

The Prime Minister's speech was designed to give a punch on the nose to his critics, as he so often does. If he had given instead some soft soap they would have slid down again on their bottoms to their benches with comfort and repose.

Churchill was specially roused by the criticism of The Times—now, according to Beaverbrook, a more expensive edition of The Daily Worker —and drafted a letter of expostulation to Barrington-Ward, its editor. Beaverbrook persuaded him not to send it:

> You told me your newspaper policy was—Square or Squash. That was a quarter of a century ago.
> You have held to it ever since.
> This letter to Barrington-Ward is a departure. It does not make any effort to "Square" and it does not "Squash". Therefore I recommend against sending it.

There was another echo from the past. Lloyd George accepted an earldom, and Beaverbrook wrote to him on 3 January 1945—for the last time:

> The people say that your genius conferred on us such benefits that we cannot make the slightest acknowledgements by conferring Earldoms. I served under your leadership and it has always been my boast that I was a Lloyd George man.

Three months later Earl Lloyd-George died. Beaverbrook paid a last tribute to him in the house of lords. He said:

> To me his greatest hour came as late as the spring of 1918, when our line of defence had been broken, our troops were in retreat, the Russian Armies were out of the war, and the American Armies had not yet come into it. . . . It was at that moment that Lloyd George penetrated the gloom of doubt and indecision. . . . It was then his leadership showed itself supreme, his courage untarnished. No other moment in Britain's recurring story of escape from disaster can surpass it, save only the decision of the summer nights after the defeat of France in 1940. . . .
> He attained an authority greater than that held by any British Prime Minister who had gone before him. He dictated to Europe; he flung out great dynasties with a gesture; he parcelled out the frontiers of races; everything was in his hands, and his hands showed that they had the power to use everything. Now all that is ended.

Beaverbrook continued to wage war against the financial proposals of Bretton Woods. He wrote to Churchill on 7 December 1944:

> This is a foolish document.
> The folly of it lies in the defence of the Gold Standard.
> . . . .
> That is the process which brought us to disaster after 1922, when we made a fictitious settlement of the American debt, followed by the Gold Standard and alterations in the price structure, although we were incapable of making the necessary reductions in the wage structure.
> For a time, we tried to meet the situation by subsidies and then we crashed.

He had another go on 19 January 1945:

> After the collapse of the currency in 1931, we were saved because we could carry with us into a sterling association important sections of the world economy. Were we, at some future date, to be forced out of the Monetary Fund because we could not obtain a sufficient margin for depreciation—or could not obtain it swiftly enough—we might find that we stood alone, a financial Ishmael with the hands of all the self-righteous raised against us.
>
> . . . .
>
> Lord Keynes said in the United States "The real purpose of the Monetary Fund is to bring back gold as a fundamental reserve currency". That is, in my judgment, a sufficient condemnation of the project from the mouth of its author.

Somewhat later, on 20 April 1945, he recapitulated his objections to Keynes himself:

> We shall find ourselves (1) tied to the Gold Standard; (2) committed to a limitation of agriculture; (3) sacrificing Imperial Preference; and (4) bringing about a change in the status of the Sterling Bloc.
>
> And after all this, we shall not be able to get our bargain with the United States.

Beaverbrook offered a clear alternative, which followed from the policy he had preached before the war. The sterling bloc should be maintained as a world-wide trading community. It should be sustained by imperial preference, and the utmost encouragement should be given to British agriculture. Certainly supplies would be needed from Canada and the United States. But "without our help they cannot sell. They do not buy from us. . . . There will be a surplus of food in Canada and the United States with no market available, save only Britain". In this matter Beaverbrook stood virtually alone with no supporters except Leo Amery and Bracken. The economists led by Keynes were all against him, and Churchill, understanding nothing of the subject, came down on the American and supposedly Free Trade side.

There was one last flash of urgency when Beaverbrook sounded a warning against the increase in German jet production. He sent Churchill a survey of German and allied jet strength on 8 January 1945 and concluded: "The Germans have achieved a degree of tactical and technical superiority which is serious". On 13 January, after an array of more figures, he wrote: "If Germany has not been beaten before July 1945 she will have dominance in the air over Germany and over the Armies during the period of good flying weather". The chiefs of staff waved Beaverbrook's alarms aside. "The jet was not the answer to the jet". In any case they must gamble on winning the war in time. Beaverbrook tried once more on 15 February 1945 for the last time. He wanted "a sacrifice in

production of other weapons, in order to increase output of jet aircraft"
and wrote to Churchill:

> The policy of sacrifice to attain essential objectives is required. It was
> the policy pursued by the Ministry of Aircraft Production with your
> approval, in May 1940, when there was a shortage of fighter aircraft.
> The jet aircraft situation demands such a course now.

This appeal to old glories met with no response. The air staff gambled
that inferior weapons would carry them through, and this time the
gamble came off.

The war was ending. Beaverbrook was now entirely occupied with
preparations for the general election. Ralph Assheton, the party chairman, was pushed aside as inadequately aggressive, and Conservative
strategy was handled by Beaverbrook, Bracken, and James Stuart, the
Conservative chief whip. Beaverbrook, despite his earlier assertion that
he was "not of the Conservative party", became in effect the party
manager. He concerned himself with all the details—the early release of
candidates and agents from the services, whether candidates could wear
uniform on the platform, extra supplies of petrol and paper for electioneering. Especially strong was his insistence that candidates must be
young and with a good service record. Presumably Beaverbrook took part
in the discussions which followed the German surrender on 8 May 1945,
when Churchill proposed to continue the National government until the
defeat of Japan and the Labour party would do so only until the autumn.
There is however nothing about this in his records, though undoubtedly
he welcomed Churchill's decision to end the coalition on 23 May. Beaverbrook remained as lord privy seal in the ensuing caretaker government
and even dreamt of a political career. For he wrote to Shirley Wolmer
on 7 June:

> There is only one honour I could have which would please me very
> much. That would be to be deprived of my peerage. I would give a good
> bit to be out of it altogether and into the house of commons.

On 16 June Beaverbrook sent to Frank Gannett a disturbing report on
British opinion about relations with Russia and added an account of
how the National government had broken up:

> I am bound to tell you that in the last few weeks a measure of distrust
> of Russia has grown up in this country. . . . I am entirely convinced that
> the feeling is no more than skin-deep. The great majority of Englishmen
> realize, as you and I do, the need for Russian friendship. They would tolerate
> no Government that pursued an opposite course.
> For my part also I feel sure that such friendship can be secured, and
> on level terms, provided always we take account of the Russian situation.
> The Russian determination to achieve an absolute measure of security is

conditioned by her experiences of invasion which neither this country nor yours have suffered. The Kremlin will insist on being the predominant partner in Eastern Europe. If we accept that position then the peace of Europe is assured. If we endeavour to contest it, then assuredly the next war will be waiting in the wings. . . .

Attlee, Bevin and Dalton all favoured continued coalition. Herbert Morrison was opposed to it. Now in the inner councils the three were far stronger than the one. But the decision had to be taken while the annual Socialist Party Conference was meeting at Blackpool, and the Party's rank and file were eager for the fray. So the three generals without an army were beaten by the one general who found an Army to fight with.

Beaverbrook's electoral strategy, not surprisingly, was to base everything on Churchill's name. In this he was not alone. Lord Woolton wrote to him on 31 May:

> The mixture we want is Churchill the war-winner, Churchill, the British bull-dog breed in international conference, and Churchill, the leader of a government with a programme of social reform that will ease the hardpressed and raise the standard of life for all. . . . We shall have to have answers on land for housing and on Coal.

Beaverbrook had also a programme of his own, compounded of the Empire and high wages. This was not a programme welcomed by most Conservatives, and in any case Beaverbrook was easily diverted into personal invective. When Attlee and Bevin abused him, he answered back—a grave offence for which The Manchester Guardian solemnly rebuked him. Beaverbrook addressed almost as many meetings as he had done during the general election of 1931. Then he had tried to run a one-man show, smuggling the Empire Crusade into the atmosphere of the financial panic. Now he was campaigning for Churchill and threw in his own record as an afterthought. It was a turbulent election, certainly rougher than 1931, and Beaverbrook enjoyed it. At Chatham he extolled Bracken, who had just become first lord of the admiralty, as the greatest holder of the office since Churchill. Legend has it that he also extolled Bracken as the greatest first lord since Nelson—an unlikely, even an impossible, contingency.[1] At Ashton-under-Lyne he evoked the memories of thirty-five years before, which can have had little relevance for most of the electors.

Afterwards, when the Conservatives had been defeated, Beaverbrook was accused of misdirecting their election campaign and, in particular, of inspiring the virulence which Churchill discharged against the Labour leaders. The charge was unfounded. Woolton, not Beaverbrook, inspired the Conservatives' election literature, and Churchill and Beaverbrook hardly met while the campaign was on. Beaverbrook had nothing to do

---

[1] This legend was invented by a Daily Herald cartoonist.

with the broadcast in which Churchill asserted that Labour would introduce a Gestapo. This was Churchill's own inspiration, settled at Chequers and approved only by Randolph Churchill and James Stuart. Nor did Beaverbrook issue any direct orders to his newspapers. Christiansen, Gordon, and Robertson could be relied on to reproduce their master's voice without hearing it. Beaverbrook's only signed article during the campaign was in The Daily Herald, and it was for him a well-reasoned piece. The only reference to his newspapers in his correspondence is in a letter of 12 June 1945 to Anderson, chancellor of the exchequer, who had expostulated against an article in The Daily Express, prophesying that the Conservatives would reduce income tax, and had asked: "What next?":

> I do not manage or control the Daily Express. . . . You ask what next. I do not know. But according to our faith, it is all mapped out for us.

Nevertheless it was Beaverbrook's newspapers, not his activities during the election campaign, which brought down on him the complaints of disgruntled Conservatives. Ralph Assheton attended later a meeting of defeated candidates and wrote of this to Beaverbrook on 25 January 1946. After expressing his own warm regard for Beaverbrook he went on:

> It was not in the mind, I feel sure, of anyone of those present to deny the enthusiasm and abounding energy which you and the papers under your control threw into the fight during the election campaign.
> The sense of the meeting was, however, critical of one aspect of your relationship to the Party. Many of the speakers at the meeting took the view that, however inadvertently, you had done the Party no small disservice in the previous formative years of public opinion by the employment on your papers of some of the ablest and most consistent Left Wing propagandists of the day.
> Their view was that if you have employed a brilliant propagandist such as Low, an amusing (but none the less deadly) propagandist in Nat Gubbins, a vitriolic propagandist such as Michael Foot, or a subtle propagandist such as J. B. Priestley, (to mention but a few) over a period of years, no whirlwind campaign of a few weeks can undo the long term anti-Conservative work of these men.

After some further comments Assheton added on his own account:

> I admit, of course, that many of these Left Wing propagandists are, journalistically, extremely talented—but taking a long term view I suggest that you can sometimes buy this type of talent for too high a political price.

Beaverbrook returned a sharp answer on 1 February 1946:

> As to the criticism of my newspapers, I can do nothing to meet it. The papers were built up on a conception of freedom which gives a hearing to every Party. In this respect they have always differed from the Daily Herald.

The cartoons are always valued on their merits and not on the opinions they illustrate. The columnists and humorists are treated in the same way. But of course the leader column is different. That is the property of the newspaper and not open to anyone who opposes the paper's policy.

But on one matter you all go wrong.

Owen and Foot never gave a left turn to the politics of the Evening Standard. This will surprise you. But an examination of the files of that newspaper will confirm what I say.

There was considerable agitation in the Evening Standard for a Second Front. This may have been misunderstood as a movement to the left. But it was no such thing. And indeed I was responsible for it, after I retired from the Government.

This was one version of events. In the first days of the campaign Beaverbrook was confident of victory. He wrote to J. M. Patterson on 15 June 1945:

Nationalisation or continued free enterprises are the alternatives between which the electors will have to choose—control for control's sake or its abolition at the earliest feasible moment.

The Socialists are afraid of two things—their own programme and Churchill. They have issued an election manifesto entitled "Let us face the future", but never has a political Party been more nervous of doing so. After five years as Ministers the leading Socialists know very clearly that the problems in front of us cannot be solved by political catchwords and ideological nostrums. They are uneasily aware that the electorate shares their knowledge.

... They know of course the hold Churchill has on the public imagination and they will stop at little to loosen it. All that they are likely to achieve however is to strengthen it yet further.

A fortnight later he was less sure. Beaverbrook wrote to Harry Hopkins on 29 June 1945:

I believe Churchill will win, with at least a comfortable majority. . . . There is a tug-of-war between two persisting factors in the electorate. There is the conviction that Churchill is the best man for the job. And, there is on the other side, a desire for change. After all, the Tories have been in for a long time.

Since the last election there has been a strong trend towards the Left. I believe that it reached its peak about the time that the Beveridge Report appeared. Since then, it has sagged perceptibly.

Polling took place on 5 July. On the previous day Beaverbrook sent to Churchill his final letter of resignation. He wrote:

You were kind enough to say that, when the election was over, I might be permitted to retire from the Government.

Now that the voting has taken place, I send you my resignation.

The altered, and happier, circumstances produced by victory in the German war give me an opportunity of withdrawing from administrative duties which it is proper I should take.

In parting, I want to give you my grateful thanks for so much personal kindness and understanding during the crowded and trying years in which I served under your leadership.

May I express, too, the profound admiration of one who had the good fortune to watch at close quarters your immense and victorious exertions for the salvation of Britain and mankind.

Declaration of the result was postponed for three weeks, while the service votes came in. Churchill went on holiday to Hendaye. Beaverbrook sent him optimistic forecasts. On 12 July he still expected that the Conservatives would have an adequate majority. By 15 July, when Churchill had moved to Berlin, he expected only a Conservative majority of 10. On 17 July Beaverbrook sent to Churchill his last official message:

The Tory party is without spirit, apologetic for having made a vigorous struggle and quite sorry it did not just take punches without giving any in return. It has no fighting disposition for the future . . . and Tory papers are frankly hostile to the administration. The only asset the Tories have got is in Berlin anyway.

Churchill returned to London on 25 July. The next day it was clear that he and his party had been routed. The result: Labour 393, Conservatives 189, Liberals 12. Churchill resigned that evening. Beaverbrook had arranged a large party at Claridge's. When the results came in, he stood up and said: "This occasion was intended as a victory feast. In the circumstances it now becomes a last supper".

The last supper indeed for Beaverbrook the statesman and party politician. Never again would he hold office or be the confidential adviser of a prime minister. Never again would he appear on platforms at a general election. This exclusion was also a release. Beaverbrook the independent observer and political hobgoblin was restored and, though he did not yet know it, a new career as a writer was opening before him. His spirit remained resilient. Unlike Churchill, who was crushed and affronted by defeat, Beaverbrook soon analysed it with detachment and understanding. On 31 July 1945 he penned two such comments. To J. P. Bickell:

The truth is that the British public have been conceiving for a long time an immense dislike of the Tory Party, the Tory Members of Parliament and many of the Tory ideas. They were bored and wanted a change.

To Joe Patterson:

The main factor in the political landslide here lies way back in the years 1938–40. It was about that time that the great mass of middle class opinion in Britain decided to punish the Conservatives. It was unfortunate that the blows intended for the heads of Mr. Chamberlain and his colleagues should fall upon Mr. Churchill.

On 8 August he made two further comments. To Trevor Westbrook:

> It was a mistake to believe that the public were thinking of the war and Mr. Churchill's record as our national leader. They were thinking of before the war and the Tory Party's association with mass unemployment.

To Theodore Yardly:

> It was Churchill that I was endeavouring to return to office, and not his party. The unpopularity of the party proved too strong for the greatness of Churchill and the affection in which he is held by the people.

Finally, on 17 August 1945 he sent a deeper analysis to Frank Gannett:

> The defeat of the Tory Party is in the nature of a delayed action detonation. The fuse was lit many years ago, in the depths of the depression, and it would have fired the charge in 1939 if the war had not intervened. . . . Once the middle class had been made up of small, self-employing business men, whose national political interest lay with the Conservative industrialists or the Liberal exporters and merchants. But now, to an increasing degree, the middle class is composed of salary-earners, whose relationship to the capital structure is precisely parallel to that of the wage-earning proletariat, although on a higher financial plane and whose future is conceived in terms of pensions, like the worker rather than investment like the capitalist.

Beaverbrook did not deeply regret the defeat of the Conservatives, however much he regretted that of Churchill. He wrote to Herbert Swope on 31 July 1945:

> The ability at the disposal of the Socialists exceeds the talent of the Conservatives if Churchill be left out of the reckoning.

On 11 October he sent E. J. Flynn a letter which showed how little sympathy he had with the new lights of the Conservative party:

> The battle within the party is fought between the Tory individualists who follow ironically enough, the creed of nineteenth-century Liberalism and the Tory Reformers who raise the banner, or rather wave the pocket handkerchief, of Disraeli's Young England. Their ideas may be described as Socialism without Socialists. But they may also prove to be Toryism without Tories. . . . I prefer the old Pretenders to the new. But that does not mean I believe the Old Guard of Tory Janissaries massed round the glorious but tattered banner of Free Enterprise are more likely to win a victory within the party or with the electorate. The suspicion clings to that splendid body that it is more concerned with freedom than with enterprise.

Beaverbrook anticipated that he might be attacked at the Conservative party meeting on 28 November. He therefore composed an impudent defence which, as he was not attacked, he did not use:

> Members of the Conservative Party attack me. They say I gave Mr. Churchill bad advice.
> I don't blame them.
> For I urged Mr. Churchill to give up the leadership of the Conservative Party and let them go out on their own.[1]
> I told him many times that I did not like the Conservative conduct of public affairs in and out of office. They have sabotaged one policy after another, including Imperial Preference. And I never could stick them.
> They never could stick Mr. Churchill until he became indispensable to them.
> I don't deny that I prefer them to the Socialists.

Beaverbrook had many reasons for disliking the Labour government. He had hoped that British foreign policy would remain firmly anchored to the two great principles which had been established during the war— alliance with Soviet Russia and cooperation, on a basis of equality, with the United States. Both principles were abandoned by the Labour government. Ernest Bevin outdid the Americans in his zest for the cold war. Beaverbrook commented wryly to Frank Gannett on 15 November: "It is now an accepted thing that when Bevin, the Foreign Secretary speaks, the Tories applaud and the Socialists remain glumly silent". The Labour ministers were abjectly convinced that Great Britain was on the brink of financial ruin. Prompted by Keynes, they accepted an American loan that involved the dismemberment of the sterling area and of Imperial Preference. The Labour government were now apparently eager to restore free trade and the gold standard—the very things, as Beaverbrook said, which brought world wide economic disaster in the twenties and thirties. Most Conservatives agreed with them.

An honourable minority, partly Conservative, partly Labour, opposed the American loan in the house of commons. Beaverbrook opposed it in the house of lords. On 18 December he forced a division. He found only seven supporters. The names of those peers who voted against the American loan are worthy of record: the duke of Bedford, the earl of Portsmouth, Viscount Bennett, Lord Balfour of Inchrye, Lord Beaverbrook, Lord Redesdale, Lord Sempill, Lord Stanley of Alderley. Lord Croft had been a great Empire man in the days when he was Sir Henry Page-Croft. He did not vote against the loan. Lord Cranborne, later Lord Salisbury, claimed to be a great Empire man. He did not vote against the loan. The Socialists and the bankers were united against the Empire.

---

[1] There is no other evidence that Beaverbrook gave this advice.

Keynes interrupted Beaverbrook's speech with the remark: "I have never heard statistics so phoney".[1] It was Keynes's statistics which turned out to be phoney.

For this is one of the few controversies which can be judged in the light of later events. We cannot say what the result would have been if the policy of appeasing Hitler had been continued or if that of resisting him had been adopted earlier. We can say what would have happened if Great Britain had not accepted the American loan. In 1947 the British government fulfilled the conditions imposed by the loan. Sterling was made convertible. The dollars obtained by the loan vanished overnight. Sales of sterling had again to be blocked. The loan might just as well have not been made except for the obligations remaining on Great Britain. Did ruin follow? On the contrary Great Britain started on the hard road to recovery. The loan proved to have been totally unnecessary. Beaverbrook had been entirely right. Keynes, the bankers, the economists and the Labour ministers had been entirely wrong.

Beaverbrook pointed the moral to R. N. Gardner, author of Sterling-Dollar Diplomacy, an admirable account of the affair (published in 1956 and republished in 1968). Beaverbrook wrote on 21 August 1956:

> My own opinion is that the Loan was bound to fail. That it was based on a complete misunderstanding of the economic facts and the economic needs.
>
> In making the destruction of Imperial Preference and its financial off-shoot, the Sterling Area, a main target, American officials were pursuing a course which made America's chief ally weaker and poorer, and America's own burden, both military and financial, heavier than it should have been.
>
> Was this wise? Was this sound politics?
>
> . . . .
>
> I believe that we are paying a heavy price for military, financial and trade policies followed after the end of the war.
>
> It is true we have been saved from the worst. The basic sympathy between the two English speaking blocs, has been an immense source of strength and security. No error has been able to destroy it.
>
> . . . .
>
> That is not, however, a safeguard which we should regard as permanent.
>
> It is better, surely, to rely on policies by which an ally respects the interests of the other, even when it regards them as prejudices.
>
> . . . You may have the idea that my opposition to the Loan was contentious or obscurantist.
>
> It was, as I see it, the attitude of one who sought to reconcile his belief in the Empire, with his hope that a strong Empire was the best ally the United States could have.
>
> Was I wrong?

[1] Beaverbrook thought Keynes had said "funny", and this word appears in Hansard.

Beaverbrook never went to the house of lords again after the debate on the American loan. His political career was at an end. He also wound it up financially. The details are characteristic and curious. He stood on his rights and then yielded voluntarily once these had been established, just as he scrutinized every item on his hotel bills before distributing lavish tips. Immediately the German war ended, Beaverbrook instructed his financial secretary to compute his net British income from all sources during the war after taxes and covenanted annuities had been paid. The answer was £37,700. Beaverbrook rounded this up to £50,000 and sent a cheque for this amount to the chancellor of the exchequer. He had lent his Grumman amphibian aircraft to the air ministry for the duration of the war. It was wrecked and became a total loss shortly after hostilities ended. The aircraft had cost Beaverbrook £15,000. He accepted £6,250 as compensation and remitted this sum to the treasury the same day. He also paid to the treasury something over £5,000 which he had received as a refund of income taxes in respect of farm losses. The total of his direct gifts to the treasury was £61,567. 14. 2.

Beaverbrook also aided the treasury by not claiming the salary and expenses to which he was entitled as a minister. He did not draw any salary when in office, thus forgoing £17,500. He paid for his own cars, secretaries and telephone calls. In addition he paid all hotel and travel expenses during his four official visits to Canada and the United States. These payments amounted to well over £5,000.

Beaverbrook made a further contribution to British finance in a more indirect way. Most of his fortune had always been in Canadian stocks. Where he himself held ordinary shares, these of course became subject to the direction of the Bank of England, which used them to sustain sterling in New York. In one of his largest holding companies, Candisle Corporation, he held only debentures, and the corporation itself was controlled by Canadian directors who were outside the jurisdiction of the Bank of England. Nevertheless Beaverbrook insisted that the corporation hand over some $1,736,000 and guaranteed this sum to the corporation out of his other resources. Further, throughout the war, Beaverbrook prevailed upon the Canadian directors to pay dividends, which they were not accustomed to do, so that the dollars could be available for the Bank of England.

In July 1946 the Canadian government secured the release of Canadian assets held by Canadians resident in England. Beaverbrook thus recovered possession of his Canadian company holdings among the assets of which were over a million dollars of US securities. These assets could now be removed from the control of the Bank of England. Beaverbrook prevailed upon the Canadian directors to relinquish these securities which remained under the control of the Bank of England until 1951, when the system ended. In the interval Beaverbrook received the income from these securities in sterling and thus forfeited many opportunities for profitable investment in the United States and Canada, to say nothing of forgoing his American pocket-money.

All these contributions to the British exchequer, direct and indirect, were made on the condition that there should be no public reference to them. This was not the first instance of such voluntary gifts. Baldwin made a similar gift after the first world war and imposed the same condition of secrecy. There was one striking difference. Baldwin soon allowed knowledge of his gift to leak out. Beaverbrook's gifts remained a secret until after his death.

CHAPTER TWENTY-THREE

THE ABSENTEE, 1946–56

On 18 March 1948 Beaverbrook gave evidence before the royal commission on the press. He was asked how he controlled his papers when he was so often away. Was it "long distance control, intermittent control, control by beam?" He replied cheerfully: "Yes, the worst kind, absentee control!" He had become a Cheshire Cat, impossible to pin down. He never stayed in one place or even one country for long, vanished overnight and reappeared with equal suddenness. He surrendered to the restlessness of his nature and then turned this restlessness into a fixed pattern which he followed from the end of the second world war until the approach of his last illness, a period of some eighteen years. Beaverbrook the public figure was in some sense diminished. Beaverbrook the man grew riper and more varied in his personality.

He had always been impatient with rules, whether political or personal. Now he disregarded them. He was his own master. He became more dictatorial and also more conciliatory. He claimed to work less, or not at all, and in fact became both more interfering and more creative. The sprite in him took control. If these last years are less significant as a record of public events, they are also the period when his friends remember him as the most beloved man they ever knew.

Beaverbrook's withdrawal had many causes which added up more or less by accident. After 1945 he had few contacts with the political world and no sympathy with the prevailing policies. The leading figures of the Labour government, Attlee, Bevin and Cripps, had always been hostile to him. Even Aneurin Bevan regarded him as an evil influence, and they do not seem to have met after 1943. Hugh Dalton and Herbert Morrison, though personally friendly, were themselves precariously placed and could not risk association with him. It was not much better with the Conservatives. Most of them held that Beaverbrook's malign influence had lost them the election. Churchill was not unaffected by this view. Brendan Bracken was now Beaverbrook's only political intimate, and he, too, had lost all influence.

Divergence over policies reinforced this personal isolation. Beaverbrook had no sympathy with Socialism even when it was voiced by Conservatives. He was even more out of step over foreign affairs. The Labour government had promoted the American loan. Most Conservatives, including Churchill, had acquiesced in it. Beaverbrook had opposed it almost alone. The swing of British foreign policy against Soviet Russia was equally abhorrent to him. He regarded the cold war as a false alarm, which many good judges now agree that it was. The consequence of close association with Europe was, in Beaverbrook's eyes, still worse. As a final blow, the death of President Roosevelt and the coming to power of cold warriors deprived him of all influence at Washington. Beaverbrook despaired and gave up for lost the causes which he had believed in. He was too old to fight again. Also, as anyone who lived through those years can testify, it was harder to champion friendship with Soviet Russia after the war than it had been to preach resistance to Germany before it.

David Farrer set down some shrewd guidance for his successor when he ceased to be Beaverbrook's secretary in August 1946:

> You should get it into your head that Lord Beaverbrook has never been an orthodox Tory. He loathed Baldwin and attacked many aspects of Tory policy between the wars. He is an all-out Protectionist and anti-monopolist in domestic affairs, and still an isolationist at heart abroad. At present he has no use whatever for "progressive" Tories like Eden, Macmillan and Quintin Hogg. He wants the Tories to oppose any and every Socialist measure. As for Churchill, he will frequently attack him in private and always praise him in public.

These public reasons for withdrawal were to some extent a cover for the personal ones which would have operated in any case. Before the war Beaverbrook constantly announced his withdrawal and almost operated it in 1939 or so he made out. Asthma overcame him after the war, and he was convinced that, apart from countless medical remedies, he needed to spend the winter months in a warm climate. La Capponcina, his house in the south of France, was restored undamaged, and he could use Canadian dollars there freely. He told his American friends that he would have liked to spend the winter in Miami and was prevented by lack of American dollars. This is puzzling. Beaverbrook had plenty of Canadian dollars and these were exchangeable into American without restriction. Maybe he felt that, since he had surrendered his American securities to the Bank of England, he had a moral obligation not to spend American dollars until these securities were released. Maybe, with the Canadian dollar standing at a considerable discount on the US dollar, it hurt his financial soul to squander Canadian dollars in this fashion. Or maybe he simply did not like Miami.

At all events Beaverbrook bought Cromarty House at Montego Bay, Jamaica in 1946 and Matthew's House, renamed Aitken House, at Nassau in the Bahamas in 1947. Both these were within the sterling area, though even so he was irked by the substantial charges which the local banks imposed for transferring sterling. Nassau was easier of access and also nearer to Miami if Beaverbrook wanted to bring over any American friends. He therefore made Aitken House his principal winter home and visited Cromarty House only occasionally. Both houses were pretty substantial residences, lavishly appointed and big enough to accommodate a full-sized house party.

Beaverbrook kept up the fiction or reality of his shortage of American dollars by only spending a week or so at a time in New York. There his dollar funds were supplied by American friends, principally Henry Luce, the proprietor of Time-Life, and Ben Smith—the famous "Sell 'em Ben" of the depression.[1] Similarly the Ford company provided him with a free car at the request of Sir Patrick Hennessy, head of English Ford and formerly Beaverbrook's right-hand man at the ministry of aircraft production. Of course his friends were reimbursed by holidays in England or the south of France. It was an odd arrangement all the same.

The circuit was completed by yet another accident. The University of New Brunswick at Fredericton, though ancient by Canadian standards, had been a modest institution before the war with less than 500 students. It had now trebled in numbers. It felt grand enough to have a chancellor for the first time, and who more appropriate than Beaverbrook? He had already given to the university the Lady Beaverbrook residence for men, the Lady Beaverbrook gymnasium and many scholarships. Beaverbrook was delighted. It is true that Fredericton was some way from Newcastle, his home town. But he had at last a real function and a foothold in New Brunswick after more than half a century of absence. The new post was created in 1946, and Beaverbrook was installed as chancellor in May 1947 at the annual degree ceremony. A Canadian fixture in May did not suit Beaverbrook. This was the time when he wanted to be in England. After a year or two, the ceremony was transferred to October, and Beaverbrook never missed an appearance until 1963.

The university got more than it bargained for or at any rate expected. In normal practice, the chancellor of a university turns up once a year, presides over the degree ceremony and goes away. This did not suit Beaverbrook. He was not cut out to be a figurehead. Despite many

[1] During the depression the bankers of Wall Street often organized a syndicate to stop the fall in share prices. Ben Smith always broke the artificial rally by selling forward. He told Beaverbrook that it was more difficult to be a bear than a bull: "In a Bull market the sky may one day really be the limit; in a Bear market there is always a bottom". Smith rode with Roosevelt to his first Inaugural and promised that he would never bear the market again. This was a shrewd operation. Ben Smith won Roosevelt's favour and, as well, divined that with the coming of the New Deal the bear market was over.

disclaimers that he would merely watch a few football matches, he resolved to play a leading part in the running of the university. Every autumn he moved in to Fredericton for six weeks or two months. He announced his intention of establishing a permanent residence there and indeed bought more than one house. None of them was to his taste, and he gave each in turn to the university after a brief trial. He made do with the Lord Beaverbrook Hotel, in which, though named after him, he held no share. Fredericton became the most fixed point in his restless life.

This was the pattern which Beaverbrook followed henceforward, a pattern immutable as the swallow's. His annual rhythm began each October in Fredericton. He presided over the Convocation, entertained the professors, advised or directed university affairs. He usually had time for a week or so in Montreal, where he discussed his own finances with his brother Allan and weighed up the leading businessmen. By the beginning of November he was ready for New York and outdid even the normal speed of that hectic city. He saw the Broadway hit of the day, talked with more businessmen and turned the New York office of The Express upsidedown. He also stocked up with pills or convinced himself from reading Time that he needed different ones. Between 1946 and 1961 he propounded 27 different remedies for asthma to Sir Daniel Davies, his medical adviser. They ranged from ACTH to chlorprophen-pryridamine and were all taken from the popular press.

Montego Bay was the next stop. Beaverbrook arrived there late in November and remained until after Christmas. He saw a good deal of the local society and sometimes invited friends from England. By the New Year he was bored with the social round and escaped to Aitken House at Nassau. Sometime in March he had another week in New York and then returned to England, at first on the Queen Mary and later by air. Though he claimed in 1950, when making a declaration of Canadian domicile, that Cherkley was "almost a ruin on account of war damage", this damage was not apparent to the naked eye, and Beaverbrook lived there in considerable comfort as he had always done. Stornoway House was truly a ruin, and Beaverbrook relinquished the crown lease.[1] The Daily Express then leased a flat for him in Arlington House at the upper end of St. James's Street. In theory his newspaper executives could hold conferences there and The Express could use the flat for other business purposes. This theory does not seem to have been applied. Beaverbrook came there from Cherkley nearly every day and often spent the night there mid-week. As well, he turned Cricket Malherbie to good use, going down to inspect his farms or using a projected visit as an excuse for avoiding tiresome visitors.

[1] Stornoway House was restored in 1959 with some internal modifications and is now the headquarters of Firth Cleveland Ltd.

La Capponcina had also to be fitted in. Beaverbrook usually went there for ten days or so at Easter and for a more prolonged stay during the late summer. But he might go there at almost any time if the English weather was disagreeable. La Capponcina was an attractive villa with a veranda where Beaverbrook could sit out in the sun. There was a small swimming pool and a private bathing-place in the sea, which was in fact a couple of rocks. The surroundings were hideous. The only walk was along a concrete path by the sea. However Beaverbrook did not mind. He drove into Monte Carlo where he kept his yacht and cruised slowly along the coast while he ate lunch. Beaverbrook's nearest neighbour was Greta Garbo, whom he never met. Instead he asked any friend who had been out for a walk: "Did you see the actress?" The south of France was no longer smart, and Beaverbrook's few acquaintances, such as Somerset Maugham, were even more elderly than he was. But he loved the place. He gave Cap d'Ail a gazebo and was delighted to be made an honorary member of the commune.

Four months in the year was about Beaverbrook's normal allowance in England. He was not a tax exile. He always paid income tax and surtax on his entire English income. What he relied on and maintained was his Canadian domicile of origin. This relieved him of British taxes on his income in Canada and the United States and was ultimately designed to secure his estate from British death duties, as indeed it did. However Cherkley was his home, though not his domicile, so far as he had one. It was by no means certain or even likely that he would be found there. This migratory way of life suited Beaverbrook very well. The constant moves were attuned to his temperament. The openings for evasion were also much to his pleasure. "Tell him I am going to Capponcina, and don't tell him where Capponcina is".

In the days before the war Beaverbrook travelled with an "entourage"— Castlerosse, Michael Wardell, two or three lady friends and a couple of secretaries. Now Castlerosse and Mrs Norton were dead. Wardell, who had risen to become a brigadier during the war, did not return to Fleet Street after it. Deciding to break new ground, he acquired a newspaper, The Gleaner, and a printing works in Fredericton and became in time a successful publisher. He was also conveniently placed to look after Beaverbrook's interests and discharge manifold commissions in New Brunswick. Though acknowledged as a brigadier by everyone else, he remained to Beaverbrook "The Captain". Thus deprived of an entourage, Beaverbrook travelled on a more modest scale—always with a chef and a valet, usually with a single secretary, sometimes without. Even when he had a secretary, he often made out that he had none and sent his letters by Soundscriber, to be forwarded by George Millar in London—another aspect of his vanishing trick. Occasionally he took with him some young man from The Express office and claimed to be grooming the youngster for stardom or even for an editor's chair. At any rate the budding journalist got plenty of practice in summarizing the newspapers and also in withstanding the proprietor's rages, simulated or otherwise.

Absentee control was no impudent boast. Beaverbrook watched every detail of his papers until the last day of his life. During his four months in England he met all the senior members of the staff and many junior ones as well so that he knew what was going on personally. He telephoned his editors two or three times a day. The conversation had an almost ritual quality. First, "what's the news?", then "what are you going to say?". If Beaverbrook did not much like the answer, there would follow "If that's your opinion you are entitled to say so". Alternatively Beaverbrook would have his own ideas. If so, he rattled out the lines for a leader straight away. Finally "Anything else?", quickly succeeded by "Goodbye to you now".

When Beaverbrook was at La Capponcina the office called him every day, and it was a terrible time for him one year when a French postal strike cut off his telephone for some weeks. When he was in Canada or the United States the calls were made twice or three times a week. These calls, too, had their own ritual. They were made from the chairman's room, and there assembled the chairman himself (at first E. J. Robertson and after 1955 Tom Blackburn), Max Aitken, A. G. Millar, head of Beaverbrook's private office, one or two editors and later Mrs. Ince to report on the buying of books or pictures. Each in turn took his place at the instrument while Beaverbrook poured out requests, instructions and complaints for twenty minutes or half an hour. Sometimes Beaverbrook lost patience, waiting for the call to come through, and rang the chairman himself. Whereupon the others were frantically summoned on the internal line and turned up at the double.

In the West Indies atmospherics made the line unusable, though Beaverbrook sometimes crossed specially to Miami from Nassau in order to put through a call. Otherwise he relied on written reports. Christiansen, editor of The Daily Express, sent him a ten-page letter every Friday, mostly of political news and gossip. Robertson, the chairman, wrote up to 40 long letters a year, dealing mainly with business affairs, though with many personal comments as well. Max Aitken and the other two editors wrote often, if less frequently. These letters, extending over nearly twenty years, provide fascinating material for the history of the newspapers and British politics. They are less relevant to the story of Beaverbrook for he rarely replied to them.

The instrument by which he principally exercised his absentee control was that ingenious device the Soundscriber. Beaverbrook's first recording machine used wax cylinders which were affected by heat, and the loss of his messages caused him much pain. The Soundscriber produced small plastic discs which came safely through the post. The machine became his constant companion—at his bedside, at the swimming pool, on a journey, even at the dinner table. It was disconcerting for the inexperienced when Beaverbrook interjected, in the middle of a conversation, some such apparently irrelevant remark as "Mr. Wintour, your Diary paragraphs are too long".

The Soundscriber enabled Beaverbrook to think aloud. As soon as an idea came into his head, he pressed the recording button and set it down— private grumbles, recollections, financial instructions and, above all, guidance for his newspapers. He went through them each day or when a batch of them arrived from England by airplane. He looked at his rivals, particularly The Daily Mail, and raised a query when he thought one of his newspapers had missed a story. The messages were identified only by the name of the person to whom they were addressed: Mr. Robertson, Mr. Junor or whoever it might be, and the name was repeated with menacing effect throughout the message. The habit so grew on him that he used it in ordinary conversation, which was also alarming for the inexperienced.

The recorded discs were deciphered in London at Beaverbrook's private office, which was directed by A. G. Millar. Beaverbrook never paid public tribute to George Millar, and his services have passed almost unnoticed. He was in fact the key figure in Beaverbrook's life, and it is hardly too much to say that Beaverbrook could not have existed without him. George Millar was the perfect secretary—devoted, efficient, with limitless discretion and almost limitless patience. He handled Beaverbrook's financial affairs, resisted Beaverbrook's wilder suggestions, knew everything and revealed nothing. All the storms fell upon his uncomplaining head. It was also a minor advantage that, being himself of Scotch origin, he was not perturbed by Beaverbrook's misuse of the English future indicative. This is a good opportunity for me to set down my admiration for his services and my gratitude for the way he handled Beaverbrook's papers and other records.

All machines need a human being in the last resort to make them work, and George Millar was the human agent in the Soundscriber system. Beaverbrook, with his usual passion for economy, would not allow the individual messages to be typed on to separate sheets. They were copied one after another, and the sheets were then cut into strips, according to the names of the recipients. George Millar kept his own messages and forwarded the others. Most of the original transcripts have been destroyed. What survives are the strips as they were sent round, and these only when the recipient pinned them to the letter in which he answered Beaverbrook's queries or complaints. They provide exasperating material for a conscientious biographer. They are on flimsy paper and vary in length from a single sentence to fifteen or twenty lines. As many as ten may be pinned higgledy piggledly to a single letter. The historian of recent times is corrupted by the easy task of reading mainly print and typescript. Beaverbrook's flimsies return him to the delights or labours of palaeography.

I have encountered another problem in dealing with Beaverbrook's later years. Until the end of the second world war his career fell into clearly defined phases, as the division into chapters shows—the Lloyd George time, the Baldwin time, the Empire Crusade, Isolation, the Churchill time. After the second world war, Beaverbrook's life was not shaped by public events. It was all of a piece, though there was, I think, also one striking development. Very few of his messages can be dated from internal evidence, and it was therefore tempting to present him by theme—Beaverbrook the journalist, Beaverbrook the university chancellor, Beaverbrook the historian, Beaverbrook the eccentric character— instead of chronologically. However I am a narrative historian, not gifted in analysis. Beaverbrook himself was a newspaper man, expecting things to happen day by day. And there was still after all a single man moving through time, not six different men, though it often seemed like it. At any rate the dates provide some sort of framework, though they are less important than they were before.

1946 was pretty much of a dead year. Beaverbrook was busy organizing his migrations to the West Indies and the south of France. He was finished with politics after the American loan went through, or thought he was. He was impotently opposed to Bevin's foreign policy and Churchill's Iron Curtain speech at Fulton. Bracken reported on 16 April: "Winston is determined to continue to lead the Tory Party until he becomes Prime Minister on earth or Minister of Defence in Heaven". Beaverbrook made no answering comment. Harold Laski took a libel action against The Daily Express for alleging that he had advocated violent revolution. He lost and had to pay £10,000 in costs. Beaverbrook wished to let him off. Robertson refused. The Daily Express, he argued, had offered to forget the affair. Laski had persisted and had boasted that he would found a lectureship at the London School of Economics with the damages he expected to receive. Now he must foot the bill.

There are two letters which illustrate Beaverbrook's attitude to his newspapers. One is to Nathaniel Gubbins who wrote a humorous column for The Sunday Express:

> I do not expect you to show me any consideration at all. I am quite sure you do right to treat me the same as any other man in public life. There is not the slightest reason for tempering your attacks on anything I stand for, of which you disapprove.

The whole purpose of the Express is to give you freedom of expression, and there will be no departure from that general policy.

Another letter shows that this freedom did not extend to editors. It is from Herbert Gunn, editor of The Evening Standard, writing on 27 May:

This is a written reaffirmation of my undertaking to submit to you before publication, all copy of leaders and other projects which you have initiated.

In May 1947 Beaverbrook was installed as chancellor of the University of New Brunswick. This interrupted his summer routine in England. It also absorbed much of his time and energy. He at once set himself up as buyer-in-chief for the university library, though without enquiry into its most pressing needs. The library got what Beaverbrook thought good for it—Calvinist theology, Knox's works, John Galt's Annals of the Parish, fine copies of the Shorter Catechism. Daily Express stringers throughout Great Britain were diverted from their usual task of gathering news and ransacked local bookshops for secondhand copies of the books Beaverbrook wanted. One instruction read: "Buy all the books listed and ship with speed". Books sent to The Daily Express for review or presented to Beaverbrook himself went the same way, as did the first editions of modern novels which he had accumulated at Cherkley. Not all the books met with Beaverbrook's approval on closer examination. He tried to read Knox's First Blast of the Trumpet against the Monstrous Regiment of Women while crossing the Atlantic on the Queen Mary and sent back the instruction: "send no more of Knox's works. There is nothing good about them except the title". Annals of the Parish, however, "stood up". What Beaverbrook liked about it was the minister's farewell sermon which stirred the emotions he had felt about his own father's farewell. Indeed he mixed the two up and once read the sermon in Annals to me as an example of his father's eloquence. The sermon comes on an early page of Annals, and Beaverbrook probably read no further.

Apparently the delights of Fredericton made Beaverbrook really think of leaving England. At any rate he put Cherkley up for sale at £75,000 and lamented (to Ashton-Gwatkin on 13 August): "Nobody will buy it because of the large acreage of agricultural land that goes with it". He claimed that he had lost all say over his newspapers and told Anthony Marlowe, the current Cross Bencher: "I am being constantly denied and contradicted by the Editors of the papers and also by the members of the Policy committee". Actually his instructions and comments on politics continued to flow freely. One to Robertson early in the year, on 14 January, showed an unusual support for the government:

It is imperative that the Daily Express and our newspapers, give help and encouragement to the Government in raising loans.

We are all dependent for our daily bread upon the favourable attitude of the public to government finance. Do you want to take the crust out of your own mouth?

Usually his comments were more critical. One was retrospective. Beaverbrook wrote to Harold Macmillan on 14 June:

If the government had listened to the advice of the Daily Express in 1938–39, then this country would have been thoroughly armed and standing out of European conflict.

When Europe, East and West, had reached exhaustion, a strong, good Britain could have imposed Peace and International Law.

He had no enthusiasm for the modern Conservatives and wrote to Leo Amery on 3 July:

The Conservative Party is not worth any support at all. . . . In my view the Socialists are doing more for the Empire than the Conservatives ever achieved. . . . I must content myself with asking over and over again the old question that John Knox addressed to the Scots lords, "Whaur will ye win, gin ain may speir?"

Evidently Knox's works left some mark.

By the autumn Beaverbrook was a little more cheerful. He wrote to Frank Gannett on 11 September:

We have a Socialist Government which is irresolute, inconsistent and insecure.

The civil servants toil but they do not spin; and Solomon in all his glory was not surrounded by such an array of non-producers. If he had been, he would never have built the Temple.

. . . Already there are signs that the leaden sky is clearing. The call for a rallying of our strength in a Commonwealth Customs Union is one of them.

Looking forward to the next election, he reported to Jesse Jones on 10 October:

Probably the Left will be cast out ferociously. The men of the extreme right will hold untrammelled power for a time.

Beaverbrook was delighted when the convertibility of sterling, imposed as a condition by the American loan, led to a run on the pound and fruitlessly exhausted the loan. Exchange control was restored along with many other restrictions, and Brendan Bracken wrote lightheartedly on 11 November:

Our white Gandhi [Sir Stafford Cripps] is enforcing a crackpot plan to empty the shops at home in order to provide for shrinking, not to say, mythical markets abroad.

Beaverbrook himself wrote to Dr. John Williams on 21 December:

> Well, now we retreat again within the defences of the Sterling Area. I am not at all surprised. The loan should never have been negotiated.
> One of our reactions will be, I think and hope, a great upward swing in our agricultural production.

Despite this triumph for his views, Beaverbrook had two worries over his newspapers in the winter of 1947–48. One sprang from the government restrictions on the supply of newsprint, which threatened to increase the cost of newspapers. The other was a royal commission on the press which was promoted by a number of Labour MPs, themselves mostly journalists. The object of the enquiry was to discredit the great capitalist proprietors and especially to expose the black list which they operated against individuals whom they did not favour. Beaverbrook commented: "I expected no better from that fellow Driberg, but I never thought Michael Foot would do this to me". One of his Soundscriber messages of this period has survived in full. Though very long, it merits inclusion as an example of the messages which he sent nearly every week. It starts with a complaint about his own lack of newspapers, goes on to newsprint and the royal commission, and ends in a helter-skelter of miscellaneous comments:

> Mr. Millar, I have had nothing since the 12th December, and here it is the night of the 22nd. No airplane tomorrow, so I suppose I will have nothing till the 24th. You see what comes of Socialisation.
> Mr. Robertson. I will be glad to hear about the Royal Commission on the Press which is one of the Government Agencies in the persecution of newspapers. Sorrow, sorrow ever more. There is nothing I can say about it except to bow my head in misery. It wouldn't be a bad thing if the Socialists cut off all newsprint entirely.
> I don't care Mr. Robertson what the Government tries to do to us. The intention is without doubt to persecute the press, but let the effect of that persecution fall more heavily upon the Govt. Press than upon the independent newspapers. Now the way to carry that situation to a conclusion is to refuse to increase your selling price, tighten your belt and let the suffering and misery descend upon the wretches who supported the Socialists in the last election.
> Mr. Robertson. Will you please try and get all our people to stop saying You must think again. It must think again. The Government must think again. In other words abolish that phrase "think again". It has been overdone in the Express for a long time. It is not good style anyway and it is commonplace to a degree.
> Mr. Gordon. I find the political notes all a most partisan production. I hope very much we shall become what we say we are—a Cross-Bencher column giving both sides with impartiality which persuades the public that our judgments on politics are entirely without bias.

Mr. Gordon. It is your duty to guide Mr. Thurtle [a Labour MP who contributed a weekly column to The Sunday Express]. He has gone off altogether in anti-Communist line. He is going to carry out a crusade against the Communists, but I am saying that a crusade against the Communists is not our line at all. That, I think, is the particular property of the Daily Mail, and of the Daily Mail group.

Mr. Christiansen. Look at the leader in the Daily Mail of December 6 on sea fishing. Who is the writer of it? It is a very good style and excellent material for the first three-quarters of it.

On 1 January 1948 there came a further message for Robertson:

I don't care whether you make money or not. All I want to see Mr. Robertson is a great newspaper, strong in reserves and so completely and absolutely set up in finance that no other newspaper can ever challenge us. Even after you and I have laid down our task Mr. Robertson.

Beaverbrook's worries over his newspapers were soon dispelled. The newsprint problem was overcome by producing smaller newspapers. The critics put up a poor show at the royal commission, and its members, who knew nothing of the newspaper industry, remained in invincible ignorance. Robertson in evidence showed that most names on the so-called black list were of persons, such as Sir Thomas Beecham and Putzi Hanfstaengel, who had taken libel actions against The Daily Express. Many had been put on at their own request. Many who were supposed to be on were not on at all. Baldwin for instance had been mentioned 1,100 times when he was allegedly excluded. Every paper kept a warning list as a natural precaution, and that was all there was to it. If Beaverbrook sometimes imposed a ban—and he did—it was to exclude a friend, not an enemy. As Jean Norton once remarked, "Marriage with publicity and divorce with privacy is what they all want", and though Beaverbrook disapproved of this wish, he often granted it.

Beaverbrook himself gave evidence on 18 March and had a field day. It was particularly agreeable for him to score off his old antagonist Lady Violet Bonham Carter, and he made the most of his opportunity. What he said was no novelty. He had said it many times before in his newspapers. But it apparently surprised the commission.

I ran the paper purely for propaganda, and with no other purpose. . . . In order to make propaganda effective the paper had to be successful. No paper is any good at all for propaganda unless it has a thoroughly good financial position. The policy is that there shall be no propaganda in the news. There is a strong, stern rule, and the most tremendous attempt . . . to carry the rule into effect. But we do stumble. It is terrible how we stumble; it is heartbreaking sometimes.

The Beaverbrook papers were united in support of the Empire. If any editors diverged from this, "I talked them out of it". On other subjects editors had their own views, as John Gordon and Frank Owen had refused to support appeasement before the war. Beaverbrook struck an affectionate blow at his principal parliamentary critic:

> I did issue very many of what were called directives. It was really advice, particularly to Michael Foot. He is a very clever fellow, a most excellent boy. And then suddenly he was projected into the editorship of the paper before he was ready for it. . . . Michael Foot himself believed that I made him a journalist. He took the view that I allowed him immense freedom of expression, and he certainly thought that he had more freedom of expression with me than he could have with anyone else.

There was really no more to be said. The truth is that a newspaper reaches and holds a circulation of more than four million only by being a good paper, presenting the news in a lively efficient way. This is what The Daily Express did.

Did Beaverbrook really believe his own statement that his editors had full freedom of opinion except on the Empire? Probably he did and he didn't, much as with his repeated statements that he had withdrawn from the newspapers or had left England for good. He never appreciated the impact of his own personality. He harassed his editors and was genuinely contrite if one of them broke down under the barrage. Peter Howard tells how he had an article battered at Stornoway House and went out in disgrace:

> As I walked away I heard the scurry and patter of slippered steps on the pavement behind me. I turned. There was Beaverbrook. "I'm sorry, Peter", he panted, "I should never have spoken that way to you. Will you forgive me?".[1]

William Barkley, the parliamentary correspondent, was similarly harassed at Cherkley. Beaverbrook complained of an article he had written, asking "What does it mean?" and ordered him to read it aloud. Barkley began and then broke off, saying: "If you treat me like this you will make me nervous and I shall be no use to you". When Barkley got back to the office, Christiansen said to him: "What have you been up to at Cherkley? Lord Beaverbrook has telephoned me and all the senior executives: Mr. Barkley must not be criticized. If you criticize Mr. Barkley it will make him nervous and he will be no use to us". It is fair to add that, after an apology of this kind, Beaverbrook still expected to get his own way.

Percy Cudlipp, who had long experience of Beaverbrook when editing The Evening Standard, gave another illustration of Beaverbrook's mock repentance.[2] It was Beaverbrook's custom to end a telephone conversation

[1] Peter Howard, Beaverbrook, 21.
[2] In The Inky Way Annual, November 1948.

by asking, "Is there anything else?" When the man at the other end began to talk, Beaverbrook would say, "Goodbye to you" and replace the receiver. He did this one day in Cudlipp's presence, and Cudlipp said, "That is a very disconcerting habit of yours, and I used to hate it". An hour later they went for a walk. They were caught in the rain, and Beaverbrook telephoned to his butler from a cottage for a car to be sent. When he had given his instruction, he went on: "Now, is there anything else you want to say to me? Just think, there's no hurry. Mr. Cudlipp is standing by my side, and I know that if there is any other matter you have to raise he would wish me to give it complete attention. You say there is nothing else. Very well, I must accept your assurance. And now I am about to say 'Goodbye to you'. Here it comes. *Goodbye to you*". Then turning to Cudlipp: "There y'are, Percy. You've accused me most unjustly. I'm the politest fellow in the world or anywhere else. ISN'T THAT TRUE?" Cudlipp had to say, "Yes".

Beaverbrook may have been pleased with his newspapers. He was still gloomy about political affairs. He had welcomed the failure of the American loan, but it brought consequences which he regarded as lamentable. The Marshall Plan gave American assistance to Europe, and it was justified by an alarm that Soviet Russia had plans for aggression. Beaverbrook was out of step on both counts. He wrote to Roy Howard on 25 April 1948:

> I was against the Loan. I am opposed to the Marshall Plan. I hate the Dole. I deplore the disintegration of the British Empire. I condemn the Socialists. And I detest the Tories who helped the Socialists to perpetrate these follies.

Beaverbrook did not believe in the supposed Russian danger. He was for peace as he had been in 1939, and this time with more reason. When Harold Clark, a friend of his in Miami, feared to come to Europe because of the war that he thought was impending, Beaverbrook replied on 24 May:

> I do not take the view that war is imminent. There will not be any fighting for years, I hope.
> There never need be any fighting on the issues that now divide the world.

Beaverbrook was again assuring his friends that he had detached himself from his newspapers. He wrote to Roy Johnson on 16 March: "When a man is away for more than six months out of every year, it is time he left to others the responsibility for conducting daily newspapers", and to Tom Clarke on 21 March: "It is easier for me in my old age to live in two continents, since I am no longer engaged in any activities". In reality he was of course as active as ever. He mobilized his newspapers against

British participation in Western Union, an early version of many such plans. Thus to Christiansen on 28 October:

> You should make it very clear that we are not opposed to Western Union. That may be very good for Europeans. Our opposition is to Britain joining Western Union. And that opposition is based on two lines of criticism:
> (1) It separates us from the Empire sooner or later;
> (2) it separates us from the United States and makes us a subsidiary instead of an equal partner.

And to Max Aitken who was then writing Cross Bencher:

> Look up the Socialist who said that Europe must be a union of Socialist states and let us hear about him in your column. There must be many such Socialists. Look up Mr. Crossman—he is sure to have said many foolish things.

Other messages of the same day contain more miscellaneous comments. To Robertson:

> The Daily Express should be making fun of Conservatives who oppose Mr. Churchill. If they lose him they lose a large part of their voting strength. The only hope of a friendly nod from many passers-by is the company they keep with Churchill. Lose that and they lose a lot.

Next a grumble to Robertson about Herbert Gunn, then editor of The Evening Standard:

> It is a weary world the life we lead, you and I.... I asked him who was the co-ordinator of Chamberlain's government, the nobleman who had been the head of the navy, but he couldn't name Lord Chatfield, but I can't blame him on that account for I couldn't name Lord Chatfield either. It's fair to say however that I am sixty nine years of age.

After this, praise to Christiansen of a columnist:

> James Cameron is a great journalist. He must not be expected to make a good pork pie every time.

Beaverbrook was always generous with his praise, particularly of the humorous features. On 27 July 1948 he congratulated Osbert Lancaster on a pocket cartoon and wrote:

> It was as brilliant a piece of work as anything I have seen in the Daily Express, and I have seen much that is good in that paper.

On 10 May 1949 he telegraphed to Beachcomber—J. B. Morton:

> I send you my grateful thanks for twenty-five years of collaboration in the Daily Express.
> It has given us a feature of such excellence that you have adorned our columns and charmed our readers throughout the vicissitudes of England's darkest age.

Beaverbrook's appreciation did not stop at letters or telegrams. On one occasion he entertained twelve of his senior executives to dinner and afterwards gave each of them 2,500 shares in Express newspapers. The total value at the time was £28,000. Twenty years later it had risen to £156,000.

When rationing was in force in England, Beaverbrook showered Canadian hams on his chief employees—so many indeed that they often had to pass on his bounty to their friends. A sick wife of an Express man was given a long holiday at La Capponcina. For the handicapped child of another, Beaverbrook found a special school and provided an annuity to pay all the education expenses. When one editor groaned at the size of his surtax, Beaverbrook offered to pay it for him, though the offer was not taken up. Another editor asked for a loan of £3,000 towards buying a house. He was told that there was a strict rule against loans to members of the staff and a few days later received the money as a gift. Another Express man became involved in a court case. Beaverbrook paid for his defence.

Beaverbrook took as much trouble over his friends as over his staff. His office kept a note of all birthdays and also drew his attention to any event in a friend's life. Beaverbrook's awareness of other people's affairs seems breath-taking until you remember that George Millar's machine was working overtime. Beaverbrook's office had sample letters for all occasions—congratulations for a title or a wedding, sympathy for the loss of a wife or child, encouragement after an illness. Looking through these letters in bulk as I have done gives at first an impression of mechanical grief. But of course for the recipient each letter was unique, and it did not detract from Beaverbrook's thoughtfulness that he also bestowed it on others. He wanted to be efficient even in his personal kindness. It was kindness all the same.

One element was missing in these first years after the war. Though Beaverbrook often talked of his past experiences, particularly at the ministry of aircraft production, he showed no sign of returning to the writing of history. Indeed he declared that he would write no more, no more. Yet interest in the past was creeping up on him. One small indication came when he wanted George Malcolm Thomson to run a weekly feature in The Evening Standard on bestsellers of 1880–1890, the period of his boyhood—"they are much more attractive than most contemporary productions". Again when Thomson reviewed the first volume of Churchill's Second World War, Beaverbrook wrote to him regarding Eden's resignation in February 1938:

> Wasn't it Eden's duty if Europe was sinking into dark night, to disclose to the public that Chamberlain refused to take the aid of Roosevelt? Wasn't it his duty to go to the people and to tell the people to reprove Chamberlain and to compel him to accept guidance from the west as well as taking decisions in our Island home.

The idea of again writing books came to Beaverbrook in a roundabout way. W. J. Brittain, an admirer and former employee of Beaverbrook's, now ran a weekly periodical The Recorder. Beaverbrook liked him and told Churchill: "He is entirely devoted to yourself and to the Conservative party so far as I can see. I can understand his devotion to you, but it bothers me how he sees the Conservative party in that favourable light". To help The Recorder, Beaverbrook allowed it to serialize his old work of worldly guidance Success. This attracted the attention of an American publisher, who offered Beaverbrook $5,000 a month for a year if he would bring it up to date. Beaverbrook was tempted by the prospect of so many American dollars and went around telling his American friends that he would soon be a rich man again. Then he revolted against the work involved, and the project vanished, taking the American dollars with it. But the seed had been sown. Going over Success started Beaverbrook thinking again about his Canadian youth and about the great political events in which he had been involved during the first world war. Nor did he neglect Success for ever. He tinkered with it, as he loved to do with all his books, added new anecdotes, and brought out a revised edition in 1954 as Don't Trust to Luck.[1] Then he tinkered still more and produced an American edition in 1956, entitled Three Keys to Success, with an introduction by Joseph Kennedy.

There was another, more unexpected opening, the significance of which Beaverbrook did not realize at the time. While returning to England on the Queen Mary, he received a note on 27 June from Stanley Morison, a fellow-passenger:

> If you aren't too occupied in telephoning, writing, dictating letters, etc., would you consider answering a question regarding the circumstances of your early proprietorial connection with the Daily Express.
>
> I need certain of these details for the chapter on the London press that forms part of the IV (and final) volume of the History of the Times—and I should prefer, with your assistance, to be accurate.

The two met. They had a lively conversation. Beaverbrook attached no importance to the meeting and indeed forgot all about it. He did not foresee that it would change the pattern of his life.

Stanley Morison was a remarkable man. He had been a conscientious objector during the first world war and claimed then to be a Communist, though he also managed somehow to be a Roman Catholic at the same time. Despite being entirely self-educated he became one of the world's leading typographers and in 1930 designed new type for The Times. His connection with the paper did not stop at typography. He soon became concerned in policy also. He had been sympathetic to Germany

---

[1] Beaverbrook gave the book to The Daily Express. It did not bring him any American dollars or even English pounds.

during the first world war and later supported the appeasement line which The Times followed when Geoffrey Dawson was editor. Once the second world war broke out, he turned violently against appeasement and became an uncompromising champion of Soviet Russia. He shared a house with Barrington-Ward, who had succceded Dawson as editor, enlisted E. H. Carr as principal leader-writer on foreign affairs, and these three men transformed The Times into the threepenny edition of The Daily Worker. After the war opinion turned against friendship with Soviet Russia. Morison sought refuge in finishing the History of The Times which Buckle had left incomplete.

The History was an important contribution to newspaper history, a subject on which Morison was a considerable authority. It was also a sustained repudiation of his earlier views and a vindication of his later ones, so much so that foreign affairs occupied an altogether excessive place in his book. He extolled at length the hostile line which The Times had taken against Germany from the beginning of the twentieth century until the outbreak of the first world war. He condemned in equal detail its policy of appeasement before the second. And something more. Radicals of Morison's stamp regarded Northcliffe during his lifetime as the embodiment of evil. Now Northcliffe became Morison's hero—the man who had saved The Times by making it pay, the greatest newspaperman of all time, and in public affairs a selfless patriot. Morison never wearied of talking about Northcliffe's achievements and about the political events of the first world war, and in time his talk struck an answering chord in Beaverbrook. Later the two developed another unexpected common interest. Morison was an amateur theologian and a Thomist. Beaverbrook admired John Knox and could master Calvinist phrases. When they wearied of Northcliffe and Lloyd George, they turned to theological dispute. As a further surprise, Morison, the former Radical, brought out the radicalism in Beaverbrook also, and the two joined in singing the Red Flag, which had not previously been numbered among Beaverbrook's favourite psalms.

This still lay in the future. The great event for Beaverbrook in 1949 was that he reached the age of 70. At 50 he had announced that he was giving his newspapers to his sons. At 60 he prepared to depart from England for ever. With characteristic perversity, at 70 it was quite the reverse. On his birthday, 25 May 1949, 600 of his employees entertained him to lunch. He announced his three resolutions:

FIRST, I will not give up my bad temper.

SECOND, I will not give up my passions. I have enjoyed them far too much to put them away.

THIRD, I will not give up my prejudices, for these prejudices are the foundation of my strength and vigour.

20

He went on:

> I give you warning that I will not be dismissed. I am continuing what
> I believe to be a necessity in journalism—a vital force, a living spark in spite
> of my years.
> The last turn in the road is the best, and I am nearing the last turn.

He told W. J. Brittain that he was now living on borrowed time and recited
the ninetieth psalm in the metrical version of the Scotch psalter:

> Three score and ten years to sum up
>   our days and years we see;
> Or if by reason of more strength
>   in some four score they be;
> Yet doth the strength of such old men
>   but grief and labour prove:
> For it is soon cut off, and we
>   fly hence and soon remove.

And he repeated: "yet is their strength labour and sorrow". Brittain said:
"I think you will still have fun". Beaverbrook replied: "So do I!"

He was right. The best years of his life were opening before him,
despite physical discomfort from asthma and other ailments—years in
which he managed to combine irresponsibility and creative work. With
the approach of the general election which must come some time in 1950,
he began to take a more active interest in politics. He had seen little of
Churchill since 1945, being completely out of sympathy with Conservative
policy. The year 1949 opened with a great row between them. On 11
February The Evening Standard published a leader, declaring that the
Liberals should run more candidates. Churchill, who had just accepted
an invitation to stay at Beaverbrook's house in Jamaica, was furious and
telegraphed:

> Leading article Evening Standard February 11 is so obviously designed
> to injure Tory chances in impending by-elections that alas I cannot while
> remaining leader accept your most kind and attractive invitation to be so
> publicly your guest in Jamaica. I am making arrangements at hotel. I do
> not exaggerate importance of your newspaper action in our affairs nor of
> course is our friendship affected. Trust you will be able to give me good
> news of your health and that we shall meet when I arrive 8th or 9th it is a
> sad world.

Beaverbrook had not seen the leader and found nothing wrong with it
when he did. Encouragement of the Liberals was an old line of his. However he assured Churchill that he would not be in Jamaica when Churchill

arrived, "so you will not be embarrassed by me". He sent a further telegram the same day:

> Personally I deplore Standard leader and I have asked Robertson for enquiry into circumstances. I can tell you more when I hear results. Surely Conservatives should grasp simple truths that Express group help their cause more than any other newspapers on account of widespread circulation and independent policy.

Churchill was contrite. He replied: "My reaction was too impulsive but I feel that all we have worked for all our lives is at stake in the near future". He agreed to come to Jamaica and then decided that he could not desert the English political field for so long.

However the two resumed their friendship when Beaverbrook returned to England in April. They went over the proofs of the third volume of Churchill's Second World War, and Churchill commented, in reference to their visit to Washington in December 1941: "You certainly, and not for the first or last time, made a 'ferment'. I am so glad to be able to pay my tribute to your services to us all". For a time Beaverbrook was cheerful about the political future. On 27 June he wrote to an old voter at Ashton-under-Lyne who remembered saying of Max Aitken in 1910, "Why, he is only a kid":

> It is my belief that Churchill will be restored to power this Autumn or early next year, and with his return to Downing Street, confidence will improve, business will pick up steadily, and manufacturing enterprise will expand.

In August Churchill visited La Capponcina for the first time. On the evening of 23 August he played gin rummy with Michael Wardell. He had a sensation of paralysis. At his bedroom door he said to Wardell: "The dagger is pointing at me. I pray it may not strike. I want so much to be spared at least to fight the election. I must lead the Conservatives back to victory. I know I am worth a million votes to them. Perhaps two million!" During the night he had a stroke. Beaverbrook kept the news from reporters. Churchill soon improved and said to Wardell: "The dagger struck, but this time it was not plunged in to the hilt. At least, I think not".

The shadow hanging over Churchill's life brought a new element into Beaverbrook's relationship with him. Beaverbrook felt that he was needed again. With physical weakness as with other troubles he was the foul-weather friend. Henceforward he guarded Churchill, concealed his illnesses from the papers, and encouraged him to stay in politics—not because it was good for the country, though he thought it was, but because it was good for Churchill. Sir Charles Wilson (later Lord Moran), Churchill's medical adviser, took exactly the same attitude.

Politically in fact Beaverbrook soon lost his shortlived faith in Churchill and told his New York office in December:

> Next year we will have a new Government, a new Foreign Secretary, and a new Colonial Secretary.
>
> Everything new except Policy, that will be as bad as ever.

Beaverbrook therefore decided to announce his own policy. On 10 October 1949 he published an article in The Sunday Express for the first time since 1946. It contained all his old beliefs: Empire Free Trade, guaranteed prices for the farmer, a floating pound, abolition of a hereditary house of lords, and a foreign policy based on Anglo-American friendship. His most novel proposal was for industry: a £6 a week minimum wage, no limitation of dividends, and reduction of taxation. Prosperity in fact secured by a permanent boom. This programme was greeted with deafening silence. The Conservatives including Churchill repudiated the minimum wage. Beaverbrook did not lead a new crusade.

There is little to record about Beaverbrook's newspapers in 1949. A few lively entries are nearly all that they offer. To William Barkley: "Be bad-tempered but never cynical". To Robertson:

> Can you, Mr. Robertson, help me to weed out that old bad habit, the survival of journalism of days gone by; that desire of critics to display themselves in favourable light in relation to many persons by mentioning their names. Help me, Mr. Robertson, help me.

And to Charles Wintour who had sent a message on Evening Standard headed paper, though trying to minimize his offence by typing his message on the reverse side: "Don't waste valuable letter paper". This was always an obsession with Beaverbrook. His secretaries used flimsy paper, and his newspapers kept special stocks of used envelopes for forwarding material to him. He protested against every lapse and wrote to the New York office some years later:

> The extent to which you make use of new envelopes in sending me old material is a distressing experience.
>
> I suggest that you use old envelopes and send me new material. Economy should be practised. It is always essential.

There was one exception to this rule. When at Fredericton, Beaverbrook's correspondence, including the copy, was on thick elegant paper. An explanation meets the eye. The paper, though headed Lord Beaverbrook, came from the hotel.

The gravest event for the newspapers in 1949 was the resignation of David Low who had supplied The Evening Standard with incomparable cartoons for more than twenty years. Low was distressed when the restrictions on newsprint cut down his space. More seriously he felt that he was getting stale and wrote to Beaverbrook on 2 December: "The Oldest Inhabitant will inevitably decline into dullness and boredom". There was no quarrel or estrangement. Indeed Beaverbrook was greatly distressed. He headed his answer to Low, Black Friday, and wrote: "Your letter is a disaster. It is unnecessary and inadvisable". However Low insisted on moving to The Daily Herald. He did not recover his inspiration. Perhaps he was unhappy in his new surroundings. Or perhaps the political world of the day no longer suited his genius. The Evening Standard, after some other experiments, found a worthy successor to Low in Vicky, whose cartoons, too, drew uninterrupted commendation from Beaverbrook.

On 15 September 1949 Stanley Morison renewed the acquaintance which he had begun on the Queen Mary the previous year. He wrote: "I am the 'clergyman' with whom you discussed very various and amusing matters on the deck of the Queen Mary last year", and he went on to ask for details of Beaverbrook's correspondence with Northcliffe. Beaverbrook answered with a four-page summary of this correspondence. Morison asked further questions about the sale of The Times after Northcliffe's death. Beaverbrook sent another long account, based on information he had received from Rothermere. In conversation Morison let slip that Lloyd George had left a large collection of political papers, which Lady Lloyd-George, to whom they had been bequeathed, had made available to him and which she might perhaps sell to The Times.

Beaverbrook made no comment. But he acted without delay. He already owned the papers of Bonar Law which had been bequeathed to him as literary executor. He announced his intention of presenting these papers to the University of New Brunswick. Now he had another use for them. The talks and correspondence with Stanley Morison had reawakened his historical interests, and he resolved to promote a biography of Law and of Lloyd George as well. There was already an official life of Lloyd George by Malcolm Thomson, one of his secretaries, which had been brought out with Lady Lloyd-George's encouragement soon after Lloyd George's death.[1] It had used none of the confidential papers and Lady Lloyd-George was eager to cooperate in the production of a more searching volume. After some discussion the simplest course seemed to be for Beaverbrook to buy her entire Lloyd George material, which he did for the sum of £15,000. With this he came into untrammelled possession of what is probably the richest single stock of twentieth-century British political papers, and that in the period which Beaverbrook had already made his own.

[1] This Malcolm Thomson, who had been one of Lloyd George's secretaries for many years, was no relation of Beaverbrook's political secretary George Malcolm Thomson.

The writing of the biographies took longer to settle. Bonar Law's only surviving son Richard, later Lord Coleraine, had long intended to write his father's life, but after some reflection now withdrew. Beaverbrook's next idea was that Robert Sherwood, the American dramatist, who had just published the papers of Harry Hopkins, should write a combined biography of Lloyd George and Law. Sherwood, after considerable discussion, also declined. His principal motive was an unwillingness to settle in England for a long period, and maybe he had had enough with one biography. All this took time, and Beaverbrook's historical work did not move much during 1950 except for some further correspondence about the circumstances of Lloyd George's fall. He wrote to Morison on 6 June:

> I think you are producing a best seller. There is nothing on Northcliffe's character approaching the account you give.
> I think you are just to him, and if anything generous.
> You do not tell us enough about George.
> I mean about George's character and his accomplishments and achievements in office.
> In gratitude for four chapters I send you four bottles.

In other ways, too, Beaverbrook's life did not move much during 1950. When the general election was fixed for February, he was in Nassau and was reluctant to return: "I should have to go against Winston Churchill". Robertson answered: "All recognize the advantage of having you on the bridge", and Beaverbrook came back. This brought little advantage. Beaverbrook's papers attacked Labour without showing much enthusiasm for the Tories, and Beaverbrook wrote to his old Norfolk friend J. F. Wright, on 11 February:

> The Tories will not do much for the Empire unless they are driven to it. Salisbury, Stanley and Butler are all at heart free traders. Eden is a weak fellow who is dragged back and forward by his Soviet.
> Remember what you and I have been through in the years of wickedness when the Tories could have given us our policy, and instead they cheated us.

Labour won the election, though with a majority of only six. Beaverbrook returned with relief to Nassau.

One miscellaneous item of 1950 is worth recording for its idiosyncrasy. The editor of The Jamaica Gleaner had boasted that there were no Roman Catholics on his board. Beaverbrook replied:

> I am sorry that The Gleaner board is not dominated by the Roman Catholics. I would rather see the influence of this religion in any newspaper office except, of course, for the Presbyterians. But if I can't have the hard teachings of Presbyterians then I wish to turn to the rigid beliefs of the Roman Catholic church.

Another letter shows that Beaverbrook had lost none of his old cunning in apologizing for something that appeared in his newspapers, or rather in not apologizing while appearing to do so. Sir Richard Fairey, once of MAP, complained of a paragraph in The Evening Standard, which implied among other things that business affairs were discussed at his house during social weekends. Beaverbrook replied on 2 June:

> If your house is given over to discussion of business affairs at all times, early and late, what a good thing it is for the country.
>
> And what a happy situation it was in 1940 when we found that you could be made to give all your waking time, not only to talking about the business of the country, but in acting also.
>
> Without your help, and without your guidance during those early days, I do not know what troubles the aircraft ministry would have encountered in addition to the many obstacles over which we stumbled.
>
> . . . .
>
> Any time that you are offended by anything in the Daily Express there is sure to be a profound and heartfelt apology.
>
> But what dispositions we can make in order to satisfy your desires I am not quite sure. My own view would be that the situation would best be served by leaving it alone and saying and thinking no more about it.
>
> Do you approve of that?
>
> We meet seldom, but always under such agreeable conditions that I think we should arrange to come together more frequently.
>
> Do you recall the occasion when we set out from Bermuda in the aeroplane. Just you and me. . . . We passed through the Valley of the Shadow of Death that afternoon. You knew quite well into what dangerous conditions we had fallen. But there was no sign of it in your conduct and bearing.

Sir Richard Fairey let the matter drop.

And here is Beaverbrook dealing with a dissatisfied contributor. J. P. W. Mallalieu complained that a review of his on Pitt and Fox had not been published. Beaverbrook answered on 19 July with a skilful historical diversion:

> You do not take account of the most interesting of all these figures, Henry Fox.
>
> He was probably a better speaker than Charles James. He certainly excelled him in conversation. He was the most brilliant wit of his time. And while he was faithful to his wife, he was faithless in every other thing.
>
> He left the Treasury Bench because he put through the unpopular "Peace at a Price". Namely, a peerage and a five year period of freedom in dealing with the funds of the Treasury Chest.
>
> The King cheated him out of the Treasury Chest plunder. And his son bamboozled the public into believing that he was Henry Fox's greater son.
>
> They were all rascals without political principles in those days.

When Henry Fox lay dying, one of his colleagues who was fond of attending funerals, called at Holland House.

"Show him up", said the old politician. "If I am alive, I'll be glad to see him. If I am dead, he'll be glad to see me".

Why don't you write a life of Henry Fox?

Mallalieu, too, was mollified.

In 1951 Beaverbrook's literary plans began to mature. Robert Blake, who had just edited Haig's diaries, was enlisted to write the life of Bonar Law, and Beaverbrook was soon announcing that the book would be "among the best biographies of the half century". With Lloyd George Beaverbrook intended to play the part of ghost, providing inspiration by absentee control as he did with his newspapers. He therefore needed a congenial journalist, not a historian, and commissioned Frank Owen, formerly editor of The Evening Standard and himself a Radical follower of Lloyd George's in the parliament of 1929 to 1931. Lady Lloyd-George undertook much of the research and provided many of the ideas. It was a harassing experience for any writer to work under the direction of two such powerful ghosts, and Frank Owen almost succumbed under it.

Frank Owen had been one of Beaverbrook's "young eagles" before the war, and Beaverbrook was glad to be working with him again. Another reconciliation brought even more pleasure. There had been considerable coolness, though not hostility, between Beaverbrook and Michael Foot, in the days when Foot, as a pugnacious Socialist MP, was attacking the great newspaper proprietors and campaigning for a royal commission on the press. In 1951 Foot turned to Beaverbrook for help. Tribune, the leftwing weekly which Foot directed, was in financial difficulties. It had lost one patron, Sir Stafford Cripps, could not find another, and was on the point of extinction. Beaverbrook gave Tribune £3,000, which he charged to The Daily Express. When Robertson objected, Beaverbrook replied: "Where should we get our recruits without Tribune?", and any one who studies the names of the prominent writers on Beaverbrook newspapers will know what he meant. From this moment the friendship between Beaverbrook and Michael Foot flourished more intimately than before. Foot took a cottage on the Cherkley estate and was the closest of neighbours in every sense until Beaverbrook's death.[1]

I told Beaverbrook one day that Michael had been educated at Leighton Park, the snob Quaker public school, and I at Bootham, the non-snob one.

---

[1] My rule in writing this book has been Beaverbrook's own: publish everything good and bad. But every rule has its exception and mine, which I know Beaverbrook would have approved, was: Nothing to hurt Michael. I therefore asked his permission to publish the story. He replied: "The transaction was creditable to Max, and most convenient to me: at that moment it saved Tribune from extinction. . . . And you can publish the sentences above, if you wish."

Beaverbrook was delighted with this and said: "You and I are sons of the people. Michael is an aristocrat".

Exchanges with Stanley Morison went on ever more intensively. Beaverbrook provided further information about Northcliffe's attempts to dictate policy during the first world war. He also read Morison's proofs on the abdication crisis, and these so excited him that he wrote an account of his own part in the crisis—the first of his later historical works. Beaverbrook intended to publish this early in 1952. Then the death of King George VI led him to put it off, and the book was not published during his lifetime.[1]

There was another less pleasant exchange with Morison. He had taken extensive quotations from the Lloyd George papers when they were still in Lady Lloyd-George's possession and had not received formal permission. When he submitted his proofs, he received a stern letter from Tom Blackburn, who handled Beaverbrook's historical business, that while he could consult the Lloyd George papers in order to check the accuracy of his own information, he could not quote from them. Morison was in despair. He had shown his proofs to Beaverbrook in the previous year, and Beaverbrook had made no complaint. Morison felt that it must all be a misunderstanding. He wrote to Beaverbrook on 24 July:

> I simply canNOT believe that you mean what Blackburn writes. . . .
> But poor Blackburn is no more to blame than poor me. He simply did not
> know because he was not told; and it was certainly not my place to tell him.

Beaverbrook groaned: "Ah, Mr. Blackburn is a hard man". But there was no relenting. Some 10,000 sheets of The Times history which had been printed had to be cancelled. Much, though not all, of the Lloyd George material was taken out. Beaverbrook also insisted, through Blackburn, that, while there could be a statement that some of the information about Northcliffe came from his own records, there must be no acknowledgement that he himself had provided information or help.

This was a characteristically Puckish prank. Beaverbrook was the most generous of men, but if someone, even a close friend like Morison, slipped, Beaverbrook chuckled at the thought of tripping him up. He might have taken a different line if Morison had been writing the book in his own name. But this was an official publication by The Times, and Beaverbrook was not sorry to embarrass that staid newspaper. Also, like other lone operators, he overrated the importance of original documents and believed that they lost much of their value if they were published elsewhere. Hence he hoarded the Lloyd George papers throughout his lifetime and refused access even to the most qualified enquiries. However the trouble

---

[1] I resurrected it, and it was published as The Abdication of King Edward VIII in 1966.

Morison had with Beaverbrook was nothing to what I had with Randolph Churchill when I proposed a pooling of our Churchill and Beaverbrook resources. It is agreeable to record that Morison bore no resentment and was indeed highly amused at the trick Beaverbrook played on him.

The refusal to take responsibility for anything in Morison's book was also characteristic. If Beaverbrook published a story himself, he took good care to have solid evidence for it and of course stood by it. If others used one of his stories, that was their affair, and he expected them to look after themselves. The others did not always appreciate this, and Robert Blake was to encounter an unexpected storm. But Beaverbrook's attitude was really quite reasonable. He had battles enough of his own, into which he went well prepared, and could not be expected to fight others' battles for them.

In January 1951 Beaverbrook's son Max married again. His previous marriages had been dissolved, and the Church of Scotland in London would not perform the ceremony. Beaverbrook was indignant at this departure from Presbyterian doctrine and was not impressed by the explanation that the Church of Scotland, having lost its own building during the war and being temporarily housed by the Church of England, had agreed to observe the Anglican ban on the marriage of divorced persons. However Max married at a Presbyterian church in Jamaica, and all was well. Beaverbrook transferred the Cherkley estate to Max on the occasion of the wedding and henceforth paid a rent for the house, thus strengthening his claim not to be domiciled in England. Also Beaverbrook, though rigid in his finances, believed in reducing his tax liability by all legal means, and the transfer of Cherkley was a first step in reducing the future death duties on his estate.[1]

All these activities were eclipsed by the affair of the American Express traveller's cheques, if we are to judge from the bulk of correspondence. This was an episode of no conceivable importance except for its illustration of Beaverbrook's ways. When out of England Beaverbrook relied for his ready money on American Express cheques in Canadian dollars. He paid a commission of $1\frac{1}{2}\%$ on buying them. When he changed them into Canadian or even American dollars, he paid no further commission. But on changing them into French francs at the American Express office in Nice he was charged $\frac{1}{2}\%$. He expostulated. The clerk replied that this was normal practice. On the next occasion Beaverbrook expostulated to the manager, who explained that it was the universal practice of French banks and that American Express must conform to it. Beaverbrook was not satisfied. He complained to the London office, which made a false

---

[1] In 1962 Max Aitken donated the house and grounds to the Beaverbrook Foundation, and Beaverbrook occupied it from then until his death on a "grace and favour" basis.

move. As a favour it refunded the sum involved, £5. 13. This produced a demand for the refund of earlier charges and of course renewed expostulations when the commission was charged on the next occasion. This time Beaverbrook wrote to the head office of American Express in New York. American Express refused to yield. Beaverbrook decreed that no employee of his newspapers should travel with American Express cheques. He wished to attack American Express in The Evening Standard, though for once his wish did not prevail. George Millar tried to explain that the American Express charge was justified. Robertson argued that the fuss was not worthwhile. It was of no avail. Beaverbrook continued to protest and did not lift the ban on American Express for some years. This was one battle which he did not win.

In politics 1951 brought Beaverbrook one piece of cheer. Bevin left the foreign office, and Herbert Morrison, one of the few Labour leaders whom Beaverbrook admired, took his place. Beaverbrook was delighted. He wrote to Morrison on 3 March: "I feel sure you will be blessed by the whole nation as well as by the British races over the seas". And to Senator Davies on 17 April:

> Bevin's career at the Foreign Office was a complete and absolute failure. He began by being hostile to Russia and he did a great deal to stir up the present situation, which appears to be such a hopeless muddle. . . .
> Morrison I predict will be a good Foreign Minister. I think he will show a capacity for negotiation which will lead us to happier days.

Beaverbrook's estimate of Bevin's work may have been justified. His expectations about Morrison were not fulfilled. As often, friendship clouded Beaverbrook's judgement.

In any case the days of the Labour government were numbered. There was another general election in October, and Labour was defeated by a narrow margin. Beaverbrook remained in England for the election and apparently advised Churchill, if only in the sense of listening to whatever Churchill was saying. But he was still out of line with Conservative policy. His own contribution was an attack on purchase taxes, an idea which produced no response. He wrote to Max Gordon on 8 October:

> I think the Conservatives will get a majority of 100. I am advocating taxation of capital gains. The Daily Express has launched an attack on purchase taxes. They are very foolish taxes which bear very heavily on poor people. In fact, they are applied to rich and poor alike, which is not the right way to impose taxation any way.

Beaverbrook proclaimed his lack of faith in the Conservatives more openly. For many years the Empire Crusader had headed the front page of The Daily Express. On 15 October 1951 the Crusader appeared in chains and so remained for the rest of Beaverbrook's life. About this time also Beaverbrook allowed his subscription to the Epsom branch of the Conservative party to lapse. He continued to send £100 a year to the Ashton-under-Lyne branch, but this was a gesture of sentiment, not of party loyalty.

The Conservatives won the general election, though with a majority of 16, not of 100. Churchill became prime minister. Beaverbrook departed for Jamaica. Kenneth Young conjectures[1] that Beaverbrook was hurt at not being offered a place in the government. This is most unlikely. It had been difficult enough to keep him in the government even in wartime, and he had always declared that he would never take on the burdens of office again. Besides he distrusted Churchill's policy however much he loved the man. An instruction to Christiansen on 1 January 1952, when Churchill was about to visit Washington, shows Beaverbrook's waverings:

> Replying to your request for guidance. The old firm is in business again. Churchill Eden Ismay and Cherwell if I remember rightly represented Britain at Yalta. Perhaps that is why we have a meeting at Washington at this time. I advise you do not overlay Churchill during negotiations. Thereafter if necessary declare John Bull is grown up and should not be bottlefed. If any pledges limiting Imperial Preference secret or otherwise I recommend fight all out.

On 14 February 1952 Beaverbrook wrote to W. J. Brittain:

> I tell you privately, that I have given up hope of a consolidated Empire.
> When you and I worked on the project, the Dominions wanted it. Now they are afraid of Britain. In the Colonies there was respect for British leadership. That has passed away.
> If the great Churchill happened to be an Empire man, a struggle for regeneration of Empire ties might be possible.
> He does not believe in the economic structure.
> It is seldom that a man of my kind resigns himself to defeat.

Beaverbrook had even less faith in Churchill's predestined successor. He wrote to Beverley Baxter on 18 March:

> Eden would make a very terrible Prime Minister. The Conservative Party would never recover from him. He is no Mr. Baldwin. Mr. Baldwin was a cunning man. Mr. Eden is not cunning. But over everything Mr. Baldwin had an element of common sense, harnessed with cunning, which made him a master of most persons. Mr. Eden is lacking in cunning, the common sense and the mastery.

Thus detached from politics, Beaverbrook found plenty of other things to occupy him. He developed plans to launch evening newspapers in Manchester and Birmingham. These plans were delayed by the restrictions on newsprint and then broke on the opposition of the unions. They were never carried out. Another project was more surprising. The News

[1] Young, Churchill and Beaverbrook, 291.

Chronicle was in financial difficulties, which ultimately killed it. Beaver-brook approached Layton, the managing director, and offered to buy both The News Chronicle and The Star. He wrote to Layton on 24 August: "Policy and production of news pages would be your responsibility. Business side would rest with me. It would be a community of interest for business and management only", and he added: "The greatest asset of The News Chronicle is the non-conformist public". Later, in 1955, Beaverbrook told Bracken:

> I told Layton I would join him in buying the News Chronicle at a reason-able price. He may direct the policy of the paper and take full credit for it. I will put in an editor and also Tom Blackburn to manage it.

Nothing came of this offer which might have saved The News Chronicle from extinction.

This did not exhaust Beaverbrook's ambitions. It is often said that he would have nothing to do with television, and he himself wrote to Christiansen on 12 March 1959:

> The reason why I have always opposed association with television is that we are newspaper men.
> If we divert our activities, we will undoubtedly damage our newspapers.

In fact, when commercial television was first aired, Beaverbrook was at once in the field. It was not clear at this time how the new system would work, and it seems to have been assumed that there would be a number of stations covering the same area, with different newspapers each giving a channel its particular character. No doubt Beaverbrook supposed that the staff of his newspapers could take on a television station as an extra assign-ment, just as he had expected the staff of The Daily Express to take on The Sunday Express also in December 1918. At any rate he applied for a television station first in London and, when this was turned down, in Glasgow. It gradually emerged that, while newspapers would be allowed to invest in a television station, they would not be allowed to determine its character. At this Beaverbrook lost interest and was soon declaring that he never had any.

Yet this was the year when he himself became a great television per-former. Morison's History of The Times was at last finished, and Beaver-brook was eager to talk about it. The BBC were willing, but they wanted Beaverbrook to be interviewed. Beaverbrook refused with his favourite phrase: I am the cat that walks alone. Television pundits believed that no man could stand in front of the cameras and hold the viewers' attention without adventitious aids. Beaverbrook insisted and was once more a pioneer. He simply stood at his lectern and delivered a television rhapsody on Northcliffe. When speaking of newspaper circulation, he roared: "I hold one fifth of the newspaper market, but (pause) Northcliffe held one *half*", and he shook the lectern in simulated rage. Morison's letter of congratulation was the best tribute:

My dear Beaver*cliffe*

Oh! Oh!! What a show!!! And how perfect you were. John Walter and all here praised you to the skies & even forgave S.M. all his sins of cooperating with personal publicity and all that. By universal consent you have now started a new career for yourself. And how jealous the Tories will be.

Above all, how N would have loved and approved you; as I do.

The comment by A. J. Cummings in The News Chronicle is also worth quoting, since Cummings was an independent journalist who shared none of Beaverbrook's political beliefs. Cummings wrote:

As I listened to Lord Beaverbrook's intimate talk about Northcliffe there occurred to me one vital point of difference in the character of these two newspaper magnates.

One couldn't "take it"; the other can.

In his rising megalomania, a political rebuff filled Northcliffe with a personal fury that deprived him of rational judgment.

Beaverbrook, too, has had his political rebuffs and disappointments. But I have never known him lose his temper or his sense of human relationships. He does not bear malice, as Northcliffe did. Rarely, if ever, does he conceal his admiration for an opponent who gets the better of the argument.

Not a common virtue in political controversy.

There was one alarm before the performance. Beaverbrook wished to show a picture of Stanley Morison, the former Communist, inspecting Karl Marx's grave. Morison wrote:

I AM MOST ALARMED.

About the Karl Marx idea.

Brilliant for you, but death for me.

The Times tell me that it would do them and me a lot of damage. As you know they don't like personal publicity of any kind. And this is a very bad kind.

Beaverbrook would not relent. Nor had he done with The History of The Times or with Morison at Marx's grave. He had more to say than he could get into 20 minutes, which is all the BBC had allowed him. He composed a further broadcast, this time for sound alone, and delivered it on his birthday, 25 May. After a preliminary tribute to Lloyd George, he plunged into the abdication crisis which Morison had covered in an appendix. With considerable ingenuity, Beaverbrook revealed that Geoffrey Dawson, then editor of The Times—Dasson, as Beaverbrook called him—was the villain of the piece. Morison did not agree. He wrote:

A journalist can pay too high a price for his information. In this case G.D. was on the side of Baldwin so completely and B. was so subtle that G.D. had virtually lost his independence. It was a masterstroke of Baldwin & Lang to use *T.T.* as they did. I agree that things would have been v. different if the paper had taken an independent line—against Baldwin & Lang.

Query—what would Northcliffe have done? Suppose *T.T. D. Mail*, *Evg News* had all challenged Baldwin? with Northcliffe ruling all. Wd he have become king? or king-president?

Morison often had wild ideas. Beaverbrook's broadcast produced an uproar from the old establishment. Wickham Steed and even the bishop of Bradford were mobilized. Beaverbrook defended himself in a glossy pamphlet, enriched with illustrations. Among these the photograph of Morison at Marx's grave received pride of place. Some two hundred copies of the pamphlet were privately circulated. Then, for some reason, Beaverbrook decided not to publish it, perhaps because it cut across his book on the abdication. He tacked on to this book his attack on Dawson and laid the whole aside.

Morison made a further gesture of appreciation. In September he presented Beaverbrook with the 1560 folio edition of Calvin's Institutes in French. He added this esoteric piece of typographical lore:

> Calvin was a great man. Have you ever reflected that but for Calvin and Knox, the Daily Express would be printed in black letter throughout?

This remark was beyond Beaverbrook, as it is beyond me.[1] He was content to reply:

> Calvin's splendour shines out through the years. And were it not for John Knox, then the vision would be much brighter and the fame far greater.

The folio itself was dispatched to the University of New Brunswick.

Frank Owen and Robert Blake were now at work on the two biographies which Beaverbrook had commissioned. Beaverbrook soon grew impatient. He seemed to think that a book, once commissioned, should come out like a newspaper next day or at any rate by the end of the week. Blackburn was repeatedly instructed "to put on the pressure" and duly did so. Blake was an independent scholar. He listened to Beaverbrook's anecdotes, accepted some of them—perhaps one too many—and then withdrew into the country to write at his own speed. Owen was more vulnerable. He was working in Fleet Street on a salary with Blackburn at his elbow and Soundscriber messages pouring in. Though without previous experience as a historian, he was expected to keep a schedule of so many thousand words a week.

Beaverbrook himself was reliving the Lloyd George period with intense

---

[1] I have recently been given the explanation by a typographical expert. Until the Reformation all printing was in Gothic "black letter". Calvin and Knox, wishing to reach a mass readership, went over to clear Roman type, and the Counter-Reformation followed their example for the same reason. Calvinist influence was strong enough in England to secure the victory of Roman. Lutheran Germany, being less affected by either Calvinism or the Counter-Reformation, retained black letter until the present century.

excitement. His messages, though perhaps not helpful to Owen, reveal what was simmering in his mind. They also give some idea of what his talk was like when he was stirred up about the past. I give one characteristic outburst:

If ever there was opportunity Mr. Frank Owen to pump water out of a well or to get water from a fountain I offer you that opportunity. But I am growing old. I can't be expected to sit round here raking up the dead past. If I am properly primed and if I am made to talk then the recollections come out naturally.

... What a rascal Haig was. One of the biggest rascals in a long time. Twisting turning conspiring against French, pushing him out, conniving with the King. Oh he is a disgraceful story. All told in his diaries.

I was in France Mr. Owen. I was driving along in my Rolls Royce and I had to pull off what is called the pavé in order to make room for a cavalcade moving down the centre of the road, with outriders and after riders and in the middle Haig who wasn't even Commander in Chief then riding about on his horse—what a way to conduct a war. A war that had become a petrol war by that time.

The man was riding along the pavé like as though he was a King of ancient times conducting a war in the 14th Century or the 15th or 16th Century.

The stuff that Haig tells about drunken Asquith must drive Lady Violet Bonham-Carter into a fury. Old Asquith has all my love but he also had all the brandy according to Haig.

Mr. Owen, there are far too many figures in your chapter, far too many statistics; in part you make it a statistical narrative. You can't stand all those figures; the public can't stand them either; nobody will want to read them.

While these works were in the making, Beaverbrook was himself threatened with a biography. Alan Wood, who had been briefly a leader-writer on The Daily Express, compiled this mainly from press cuttings. He certainly did not use Beaverbrook's own archives. Wood had previously written a novel, Herbert, with a portrait of a press lord sufficiently like Beaverbrook to be highly libellous. At first Beaverbrook affected not to care and merely remarked: "He wrote a novel about me. No doubt he is now writing another". Beaverbrook was then stirred into action by the life of Baldwin which G. M. Young had just completed. This contained some grotesquely inaccurate statements about Beaverbrook, for example that he had been in favour of war at the time of the Chanak crisis. Beaverbrook secured the removal of these statements from the proof, and the publishers were warned: "There is no mood to overlook the publication of offending matter".

At this, the publishers of Alan Wood's book took alarm and refused to publish it. Wood laid the book aside, no doubt intending to publish it after Beaverbrook's death. However he died first, in 1957, and it was published incomplete in 1965 with a postscript by Blumenfeld's son, Sir

John Elliot. As a matter of fact, Wood's book was by no means unfriendly. In particular Wood brought out the Radical side of Beaverbrook's character, though he went too far when he suggested that Beaverbrook would have been happier in the Labour party.

Soon after this, another publisher suggested to Tom Driberg that he should write a biography of Beaverbrook. Driberg was keen; Beaverbrook was willing on condition that the book should be an entirely independent work. Driberg was told that he would have a free hand. Beaverbrook wrote to him on 3 December:

> The late Lord Northcliffe would not print anything in criticism of himself. He would always print the words of praise. Even from the publicity point of view, he was wrong.
> I regret to say that there is real advantage in attack. A newspaper is helped on that account. But I must not misrepresent my own views. I am not printing attacks for the purpose of furthering the publicity of the Express. My attitude, briefly stated, is that I can give it and I can take it.

Thus encouraged, Driberg went ahead. In Canada, Wardell was sent round New Brunswick, collecting anecdotes from old people about Beaverbrook's early life. When Driberg produced the first four or five chapters, Beaverbrook was delighted and bought the serial rights for £4,000. Then he said: "*Now* you'll have to attack me much more fiercely!". Beaverbrook was thus inspiring three biographies—Lloyd George's, Bonar Law's and his own. Admirable enterprises, but he was also beginning to regret that he was not writing the books himself.

Some minor items conclude the record for 1952. At Easter Beaverbrook was at La Capponcina with E. J. Robertson and was visited by Viscount Jowitt, who had been lord chancellor in the Labour government. Beaverbrook made this record which has considerable historical interest:

> Lord Jowitt told us that the Law Lords had been divided on the Lord Haw Haw case.[1]

[1] Lord Haw Haw was the nickname of William Joyce who broadcast from a German station during the second world war. Joyce was born in New York. His father was a naturalized American citizen. Joyce never acquired British nationality, though he spent most of his life in England. In 1938 he applied for and obtained a British passport, stating falsely that he was a British subject. In August 1939 he renewed this passport for one year and went to Germany. In September 1940 he became a naturalized German. As Joyce had never been a British subject, he seemed secure from a charge of high treason. However it was argued that he had sought the protection of the Crown by acquiring a British passport and therefore owed allegiance while he retained it. No evidence was produced that he had used the passport once he was in Germany or that he had broadcast for the Germans during the period of its validity. Joyce was convicted and sentenced to death. He appealed to the house of lords which dismissed his appeal. Joyce was hanged without being informed of the grounds on which his appeal had been dismissed.

He said two were for acquittal (Lords Macmillan and Porter) and two for conviction (Lords Wright and Simonds) while he held the balance.

He said that he was for conviction but, of course, there were difficulties as the prisoner had made a considerable case in favour of American citizenship.

Jowitt said that when the disagreement took place he invited his colleagues to join him in his private room and there they carried on an intimate conversation.

The upshot was that Lord Macmillan changed his mind but Lord Porter remained firm.

The decision was taken to hang the prisoner.

Lord Jowitt in his conversation with Robertson and me indicated that he had doubts about the verdict—as he recognized there was a good case for alleging American citizenship.

When I remarked that public opinion would have been outraged by a verdict of not guilty, Jowitt responded that of course public opinion had to be taken into account.

Jowitt appeared to indicate that Lord Porter's unwillingness to bring in a verdict of guilty was based on the fact that there was no evidence that Haw Haw had ever used his British passport, although he had secured one.

The next item is of a more agreeable nature. Beaverbrook's farms in Somerset had a good year and his cattle won many prizes. Boasting of this to Sir Patrick Hennessy, once of MAP and now head of the English Ford company, Beaverbrook added: "as for tractors, my Somerset farms have so many that I am thinking of setting up as an independent Ford Dealer". Hennessy, much impressed, went to "count these legions" and found there was not one. This was an innocent piece of flattery which miscarried.

Finally a rather pathetic entry. Though Beaverbrook was "Max" to innumerable friends, he remained "Lord Beaverbrook" to all the staff of his newspapers, however senior. Blumenfeld of course had used "Max", and Max Aitken wrote "My dear Boss". The other, including even Robertson who had been managing the papers for thirty years, never wavered from "Dear Lord Beaverbrook". With one employee Beaverbrook tried to change things. J. B. Wilson, the news editor, was the only journalist who had been on the paper before the young Max Aitken arrived in England. On 5 September Beaverbrook sent him good wishes and concluded: "And now I subscribe myself by my Christian name which I hope you will use". Wilson kept up "Max" for some six months and then relapsed into the old formality. Beaverbrook never tried again.

Beaverbrook saw Churchill occasionally when he was in England during the summer of 1952. The two, though now very friendly, were still far apart in politics. Beaverbrook viewed with alarm Churchill's attempts to draw closer to Europe. On 18 December 1952 he sent a message to Robertson from Jamaica:

> I can't see that there can be any way of avoiding an attack before very long. Something has got to be done about the bits of Empire Policy even if we only leave a glimmering of candle's light until some new situation arises where Britain .. will take up the cause once more and perhaps bring the sterling block into a united group for trading and financial purposes.
>
> . . . .
> I do not think we dare neglect the responsibility of leaving a glimmering light behind, and hope that one day there may be a new movement and a movement far more successful than our own which has been struggling for breath for some time. Like myself the movement has had asthma for years past.

Robertson tried to dissuade Beaverbrook. He replied on 6 January 1953:

> Sorely as we are tried by Mr. Churchill's attitude, it would be quite useless and quite wrong of us to resort to a personal attack which would endanger the much admired personal relationship which developed between him and you during the war and which, notwithstanding many stresses on either side, has endured ever since.
>
> As things stand, your names go into history securely linked as two men who did most to secure victory, and in our view no temporary exasperation should be allowed to spoil the picture. A personal attack would probably be more injurious to you than to him.

Beaverbrook seems to have accepted this advice, though no doubt reluctantly, and his paper attacked the move into Europe and the cold war without mentioning the prime minister. There was a deeper motive for this. Churchill had another stroke in June. Beaverbrook was soon at his bedside and in September lent him La Capponcina for a fortnight's holiday. Beneath the surface, Beaverbrook remained discontented. When the British troops were withdrawn from Bermuda, he wrote to Sir Richard Fairey on 2 March:

> What a scandal when a Conservative government sends troops to Germany and refuses to continue the small garrison in Bermuda!
>
> I wish Churchill knew what was going on. But he takes his dope from Anthony Eden and he is influenced by the opposition of Lord Salisbury who lives on a tradition of hatred for everything connected with the late, great Joseph Chamberlain.

On 7 April he composed, though he did not send, a letter attacking the support which the editor of The News Chronicle gave to the United Nations:

> Cruikshank gives us the old League of Nations Union racket all over again.

The columns of The News Chronicle were filled with such stuff and nonsense a quarter of a century ago.

The News Chronicle made Eden. Now they try to sustain him. No use.

Turn to the Empire, Cruikshank, turn to the Empire, Cruikshank, before it is too late.

These were trivial outbursts. Beaverbrook's messages to his papers this year rarely touched on politics. Thus, to Christiansen on 22 January:

I do hate this highbrow "criticism". We are not a highbrow paper, and we ought to have some regard to what the ordinary individual likes in the way of his music and his films.

Now sack me, Mr. Christiansen.

And a little later, in reference to the coronation:

It seems to me a form of idolatry.... And idolatry, Mr. Christiansen, is "Excess of attachment, or veneration of any person or thing". Mr. Christiansen that is the dictionary definition.

Beaverbrook was again in a mood of announcing his withdrawal from public affairs. In July The Evening Standard serialized Success, which was published as a book in the following year, and Beaverbrook introduced it with these words:

I have no regret for the past and no hope for the future. There have been pitfalls, of course. Frequently I have stumbled. Henceforward I do not intend to put grave issues to the test. Younger men must carry the lance and the breast-plate.

Similarly, when William Gerhardi offered an article entitled If I were Lord Beaverbrook, Beaverbrook wrote to him: "That fellow gets too much space in The Standard", and rejected the article. A message to Robertson of 28 May struck a very different note:

Mr. Robertson. I saw a very good acct in the Evg Std by Dick Law about my service for Bonar Law. It seems to me that it might have been reprinted in the DX and also in the SX. Or at any rate, similar statements.

I don't see why you miss opportunities of that sort to advance the fortunes of myself, considerg that I am so closely identified with the DX, and also tkg into acct the fact that no other newspaper will print it.

Robertson replied contritely:

I can assure you that our newspapers rarely miss an opportunity of printing personal publicity about you. So far in this month of May there have been 14 references to you in our three newspapers.

One piece of news about Beaverbrook bulked large though only in the Canadian newspapers. The president of the University of New Brunswick resigned, and it was necessary to appoint a successor. The normal practice was for the government of the province to make the appointment from a list put forward by the nominating committee of the university. In the spring of 1953 Hugh John Flemming, the prime minister of New Brunswick, was in England, and Beaverbrook suggested Colin Mackay, a young New Brunswick graduate who was now a lawyer in Halifax, as the next president. Beaverbrook also claims to have added that, as chancellor, he would support any candidate nominated by the government and the senate. He further told the nominating committee that, while he favoured Mackay, he would not put the name forward if the nominating committee were against it. Flemming, who was no doubt in more awe of the chancellor than he was of the university, told the nominating committee that it need not put forward any names, as the government had already made up their minds, and Mackay was appointed. The graduate assembly of the university protested at this disregard of constitutional procedure. Beaverbrook defended his conduct and announced that, since he had lost the confidence of the university, he resigned as chancellor. Here was a fine mess. The members of the university, though angry at being disregarded, had no wish to lose their beneficent chancellor. A complicated way out was found. An act of the New Brunswick legislature appointed Beaverbrook honorary chancellor for life, and he graciously accepted.[1] Since the appointment was honorary in any case, there was no difference, but appearances were saved. Beaverbrook, as so often, had taken a short cut. He imagined that he could appoint a university president just as he appointed a newspaper editor, and the event showed that he could. Mackay proved to be an energetic president, devoted to Beaverbrook's interests.

In 1954 Beaverbrook reached the age of 75. On his birthday, 600 of his employees entertained him to lunch. Once more he made the gesture of withdrawal, this time, from a legal point of view, more effectively. As a preliminary, the name of London Express Newspaper Limited was changed to the more appropriate Beaverbrook Newspapers, the name they still hold. Beaverbrook then transferred all his voting shares to the Beaverbrook Foundation which he set up.[2] The value of these shares was about £1,500,000, and they gave the Foundation 51% of the votes. Holdings by members of his family, principally his son Max and his daughter Janet, raised this control to 74%. The Foundation was to promote scholarships in New Brunswick to and from the United Kingdom;

---

[1] This was the occasion when he was described as "a native son of New Brunswick".
[2] There was at first some doubt whether, since Beaverbrook was to be chairman of the trustees, the settlement was effective for escaping death duties. Beaverbrook therefore transferred only 250,000 of his shares to the First Foundation. By the autumn the legal hurdles had been overcome, and Beaverbrook transferred his remaining 583,036 shares to a Second Foundation. The purposes and deeds of both trusts are identical.

to assist the Presbyterian Church of Scotland, England and Wales, and in New Brunswick; to build hospitals in the United Kingdom or New Brunswick; to buy books, manuscripts, works of art, etc., for libraries and galleries in New Brunswick; and to promote such other charitable purposes as the trustees might think fit—a clause which, after Beaverbrook's death, fortunately embraced the Beaverbrook Library. The trust deed also expressed the wish that the trustees should sustain "the Empire policy which has been advocated by the Settlor for many years". Subsequently Beaverbrook gave away his non-voting shares also—some to the Foundation, the rest to members of his family. He could truthfully announce: "I do not own a single share in the newspapers".

The financial purpose of the Beaverbrook Foundation was clearly to protect Beaverbrook Newspapers from the impact of death duties and to ensure that the policy and control of the newspapers remained unchanged. Beaverbrook was to be chairman for his lifetime and Max Aitken after him. In filling any vacancy the trustees were to ensure that "only persons who support the said Empire policy are appointed" and they were to consider "the suitability of any lineal descendant whether male or female of the Settlor . . . who in the opinion of the trustees supports the said Empire policy". Other newspapers, such as The Observer and The Guardian were protected by similar trusts. There was one striking difference. The Beaverbrook Foundation alone was essentially a charity. Its income went to the various charitable undertakings which Beaverbrook had promoted. It is ironical that the newspapers most dedicated to the virtues of capitalism and private enterprise are also the only ones in Great Britain the entire revenues of which are devoted to public welfare.

In theory establishment of the Beaverbrook Foundation also implied that Beaverbrook had relinquished control of his newspapers. The words, "controlling shareholder: Lord Beaverbrook", disappeared from the head of The Daily Express. The trustees met regularly at Arlington House, and Beaverbrook presided over their deliberations, which is more than he had ever done with the board of directors. In practice the abdication did not make a ha'p'orth of difference. The Foundation took over Beaverbrook's charities and ensured that they would continue after his death. Otherwise, as he wrote to Henry Luce: "I no longer control. I still dominate". Beaverbrook directed his newspapers in great things and small until the day before his death. He determined policy, dictated leaders, contributed Diary paragraphs, and criticized omissions. He appointed the members of the staff and fixed their salaries—usually pushing up the salaries against Robertson's protests. He scanned the balance sheets, complaining when the newspapers made too much money. He carped against top-quality letterpaper, staff cars and high expense accounts. The most senior men, including even Robertson, Blackburn and Max

Aitken, still asked his permission before being absent from the office for a single day. Beaverbrook complained if any of the top men were away even on a Saturday morning. Demanding Max Aitken, he would ask: "Where's the young squire? I suppose he is yachting (pronounced yatting)" and there followed inevitably: "Who is in charge of the clattering train?"[1]

Beaverbrook was fond of quoting Isaiah, xxi. 8: "I stand continually on the watch-tower in the daytime"—and at night-time also. Every writer in Beaverbrook newspapers was conscious of this scrutiny. Malcolm Muggeridge, who wrote many foolish and hostile things about Beaverbrook, made one true remark.[2] He recorded that one Express writer, when asked which section of the vast readership of the Beaverbrook newspapers he particularly aimed at in his articles, replied: "I write for one little old reader". This was the secret of the newspapers' success and always had been.

Beaverbrook took further steps towards tidying up his affairs against the event of his death. The annuities which he had granted to old friends and dependants in England amounted to over £20,000. As the seven-year covenants ran out, he transferred the obligations to Max and Janet, endowing each of them with the necessary capital sums. He also sold the Lloyd George papers to Beaverbrook Newspapers.[3] This was not all that the newspapers had to pay for Lloyd George's sake. Beaverbrook had a belief, which Robertson did not share, that the Lloyd George biography would arouse great interest and win many readers when serialized in The Sunday Express. The newspapers therefore should foot the bill. They not only paid £15,000 for the Lloyd George papers. They were also charged with Frank Owen's salary while he was writing it, Lady Lloyd-George's salary while she was researching, and the salaries of Beaverbrook's secretaries while he was making comments—a total of £42,000. The newspapers recovered £10,000 in royalties. The book, when serialized, did not put on sales.

The Lloyd George biography renewed Beaverbrook's contacts with Churchill. Beaverbrook wanted permission to print some of Churchill's

[1] Beaverbrook's quotation was not quite accurate. The poem goes:
> Who is in charge of the rattling train?
> The axles scream and the couplings strain
> And the pace is hot and the points are near
> And sleep has deadened the driver's ear,
> And the signals flash through the night in vain
> For death is in charge of the rattling train.

[2] New Statesman, 24 December 1955.
[3] In 1970 Beaverbrook Newspapers sold the Lloyd George papers to the first Beaverbrook Foundation.

letters to Lloyd George. Churchill was reluctant. Like his son, he never liked parting with his precious papers. He raised particular objection against a letter of December 1911 about female suffrage because it might lose him the women's votes and against another of September 1919, defending intervention in Russia, which would cut across his attempts at reconciliation with Stalin's successors. Beaverbrook lost patience and told Frank Owen to cut out most of Churchill's letters. Churchill added a political note on 30 March:

> I grieve that you continue to oppose so violently the rearmament, under proper limits, of Western Germany. It is going to happen any way and it is better to have them on our side than against us.

Beaverbrook did not reply. His newspapers continued to oppose German rearmament. Churchill's retirement was supposed to be imminent. Beaverbrook reflected on his successor and on the successor to his successor as well. He wrote to Malcolm Muir on 9 September:

> It is widely assumed that Eden will be the next Conservative Prime Minister and Macmillan his Foreign Secretary. Always remembering that when a man becomes Prime Minister he sometimes surprises his friends, it may be agreed that Macmillan could make a strong claim to the post.

Beaverbrook's forecast was to be fulfilled, though not in the way that he expected.

He knew that he would not be consulted. Gone for ever were the days when he was the kingmaker. The Empire cause in which he believed seemed to have perished also. When he left for Canada in October 1954, he announced in The Daily Express:

> I go in gloom and sorrow. The Empire is now being liquidated and the British people don't care.

In December he informed the shareholders of Beaverbrook Newspapers that the joy of commercial success had turned to ashes:

> Miserable and wretched Governments—Liberal, Socialist and Tory— have brought us to a disintegrating Empire with a ruthless liquidation of Imperial interests. And at the very moment of our degradation, our country is involved in disastrous commitments in Europe, separating us from the Dominions and divorcing us from the joint obligations we formerly shared with the United States of America.
>
> Britain is committed to this foolish venture for nearly half a century. U.S.A. is free to determine its obligations in Europe almost without notice.
> Our cause has failed.

Thus detached from politics, Beaverbrook found an outlet for his energy in literary affairs. He started a book-publishing department of

Beaverbrook Newspapers, which brought out among other things an admirable series of illustrated works on art. He wrote surprisingly to Blackburn: "I have always wished we had a magazine like the T.L.S."—a highbrow ambition out of his usual character. Still more surprisingly he proposed to launch an intellectual quarterly devoted to the ideas of the Reformation, and especially those of Calvin and Knox, with Morison to edit it at a salary of £100 a month. Since Morison was a rigid Roman Catholic, the result would have been curious, to say the least. The project got as far as a contract drafted by Morison and then vanished from sight.

The books which Beaverbrook had inspired were now all on the point of publication. Frank Owen's came out in 1954, Blake's in 1955, Driberg's in 1956. All proved disappointing to Beaverbrook for different reasons. Frank Owen's life of Lloyd George was a rush job, written by one who had no previous experience of historical work and only scratching the surface of the vast Lloyd George material. A satisfactory life of Lloyd George remains to be written. Blake's book was a first-rate production, which has stood the test of time as the standard work on its subject. But it failed to do what Beaverbrook wanted. He would have liked more drama—with a short "a", particularly over the story of Baldwin's succession to Bonar Law, which Blake revealed for the first time. Beaverbrook had hoped that Blake would do what he himself had never quite accomplished and show Bonar Law as a great dramatic personality. Instead, at the end of Blake's book, Bonar Law was till The Unknown Prime Minister.

Also there was the tiresome affair of Asquith's bridge game.[1] Beaverbrook advised Blake not to reply to Lady Violet Bonham Carter: "He rejected my advice. Thereafter her ladyship spent more time and effort in pulling him down than he could give to building up the story".[2] Eventually Beaverbrook was drawn in, much to his discontent. Asquith's champions made much play with the fact that the visitors' book at The Wharf, his country home, had the names of only two ladies during the critical weekend. Therefore he could not have been playing bridge with three ladies. Beaverbrook put his mind back and managed to recall what Law had told him: one of the three was Lady Tree, whose name was not in the visitors' book. A brief letter announced this in The Times. The letter must have been incomprehensible to most readers of The Times, but it finished the controversy. Lady Tree was the most inveterate bridge player of the day. The visitors' book was shown to be unreliable. Moreover if she was at The Wharf that Whit Monday morning, and she was, it was certain that bridge was being played. This was a remarkable score for Beaverbrook's memory fifty years afterwards.

[1] See pp. 97-98n.
[2] Beaverbrook to Christiansen, 7 August 1961.

Driberg's biography of Beaverbrook caused the greatest trouble. Driberg, as the preliminary correspondence shows, had been given a free hand. His book was to be, in his own words, "unauthorized and independent". Beaverbrook had however paid £4,000 for the serial rights and when the book was not to his taste complained, most unreasonably, that Driberg had got money out of him under false pretences. Mutual misunderstanding would have been a fairer phrase. It is a risky thing to write a man's biography during his lifetime, particularly when the man has his own version of events, as Beaverbrook had. There were some unnecessary and unjustified remarks about Beaverbrook's private life. There were some mistakes as there were bound to be when Driberg, too, was working under pressure. Most of all there was, particularly in the later part of the book, an unsympathetic approach. Like many Socialists, Driberg regarded the making of money as intrinsically wicked and, in his anxiety not to appear a Beaverbrook stooge, leant over backwards in the other direction. Driberg's Beaverbrook is certainly not my Beaverbrook, either as I knew him or as I have learnt to know him from his records.

Driberg called his book a Study in Power and Frustration. These are not the words I should choose. Beaverbrook was not interested in power except in the sense of being able to ensure that his orders were carried out. What interested him was achievement—achievement in making Lloyd George prime minister, achievement in producing fighter aircraft, achievement in bringing out successful newspapers. Frustration? Beaverbrook was frustrated by his failure to carry Empire Free Trade. But he was equally frustrated when he failed to tune his television set or to get through on the telephone. In fact he was perpetually frustrated by the refusal of events, great and small, to move as fast as he wanted them to. Excitement, fun, friendship are words which come into my head. Max Aitken said to me: "Charity was the strongest force in my father's life". This, though perhaps too emphatic, was a good deal nearer the truth than Driberg's judgement. In revenge Beaverbrook passed a judgement on Driberg. He quoted a nineteenth-century piece of American invective: "Mankind fell in Adam and has been falling ever since, but never touched bottom till it got to Henry Ward Beecher", and substituted Tom Driberg's name.

Beaverbrook was pulled two ways. He told Bracken fairly enough: "The book is not a Citizen Kane.[1] It is made up of much praise of me with a Jekyll and Hyde theme". Beaverbrook had always taken the line that he was prepared to accept criticism and stuck to this line now. The next moment anger overcame him. He was angered that Driberg had resurrected the charges which had been made—and in Beaverbrook's opinion

[1] Orson Welles's film Citizen Kane depicts a newspaper proprietor mad with power. Welles made it many years before he met Beaverbrook and denies that there is any resemblance between Beaverbrook and Citizen Kane.

discredited—at the royal commission on the press. He was angered that Driberg had not, as he thought, done him justice over his battles with Baldwin. Most of all—to Driberg's bewilderment and that of others—he was angered that Driberg had presumed to find minor faults in his account of the great political crisis in December 1916.[1] Even so Beaverbrook could not bring himself to decree that the book should not come out. Innumerable messages to Robertson from Nassau showed his dilemma. This is a wicked book; we must condemn it. But we have paid £4,000 for it, so we must get Driberg to revise it. No, he is a rascal; we will have nothing to do with him. And so on, round and round.

A long message to Robertson of 14 December 1954 gives a taste of the rest. Here are some of the concluding sentences:

> I am not going to let Driberg get away with the impression that he can write what he likes about me without having a considerable row.
>
> But on the other hand if he does finish the book and is willing to make such alterations as to confine himself to a hostile book without base and gross insinuations, then perhaps the best thing to do is to send him with the chapters to me for such revision as may be necessary in order to secure our co-operation.
>
> But the real point is that you will have to settle whether I am going to go on with this fellow now that I have got into this mess or am I to crack down, say nothing and let him do what he pleases.
>
> Mr. Robertson. I am very sorry to give you all this trouble. It is my own fault. I have made so many errors in life. I seem to be continuing them like some others I could mention. The older I grow the more frequently I blunder into mistakes.
>
> But this fellow with cunning persuaded me to help him with his project in the belief that he was doing something that would be critical but fair, instead I find that I am subjected to accusations of a very disagreeable character. And I want to make it plain, Mr. Robertson, that in order that you may form a fair judgement as far as my folly is concerned that I don't mind a bit, that I would just as soon go one way as the other. I get vexed at having fallen into a trap but that is all. I don't mind, I can scramble out all right.

[1] Driberg made two points. He criticized Law for not giving Asquith a copy of the resolution agreed by the three C's on 3 December. This misled Asquith into believing that the leading Unionists were against him. In my view Driberg himself is mistaken in attaching importance to this point. Law read the resolution to Asquith who grasped its purport clearly. On 3 December Asquith was still set against resignation, and Law sustained him. The alternative was compromise with Lloyd George which Asquith achieved later that same day. The political crisis really began only on 4 December when Asquith went back on this compromise, and the encouragement to provoke a crisis came solely from his Liberal associates, especially Runciman.

Driberg also denied that the three C's saw Asquith on 4 December. Here he was certainly right and Beaverbrook certainly wrong. However Beaverbrook was angrier at being told he was wrong when he was than at being criticized undeservedly.

No use in telling me, Mr. Robertson, which several persons have a right to do, no use in telling me that I was warned, for indeed I was. Plenty and plenty of warning. But in vain—in the face of the bird is the net of the fowler displayed.

Robertson was one of those who had advised against the book from the beginning.

Proofs were sent to Beaverbrook at Nassau and came back with many angry comments. Driberg himself went to Nassau with the two final chapters. Aitken House being full of guests, he put up at the nearby hotel, where next morning he received an order to leave at once. Three sets of lawyers—Beaverbrook's, the publisher's and Lloyds'—wrangled over the book for months. Robertson and Max Aitken had in it a full-time occupation. As a further misunderstanding, they thought their main duty was to cut out offensive personal references, whereas Beaverbrook was more provoked by Driberg's failure to appreciate his political conduct. In the end Beaverbrook got bored with the controversy as he often did and allowed the book to appear. He prepared some articles for The Daily Express giving Driberg "what for" and then killed them. Instead the book was serialized under the heading: "Lord Beaverbrook: a hostile biography", and footnotes drew attention to Driberg's mistakes, sometimes to his discredit. Kingsley Martin commented to Christiansen: "Driberg is a funny chap. He honestly believes that he can bite the hand that feeds him and be thanked for it".[1]

Beaverbrook's resentment did not last. In 1959 Driberg was invited to the farewell dinner to Christiansen, and in 1963 Beaverbrook wrote to him: "If the Socialists should come to power, which I very much doubt, I hope you will have a high office". Driberg was also a guest at the great dinner to Beaverbrook on 25 May 1964. In the last resort Beaverbrook could not resolve to suppress a book about himself, however hostile. Also by 1955 he was no longer interested in other people's books. His last and most creative period had opened.

[1] Christiansen, Headlines All My Life, 253.

CHAPTER TWENTY-FOUR

WRITING GOOD BOOKS..., 1956-63

In 1962 Beaverbrook said to his publisher, when passing the proofs of his last book: "Writing good books, that's my passion now". Here was the great new theme of his last years. Beaverbrook had not produced a book since 1932 other than the two revised versions of *Success*. Between 1956 and 1964 he published six, all in their way remarkable: two works of history, two biographies, an account of his own early life, and an essay on Christ's teaching. Not many men have shown such fertility or originality after they have passed the age of seventy-five. It was this which at the end gave him most satisfaction. He told Charles Wintour in May 1963: "In ten years' time, if I am remembered at all, it will not be for my newspapers. It will be for my books". I hope this is true.

Having constantly announced his withdrawal when he was relatively young, Beaverbrook became increasingly active as age advanced. He meant to live fully till the last moment. He wrote to Sir Ben Smith in 1956:

> You and I have reached the Age of Discretion.
> For my part I do not mean to be bound down or fenced in by any limitations. I mean to lead my life as though I were seventeen, instead of seventy seven.

And to Sir William Stephenson in 1959:

> I am not unemployed and I do not intend to be unemployed because it is not good for old men to neglect their opportunities to work, nor, for that matter, young men either.

Beaverbrook did not lay aside his other activities in order to write books. He merely added their writing to his other activities. Until he was nearly eighty he still went swimming. Until he was eighty-three he still moved from one continent to another. He controlled his papers in as much detail as ever, though, owing to his long absences overseas, he perhaps criticized more and directly contributed less. In almost the last year of his life, he conducted a political campaign successfully to his delight and surprise. He married again. He founded an art gallery and became for the first time a patron of the arts.

There were changes of emphasis during Beaverbrook's last eight years. He became less involved, though not less interested, in political affairs. This was partly the old story that the cause of Empire Free Trade was lost. Beaverbrook wrote to Humphry Berkeley on 26 May 1955:

> I have retired from politics now since I have been crushed and broken by the failure of the cause, to which I dedicated a lifetime.
>
> At last I have come to realize that there is no use in beating a dead horse.

Beaverbrook's detachment had also personal causes. Churchill finally resigned as prime minister in April 1955, and this cut Beaverbrook off from politics at the top. He had few contacts with Eden, Churchill's successor, despite a long personal friendship, believing that Eden favoured the United Nations and British involvement in Europe. Nor was he at first more sympathetic towards Macmillan, though their relations grew closer before Macmillan left office. On the other hand Beaverbrook became friendly with Hugh Gaitskell about 1960, and this gave him an insight into Labour politics which he had never had before.

Churchill and Beaverbrook continued to see much of each other, more indeed than in earlier years. Churchill was often at La Capponcina. After one such visit Beaverbrook wrote to him on 27 August 1958:

> I have had many benefits and advantages in life, sitting in reserved seats while the comedy was being played out during the years.
>
> But, never was I written off completely.
>
> Because I was one of Churchill's Ministers in the hour of trial. And, with my reputation for mischief I could never have carried through this role had I not been sustained by your confidence and support.
>
> Now, looking back on that year filled with anxiety, when we knew that we would be hanged to lamp-posts, I acknowledge that it was the most glittering, glorious, and glamorous era of my whole life.
>
> I packed more into twelve months of danger and escape than into just on eighty years of a not unexciting existence.
>
> All that I owe to you.

Nevertheless their relations changed. Churchill's mind was sinking into oblivion; Beaverbrook was as zestful as ever. Churchill was no longer the patron and protector. He was a dwindling force which Beaverbrook laboured to restore. Beaverbrook asked questions about the past, retold his best stories, laughed and joked, in the hope that Churchill would respond. Often Beaverbrook sat thus for two or three hours at a stretch before Churchill showed any awareness of his presence. When Churchill at last threw in a sentence, Beaverbrook went home content. This was his last service to Churchill as a foul-weather friend.

Illness and death brought changes for Beaverbrook also in his newspapers. In July 1955 E. J. Robertson had a stroke and never recovered though he lived on for another five years. He had been in newspapers with Beaverbrook almost from the beginning and had carried the burden of their management for over thirty years. He indeed was faithful unto death, serving Beaverbrook with unshakeable loyalty and yet tempering his whims. Now Robertson's kingdom was divided. Tom Blackburn, his chief assistant, became chairman of the company. A new post, as chairman of the board, was created for Max Aitken. Beaverbrook professed great confidence in the two chairmen and for instance wrote to Max Aitken in February 1957: "Your conduct of the newspapers convinces me that I need never visit England again except for the opportunity of enjoying the pleasing company of my old friends". This was hardly how it appeared to Blackburn or Max Aitken. Maybe Beaverbrook thought that two men were needed to perform the tasks which Robertson had performed alone. There was also an element of divide and rule. The more Beaverbrook felt life slipping from him, the more resolutely he clung to his absolute power.

Editors also changed, though usually without trouble. In 1952 John Gordon became editor-in-chief of The Sunday Express, a more or less titular dignity. He continued to write his own column, and this continued to give Beaverbrook satisfaction. When an influential friend complained of one paragraph, Beaverbrook replied sharply:

> Our John Gordon is an independent columnist. His vigorous voice is his own. He may blast and praise as he pleases—providing he does not break the laws of common decency, a thing I know he would never do.

After a brief period of experiment, John Junor became editor—another Scotchman at sea over "shall" and "should", a believer in Empire, with a ready appetite for controversy. He too gave satisfaction, even though he refused to serialize one of Beaverbrook's books. Beaverbrook recorded the results in 1963. In June 1928, when John Gordon took over The Sunday Express, its circulation was 586,740. On 5 October 1954, when Junor succeeded, the circulation was 3,291,000. In September 1963 it was 4,370,865.

The Evening Standard also gave Beaverbrook little anxiety. In 1950 he fell out with Herbert Gunn, the then editor, who wished to make The Evening Standard more sensational and popular. Beaverbrook was determined that it should remain sophisticated. Gunn resigned without recrimination or bitterness. Percy Elland kept the paper as it was, and so did Charles Wintour, who succeeded him in 1959. Beaverbrook sent few messages of criticism and many of praise. There was one such from Nassau in 1955: "Mr. Elland, there is nothing I miss so much as The

Evening Standard when night comes and I am waiting for dinner. I am sure many of your readers feel the same way". Of course a few pinpricks accompanied this:

> In Friday's ES there are three turnaways. You should cut down your turnaways into the inside of the paper. You should never have three stories that have to be turned over, except in great crises, immense events. In the ordinary course of the news, there is nothing that will justify three turnaways.
>
> Mr. Elland I do not admire your front-page cartoon but evidently you do so I bow to you and bend the knee and submit and do it gracefully at that.

At Beaverbrook's prompting The Evening Standard ran campaigns against the British Council and against the practice of the National Trust in taking over historic houses, while allowing the owners to live in them. Essentially it remained a Fun paper.

It is symptomatic that Beaverbrook did not brood over the circulation progress of The Evening Standard as he did over the two Express papers. The Daily Express was always Beaverbrook's first concern. He used it for propaganda, but he put the news first. The Daily Express had to be the outstanding newspaper, always first with the news and presenting it in the most effective way. Christiansen, its editor, had been a genius of presentation and an inspiration to his staff for more than twenty years. Here trouble struck Beaverbrook hardest. In July 1956 Christiansen had a heart attack, actually while with Beaverbrook at La Capponcina. He recovered but his stamina had gone. He was no longer fit for full-time work and refused to recognize it. This was a sad story. Christiansen's life was wrapped up in The Daily Express. All he asked was to return to it. Beaverbrook, Blackburn and Max Aitken treated him with great consideration. They kept his place open for him at The Daily Express. They suggested that he might move to lighter work at The Evening Standard. The one thing they could not do was to place him in a position of decisive responsibility when he was no longer fit for it. Tasks were invented to give him the illusion that he was still active. He was appointed editorial consultant, to comment on yesterday's newspaper. He was employed to direct the syndication of The Evening Standard features, and Beaverbrook wrote to him flatteringly:

> I have always had an advantage over some other journalists, because I knew both the commercial and the editorial side of newspapers. When you emerge from your contact with The Evening Standard you will roll me over in commerce as you have always done in journalism.

It was no use. Christiansen felt that he was being pushed aside. He came to believe that Beaverbrook was jealous of him. In 1957, when he was convalescing with Beaverbrook in Jamaica, Francis Williams's book on journalism, Dangerous Estate, arrived. There Beaverbrook read that

Christiansen "had stamped his personality on the *Express* only a shade less indelibly than Beaverbrook himself".[1] The next morning Christiansen found a letter on the breakfast table, telling him to return to England and resume work. Such was Christiansen's story, and there is no reason to doubt it. Beaverbrook exploded over something or other a dozen times a day, but his rage passed like a summer shower and the sun shone again. So it was with Christiansen. Beaverbrook was soon seeking new ways of keeping him busy. Incidentally Francis Williams's remark was by no means unfair. In character Beaverbrook's newspapers remained unchanged from beginning to end. The one change was in more vivid presentation and this was Christiansen's doing.

By May 1958 Christiansen could no longer deceive himself. He exploded in his turn and resigned. Beaverbrook was truly grieved. When Christiansen said farewell at Arlington House, both men were in tears, and Beaverbrook said, as he pressed the button of the lift: "Well, goodbye, Chris. Sorry to see you going down". Christiansen received a generous settlement—a pension of £3,000 a year and £35,000 in cash. He remained disconsolate and wrote to Beaverbrook late in 1959: "I still want to come *home*, and home to me means beside you". There was nothing Beaverbrook could do for him. In the last resort the head of any large concern has to put its interests before that of any individual, however great his past services. Beaverbrook was softhearted and always tried to avoid wielding the axe himself. But it sometimes had to be used.[2]

Christiansen left a place which proved difficult to fill. Three successors were tried in turn—Edward Pickering his former deputy, Robert Edwards, Roger Wood, Robert Edwards again. None of them came up to Beaverbrook's requirements. One was too gentle with the staff. One could not stand up to Beaverbrook's harrying. The Daily Express did not find a stable editor in Derek Marks until after Beaverbrook's death. Until then it ran on his promptings and on the momentum which Christiansen had given it. Even so it continued to give satisfaction. Beaverbrook contemplated the results in 1963. On 24 March 1924, when Baxter became managing editor, The Daily Express had a circulation of 735,137. On 31 October 1933, when Christiansen took over, its circulation was 1,851,748. On 31 August 1957, when he officially resigned, the circulation was 4,178,911. And in September 1963 it was 4,344,429.

A little earlier, in 1960, Beaverbrook also contemplated what would have happened to £100 invested in newspaper shares in 1930. In Beaverbrook

---

[1] Francis Williams, Dangerous Estate, 220. The entire chapter is an exercise in denigration of Beaverbrook, usual with journalists who were less successful than he was.

[2] Francis Williams retails Christiansen's grievances in Nothing so Strange, 300–4. A sick man can be forgiven for having delusions of persecution. It is harder to forgive a presumably detached observer who takes these delusions seriously.

Newspapers the £100 would have become £983; in Odhams £786; in The Daily Mirror £500; and in Associated Newspapers £171. This was not a bad record for a proprietor who claimed not to concern himself with dividends.

Newspapers did not impede Beaverbrook's discovery of new outlets. One was provoked by the presence of his old friend Sir James Dunn at the convocation of the University of New Brunswick. Dunn had been an art connoisseur throughout his life and was now a generous art patron of Dalhousie University. Beaverbrook took up the challenge to be an art patron in his turn. He had run through the interest of providing books for the University of New Brunswick and the town of Newcastle. Pictures would be a new field of endeavour. At once he gave orders for the building of an art gallery at Fredericton, an enterprise conducted with his usual hurry and impatience. Mrs. Ince, who had organized the buying of books for New Brunswick, was switched over to buying pictures and became a considerable expert.

It cannot be said that Beaverbrook himself had a cultivated taste. He liked the folk-art of the German-Canadian painter Cornelius Krieghoff, whom Dunn dismissed as not an artist at all. He liked paintings of the English countryside and the luscious females of Boucher and Fragonard. Otherwise he bought pictures much as he made up his investment portfolio, never acquiring many by the same artist, with the exception of personal friends—Orpen, Sickert, Graham Sutherland and Churchill—and, oddly enough, William Etty. He rejected a Turner with the words: "I've got enough of that fellow" and issued a general instruction: "We must have big pictures in the gallery". He was determined always to get a bargain and so missed many. He asked the owner to state a price which he then tried to beat down. If another patron entered the field and bid up the price, Beaverbrook at once withdrew. The result was a remarkable, though uneven, collection of British and Canadian pictures. Beaverbrook seems to have assumed that, with his collection, the gallery was complete. At any rate he made inadequate provision for expansion or for further purchases. He intended the gallery to remain exactly as he had made it.

Another new enterprise was the giving of pensions to ministers of the Presbyterian Church, a truly pious gesture to his father's memory. Beaverbrook wrote to Bracken on 25 January 1956:

I am now giving the retired Ministers of the Presbyterian Church in the Maritime Provinces and the widows of Ministers $300 a year each. Would you believe that that trifling sum is an amount of money to which each and every one of them attach extreme importance.

It appears to me that the complete failure of Christianity will come to pass because the Ministers now in the church will die off swiftly of worry and new men will refuse to enter upon a career of poverty.

A couple of years later the pensions, this time of £200 a year each, were extended to ministers of the Presbyterian Church of England. Beaver-brook also offered to provide homes for them in Cornwall, though this does not seem to have been taken up. He recorded one anecdote which gave him pleasure:

> A retired Minister called to see me. He asked me how old I was. He looked me up and down with close attention, almost a medical examination—asking what's your blood pressure.
> And after more than two minutes silence he said: "Do we get it now or do we have to wait?"
> I replied: "Now".
> He smiled ever so pleasantly and declared: "I hope you will live for ever".

Even the Presbyterian Church did not always meet with Beaverbrook's approval. In 1955 he learnt to his dismay that the new Draft Catechism was proposing to tamper with his most prized instruction, the interpreta-tion of the eighth commandment as an encouragement to worldly wealth. Beaverbrook wrote sternly to the erring minister:

> The departure from the Faith is much more sweeping than I had expected from my experience of the Church. . . .
> For example the Old Catechism says flatly that the Eighth Command-ment requires the "lawful procuring and furthering" of wealth.
> The New says "possessions" are a "trust" for which man is responsible to God.
> There is a vital difference between "furthering", which is an active pursuit, and "possessing" which is a passive acceptance of wealth.
> . . . .
> I can guess why the emphasis is changed from procuring wealth to dis-charging a trust. But it is not a fearless attitude towards property.

This theological essay owed something to Stanley Morison's inspiration—a curious exercise for a former Communist. Beaverbrook recorded his own conviction: "Calvin was the founder of capitalism. He never en-couraged or countenanced the monopolist or the usurer".

These countless activities were a diversion from Beaverbrook's main enterprise: his return to authorship. This had been simmering as he watched the wealth of sources being dissipated, as he thought, by Blake, Owen and even Morison. He was convinced that they had gone wrong on many points, perhaps from not listening carefully to his guidance. For instance, he was sure from his recollections of the time that the dispute between Bonar Law and Lord Cunliffe, governor of the Bank of England, in 1917, had not ended as simply as Blake presented it. He ransacked the Lloyd George papers for further evidence and this proved that

Beaverbrook was right.[1] Again Morison had written an account of the relations between Northcliffe and Colonel House, and once more Beaverbrook disputed the version. He noted:

> Of course House is a foolish man. He never had any sense. If he had known or understood human nature, he would have realized that Northcliffe was concerned with overlaying George. He would have realized that Northcliffe's promises to support House and House's American policy depended entirely upon whether George was opposing House and House's American policy.[2]

Beaverbrook also looked forward to showing that Lloyd George's War Memoirs were often inaccurate or evasive. Above all, he wanted to display in all its drama Lloyd George's conflict with the military leaders and the king.

Beaverbrook began to work on his new book in 1954 and it was finished in 1956. Much of it was dictated to secretaries; some of it was drafted by these secretaries and then revised by Beaverbrook; some of it he wrote in his own hand. The drafts and subsequently the proofs were scattered between Cherkley, Fredericton, Nassau and Jamaica, and it is amazing how Beaverbrook or his secretaries managed to coordinate the amendments which he had made at the ends of the earth. The central figure of the system was Sheila Lambert, Mrs. Geoffrey Elton. She began by making a detailed calendar of the Lloyd George papers, which researchers at the Beaverbrook Library now find of inestimable value. She explored the royal archives at Windsor. As well she found time to act as secretary to the Beaverbrook Foundations—all on a part-time basis. Beaverbrook regarded her justly as "a very remarkable woman". Other secretaries explored the House papers at Yale. All of them were kept busy reducing Beaverbrook's drafts to order. In 1963 Beaverbrook described his methods to Robert Pitman:

> H. G. Wells wrote: There but for the grace of God, I say, goes a fine novelist—not a fictionist I mean but an appraiser of conduct and character.

---

[1] Blake's account is in The Unknown Prime Minister, 351–54, Beaverbrook's in Men and Power, chapter III. According to Blake, Cunliffe signed a full recantation of his defiance of Bonar Law on 13 July 1917. Beaverbrook showed that Cunliffe held out until 12 August and even then did not withdraw fully. In my opinion, even Beaverbrook exaggerated the completeness of Cunliffe's defeat. It is true that he ceased to be governor of the Bank of England in November 1917. But he survived to make in 1919 a grossly inflated estimate of Germany's capacity to pay reparations and also to write a report which ultimately shackled Great Britain to the gold standard. These lamentable achievements were evidence of his continuing power.

[2] Morison wrote his account of House and Northcliffe too late for it to be included in his History of The Times. It appeared in Essays Presented to Sir Lewis Namier, edited by Richard Pares and A. J. P. Taylor (1956). Beaverbrook's account is in Men and Power, chapter II.

... It has often been suggested that I should get a university man to do the research for me. But then the books wouldn't be mine. I prefer to manage with the young women, my secretaries. Their only trouble is that they get married. Sometimes I think that the best way for a young woman to make sure of getting married is to come and work with me on one of my books.

Mrs. Ann Cousins, one of these young women, duly married again and went to Australia, where she helped Sir Earle Page in the writing of his autobiography. In 1961 she wrote an account of her work with both men which she sent to Beaverbrook, together with a request that he should write a preface to Page's book.[1] Her essay provides a first-hand description of Beaverbrook's methods:

In working with any participant of history, the question of sharpness and reliability of recall provides the key to the quality of the record. It was this, more than any other factor, that for me, placed Lord Beaverbrook in the first rank of the participant historians. Checking his recollected account against his own diaries of engagements[2] and the correspondence of the period, I would meet again and again this remarkable precision and accuracy. There were, indeed, many occasions when his memory of an incident, persisting fiercely in the face of conflicting published evidence, would triumph over the united resistance of the archivist and myself when the corroborating evidence would turn up among the files. He was always the last to give up in his insistence that a document was there, and he was invariably right. Nor were these feats of memory the performance of one who has come to live predominantly in the past. They were carried on against the hectic and immediate background of newspaper direction.

It was this remarkable memory which provided the structure and method by which we worked. By normal research methods, we operated in reverse. In long conversations, Beaverbrook would recreate the outline and atmosphere of a political incident and illuminate with stories and lively anecdote the personalities involved. A born raconteur, with a flair for the pungent phrase, his staccato style was contagiously easy to acquire. Against this framework I would consult the secondary sources and draw together the archival evidence and from this collection the draft chapters emerged. These drafts, taking at times new direction or elaboration of Beaverbrook's original account, in turn stimulated him and the result resembled an exciting snowball thrust back and forth with increasing pace. And in this Beaverbrook's extraordinary energy and stamina and his need for little sleep, left him always in the forward position. Casting back, the problems of serving as a "ghost"

---

[1] Ann Mozley, as she then was, later published this essay in the Journal of the Royal Australian Historical Society for March 1965 as The Participant and the Writing of History: Recollections of Being a Ghost.

[2] This phrase confirms my belief that Beaverbrook never kept a diary, except for a few weeks at the beginning of 1906. What he had was an engagement book, recording most of his visitors during the day as well as his guests at lunch or dinner, and he really had this book in mind when he referred to "my diary".

do not seem to have been academic ones, but how physically not to become one!

Beaverbrook's knowledge of the personalities and incidents, moreover, gave him a mastery over the documentary material that no historian working systematically through those records could hope to achieve.

. . . .

Accepting Beaverbrook's conception of political history as the arena for the struggle for power, his unique reliability as an eye-witness recorder depended upon two facts. The first was his abiding curiosity. Here was an enormously curious man, forever building up impressions, jotting down notes and the fragments of conversations, and, in the widest sense, picking the minds of others. The second was the important fact that, unlike such reporters as Lloyd George and Churchill, he was not a principal participant in the events he described and had no vested interest in the concealment of the facts. To this failure to reach himself the heights of political power, one critic has suggested, can be attributed the sharpness and reliability of Beaverbrook's account. "For men surfeited with power seldom leave reliable records of the events they shape. It is the hungry who remember best".[1]

When Beaverbrook wrote to thank Mrs. Mozley for her essay, he made one criticism: "You are indeed a most competent and valuable researcher, but I have never made use of ghosts". Enclosed in Beaverbrook's letter was the preface to Sir Earle Page's book which Mrs. Mozley had asked for. This preface had been drafted by Mrs. Mozley and amended by George Malcolm Thomson. Beaverbrook did not contribute one word except his signature. Indeed he could not remember who Sir Earle Page was.

Mrs. Mozley omits one element in Beaverbrook's art to which he attached great importance. He called it "Balancing". At a late stage in the process of drafting and redrafting, he livened up the narrative, whenever he felt that it was becoming pedestrian, with a vivid phrase or an anecdote, sometimes I fear invented for the purpose. Here is one example. In the first chapter of Men and Power he describes how he asked F. E. Smith what Lloyd George should do to counter the obstruction from Sir William Robertson, chief of the imperial general staff. The draft had only this staid sentence: "F. E. Smith recommended an immediate reorganisation of the high offices in the military command at the War Office". Not much drama here. Later Beaverbrook added the sentence: "Then, "Sack him now," said F.E. in effect". The "in effect" is a warning to the wary that F. E. Smith did not in fact say "Sack him now".[2] I will give another example of balancing later.

In one instance Beaverbrook showed unusual restraint. He often described in conversation how, as minister of information, he had been

---

[1] Paul Johnson, reviewing the new edition of Politicians and the War in The New Statesman.

[2] Men and Power, 52.

attacked in the house of lords and had defended himself effectively.[1] His printed account was more anodyne:

> It was said that Lord Salisbury and Lord Beresford would raise the issue in the House of Lords. I attended quite often while expecting a motion on the Order Paper.
> I was determined to show myself to my foes, and to give them a chance to join battle at the earliest moment. But the hullabaloo died down.[2]

This was always Beaverbrook's practice. He was ready to pitch things too high in conversation. He knew how to be accurate when he came to write. I ought to have remembered this before swallowing this particular story.

Beaverbrook had plunged into exploiting his new material without considering how it would work out. For some time the drafts were known as Politicians and the War, volume III, or even simply as Crisis. Men and Power was hit on by one of Beaverbrook's associates only when the book was in page proof. It was a more appropriate title. The book was not a sustained narrative. It was a series of independent episodes, each centred on a single man—Carson, Robertson, Rothermere, Maurice and so on. Some critics complained, when the book came out, that it told sordid stories of intrigue and personal ambition. But the struggle for power is an essential part of politics, never more so than in wartime. At any rate Beaverbrook was justified in his final claim: ' I have written with complete impartiality and entirely independent of party or personal affiliations". He could have added that he had also written with an unfailing sense of fun.

As always Beaverbrook doubted his literary gifts and trembled at the book's reception. He gave all the rights in the book to The Daily Express according to his usual practice and insisted on a small print, 3,000 copies, to avoid the danger of its being remaindered. Actually the edition was soon exhausted, and the book went on to sell a further 20,000 copies in a cheap edition. Reviewers gave the book an enthusiastic reception to Beaverbrook's amazement and delight. My own review in The Observer, it seems, gave him most pleasure though I did not know this at the time nor did Beaverbrook ever mention it when we became friends later. I paid him only a deserved and impartial tribute. Now it moves me greatly that I once gave pleasure to a man who gave me so much. My review was the first occasion when Beaverbrook was taken seriously by a professional historian[3] and the acknowledgement stunned him. Michael Foot,

[1] See pp. 141–42.
[2] Men and Power, 288.
[3] Actually Sir Robert Ensor also praised Men and Power in The Sunday Times, though more grudgingly. He wrote of "a mind at once attractive and repellent" and called the book "a serious contribution to knowledge".

who was with Beaverbrook when he read the review, assures me that it changed the whole course of Beaverbrook's life. He himself said as much to Robert Pitman in 1963:

> I first became enthusiastic about my writing when I saw the report of a publisher's reader placing a high value on my book Men and Power. Then I saw A. J. P. Taylor's glowing review of the book in The Observer. It was a new event in my life. I was fascinated by the spectacle of success in a world that was not mine.

Beaverbrook was even more emphatic when he talked to George Gale on the eve of his last birthday in 1964. Gale asked what single recollection gave him most pleasure. "Without hesitation he replied: I think the review of my book by A. J. P. Taylor in The Observer. It came to me as a great surprise". I add the impudent description Beaverbrook gave Gale of how leaders were written for The Daily Express, even though it is irrelevant to the present subject:

> We have a system you know. I speak at this end and there is a machine at the other end and it comes out as a leading article.

Men and Power began my friendship with Beaverbrook, though not directly because of my review. I had sometimes answered questions of historical fact addressed to me by one of his secretaries. We had never met. In reading Men and Power, I was curious about one point in the account of how Lloyd George imposed convoy on the admiralty: "The Prime Minister descended upon the Admiralty and seated himself in the First Lord's chair".[1] This seemed to me unlikely. Lloyd George's descent upon the admiralty was in the nature of an informal call, and the board of admiralty did not meet that day. I wrote asking Beaverbrook for his evidence, and he invited me to lunch. I got little satisfaction on my specific point. Beaverbrook, when pressed, said: "I'm sure it happened. I'll ask Churchill when I see him next". Of course he never did. And of course the incident never happened. As I have now discovered when going through Beaverbrook's proofs, it was another balancing act, inserted for vivid effect at the last moment. All the same it was symbolically true— truer, I think, than the version sustained by the great authority of A. J. Marder that Lloyd George was greeted on arrival by a bevy of admirals enthusiastic for convoy.

Beaverbrook did not forget my inquiry, though he never referred to it again. Some years later we were talking about the conspiracy against Baldwin in 1923 when the old coalitionists met for the last time.[2] I

[1] Men and Power, 155.
[2] See p. 218.

remarked that Arnold Bennett had unwittingly spoilt the plot by mentioning the meeting to a Daily News reporter—an idea which had not struck Beaverbrook before and which he at once expounded in The Evening Standard. He described to me the meeting in the drawing room at Cherkley: "Churchill sat hunched over there. Chamberlain was here—oh, dear, he was a dull fellow. F.E. was looking out of the window with his hands in his pockets. And George—George sat in the centre. Wherever he was he always dominated". I said: "as at the admiralty board", and he replied: "I'm glad you've come round to seeing things the way I do". He certainly saw things. As soon as he mentioned the meeting of the conspirators or the earlier meetings at Cherkley between Asquith and Law, the men were back in the room with him. He had total recall, though I daresay some of the incidents he recalled had grown more dramatic with the passing years.

On our first meeting Beaverbrook asked questions all the time. No doubt he wanted to size me up. But I think his questions sprang mainly from an insatiable curiosity. He simply wanted to know and would switch quite happily to questions about other people. Of course he jotted down a good story for use in The Evening Standard Diary, but he asked most of the questions for their own sake. Some people were disappointed because he did not appear as interested in them on a second meeting. He did not need to be: he had got all the answers first time and never forgot them, as I sometimes noticed to my embarrassment. I was fortunate. I was writing a book on his period in history. The events were almost as vivid in my mind as they were in his. Sometimes I tried to catch him out. It was no use. His mind moved as fast as mine, even though I was a whole generation younger. I raced from the abdication to home rule, from home rule to the Suez crisis, and he always had an answering anecdote. If I questioned some fact, he would turn to his Soundscriber and say: "I've got Mr. Taylor here. He says so-and-so. Now look it up for me". He was always too much for me after our first encounter. He left me one little puzzle. We were talking about the Marconi scandal of 1913, and he suddenly said: "It wasn't American Marconi they speculated in. It was Canadian Marconi". I am sure he was wrong. I have never looked it up for fear he may have been right.

Beaverbrook had two characteristics which I had not been prepared for. Everyone noticed his zest and gaiety. But many people called him brash. What surprised me was his old-world courtesy. He was a gentleman in the fullest sense of the word, and very gentle at that. He knew the tastes and interests of each guest and never let anyone feel left out. When you came for the night, he struggled upstairs with you to ensure that the bedroom was in order and the bathroom properly equipped. When you left, he came with you to the door and stood bareheaded in the rain or cold until your car went down the drive. Though he had an unfailing tolerance, he had also a strict sense of propriety. No one talked bawdy in Beaverbrook's house. He had his whims. He did not like women smoking and, though he put up with it, he left his women guests to provide their own cigarettes. Cigarette boxes were scattered all over the house, but they were always empty. As a boy he had resolved to drink champagne every day of his life when he became rich. I do not think he liked it. He was happier at the end of his life when he went back to drinking whisky after a token glass of the champagne or, in my case, claret which he provided for his guests.

His other characteristic is more difficult to speak of. Everyone has remarked on his charm. Many succumbed to his fascination. Only a few loved him. He was usually presented as a strong man. To me he seemed fundamentally insecure or, if not insecure, deeply sensitive. He needed reassurance, and only love could give it to him. Affection meant more to him than admiration, yet he doubted whether he could win it. He always suspected that others liked him for his money or his power or because he flattered them. His most tragic sentence, and one quite untrue, was the one he wrote about Arnold Bennett: "How I loved my Arnold and how he loved my champagne". In fact his secretaries loved him most even though he bullied them and tried to drive them at his own pace. I doubt whether I ever convinced him that I loved him simply for himself. Perhaps only Michael Foot succeeded. After his death a friend asked me: "Was Beaverbrook a great man?" I replied: "I cannot say. I only know I loved him more than any human being I have ever met". For me Max could do no wrong.

The success of Men and Power encouraged Beaverbrook to go on as an historian. His correspondence with Blackburn was full of instructions to "go after" this collection or that—Hankey's papers, Gwynne's, Hore-Belisha's, and Asquith's letters to Venetia Stanley. He did not have much success. As with pictures, he always tried to bargain. He asked the price of a collection of papers, tried to beat it down and turned abruptly away when his offer was refused. His only important acquisition was the papers of Lord Curzon in which Curzon's widow had a life interest. Beaverbrook paid £2,000 for a five-year lien on them. It was also a handicap in his search for papers that he had a deserved reputation as a monopolist. Once he acquired papers he kept them to himself. I had great difficulty in prising a few Lloyd George papers from his grasp. Only A. M. Gollin got past his guard—another unique stroke by that incomparable researcher. Occasionally Beaverbrook set someone else on exploiting the material as he had done with Frank Owen and Lloyd George. Leonard Mosley wrote a life of Curzon at Beaverbrook's direction, and when James Cameron published an admirable book on the first months of war in 1914, Beaverbrook set him to write another on 1916, a book which gave satisfaction to neither author nor patron.[1]

Beaverbrook had one brief experience of being taken seriously as an historian even in academic circles. After Men and Power was published Robert Mackenzie addressed some questions to him about the events of 1917. In reply Beaverbrook invited Mackenzie and his class of twelve to dinner at Arlington House. After dinner Beaverbrook conducted a seminar on 1917 for three hours. Otherwise, so far as I know, no British university acknowledged him until the very end of his life when St. Andrews offered him an honorary degree. He accepted with delight but was never well enough to take it.[2] He was never invited to deliver an academic lecture, though he was an inspired lecturer as well as a learned historian. This was curious, though no doubt only what was to be expected from British universities.

Writing Men and Power would have been a full-time task for any ordinary man, particularly when he had also newspapers to run, an art gallery to create, and a university to interfere with. Beaverbrook was not an ordinary man. Any undertaking made him want to undertake another. Also he became bored even with writing Men and Power. His way of escape from the boredom of writing one book was to write another. Driberg's biography revived his interest in his early days, and he turned to the draft of My Early Life which Maurice Woods had written some thirty years before. He "balanced" it with new anecdotes and also added some about the Empire Crusade and the second world war which were entirely remote from his theme—a stroke of self-indulgence. The first nine chapters were ready at about the same time as Men and Power. Once more he doubted whether anyone would want to read the book. This time he decided not to publish it in England at all. Instead he sent the chapters to Brigadier Michael Wardell for publication in the Atlantic Advocate, a periodical which Wardell had just launched. Accompanying the chapters was this letter of 9 May 1956:

Dear Captain.

Here is a birthday present for you if you want it very much.

In case you want it, I would be glad to hear any suggestions for changes or alterations that you may think desirable or expedient.

---

[1] James Cameron had been a highly successful Beaverbrook journalist. In 1951 he resigned in protest when The Daily Express during the American witch hunt suggested that John Strachey, a former Communist, was a security risk as secretary of state for war. This puzzled me. At any rate I thought it ill became Strachey, a former Leftist, to bestow his superior scorn on those who remained Left.

[2] Beaverbrook prepared a highly idiosyncratic speech of thanks for the degree which was published in the St. Andrews Alumnus Chronicle for June 1970.

It is on the whole a self-revealing document and I think all the better reading on that account.

. . . .

I hope you will like this present, because I have worked hard on it. But don't hesitate to send it back to me for more work, or as a rejected manuscript.

You may announce it as a birthday present.

I am only keeping a rough copy here, and when it is set in type please see that I get proofs.

The modest tone of this letter was of course no guarantee that Beaverbrook would not hack at the proofs as indeed he did. The nine chapters duly came out later in 1956. The remaining seven remained, for the time being, untouched.

There is not much to record about Beaverbrook's other activities in 1956, ceaseless as these were. His grumbles continued. On 19 March he wrote to Blackburn about his flat at Arlington House:

Your company provides the flat here for use as an office.

In my labours for the newspapers I make much use of the accommodation you make available.

But I must tell you that unless you can do something quickly to improve the amenities for me and for your staff who work here, I will no longer be able to put up with the discomfort and inconvenience with which I am faced at present.

. . . It is certainly a great trial to an old man who labours so hard and so continuously for your newspaper.

There was also an instruction to reviewers, actually of 5 February 1957:

(1) Name—author-publisher (2) What the book is about. The story if possible (3) The Author and his idiosyncrasies (4) Is it worth reading (5) Wisecracks if good. But not any clever quips if commonplace.

Never Never Never Neglect News values if any—Critics must be Reporters First.

I am glad that I never yielded to Beaverbrook's promptings that I should review books for his newspapers.

In politics Beaverbrook claimed only to be a detached observer, exchanging lighthearted comments with Bracken. When Harold Macmillan became chancellor of the exchequer Bracken wrote to Beaverbrook on 17 January 1956:

For more than a quarter of a century the officials of the Treasury had the misfortune to be perpetually mistaken. They were wrong about the gold standard in 1924, they were totally wrong in the way they met the scarifying depression of the nineteen-thirties, they were wrong about Bretton Woods, the second American loan, the management of our attenuated gold and dollar reserves and the inflexible fiscal and trading politics they have ordained for a succession of Socialist and Tory ministers since the war ended. . . .

Macmillan may be the witch doctor we need. . . . The need is for a financial Mary Baker Eddy and Macmillan has plenty of affinities with that most successful lady.

Beaverbrook replied on 23 January:

You remember Macmillan served with me.

He will do strange things and I am sure he will live to perpetrate a great deal of mischief.

On 21 February Beaverbrook wrote again:

Be sure that Macmillan will make trouble if he has the power. As long as he is kept in order he will be all right. When he gets up he will be all wrong.

Beaverbrook entirely changed his opinion about Macmillan later. It was not only Conservative ministers who attracted his criticism. On 14 February he wrote to Woodrow Wyatt:

What exciting times you have in the Labour Party. You have a lively gentleman in Mr. Wilson. He is an amphibian. Sometimes on Mr. Bevan's water; then on Gaitskell's land. He may end up in the mud.

This was a warning which might well have been heeded.

1956 was the year of the Suez crisis. This was really remote from Beaverbrook's oceanic conception of Empire. It is true that he was no longer anti-Zionist. As he told the Jewish Chronicle in 1962:

I was anti-Zionist along with many prominent Jews. . . . My views have changed. Israel has brought intelligence, efficiency, progress and internal stability into a part of the world where instability has prevailed. It is indeed one of the outstanding accomplishments of the twentieth century.

But Beaverbrook had always opposed British commitment in the Middle East. In 1922 he demanded British withdrawal from Egypt and Irak even at the risk of quarrelling with his hero Bonar Law. During the second world war he questioned the value of the North African campaign —this time provoking the anger of Churchill. Logically therefore he might have welcomed British withdrawal from the Suez canal and condemned the attempt to reconquer it. But Beaverbrook was not logical. Once the British Empire was, as he thought, challenged, he rallied to its defence, and he supported the Suez war just as he supported the second world war, which had also met with his disapproval beforehand. He inserted a declaration into My Early Life:

I am a pacifist. . . . But when the Empire interests are threatened, as in the case of the Suez Canal, which does not belong to Egypt but to the Empire, then, in the words of John Galt: "We shall not sheathe the sword until. . .".

The Beaverbrook newspapers duly championed the Suez war. Beaverbrook himself took no part in the campaign. He remained in Nassau and New York throughout the crisis and was content to approve the line of his papers from afar. No doubt the affair moved too fast for him to do anything else. His correspondence provides only marginal comments. Bracken wrote to him on 5 November 1956:

> The Socialists who thought Eden a charming milksop now hold him to be a blood lusting monster. Vanity is a great toughener.

Beaverbrook, like many others, blamed the Americans for the British humiliation when the war had to be abandoned. He wrote to Stanley Morison on 30 November:

> The British crash fills me with despair. My first thought on waking is—"What's wrong?" Then the recollection.
> I hope Britain will not rely upon friendly consideration from U.S.A. again. Eden should not be blamed for misreading the American mass opinion anxious to take over Britain's colonial trade. He believed that the President had some responsibility for American policy. Not so.
> Will we ever recover? It requires a measure of optimism given to few old men to believe in Britain's future.

And to Bracken on 2 December:

> The Americans are exceedingly hostile to Britain. The only reason they hold on to us is because of the need for support in their impending war with Russia.

Bracken replied on 7 December:

> Eden is the best of the Tories. . . . The alternatives are the crackpot Macmillan or Butler, who is a curious blend of Gandhi and Boss Tweed.

Beaverbrook shared this new-found enthusiasm for Eden and, when he resigned, wrote to him on 23 January 1957:

> This is a letter of admiration.
> You have shown courage and devotion to your duty with all the world against you—except only your own countrymen.
> Now all the world is realizing that you were right and they were the victims of wicked propaganda promoting hysteria.

Beaverbrook had often criticized Eden in earlier days, particularly in the time of the League of Nations. He became a loyal friend as soon as Eden was in trouble. Thereafter Beaverbrook's flat in Arlington House was always available for Lord and Lady Avon when they passed through London, and his car was always waiting for them at the door. He lent them his house in Jamaica until they found one of their own and accompanied every such offer with a letter of warm affection. With Lord Avon, as with so many others, Beaverbrook was a foul-weather friend.

Beaverbrook disapproved of Eden's successor on curiously constitutional grounds. Perhaps he was annoyed that, though absent from England, he was not consulted about the appointment. He wrote to Roy Howard on 16 January 1957:

> Macmillan is not the choice of the people. He was selected by Churchill and Lord Salisbury. He is the wrong man. Butler should have been taken.
>
> Eden's policy was correct. It failed. The policy is reversed. But Macmillan was the protagonist of Eden's policy. Butler was the opponent. Naturally, they all stand together because their party is more important to them than peace of mind.
>
> However a reversal of policy called for Butler as the Executor instead of Macmillan.

Beaverbrook's resentment against Macmillan, if it existed, did not last. On 8 April the two had a long and friendly conversation, when Macmillan spoke strongly in favour of the sterling area and described Eisenhower as "an aged Monarch playing favourites—now one and then another Minister or adviser".

Beaverbrook made one new political acquaintance in 1957. He entertained James Callaghan, a leading Labour MP at Cherkley and presented him with a copy of The Troublemakers, a book of mine about dissent over foreign policy which had just come out. The book gave Beaverbrook great pleasure, as demonstrating the confusion of the Left over foreign policy before the second world war. He said to me: "Theirs was a terrible record". I replied, mistakenly as I now believe: "The record of the Beaverbrook newspapers was not all that good either". Callaghan wrote to Beaverbrook on 18 May:

> How nice to be seventy-eight and keep a sense of fun and not to be a stuffed shirt.
>
> I suppose really it is only the mediocre who have to hide their nakedness behind their dignity. Thank you too for The Troublemakers. The Dissenters so often have the noble cause—but their priggishness puts me off. But I'm on their side even when I don't march in their ranks.

Callaghan had evidently complained about the vendetta which Beaverbrook's newspapers were supposed to conduct against Earl Mountbatten. Beaverbrook replied by sending cuttings from The Express newspapers in which Mountbatten had been praised, and Callaghan wrote on 24 May:

> In face of all the evidence you send me about Mountbatten, what can I do but withdraw.

Beaverbrook certainly claimed that he criticized Mountbatten only on public grounds. Thus he answered an expostulation from Wardell, an old friend of Mountbatten's, on 30 June 1955:

> He is subject to the same measure of attack as any other public man who may transgress the high principles which the Express sets in all matters concerning the British Empire.

In July 1959, again writing to Wardell, Beaverbrook ascribed his hostility to Mountbatten:

> Over what I believe to be the betrayal of Burma, refusal to let the Dutch back into Indonesia. And over everything the sack of India. The bright jewel in Queen Victoria's crown.

On other occasions Beaverbrook attributed his hostility to the attempt on Dieppe in 1942. Thus he wrote to Max Aitken on 20 April 1958:

> Print these statements, simple statements. Don't Trust Mountbatten in Any Public Capacity. Together with a further quotation from Mountbatten's speech in Canada where he said he took full responsibility for Dieppe. Four thousand set forth and three thousand did not return.

It is difficult not to feel that more lay behind. None of Beaverbrook's friends could discover what it was. Something about Mountbatten touched Beaverbrook on a raw nerve. However the troubled story had a happy ending. In 1963 Macmillan brought the two men together, and they were reconciled.

During 1957 Beaverbrook's personal life took an unexpected turn. His old friend Sir James Dunn had died on 1 January 1956. Dunn's wife Christofor, as she was known to her friends, had tended him with loving care for many years. His death plunged her into despair. She went into deep mourning and talked of retiring to a convent. Beaverbrook determined to bring her back to life. Not for nothing was he a fisher of men— and of women too. Beaverbrook paraded the sorrows of old age. He, too, needed loving care and companionship. Christofor Dunn was won over. She visited him at La Capponcina and at Cherkley. They separated only when they came to New Brunswick. Beaverbrook stayed in Fredericton, while Christofor went to her own home at Dayspring, Saint Andrews. Even then she was often summoned to Fredericton. In 1961 I was the appreciative hearer of a telephone conversation which Beaverbrook had with her. Christofor complained that she had travelled the eighty miles between Saint Andrews and Fredericton twenty-nine times in the course of the previous three weeks. Beaverbrook said: "It was only twenty-seven times. I have here some data", and he went remorselessly through each meeting according to his engagement book. Christofor replied that she had come over once to have her hair done. Beaverbrook said triumphantly: "You see, I was right, it was only twenty-seven times".

Friendship with Lady Dunn brought Beaverbrook great satisfaction. He boasted that she was the first lady friend he had had who was richer than he was: "She must love me for myself alone". Of course he switched Christofor on and off just as he did with everyone else. She had to be there when he wanted her company and disappear when he did not. And of course the idea of diverting the Dunn millions from Dalhousie University to the University of New Brunswick was not absent from his thoughts.

The writing of history was still Beaverbrook's main interest. The success of Men and Power stimulated him to further achievements. The Lloyd George material which he had acquired somewhat threw out his earlier plans. He originally intended to present Lloyd George's fall and the brief reign of Bonar Law as preliminary chapters in a large work on The Age of Baldwin. Now he decided that the decline and fall of Lloyd George demanded a book in itself. The mighty machine went again into action. Secretaries began to research; Beaverbrook began to dictate draft chapters. As always his mind could not stay on a single subject. Unused episodes from My Early Life echoed through his head. Also he had acquired the papers of R. B. Bennett—the only papers incidentally which he permanently deposited at the University of New Brunswick—and was anxious to use them. Bennett had been Canadian prime minister at the time of the Ottawa conference and, in Beaverbrook's opinion, had been outwitted by Baldwin. A life of Bennett would be an appropriate receptacle for the jumble of recollections which thronged Beaverbrook's mind.

Beaverbrook worked on this book about Bennett off and on throughout 1958 and published it in 1959. Friends, as Beaverbrook called the book, is not a good biography. Indeed it is not a biography at all. The sub-title described it correctly: Sixty Years of Intimate Personal Relations with Richard Bedford Bennett. It is a sort of magic-lantern show: brightly lit when Beaverbrook and Bennett were on close terms and with long stretches of obscurity when they were not. There is little about Bennett's political career before he became prime minister and virtually no explanation of his position in Canadian politics. At the end he is ranked far ahead of Baldwin and Mackenzie King, the two men who in different ways defeated him. "He was good. He was great. And in the fullness of time his reputation will grow and expand". The reader remains unconvinced.

The best passages are the personal descriptions of Bennett where Beaverbrook gave free rein to his gifts as an Aubrey. When the book came out Stanley Morison wrote to Beaverbrook:

> You write sympathetically, loyally and generously. In fact you do every-thing for Bennett but produce an attractive image of this Methodist who objected to champagne "on principle" and thought creme de menthe, which he enjoyed, was a "soft" drink. No; you don't succeed in making him an

attractive character. Despite your good writing the reader does not say, "Oh what a pity I never met R. B. Bennett"!

Beaverbrook replied:

There must be some fault in my purpose. For I meant to make Bennett an attractive figure—which he was.

Again the reader is not convinced. Much of the book is very funny as only Beaverbrook could be. Once fun overcame him he could not write an orderly biography.

Two other old friends enter the record for 1958. Beaverbrook and Aneurin Bevan do not seem to have met for many years past. Now Bevan gave a Sutherland drawing of Churchill's hands to the gallery at Fredericton. A little later he lightheartedly remarked to Sir Patrick Hennessy that he would like in exchange a Lowry which, he thought, Beaverbrook did not particularly want. Hennessy passed on the message. Beaverbrook was furious and ordered the Sutherland drawing to be returned. Bevan had to explain that his remark was facetiously meant, and there was a sort of reconciliation. Beaverbrook wrote to Bevan on 4 April:

I miss seeing you. The friends of years ago are all departing and only two or three trees are left in the clear-felled forest. Brendan's last days are dragging out in pain and agony. He has the strength and the courage of the heroes of his race.

However there was no renewal of friendship. Beaverbrook never saw Bevan again and jotted down on the back of a discarded letter: "Bevan Done and lost his friends—one-quarter Bloody Revolution one-quarter Pacificist one-half Same policy as Tories but with jobs".

Brendan Bracken was indeed dying. On 5 August 1958 he wrote his last letter to Beaverbrook:

It is becoming an effort for me to walk short distances. I must fight this with all my might. If I don't I could quickly enter into a life of invalidism.

A postscript on Eisenhower showed that Bracken's spirit was undimmed:

A synthetic general was needed to launch soldiers and armies of great pugnacity and here was Ike "waiting to hand". To win the last election, and the one before, the Republicans needed a synthetic President who was all things to all men. Perfection was found in Ike. No one knew where he stood on anything. Ike is, in fact, the Dale Carnegie of generals as well as politics. A wonderful world we live in!

Bracken died three days later. He had been Beaverbrook's most intimate friend for years past. He was also, though an unorthodox Conservative, Beaverbrook's only close friend in Conservative circles, and his death pushed Beaverbrook further into political detachment.

Not that Beaverbrook was politically inactive. 1958 saw his first political article in The Sunday Express since 1950, and the theme was the same: peace and good relations with Soviet Russia. Beaverbrook wrote on 23 March:

> The Sunday Express is a pacifist newspaper. . . . Peace, at almost any price, must be the watchword in this office.
>
> . . . .
>
> Can national animosities between Britain and Russia be reconciled?
> Yes, of course. They can be obliterated and forgotten if wise policies are pursued.
>
> . . . .
>
> The British Empire should not be influenced in its decisions by German foreign policy or German desires.

Beaverbrook ended by urging that, if President Eisenhower would not go to Moscow, Macmillan should go alone.

On 2 April Macmillan wrote to thank Beaverbrook for his encouragement and added:

> I do not intend to accept a peerage. When I retire, I shall retire with my own name and go back to my business. But I do not intend to retire for at least sixteen years; that will bring me to eighty, which, I think, is now the accepted age for Leaders of the Conservative Party to lay down their burdens.

Later in the year Beaverbrook showed that he remained faithful to another of his old beliefs. On 12 November he gave an interview to an American journalist, Lawrence Fertig, who recorded:

> Full employment—and he means *brimful* employment should be the prime objective of every government (and he added, every newspaper).
> . . . Suppose, I said to him, that in trying to achieve full employment you necessarily get inflation and rising prices. Which do you sacrifice? His answer was that full employment first, last and always, must be the objective.

Roy Howard, Fertig's employer, could not believe that Beaverbrook was serious and wrote to ask whether Fertig's report really represented Beaverbrook's views. Beaverbrook replied on 11 December:

> It is my view that our primary responsibility is to the working man. If he is willing to work he must be provided with a job.
> . . . If eggs must be broken to make that omelette let us break them. But as few as possible.
> The "right to work" is a slogan which should be accepted by every democracy.

In this year also Beaverbrook displayed his loyalty to an even older cause: the Presbyterian Church of Scotland as he had known it in his youth and as he interpreted it. For its sake he launched his first full-scale campaign since the days of the Second Front. The campaign was conducted solely in The Scottish Daily Express and therefore went almost unnoticed elsewhere. Beaverbrook conducted it with great energy all the same. His target was the proposal, then widely mooted, for a union of the Presbyterian Church with the Church of England and the institution of bishops which that would entail. The Scottish Daily Express did not only run articles against this proposal. It also circularized all the ministers of the Church of Scotland and inspired public meetings. Beaverbrook's letters to A. C. Trotter, editor of The Scottish Daily Express, indicate his outlook. Thus on 22 April:

> There are many in Scotland who are willing to sell the pass.
> You might wish to warn the Church that if there is any further effort in the direction of the movement for bishops the Church may suffer another "disruption".

And on 25 May:

> Please turn up the denunciation of bishops by John Knox. Then having printed it conclude with the final sentence of the Scots Confession of 1560, written by John Knox with the aid of other ministers:
> "Arise, O Lord, and let thy enemies be confounded. Let them flee from thy presence that hate thy godly name: Give thy servants strength to speak thy word in boldness; and let all Nations attain to thy true knowledge."

Like all Beaverbrook's campaigns, this was an appeal to the people against their leaders. Many prominent Presbyterians favoured the proposal. Most ministers of parishes were against it. When it came before the general assembly, it was rejected. The last leader Beaverbrook wrote on the subject concluded with the words: "Glory Hallelujah!"

His general directions to his newspapers continued unabated. One is a good example of the way he mixed together general advice, corrections of historical fact, and personal complaints. On 20 April Beaverbrook sent a message to Max Aitken from Montreal:

> I must say that I would hope very much that we will get somebody on the leader column who thinks straight and with simplicity and at the same time writes vigorously. I do hope it will come to pass. I do wish that you'd let me know what you're going to do, what you're proposing as a remedy and relief.
> . . . .
> I see in the DX that the last German head of state to visit Britain was Kaiser William in 1907. I don't think that's right. I think Kaiser William came in 1911. And unveiled the monument to Queen Victoria. But I'm not sure, look it up and let me know if there's been some mistake there. Or if I am wrong. I hope I am wrong.[1]

----

[1] Beaverbrook was right or almost so. The monument was unveiled by King George V on 16 May 1911. Kaiser William attended the ceremony.

Max Aitken, I called you on the telephone, it's taken now about five minutes since I've been brought to the line, about five minutes and you're not coming on the line. Now that's bad organisation, surely, I want you to put it into shape please.

A piece of advice I want you to remember all your life. Never, never attack the private life of any man. Never touch it.

This last was a principle from which Beaverbrook never wavered. With his relentless curiosity, he liked to know every man's secrets from financial affairs to marital tangles. He always kept this knowledge to himself and used it in his newspapers only if it became public property by, say, a divorce case or a statement about death duties. He wrote to the assistant editor of The Sunday Express a little later:

I assume from your note that X was not born in wedlock.

I am sure I have no need to tell you that that is a subject the SX will not touch on any account. That has been our policy since the paper was founded.

Similarly Beaverbrook never allowed his newspapers to say that so-and-so had been divorced or had divorced her husband. In his view divorce was merely the termination of a contract and there were no "guilty" or "innocent" parties. The only phrase he permitted was that so-and-so's marriage had been dissolved.

In 1959 Beaverbrook reached the age of 80. He might have been expected to celebrate his birthday with a grand dinner as he had done when he became 70 or 75. Instead with fine perversity he went to Fredericton for a brief visit, where he attended a military parade and had a quiet dinner with a few friends at the Lord Beaverbrook hotel. This was perhaps a gesture of loyalty to the art gallery which was now approaching completion. It brought him one final trouble. The opening was fixed for September. In the preceding July Queen Elizabeth was to visit Fredericton. Beaverbrook sent Wardell stern instructions that she might be admitted to the gallery, but no one else. He wrote on 30 June:

I am spending a great deal of time and money in making arrangements for an Opening which will bring to the Capital many distinguished visitors from Foreign lands.

But the labour is considerable and the expenditure might be described as substantial.

I will certainly give it all up if the Gallery loses its virginity now....

I am bound to say that it would be a relief to be rid of the trouble.

Strange how men pay to make trouble for themselves.

Beaverbrook's anxiety proved to be unfounded. The queen had a full programme in Fredericton without inspecting the art gallery. Beaverbrook was hurt that, as chancellor of the university, he had not been invited to Fredericton to meet the queen. He wrote to Wardell: "I take it all this arises from my support of the Duke of Windsor when he was Monarch". No doubt this suspicion was also unfounded. The art gallery was duly opened on 18 September by Dr. William Constable, formerly curator of the Boston art gallery and a descendant of the great English painter, some of whose works graced the gallery. The creation of such a collection within the space of three years was certainly a great achievement, even if it owed as much to Mrs. Ince as to Beaverbrook himself.

Though Beaverbrook still maintained his energies undiminished, he made this year one concession to old age. He abandoned his houses in Jamaica and at Nassau, where among the last visitors were T. S. Eliot and his wife. Lord Kemsley bought Aitken House, Nassau. David Brown of the Brown Motor Corporation bought the house at Montego Bay, Jamaica. Beaverbrook gave out that he had deserted the West Indies so as to be nearer his medical advisers. This did not prevent his taking a prolonged tour of the West Indies by chartered airplane with Christofor, Lord Rosebery and a large party of friends in the following year. In fact he had never liked Jamaica and now found that Nassau, once a haven of peace, was also becoming too popular for him. As well Christofor disliked the West Indies and welcomed his withdrawal from them.

Christofor's influence was shown in other ways. With Bennett's life finished, Beaverbrook sought a new distraction and decided to write the life of Sir James Dunn. In exchange Christofor placed three paintings by Dali in the Beaverbrook art gallery. The new biography was again very much a personal account. Beaverbrook bombarded Christofor with questions about Dunn's habits. Thus he wrote on 20 October:

> Will you tell me, please, did James read slowly? Did he skim? Or did he read to a finish every book he began?
> What was his habit of reading newspapers and magazines?

Christofor had kept a detailed diary and could provide plenty of anecdotes. Beaverbrook made full use of them. The result, Courage, was again not a good biography in the accepted sense. Christofor herself hated it. Dunn did not emerge as a great man or an important public figure. The personal portrait is Beaverbrook's most accomplished work in this vein, another stroke worthy of Aubrey.

Another step in 1960 owed something to Christofor. Beaverbrook was fond of quoting a saying of Andrew Carnegie's: "A man who dies rich dies disgraced". He was impressed by the Sir James Dunn Foundation which Christofor had created and decided to do something similar. This would secure the Canadian fortune which was the bulk of his wealth. For by Canadian law an estate was exempt from death duties if it were bequeathed to a charity. But the charity must be already in working existence. Beaverbrook therefore set up a Canadian Beaverbrook Foundation with some of his American holdings, amounting to rather more than $1,300,000. As a minor advantage, the Foundation, being a charity, was also exempt from the 15% withholding tax levied on non-American citizens which Beaverbrook had to pay.

Thus Beaverbrook kept most of his Canadian fortune—some $4,500,000 in American securities and $10,000,000 in Canadian—under his own control until his death and yet made it safe from death duties. In theory the foundation took over most of his charitable obligations in Canada. In practice its income was not enough to cover the payments, and Beaverbrook made up the deficiency, amounting to $80,000 a year, from his own funds. The main payments went like this: a prize fund at Harkins Academy; a new village school at Beaverbrook; maintenance of the Sinclair Rink, the theatre and the town hall at Newcastle, the Beaverbrook art gallery at Fredericton and the civic centre at Chatham; scholarships to the University of New Brunswick; and pensions for retired ministers of the Presbyterian Church and their widows in the Maritime Provinces. It is not surprising that in 1962 the legislature of New Brunswick established 25 May as Beaverbrook Day and a provincial holiday.

By 1960 Beaverbrook was becoming impatient that his serious historical work was taking so long. He decided to make, as it were, a payment on account and refurbished Politicians and the War which had been out of print for many years. His first intention was to prepare a completely revised edition, drawing on the many books which had come out since he wrote. His secretaries collected much material which he contemplated with dismay. The revision was regretfully abandoned. Beaverbrook also thought of changing the title to War and 10 Downing Street. Fortunately he abandoned this also. Politicians and the War came out unchanged in 1960, except that the two volumes were bound up as one. This time reviewers did not stint their praise. One wrote: "This is Suetonius or Macaulay presented with all the visual techniques of Alfred Hitchcock", and another found it "terse as Sallust, pithy as Clarendon". After these, my own description that it was "Tacitus and Aubrey rolled into one" seems modest. The entire edition of 3,000 copies was exhausted within a few months—another gratifying and unexpected success.

Beaverbrook's new political interest was in reconciliation with Soviet Russia. He offered Khrushchev an honorary degree at the University of New Brunswick. Khrushchev accepted and then withdrew when Diefenbaker, the Canadian prime minister, attacked him in a public speech. In the following year Cyrus Eaton, also an enthusiast for reconciliation with Soviet Russia, urged Beaverbrook to go to Moscow as the emissary of disarmament. Beaverbrook did not respond to this invitation. Instead he gave Krishna Menon an honorary degree in the hope that he would attack both Soviet Russia and the United States, which he duly did. Beaverbrook also exploded when The Daily Express missed the significance of a conciliatory speech by Khrushchev. He sent a message on 3 July:

> What is wrong, what is wrong, what is wrong. I require a full report on this subject. Will you please give me a full report on this extraordinary situation.
> Don't put me off with explanations that are not complete. Go to the bottom of the questions, go to the bottom of the answers to the questions. I ask you and do not disappoint me with your answers.

I was with Beaverbrook at Fredericton for a fortnight in the autumn of 1961. He took the chair for me at a public lecture and said sternly to the audience: "Alan Taylor has come a long way to lecture to you, so listen very attentively". Afterwards he told me it was the finest lecture he had ever heard. When I asked him whether he had heard many others, he made his usual reply to my provocations: "Ah, you're a very clever fellow". He had taken over the flat in the art gallery, designed for the curator, and spent his days there. It was strange to see this wealthy man, with his comfortable houses and large domestic staffs, living alone in a single semi-basement room. One door opened directly on to the river bank, and the other into the kitchen. The room was piled high with books, galley proofs and company accounts. From this cell Beaverbrook ruled his empire. He waited impatiently each day until the call came through from London. Later he grew impatient again and rang the New York office of The Daily Express in order to ask "What's the news?" Later still he rang Montreal in order to find out how the markets had closed. We walked by the river and talked about Lloyd George. Beaverbrook would greet any elderly man as a boyhood acquaintance—not always, I think, accurately.

He had little company except of course on the great day of convocation. Sometimes he summoned "The Captain", Brigadier Wardell, or President Mackay. Otherwise he was a lonely old man. He took me round the university and showed me the Bonar Law-Bennett Library, empty except for the papers of R. B. Bennett.[1] One day we went to Newcastle. On the way he encouraged the driver to exceed the speed limit, universal in New Brunswick. He rubbed his hands at the thought that a traffic policeman might stop us. He told me: "They caught me once. I went to the lieutenant governor and said: 'I've given twenty million dollars to the province. You ought to leave me alone'. They did". No traffic policeman appeared. We walked in The Enclosure which Beaverbrook had endowed as a nature

---

[1] Beaverbrook sent the Bonar Law papers to the University of New Brunswick library for a time. He snatched them back when he wanted them for his own work, and they are now in the Beaverbrook Library.

reserve and drank champagne on the graves of the early settlers. Beaverbrook showed me the Old Manse, the town square which he had restored
to its eighteenth-century character, and the office at Chatham where he
had started his brief legal career. He also showed me the remote farm
house which he had acquired for his ultimate retirement. He said: "I
don't think I'll be here for some years yet". He was restless to be again
on the move and said when he saw me off at the airport: "I'm glad to say
I'll be following you soon".

He did not follow by air though he had planned to do so. He had an
attack of dizziness and for a time lost control of his limbs. Sir Daniel
Davies was flown over from London and diagnosed Ménière's disease.
Beaverbrook, though liking the exotic name, decided that he was merely
suffering from overdoses of cortisone. However he returned to Great
Britain by sea, and Christofor with him. Arriving at Glasgow, they took
the opportunity to visit Torphichen and in the church there plighted their
troth. Beaverbrook told Christofor that this was a "marriage by declaration" according to old Scotch custom. I doubt whether this was correct
without the presence of witnesses. I wonder also whether Beaverbrook,
like other men, was not ingeniously putting off the day when he actually
married again. At all events, it was a romantic gesture which gave them
both pleasure.

When Beaverbrook returned to London, the move to carry Great
Britain into the Common Market was in full swing. He responded to the
old challenge and defended the cause of Empire for the last time. His
newspapers conducted a campaign of resistance under his direction. He
paid for a series of advertisements against the Common Market, one of
which he wrote himself. It was his last political pronouncement:

> What does the Common Market mean to us? It means political subjection.
>
> ....
>
> Once in the Market we shall cut overselves off from the great Dominions.
> We and they have everything to unite us. We have the one God, the one
> loyalty to the Crown, the one language, the one law. The Dominions are
> untainted by Communism. Their military strength is greater than that of
> most of the Common Market countries. And they will fight on our side
> without question as they have always done.
>
> ....
>
> Let the people demand that our ties with the Dominions be strengthened
> and not cut off. We must not abandon those great nations which sent their
> sons to die for us.
>
> We must stand by them and work together to advance the greatest achieve-
> ment in civilisation and brotherhood that the world has ever known.

Beaverbrook consulted Hugh Gaitskell, leader of the Labour party, about
others who might be invited to write similar pronouncements. Gaitskell

suggested Sir Jock Campbell, Sir Arthur Bryant, Viscount Montgomery, and Earl Attlee, all of whom were duly invited and all of whom accepted. Their contributions, though marked "paid for by Lord Beaverbrook", were in fact paid for by The Daily Express. Beaverbrook remarked: "The Express exists to promote the cause of Empire".

In the old days Beaverbrook had no qualms in fighting Baldwin. Now he regretted having to oppose Macmillan and wrote to him on 7 March:

> There is every intention to support you in everything but that blasted Common Market, which is an American device to put us alongside Germany. As our power was broken and lost by two German wars, it is very hard on us now to be asked to align ourselves with those villains.

And to Lord Lambton on 17 August:

> I really cannot be too hard on Macmillan. You know we were together in the Government, and when Churchill was reluctant to appoint him, I argued very strongly in his favour. He has never forgotten it, and I find it very hard to forget my association with him.
>
> . . . If the Government goes into Europe, the voters will pull them out again.

However this did not prevent his trying to stir up discontent within the Conservative party. He wrote to many of his old supporters in Norfolk and, as a local landowner, investigated the Somerset seats, offering to pay £1,000 towards the expenses of "any good candidate".

He continued to harass his newspapers. Here are two messages to Tom Blackburn. On 2 January:

> Can we devise some system, Mr. Blackburn, by which your end of the telephone does the waiting instead of my having to wait on the machine. Sometimes I wait as much as three or four minutes, or possibly even five minutes after I have been told that the call is on. And I think that I should be allowed some freedom.

On 5 March:

> Tell your accountants not to send me detailed costs any more. I have tried to take things up for the advantage of the paper, but nothing comes of it, so therefore we had better save, at any rate the little bit of money which will accrue from my decision to do without details from the account-ants. It is what is called "losing at the bunghole and saving at the spigot".

Attached to this note was a complaint that the holidays taken by the editors were too long. To Edward Pickering on 10 March:

> We must be on the side of the angels and the angels are always protec-tionists. Never never depart from that general principle.

To Max Aitken on 24 August:

> See that the writing is light and not lacking in vividness. Never fail to supply readers with constant surprises, and to your staff show that you are the only one to be pleased.

A little later a rebuke to Charles Wintour: "In a diary paragraph I read 'often closing his eyes and looking towards heaven' ". Beaverbrook rarely closed his eyes.

In 1962 A. G. Millar totted up for Beaverbrook the money he had given away over the years. In England he had given nearly four million pounds to charities and private endowments, of which one and a half million pounds represented the newspaper shares transferred to the Beaverbrook Foundations. He had in fact run through his entire British fortune with the exception of the farms in Somerset which were valued at some £300,000, and even these he sold shortly before his death to Max Aitken, in order to provide himself with spending money.[1] In Canada Beaverbrook had given ten and a half million dollars, the largest single gift being to the art gallery at Fredericton for building, pictures and endowment. Beaverbrook added a new project to his charities. He and Lady Dunn jointly undertook the provision of a theatre at Fredericton, which was incomplete at the time of his death. In his last two years Beaverbrook gave away a further two million dollars.

The Decline and Fall of Lloyd George was nearly finished. Beaverbrook again grew impatient and made yet another payment on account. In 1925 he had written an essay on Christ, entitled The Divine Propagandist. Tim Healy objected that it was doctrinally unsound, and Beaverbrook laid it aside. He wrote: "Tim was my very dear friend. He was my teacher too. . . . I could not endanger our association by hurting his deep religious principles". Now Healy was long dead. Beaverbrook took The Divine Propagandist from its box. He never claimed to have thought much on religious subjects. Years before William Gerhardi questioned him as to his views on immortality:

> He replied that he had neither studied the question nor given it any sustained thought; that one had either to be in possession of a philosophical mind, if one wished to probe this subject, or if one were not so endowed, leave it alone.[2]

This was still Beaverbrook's position.

---

[1] The farms qualified for the agricultural reduction of 45% on the otherwise effective rate of death duty. It was assumed that this rebate had been lost by the sale to Max Aitken, and the executors paid the full duty—£187,000. The Inland Revenue belatedly discovered that, because of a recent legal decision, the debt from Max Aitken qualified for the rebate after all, and 45% of the £187,000 was refunded to the executors.

[2] Gerhardi, Memoirs of a Polyglot, 243.

One can understand Healy's objections. Beaverbrook rejected the Pauline interpretation of Christianity. For him "Jesus was the missionary of joy. . . . His desire was to spread happiness, not to sour life. . . . He came to preach to us good tidings and the good news that man can be cheerful and happy on earth by fulfilling the manifest destiny within the spiritual code". Stanley Morison, a Roman Catholic like Healy, was better qualified to pass judgement on the book than I am. He wrote to Beaverbrook on 1 June 1962:

> It is my conviction that you have performed a great service and shown a highly courageous example. Most men would be well advised to follow you and set down their ideas, beliefs and thoughts concerning the character, life and message of the greatest of all ever to have taught the human race.
> But the hearts of most of us are less stout than yours and we weakly evade taking issue with Christ and with ourselves.
> . . . .
> Theologians will assuredly find untheological expressions in the Divine Propagandist. But what you offer is not theology, nor orthodoxy. You give insight and courage.

For once Beaverbrook risked a fairly large edition. 10,000 copies were printed. When nearly seven thousand had been sold, the remaining three thousand were sent free to schools and to Presbyterian ministers in England and Scotland—at the expense of The Daily Express. Thus an organ of propaganda served the greatest propagandist of all.

Beaverbrook grew increasingly anxious as The Decline and Fall of Lloyd George neared completion. His constant timidity as an author made him feel that this time he had really lost his gifts. It is true that the book was less of a unity than his previous works. The earlier part, describing Lloyd George's increasing difficulties, was new. Apart from Beaverbrook's own materials, it drew largely on Frances Stevenson's diary. The later part, beginning with the re-emergence of Bonar Law, derived almost entirely from a draft which Maurice Woods had written long ago, and Beaverbrook merely "balanced" it here and there.[1] He pressed the book on Robert Pitman, George Malcolm Thomson, Michael Foot and others, hoping that they would urge him to publish it and fearing they might not. Finally he turned to me and wrote on 31 May:

> If this book is not up to the standard of "Politicians and the War" and "Men and Power", I will not bring it out.

---

[1] One balancing act miscarried. Beaverbrook meant to end the book with the words: "Lloyd George and I as pallbearers walked together on the way to burial of Bonar Law's ashes in Westminster Abbey". Fortunately he discovered that Lloyd George was absent in America and that it was Carson with whom he walked as pallbearer. This did not appear as the pay-off line.

My firm resolve is not to publish unless it is up to the standard of the previous works.

Of course much of the rewriting was done in my 83rd year and certainly I do not have as much vigour as I possessed a few years ago.

Beaverbrook offered me a fee which naturally I did not accept. Instead I struck a bargain: Whatever my advice, he should take it. If I said, publish—no more doubts; if I said don't publish, he would put the book aside. Beaverbrook grumbled: "I don't like being dictated to". However he agreed. I said, publish, and like to think that, even if this was not decisive, at any rate it helped towards publication. I also told Beaverbrook that there were some irrelevant passages which he ought to cut. Again he accepted my advice and then cheated me by putting most of the condemned passages in Appendix 63.

At the beginning of August 1962 Beaverbrook went, as he usually did, to La Capponcina. He had been feeling generally unwell and was also troubled by the gout which racked him for the rest of his life. On 31 July he summoned Sir Daniel Davies who told him he had cancer of the bladder. Beaverbrook, in his own words, "disputed the diagnosis". At the front door, Sir Daniel stood in silence for some time and then said:

> Oh God thou was a little unkind
> To make these hills and dales
> So beautiful,
> And the days of a shepherd
> So few.

The next day Beaverbrook flew to the south of France. A little later a well-known surgeon called and "ridiculed the diagnosis". Lady Dunn, who was with Beaverbrook, resolved to keep the truth from him. He was soon convinced that he was not suffering from cancer or maybe secretly decided that the only sensible thing was to behave as though he were not. He remarked only of his conversation with Sir Daniel Davies: "It was a tough poem in the circumstances, wasn't it?"[1]

I am not competent to judge in this matter. Beaverbrook suffered all kinds of pains and weakness when he was bored and shook them off as soon as he became interested or excited. Whether this is compatible with cancer I do not know. My own view is that his maladies were deeply rooted in his psychology, but this may be an ill-informed guess. He certainly remained unshakably active both mentally and physically for the rest of the year. He went to Fredericton in the autumn, when my old friend J. I. M. Stewart succeeded me as visiting lecturer. Beaverbrook complained that Stewart's literary views "were rather on the orthodox side". Beaverbrook presided over the convocation and went for long

[1] C. M. Vines, A Little Nut-Brown Man (1968), 131–32.

solitary walks by the river. He returned to Cherkley for Christmas and prepared to go to La Capponcina.

Then the snow fell. Cherkley was almost cut off. Beaverbrook developed influenza and bronchitis. For some days he lay at the point of death. Christofor nursed him devotedly day and night, as she had previously nursed Sir James Dunn. She literally saved his life. By February 1963 he was well enough to go to La Capponcina. Mentally he was as alert as ever. Physically he never recovered. Gout caused him continual pain. He walked only with difficulty. From this moment he knew that he was living on borrowed time.

CHAPTER TWENTY-FIVE

LATE NIGHT FINAL, 1963–64

Early in 1963 Beaverbrook wrote to a friend: "I am now in my eighty-fourth year and that is approaching the moment when I must bring out my Late Night Final". This phrase was constantly with him. Far from discouraging or depressing, it enlivened him. He meant to make his last edition a good one. Sometimes, as with the books he planned to write, he seemed to assume that he would live for many years. More often he was busy planning for his direction to continue unabated when he had gone. Old age no doubt meant "pills and pains, pains and pills". But it also meant going through the newspapers, gathering material for his next books, entertaining friends and political leaders, and for ever asking "What's the news?". Underlying this was perhaps a feeling that, if he ever stopped, he would not start again. Beaverbrook's last words to his secretary, who had urged him to rest, were: "But, maybe, I wouldn't wake up".

In January 1963 he was on to his editors again as soon as he could get out of bed. He telephoned the editor of The Daily Express: "Ah, I'm better! Your stories on the feature page are too long! While I've been ill they've grown and grown—and now I groan and groan oh dear oh dear!" He telephoned Charles Wintour at The Evening Standard with some comment and added: "It looks as though I've got better! That's bad news, isn't it!" On 15 January he sent a message to Tom Blackburn:

> Do we take down the 6.0 news on the BBC and also the 7.0. news. If we don't take it down give an order at once that news is to be taken down and rammed down the Editor's throat, without any doubt at all. And then answer me, let me know that it is accomplished, that you accepted my advice in that respect, put this into effect and told the Editor that he is expected to read the news every night.

Beaverbrook had always been impatient and abrupt in his judgements. Now, in constant pain and aware that he had little time, he forgot to add the occasional balm of praise.

In February 1963 he was well enough to go to La Capponcina. His rebukes came from there in ever greater number. One even fell on Charles

Wintour who was usually above criticism. The Evening Standard published a leader supporting the unification of the Anglican and Methodist churches. Beaverbrook wrote to Wintour on 1 March:

> Next we'll have a leader saying that there should be an amalgamation between the Evening Standard and the Evening News.
> What will be the result of that?
> The circulation of one or the other will disappear.
> And that is what will happen to the church congregations if they unite.
> I think you must be a Baptist or a Second Day Adventist. They will gain when Methodists become Episcopalians.

Wintour replied that he had thought the agreed policy of The Evening Standard was to support the established church, to which Beaverbrook retorted:

> The Evening Standard should certainly support the Church of England. I am unable to do so. But I bow to the superior judgement of the Editor.

As the rebukes increased Max Aitken was moved to expostulate for the first and last time. On 25 April he wrote this fine letter:

> I respect your judgement and along with all Fleet Street acknowledge your absolute leadership in journalism. For some thirty years I have gratefully accepted your criticisms, usually I hope with good grace. But lately all we do or don't do is muddle and muddle. I agree some of our mistakes are silly but some of our successes are magnificent.
> You say "I wearily said anything else" and you are right. Sometimes I am weary. Weary from trying to lead with enthusiasm and with a critical eye and with justice.
> Weary from trying to patch up oversensitive and deeply loyal feelings hurt by constant criticism seldom if ever tempered by a little praise.
> Some men are not much affected by criticism—you are one—Blackburn is not. I believe all men react to a measure of praise. The Daily Express is in a proud position—that is no accident—it has been achieved by the hell of a lot of hard work by Blackburn and the editorial staff.
> When you used to work at the office with your coat off you drove everyone hard but you also made them laugh and feel that they were on the "sunny side of the street".
> This is still necessary and some of it must come from the master however far away he may be.
> Therefore I hope you will continue to hold us by the hand each and every day and beam an occasional smile our way.

Beaverbrook did his best. Thereafter his criticisms were made in a gayer tone, and when he returned to England in May he put himself out to entertain the senior members of staff in turn at Arlington House.

Beaverbrook had two triumphs in the early days of 1963. The first was the failure of the British attempt to enter the Common Market. This gave him little joy. He realized that it had been caused by French objections and not by the campaign against it which he had attempted to inspire. He remained discontented with the political situation. He had admired Hugh Gaitskell who died suddenly. He had no faith in Harold Wilson, Gaitskell's successor. Beaverbrook wrote to John Junor on 27 March:

> I think that his whole career shows that he has not got the balance and the understanding and the steadfastness that a political leader should have.

Later events did not belie his judgement. In Beaverbrook's eyes the Conservatives were little better. He wrote a little later:

> I have the greatest difficulty in supporting Mr. McLeod and Mr. Heath. They are the favourites of our wonderful Prime Minister. He has himself strayed far from the principles of the Tory Party.

These troubles were forgotten when The Decline and Fall of Lloyd George was published.[1] Beaverbrook worried over it until the last moment. He insisted on references to it in The Daily Express and The Evening Standard every day for a week before it came out and explained to the reluctant editors that propaganda, to be effective, must increase in volume and strength "until it reached a level not far removed from violence". Beaverbrook's worries proved unnecessary. Old friends and old enemies combined to praise The Decline and Fall: Earl Attlee, Roy Jenkins, Robert Blake, Lord Longford, Sir Charles Snow, Lady Violet Bonham Carter, Dick Crossman, Denis Brogan. Snow emphasized "the sarcastic, self-mocking humanity that gives these histories their flavour and their bite". Beaverbrook's lifelong antagonist, Lady Violet, delighted him most, particularly with her paragraph:

> Outspoken critics of Lord Beaverbrook, who are often warned by their well-wishers that he can be a very dangerous enemy, will find some reassurance in these pages. However dire the dangers of his enmity may be, they pale before the perils of his friendship.

This, though more clever than true, might have been written by Beaverbrook himself. At any rate he was vindicated as a historian. He wrote to thank every reviewer. Over 14,000 copies were sold before his death.

Kenneth Young has called Beaverbrook's Decline and Fall of Lloyd George "the finest of all his writing". Though I, too, said as much at the time, I now do not put it quite so high. It is an amazing book for a man of over eighty to write. It has a boy's gaiety and an unfailing fairness. The use which Beaverbrook made of Frances Stevenson's Diary was particularly ingenious. He slipped in many anecdotes from it, not claiming them

---

[1] Beaverbrook had intended to call the book And Great Was The Fall Thereof.... His publisher persuaded him to adopt a more comprehensible title. But he kept his original choice as the sub-title.

as his own but also not indicating where they came from. There is in the book a deep inner equivocation which always troubled Beaverbrook and which had already appeared to a lesser extent in Politicians and the War. He was torn between Lloyd George and Bonar Law. He knew that Lloyd George was the greater man, indeed the most dynamic British statesman of the twentieth century. Yet, for one reason or another, he would never commit himself to Lloyd George. Hence he built up Law as a way of escape. Beaverbrook's own role in The Decline and Fall remains obscure, whether he appreciated this or not. Was he trying to sustain Lloyd George or to overthrow him? Apparently sometimes one, sometimes the other. Again, was he always hoping to bring Law back? And if so, was it to help Lloyd George or to ruin him? The Decline and Fall is, among other things, a fascinating human document. This adds to its appeal, even if it makes for confusion as a historical record.

The Decline and Fall has, I think, another flaw. It should have ended, as the title implies, with the fall of Lloyd George. Once Law became prime minister, the story was finished. Law's brief reign and the subsequent elevation of Baldwin belonged to Beaverbrook's next book, The Age of Baldwin, for which they were originally intended. Beaverbrook brought them in irrelevantly for a characteristically artistic reason. He wanted to end the book with a joke at his own expense: his hope that Law would bring in Empire Free Trade and the way in which this hope was disappointed. He was confessing, perhaps unconsciously, that the hero whom he served in fact betrayed him. And of course he wanted to include the final stroke when he reconciled Lloyd George and Law shortly before Law's death.

Beaverbrook, though pleased by the chorus of praise, remained modest about his historical gifts. When Crossman sent him a book inscribed: "To a great historian from an admiring journalist", he replied: "you neatly reverse the truth: for you are the historian and I am a journalist. A journalist who has become a chronicler but is essentially—and even proudly—a journalist still". Journalist or historian, he was impatient to get on with the further books which he had announced: The Age of Baldwin and Churchill's Victory.[1] He and his secretaries once more set to work. What he called "accumulating material" was in fact recalling,

[1] This projected book had many changes of title. Originally it was called Churchill: His Character and Conduct. At this stage Beaverbrook intended to cover the highlights of Churchill's entire career. Particularly he wanted to bring out the contrast between Churchill's earlier failures and his triumphs in the second world war. Gallipoli, intervention in Russia, return to the gold standard, opposition to the constitution of India bill and the Abdication crisis would provide a paradoxical prelude to the time when Churchill became the saviour of his country. Later Beaverbrook decided to concentrate on the second world war. The project became Churchill's War and finally Churchill's Victory.

with fantastic accuracy, letters or articles he had written thirty or forty years before and pulling them out of the files. His secretaries wrote a few connected narratives. Here and there Beaverbrook "balanced" them.

Not much got to finished form. Baldwin's beginnings were charted: his gradual rise to power; the American debt settlement and the conspiracy against him by Lloyd George and others in the autumn of 1923. Beaverbrook published a fragment from this last theme in The Evening Standard as a two-part tribute to Arnold Bennett, the man who, he now thought, had unwittingly wrecked the plot. Towards the end of Baldwin's career there was an account, written out in full, of the Hoare-Laval plan and a narrative of the abdication crisis which was published separately after Beaverbrook's death. In between there was nothing except the story of Churchill's receiving office in 1924 and an account of the general strike which was again mostly about Churchill. Beaverbrook never tackled the central episode of the Empire Crusade, and for a characteristic reason. He believed, with some justification, that Baldwin had outwitted him. This so exasperated him that, every time he thought of writing about it, he broke off in a rage.

Churchill's Victory was held up for a different reason. Beaverbrook declared that he could not write it until after Churchill's death which in fact he did not live to see. For, though he meant to build up Churchill's greatness, he also meant to reveal Churchill's failings. Beaverbrook wanted to bring out Churchill's strategical mistakes from Norway to Singapore and to emphasize the drama of Churchill's precarious hold on power. Also he meant to fight the battle of the Second Front over again, and this time no doubt to win it. None of this could be even contemplated while Churchill was alive. As a result, Beaverbrook only developed a few isolated episodes from the early days of Churchill's government—the row with Dowding, the visit to Tours on 13 June, and the attack on the French fleet. He wrote an account of how Churchill became prime minister when everyone, except the British people, wanted Halifax. This appeared in The Sunday Express for 1 December 1963 as The Great Silence that saved Britain. It was appropriately the last article which Beaverbrook published.

Beaverbrook told Robert Pitman how he proposed to treat his subjects:

> Everyone thinks I will try to tear Baldwin to pieces. But I won't. Not at all. Rancour is the worst fault. Churchill is essentially a man without rancour. He has been accused of being bad-tempered. It isn't true. He could get very emotional, but after bitterly citicizing you he had a habit of touching you, of putting his hand on your hand—like that—as if to say that his real feelings for you were not changed. A wonderful display of humanity.

And a wonderful bit of observation on Beaverbrook's part. He would, I think, have treated Baldwin with fun, not with animosity. As to Churchill, he told John Grigg: "Churchill was always a better friend to his friends than they were to him". And he applied this even to himself.

Two books might have provided enough work for any ordinary man. Not for Beaverbrook. Only half of My Early Life had gone to Wardell in 1956. Beaverbrook wanted to get the rest of it into shape while he had time. Most of it was again Maurice Woods's old draft with some irrelevant anecdotes added. Beaverbrook planned a larger addition. The draft ended with his arrival at Ashton-under-Lyne in 1910. The Canada Cement story was left hanging in the air. Beaverbrook dug into his old records and composed a detailed narrative almost to the point of Fleming's final discomfiture. This was a decisive vindication. But there was one flaw. At the very end, Beaverbrook would have to confess that he had paid Danegeld after all. When Fleming was totally defeated, Beaverbrook contributed $20,000 to help him out, solely out of softheartedness. The recollection now infuriated him. He could not bring himself to set it down. He locked his narrative away and sent the old draft to Wardell. Instalments of it were published in The Atlantic Advocate and it came out as a book shortly after Beaverbrook's death. It makes a delightful exercise in autobiography and deserves to be known by a wider public.

I had a little experience of Beaverbrook's zest for history, an experience which also taught me something of his genius as a foul-weather friend. I went to Cherkley one gloomy evening. Beaverbrook was very low. He was in great pain from gout. He had to be assisted to the dinner table. There his chin often sank on to his chest. I, too, was depressed. I was trying to write a book about recent English history. I had reached the year 1931 and was stuck: economic affairs failed to excite me, foreign affairs I had written about already. After dinner Beaverbrook asked listlessly: "What are you doing now, Alan?" For want of anything better, I began to talk about my troubles. As I did so, an extraordinary transformation came over Beaverbrook, a transformation which passed belief. When he realized that I needed help, his face lit up. He kicked off his gout shoe and walked up and down without the aid of his stick. He declaimed about the exciting episodes of the nineteen-thirties—the making of the National government, Ottawa, the Hoare-Laval plan, the abdication. The name of Baldwin occurred again and again: "What a rascal! He was cunning. He dethroned a monarch. He tricked us all". And then with a roar of laughter: "His private life was beyond reproach". After that he said: "Now let's have some more whisky" and marching across the room, he rang the bell.

For the rest of the evening he was boyishly gay. He told me about his meeting with Sir Charles Dilke in 1911. Then he switched to the battle for Macmillan's succession, a topic which gave him high delight. I was gay too. Beaverbrook had not given me any new ideas. Indeed I thought much of what he said greatly mistaken. But he inspired me. I thought:

"If this frail old man can be so excited about history, shame on me if I cannot be excited too". That night Beaverbrook saved my intellectual life. I went home, sat down at my typewriter and did not pause again until my book was finished. English History 1914–1945 was a payment on account. The full debt of gratitude I shall never repay. Not that I always survived unscathed. I incurred Beaverbrook's wrath when I reviewed John Terraine's study of Haig not altogether unfavourably and failed to review Alan Clark's The Donkeys favourably enough. Beaverbrook was not mollified by my explanation that I was concerned to assess a book's historical merits, not to plunge another dagger into Haig's back.

I add another story with some embarrassment. Martin Gilbert projected a volume of essays for my sixtieth birthday in 1966. I suggested that he should invite Beaverbrook to contribute, in the hope of extracting a fragment from The Age of Baldwin. Beaverbrook outwitted me by writing instead a paean in praise of me. Once written, he could not wait until 1966 and published the essay at once in The Evening Standard. Then he sent for Martin Gilbert and unknown to me or to anyone else, arranged alternative endings: one to be used if he were still alive, the other if he were dead. The second ending appeared when the essays were published. In small things as in great, Beaverbrook made plans against his death as he would for any other journey.

While Beaverbrook praised me, others criticized him. He reacted as usual first with anger and then with amusement. In 1962 Lord Boothby took part in Any Questions, a radio chat-programme. A question was asked about Beaverbrook's newspapers. The chairman rashly encouraged the team to say just what they thought. Boothby first implied that the staff of the papers were writing against their convictions and then asserted that all the Canadians in England should be shipped back to Canada. Half-recalling a jingle by Chesterton he lamented the influence of Borden and Morden and Beaverbrook and threw in Lord Thomson for good measure. Members of the staff took action and each of them received damages.

Beaverbrook put in his own claim for £5,000. Boothby then sent a private letter of humble apology, claiming that he had always admired Beaverbrook's political activities and adding that, as rector of St. Andrews University, he had nominated Beaverbrook for an honorary degree. Beaverbrook was appeased. He minuted: "Send this letter from Boothby to the lawyers and tell them to lay off him". Beaverbrook lowered his claim for damages to £2,000 on condition that the BBC paid the entire sum and in addition paid all his own and Boothby's costs. The BBC agreed. Beaverbrook paid over the £2,000 to the Canadian War Veterans' Association.

Boothby was a glutton for punishment. After Beaverbrook published his final tribute to Churchill, Boothby wrote to the editor of The Sunday Express and accused Beaverbrook of supporting not only the Munich agreement but also "the filthy Nazi regime". Beaverbrook again contemplated action: "I think it might be quite interesting to go after the fellow again and this time to bankrupt him if I can". Researchers set to work. They reported that Boothby had himself voted for the Munich agreement[1] and had said of Neville Chamberlain on 1 November 1938: "The Prime Minister had no alternative at Munich but to make the best terms he could. . . . That action was courageous and he deserves the profound gratitude of the people of this country". This information delighted Beaverbrook, and he took no further action.

Malcolm Muggeridge was at this time principal book-reviewer on The Evening Standard. This did not deter him from publishing in Maclean's Magazine an account of the near-idolatry with which Beaverbrook was treated in New Brunswick. The article contained, among other exaggerations, the remarkable statement: "memorials to the Beaver outnumber churches". Wardell reported that there were in fact twenty churches in Fredericton alone and two memorials to Beaverbrook: a statue paid for by voluntary contributions and a bronze head paid for by the Friends of the Art Gallery. There was also a bust at Newcastle paid for by the town. This was not an extravagant return for the ten million dollars which Beaverbrook had given to the province. Thus vindicated, Beaverbrook reacted with good humour. He wrote to Charles Wintour:

> I don't sing hymns—I sing psalms. Any other mistake I don't mind, but when he mixes up hymns and psalms, that is too much.
>
> I make no objection to Muggeridge's attacks. On the contrary, I find them amusing. But it is all old stuff. I could have helped him with some fresh material.
>
> No one is asked to look after my reputation. That stands on the foundation of fifty years of hard work. Errors there have been. Many mistakes. Much service.

Muggeridge's contract was not renewed at the end of the year. Michael Foot, who had fortunately just left The Daily Herald, became principal book-reviewer on The Evening Standard. For Beaverbrook this was very much a case of all's well that ends well.

7 June was the anniversary of Christofor's marriage with Sir James Dunn. On 7 June 1963 Beaverbrook provided her with an unexpected celebration of the day. Early in the morning Max Aitken and A. G.

---

[1] This was not correct. Boothby voted against the Labour amendment which demanded support for collective security and the summoning of a world conference to consider the removal of economic and political grievances. He abstained on the motion approving the government's policy.

Millar arrived at Cherkley in Max's estate car. Beaverbrook and Christofor got in. They drove to Epsom registry office where Beaverbrook and Christofor were married. Beaverbrook was crippled with gout and therefore kept the news from the press so as to avoid photographs. Perhaps too he was reluctant to confess that he had been led into matrimony after so many years of evading it. When he had been married for a week he let out the news to the Canadian press, or maybe Wardell leaked it. Beaverbrook said contentedly: "It is quite something to have a woman still interested in you when you are eighty-four". It was too late for him to become a model husband. For a few weeks Christofor ordered the meals. Then things slipped back as they had been before. Nor was Christofor any better informed than the secretaries as to when Beaverbrook would go to La Capponcina or return from it.

Christofor was drawn into Beaverbrook's plans for the future— another agency which would continue to operate when he had gone. She became a trustee of the Beaverbrook Foundations and was put on the board of Beaverbrook Newspapers. Beaverbrook had also a special role for her. Cherkley was to become "a centre for historical material on the first and second world wars" and Christofor was to be the custodian. After his death the house was to be turned over for the use of historians and students. Beaverbrook's own papers were already at Cherkley, and the rest of his collection was now moved there from London. The Lloyd George papers were placed in what had been the cinema, and the Bonar Law papers in what had been the nursery. This was a very mistaken project. The papers were not secure from either fire or damp. Cherkley was over a mile from the nearest station. There was no suitable place for researchers to work and nowhere at all for them to eat lunch. The books, which Beaverbrook dignified with the name of the War Library, were a scratch collection left over after he had dispatched most of his books to the University of New Brunswick. Sheila Elton, who had controlled Beaverbrook's historical collections, resigned in protest and was justified in doing so.

While Beaverbrook's intellectual activity continued at full pressure, physically he was running down. He could hardly walk. He fought against weariness. He lost interest in the projected theatre at Fredericton. He had never cared for it much, gloomily anticipating the time when he would have to attend a performance there, and he lost patience when the difficulties always attendant on his building enterprises duly broke out. On 16 April 1963 he wrote to Wardell:

> For your private information, and solely for your information and not for disclosure to anybody else, I am not greatly concerned with the future in New Brunswick for obvious reasons.
>
> Frankly, Captain, I am a lame duck and that's that.

In September Christofor was due to open the Sir James Dunn International Art Exhibition at Fredericton. Beaverbrook was not well enough to go with her. In October he had to miss the convocation of the University of New Brunswick for the first time since he became chancellor. In November he wrote to Roy Howard:

> Swift complained that he was like a great oak tree, dying at the top. I am a humble admirer of Swift. But I differ in this respect. I am dying from the legs and the top is still quite all right.

A new political excitement served to revive him. Macmillan fell ill and the choice of the next prime minister was not an easy one. Macmillan had brought trouble to Beaverbrook earlier in the year. John Junor, editor of The Sunday Express, lost faith in Macmillan during the Profumo affair and refused to support him any longer. Junor complained that The Sunday Express was taking a "soft" line quite out of character. Beaverbrook would not go against Macmillan. Junor resigned. This was a considerable blow to Beaverbrook who had come to count implicitly on Junor's devotion. He contemplated the problem of a successor with dismay. Macmillan's resignation came just in time to get both Beaverbrook and Junor out of their difficulties. Junor withdrew his resignation and received the welcome of a prodigal son.

Even so, Beaverbrook would have liked Macmillan to stay on, in the belief that he alone could get on better terms with Soviet Russia. Beaverbrook wrote to Macmillan on 16 November:

> If you came back as the Prince of Peace, I, for one, am persuaded that you would carry the country in the election, and perhaps by a fine majority.
> Between us lies only the shadow of the Common Market. But that is over now and, I hope, done with for ever!

However Macmillan resigned. Beaverbrook followed the ensuing battle with relish. Of course he remembered the time when he had made prime ministers instead of merely waiting for news about the succession. Perhaps he even hoped that someone would consult him. At heart he did not really care. All he wanted was a ringside seat, and Randolph Churchill, who was running Quintin Hogg, provided him with one.

A message to Blackburn at this time recaptures his impatience in an exaggerated form:

> I have been ringing the Express, Mr. Blackburn, at 25 minutes to one for about five minutes, 8000 on this day Sunday, and getting no answer. What is to be done about that exchange by putting men on duty who will answer the telephone. This complaint is not to come from me. I have enough trouble without being made responsible for all these inadequacies in the organisation, that is your responsibility.

I am now ringing again, and the response seems to be no better. What is wrong, what is wrong, what is wrong? ... Here I am again at the telephone at five minutes after five with the same result, bell ringing, ringing, ringing, I can hear it ringing but no reply.

In this hot news period when it is wellknown that I am doing everything I can to further the interests of the newspaper why am I not given better service?

Such was the old man alone on a Sunday afternoon, angrily shaking the telephone and probably dialling the wrong number.

The elevation of Sir Alec Douglas-Home, formerly fourteenth earl of Home, afforded Beaverbrook great amusement. He declared with mock indignation: "Fourteen earls of Home have oppressed fourteen generations of Aitkens". When Sir Alec was invited to form a government, one of Beaverbrook's companions expressed doubt whether he would succeed. Beaverbrook answered from his accumulated wisdom: "He has got the loaves and fishes. There is no stopping him now". So it proved. Sir Alec Douglas-Home became prime minister. Beaverbrook continued to get fun from the situation. When his secretary asked what his future line would be, he replied: "It all depends on the belted earl! If he goes for the Common Market, we go in the other direction! If he goes for Polaris, we go in the other direction!" A little later Chapman Pincher sent Beaverbrook a brace of pheasants together with regret that they had not been shot in the company of the fourteenth earl. Beaverbrook thanked him and added:

> Of course I am one of the multitude in Britain to whom pheasants shot by the fourteenth Earl must necessarily be better than pheasants shot by Chapman Pincher.
>
> Of course there is another step above the fourteenth Earl—the Duke of Edinburgh. Think of that! A pheasant shot by him, or Prince Charles, or better still the Duke of Snowdon!

Beaverbrook's sincere admiration was reserved for Macmillan, to whom he wrote on 17 March 1964:

> I make bold to say that your Premiership will hold a most distinguished place in history—in fact I rank your triumphs in handling the tangled affairs of the country next to the Old Warrior himself.

From Beaverbrook there could be no higher praise. When Macmillan came to write his autobiography, he wrote of Beaverbrook: "While I served him and until the end of his life I received from him nothing but kindness, and was never asked to make any kind of repayment in any form. Perhaps I was fortunate, but this was my experience".[1]

---

[1] Macmillan, The Blast of War, 145.

In February 1964 Beaverbrook went to La Capponcina for a month. He was visibly slowing down. He could walk only a few steps and that with difficulty. He turned over his historical records without adding any new anecdotes. In other ways he refused to relax. He remained vigilant against the Common Market. When Edward Heath, the leading advocate of the Common Market, came out against retail price maintenance, The Daily Express at once received instructions to number retail price maintenance among its principal causes. Beaverbrook even found a new Empire champion. An all-party group of MPs set up a Commonwealth League for Economic Cooperation, with Geoffrey Rippon as joint president. At first Beaverbrook was not impressed and wrote to John Rodgers on 2 November 1963:

> Rippon goes through all the notions [?motions] about Empire trade, but he neglects the emotions.
>
> He cannot be on the side of Europe and the Empire with any hope of attracting a devoted following.
>
> He repeated over and over again that he is against nothing and for everything. That won't do. He must have targets to bombard. And those targets must be the European Common Market.

Later Beaverbrook decided to make the best of things and welcomed Rippon as a convert. He wrote to Rippon on 24 February 1964:

> I wish you great success—and I hope that you may persuade the country that the Tory Party means business at this late hour.
>
> Heaven knows they have turned down their opportunities often enough in the past. But after all, there is now a new brood—you and Rodgers and others.
>
> There is a hymn in our church which goes:
>
> > "And while the light holds out to burn,
> > The vilest sinner may return".
>
> The vilest sinner, in this case, was the Tory Party—before you and your young fellows came along.

Beaverbrook did not foresee that Geoffrey Rippon himself would stand high among the sinners.

Whether in England or the south of France, Beaverbrook still kept tight hold on his newspapers. His messages rode all the old hobbyhorses. Thus he preached the power of propaganda to William Davis, then financial editor of The Evening Standard, on 12 January:

> You say "Repetition dulls impact".
> Not true.
> Repetition is the principal secret of successful propaganda.
> You say "I believe tobacco shares will survive their new test, as they have done before".

But repetition will kill cigarette habits. You may be an old man with a beard by the time the cigarette habit is destroyed, but destruction is inevitable. *That is the opinion of a reader—you don't need to take notice of it.*

On 15 January he wrote to Blackburn:

I'd spend less money on foolish propaganda, and more money on wise propaganda, Mr. Blackburn. I called yesterday for projects please, for the advertising in the Daily Express. Please get a march on there.

Another old cause raised its head to Blackburn on 9 April:

I have been surprised to see the heavy embossed notepaper in use by the Daily Express.

I would like to know how far this measure of extravagance has spread.

Kindly give me a clear statement and take immediate steps to put an end to this extravagance.

The Scottish Daily Express ran into trouble when it rejected an advertisement from the Free Presbyterians. Beaverbrook wrote on 25 March:

The Daily Express accepts the Presbyterian doctrine. The Principal proprietor is a devoted supporter of the church. The Editor in Glasgow is an elder. But The Scottish Daily Express will not exclude any religious institution wishing to advertise in its columns.

The paper will never attack any form of religious teaching—Mormons, the Salvation Army, the Seventh Day Adventists, and the Free Presbyterians.

In April a reader who had moved to Aberdeen from London wrote to him complaining that The Scottish Daily Express was not as good as The Express she had received in London. Beaverbrook had the Scottish paper sent to him for a week, wrote twice to the Scottish editor and then sent a long letter of defence to the lady in Aberdeen.

On 12 May Beaverbrook telephoned Robert Edwards, editor of The Daily Express, at 3.20 in the afternoon and was told that the editor was still at lunch. Beaverbrook dictated this message, throwing in a warning that The Daily Herald was soon to begin a new career as The Sun:

Mr. Edwards, I telephoned you at 3.20 p.m. today and I was told that you were still at lunch.

My goodness the staff of the Daily Express eat a lot. But thank goodness you don't eat in the canteen because it would impoverish us.

> Now's the day and now's the hour
> See approach proud Edwards' power!

—or I hope we're in that position because in the month of September The Sun will be started. And if we lose much sale the sun won't shine for me any more.

> If there would be a coward here,
> Let him turn and flee,
> For who would fill a traitor's grave
> Who would be a coward's knave?

On 19 April, when he had only eight weeks to live, he rebuked Henry Luce for retiring at the age of sixty-six:

> That is not very good business. On the eve of my eighty-fifth birthday I am still working in much the same manner of twenty-five years ago.

Beaverbrook would be eighty-five on 25 May. Lord Thomson of Fleet, a fellow Canadian and newspaper proprietor, projected a great dinner in Beaverbrook's honour with six hundred guests. Hugh Massingham interviewed him a few days before the dinner for The Sunday Telegraph. The piece gives an incomparable picture of Beaverbrook in his last days, a Beaverbrook essentially unchanged from the mischievous boy in Newcastle, New Brunswick.

> Without warning, there slowly descends from the ceiling an extraordinary contraption that might, I suppose, be called a lift. Out of this crawls a little old man, leaning on a stick. He has on brown felt bootees, which he kicks off as soon as we are seated.
>
> The old man's mind is like an echoing gallery through which stump all the great figures of half a century—Churchill and Lloyd George and F. E. Smith and Bonar Law and Stalin and Arnold Bennett.
>
> Beaverbrook remembers Stalin very clearly. "Ah, yes, he was a proper villain, but I liked him. He was a very jovial man, full of fun. He made lots and lots of jokes. Yes, he was a fine fellow. Drank a lot".
>
> · · · · · · · · · ·
> "Lord Beaverbrook, do you still read the Bible?"
>
> "Well, no, I don't. You see, I have a lot of othert hings to read—memoranda and files and papers and God-knows-what. Just look over there", he says, pointing to a pile on the desk by the window. "That's all got to be read. It's my Baldwin file. I'm working on it for my new book—'The Age of Baldwin' ".
>
> "And do you pray, Lord Beaverbrook?"
>
> "Pray?"
>
> "Do you pray?"
>
> The old man considers. "Well, no. I leave all that to the Moderator of the General Assembly of the Presbyterian Church in Canada".
>
> He is funny, reverent, irreverent, spritely, sad—quicksilver in fact.
>
> · · · · · · · · · ·
> "Lord Beaverbrook, you who have been a journalist, a politician, an author, what are you most proud of in your life?"
>
> "Well, I'm very proud of my son. He's a fine fellow". The mood instantly changes from gay to sad. "He's a nicer man than ever I was", he says. "A much, much nicer man".
>
> · · · · · · · · · ·
> "Somewhere or other you have described Baldwin as a humbug and a hypocrite. Is that going to be the theme of your book?"
>
> "No, let us put it like this. I'm going to describe various scenes in which the reader can draw his own conclusions". Once more he squirms with

laughter. "You see, Baldwin . . ." He shakes his head and reaches for a handkerchief. "The fact is, you see, he betrayed me over the negotiations for Empire Free Trade. He posed as the martyr. He collared the Crown of Thorns. In a way it's rather funny. I got what was left. I was the real martyr".

. . . .

And what has he enjoyed during his life? Food?

He nods.

"Drink?"

The old boy sparkles. . . .

And the regrets? The disappointments?

"Well, I suppose, life itself. I don't consider", he goes on in a moment of melancholy, "that I have made a great deal out of my life. They say I've had a lot of influence. But I haven't. They say I'm a historian. But I'm not. I'm a chronicler. It's all nonsense".

"But, surely, the greatest disappointment of your life must have been the failure of the Empire Crusade—this idea of creating a free trade area within what is now known as the Commonwealth?"

One suddenly becomes aware of the ticking of a clock in the unexpected silence. And one suddenly realizes that the old man is weeping. It is what he feels is the real failure of his life, and there he sits in his stockinged feet, fishing for a handkerchief and weeping over what he thinks was a personal failure. "I was unworthy", he says. "Yes, I was unworthy. It touches me very deeply. If I had been a better man. . . . Ah, if only I'd been a better man".

"Surely you oughtn't to blame yourself? Personally, I never believed it was a starter".

"No, I was unworthy. I thought I could carry on the great policy of Joe Chamberlain. But I failed, you know. I failed".

We crawl into another room and Lord Beaverbrook goes off to the lavatory. Later he returns in a more cheerful mood. "Did I ever tell you", he says, "about an old Canadian of 80 whom I went to see when I was young and first came over to England? 'I can't piss', he said". He lowers himself on to the sofa. "Well, I can piss, but I can't walk. That's the trouble".

The talk turns on his newspapers. He remembers as if it were only yester-day how he started the *Sunday Express*. The first print was 300,000 and it sank little by little to 160,000. Then the Beaver wrote a series of articles that he afterwards turned into the book called "Success". And the sales recovered. The miracle was born.

"But you don't want to take 'Success' too seriously", he says. "It's only newspaper stuff".

Then he hobbles through the hall, past the lift, and out into the garden. He has lived here for 53 years and loves every stone of it.

There he is—romantic dreamer, coolheaded realist, weeping over his past failures and gay over his present troubles; in the end still elusive, a sprite vanishing into the garden.

The great dinner threatened to be an ordeal beyond Beaverbrook's strength. He would be unable to walk to his place, let alone make a speech.

For days beforehand, he scribbled fragments of his speech on bits of paper which were still scattered over the house after his death. When the day came, he was urged not to go. He tried to make a recording of his speech which could be played to the assembled guests. It was no good. His voice was too feeble. He pushed the machine aside and said: "Never mind. I'll be there anyway". In the late afternoon he was driven to the Dorchester and taken upstairs in a wheeled chair. When the moment came, he rose from his chair, balanced himself on Max Aitken's arm and walked sturdily to his place practically unaided. At dinner he ate heartily and outshone all others in gaiety. He listened appreciatively to speeches by Lord Thomson and Lord Rothermere.

It was Beaverbrook's turn. He stood upright and spoke in strong firm tones. His theme was that he had always been an apprentice. First an apprentice to finance in Canada. That was a life of daring adventure. Then London. "And there I decided to become an apprentice in politics". "After war I became an apprentice in Fleet Street. And that was a real exciting experience".

At last, I thought, I will be a Master. Fancy free. Instead, I became the slave of the Black Art. I did not know freedom again for many a year.

Beaverbrook laid down the journalist's code as he saw it:

First, he must be true to himself. The man who is not true to himself is no journalist. He must show courage, independence and initiative. He must also, I believe, be a man of optimism. He has no business to be a pedlar of gloom and despondency. He must be a respecter of persons, but able to deal with the highest and the lowest on the same basis, which is regard for the public interest and a determination to get at the facts.

For himself, "I take more pride in my experience as a journalist than in any other experience I have had in my long and varied life".

Beaverbrook spoke frankly of the Empire Crusade and its failure, this time without repining. He compared his fate with that of Montrose and added:

Montrose was let down, strange to say, by the Earl of Home, and I was let down by the present Earl of Home's predecessor. You know who I mean. I am happy to say that the comparison stops there. Unlike Montrose, I was not let down at the end of a rope.

The Second World War, and once more an apprentice. This time to Industrial Production, under Churchill's guidance, and he sustained me. Without his support I would have failed completely in my task. I didn't stand a chance without his backing.

Then Beaverbrook gently teased Lord Thomson about his title:

What a fine title—Lord Thomson of Fleet! How did Northcliffe and Rothermere, Riddell and Lord Dalziel, and I and some others give him the opportunity of taking that title? I cannot make it out. We could have been in before him.

Beaverbrook drew towards his close. Everyone present knew that he was near to death. With one half of his mind he knew it himself; with the other he was determined to go on. A few false words, and the evening would have ended in melancholy. Instead he announced his future intentions so gaily that we hardly noticed their implications:

> Here I must say, in my 86th year, I do not feel greatly different from when I was 85 [?84]. This is my final word. It is time for me to become an apprentice once more. I have not settled in which direction. But somewhere, sometime soon.

These sentences were his final masterpiece. We sang For He's a Jolly Good Fellow and followed it with Land of Hope and Glory, of which few present knew the words.

Beaverbrook walked from the room as sturdily as he had entered it. He was driven back to Cherkley and put to bed. He came down once to dinner which he could not eat. Otherwise he stayed in bed or sat by his bedroom fire. He dictated letters of thanks to all those who had sent good wishes or had written articles about him on his birthday. He still struggled through his newspapers and kept up a flow of messages. These, unimportant in themselves, are the last which have survived. To Charles Wintour on 2 June:

> I would advise against sending Randolph [Churchill to the Republican convention at San Francisco] unless you are looking for trouble.

To Tom Blackburn on 5 June:

> The last time I looked at your balance sheet reserves it stood at £1 million but now there is only £600,000. Where did the rest go?

And there followed a complaint against the number of company cars and private aircraft used by his newspapers.

On 7 June he had The Sunday Express read to him for the last time. But he did not forget that it was the anniversary of his wedding with Christofor. At dinner he ate a few strawberries. He filled a glass with champagne, raised it towards Christofor and said: "To my beloved". Then he exclaimed: "Come on. Let's be cheerful. Let's sing. What do you know?" Michael Wardell and Christofor joined him in singing the songs of the first world war, finishing with Pack up Your Troubles in Your Old Kit Bag, and Smile, Smile, Smile.

On 8 June he could eat nothing. The next morning he was sinking into unconsciousness. Before he did so, he handed to Max Aitken his box of "secret" papers. Max and George Millar took them out on the hillside and burnt them. Beaverbrook died in Christofor's arms at a quarter to four on the afternoon of 9 June. For five days he lay in state in the great saloon which of late years he had hardly used. Then he was privately cremated in the presence of his family. On 24 June there was a memorial service in St. Paul's Cathedral. Lord Rosebery spoke of Beaverbrook as "one of the most remarkable men who has lived in our time". He praised Beaverbrook's achievements in the second world war and then passed to something "not so well known"—his charity. Rosebery said:

> Lord Beaverbrook was a rich man, and it is written that it is easier for a camel to pass through the eye of a needle than for a rich man to enter the Kingdom of Heaven. But if any man deserves to do so, that man is Max Beaverbrook. He used his wealth unostentatiously, sometimes not even letting his right hand know what his left hand did. He helped many in distress. I have known even his enemies, of whom he had many, to be helped by him anonymously when he heard that they were in an impoverished condition.

Beaverbrook's ashes were taken to Canada. On 25 September Christofor placed them in the plinth of the bust by Oscar Nemon which stands in the town square, Newcastle, New Brunswick. The citizens of Newcastle and the Aitken family joined in singing Onward Christian Soldiers. The son of the manse had achieved his ambition. He had come home for the rest which he had neither found nor wanted in life.

Beaverbrook left few personal bequests: a trust fund of $500,000 for his grand-daughter Lady Jean Campbell and other trust funds for Peter Aitken's two sons. Christofor received nothing apart from the portrait of Beaverbrook by Graham Sutherland, a head of him in bronze by Oscar Nemon, and all his gold and silver boxes and musical boxes. Beaverbrook wrote in his will: "Lady Beaverbrook, having ample resources of her own, has asked me not to make any provisions for her in my will".[1] Max and Janet also received nothing "because I have amply provided for them both in my lifetime".

The dispositions on which Beaverbrook had laboured so long worked out successfully. The British Inland Revenue agreed after some dispute that Beaverbrook had retained his Canadian domicile. In consequence $12,600,000 passed to the Canadian Beaverbrook Foundation without any payment of death duties. In England the estate paid £100,000 in death duties on the money which Beaverbrook had received from Max Aitken for his farms in Somerset. Thus all ended well. Beaverbrook had once possessed some forty million dollars and, though he could not take them with him, he did the next best thing: he ensured that all except £100,000 went on deserving causes of his own choice and not to the inland revenue in either Great Britain or Canada.

[1] Christofor says Beaverbrook never discussed his will with her.

Max Aitken said as he left his father's deathbed: "As long as I live there will be only one Lord Beaverbrook" and at once took steps to renounce the title. The baronetcy, to which Beaverbrook himself had wished to return, remained to him. As Sir Max Aitken he appointed himself chairman of the trustees of the Beaverbrook Foundations. When Tom Blackburn reached retiring age, Sir Max united the post of chairman of the company with that of chairman of the board. Beaverbrook had no doubt planned to play off Christofor against Max after his own death. Christofor felt that she had done enough for Beaverbrook while he was alive and tactfully withdrew from all connection with the newspapers. Sir Max Aitken alone personified Beaverbrook Newspapers as his father had done before him.

The project of making Cherkley a centre of historical research was also, I am glad to say, abandoned. Christofor had no desire to be its custodian. The trustees of the first Beaverbrook Foundation moved the papers to London and provided a splendid home for them in St. Bride Street. The portrait of Beaverbrook by Sickert was rescued from its exile in Manchester and now looks down on the eager researchers.

When Beaverbrook was 81 Churchill gave him an engraved silver box which he sent to the University of New Brunswick. He wrote to Churchill: "Many will see it and they will say 'Our Boy' must have been a 'Somebody' ". Max Aitken Lord Beaverbrook was quite a Somebody. Those who loved him have one dream in life: that the telephone will ring again and the familiar voice ask, "What's the news?".

SOURCES

Most of this book rests on Beaverbrook's own records which run almost uninterruptedly from 1903 to 1964. When Aitken set up Royal Securities Corporation in 1903, he took on a secretary who conducted all his correspondence by typewriter and kept carbon copies. Aitken himself became, as it were, part of the corporation and even his family letters remain in the files. Later in England Beaverbrook often concluded a highly personal letter by apologizing that he had not written it in his own hand. Occasionally he wrote a brief note by hand, and most of these have not survived. He himself destroyed almost all his correspondence with his first wife and with Mrs. Jean Norton. He may have destroyed correspondence with other intimate friends, both men and women. I have deliberately not looked at the boxes of Beaverbrook's correspondence with his children, Janet, Max and Peter, which seemed to me their affair, not mine. Hence my book gives perhaps a misleading impression that he had no private life.

Between 1903 and 1910 there are 46 boxes of correspondence, kept by Miss de Gruchy, Aitken's secretary. Business, politics and family affairs are all mixed together. When Aitken came to England, S. W. Alexander, the London secretary of Royal Securities Corporation, looked after the correspondence in much the same way. In 1919 Beaverbrook disposed of Royal Securities Corporation and thereafter had no single working base for some time. Maurice Woods, Beaverbrook's principal ghost, seems to have looked after such correspondence as was preserved, but the files are thin between 1919 and 1928. In 1929 Woods died. About the same time Beaverbrook stopped going to The Express office in Fleet Street. He set up his own private office, first at a suburban house in Fulham, then at Stornoway House and finally in The Express building. His correspondence was looked after more systematically, though much of it had to be re-assembled from wherever Beaverbrook happened to be. Altogether there are 161 boxes of Social and General correspondence between 1911 and 1964.

At various times correspondence with political or literary figures was abstracted from the general boxes and put into individual folders. There are now 86 boxes of these Persons. Beaverbrook also put the original letters from many important individuals into albums. Transcripts of these letters were left in the original files, and the albums need not be consulted except by the student of handwriting.

The boxes dealing with Beaverbrook's newspapers start fairly late. There is one box dealing with the business affairs of The Express newspapers up to 1928 and another dealing similarly with The Evening Standard. The detailed correspondence then begins: 62 boxes for The Daily and Sunday Express, 20 for The Evening Standard. The bulk of this correspondence comes from the years after the second world war when Beaverbrook was often out of England. His Soundscriber messages, which I have described in the text, have not been preserved systematically.

Some topics were filed separately. There are 9 boxes dealing with constituency affairs at Ashton-under-Lyne between 1910 and 1912, and a few further papers for the years between 1913 and 1916. For the first world war there are 5 boxes on Aitken's work in England for the Canadian government, mostly concerned with the Canadian war records; 12 on the ministry of information; and 2 on his promotion of news films. The correspondence on the Empire Crusade, which was originally filed separately, has been amalgamated with the general files for 1930 and 1931. There remain office files on the Empire Crusade which I have not explored: 6 of office business, 7 of correspondence with the districts, 2 dealing with possible candidates, and 7 concerned with raising money for the Crusade. There are also 2 boxes on the Agricultural party and 6 covering miscellaneous campaigns waged by Beaverbrook between 1921 and 1963.

The second world war papers are in confusion. It seems that Beaverbrook's own private secretaries made one collection and those provided by the civil service made another. The first amounts to 14 boxes, the second to 22. The two collections often duplicate each other and sometime must be amalgamated. The papers, though dealing with official matters, are themselves mostly private drafts and letters. The only ones which might qualify as secret are weekly returns of aircraft strength. Beaverbrook did not bother to keep his war cabinet papers except when they concerned his own ministry, or maybe he returned them when he left office. There are also 27 boxes of unofficial correspondence which Beaverbrook maintained during the war, and 8 dealing with various political topics, which seem to have been compiled for Beaverbrook by members of The Daily Express staff. There are 17 boxes concerning negotiations with the United States over the future of civil aviation and 4 concerning similar negotiations over oil. I have not examined these two latter collections.

There are other series which I have skipped after satisfying myself from a quick dip or two that they were not for me. The bulkiest was the 169 boxes of Canadian affairs after 1947, dealing entirely with Beaverbrook's charitable activities in Canada, especially the art gallery at Fredericton. Over a hundred boxes of unimportant material have been abstracted from the general files and kept separately. These cover such topics as newsprint, household receipts, properties, yachts, private air-craft, and innumerable firms in which Beaverbrook was interested at one time or another. I have looked only at those which seemed of some general interest, such as the Canada Cement Company. Finally there was some material which illustrated nothing except that Beaverbrook was a hoarder of papers: hotel and travel reservations and stuff of that kind. We have disposed of all this.

I have mentioned the destruction of Beaverbrook's "secret" box on the day of his death. There is really no mystery about what it contained. Indeed there are 11 boxes of papers which Beaverbrook fed back on to the open shelves as no longer needing secrecy. Nearly all of them deal with other people's financial affairs—moneylenders, bankruptcies and so forth, usually ending with considerable financial assistance from Beaverbrook. Some of them are marriage settlements of distinguished ladies where Beaverbrook acted as a trustee. A few are records of court cases in which his friends or members of his newspaper staff were involved, again usually ending with financial assistance from Beaverbrook.

I do not think that Beaverbrook kept secrets about himself. One episode is recorded on the file by his secretary. In 1961 she found a number of letters written many years before by a society woman who demanded money from Beaverbrook on the ground that her husband had covered up for Beaverbrook by appearing as sole co-respondent in a divorce case. The secretary suggested that the letters should be destroyed or transferred to the "secret" box. Beaverbrook said: "Leave them in the open file. I don't give a damn" and added with a chuckle: "She didn't get anything, anyway".

When Beaverbrook was working on a book, his secretaries took the relevant material from the files and kept them in a tin deed-box. To this was added any correspondence Beaverbrook had with those who had participated in the events he was writing about, material contributed by others, and many sets of proofs, some marked by Beaverbrook and some by those he consulted. The contents of these deed-boxes were not dis-persed when the book was finished. Hence much important material has to be sought in them and not in the general files. For a long time there were only three boxes, all assembled by Maurice Woods; one for My Early Life and two for Politicians and the War. When Beaverbrook took up writing again he added more boxes, and there are also some which contain material collected for others—Bonar Law material for Robert Blake and abdication material for the duke of Windsor. The boxes now amount to 20 in all. As well as those covering the books he actually wrote there are others indicating the books he thought of writing: the Age of Baldwin, British politics between 1910 and 1914, the Canada Cement Company affair (two boxes for this), and the first Lady Beaverbrook. This last box is almost empty. Evidently Beaverbrook destroyed most of the contents. What remains he must have preserved deliberately, and I have therefore felt entitled to use it in my text.

The visitors' book at Cherkley was kept from 1911 to 1964. This is mainly interesting as a collection of autographs. Beaverbrook's engagement books from 1922 to 1964 are fuller. They record everyone who came to see him during the day as well as his guests at lunch or dinner. These books do not of course cover Beaverbrook's calls on others, and they are blank when he was out of England. The cellar books indicate the character of Beaverbrook's lunch or dinner parties. Many of them were lost when Stornoway House was bombed. From 1929 to 1964 A. G. Millar kept a cash book recording each day the cheques which he drew for Beaverbrook to sign. The payments are under various heads: groceries, household supplies and so on. The heading, Donations, indicates Beaverbrook's gifts of money to charities and private persons.

Newspaper cuttings provide another substantial source. 65 volumes cover every aspect of Beaverbrook's life from 1910 to 1964—politics, personal events, travels, attacks on him and articles about him. I have lifted many anecdotes from these last. 4 volumes contain Beaverbrook's own articles from 1919 to 1963, mainly in his own newspapers. Some of these, particularly in the earlier years, are fragments of contemporary history which he did not use in any of his books. Thus there is an account of how Baldwin became prime minister in 1923 and another of how Lloyd George and Austen Chamberlain combined to defeat the Labour government in 1924. 8 volumes contain reviews of Beaverbrook's books with the exception of Politicians and the War. Perhaps to compensate for this there is a volume of the reviews of Tom Driberg's Beaverbrook. There are also 23 volumes of Canadian cuttings from 1919 to 1964 which I have not examined.

I have discussed Beaverbrook's books in the text. I list them here for convenience:

Canada in Flanders, two volumes, 1915 and 1917. (The two later volumes were written by C. G. D. Roberts and others.)
Success, 1921 and many later editions under various titles.
Politicians and the Press, 1925.
Politicians and the War, two volumes, 1928 and 1932, reissued as a single volume, 1960.
Men and Power, 1956.
Friends, Sixty Years of Intimate Personal Relations with Richard Bedford Bennett, 1959.
Courage, The Story of Sir James Dunn, 1961.

The Divine Propagandist, 1962.
The Decline and Fall of Lloyd George, 1963.
My Early Life, 1964.
The Abdication of King Edward VIII, 1966.

Having so much material of Beaverbrook's, I have not worked system-atically through other archives. The Lloyd George and Bonar Law papers, both in the Beaverbrook Library, mainly provide duplicates of the Beaverbrook correspondence. There are a few letters to Law from leading Unionists, protesting against his friendship with Beaverbrook, and the Lloyd George papers gave me some additional details about the purchase of The Daily Chronicle. I went through the Beaverbrook files in Churchill's papers with the cooperation of Martin Gilbert and found a few drafts and handwritten letters. Where there was indication of a handwritten letter by Beaverbrook, of which there was no copy in his own files, I tried to recover it from the archive of the recipient, usually without success. I also examined Asquith's papers in the hope of finding letters from Earl Grey denouncing Beaverbrook. I found none.

Full bibliographies of the period are given in many works of recent history, beginning with my own English History 1914–1945. I give here books directly concerned with Beaverbrook, listed in order of publication:

F. A. Mackenzie: Lord Beaverbrook: An Authentic Biography, 1931.

Though Beaverbrook claimed to have nothing to do with this book, he clearly provided newspaper cuttings and perhaps some personal information. The author had worked on The Daily Mail, but not on any Beaverbrook newspaper.

Edgar Middleton: Beaverbrook: The Statesman and the Man, 1934.

The author was active in the Empire Crusade. His book adds nothing to Mackenzie's.

David Farrer: The Sky's the Limit, 1943.

This is an account of the ministry of aircraft production which Farrer wrote under Beaverbrook's direction.

M. M. Postan: British War Production, 1952.

This introductory volume to the official histories of British war production during the second world war was closely scrutinized by Beaverbrook, and some amendments were made at his suggestion.

J. D. Scott and Richard Hughes: Administration of War Production, 1955.

This volume in the official history adds some details especially on Beaverbrook's time at MAP.

Tom Driberg: Beaverbrook. A Study in Power and Frustration, 1956.

Driberg was the first and most long-lived "William Hickey". The book began with, but did not retain, Beaverbrook's blessing.

William Kilbourn: The Elements Combined. A History of the Steel Company of Canada, 1960.

Beaverbrook provided the author with information about the founding of the company, and this information is confirmed in an appendix with documents from the company's records.

Arthur Christiansen: Headlines All My Life, 1961.

The author was editor of The Daily Express from 1933 to 1956, and his book is almost as much about Beaverbrook as about himself.

Peter Howard: Beaverbrook: A Study of Max the Unknown, 1964.

The author had been a writer on The Evening Standard and then became the leader of Moral Rearmament. His book, which was much revised by Beaverbrook, is a series of sketches rather than a biography, with an implication that there was still time for Beaverbrook to become an Oxford Grouper.

Alan Wood: The True History of Lord Beaverbrook, 1965.

The author was for some time a Beaverbrook journalist and then became a fulltime writer. He broke off his book in 1952 from fear of a libel action and died in 1957. The book has an epilogue by Sir John Elliot.

Kenneth Young: Churchill and Beaverbrook. A Study in Friendship and Politics, 1966.

This book derives from the correspondence between Churchill and Beaverbrook in the Beaverbrook papers. The emphasis is on the personal friendship, and Kenneth Young does not stress as much as I do the wider reasons underlying the differences between Churchill and Beaverbrook during the second world war.

George Malcolm Thomson: Vote of Censure, 1968.

The author was Beaverbrook's political secretary for a long period. His book presents the political crises of 1942 in somewhat muffled tones.

C. M. Vines: A Little Nut-Brown Man. My three years with Beaverbrook, 1968.

The author was one of Beaverbrook's secretaries from 1961 to 1964. He lived in a state of perpetual bewilderment with his employer, a state which Beaverbrook rejoiced to enhance. This strange conflict has produced, in my opinion, the best portrait of Beaverbrook in his latter days. Here was a great humorist at work. Thanks to Beaverbrook, the book rivals The Diary of a Nobody as the funniest in the English language.

David Farrer: G—for God Almighty. A personal memoir of Lord Beaverbrook, 1969.

This book is also funny, though more consciously so. It covers the author's period of employment with Beaverbrook as a private secretary from 1940 to 1946.

Many memoirs of the period, both social and political, have references to Beaverbrook, few of much interest. He appears either as a sort of sinister noise off or as a fairy godfather. The anecdotes about him usually derive from himself or from one of his associates, especially Percy Cudlipp, and do not acquire greater authenticity from being constantly repeated. As well memorialists writing in old age remember what they have read in other books more than what they actually experienced. The only contemporary account I found of any value was in Memoirs of a Polyglot by William Gerhardi (1931). Gerhardi also presented an attractive picture of Beaverbrook as Lord Ottercove in some of his novels. Otherwise Beaverbrook was not used seriously in any novel except those by Arnold Bennett and H. G. Wells which I have discussed in the text. I have Evelyn Waugh's authority for stating that Beaverbrook was not the original of Lord Copper.[1]

There are 61 albums of photographs in the Beaverbrook Library and also albums containing every cartoon in which Beaverbrook appeared however humbly. Even in photographs he was the cat that walked alone: there are far more of him on his own than with other people. To the best of my knowledge, there are only two full-scale portraits of Beaverbrook: by Sickert, painted in 1935, now in the Beaverbrook Library, and by Graham Sutherland, painted in 1952, now the property of Lady Beaverbrook. The best likeness is the famous drawing by Low, though it makes Beaverbrook misleadingly small.

[1] Beaverbrook professed not to have read any of Evelyn Waugh's books. When I told him that Evelyn Waugh was in my opinion the greatest novelist of the age, he replied: "Is that so?"—his usual way of refusing to discuss a subject. If he had really not read Waugh's novels he must have had a sixth sense. I heard a journalist try on him the immortal phrase: "Up to a point, sir". He replied cheerfully: "The idea's no good, eh?".

ACKNOWLEDGEMENTS

I thank the following for permission to publish copyright correspondence and articles:

Sir Max Aitken
Rt. Hon. Julian Amery, MP—L. S. Amery
Associated Newspapers Group Ltd.—A. J. Cummings
Rt. Hon. the earl of Avon
Earl Baldwin of Bewdley—Stanley Baldwin
The earl of Balfour—A. J. Balfour
Rt. Hon. the Lord Balfour of Inchrye
Mrs. George Bambridge—Rudyard Kipling
Sir Patrick Hamilton Benn—Sir Ion Hamilton Benn
Mrs. Dorothy Cheston Bennett—Arnold Bennett
The earl of Birkenhead—The 1st earl of Birkenhead
The Hon. Mark Bonham Carter—The earl & countess of Oxford & Asquith
Viscount Bridgeman of Leigh—W. Bridgeman
Mrs. Collin Brooks—Viscount Rothermere
Mr. Alan Bullock—Ernest Bevin
Rt. Hon. James Callaghan, MP
Mr. D. N. Chester—Herbert Morrison
Churchill College, Cambridge—Brendan Bracken
Rt. Hon. the Lord Clitheroe of Downham
Dame Isobel Cripps—Sir Stafford Cripps
C & T Publications Ltd.—Sir Winston Churchill
Mr. Michael Cummings—A. J. Cummings
Viscount Davidson of Little Gaddesden—J. C. C. Davidson
Lord Davies of Llandinam—The 1st Baron Davies
The earl of Derby—The 17th earl of Derby
The Dominion Archivist, The Public Archives of Canada, Ottawa—Sir Robert Borden
Mr. Gordon Duncan—Sir Andrew Duncan
Lady Beatrix Evison—A. V. Alexander
The First Beaverbrook Foundation—Lord Beaverbrook, David Lloyd George, Andrew Bonar Law
Mr. Michael Foot, MP

Lady Forres—The earl of Woolton
Lord Grantley—Lady Grantley
The Hon. Raymond R. Guest—F. E. Guest
The Harriet Irving Library, University of New Brunswick—R. B. Bennett
Dr. T. M. Healy—Tim Healy
Vice-Admiral I. L. T. Hogg, CB, DSC—H. A. Gwynne
Lady Ismay—General Ismay
Mr. J. R. Lamberton—Sir Robert Horne
Professor Ann K. S. Lambton—Viscount Cecil of Chelwood
Rt. Hon. the baroness Lee of Asheridge—Aneurin Bevan
Mrs. Dorothy Lindsay—Sir Andrew Macphail
The Literary Executor of the late Stanley Morison—Stanley Morison
Mrs. Stephen Lloyd—Neville Chamberlain
Mr. David McKenna—Reginald McKenna
Mrs. Mary McManus—W. P. Crozier
Rt. Hon. Harold Macmillan
Major Maxse—L. J. Maxse
Sir Oswald Mosley
Mrs. Moyal
Mr. P. E. Paget—Lord & Lady Templewood (Sir Samuel & Lady Maud Hoare)
Captain S. W. Roskill, RN—Sir Maurice Hankey
Sir Edward Spears
The Sunday Telegraph—Lady Violet Bonham Carter
Hugh Massingham
Professor J. P. M. Tizard—Sir Henry Tizard
Mr. T. C. Usher
Lady Vansittart—Sir Robert Vansittart

I also acknowledge with thanks permission to use copyright material from the following books:

The earl of Avon, The Reckoning, Cassell & Co. Ltd.
Lord Beaverbrook, My Early Life (Brigadier Wardell)
Politicians and the War 1914–1916 (Beaverbrook Foundations)
Men and Power 1917–1918 (Beaverbrook Foundations)
Friends (Beaverbrook Foundations)
The Decline and Fall of Lloyd George (Beaverbrook Foundations)
Arthur Christiansen, Headlines All My Life, William Heinemann Ltd. (Mr. Michael Christiansen)

Randolph Churchill, Winston Churchill, Companion Vol. II, Part 2, William Heinemann Ltd. (C & T Publications Ltd.)

Lady Diana Cooper, The Rainbow Comes and Goes, Rupert Hart-Davis.

David Farrer, The Sky's The Limit, Hutchinson & Co. Ltd.
                    G—For God Almighty, George Weidenfeld & Nicolson Ltd.

William Gerhardi, Memoirs of a Polyglot, Gerald Duckworth & Co. Ltd.

Sir Roderick Jones, A Life in Reuters, Hodder & Stoughton Ltd. (Lady Jones)

Thomas Jones, Whitehall Diary, II, Oxford University Press (Mr. Tristan Jones)

Air Chief Marshal Sir Philip Joubert, The Third Service, Thames & Hudson Ltd. (Lady Joubert)

Iain Macleod, Neville Chamberlain, Frederick Muller Ltd. (Baroness Macleod of Borve)

Harold Macmillan, The Blast of War, Macmillan & Co. Ltd.

Leonard Mosley, Backs to the Wall, George Weidenfeld & Nicolson Ltd.

Sir Frederick Pile, Ack-Ack, George G. Harrap & Co. Ltd.

Sir Edward Spears, Assignment to Catastrophe, II, William Heinemann Ltd.

Viscount Templewood, Nine Troubled Years, Collins (Mr. P. E. Paget)

The drawing of Beaverbrook by David Low was published in Lions and Lambs (Jonathan Cape, 1928) and is reproduced from the original by arrangement with the Low trustees. The drawing by Graham Sutherland is reproduced by permission of Lady Beaverbrook. All the photographs are taken from Beaverbrook's private albums. I express humble apology if I have unwittingly infringed any copyright.

INDEX